WORLD'S COOLEST MOVIE STAR

VOLUME ONE: TRAGIC DRIFTER

WORLD'S COOLEST MOVIE STAR

THE COMPLETE 95 FILMS (AND LEGEND) OF

Jean Gabin

VOLUME ONE

∞ Charles Zigman ∞

With a Foreword by Michele Morgan

ALLENWOOD PRESS

For information contact Allenwood Press
www.allenwoodpress.com
publisher@allenwoodpress.com
www.jeangabinbook.com
author@jeangabinbook.com

ISBN 13: 978-0-9799722-0-1
ISBN 10: 0-9799722-0-5

Library of Congress Control Number: 2007907374
Library of Congress Subject Headings:
Film; Biography; France.

Book design by Michael Kellner

Second Edition (2009)

Published by Allenwood Press
Los Angeles

2.0

This Book is for My Aunt,
Shirley Marilyn Zigman Rothstein
(1927-2004)
Who Introduced Me to the Films of Jean Gabin

WORLD'S COOLEST MOVIE STAR

VOLUME ONE: TRAGIC DRIFTER

TABLE OF CONTENTS

Volume One: Tragic Drifter

The Films: 'Cycle One'
1930—1933, Film Nos. 1 to 15: On the Verge of Stardom

* Housekeeping Note about Films Eight, Thirteen and Fifteen:
The three feature films *La Foule hurle*, *L'Etoile de Valencia*, and *Adieu les beaux jours* are the only three of Jean Gabin's ninety five movies which today do not exist: Each one is considered to be a lost film (two of them were even destroyed, by the Nazis) and has not been seen for decades. However, in each of these three cases, there is, thankfully, a still-existing and identical 'alternate' version of the film,

which the producers filmed simultaneously with, or shortly thereafter, the Gabin version, in another language. Each one features another actor in the role which Gabin played in the French version, and so, for these three chapters alone, I have viewed, and substituted, these alternate versions.

THE FILMS: 'CYCLE TWO'
1934—1941, Film Nos. 16 to 31: Tragic Drifter

THE FILMS: 'CYCLE THREE'
1942—1944, Film Nos. 32 & 33: Hollywood

THE FILMS: 'CYCLE FOUR'
1946—1953, Film Nos. 34 to 46: After the War

Gabin Returns to France After Two Years in America, and After an Additional Two Years in the Free French Navy. He Makes Twelve Films, but the French Public Ignores Him, Feeling that he Deserted Them, When He Left for America.

A FOREWORD BY MICHELE MORGAN

The legendary French actress co-starred with Jean Gabin in
Quai des brumes (1938), Le Recif de corail (1939), Remorques (1939/41), La Minute de verite (1952).

"T'as de beaux yeux, tu sais…"

La replique de Carne et Prevert a fait le tour du monde. Dite par un autre que Jean Gabin, aurait-elle eu le meme charme? Je l'ignore, mais ce que je sais, ce dont je suis consciente, c'est d'avoir appris mon métier face a des acteurs de la dimension de Gabin… Il n'y avait qu'a observer la facon dont Jean jouait la comedie, comment il abordait chacun de ses roles de maniere different, il n'y avait qu'a regarder ses yeux, qu'a ecouter sa voix. Je n'y ai pas manqué et bien des annees après, la lecon demeure presente a mon coeur et a mon esprit. Il y a certes aujourd'hui de grands comediens, mais Jean Gabin demeure inoubliable. Grace a ses films et la television qui les diffuse, les jeunes le connaissent. Eux non plus ne l'oublieront pas.

"You have beautiful eyes, you know…"

That phrase, written by Carne and Prevert, traveled around the world. Said by anybody else other than Jean Gabin, would it have had the same charm? I don't know. But what I know, is that I learned my profession facing actors like Gabin… You just have to observe the way Jean was acting, the way he would approach each of his roles in a different way. You just have to look at his eyes and listen to his voice. I didn't miss that lesson, and a lot of years later, the lesson stays present in my heart and mind. There are, nowadays, great actors, but Jean Gabin remains unforgettable. Because of his movies, and television which shows them, people will always know him, and will never forget him.

MICHELE MORGAN
Neuilly, France

AUTHOR'S NOTE: Michele Morgan begins her foreword to this book, by quoting a line of dialogue from director Marcel Carne's 1939 film, *Le Quai des brumes* (in English, *Port of Shadows*): "You have beautiful eyes, you know" is spoken by Jean Gabin to Michele Morgan during that film's most romantic moment and, to this day, it remains one of the most famous lines of spoken dialogue in the entire history of French movies—a line which is just as mythic in France as, "Frankly my dear, I don't give a damn," from *Gone with the Wind* is, in the United States. (The screenplay for *Quai des brumes* was co-written by Carne, with the screenwriter and poet, Jacques Prevert.)

PREFACE

Jean Gabin, in a nutshell

THE FRENCH ACTOR JEAN GABIN (1904-1976) REMAINS, TODAY, ONE OF THE MOST popular movie stars in the entire world.

Everywhere else in the world except in the United States, he in considered to be one of the entertainment world's biggest icons of all time, on the same level as Marilyn Monroe, Elvis Presley, or James Dean. Gabin made ninety-five movies, between 1930 and 1976.

He is known in America today only by serious film enthusiasts, and only for a handful of very serious French movies in which he played a silent, somber, world-weary (and yet life-loving) 'tragically-fated drifter.' These movies were made between 1934 and 1941, and the two movies he is mostly known for in America today, which were made during this period, are 1937's anti-war epic *Grand Illusion,* and that same year's gangster classic, *Pepe Le Moko.*

The thing is: Between 1930 and 1933, and also between 1946 and 1976, Jean Gabin made seventy-five additional movies which, today, are completely unknown in the United States. In these movies, very often, Gabin's characters are not tragic drifters at all. Sometimes, they are smooth, soft-spoken gentleman-criminals, *a la* Michael Corleone, in *The Godfather,* or else they are wealthy, immaculately-dressed, *bourgeois* captains-of-industry with huge families to deal with (*a la* J.R. Ewing, from the '70s television drama, "Dallas"). In many of these movies, not only are Gabin's characters not tragically fated, but very often—they'll even smile, laugh, and break into song!

If you are an American, this book will either introduce you, or re-introduce you, to Jean Gabin. If you are French, or if you're from the other countries in which Gabin continues to be venerated today, you're in luck as well, because even in your countries, while there are printed biographies dealing with Jean Gabin's life, there has never been a concise study of each of his ninety-five films, in which a separate chapter has been given over to the study of each one. (In France, there was once a book about 20 of his films, but there is no book about all 95.)

And there has never been any book about Jean Gabin in English, at all. Ever.

But now there is. (You're holding it...)

| |

INTRODUCTION

Who is Jean Gabin and why does the world need this book?

"Like so many foreign stars, Jean Gabin was considered to be a huge star in America in the 1930s and '40s, on a par with Bogart and Gable. Thanks to the industry's selective memory, he's been heavily forgotten in the U.S. today, despite remaining the most popular star of all time, throughout the rest of the world."
— *Author's Interview with Mark Gallagher, Ph.D, author of "Action Figures: Men, Action Films, and Contemporary Adventure Narratives" (Palgrave MacMillan, 2006), Lecturer in Film Studies, University of Nottingham, England*

"Come with me to ze Casbah. We will make ze beautiful muzeek togezaire, no?"
— *A line famously attributed to movie star Jean Gabin—a line which he never actually spoke...*

I MAGINE A FICTITIOUS MOUNT RUSHMORE, IN WHICH THE GREATEST AND MOST LUMINOUS movie stars of the past have all been carved in stone: There's Humphrey Bogart, Bette Davis, James Cagney, Barbara Stanwyck, Edward G. Robinson, Jimmy Stewart, Spencer Tracy, Glenn Ford, Gary Cooper, and—I know, I know: The real Mount Rushmore only has four presidents, but this fictitious 'Movie Mount Rushmore' just seems to keep going on forever. I know! (Just go with it!)

Now:

Imagine that there's a large, gaping hole in our mountain; one of the heads is missing and hopefully, it hasn't been vandalized. Who belongs there? Well, if you're just your average American movie fan, nobody does: You'd probably just drive by the monument, absently remark, "Nice hole," and move along, without even giving the void so much as a second thought. In fact, you might even throw your recyclables into it.

Anyway, you'd be driving away without realizing that this is the space which should be occupied by the Greatest, and Coolest, Movie Star of All Time:

Of course, I'm talking about the incredible, iconic French everyman/anti-hero, Jean Gabin

(1904-1976), an actor who, even today, more than thirty years after his death, remains one of the biggest and most recognizable movie stars of all time, everywhere on earth *except* in the United States, where he used to be super-popular decades ago, in the late '30s and the mid-'40s, but where he's now been largely forgotten by a good portion of the general public.

How cool is Jean Gabin? *Check this out:*

■ The Warner Bros. cartoon character Pepe Le Pew, created by Chuck Jones, was based upon actor Charles Boyer's portrayal of the gangster Pepe Le Moko in the 1938 film *Algiers*, a remake of Jean Gabin's 1937 classic, *Pepe Le Moko*. Whenever any old movie or cartoon character from the '40s and '50s says, "Come with me to the Casbah… we will make ze beautiful muzeek togezaire," they are directly referencing what is supposed to be the most famous line from those movies, although neither actor ever actually said it—in the same way in which Cary Grant never actually uttered, "Judy, Judy, Judy;"

■ In the December 2007 theatrical release *Atonement,* actor James McAvoy runs into a World War II-era movie theater, where he comes face-to-face with a giant, silver-screen representation of Jean Gabin and actress Michele Morgan, from the 1938 movie, *Le Quai des brumes;*

■ Johnny Depp told interviewer Emmanuel Itier in a July 10, 2006 interview, in connection with the release of the second *Pirates of the Caribbean* movie, that one of his biggest regrets in life, is that he will never be able to work with Jean Gabin;

■ "His Face was His Passport:" In an MGM pressbook from 1946 (the studio was releasing one of Gabin's French films in the U.S.), the writer mentions that, "during World War II, when nobody could move ten steps in France without showing identification papers, Jean Gabin was never asked for them. Invariably, before the star could reach into his pocket, French and even German military personnel would wave him across with a shout of, 'Oh, it's okay! It's Gabin!'"

■ ROCKIN' WITH GABIN #1: One of France's current rap artists is 'MC Jean Gab'1 (pronounced, 'MC Jean Gabin');

■ ROCKIN' WITH GABIN #2: In N.Y. and L.A. clubs, today's trendy young notables are often seen dancing to Italy's big, techno band 'Gabin' (their CDs are available in the U.S., on Astralwerks records), whose two front-men, DJ Filippo Clary and bassist Max Bottini were childhood friends who grew up loving Gabin's movies, and calling each other 'Gabin!'

■ ROCKIN' WITH GABIN #3: Similarly, the '70s band Styx named its 1977 hit, "Grand Illusion," after the 1937 Gabin movie of the same name;

■ ROCKIN' WITH GABIN #4: And speaking of *Grand Illusion*, Madonna loves the Jean Gabin movie so much, that when she wrote and appeared in those shocking photographs for her notorious 1992 book *Sex*, she named her alter-ego/character in the book 'Dita,' after Dita Parlo, Gabin's handpicked female co-star from the classic movie. (On a similar note, rocker Marilyn Manson's ex-wife, the burlesque dancer Heather Sweet, re-christened herself as 'Dita von Teese,' after she watched *Grand Illusion;*)

■ ROCKIN' WITH GABIN #5: Members of the '80s rock band, The Clash, are such huge Jean Gabin fans, that they were inspired to come up with one of its biggest monster hits, "Rock the Casbah," after repeated viewings of *Pepe Le Moko*, Jean Gabin's *film noir* production which set its scene, famously, in the dark, dank Casbah section of Algiers;

■ Woody Allen is such a big fan of *Grand Illusion,* that he's even name-checked it, in two separate movies: In 1977's *Annie Hall,* Woody's in attendance at Paul Simon's swank Hollywood party, and a stoner on a couch tells him that *Grand Illusion* is "a great film to watch when you're high." In 1979's *Manhattan,* Woody tells Diane Keaton that he never misses the opportunity to see *Illusion,* whenever it appears on television;

■ *Grand Illusion* continues to appear on the American Film Institute's list of the 100 greatest films ever made;

■ Gabin's 1937 film, *Pepe Le Moko,* is widely considered to be the very first *film noir* movie (by definition, what makes a movie '*film noir,*' is when its tragic characters exist in 'dark underworlds,' and are beset by forces beyond their control);

■ Jean Gabin Has Changed the Way We Wear Clothes: In 1937, when Gabin played Pepe Le Moko, he was movie history's very first star to dress, on-screen, in a black shirt and a light-colored tie, a look which director Martin Scorsese would crib fifty-eight years later for Robert De Niro's Las Vegas kingpin character, Sam 'Ace' Rothstein, in his 1995 film, *Casino.* (Of course, 'the dark shirt and light-colored tie' look remains popular today among the *cognoscenti* of 'Young Hollywood;')

■ Similarly, in a 1939 picture called *Le Jour se leve,* Jean Gabin was the first-ever screen star to make 'brooding around, in a black leather jacket' look cool, and this is eleven full years before Brando attempted leather jacket coolness in *The Wild One,* and a full seventeen years before James Dean did it, in *Rebel without a Cause;*

■ Now that The James Dean Museum is gone, Jean Gabin and James Stewart are the only (non-cowboy) movie stars in the world with museums which are completely dedicated to them: It's Meriel, France's two-story *Musee Gabin*;

■ Between 1980 and 2007, the annual award for the year's best new film actor, awarded by the French critics, was called the *Prix Jean Gabin.* Some of the big winners whom you may have heard of, include Thierry Lhermitte, Tcheky Karyo, Jean-Hughes Anglade, Lambert Wilson, Vincent Perez, Matthew Kassovitz, Guillaume Depardieu, and Jeremie Renier;

■ The *Christian Science Monitor's* film critic David Sterritt has reported, in correspondence with this author, that Jean Gabin was Jack Kerouac's all-time-favorite movie actor;

■ Gabin also happened to be director Sergio Leone's all-time-favorite movie actor, even though the two men never actually got to work together. In 1973, Leone tried to get his film *Once Upon a Time in America* off-the-ground, announcing at that year's Cannes Film Festival that Jean Gabin would be appearing in the picture; unfortunately, it took Leone ten years to raise the financing for his movie, and by the time he did, Gabin had already

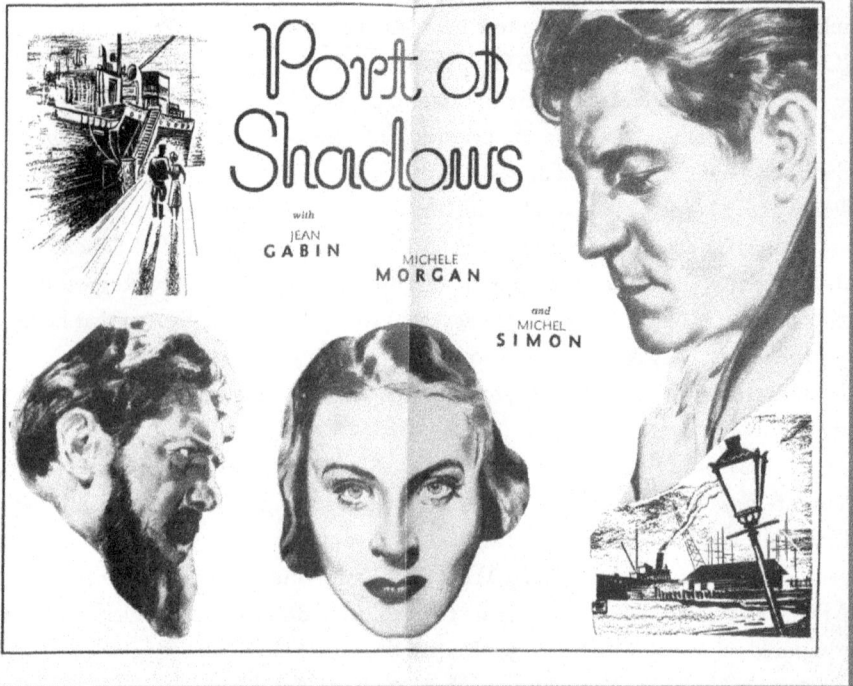

passed away. The role which Gabin was supposed to have played, was instead played by James Woods;

■ Gabin's daughter, Florence Moncorge, has told this author, in correspondence, that her father is synonymous with France and French values (*'libertie, egalitie, fraternitie'*) in exactly the same way in which John Wayne has always been associated with America and American values ('peace,' 'strength', 'hard-work,' *etc.*). Surely, when you watch both Gabin and Wayne on-screen, you can see that Jean Gabin is all about freedom and fraternity, while Wayne is about peace and strength (not to mention,' peace through strength');

■ February, 2007: Composer/Conductor Ennio Morricone electrified audiences by conducting the eponymously named "Jean Gabin Theme" from Gabin's 1969 Mafia thriller, *Le Clan des Siciliens* at the UN (on 2-2-07), and then for a second time, at Radio City Music Hall (on 2-3-07);

■ Walt Disney considered Jean Gabin to have been his favorite French movie star of all time. In 1960, when Disney produced his big Jules Verne epic, *20,000 Leagues Under the Sea,* he hired Jean Gabin to read Verne's story on the French-version of the Disneyland Records soundtrack album;

■ The race car-driving city of Le Mans (in northwestern France, popularized by Steve McQueen, who used to race there, and who even made a great 1971 documentary about the town) is home today to France's third biggest racing track, the Jean Gabin Hippodrome;

■ In 2004, the Champagne region of eastern France became the home of France's first all-digital cinema multiplex, the Jean Gabin Cinemas;

■ And speaking of champagne: Jean Gabin is the only movie star in the world who has a continually produced brand of champagne named for him—*Cuvee Jean Gabin;*

■ Author Robin Buss, writing in his 1994 book *French Film Noir*, maintains that in his view, France has only ever created "three real exportable movie stars:" Jean Gabin, Jean-Paul Belmondo, and Gerard Depardieu;

■ Two great French directors both "got their starts" as assistant directors on Jean Gabin movies: Louis Malle shot underwater footage for a 1954 Gabin picture called *Port du desir,* and Costa-Gavras was A.D., on a 1962 Gabin picture, called *Un singe en hiver;*

■ In Eastern Europe, Jean Gabin has always been, and continues to be, worshipped almost as a god: There are Polish and Romanian-language picture books about Jean Gabin, and Czechoslovakians know him as '*Jeanem Gabinem.*' In 1972, Russian Cosmonauts, orbiting the earth, wanted only to speak, *via* satellite, to Jean Gabin. (They didn't, but they tried!) In fact, in 2005, Russia released twenty Gabin movies on DVD, with Russian subtitles.

And believe it or not, once upon a time, a group of five of Jean Gabin's French movies, all of which were made in the mid-to-late 1930s, and in which the actor played movie history's pre-eminent world-weary, tragic drifter (*Pepe Le Moko, Le Grande illusion, La Bete*

Humaine, Quai des brumes, and *Le Jour se leve*) were so beloved in the United States, that people who would never in a million years go and see a film which was (heaven forefend!) 'made in another country,' lined up to see Gabin's mega-cool flicks and, correspondingly, at the beginning of 1941, important Hollywood movie executives even flew the actor out to Los Angeles, in the hopes of molding him into a major star of American movies, on the order of a Humphrey Bogart or a Spencer Tracy. In fact: Jean Gabin has always been known by American film scholars as 'The French Spencer Tracy,' and if you like Tracy—or Humphrey Bogart, or Gary Cooper, or Clint Eastwood—then you'll love Jean Gabin just as much, or maybe even more, because he's cut from the same cloth as those other guys, which is to say that, like them, he's a quiet tough-guy, and he's both quieter and tougher than all of them put together. (This author isn't sure if Tracy and Gabin were actually great friends, but according to a 1946 MGM press release which was issued in connection with the North American release of one of Gabin's French films, 1941's *Remorques,* the two actors were on friendly terms.)

While Gabin has been forgotten by most 'regular' Americans, today (even though he remains beloved throughout the rest of the world), he's still remembered in the United States by your grandmother, by the film studies professor at your local college and, most importantly, by the *couple of thousand moviegoers* who lined up for two Jean Gabin Film Festivals in 2002, which took place simultaneously at the Los Angeles County Art Museum and at the Walter Reade Theatre, in New York.

Okay. *So:*

If what I'm saying is true, and Jean Gabin is as great as Bogart and Tracy, then what's the problem with Americans? Why aren't Gabin's movies, which are just as great as the greatest pictures made by any of the biggest American movie studios, turning up on Turner Classic Movies every day of the week? There are a lot of reasons, but a good one to start off with (and forgive me for sounding academic), relates to the whole concept of 'selective memory,' and it's relationship to popular culture,' and what I mean by this, is: For every once-famous personality from long ago whom we *do* remember, there's always another person, of equal or even greater stature, whom many people have forgotten today. *Example:* Today, admirers of classic movie comedy remember the Marx Bros., the Three Stooges, Abbott and Costello, and Laurel and Hardy, with great fondness. But who (under seventy) remembers Joe E. Brown, the Ritz Brothers, or Wheeler and Woolsey, who were almost as popular as the Marxes and Laurel and Hardy at the U.S. box-office, back in the 1930s and 1940s?

An even bigger reason why Gabin's movies aren't as popular in the U.S. as they continue to be in the rest of the world, is that ninety-three out of the ninety-five feature movies in which Jean Gabin appeared during his incredibly prolific forty-six-year film career, which spanned from 1930 all the way up to his death at the age of seventy-two in 1976, are in *French,* and Americans (at least, this is what Hollywood executives have always told us) just aren't interested in reading subtitles. And it's too bad, too, because most of Gabin's films—in fact, I would even wager to say eighty-three out of Gabin's ninety-five films—are fantastic, and 'regular, old' American moviegoers would love them too, if only they'd have the chance to see them: Every movie star has his good movies and his clinkers, but a whopping 87% of Jean Gabin's movies are great and, for my money, that's the highest good movie-to-bad movie ratio of any other star, in any era, in any country. (Gabin told a television interviewer once, that he felt that he owed a great movie to the people who came to see him, because he knew that the money which his audiences spent at the movie theater to see his movies was hard-earned.)

Relatedly, the small 'boutique' American film distribution companies which have always released foreign language films in the United States (it's been changing for the better over the past few years, but it used to be like this) have mostly always stuck with the pretentious/abstract/'artsy-craftsy' fare—the Kurosawa, Bergman, Antonioni, and Fellini pictures. And Jean Gabin movies are anything but pretentious! They're (mostly, all) fun, engrossing, crowd-pleasing, genre pictures—cop movies, action thrillers, comedies, and hot-blooded romances—the majority of them existing in that same pantheon, both dramatically as well as technically, as anything that's ever emerged from the American studios. In other words, Jean Gabin's movies are definitely the kinds of pictures of which all admirers of great movies deserve to be aware, and one of my (many) hopes for this book, is that it will find its way into the hands of some forward-thinking soul who works for one of those presently-operating American companies which release foreign-language films in the United States, and here, I'm talking about a Rialto, a Magnolia, or a Strand, and that, that person will get so excited about one, two, or, maybe even half-a-dozen movies which he reads about in this book, that he will acquire them for proper theatrical and/or DVD distribution, in the United States. (I can dream, can't I?)

But if I were only writing this book for a tiny audience of movie distribution people, I'd be heavily remiss. This book is for everybody! If you're a young(er) American reader— say, if you're in your twenties or your thirties, and you're only nominally familiar with Gabin (if, in other words, you picked up this book because you've seen him in *La Grande illusion* and you want to learn about what else he did, or if you heard your high school French teacher talking about him, or if you saw the two famous movies for which Gabin continues to be known today in the United States, 1937's double-header of director Julien Duvivier's mind-bogglingly great *film noir Pepe Le Moko*, and director Jean Renoir's intense, anti-war classic *La Grande illusion*)—this book will give you a proper introduction to him because, in this book, I have dedicated individual chapters to each and every one of the actor's ninety-five movies, describing them in great depth, one-by-one and chapter-by-chapter. Since two-thirds of Jean Gabin's movies are currently, at least at the time this book is going to print, unavailable in English-subtitled or English-dubbed versions, these chapters will contain complete, written synopses of each film (as complete as I've been able to make them) and, as you'll see, I have attempted to replicate the tone of each film with my writing style, so that you can feel like you're 'seeing' the films in English, or whatever non-French language in which you happen to be reading this book, even if you haven't seen them at all.

If you're French and you're reading this book, then *bienvenue, mes amis!* (Welcome, friends!) I'm glad you've joined me: Even in Jean Gabin's native France, where there already exist a few great published biographies about Gabin's life, as well as some photo-books, and some books of memories which were written by his kids (*and* a fantastic book consisting of his famous quotes), there has never been a single, solitary book which concentrates solely on his complete, ninety-five-films. And if you're from the myriad other countries where, even today, Gabin continues to be worshipped, celebrated, deified, and propitiated like the god he is, then let me now welcome you in your own indigenous tongues: *Bienvenidos!* (Mexico); *Vitejte!* (Czecholslovakia!); *Bun Venit!* (Romania); *Irashaimasu!* (Japan!) *Witajcie!* (Poland!); *Benvenuti!* (Italy!); *Wilkommen!* (Germany); *Khosh Aamadid!* (Iran!); and *Dobro Pozhalovat* (Russia, the country where they love Jean Gabin so much that, in 1968, according to the April 24ᵗʰ issue of *Variety* that year, they actually offered to buy him his favorite animal, a racehorse, and to ship it to him, directly!) Go to any of the countries I've just mentioned and get a good look at the postcard racks at the local gift shops: I can almost guarantee that you'll see Gabin right up there with other important showbiz figures like Johnny Depp, Elvis, Marilyn Monroe, and—to paraphrase Woody Allen, in *Annie Hall*—the Pope...

As I have mentioned, even though Jean Gabin made movies between 1930 and 1976, he's known in America today mostly for a small group of fantastic movies which he made in the mid-to-late '30s, in which he played movie history's ultimate, 'world-weary, born-having-seen-it-all, working-class, tough-guy/tragic drifter,' and these uniformly excellent pictures all share the same basic storyline: In each picture, Gabin's characters have, almost invariably, committed a murder, or have been *accused* of committing a murder (or have deserted their army posts) before the film has begun and, right after the opening credits have completed themselves, he is already on the run in other parts of France, or in other countries, from the authorities, involving himself in two-fisted adventures while, at the same time, romancing every hot brunette he can get his mitts on. (Just because you're in-hiding, it doesn't mean you can't have fun!) This pre-World War II period also represents the actor's ruggedly-handsome Matinee Idol Cycle, during which the ladies of the world were lining-up at the world's box offices (including in the U.S., where the pictures were released a few years after their French releases) to gawk at him, in the same way in which today, they line up (for example) to see Brad Pitt. In October of 1938, a one-off Jean Gabin fan magazine called *Jean Gabin: Sa Vie/Ses Films* (*Jean Gabin: His Life/His Films*) even hit French newsstands, and its full-color cover is *a real hoot* because, on it, Gabin is holding a woman in his arms, and staring dreamily into her eyes. (It looks, for all the world, like the cover of a *Harlequin Romance* novel.)

What makes Jean Gabin's swarthy, tough guy-character a bit different than his American counterparts—Bogart and Cagney and Cooper—is that, while Bogart and Cagney and Cooper own their own destinies, Jean Gabin is a Frenchman through-and-through, and so his characters, although they are similarly strong, will always ultimately be ruled by, and resigned to, their fates. (If a hot brunette is Gabin's co-star in each of these films, then 'Lady Fate, Herself' can always be seen to be each individual film's third lead.) Relatedly, at the end of each of these pre-WWII Gabin films, Jean Gabin's characters will almost always be killed, jailed, or even worse: In many of the films, the actor's doomed characters will just walk away, alone—tiny, solitary figures (dots, really) in the middle of giant, expansive movie frames which threaten to swallow them up whole, jaunty berets and all.

While Gabin's on-screen persona was always that of a loner (and not just in the films he'd make in the 1930s, but also, in many of the films in which he would appear in the '40s, '50s, '60s, and '70s), they were mostly friendly loners, men who were always living for those rare moments in which they could truly connect with other people. So it's no surprise, then, that in almost all Jean Gabin movies, no matter which decade in which they are made, friendship is the single most important thing in the world and, very specifically, the friendship between men: In forty-six years worth of Jean Gabin movies, the lasting and enduring friendship between men will always be more important than the love between men and fickle (but *always hot*) women because, while the women in Gabin's movies will always try to hurt (and betray, and deceive) him, his male pals never want anything out of him, and they've always (as we say today, in the lamentable argot of our present day) 'got his back.'

When I make a statement like the one I've just made ("Men, good! Women, bad!"), I'm not coming from a misogynistic place: Check out the North American DVD restoration of Jean Gabin's great 1954 crime picture, *Touchez pas au grisbi* (*Don't Touch the Loot*), which was issued by the Criterion Collection, in 2004. In the picture's original French trailer, which has been added to the DVD as an 'extra,' the *gravitasy*-voiced narrator explicitly states the theme of nearly every Gabin movie: "The friendship of men! The fickleness of women! This is the true theme of our times!"

And it's not just anybody who could be Jean Gabin's friend, in real life and in his films: Jean Gabin was a man who did not suffer fools (and for that reason, he was sometimes branded, in the movie world, as being "difficult" and a "complainer"), so if you're a pretentious, pompous, phony hypocrite, stay away! But if you're a 'real' and 'good' and 'nice' person, sit down and have a drink, *mon ami*, because if you have all of those qualities—Jean Gabin Wants You!

The actor was always quiet and reclusive, and he told an interviewer in 1969 (Leon Zitrone, who interviewed him for French television) that he wasn't interested in having too many friends, outside of his children, because he had always found friendship to be debilitating, but he was probably just being surly when he said that, because Jean Gabin always had a lot of great friends who really enjoyed spending time with him and *vice-versa,* and not just the usual farmers and other working people whom he had always claimed to be his compatriots (and he wasn't lying, because they were), but also his lifelong movie friends, those few men whom he believed to be as real, non-phony, non-pretentious, and straight-forward as he was—men like France's great movie stars Fernandel and Lino Ventura, and character actors

Bernard Blier, and Paul Frankeur, as well as Michel Audiard, a genuine cult figure in France who wrote the screenplays for nineteen of Gabin's movies throughout the 1950s, '60s, and '70s. In the same 1969 television interview, Leon Zitrone tells Gabin that the one quality which he has always appreciated about the actor, is that Gabin always seems to have been faithful with his friends, to which Gabin replied that he never had too many, which is why he was always able to be so faithful with them. (And here's a fun-fact about just how tiresome Gabin thought friendship could sometimes be: In later years, when guests came to stay at his home, he'd intentionally put them in guest rooms with short beds, so that they would get uncomfortable and leave, and sooner rather than later!)

––––––––––

And it's not just Gabin's friends who were always trying to protect him from *His Bad Moviefates* either, but also the characters of his neighbors, who were always portrayed, in the pictures, as having emerged from similar, working-class backgrounds, and this is the case even in those movies in which Gabin's characters had actually perpetrated the crimes for which they had been accused. To wit, in a 1936 picture called *Les Bas-fonds* (or in English, *The Lower Depths*), Gabin's character has killed a man. His neighbors know that he has committed the crime only in self-defense, and so they all link arms, forming a human barricade (the French love those things!), to protect him from the long arm of the law.

Another thing which makes Jean Gabin so unique among movie stars, is his *Mona Lisa*-like enigmatic quality: Even at a young age, his face, although it registered the occasional smile (and could very occasionally, even be capable of great joy, *especially* when he was with one of those hot, on-screen brunettes!), was very famously stoic, world-weary, and expressionless, as if he was born 'having already seen it all.' Gabin, on-screen, was always the ultimate quiet reactor, usually permitting the other actors with whom he was sharing his scenes to receive the lion's share of the dialogue, in fact, Gabin was so quiet in most of his movies, that when you watch a Gabin movie, it isn't simply 'washing over you,' because his legendary on-screen quietude is making you, the film's viewer, an active participant in the unfolding drama, and here's what I mean by that: Typically, in most Gabin movies, another character will say something to Gabin's character, and we'll next see Gabin's expressionless reaction shot. He makes no answer, but we always seem to be able to know exactly what he's thinking, as well as what his response would probably be, were he to actually verbalize it, because Jean Gabin was The Ultimate Everyman, and 'his thoughts are our thoughts'—at least, he always wanted his fans to feel that way.

Once in almost every film (and on occasion, even two or three times), however, Gabin would stop being quiet and, very famously, go ballistic, in what critics and audiences have always referred to as being the actor's trademark 'Gabin Outburst-Scene:' This is the scene, in most of Jean Gabin's movies, in which he always made it eminently clear to the other characters that, in spite of his silence, he really knew the score. The Gabin-Outburst is, additionally, the moment in each film in which the actor's characters unleashed their hatred for hypocrisy, not to mention their disdain of everything that was false, pretentious, mean-spirited, and inhumane in the world, in a barrage of invective-spewing, head-shaking, shoulder-bobbing glee, which was, customarily, always punctuated by the equally famous 'Gabin-Scowl' (the most famous grimace in the world), in which his mouth, which was clenched tightly, resembled an upside-down, and lipless, parabola. Even today, on French television, whenever comedians scowl, the audience knows automatically, and without any kind of a verbal set-up or prompt, that those comedians are perpetrating full-on Gabin imitations. Since Gabin always had between one and three big Outburst Scenes in almost every picture (but normally, just one), French audiences believed that these supercharged moments were actually written into his movie contracts but, of course, they were not, and he just performed them because he knew that his audiences expected him to.

In Jean Gabin's movies, female characters (usually, of the *femme-fatale* variety) were always drawn to his patented 'interested indifference' to them (he definitely had his whole, combination 'come hither/go away' *shtick* down to a T), and they would always, rather compulsively, tell his characters their whole life stories, only about three seconds after having just met him, and even after he had already assured them that *he just wasn't interested*. Well, of course he was interested! He only feigned disinterest to make the lovely ladies more interested, and of course (*natch!*) it always worked like a charm.

But of course, the number one thing which always got Gabin's female co-stars attracted to him in the first place, was his rugged (5'10, 170-pound) good looks: When Jean Gabin was at the peak of international stardom (even in the U.S.) back in the 1930s and 1940s, he had, even though his movies were in black and white and you couldn't actually see it, blonde hair—hair which one of his best-known co-stars (and real-life lovers), Michele Morgan, once compared, very favorably, to lush wheat (and, of course, his '*whole-wheat hair*' was set-off by his equally-famous blue eyes). Today, in fact, it is Jean Gabin's eyes which adorn the letterhead of France's Jean Gabin Museum.

While in America, today, Jean Gabin is remembered only for playing that somber tragic drifter-character which I've already described, the fact is, that he mostly only played this character between 1934 and 1944. Between 1930 and 1933, and between 1946 and 1976, he played other kinds of characters, and in more than seventy-five of his ninety-five movies.

In Jean Gabin's fifteen earliest pictures, the ones in which he appeared between 1930 and 1933, when he was between twenty-six and twenty-nine years old, he hadn't yet begun to portray his famously-somber, tough, and moody tragic drifter-character; indeed, in these movies, he was constantly smiley, and even happy-go-lucky. In many of these movies, there was even a moment in which Gabin (who in real life, began his acting career, singing and dancing on the French vaudeville stage) actually stepped out of the dramatic storyline, even when he was playing cops or soldiers, to warble a show-tune in a smoky bar, and yet, very importantly, his characters' ebullient singing never detracted from his tough, masculine image, in fact, 'The Singing Gabin' even enjoyed a number of hit records in his native France in the early 1930s, records which capitalized on, and 'worked synergistically with,' his ever-burgeoning box-office appeal. (In early 1930s France, Gabin was a very early example of entertainment business 'cross-promotion:' His movies promoted his music, and *vice-versa*.)

In 1942, Gabin starred in the only two American films which he would ever make for Hollywood studios and in English, 20th Century-Fox's *Moontide* and Universal Pictures' *The Impostor* (released in 1944), two pictures which copied the tragic drifter-trope of his world's famous classics of the mid-to-late-1930s, however, today, both of these films are unknown in America, the very country in which they were made!

From 1946 through 1976, the final thirty years of his career (agewise, at this point, Gabin was in his own 40s through his 70s), Gabin played a new kind of recurring character, and one which was rooted in his previous, 1934-1944 recurring character: In the movies in which he would star from 1946 on, his persona was still the same, which is to say that Gabin's movie characters remained as quiet and tough as ever, still getting in their usual couple of mercurial Gabin-Outbursts in each picture, but now they were working-class men less frequently: Older now, Jean Gabin would, at this stage of his career, begin playing wealthy, patriarchal, captain-of-industry-types, men who, in most of the pictures, have risen up to power from humble, working-class upbringings. (Because of this fact, the screenwriters of the films would [most of the time, anyway] make sure that Gabin's 'moneyed' characters were usually treating their working-class employees with a great deal of respect.) In others of these post-1946 films, Gabin would, relatedly, begin playing the bad-guy correlates of these wealthy, captain-of-industry characters, namely, 'calm, classy, smoothly-dressed, gentleman gangsters,' men who, just like *The Godfather's* Vito (or Michael) Corleone, treated their disreputable businesses as if they were above-board and respectable. (Today, of course, with companies like Enron and Exxon [and Halliburton, and Arbusto Oil], the line blurs!) In these pictures, Jean Gabin's smooth, Parisian crime bosses usually spent just as much time dousing the fires which had been set by their own crooked and double-dealing underlings, as they did in dealing with the problems which emerged 'from without.' (Read: Problems with the cops!)

While almost all of Jean Gabin's post 1945 efforts (60 of his 95 films) are unknown in the United States today (with three exceptions—1952's *Le Plaisir*, 1954's *Touchez pas au grisbi*, and 1955's *French Cancan*), a number of Gabin's films from this period were, once upon a time, released theatrically in the United States with either English subtitles or English-dubbing, and usually only at one 'art-house' cinema in New York City and, very occasionally, one more, in Los Angeles, as well. Only one or two English-subtitled prints were ever struck of each film, and when the small distribution companies which released the pictures in America went out of business, they would, almost invariably, take the one English-subtitled print ever made with them into oblivion, the result being that most of Jean Gabin's post-World War II movies haven't been seen in English since their initial, *and teeny-tiny, token*, North American releases, forty and fifty years ago. For me, it meant that, when it came time to watch many of the films for this book, I had to rely quite heavily on French language-only DVDs from Europe, which feature no English subtitles or dubbing, at all.

What you notice about Gabin's face in the movies which he'd make when he was getting older (1946 to 1976) is that, while it was never all that expressive to begin with, as he began aging, his famous 'Gabin-Scowl' had become a more or less permanent fixture. (Remember when your mom used to say, "Don't frown, or your face will freeze like that?" That's Gabin!) But Jean Gabin didn't frown one hundred percent of the time: When he smiled—which he tried to do at least once in each picture, no matter what decade in which it was made (and a lot of these smiles usually came when his characters knew they were about to *make it with chicks*), it was always unexpected, so it always lit up the room because, just like with those Gabin-Outbursts, you never knew exactly when the smiles were going to be happening.

And even though Gabin was mostly playing *bourgeois* characters, post World War II, there was occasional overlap: A few times during his older period, he would ditch his characters' expensive boss-togs, in favor of wearing overalls, occasionally, again, playing working-class characters, just like he used to do in the 1930s. In these post-1946 pictures though, his working man-characters weren't usually tragic drifters, as they had been in the pre-World War II pictures, but just solid family men, and frequently, men who, just like his captain-of-industry characters, usually had grown, and often rebellious, kids. (Gabin would play these working-class men only a few times from 1946 on, to remind his beloved French audiences from whence he came, and also to reward them for remaining with him throughout roughly eighty-percent of his career, which, as you'll soon learn, they did, even when, very often, the critics did not.) While Jean Gabin *did* make French movies between 1946 and 1953—twelve in all, in fact—it took nine years, until 1954, before he would become the country's #1 Star again, just as he had previously been, before the War.

In the 1950s and the early 1960s, while Gabin was playing his spate of *bourgeois* men, as well as the very occasional working-class guy, he would additionally start playing a completely new kind of character, and one which he had never played on-screen before: For the first time in his career, and starting in about 1956, Jean Gabin would also begin appearing in a number of truly uproarious, and brilliantly rendered, comedy farces. While a few of Gabin's earliest movies (the ones he made during his First Cycle of films [1930 to 1933, in which his characters were still 'happy,' and hadn't yet become tragic drifters]) were light entertainment, and were often very funny, Gabin was very young when he made them, and in them, he was mostly 'playing it straight.' But in his new 1950s and 1960s comedies, and for the very first time in his career, he would actually begin playing each moment very specifically for the laugh, and would be quite verbose throughout each picture. In his comedies, Gabin always got lots of dialogue, and he was never, for a single moment, quiet. In these fun and funny comedies, Gabin typically played a loud/unruly/boisterously-hilarious voice-of-reason, his non-stop inflammatory harangues always serving to 'call the other characters to the mat,' on their seemingly boundless pretentiousness. (In other words, in Jean Gabin's comedies, the 'Gabin-Outburst' is the entire movie.)

| | |

A COUPLE OF (BRIEF) HOUSEKEEPING NOTES

A S IF YOU HAVEN'T FIGURED THIS OUT, THE TONE OF THIS BOOK IS *LIGHT-HEARTED*. As I've already mentioned, I *hate* academic books which turn movies, the world's most 'fun' medium, into soporific, pedagogical exercises. Gabin's movies are *not* art movies: They're (mostly) fun, engaging crowd-pleasers and so, with that in mind, I have decided to write this book in, if not exactly a fun style, then at least, in a style which you will hopefully find to be non-pretentious. If you think this book is too flippant, *write your own book about Jean Gabin,* and I don't mean that frivolously: One of the reasons I decided to write this book is because, hopefully, it will serve as a jumping-off point for other people to write more books about Jean Gabin, in English or in any other languages where presently there are few (or, even *no*) Gabin books in print.

If you see any mistakes in this book—informational, typographical, or otherwise —they are one hundred-percent mine, and you're very welcome to e-mail me at author@JeanGabinBook.com, and I'll try to correct them for the next edition. Much of the research material I used for this book, including the films, was in French, and I don't speak French (I barely speak English!), so I did the best I could. Also, it is important for me to note, here, that some of the initial VHS versions of Gabin's films which were issued in America back in the 1980s often featured English-subtitled translations which are wildly at odds with the translations that are used in the most current DVD versions— sometimes frustratingly so, because in the case of a few films, the 'old subtitles' seemed to completely re-write some of the films' stories and characters—so I've also tried my best to get the most correct translations.

While I've spent more than six years trying to make this book complete, as far as giving you every bit of information about every movie is concerned, there is, sadly, some information which is today unknown: Specifically, each chapter of this book concentrates on a separate Gabin film and, at the head of each chapter, I have tried to provide you with the names of the important, behind-the-scenes people who worked on each film, including the directors, screenwriters, cinematographers, editors, composers, and art directors but, *alas,* for eleven of Gabin's earliest films, mostly from the early thirties, the names of the films' editors are not mentioned in the film's credits, nor are there any French books which mention who they are; in fact, in one very early Gabin picture, 1931's *Pour un soir..!,* most of the behind-the scenes names associated with the film's production have always been unknown, and are uncredited in the film's opening-title sequence.

Relatedly, at the end of each chapter, I've tried to quote from some original newspaper and magazine reviews which were written by both European and American film critics at the time when the films were first released, so that you can read about what people thought about the films, 'back in the day.' The New York *Times* and the Hollywood trade paper *Variety* reviewed many of Gabin's earliest, 1930s' films, but their critics very often utilized only initials or nicknames ("H.T.S.," "Ravo," "Rick," *etc.*), and for some of these critics, their full names are no longer known—not even by the archivists of The New York *Times* and *Variety,* who were very nice when I bothered them with my constant phone calls and e-mails. In fact, some of the ancient newspaper and magazine reviews from which I've quoted in this book, both European and American, aren't attributed to any authors, at all. (I can only surmise that their publications wanted the writers to be invisible.)

Gabin, age 9.

IV

BIOGRAPHY, PART ONE: 1904 TO 1953

Tragic Drifter

O N MAY 17ᵀᴴ, 1904, JEAN GABIN (A/K/A, THE WORLD'S COOLEST MOVIE STAR) WAS born Jean-Alexis Moncorge to French musical hall performers Joseph Ferdinand Moncorge and his wife Helene Terpse, in Paris' 18ᵗʰ District (on Rochechouart Street) and almost immediately, this youngest of seven children was shuttled over to the family's second residence, a two-story home in the small town of Meriel-Val d'Oise, twenty-two miles north of Paris. (Today, Meriel is home to the *Musee Jean Gabin* [the Jean Gabin Museum].) Joseph and Helene really loved their little boy but, due to their hectic performing schedules, they were usually absent from his life, and so he was raised primarily by his devoted older sister Madeleine, who was fifteen years his senior. (In a 1946 Gabin picture called *Martin Roumagnac,* a project which Jean Gabin initiated, he played the role of a fortysomething construction worker who lives with his older sister, a kindly spinster who's devoted her entire life to taking care of him.) It's possible that young Jean may have even considered Madeleine to be more of a mother to him than his real mother was, because Madeleine was always attentive to him, while Helene was meant to have been very distant, and not just physically (because she was always away, performing on stages throughout France with her husband, but emotionally, as well; a large part of Jean Gabin's Recurring Movie Persona, which we'll be seeing in almost every one of the actor's films is that, while Gabin always comes across as being friendly and likeable whenever he's meeting real and unpretentious people, he is, at the same time, cool and distant, whenever he meets anybody who's fake and pompous. And since Gabin is supposed to have been the same in real-life as he was in the movies, it's possible that he inherited his famous no-b.s. personality from his mother). Gabin's son Mathias Moncorge, who was interviewed for French television by the film historian and television presenter Philippe Labro for a Jean Gabin Special which was aired in 2005, remarked that in his opinion, his father may have been unplanned, or even worse—unwanted.

Madeleine Moncorge loved to paint, and she instilled her younger brother with an appreciation of the arts, even when he was very young. As a child, however, Jean demonstrated more of an interest in the things which all little boys love: In particular, he had soft-spots for soccer (as a grown-up movie star he would, in 1933, take on the role of a soccer player, in a great, D.W. Pabst-directed movie comedy, *Du haut en bas* [*From Top to Bottom*]) and bicycles. (Bikes will appear in all their glory in two Gabin pictures, both of which were made in 1959: *Rue des Prairies* and *Les Vieux de la vieille.* In fact, of Gabin's best boyhood friends from Paris and Meriel—Andre Leducq, Georges Speicher, and Charles Pelissier—would even grow up to be very prominent French bicycle champions.)

Young Jean was also interested, in no particular order, in trains, nature, the military, and boxing, and obviously this is because he was in such close proximity to all of the above. His interest in trains was fostered by the fact that his boyhood home in Meriel was, and continues to be, located directly across from a bustling train station (today, a family from Togo lives there), and he would often spend his evenings staring out of his bedroom window at the passing locomotives, always dreaming of hopping-aboard one of them, and setting off on action-packed adventures. (It didn't exactly hurt that Jean's maternal grandfather, Louis Petit, was a locomotive mechanic/engineer, and little Jean apparently loved nothing more than quizzing the older man about his life on the rails: Yes, even as a child, the peripatetic, roaming life of the railman seemed great and really freeing to young Jean who, as a grownup, would achieve his biggest international movie fame playing peripatetic drifters, men who would never be too long for one place. In two great pictures, 1938's *La Bete humaine* and 1951's *La Nuit est mon royaume*, he would even play train engineers.)

In fact, young Jean much preferred *train-spotting* to hanging around in his teacher Mr. Dervelloy's class, and it's been verified by boyhood friends that he would often spend more time playing hooky from school than he did in actually attending it. The purpose of this planned non-attendance wasn't just because the boy wanted to groove on the passing trains, but also because he always seemed to be wandering around in the woods, commiserating with nature. (Another hallmark of Jean Gabin's personality, both in his movies as well as in his real life, is that he was a man who really loved the land: In fact, as an adult, after he had already become a movie star, he bought an almost three thousand-acre farm in Normandy, and would even play farmers in a couple of pictures.)

In the 1940s, and for about five years, Jean Gabin would, very famously, date Marlene Dietrich, and Dietrich's biographer Charles Higham commented on Jean Gabin's much-vaunted love of farming and nature in his book, *Marlene: The Life of Marlene Dietrich:*

"He [Gabin] loved the bustle of ports, the smell of the sea, the clank of cranes, the roar of locomotives, and the tooting of horns. He loved the land, the fields, [and] the creatures of the land."

Little Jean played so much hooky, in fact, that whoever he happened to be living with at the time, whether it was his parents or his sister, always seemed to be punishing him—even when he was a teen-ager—and his very biggest hooky-infraction of all time seems to have happened in 1916: Europe was now two years into the throes of the First World War, and when French soldiers marched through Meriel, on their way to the front, twelve-year-old Jean often spent his days following them around. Apparently, the soldiers really enjoyed the company of this bright and fearless boy, but Jean's fun days with the fighting men would end,

Gabin, age 5, with his father.

invariably, with the police, who had been summoned by Madeleine, dragging the rebellious boy home. It's not known, today, what specific form his punishments took, but whether he received a *potch* on the *tuchus,* or just a stern chewing-out from *big sis,* he would always, apparently, get through his punishments with a smile, because his friends all idolized him for being ballsy enough to skip school and hang out with the fighting men, while they were all stuck in their hot, cramped, airless classrooms. Just like the rugged individualist characters whom Jean Gabin would one day be playing in the movies, Gabin, as a boy, never did anything less than exactly what he wanted to do, at all times, and damn the consequences.

In 1917, the invading Hun was closing-in on Meriel, and Madeleine reacted by packing thirteen-year-old Jean up, and sending him off to live with Joseph and Helene, in Paris. Still too busy to take care of their boy properly, however, Joseph and Helene sent their teen-aged son off to the Janson de Sailly boarding school and, of course, Jean hated school in Paris, just as much as he did in Meriel.

Jean's mother Helene passed away in February of 1918, when the boy was fourteen years old, and his mother's untimely passing would also mark the end of his relatively brief career as a student. At his father's behest, Jean returned to Meriel, and even though he was now an adolescent, he was still excited about the prospect of having his adoring older sister all to himself, and so it's no wonder that he became enraged at first, when Madeleine announced her engagement to Jean Poesy, a strapping young local boxer. At first, Jean was resentful of their union, Oedipally-feeling that this man would be stealing his sister (who, in effect, was more like his 'mother') away from him. But gradually, Jean really came to like Poesy, who became the 'present' father-figure which his own real father, Joseph, could never be. Poesy was a man whom Jean truly idolized, because he was the only male adult who had ever taken the time to engage in father-and-son-type activities with him, and when Poesy opened up his own training camp for boxers, in Meriel, he also held classes for children and teen-agers, and Jean, who attended them (this is the only kind of schooling he could abide) took to 'the art of *le box*' like a fish to water and, by all accounts, he was very good at it. (In 1954, at the age of fifty, Jean Gabin paid tribute to Jean Poesy, and to the art of pugilism, in a 1954 picture whose production he initiated, called *L'Air de Paris* [*The Air of Paris*] in which, by design, Gabin played a Poesy-like boxing instructor who takes lost, young souls off of the streets, and trains them to be, per the U.S. Army, 'the best they can be!') Teen-aged Jean loved mixing it up in the ring, even in spite of the fact that one of his opponents very famously broke his nose, which is what accounted for what some of Gabin's French biographers have always referred to as being the actor's famous, beaten-up look. Jean wouldn't be training with Poesy for long though because, in the late summer of 1918, Poesy left Meriel to join the army during the waning days of the War, and when he returned to Meriel a few months later, not only was the War over, but so was his boxing career: Poesy had been wounded in battle, and was forced to face the indignities of an amputated leg.

Needless to say, fourteen-year-old Jean, like most young men, or like most *people* of any age, had no idea what he was going to do next. He spent the following two years mixing cement, at twelve francs per day, for a Paris construction company, he marked time as a shop clerk, and he even labored as an office boy in an electrical-supply house. Then, his father Joseph came back into the picture, after years of being 'in and out'—and mostly, *out*. Joseph was in-between performing jobs, and was well-aware that his son, who was quickly becoming a very handsome young man, had a reputation, in spite of always being quiet and even stoic in private, of being a cheerful 'life of the party,' in social situations: Seventeen-year-old Jean, with his thick mane of blonde hair, was a favorite of the girls because, aside from his burgeoning good looks, he had also developed a rather dynamic singing voice and, apparently, he was no slouch in the dancing department, either. So, at this relatively late

Gabin, age 10, with his mother and sisters.

stage of his son's adolescence, Joseph decided to become a stage-dad, valiantly pushing his son toward the inevitable. (In Jean Gabin's best movies, fate will usually be seen to inform the choices which his characters will make, and fate always seemed to have been a pretty important determining-factor in Gabin's real-life, as well.) Of course, Jean, in spite of his talents, still evinced absolutely zero interest in show business, feeling that any man who wore make-up and costumes really wasn't in any position to be calling himself a man; indeed, at this point in his life, Jean entertained only one dream: He wanted to own his own farm (a dream, as I've already mentioned, which he would one day realize, as an adult). Young Jean also had a back-up plan, in case his farmer-daydream didn't work out: He told his friends that he'd settle for being an auto mechanic. ("Anything," he was often heard telling them, "except [for] an actor… or a bureaucrat!")

It's no surprise, then, that at the age of seventeen, in 1921, Jean complained vociferously, the day his father took him down to Paris' famed *Folies-Bergere* Theater, and introduced him to the theater's director, Pierre Frejol, in the ardent hopes that Frejol might offer Jean some (*any*) employment, behind-the-scenes. When Jean arrived at the theater, he changed his negative opinion about a possible career in show-biz almost immediately, because of something that he noticed the second he entered the building:

The place was crawling with women. And many of them were *hot!*

This is the moment when Jean changed his mind, and decided to give show business a fair shake and, aside from the girl factor, it's pretty obvious that he was choosing this course to please his father: Even though Joseph Moncorge wasn't necessarily the nicest or the most available guy around, Jean didn't want to disappoint him and, anyway, as Jean was now rationalizing, "Show business is stupid—but it's easier than the factory…"

Jean spent the next five years of his life at the *Folies,* learning his craft—first, backstage and then, secondly, on-stage, when Frejol began asking him to fill in for some of the minor and (soon) 'major' actors who had taken ill: The creative team at the *Folies* loved Jean so much that, slowly at first, and then more frequently, they began adding him into the cast of one show after another, and his roles began growing larger and larger. Audiences were beginning to take notice.

Only eighteen years old in 1922, Gabin was now playing the fourth, third, and sometimes even second male leads in a number of shows at the *Folies* and, by all accounts, according to newspaper clippings from the time, audiences were already beginning to buzz about him, even during those instances in which he was acting opposite unqualified 'huge' stage-stars like Maurice Chevalier. Gabin, as I'll only be mentioning a few million times throughout this book, was a serious guy and, therefore, it's no end of funny that he, a guy who would eventually make his name in movies by playing movie history's most famous 'quiet, tragically-fated tough guy,' would begin his show business career, singing and dancing on the stage.

When you're talking about the theater in 1920s'-Paris, what you're really talking about is *operetta*—a/k/a, comedy interspersed with showtunes. (It's a genre of theater which mutated, in the U.S.A., into 'musical comedy.') Very quickly, other theater companies outside of the *Folies-Bergere* now began enlisting Jean to lend his uniquely-charismatic and insouciant *elan* to their own productions: At the *Bouffes-Parisiens* (today, it remains one of Paris's premiere theaters [it's on Rue Monsigny, near the Champs d'Elysee, and many of France's 'big, important plays' continue to open there]), in December of 1923, Gabin impressed the theater's director, the playwright Albert Willemetz, to such an extent that, at the age of nineteen, he even played Maurice Chevalier's young sidekick in a popular attraction called *"La-Haut"* (*"The Top"*), in which horny bachelor Chevalier winds-up at the Pearly Gates before his time, and Gabin's young, handsome *Saint Peter* (!) allows him to return to earth, but only on the condition that Chevalier's character will 'bring him along for the ride.'

(How the play shapes up, is: Chevalier and Gabin pose, on earth, as aviators and they, very promptly, begin working their way through all of Paris's pert, young *wimminfolk*.) Jean's next *Bouffes-Parisiens* outing was a 1923 musical by Yves Mirande, Maurice Yvain, and Lucien Boyer called "*Les Dames en decolette*," in which he played the small but meaningful role of the handsome, young bartender whom all of the ladies in the play craved. (Think: Tom Cruise in *Cocktail*, circa 1923.) "*Decolette*" is the story of a wealthy young widow who's afraid that her new fiancé, a high-ranking government official (who also happens to be the son of a prominent judge), will be calling off their wedding, because of her fiscal irresponsibility: She was apparently quite wealthy at one time in her own right, but her scheming business manager gambled-away all of her money, and her only remaining possession in the entire world, was the cleavage-revealing dress of the play's title. The *Folies-Bergere's* Pierre Frejol attended a performance of "*Decolette*" with Jean's father Joseph and, during the performance, Frejol apparently leaned over to Joseph and whispered, "To be a successful actor, you need to be good at acting, singing, and dancing—and your son is brilliant at all three." It is at the *Bouffes-Parisiens* that Gabin would meet, and fall in love with (and also perform with, in two big shows, "*La Nouvelle revue de RIP*" and "*L'Amour a Paris*") a young actress by the name of Camille Basset who, like Jean, would soon be enjoying a pretty great film career of her own a few years later, when she changed her name to *Gaby* Basset.

After seven years at the *Folies*, at the *Bouffes-Parisiens,* and also at a third theater, the *Vaudeville*, Gabin (it should go without saying) had really grown, in spite of his initial resistance to it, to love both acting and actors. But as much as he loved performing for audiences, he loved his country just that much more (which is why today, in the 21st century, the French people continue to love Jean Gabin, right back), and even though France was currently in between wars, he felt like he would be happier serving his country; and so it was that, in 1924, twenty-year-old Jean Gabin enlisted in the French Navy, where he put in a year's service as an officer's steward, in Brittany (France's major port in the northwest, on the English Channel) and after his release about a year later, he would marry Gaby Basset, and return to the Paris stage. This period of Gabin's life is of particular importance because, for the first time, the actor was billing himself on stage, *not* as 'Moncorge,' which is what he had been doing since the beginning of his career, but under the stage name which had always been used by his parents, 'Gabin.' (According to Jean Gabin's daughter Florence, in correspondence with this author, the name Gabin is a French-derivation of the name of the Catholic Saint *Gabinus* who, in life, was a priest and a Roman noble. Gabinus, who was the brother of the twenty-ninth Pope, St. Caius, was murdered in Sardinia in 296 A.D. by the bloodthirsty Emperor Constantine, a tyrant who enjoyed killing all of the Christians who wouldn't join his armies because fighting, for any reason, was against their beliefs. Today, St. Gabinus is honored once a year on his Feast Day, every February.)

March of 1925 found Jean, who was now 21, lighting up the stage of the *Bouffes-Parisiens* once again, in the enticingly-titled confection, "*Trois jeunes filles neues*" ("*Three Young Nude Girls*"), which was written by Yves Mirande, Raoul Moretti, and Albert Willemetz. In this play, his character, a sailor-on-leave (therein lies trouble!), falls in lust with the hottest of four sisters, all of whose names begin with the letter 'L' (!)—four sisters, whose mother has handed them all over to a shady priest for their education, although behind her back, *the horny cleric* has really been training them to be nightclub strippers! After this popular show ended its run, Jean packed Gaby up, and the two of them headed-off for a year in South America, where they became part of an itinerant theater troupe: In the 1920s, scores of wealthy westerners (Frenchmen, Englishmen, and Americans) were living high-on-the-hog in Venezuela, Colombia, Peru, and Brazil, because there was a great deal of money to be made in that part of the world from the mining of coal, copper, nickel, uranium and (everybody's favorite mineral) *bauxite,* and theater troupes who spoke their languages were needed to keep them all entertained; for Jean Gabin, this meant doing a lot of what was supposed to have been his pretty mean Maurice Chevalier imitation!

When Gabin and Basset returned to Paris in 1928, Gabin was immediately signed to appear on stage opposite fifty-six year-old Mistinguett (she was born Jeanne Bourgeois, in 1872), France's mega-famous lady-singer at Paris's famous *Moulin Rouge* theater. Mistinguett was the bold n' brassy diva who was, in effect, the Cher/Bette Midler/Mae West of her time, an ageless woman who performed bawdy songs and lusty ballads while adorned in oversized headdresses and exotic costumes, all the while flirting with the actor who played her young servant boy, Jean Gabin, who at twenty-four, was more than thirty years her junior. The play in which they performed together was called "*Paris que tourne*" ("Paris, When It Turns") and, luckily for us, much of it was actually recorded for posterity. The big show-stopping duet which they performed together in that show, a song called "*On m'suit,*" ("Follow Me"), became a hit record in France, and continues to be available today on a variety of 'The Best French Music of the Past' CDs, along with many of the other songs from the show which Mistinguett and Jean Gabin performed together. (Indeed, Mistinguett kept performing right up until her death at the age of eighty-three, in 1955.)

1929 began with Jean turning in more than four hundred performances, at the *Bouffes-Parisiens*, of yet another exceedingly popular stage musical, "*Flossie,*" by Marcel Gerbidon, in which a young French girl travels to Britain with her father—a priest—and falls in love with William (Gabin), a British (!) bartender. (Whenever play producers needed a handsome young guy to play a bartender, they always turned to Gabin!) During the run of this show, Gabin became enmeshed in a torrid affair with the play's lead, Jacqueline Francell, and needless to say, this affair didn't sit too well with Jean's wife Gaby Basset, who dissolved their marriage in 1931, although Gabin and Basset would continue to be lifelong friends. (In fact, in a lot of the later movies in which an older Gabin would star in the 1950s and 1960s, he'd always make sure that the producers would hire Gaby, whenever they had a supporting role for 'an older woman' to fill. Usually, she was called on to play Gabin's matronly chambermaid, a gesture which she apparently always took in bemused good spirits.)

In July of 1930, Jean Gabin would appear in his final stage operetta, "*Arsene Lupin, le banquier,*" in which he played the role of a young general. *Lupin* was the well-received musical

Gabin performed in vaudeville with the legendary Mistinguett.

version of author Maurice Leblanc's eponymous legendary gentleman bandit/French Robin Hood-character, an all-time-favorite pulp character in France, who has appeared in more than twenty-five novels, and who remains as popular in France today as Sir Arthur Conan-Doyle's Sherlock Holmes is, in all of the various English-speaking countries. (A new *Arsene Lupin* movie was even made in France in 2004, and it co-starred Kristin Scott-Thomas, Romain Duris, and 'Bond girl' Eva Green.) The song which Gabin made famous in the play, "*Quand on a ça,*" ("When You've Got It") was recorded (by him), and it became a big hit, introducing the actor to 'the rest of France'—to people far away from Paris, who couldn't make the trip to Paris, to see shows. (Like "*On m'suit,*" the song which Gabin had recorded with Mistinguett, "*Quand on a ça*" surfaces today, very frequently, on CD compilations of old French music.)

Even though Jean Gabin was, at this point in his life, becoming known throughout France for captivating audiences in his second and third male-lead roles in musicals, and for his songs from those musicals, he was now growing tired of all of the singing and dancing, and longed to lend his talents to more serious (read: more dramatic and more challenging) fare, but he couldn't, because there simply wasn't any: In the 1920s (and just like today) legitimate theater throughout the world gleaned most of its profits, not from serious drama (in other words, from Shakespeare and Mamet), but from giant, overly-produced musicals and spectacles. (*Cats, Hairspray,* or '*Les Miz,*' anyone?) But, then, fate suddenly threw Jean Gabin a very interesting curve-ball: While the Paris stage was unable to offer Jean anything 'serious,' a pretty new (three years old, at this point) entertainment medium, '*talking movies,*' could:

THE FILMS, 'CYCLE ONE'
1930 — 1933. Film Nos. 1 to 15: On the Verge of Stardom.

RAYMOND DANDY (WHO WAS BORN RAYMOND FRAU) WAS A PROMINENT, BAGGY-PANTS vaudeville comedian who had appeared with Gabin in an assortment of stage productions throughout the 1920s, and when a French film director, Michel du Lac, starred Dandy in two short films—the first was called *Ohe! Les Valises* (a/k/a, *L'Heritage de Lilette*), and the second, *Les Lions* (a/k/a, *On demande un dompteur* or, in English, *I Demand a Trainer*)—the laughmaker personally requested Jean Gabin to be his co-star/straight-man. (Gabin does *not* appear, as it has sometimes been reported, in a third short, director/actor Charles Vanel's 1932 effort, *Le Coup de minuit.*)

Ohe! Les Valises and *On demande un dompteur* have both, like more than half of the movies which were made throughout the world, prior to 1950, been lost to the ravages of time, however Raymond Dandy's grandson, Laurent Frau, illuminated this author as to the plots of these two productions:

"*On demande un dompteur* is the [1930 film version] of one sketch from the popular 1929 stage-review in which Gabin and Dandy had both appeared at the Moulin Rouge Theatre, '*Allo... Ici Paris.*' In both the play and the film, a circus places an advertisement in the want ads, seeking a lion trainer. Several people, including Gabin, present themselves for the job. Each potential applicant enters the lion's cage and each one, in turn, leaves, sporting torn clothing. Dandy is the last one into the cage. Human screams mixed with frightening lion-roars are heard, and when he emerges from the cage a few moments later with his chewed-up clothes, he's carrying a sign which reads, '*On demande un dompteur!*' ['We need a trainer!'] Apparently, this bit received big laughs, both in its stage and film versions.

"All that is known about the second Dandy-Gabin short, *Ohe! Les Valises!,* is that it takes place in the kitchen of a restaurant..."

One of France's biggest feature film producers, Bernard Natan, saw the two short films, and took immediate notice of young Gabin. In 1929, Natan had taken control of France's biggest film production company, *Pathe-Freres* (Pathe Brothers), from the company's surviving member, sixty-seven-year-old Charles Pathe (Charles' brother, Emile, had already passed away), rechristening the operation as Pathe-Natan; and now that sound movies had arrived with the international release of Al Jolson's *The Jazz Singer*, Natan has a vested interest in discovering a hearty French leading man who could bring women into the cinemas—somebody who could go head-to-head with that first wave of handsome, new leading men who were populating the first American sound movies, films which, at the time, were very popular in France. (These 'Yank-thesps' included Paul Muni, Frederic March, Douglas Fairbanks, Jr., George Raft, and Clark Gable.) Natan recognized twenty-six-year-old Jean Gabin's potential and, as luck would have it, Gabin had just rejected a contract from a German film company which had been lobbying for his services. (Gabin, who was a patriotic Frenchman to the core, had no desire to work in Germany, or anywhere else in the world, for that matter.) And so it was that, in 1930, Jean Gabin signed a one-picture contract with Pathe-Natan, and Bernard Natan immediately starred him alongside Gaby Basset, his soon-to-be ex-wife, in the actor's very first feature film, a musical comedy called *Chacun sa chance* (*Everybody Gets His Chance*), in which Gabin's character, a charming, head-in-the-clouds haberdashery clerk, spends the week dreaming of Friday nights, because Friday is the one night each week when he gets to blow off steam, by heading off to the local theatres to watch performances of his favorite kind of theater—*operetta!* In *Chance*, which was not only Jean Gabin's first feature film, but also his very first film as a leading man, he hadn't yet developed his trademark world-weariness (he'd add that into his bag of tricks in the movies which he would make when he was France's #1 Movie Star, between 1934 and 1941). On the contrary, in these, Jean Gabin's first fifteen movies, audiences across France were really beginning to enjoy him even though he wasn't yet 'super-famous,' and in them, he'd even (frequently) burst into ecstatic song.

Even before *Chacun sa chance* was released in France in December of 1930, French movie executives who had already previewed the film were so impressed with Gabin, that they immediately signed him to appear as either the first, second, or third (or seventh, in the case of a 1931 movie called *Coeur de lilas*) male lead, in more movies, and were responding to him for the same reason that audiences had already been enjoying him on the stage: Namely, Gabin could sing, dance, and act and, most importantly, he could 'scale it down' for the movies, a more intimate medium in which actors didn't need to project as much as they had to do, in the theater. Women who attended screenings of *Chacun sa chance* responded to Gabin's dreamy eyes. (Just like how American movie fans today deify Bette Davis' legendary eyes, so, too, have the French always lionized Gabin's *'yeux bleus,'* in fact, today, written correspondence from the Gabin Museum in France always arrives on letterhead which displays *only* Jean Gabin's eyes.)

A four-part, two-hour-and-forty minute detective serial, which was also released as a long feature film, 1931's *Mephisto*—in which Jean Gabin's cheerful, young Detective-character solves the crime, while actually warbling a whimsical song called (I kid you not), "I Love Fat Ladies" (!!!)—followed *Chacun sa chance,* and after *Mephisto,* the actor began toiling in the service of an impressive roster of young, soon-to-be-famous film directors who were coming up during the same time period during which Gabin was making his own cinematic ascendancy, including Jacques Tourneur (the future director of America's classic 1941 horror feature *Cat People,* and of 1946's velvety-smooth Robert Mitchum-Jane Greer *noir, Out of the Past*), as well as the young Anatole Litvak, a man who, one decade later, would become one of America's great 'house directors' for the major studios. (House directors were those guys who were equally adept at making great movies in any genre, and they were always on-call, from the heads of the various major studios; in 1948, Litvak would churn-out both Olivia de Haviland's mental-hospital classic *The Snake Pit* as well as the tense Barbara Stanwyck/ Burt Lancaster *noir, Sorry Wrong Number.*) In Litvak's February 1932 release, *Coeur de Lilas* (Gabin's ninth picture in only two years, and one in which the actor played a supporting role as a tough-as-nails nightclub bouncer), we see, for the first time, that Gabin had already developed one of his most known physical trademarks: In *Lilas,* Jean Gabin's face (although in this early part of his movie career, it would still produce the more-than-occasional smile, laugh, and even *show-tune*) had now, without warning, begun its metamorphosis into it's famous, world-weary mask, a mask which usually happened to have an omnipresent cigarette dangling from it. (Jean Gabin, beside being moviedom's *World's Coolest Movie Star of All Time*, was also a fond practitioner of France's greatest second greatest sport after bicycle racing, *cigarette-smoking,* a compulsion which would contribute to his death in 1976, at the relatively early age of seventy-two.)

1933: On November 20th of that year, just when Jean Gabin was on the verge of becoming France's first mega-watt movie superstar, he married the second of his three wives, Jeanne Mauchain, a stripper who lost her laundry nightly at the Casino of Paris, where she danced under the pseudonym of 'Doriane' (and if you want to know what Jean's father Joseph thought about his son's having just married a stripper: Three days before Jean married Jeanne, Joseph Gabin was found dead in an armchair, of a massive heart attack). Jeanne was as intelligent and as strong-willed as Gabin himself was, and their marriage, as hot, sexy, and tempestuous as it was, was also fraught with arguing—not to mention, with both sides frequently hurling invectives, and heavy objects, at each other.

THE FILMS, 'CYCLE TWO'
1934 — 1941, Film Nos. 16 to 31: The Tragic Drifter Cycle.
Gabin's movies during this period make him famous, for a brief time, even in the United States.

GABIN'S SIXTEENTH PICTURE, DIRECTOR MARC ALLEGRET'S 1934 *ZOU ZOU*, IN WHICH he co-starred with the legendary African-American entertainer Josephine Baker (who had moved to France to jump-start the career which had been flagging in her own unappreciative [read: *racist*] home-country) would begin what I've characterized in this book, as being the mega-important 'Second Cycle' of Jean Gabin's five-cycle movie career, the stage in which he shifted from being the happy-go-lucky/light comedy-guy (the character whom he had portrayed in his first fifteen pictures) to being the working-class, world-weary, tragic-drifter-character who would capture the world's imagination. In this series of fifteen French movies, many of which are dark and depressing, and in which Gabin starred between 1934 and 1941, he made five of the eight movies for which he continues to be known in the United States today, and in this cycle of films, the storyline is always pretty much the same: Gabin typically plays a character who has committed a crime (or else, he plays a character who has been accused of committing a crime, *or* a character who has deserted his military post) before the film began. He knows fate has dictated that he'll soon have to die and so, on the way to his characters' inevitable conclusions, he'll always be romancing hot brunettes, and engaging in pulse-pounding adventures. And as each of these films end, he'll always (if his characters are still alive, that is) 'go quietly,' whether his characters have committed the crimes for which they have been accused, or not. Most of Gabin's 1934-to-1941 films were part of a style of French cinema known as 'Poetic Realism,' and Jean Gabin was more closely identified with this mid-to-late 1930s' French film movement than any other actor in his country, so much so, in fact, that many critics at the time even referred to him as The King of Poetic Realism. Poetic Realism is exactly what it sounds like, and its chief filmmakers, all of whom would be directing Gabin during this period (principally, Jean Renoir, Julien Duvivier, Marcel Carne, and Jean Gremillon), utilized this style, to portray the dark poetry of everyday life, and to deal, in a frequently unblinking manner, with the trials and tribulations of working-class characters, often elevating these characters to mythical status.

Whenever a country is enduring difficult times, that country's cinema usually reflects it, becoming similarly dark (Expressionism in Germany; Neo-Realism in Italy; *film noir*, in America), and French Poetic Realism is a visual style of filmmaking which emerged in France in the mid-to-late 1930s, in answer to any number of problems which the country happened to have been facing, during that point in time: If Jean Gabin's on-screen characters from the 1930s always seem to have been resigned to their cruel fates, then so, too, during that decade, as historians have always been quick to point out, was France, as a country, resigned to her own: In 1931, France had finally started feeling the effects of America's 1929 stock market crash (a bit later than the rest of the industrialized nations of the world), and tens of thousands of Frenchmen were unemployed. France was the only country in Western Europe which, at that time, hadn't yet turned fascist, and with Hitler's ascendancy as Chancellor of Germany in 1933, they could feel it coming, but weren't ready to deal with it: According to author J.B. Duroselle, in his outstanding French-language book which covers that decade, *La Decadence* (1979), even in the early 1930s, France was still reeling from the heavy losses which it had sustained during the First World War, and the French just didn't want to fight anymore. (Many historians maintain that the French had a defeatist attitude during this period, but really, this collective national attitude was not defeatist in nature, so much as it was *pacifist:* The French just didn't want any of their own people to get hurt anymore—and that's an ideal, to which we can all aspire!) Regular French citizens, according to Duroselle, felt helpless and transitional, never knowing what to expect next, and it was these dark, insecure feelings, which manifested themselves in the kinds of movies which the country made in the 1930s. Jean Gabin's recurring tragic-drifter character, in his very dark and pessimistic series of 1934-to-'41 films, is considered to be 'the living embodiment' of France's own 1930s' darkness.

So when I'm talking about the difference between Humphrey Bogart's and Jean Gabin's recurring on-screen characters, what I'm really talking about, is a basic historic difference between America and France: America, of course (from 1776, and right up through this year's Super Bowl), has always been 'all about the winner;' Americans (to paraphrase George C. Scott, paraphrasing George S. Patton) will not tolerate defeat, and the French meanwhile, while they too have always been a strong people, just like their famous countryman, Jean Gabin, have sometimes, throughout the course of history, had to surrender some of their freedoms, in order to avoid losing all of them.

Many of Poetic Realism's greatest movies were even written, or co-written, by an actual, verse-spewing poet, France's legendary (unofficial) poet-laureate, Jacques Prevert, who doubled as one of France's great screenwriters. The most concise way to describe the film movement known as Poetic Realism, is to use one of Prevert's best lines of dialogue from the 1939 Jean Gabin classic which he co-wrote with Jacques Viot, *Le Jour se leve*: "When reality is grim… dreams help."

———————————————

Gabin followed *Zou Zou* up with a 1935 picture called *Maria Chapdelaine*, which was his first *ultra*-major hit in France, and *Chapdelaine* represented the first time that movie audiences were actually queuing up outside of cinemas very specifically to see a Jean Gabin picture: *Chapdelaine* garnered the *Grande Prix du Cinema* (France's Best Movie of the Year award), and when his character, a steely fur-trapper, died at the end of the movie, some audience members apparently became distraught, really feeling as though they had lost a close friend. (Because Gabin always dies or gets arrested at the end of his Poetic Realism pictures, there was always a rumor that his movie contracts stated his characters had to be 'ill-fated,' something which the actor always denied very categorically, throughout his life.) Author Remi Fournier Lazoni, in his 2002 book *French Cinema*, has provided some insight into *France's Big Gabin Phenomenon*, when he claims that one huge reason for Gabin's super-popularity with European audiences in the 1930s is that, at that point in time, Gabin was the only European movie actor to be routinely photographed in Hollywood-style close-ups: Close-up camera shots of any actor's face, as any pretentious first-semester film school student will tell you, engender an audience's familiarity with the actor on screen, since the audience, in being able to see right up the actor's nostrils, presumes to be able to tell what the actor on-screen is thinking. Most European movies from the 1930s, before Gabin arrived on the scene, were filmed with the camera positioned far away from the actors, in long master shots, and audiences identified with the friendly-looking Gabin so much, that old French movie magazines from the time have referred to him, variously, as 'The People's Star,' 'The Proletarian Star,' 'The Man of the People,' and even (this author's personal favorite), 'The King of France.' And this is not mere hyperbole: In the mid-to-late thirties, at the height of Gabin's brand-new French mega-popularity, people loved him and treated him like a real king, as if beneficent monarchy had been restored to France, right under everybody's nose. But while, to paraphrase Mel Brooks, "it's good to be the king," Jean Gabin always (and not just in his movies, but in real life as well) remained 'down-to-earth,' preferring, in his adulthood just as he did when he was a child, the company of 'real,' working-class people (and especially *farmers*) to that of celebrities, although he did have a few good celebrity friends whom he would keep throughout his life. On that same note, the French actress Nadia Gray, who would appear opposite Gabin in a 1953 melodrama called *La Vierge du Rhin*, directed and narrated a one-hour documentary about him for French television in 1978, in which she stated that, in her opinion, "… Jean Gabin was an anti-intellectual intellectual—a man who read and who knew a great deal but who, nevertheless, preferred the friendship of everyday country people, over pretentious geniuses."

In 1935, Gabin took on a small, supporting role, for his *Maria Chapdelaine* director Julien Duvivier, in a Biblical picture called *Golgotha*, the big-screen's very first ever sound movie about Jesus made in any language, and in this movie, the actor played the role of Pontius Pilate. (*Golgotha* represents the only time in his early career, in which Jean Gabin would play a small supporting role, appearing in only seven scenes, as a favor to his friend Duvivier, and obviously to bolster the box-office of what otherwise might have been considered to be a turgid costume drama.) After this, Gabin re-teamed with Duvivier for a third time, to appear in *La Bandera*, in which the actor played the leading role which would establish him, for all time, as a romantic adventure-hero in which Gabin's usual 'tragic-drifter Frenchman-character' escapes to Spain, joining the Spanish Foreign Legion, with some pretty harrowing results, namely: Gabin, unable to escape from his Fate, gets killed at the end of the picture. After *La Bandera*, Gabin and Duvivier re-teamed yet again, for a wonderful ensemble comedy called *La Belle equipe*, a film about five friends who win the lottery, and *La Belle equipe* is one of the many Gabin films which illustrated, just like a lot of the actor's movies did, that the friendship between men is often more honest, and more lasting, than love affairs between men and women. And after appearing in these films, Gabin teamed-up for the first of four pictures which he would make—three in the 1930s, and one more, in the 1950s—with the director who has always been considered to be Poetic Realism's great humanist of all, Jean Renoir. Renoir's Poetic-Realist movies, while they were almost as depressing as every other directors' Poetic Realist movies, were always, at the same time, a bit more uplifting than the other directors efforts, because Renoir's movies, in particular, always concentrated on the inherent goodness of all people, and the first Renoir/Gabin collaboration was a contemporary adaptation of Maxim Gorky's 1902 Russian play, *Les Bas-fonds* (*The Lower Depths*). And even though, at this point in time, Gabin had already begun earning a lot of money as a movie star, he always considered himself to be a real, working-class fellow, aand so initially, he was hesitant to work with Renoir, whom he believed to be, and to carry himself like, an aristocrat. The two men would ultimately become great, lifelong friends though, each man, apparently, always trying to impress, or 'one-up,' the other, and it didn't exactly hurt that Jean Renoir happened to be the son of the painter Auguste Renoir, whose works Gabin had always admired, in fact, when Gabin started earning his big movie salaries, in the mid-'30s, the first fine-art piece which he ever purchased, was an Auguste Renoir painting. Apparently, throughout the forty years of their friendship, which continued until Renoir's death in 1971, Gabin always demonstrated a special fondness for, as the Brits say, 'taking the piss' out of his good friend, usually addressing Renoir—and this must be some kind of a 'Gabinian Term-of-Endearment' (although, truthfully, it's hard to tell what was so endearing about it), as "the fat one."

In 1937, Gabin next starred in the two French/Poetic Realist classics for which, even today, he continues to be the most known in America—Duvivier's *Pepe Le Moko,* and Renoir's *La Grande illusion. La Grande illusion* was the very first non-English-language film to receive a nomination for the Best Picture Oscar at 1938's American Academy Awards ceremony, and although the picture lost-out to director Frank Capra's charming Jimmy Stewart/Jean Arthur comedy, *You Can't Take it With You,* its nomination turned out to be wonderful publicity, because when the picture was released in America in '38, it ran for an unheralded (for a foreign film, anyway) six months at what was, at that time, New York City's premiere art-house cinema, the Filmarte. In 1938, too, American critics uniformly hailed *Illusion* as being the year's best foreign film, and the twin successes of *Pepe Le Moko* and *La Grande illusion* led to three more of Gabin's late-1930s' movies performing spectacularly at America's few art-house cinemas—*La Bete humaine, Quai des brumes,* and *Le Jour se leve.* For a brief period, in the late thirties through the early-to-mid forties, Jean Gabin's name was actually being bandied-about by sophisticated Americans, just like the names of any other important personalities in the arts.

In France, *La Grande illusion* was already 1937's #1 box-office champ, its success establishing Gabin, who had already been France's biggest movie star since 1935's *Maria Chapdelaine,* as something more than just an important figure: The picture made him an *icon.*

In fact, Jean Gabin was so popular in France during the late 1930s that, at that particular point in time, he was the only movie star in the entire world who was able to pick his own directors, screenwriters, and even film projects, because in America, stars wouldn't be enjoying that much power for at least another decade; in the Hollywood of the 1930s, even the biggest stars, whether we're talking about Bogart or Bette Davis, were forced to appear in whatever productions the studios told them to appear in, and if they didn't, they faced suspension from their contracts and, even worse, outright dismissal. In fact, fashioning himself after the rebellious characters whom he had often played in his movies, Gabin always went out of his way to pick other rebels to work with, and this is how, during this same period of his intense worldwide fame, he began his long association with director Marcel Carne and

Carne's preferred screenwriter, Jacques Prevert, the team which would guide Gabin through two of the actor's best and darkest Poetic Realist classics of the late '30s, 1938's *Quai des brumes* (*The Port of Shadows*) and 1939's *Le Jour se leve* (*Daybreak*). Carne and Prevert, who are recognized today as being two of France's greatest filmmakers, weren't exactly popular when Gabin hired them and, in fact, when he put them on the payroll, they were actually considered to be box-office poison: In 1937, that banner year during which Gabin made both *Pepe Le Moko* and *La Grande illusion,* Carne and Prevert were busy making a movie of their own, *Le Drole de drame* (literally, in English, *The Comedy in Drama*), an 18th-century-set costume drama which critics today consider to have been ahead of its time, because it was one of the first movies ever made to traffic in what elitist movie critics have always referred to as being 'genre-subversion.' In other words, *Drole de drame,* which was released in a couple of U.S. art-house theatres as *Bizarre, Bizarre,* was one of the first movies ever made which played with audience expectations regarding what an audience thought it should be seeing in a dramatic picture: *Drole de drama* was a crime film in which nobody tried to solve the crime, and French audiences who saw the movie were apparently so infuriated that, at one Paris cinema in particular, enraged viewers are reported to have torn bolted-down chairs out from the floorboards, actually hurling them right through the windows of the projection booth!

Aside from being able to make any movie he wanted, Gabin could naturally, at this point in time, also *make any woman he wanted* and, in the 1930s and 1940s, this meant that he was able to engage in torrid affairs with two of his most beautiful co-stars—Mireille Balin, with whom he had already starred in two films, including *Pepe Le Moko,* as well as the striking Michele Morgan, with whom he would co-star in four movies. Morgan truly loved Gabin but, as you might expect, all of this extra-curricular dating didn't sit too well with Gabin's wife, Jeanne 'Doriane' Mauchain, who had been married to him since 1933, and so in September of 1939, the couple divorced, and *talk about why you should always get a pre-nup:* Gabin wound-up having to pay Mauchain the kingly sum of sixty million francs, which was, at that time, the largest divorce settlement in the history of the French Republic. (The only other set-back to Gabin, during this period of his biggest international fame, came in the fall of 1939: When Hitler invaded Poland on September 1st of that year, France thought it would be next country to fall, and during the shooting of Gabin's final Poetic Realist epic, director Jean Gremillon's *Remorques,* or in English *Tugboats,* the actor was conscripted into the French Navy for the first time since 1924, for a period of six months. In the early spring of 1940, when Gabin was released from his seagoing duty, he was able to complete his filming on *Remorques,* which meant that the film did not see release in France until 1941.)

Because Jean Gabin was the most popular movie star in France, and because several of his French movies were doing considerably well at U.S. art-houses, it was only natural that executives at a number of the big American movie studios were now beginning, like the Pathe company's Bernard Natan a decade before, to take notice: In particular, 20th Century-Fox's President, Daryl F. Zanuck, believed that he could fashion Gabin into a big leading man for American-made/English-language movies, a 'hunk' on the order of a Clark Gable. But Jean

Gabin evinced absolutely zero interest, believing that there was no reason for him to venture to America, where he would be just another cog in the Hollywood Studio Talent Stable, albeit an extremely highly-paid one, when he was already the #1-biggest movie star in his own country, although fate, just like it always seemed to do in his movies, would ultimately wind up making the decision for him: When the Nazis invaded France in July of 1940, the invading Germans didn't merely cripple the French government, but they also, under the watchful eye of Hitler's Minister of Propaganda, Josef Goebbels, took over the day to day operations of the French movie business, because Hitler was exceedingly worried about anti-German sentiment getting cranked out of French cameras. And so it was that Gabin, and a great many other members of Western Europe's film community, all of them acting in opposition to the Nazis, headed to America at the beginning of 1941, seeing the land of the free as representing their only hope of continuing to work in the movies. Ethically, Jean Gabin felt that he couldn't remain in France during this uncertain period, and other film professionals who moved to the U.S. when he did, included some of the men who had directed him in the French pictures which he had made throughout the 1930s, principally, Julien Duvivier, Jean Renoir, Anatole Litvak, and Jacques Tourneur. Just like in 1930, Gabin was now, as 1941 was beginning, offered a rather lucrative film contract by a German film company, Continental Films, but he turned the offer down flat, in reluctant favor of trying America on for size.

Of course, in order to actually *get* to Hollywood, Gabin and his Nazi-defiant film-industry compatriots had first to sail to New York, but because the Germans had already taken over the port at Brest, which was the mooring-place of all of the big U.S.-bound ships, they were all forced to set-sail from Portugal. When Gabin arrived in New York in February of 1941, he carried with him only a few of his favorite possessions—his racing bike, an accordion, and three paintings, one by Jean Renoir's father, Auguste, a second (a pastoral piece) by Maurice de Vlaminck, and a third by the Impressionist, Alfred Sisely. Apparently, Gabin's bulky racing bike caused no end of problems, when he tried to squeeze it through the turnstiles at Ellis Island's narrow immigration area!

Daryl Zanuck, in his majestically appointed office 'The Z Room,' quickly introduced Gabin, at Gabin's own request, to the actor's favorite American director, Howard Hawks, who was placed in charge of grooming Gabin, and of Americanizing Gabin's tragic-drifter screen persona which the actor had been playing in his most of his recent French films. (Nine years earlier, in 1932, Gabin had starred in *La Foule hurle*, a scene-for-scene and shot-for-shot French remake of Hawks' American-made, James Cagney race car picture from that same year, *The Crowd Roars*.) But because no film projects were immediately forthcoming, Gabin spent much of 1941 *just hanging out*, and usually, at the famous Mocambo Room on Sunset Boulevard, with all of his other European ex-patriot movie friends—and not just with directors Julien Duvivier and Jean Renoir, but also with Germany's great director (of 1927's *Metropolis* and 1930's *M*) Fritz Lang, as well as with Michele Morgan. (Interestingly, for architecture [and murder!] buffs, it was Morgan who designed and built [for her own use] the estate at 10050 Cielo Drive in Beverly Hills where, in 1969, the famous Manson Family murders, which involved Roman Polanski's young actress-wife Sharon Tate and her friends, took place. [The house which stands on that lot today is a newer one, built in the 1980s.])

At this point, besides hanging out at swanky Hollywood nightspots, Gabin was also enjoying the company of any number of the famous American movie actresses whom he had always admired from afar, particularly Ginger Rogers, and he also spent some of his free-time riding horses, resting, cultivating an L.A. tan, tooling around town in his newly-purchased convertible, helping out in the kitchen at the Hollywood Canteen (the nightspot created by the American movie star John Garfield, where the U.S. Army sent its G.I.'s to dance with hot movie starlets, as pre-amble to sending them overseas to get their heads blown off!) and, most importantly, learning English: When Gabin arrived on American shores, he spoke almost no English at all, and part of the reason that he would only make two out of his ninety-five movies in America, and in the English-language, during the entirety of his forty-six-year film career, is because unlike other French stars who made a lot of American movies, and who are, resultantly, more known to Americans (Maurice Chevalier, Charles Boyer, Yves Montand, Louis Jourdan), Gabin felt very self-conscious when it came to speaking English, never feeling entirely comfortable with the language.

It is in Los Angeles, too, that Jean Gabin would embark on the romantic affair which he would always acknowledge to be the love of his life, his five-year romance with Marlene Dietrich, and apparently the feeling remained mutual throughout both of their lives, even though they never saw each other again, after their five year relationship ended, at the beginning of 1947. In her 1970 autobiography *Marlene*, the German actress waxed-eloquently about her great love:

"Gabin was *the man,* the Superman, [a] 'man for life.' Nothing in him was false. I loved him as I did my own child; indeed, for a certain period of time, he took the place of my daughter. He was gentle, tender, and had all the traits a woman looks for in a man. The tough-guy façade and the macho stance were put-ons. He was the most sensitive man I know, a little baby who liked best of all to curl up in his mother's lap and be loved, cradled, and pampered. He clung to me like an orphan to his foster mother, and I loved to mother him, day and night. I was his mother, his cook, his counselor, his interpreter, his sister, his friend, and more. He was the ideal being—the one that appears in our dreams. My love for him has always remained strong and unfading. He never asked me to prove it. *Gabin was that way.*"

Dietrich had already been living in Los Angeles and making American movies since 1931, preceding this new, War-displaced crop of European arrivals by a full decade. When Marlene recognized that Hitler was about to become Chancellor of Germany, which he did in 1933, she got the hell out, becoming one of the entertainment world's first conscientious objectors to Nazism: In effect, Dietrich was the European movie industry's premiere 'Goodwill Ambassador in Los Angeles,' and it became her self-imposed job, to meet-and-greet the new European arrivals as soon as they arrived in L.A., taking whatever steps she deemed necessary to make them feel at home (and you can read whatever you want into

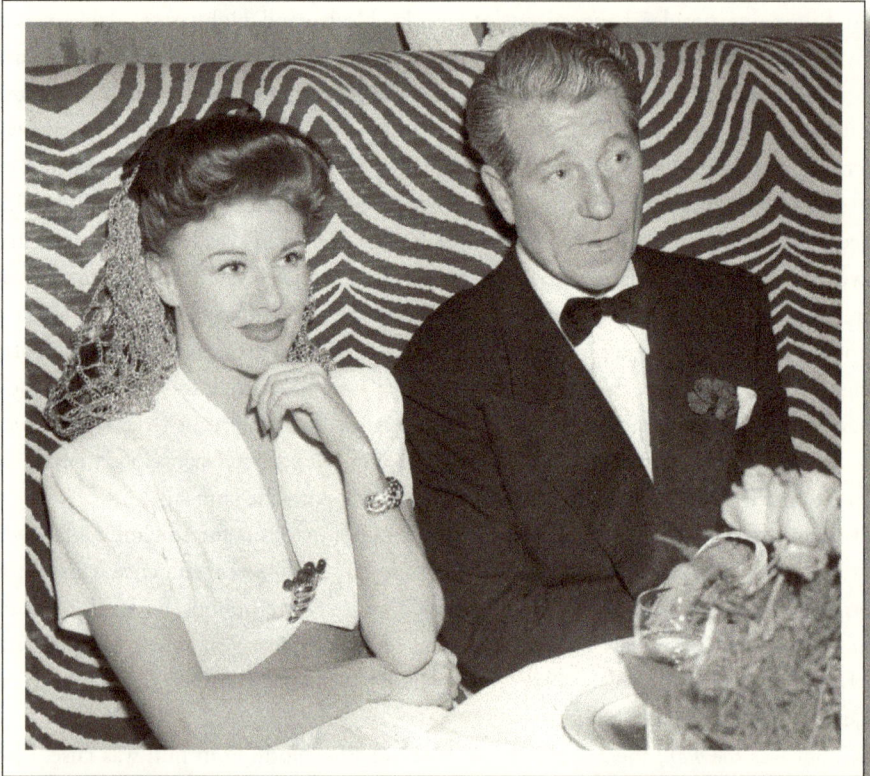

Ginger Rogers and Gabin on a date in L.A., 1942.

that, because Dietrich was just as famous for the innumerable romantic liaisons in which she participated throughout her life, with men and with women, and so whatever you're thinking right now—it's probably true). While Dietrich had been married, since 1923, to a German assistant director by the name of Rudolf Sieber, and while Dietrich and Sieber would never divorce (in fact, they remained married until Sieber passed away on the chicken farm which he owned in Los Angeles's San Fernando Valley in 1977), theirs was mostly a 'brother-sister' type of a relationship, a marriage-of-convenience which, nevertheless, produced Dietrich's only daughter, Maria. In fact, on many occasions in which Dietrich and Gabin were separated by geography, Marlene even asked her husband, Sieber, to help her to arrange 'play-dates' with Gabin, which Sieber always did—if not gladly, then, at least, dutifully.

In spite of the scads of simultaneous lovers whose attentions Marlene had enjoyed in Los Angeles throughout the 1940s, not only with actors like John Wayne and George Raft, but also with the noted U.S. General John Gavin, the 82nd Airborne's famous young 'Jumping General' (who was portrayed by Robert Ryan, in Daryl Zanuck's 1962 invasion-of-Normandy epic, *The Longest Day*), she always felt the most comfortable and 'at home' with Jean Gabin and, one might say, very literally so: After Gabin had already been 'shacking-up' with Dietrich for some time, in her rented Beverly Hills Hotel bungalow, the two decided to take a house in Brentwood together, renting it out from the only other European film actress in cinema history who is today considered to be equally legendary to Marlene herself, *Greta Garbo*, whom Dietrich and Gabin would both claim to see on more than one occasion, 'haunting' the property standing on garbage cans and peering over at them from the second adjoining home which she also owned next door, making sure that her rental property was being well cared for.

The Gabin/Dietrich affair wasn't all *hot sex*, however, and apparently, *there was just as much fighting as there was fooling-around:* One of Dietrich's biographers, Charles Higham, made this observation, in his 1977 book *Marlene: The Life of Marlene Dietrich:*

"Gabin was not an easy man to know. He could be stingy, mean-tempered, and harsh. He was not an intellectual. He despised opera and ballet, which Marlene loved. One night, [Marlene and Gabin] went to the Hollywood Bowl to see an opera. Suddenly, Gabin shouted out, 'I don't like opera! Nobody sings when he's dying!' Part of the reason for his stubbornness may have been that he just hated Los Angeles. He was bored as hell, sitting around waiting for projects [to materialize, unlike in France, where producers always had one movie after another ready for him to star in]... He felt like a castrated bull."

THE FILMS, 'CYCLE THREE'
1942 — 1944, Film Nos. 32 and 33: Hollywood.
Gabin makes two movies in America.

IN NOVEMBER OF 1941, AFTER NINE MONTHS OF *SITTING ON HIS ASS*, JEAN GABIN FINALLY began shooting the first of his two consecutive American-made/English-language pictures, 20th Century-Fox's production of *Moontide*. He was, apparently, completely terrified of the experience because, even after ten months of eight-hour-a-day English lessons, and also after conversing with his Filipino houseboy, and after watching daily film footage of President Franklin D. Roosevelt in an effort to ape the President's diction (and, per Ginette Vincendeau, in the 2006 book which she co-wrote with Alastair Phillips, *Journeys of Desire: European Actors in Hollywood, a Critical Companion*), hanging out in 'grotty' parts of Los Angeles where he could learn 'American slang,' he still felt as though he couldn't speak the language, properly. What didn't help, is that a bunch of studio jokesters, under the guise of 'being helpful,' taught Gabin that all he really needed to get by in English, were what they told him were a few key American phrases, which included, "It stinks!," "It's terrific!," "Snake eyes!," "Little Joe from Kokomo!," "Fever in the South!," as well as that *sine qua non* of 'how-do-you-do's'—"*Get the fuck out of here*," which, they assured him, was a standard American greeting! Gabin had already begun to irk Daryl Zanuck, because the thirty-seven year old actor's blonde hair had very suddenly begun to streak with gray, and he refused to let 20th Century-Fox dye it.

Directed Fox's utilitarian house director Archie Mayo, with some scenes directed by an uncredited Fritz Lang, *Moontide* disappeared from American theaters just as soon as it was released in May of 1942, and it sank like a stone in France as well, when it was finally released there in 1946, although when you see the film today, it's easy to recognize it as a great movie—a true lost classic. *Moontide* shared its basic story-line with Gabin's world's-famous French 'Poetic Realism/tragic-drifter' classics of the late thirties, in which a guy has committed a crime before the movie started, and he spends the whole movie on the lam, in an exotic locale, romancing a brunette while waiting for his inevitable fatalistic downfall. The second of Gabin's two American/English-language films, and the one which followed *Moontide*, Universal's up-to-the-minute WWII adventure *The Impostor*, which was directed in 1942 by Julien Duvivier but not released in the U.S. until 1944, also followed the usual tragic-drifter-trope: Off-screen, before *Impostor's* beginning credits, Gabin's French military man-character has murdered a man from his own battalion and, when we first meet him, we see that he's just escaped from his own execution although of course, sly Lady Fate will make sure that he's going to be meeting his usual 'Gabinian Bad End.' *Impostor*, just like *Moontide*, was a commercial failure, both in the U.S. and Europe.

In spite of the fact that Fox's *Moontide* and Universal's *Impostor* were both box-office losers, RKO Pictures was still very excited, in the autumn of 1942, about the prospect of having Jean Gabin headline one particular property which the studio owned, a love story entitled *The Temptress*. Gabin, erroneously believing that he had the same clout in America which he had enjoyed in France, immediately began throwing his weight around, and trying to intimidate even the biggest studio suits. Not only did he demand one script change after another, but he also insisted that Marlene Dietrich should be hired as his co-star. The RKO execs, however, rejected Dietrich, and for a very bottom-line, dollars-and-cents reason: While the initial group of movies in which Marlene had starred for American studios in the early '30s were huge hits (*Morocco*, *Shanghai Express*, *Desire*), some of her late 1930s' entries, especially *The Devil is a Woman*, although they were of a similar high quality, were box-office bombs. The more cosmopolitan/cultured/hip/urbane moviegoers of New York and Los Angeles continued to love Marlene but, in the heartland of America, where 'the real money' was made, regular people couldn't make heads-or-tails of her extreme European-ness, and some were confounded by it, even to the point where, in 1938, the nation's movie theater owners took out a full page ad in the movie industry's big trade paper, *The Hollywood Reporter*, imploring the studios to please not send them any more Dietrich product. The RKO execs, who were unused to dealing with any kind of 'guff' from anybody, solved their

Gabin Problem, by paying Gabin's contract for the picture off, canceling the project, and assuring the actor that he would never eat lunch in this town again, and it's no surprise that Gabin, who could barely abide working in America in the first place, didn't even care, because he couldn't bear the two movies which he had made in the U.S. Gabin, who was famous for not speaking too much in his French movies, was given much more dialogue than he was accustomed to in *Moontide* and *Impostor,* which was doubly-hard for him to learn, since the scripts were written in English, and worse, both Fox and Universal made him wear his hair in a giant, wavy perm (unlike the more close-cut look which he always wore in his French pictures)—a style which he thought to be patently ridiculous. At this point in his life, he was beginning to grow extremely homesick for France, and was much more interested in returning home, to join up with the Free French Armed Forces, which General Charles de Gaulle had created in opposition to Hitler, because France's actual army had been forcefully disbanded by the Nazis, when they had invaded France. Gabin could no longer abide hearing about how the Germans were decimating France and the rest of Europe, and he wanted to help out personally, just like Clark Gable and James Stewart had already been doing. (Those two American movie stars had already taken hiatuses from their brilliant careers, in order to serve in America's own armed forces.) In Gabin's mind, by leaving his country for America, he had deserted his own people, the good and heavily working-class French people who had loved him, and who had made him their country's biggest movie star in the years which had immediately preceded the War. He believed that, in spite of the fact that he was a rich, powerful movie star, that 'regular' French people really believed him to be 'one of them,' based on the kinds of working-class characters whom he had always been playing in his movies, and he just didn't want to let them down.

Weirdly, however, the final deciding factor in Jean Gabin's deciding to leave L.A., wasn't anything that happened in real-life, but something which he had seen in a movie: It was late 1942, and Gabin was sitting in a Warner Bros. screening room, catching an afternoon preview screening of director Lloyd Bacon's contemporary/up-to-the-minute World War II docudrama *Action in the North Atlantic,* which wouldn't be released in the U.S. until May, of 1943, in which Humphrey Bogart's character, a brave American Merchant Marine Lieutenant, was valiantly fighting the Germans. Fired up by Bogart's on-screen bravery, a cocky Gabin apparently thought to himself, "If Bogart can do it... I can do it!"

It should go without saying then that, in February of 1943, Gabin was over the moon, when the call-up papers from the Free French Navy, which he had requested months before, finally showed up on his and Marlene's Brentwood doorstep. And so it was, that Gabin left the United States, never incidentally to return, ever, from the port of Newport News, Rhode Island. Marlene, with a great deal of sadness, personally escorted Gabin to the tanker which delivered him back to Europe, promising to look after his favored possessions—his three paintings, his bicycle, and his accordion. In his 1999 book *The Ultimate Bogart,* author Ernest W. Cunningham mentions that, just before Gabin left America to return to France, Warner Bros. had offered him the lead role in another of its contemporarily-set World War

Tank-commander Gabin, Algeria, 1944.

II pictures, *Passage to Marseilles*, but that the studio was never really serious about its offer: As it turns out, Humphrey Bogart, who had been under contract to WB, was itching to play the lead in *Marseilles*, but the studio chiefs informed him that he could only do *Marseilles* if he would also agree to star in a second movie, and one which he didn't want to make—director Curtis Bernhardt's *Conflict*. Jack Warner told Bogart that if he didn't perform in *Conflict*, he'd hand the role which Bogart had coveted in *Marseilles*, to Jean Gabin. (Warners even went as far as to hire Gabin's frequent co-star, Michele Morgan, to play the female lead in *Passage to Marseilles*, which she did.) Bogart wound-up starring in both *Conflict* (a bad movie) and *Passage to Marseilles* (not that much better) and, as it turns out, Gabin couldn't have starred in *Passage in Marseilles* anyway because, while it was being filmed in 1943, he had already left the U.S., to return home to France.

Because Gabin already had a year of Naval experience back in the 1920s, when he was in his own twenties, Admiral Jean de Laborde, who was Commander of the Free French Navy, instantly saw fit to appoint Gabin, whom he had deemed to be 'very good with guns,' as the Weapons Captain of the *Elorn,* a small ship whose duty it was to escort other French war ships through the North Atlantic. (In the film *Impostor,* Gabin had played a military man serving in the Free French, and now he was one in real-life!) South of the Azores, off of the coast of Africa, the *Elorn* was attacked by a German submarine, and Gabin and his men, by all accounts, put up a great fight. The enemy quickly retreated, although not for long: As the *Elorn* neared the Straits of Gibraltar, off of the coast of southern Spain, she was next strafed by the German Air Force, and apparently, during this attack, according to some of the men in Gabin's outfit who had been interviewed over the years, the actor was really trying to keep his cool, but his comrades knew he was scared, because they could see his teeth chattering, and as Gabin himself would confess many years later, the only thing on his mind during that auspicious moment was, "What would that asshole Bogart do now?" (Apparently, Gabin wasn't too fond of other by-products of being attacked, either—especially, fires and electricity!) The *Elorn* didn't survive this particular bombing, but Gabin and His Merry Men did, living to fight another day.

In May of 1943, Gabin and his platoon arrived at the Port of Algiers, which is where he had previously come, to act in *Pepe Le Moko,* eight years earlier. Louis Jacquinot, who was Minister of the Free French Naval Forces, offered to place Gabin in charge of his Artistic Propaganda Squadron, but Gabin wouldn't hear of it, telling Jacquinot that, for him, it was either the front lines, or nothing at all. (An incredulous Jacquinot apparently asked him, "At your old age [Gabin was, at this point, only 39], you *still* want to play the hero?!") The two men eventually reached a compromise which was satisfactory to both of them: Jacquinot appointed Gabin to be a shooting instructor at the *Sirocco,* the Free French's Algerian-based school of marksmanship.

Gabin had to wait until the fall of 1944 to return to his preferred front lines, and it wasn't long before he was appointed as a tank commander in General Jacques Leclerc's black-bereted Second Armored Tanks Corps. of the *Fusiliers Marins,* the Free French Navy's land-based infantry operation. The name of the tank in which Gabin traveled was the *Souffleur II.* (A '*souffleur*' is the guy who stands in the wings during a stage production, holding up the cue cards.)

It's important to note that on two separate occasions during Gabin's military service, did Marlene Dietrich show up, right on the battlefield, to surprise him:

"**Dietrich, Surprise Visit, #1:**" By 1943, Marlene had already signed-up with the U.S. Army's traveling entertainment unit, the U.S.O. (the United Service Organization), and while her stated goal in doing so, was to entertain the American G.I.'s, her not-so-ulterior motive was, obviously, that she just wanted to find Gabin. All of Dietrich's assorted biographers have painted the same tableau of that not-so-fateful day that year, when Dietrich was observed running alongside the Free French tanks in Algeria, dressed in full U.S. military regalia: Apparently, when she caught-up to Gabin's tank, and he popped out from under the hatch and saw her, his only comment was a confused but happy cry of, "Oh, shit!" (One of the entertainers with whom Marlene had been traveling on this particular U.S.O. tour was the American comedian and future star of his own successful 1950s' t.v. sit-com *Make Room for Daddy*, Danny Thomas, who witnessed the whole thing first-hand, and spoke about it to Dietrich's biographer, Eamon Williams: "They [Gabin and Marlene] attached themselves to each other so amorously that the GI's cheered for at least five minutes. They clutched and kissed, in full view of everyone!")

"Dietrich, Surprise Visit, #2:" On May 7th, 1945, Gabin was part of the grouped Allied forces which swept heroically into Paris, liberating the city from the (now almost 100%-defunct) German army. When Gabin popped-up out of the turret of the *Souffleur*, there was Marlene again, and the two now enjoyed another very sweet reunion. Even though the men in Gabin's outfit loved him, and definitely considered him to be 'just one of the guys' (that is to say, he never pulled any movie star ego-trips on them), they still, apparently, enjoyed poking the occasional gentle fun at him, for dating Marlene Dietrich, due to her *Extreme Teutonic-ness*.

Two days after 'The Second Big J.G./M.D. Reunion,' came May 9th, V-E (Victory in Europe) Day, the date upon which the war in Europe had been declared officially over. It was on this day, that Gabin was part of a special envoy which had been sent on a mission to Hitler's Berchtesgarden residence: Now, of course, Hitler had already committed suicide on April 30th, but Gabin and several other troops were there anyway, scouting the property in search of the *Fuehrer's* second-in-command, *Reichsmarschall* Hermann Goring, in order to bring Goring to justice. (Of course, they didn't find Goring, who would eventually be tried for war crimes, in Nuremberg.) Two months later, in July of 1945, after Gabin had been released from military service, General Charles de Gaulle awarded him both the *Croix de Guerre*, "for bravery in battle, against enemy forces," as well as the very rarely-awarded *Medaille Militaire*, one of the French military's most important leadership honors.

By August, Gabin was back in Paris, sequestered at the Ritz Hotel, and Marlene Dietrich had moved in with him, and what's odd, is that when Gabin left France for the United States at the beginning of 1941, he was his country's biggest movie star of all time, but when he returned home in mid-1945, having performed heroically for his beloved French countrymen in the field of battle, most movie producers, and much of the press, completely ignored him, and would continue to do so for about nine years: As it turns out, the French people were actively angry with Gabin, just like they were also upset with everybody else who had left France during the outbreak of the war: Even though Gabin had spent most of 1943 through about half of 1945 fighting for the French people, and on their behalf, they just couldn't forget that, during the early years of the German Occupation in 1941 and in 1942, he had, in the collective opinion, betrayed them, by 'deserting France in her darkest

With Dietrich on V-E Day, May 7, 1945.

hour,' for Hollywood. The majority of Gabin's now-'ex' fans felt that, while they were forced to stay in France, suffering the privations of the War (rationing and poverty, not to mention thousands-upon-thousands of Frenchmen getting killed, and not just on the battlefield, but civilians, as well), that he was off, on the other side of the world, living it up! (So, apparently, the French loved it when Jean Gabin was playing a deserter in his pre-War movies like *La Bandera, Le Quai des brumes,* and *Le Jour se leve,* but they didn't much care for it when he [they felt, anyway] deserted them, in real life.) He was starting to get depressed about his lack of employability, and his depression very quickly compounded itself because, during those two-and-a-half years between January of 1943 and May of 1945 in which he was away from both French and American movie cameras, fighting in the Free French Navy, he looked to have aged about twenty years, owing, no doubt, to the horrors which he had witnessed on the battlefield: His hair had now morphed from its famous 'matinee-idol blonde,' to an avuncularly-premature, snowy white. (Plus, with no work forthcoming, *gourmand Gabin* apparently spent more time than ever eating and smoking, so that while he was still ruggedly handsome, and would remain so for the final thirty years of his life, he had now begun to *pack on the pounds;* he now looked paternal, instead of like 'a young lover,' although he would always retain his movie star handsomeness, and would continue to play romantic roles.)

Marlene, to her great credit, kept Gabin sane during that uncertain second half of 1945, making sure that the two of them spent all of their free nights networking (and partying, everywhere they could be seen) at plays, hip cafes, and trendy nightspots, and hanging-around with the people who she felt could make things happen for both of them. Two of the people with whom they associated during this period, included the *veddy proper* British hyphenate (filmmaker, raconteur, playwright) Noel Coward, as well as the genius *avant-garde* filmmaker Jean Cocteau, with whom Jean Gabin would never work, but who would soon, in 1946, make one of the films for which he would always be the most remembered throughout the world, the beautifully-hypnotic *Belle et la bete* (*Beauty and the Beast*).

One evening, Gabin, Dietrich, Coward, and Cocteau were out-and-about, enjoying author Roland Petit's popular World War II-set play, "*Le Rendez-vous,*" the story of a man who carries on a relationship with a housewife whom he has met in the subway—a housewife who turns out to be 'the living embodiment of fate.' Apparently, our four famous theatergoers all hit upon the same idea at the same time—namely, that this entertainment property, because it dealt with *fate*, the most important theme in most of Gabin's movies, would make a great Jean Gabin comeback movie and, moreover, that it would additionally be an ideal Gabin/Marlene Dietrich team-up-picture. (In fact, it would be the screen's very first Jean Gabin/Marlene Dietrich movie, ever.) Gabin immediately enlisted Marcel Carne and Jacques Prevert to head the project up, because they were the men who gave Gabin two of his biggest pre-War hits, 1938's *Quai des brumes* and 1939's *Le Jour se leve,* both of which French audiences adored. Pathe Pictures committed itself to making the film version of "*Le Rendez-vous,*" which Carne and Prevert had now re-christened as *Les Portes de la nuit* (*The Doors of the Night)* but, as he had already done with RKO on *Temptress,* Gabin was now reportedly making one diva-like demand after another, believing that he had the same power in France which he had before the War: Mostly, he was insistent that Carne and Prevert should keep making alterations to their script (and they started to get pretty pissed-off at him, about it), because he felt that they weren't really getting Marlene's part right. Plus, Gabin had begun to grow increasingly uncomfortable with the script in general, even though it was he, himself, who had initiated the project, and also, even though Carne and Prevert had honed the script to the point where Gabin really liked it, because one of the story's major sub-plots involved the still-taboo (in post-War France) issue of French-German Collaborationism; suddenly, Gabin was no longer sure that he wanted to make a movie which trafficked (pun intended) in that kind of 'dicey' subject matter. Eventually, Gabin and Dietrich pulled out of *Portes de la nuit* altogether, a move which wound-up souring the Gabin/Carne/Prevert friendship for nearly a decade, and the following year, the film would be made anyway, co-starring not Jean Gabin and Marlene Dietrich but, instead, Paris's newest twenty-five year old nightclub singing sensation, Yves Montand, alongside a young actress by the name of Nathalie Nattier. (*Portes de la nuit* received lukewarm reviews in France, dying quickly upon its first release, but if you see it today, as it's available on DVD in France, the first thing you notice about it is that, like a lot of other movies which I'll be mentioning in this book, which were also dismissed when they were first released, it's actually very good.)

While the motion picture *Portes de la nuit* has always been an unknown quantity in the United States, most Americans today, young and old, are familiar, even if they don't know they are, with the picture's lilting theme song, "*Les Feuilles mortes*" ("Dead Leaves"), a song which is known in the U.S. as "Autumn Leaves," and which continues, even today in the 21st-century, to be a piped-in Muzak favorite, in every elevator in America! The American tunesmith Johnny Mercer tricked the song out with English-language lyrics (Jacques Prevert had penned the original French ones), and composer Joseph Kosma's lilting tune, as re-recorded by Nat King Cole, was introduced to Americans in a second, and completely different, motion picture, a 1956 Joan Crawford/Cliff Robertson/Lorne Greene (!) soaper which was also called *Autumn Leaves*. (Prevert, Kosma, and Mercer are all credited in the opening titles of the Crawford picture.)

THE FILMS, 'CYCLE FOUR'
1946 — 1953, Film Nos. 34 to 46: After the War.
Gabin returns to France after two years in America, and two years in the Free French Navy. Makes twelve films, but the French public ignores him, feeling that he deserted them when he left for America.

IN 1946, AFTER FOUR YEARS WITHOUT ACTING IN ANY MOVIES AT ALL, GABIN FINALLY received a contract, when a production company called Alcina agreed to finance two Jean Gabin movies—two very good movies, both of which were nevertheless considered to be box-office stiffs, when they were initially released: First out of the gate, was director Georges Lacombe's haunting melodrama *Martin Roumagnac,* and the second was Raymond Lamy's action-packed gangster-thriller, *Miroir*. In fact, between 1946 and 1953, Gabin starred in twelve movies in all, for which French audiences just wouldn't show up, and this is the period of his career which I have decided to call 'Cycle Four.' During this cycle, Gabin will once again be making movies in France, but for a full nine years, and until 1954 with the release of a single film called *Touchez pas au grisbi* which changed his luck for the better, the public just wouldn't show up to see any of them, since they were still unable to get rid of the anger which they felt toward him for leaving them, during the War. Of the twelve films which Jean

Gabin made during this period, four were as fantastically-brilliant as the best of his 1934-to-'41 Poetic Realism classics (these great post-War pics are called *Au-dela des grilles* [1949], *La Nuit est most royaume* [1951], *Le Plaisir* [1952], and *Leur derniere nuit* [1953]), while others were of varying quality: Some were good, and a few others weren't as good, but irrespective of the quality of each individual film—the French just didn't care.

For the final thirty years of Jean Gabin's career, between 1946 and 1976, while the actor would occasionally play the same kind of working-class men upon whom he had built his reputation before the War, his characters would now, in most of his newer films, move over to the other side of the social spectrum: Now, in some films, he would begin playing rich-*bourgeois*-'proto-Donald Trump-type' businessmen, and in other films, he would play the bad guy-correlate of businessmen—smooth, well-dressed gentleman-gangsters. (Even in the films in which Gabin's characters were meant to be rich, the screenwriters usually took great pains to notify us that they were guys who came up from nothing and so, in most of those pictures, we still like Gabin a lot, anyway.)

Extremely important: Even when Gabin was older, and playing moneyed men, he was still making his movies for his favorite audience—regular, working-class people. And so, even while he was taking the characters quite seriously, a great number of these films, in spite of the fact that they were outwardly serious dramas, were intended by their filmmakers to be subtly-satiric jabs at the pretensions of the rich. *Example:* In one of Gabin's movies from this period, 1956's *Le Sang a la tete* (*Blood to the Head*), Gabin's *bourgeois* captain-of-industry character actually tells us, the movie's audience, in a winking kind of voice-over narration, that, "The job of us *bourgeois,* is to be able to take a lot of shit, in style!"

And even though Gabin would now be donning the vestments of rich guys in his films, his basic screen personality remained the same, which is to say that, whether he was playing poor guys or rich men, his characters were still quiet and world-weary, evincing only occasional moments of great joy, just like in the old films in which he was also a loner—a loner who was, nevertheless, friendly toward nice/real/pretension-free people (*and brunettes*)!

Jean Gabin's switch from playing proletarians, in his 1930-to-1944 films, to playing wealthy men in his 1946-to-1976 films (in no movie is Gabin's character ever merely middle-class) is easily explainable, however, when you understand how ingrained the class-system has always been in France, a country in which even movies that are made for the widest possible audiences have always found their dramatic conflicts in issues pertaining to the eternal war between the classes.

1946's *Martin Roumagnac* represented the only film in which Marlene Dietrich and Jean Gabin would ever appear together, and yet this combustible team-up didn't lure too many *French derrieres* into theater seats. A victim of unfairly lukewarm reviews (it's actually very good), the picture, which deals with an excitement-deficient working-man (Gabin) who gets duped out of his life's savings by a hot courtesan (Dietrich), opened and closed in France, and it was also a complete non-performer in the United States, where it was trimmed by forty-five minutes and released two years later, in 1948, at one New York City art theater, and

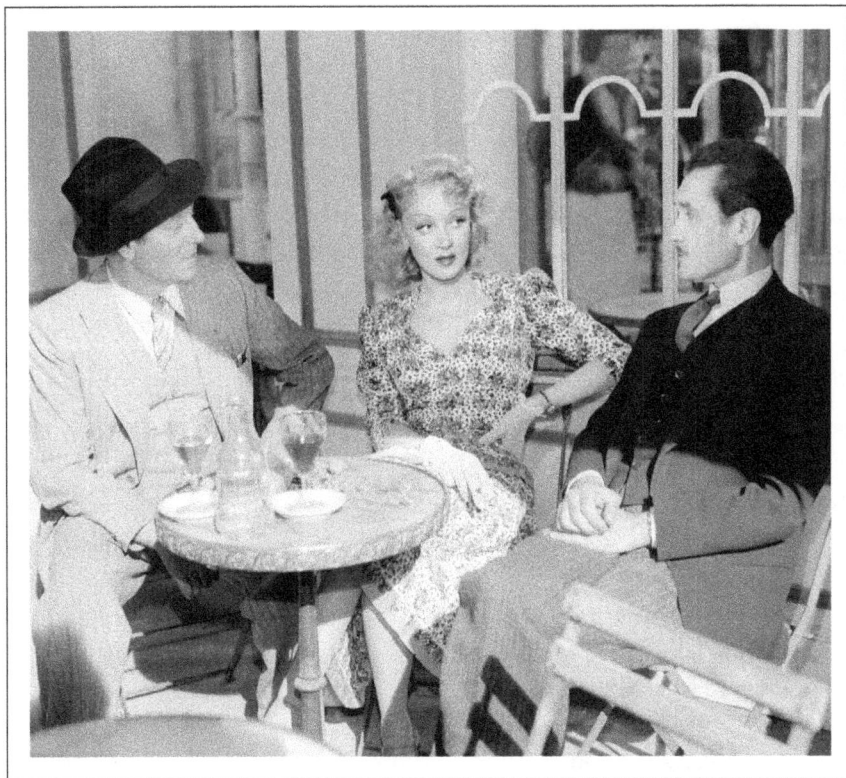

With co-stars Marlene Dietrich and Lucien Nat in the 1946 film,
"Martin Roumagnac."

to no fanfare whatsoever. (And the picture hasn't been shown in America, since '48.)

Martin Roumagnac completed its principal photography in the fall of 1946, and the night of the film's world premiere in Paris, in January of 1947, marked the end of Jean and Marlene's torrid five year relationship. It also represented the very last time that the couple would ever see each other in the flesh, again: Gabin had a keen interest in marrying Dietrich, and in starting his own family with her because, at the age of 43, he still didn't have any children of his own; but while Dietrich continued to love Gabin just as much as he loved her, she was completely unwilling to divorce Rudolf Sieber, even though she and Sieber were strictly platonic. (Plus, very importantly, Dietrich was medically unable to bear more children.)

Unwilling to be just another member of that increasingly large pantheon of 'men who used to be romantically involved with Dietrich, but who were now just her friends,' he decided, although it was, by all accounts, one of the most painful decisions he ever made in his entire life, to never see Marlene again. (At one point, Gabin reportedly even bought-up, and then physically destroyed, every print of *Martin Roumagnac* he could get his hands on, because the film reminded him of his love of for her, which might help to explain why, after 1947, the film remained unseen in France, for a full fifty-six years.) Noel Coward wrote, in one of his many books of memoirs, that when he visited Marlene in Paris in 1956, a full decade after her break-up with Gabin, she wanted nothing more from Coward than to just talk to him about her enduring love for Gabin, and she even insisted, on one particular evening, that Coward should escort her to a local Jean Gabin Film Festival. (Coward recounts the story of how, on more than one occasion, Marlene asked him to sit beside her on a bench, across the street from Gabin's Paris apartment where, according to Coward's account, she and Coward just lingered for hours, waiting for the most fleeting glimpse of Gabin—a glimpse which neither of them would ever catch.)

1948, just like 1945 before it, offered absolutely nothing in the way of movie work for Jean Gabin, and this is the year in which he decided to concentrate on starting the home and family of which he had always dreamed, purchasing a nearly three thousand-acre farm in Laugle, Normandy, which was called *La Pichionniere* (the farm was named after its previous owners, who were surnamed 'Pichion'), and building a house on the property, which he named *La Moncorgerie*, after his real surname, '*Moncorge*.' Gabin even imported two hundred and thirty cows to raise, not to mention a dozen of his all-time favorite animal—racehorses. Gabin's lifelong wish of owning his own farm had finally come true.

On March 28, 1949, Gabin married for the third (and final) time in his life, and his new wife, Dominique Fournier, was one of the Lanvin department store's most popular models. Known as 'Christine' by her friends, Dominique bore Gabin three children, and it is his children—daughters Florence (born in 1949) and Valerie (1952), and son Mathias (1956)—which Gabin always considered to be the greatest accomplishment of his life. ('Mathias,' like 'Gabinus,' is the name of a Catholic Saint, which means that Jean Gabin's son was named for not one, but *two*, saints. [If this guy isn't going to Heaven, nobody is!]) Gabin would also, at the time he married Dominique, become stepfather to her son from her previous marriage, a feisty little boy named Jacky, who was apparently so hyperactive, that Gabin gave him a new nickname, '*Le Frelon*' ('The Bumblebee'). Gabin really took to being a father, even though his kids have all mentioned (as adults, and in various interviews) that he was never all that warm with them, but this didn't mean that he didn't love them: In the 21st-century, where today's feminized men wimpily assist with the diapering, we're beginning to forget that, in the 'pre-Alan Alda/Dr. Phil/Phil Donahue/"I'm O.K., You're O.K./"Free to Be, You and Me" World' of six, seven, and eight decades ago, and especially in Europe, the men went to work, and it was the mothers alone who were the caring nurturers, and that just because the men weren't always hugging and emoting 'I love you' all the time, it didn't mean that they loved

Gabin marries Dominique Fournier, 1949.

their children any less. (That's right, friends: Back in 'the Gabin era,' *women knew how to be women, and men knew how to be men*. In other words—everybody knew his or her place!)

Deciding to bring his own children into the world may have given Gabin a dose of good Karma because, not so long after he started his own family, he was offered a big movie role by the Italians, who had never stopped loving him, in an Italian/French co-production, which was filmed in French, called *Au-dela des grilles* (literally, *Beyond the Gates*, but released in the U.S., as *The Walls of Malapaga*), a terrific film which also happened to have a truly stellar pedigree: Not only was the picture co-authored by Cesar Zavattini, who had already penned director Vittorio di Sica's Italian Neo-Realist classic, *Ladri di biciclette* (*Bicycle Thieves*), but it was also helmed by a great, up-and-coming director, the then-twenty-five year old Rene Clement, who would eventually make two French classics—1952's *Jeux interdites* and 1963's *Plein soleil*. (We might consider screenwriter Zavattini to have been 'the Jacques Prevert of Italian cinema,' because Zavattini, like Prevert, was well-regarded for his ability, in his writing, to portray 'the poetry of contemporary life.') *Au-dela* is a film in which Gabin, by design, and in an attempt to regain his pre-World War II French audience, took a break from portraying *bourgeois* men (captains-of-industry, smooth criminals), to return, for one final go-around, to playing the kind of role which had earned him the title of the King of France between 1934 and 1941, that of 'a working-class tragic drifter who's hiding out from the law, because of a crime which he committed before the film began.' (In *Au-dela*, as in many of Gabin's pre-War pictures, his character gets to romance the obligatory brunette, before spiraling toward his inevitable fatalistic downfall.)

While the truly-outstanding *Au-dela des grilles*, like the very good *Martin Roumagnac* and *Miroir* before it, was mostly ignored in Gabin's native France when it was first released there (today, the French consider it to be one of Gabin's great classics), it became an astounding smash in other countries, even taking home a few very prestigious awards. Gabin won the Best Actor prize for the picture at 1950's Venice Film Festival, and Rene Clement took home the Best Director trophy at the same year's Cannes Festival. Most importantly, *Au-dela des grilles* won the Best Foreign-Language Film Oscar, right here in the United States, at 1950's Academy Awards! (Now, this should really show you just how much Jean Gabin can sometimes be underappreciated—or just plain unappreciated: Every movie buff in the world knows that *Bicycle Thieves* was Oscar's Best Foreign-Language Film winner in 1949, and that Kurosawa's *Rashomon* garnered that prestigious honor, in 1951. But no American today remembers the great movie which won the Motion Picture Academy's Best Foreign-Language Film-award, in-between *Bicycle Thieves* and *Rashomon,* in 1950.)

While *Au-dela des grilles* is an amazing, fantastic, four-star classic, on a par with Jean Gabin's earth-shakingly amazing 1934-to-1941 efforts, and while it was the kind of movie which Gabin's French audiences *used* to like to see him in, Gabin was still unable to attract any attention in France, and not just for this movie, but for any of the movies in which he starred between 1946 and 1953 as well, and this is when what he thought was a great idea suddenly came to him, like a bolt from the blue: In an effort to try and regain his French audience, he decided that he would reach all the way back to the beginning of his career, returning to the stage for the first time since 1930, which is where the French people had originally begin to love him, for the one and only time during his entire moviemaking career: In 1949, Gabin's friend Henri Bernstein, who wrote a very good, and never-seen-in-the-U.S., Poetic-Realist Gabin movie, 1937's *Le Messager* (*The Messenger*), owed Gabin a favor: When the Nazis invaded Paris, in 1940, Gabin had aided Bernstein in booking-passage to the U.S., and now Bernstein sat down and wrote Jean Gabin 'the serious, dramatic play' which the actor had always dreamed of starring in back in the 1920s, when he was appearing on stage only in light, fluffy operettas. Bernstein's original play, "*La Soif*" ("*The Thirst*"), a three-act piece concerning the life of a middle-aged artist (Gabin), was performed at Paris's Ambassadors Theater in 1949, and it starred Gabin alongside Madeleine Robinson and Claude Dauphin. (Dauphin, one of France's most legendary actors, who was also an important member of the *Comedie Francaise* theatrical troupe, has always been known to Americans for one role: He played 'The President of Earth' in the psychedelic 1968 Jane Fonda classic, *Barbarella*.) Unfortunately, however, "*La Soif*" bombed-out with audiences and critics alike.

Marginally more successful than "*La Soif*," was a dramatic radio program with music which Gabin narrated on January 12th, 1951, for France's Radio Diffusion Francaise, *De sacs et des cordes* (*Bags and Cords*). The pre-cursor to most concept albums, the sixty-plus-minute long *De sacs*, which aired on February 5th of that year, is the harrowing story of a charismatic but perpetually lonely young man—a typically Gabinian drifter—who leaves his home in the poor area of a city (could be Paris, could be a town near the Atlantic) to join the Navy. He becomes a petty thief, befriends a singing shoeshine man, and falls in love with a gypsy girl who, in turn, falls in love with a clown. Our young man endures his first disillusionment about love and finds himself on a military ship sailing the southern seas, searching for bandits. When the entire crew dies at the hand of the pirates, our man is captured, becomes one of them, and falls in love with the pirate-captain's daughter. Eventually, he winds up in London as a paperless immigrant, and a new woman tries to convert him to religion, however music—especially the shoe shine man's tune—becomes his only true savior, and he becomes famous. Friends of the regular and 'fair-weather' variety swarm around him, but like many of Jean Gabin's movie characters, he is ultimately alone—even in death.

Like a number of the films which Gabin made during this period, *De sacs*, which was composed and arranged by another French legend, the musician Leo Ferre, was heavily ignored in its day, but when one listens to it now (it was issued on a CD in France, in 2004— Le Chant du Monde Records, #874 1165), one notices that is a powerful and haunting achievement, that Ferre's rhymed/slang-laden verse, as narrated by Gabin and sung by Radio Diffusion's chorus, recalls imagery from Baudelaire and Rimbaud, and that the whole endeavor is much more than simply a minor footnote in the career of Jean Gabin.

But you know how they (whoever 'they' are) always say that, if you just stick around long enough, good things will happen? Well, good things *did* start to happen for Jean Gabin. In 1954, France changed its collective mind quite suddenly, making him its #1 Movie Star for the first time in fifteen years (since the pre-War//Poetic-Realist/*Pepe Le Moko/Grande illusion*-period), and all because of a single movie. In fact, from 1954, and right up through his death twenty-two years later in 1976, Jean Gabin would make forty-eight out of his ninety-five movies, sometimes even starring in four or five films per year, and for the rest of his life, the French public, and occasionally, even the *critics*, would always be with him, turning out in droves for every film he'd make, and restoring him to the Legend which he continues to be in his own country, today...

❧

THE FILMS
CYCLE ONE

On the Verge of Super-Stardom; 'Getting There'

FILM Nos. 1 to 15, 1930 — 1933.

I N THESE, JEAN GABIN'S FIRST FIFTEEN FILMS, HE IS SOMETIMES THE FIRST male lead but, very often, the second, third, or fourth. (In the case of one of the films made during this cycle, *Coeur de Lilas,* he's the seventh credited lead, portraying a nightclub bouncer.) In any case, what all of these movies have in common, is that no matter who the main star happens to be, Gabin is always the guy you're looking at. The fifteen movies which Jean Gabin made during this 'first cycle' are unknown today outside of France, although one or two of them were released briefly in the United States, at one or two art-theatres, back in the early '30s, and haven't been exhibited in the U.S., since. This is the cycle of movies which Gabin made right after he finished his career in musical comedy on the Paris stage. In these movies, he hasn't yet become the stoic, serious, tragic-drifter-who's-fated-for-a-bad-end-character for whom he would become famous all over the world. In these first fifteen films, many of which are light comedies, Jean Gabin is frequently happy, smiley, and cheerful. In some of them, he'll even break into song.

1

With his real-life first wife, Gaby Basset, in "Chacun sa chance."

FILM 1

CHACUN SA CHANCE

France, 1930

(Literal English Translation, "EVERYBODY GETS HIS CHANCE") Directed by Rene Pujol and Hans Steinhoff. Produced by Marcel Hellman and Bernard Natan. Screenplay by Richard Arvay, Rene Pujol, and Charlie Roellinghoff. Based Upon a Story by Bruno Hardt-Warden. Directors of Photography (black and white), Victor Armenise and Karl Puth. Music by Nico Dostal and Walter Kollo. Songs by Paul Abraham. Production Designer, Jacques Colombier. (GENRES: COMEDY/ OPERETTA) Running Time, 1 hour 16 minutes. A Production of Pathe-Natan Films, Released in France by Pathe-Consortium, on December 27, 1930. Never Released Theatrically in the United States.

"I'd jump off the cliff, but it's full."
— Hosiery clerk Jean Gabin tells it like it is, in "Chacun sa chance"

Jean Gabin's very first feature film is billed, in its opening credits, as a "filmed operetta," and it was very smart of the film's producers, Marcel Hellman and Bernard Natan, to introduce him to movie audiences in this kind of a picture, because Jean Gabin, before his movie career began, started out in operetta, on the stage, and was a fantastic singer.

As the beginning credits complete themselves, co-directors Pujol and Steinhoff take us into the theater, where an orchestra is in the middle of striking up a jaunty overture. An Emcee emerges through a flap in the curtains (this is thirty-some years before Johnny Carson started doing the same exact thing, on American t.v.), shushes the orchestra and cries out, "Enough with the opening credits!" Instead of continuing with the film's printed opening titles, our gracious host then vocally introduces the actors who appear in *Chacun sa chance* by name, one at a time, "including," as he makes sure we know, "last but not least... Monsieur Jean Gabin!" Gabin, 'as himself,' then makes his appearance on stage with a big grin, and takes a bow, after which the film-proper begins:

Alma's Department Store: Gabin is now in character as 'Marcel Grivot,' and Marcel's harried Store Manager boss (played by Hubert Daix, and if it were 1960, he'd be "The Lucy Show's" irascible Gale Gordon) informs him that he's going to have to stay late this evening, to rearrange the hosiery department. Marcel looks right into the camera (here, Gabin is 'breaking the fourth-wall' fifty years pre-*Seinfeld*) and starts talking directly to us, the movie's audience: "Yeah, that's my duty in life—to rearrange everything. I wanted to go to the theater and see some operetta, but [with his very first big Gabin-Shrug], *whatever*. That's life." Even in his very first line, in his very first movie, Jean Gabin is already quietly accepting of the fact that life is going to be throwing us a lot of *sucky parts,* to go with the laughter and the orgasms.

Dutifully arranging the ladies' leggings, Marcel now warbles a song about how life sucks a lot of the time but that, since all of our lives have all already been pre-determined by Fate, and we can't do anything about it even if we want to, that we should just try to be happy anyway, and while the lyrics are somber, the music is as relentlessly upbeat as are any of the songs in any of the pictures made by that other, almost-as-great, French movie star of the same time era—Maurice Chevalier:

> "I'm good looking and I have no pretense/I hate my destiny/Since childhood
> I have had no luck/I think about it at night/ It's a dog's life /I'd jump off the
> cliff, but it's full!/I'm wasting my life! /La la la la la [*etc.*]"

Marcel's the only working-class guy in a storeful of customers, people whom you'd definitely consider to be upper-class 'swells.' (French movies love to rub the different social classes up against each other to see what kind of conflict drips out of it.) Since nobody is paying attention to Marcel anyway, outside of when they ask him where they can find the stuff they need to buy, he starts pretending *he's* rich too, and hilariously, he starts chatting-up two smartly-dressed mannequins, one male and one female, in a hoity-toity, upper-class accent. He even goofily impugns the masculinity of the male mannequin, comically feigning jealousy, because the male mannequin gets to be with the *hot lady mannequin,* and he doesn't. (Marcel actually looks at the female mannequin and coyly smiles, "Aaay, what's he got that I haven't got?") While Marcel's not even getting a *synthetic* woman, Hubert Daix's nebbishy Store Manager, who happens to be a married man, gets to flirt with a woman who's 100% real—a smoking-hot number by the name of Colette (Odette Josylla). Colette's the Manager's mistress, and a lot of the Manager's life involves making sure that she's never in the same room whenever his wife, Marie-Ange (played by Germaine Laborde), is around.

Fortunately, Marcel finishes his work earlier than he thought he would, and now he gets to go and see some operetta. (It's the one, great weekly joy which he allows himself, because it allows him to forget about his own troubles, and to pretend, at least by association, that he's one of the rich swells of whom he's always making fun, but whom he secretly wishes he could be, not because he likes them (because he knows that they're mostly dopes), but because rich guys always get *the hottest, sexiest babes!* Only problem is: Marcel doesn't own any evening clothes… but he *is* a great improviser: So he borrows a tux and a pair of binoculars off of one of the male mannequins (which might not be the best idea, because it happens to be the

Store Manager's own, personal tux, which the Manager keeps in his store, on Mannequin #3, as an always-ready change of clothing for his secret tryst evenings with Colette). And if you've already figured out that Marcel's going to be running into his boss at the theater tonight, then *give yourself two points, mon [or ma!] ami[e]!*

In the theatre's lobby, the cigarette and chocolate-selling girls are already dispensing their artery-clogging/lung-destroying wares, and the most beautiful among them is Simone, who's played by Jean Gabin's real-life wife, Gaby Basset. The theater company's hot-headed Impresario (Raymond Cordy) is on-the-scene as well, and he's *freaking out heavily*, because these 'pre-aerobics' cuties are eating up all of his profits, instead of selling them. (Ultimately, though, he can't get too mad at them, because they're all hotter than August!)

Arriving at the box office, Marcel, who looks 'Gabin-Dapper' (*'Ga-dapper?!'*) in his boss's tux, tells the Ticket Girl that he's looking for a 'lodge,' and she looks confused because, in French, the word *'loge'* (lodge) means 'balcony,' but it also means '*Masonic Lodge.*' Humorously, some old Freemasons who've overheard him start welcoming him a little bit *too*-warmly, believing him to be part of their age-old 'craft.' Since the only seat that the Ticket Girl is able to offer him is, what we would call today, an 'obstructed-view seat' he then tries to flirt his way into a better seat: "Haven't you got a good seat for me, *ma belle?* I'm in a group against vivisection!" Charmed by this handsome stranger, she very promptly comes up with an excellent balcony seat, guaranteeing that Marcel will soon be rubbing shoulders with the *crème-de-la-crème.* When Marcel arrives in the balcony, the moneyed-types, who are already seated, welcome him like family, especially, since he's wearing such a fancy tux.

One of the 'Balcony Swells' who's sitting close to Marcel is the regal-looking Baron of Monteuil (Monteuil's a section of Paris, and the character is played by the actor Andre Urban). The Baron's *little wifey*, the very fetching Baroness (Renee Heribel), sits beside her husband, and when she immediately casts her sights on handsome, young Marcel, we can tell from the leering way in which she's checking him out, that she's trying to figure out how she can 86 her hubby, and hang out with this alluring, new stranger, instead. When the Baron turns around to glad-hand some chums, the Baroness and Jean exchange a few, brief pleasantries, and she then, quickly, returns to her husband's side.

During Intermission, when he's hanging-out in the lobby, Marcel keeps his cool, when he catches his boss, the Store Manager, in the act of whispering sweet nothings to his mistress, Odette. And then (we could definitely see this coming), the Manager's wife, Marie-Ange, who *never* attends the theater with her husband, but who has decided to show up tonight on a whim to surprise him, spots them together! Thinking fast, the Manager grabs Marcel, whom his wife has never met (since she never comes into the store), pretending that he's been talking with *him*, instead of canoodling with his mistress. The Manager pretends that Marcel is "a business associate from America," the director of an American clothing manufacturer (!), and Marcel, to help his boss keep up his ruse (the 'Guy Code,' even in 1939, determined that 'guys always help other guys'), starts speaking goofy, *faux*-English to Marie-Ange, but he bungles it, and rather badly. "For an American, you sure can't speak English," she laughs, just as entranced by Marcel as are all of the other women, in the picture. Marie-Ange drags her husband away (she hasn't figured out that the lady he's with, is his mistress), leaving Maurice alone with Odette, but, before Maurice can hit on her, the Baron approaches them, with his own wife now, safely, out of eyeshot, and hits on her first, totally *cock-blocking* Gabin. Meanwhile, Simone the Chocolate Girl is off in a far corner of the lobby, hanging with a few of her cigarette-girl friends, and they're all checking Marcel out. Simone thinks Marcel is *the hottest thing on three legs,* but tells her friends, almost tearfully, that she knows she has no chance with him, and she has no idea that he's just a hosiery clerk: Like everybody else in the theatre, she thinks that he's, if not a Baron, then at least, part of the *hoi polloi,* and in France, of course (at least, the France of 1930, when this movie was made), *the classes never mix.*

While Simone believes she's not highfalutin enough to hang out with Marcel, she *has* cultivated a very warm relationship with the show's leading Actress, who's played by Jane Pierson, mostly because one of Simone's most important duties, is to keep the *diva* supplied with chocolate. Simone tells the Actress that she's just met "a cute guy," but that he's probably somebody rich, or a Baron, and that she *wishes* she could go up and talk to him, but that she'd probably just get too nervous. (Remember when Marcel was behind the counter at the department store, wishing he could be 'on the other side,' chumming-it-up with all of the fancy people? Well now, very bittersweetly, Simone is going through the same thing). The Actress tells Simone, in today's parlance (or, at least, in the parlance of 1975) that she's going to have to 'fake it 'til she makes it:' "If you want that handsome Baron, I will dress you to play the part."

And 'dress her,' she does: After the intermission, when everybody's returned to his or her seat, Simone is now gussied-up like a countess, replete with a massive Indian-maiden head-dress, just like the legendary Mistinguett, Jean Gabin's real-life vaudeville co-star of the '20s. Marcel invites Simone to sit down, and each one is nervous around the other, each regarding the other to be royalty. Simone asks Marcel if she can borrow his binoculars, but they're fake binoculars which he's borrowed from one of his store's mannequins, and are without lenses. So, he (white) lies to Simone, telling her that he recently took the lenses out to clean them, but that he forgot to put them back in. He next tries to change the subject, by complimenting her on her dress: "I know fabric very well, because I am the head of a large fabric company!" Now matching him lie-for-lie, she sweetly bullshits him about how her father owns a candy company and, in the few moments before the lights dim and the second half of the opera begins, Marcel puts on a fake mustache, nose, and turban, pretending to be a Wily Oriental Gentleman, to make her laugh. The two of them are both trying too-hard to impress each other, not realizing, per *Jerry Maguire,* that they both already 'had each other, at hello.'

The operetta performance which has now resumed, naturally resonates with all of the various dramas which are going on, in the audience. (Characters sing, "Don't call me Baron, it's embarrassing!" and "Don't call me Countess, it's embarrassing!") At the end of the show, Marcel and Simone are in the lobby together, and he wants to make a date to see her again, but feels embarrassed that he's had to lie to her; and so, finally, he tells her the truth, which is that he's not a *for-real Baron*, but just a hosiery clerk in a department store, and that he's "only worth two hundred francs in the whole world." She confesses her own secret, too and they, then, start talking, excitedly, about what they plan to do the next time they see each other:

> SIMONE: I'm in your hands, Marcel. But remember: Don't be too rough with me. I'm just a young girl!
> MARCEL: (smiles, making her laugh): Oh, don't worry, I won't be: *I'm a young girl, too!*

Elsewhere in the lobby, the Baron de Monteuil is now making kissy-face with his mistress, Odette, telling her that he expects to be calling on her, at her home (one of these days, when his pesky wife isn't around!), and that, when they get together, his most fervent hope is that they'll be able to engage in a little role-playing game—a little comic roundelay, in which she'll play the 'maid' and he can be the 'butler.' (Rich people *get hot*, when they're pretending to be poor.) As all of this is transpiring, Marcel's boss, who's been forced to attend the performance dressed in Marcel's ratty-old day clothes (as Marcel showed up in the Manager's tux), gets tossed out of the theater by cops, who think he's a vagrant, and who also believe Marcel and Simone to be a proper Baron and Baroness. The cops even apologize to Marcel and Simone for the unpleasantness which they've just had to endure, at having just accosted a man whom they've perceived as being a 'dirty bum!'

Come Monday, Marcel's back at work behind the hosiery counter, and the Manager is on the trail of his missing tux, and obviously, this guy's not smart enough to have figured out that it was the same tux that his happy-go-lucky employee, Marcel, was wearing, at the theater. The Manager confides in Marcel that he thinks his wife, Marie-Ange, is cheating on him with the Baron de Monteuil, and just as he's saying this, Marie-Ange enters the store, herself (it's the first time she's ever been at her husband's place of work), and confesses to him that she kissed the Baron last night, but only to get back at her husband for of his affair with Odette which, as she's telling him now, she's actually known about, and for quite some time: "I wanted to sleep with him, and to cheat on you, but I couldn't. You're my husband, and I love you too much to do that!" Then, Marie-Ange recognizes Marcel: "Hey! He's not an American! He works for you!"—and all three of them share a laugh about it. As the film ends, the Manager promises Marcel that he'll soon be promoting him to a better job. We don't get to see what happens with Marcel and Simone the Chocolate Girl, but we can pretty much tell that they'll probably be living happily, ever after—especially because the movie got some pretty stellar reviews. Including this one:

What a Critic Said at the Time: "… entertaining, and goes well with the fans. Exceedingly clever. Jean Gabin plays acts the part of the salesman exceedingly well, although he should refrain from using Chevalier's mannerisms. There is a certain vague likeness between them, and Gabin's acting makes it worth his while to develop a personality of his own." (*Variety*, 1-17-31 issue, Critic: "Maxi. [Edward (Maxwell) MacSweeney.]" Reviewed in Paris.)

Chacun sa chance turned out to be a great first movie for Jean Gabin, because it showed off the immense likeability which he had been projecting on the vaudeville-stage, for the last nine-or-so years. Audiences were really beginning to take notice…

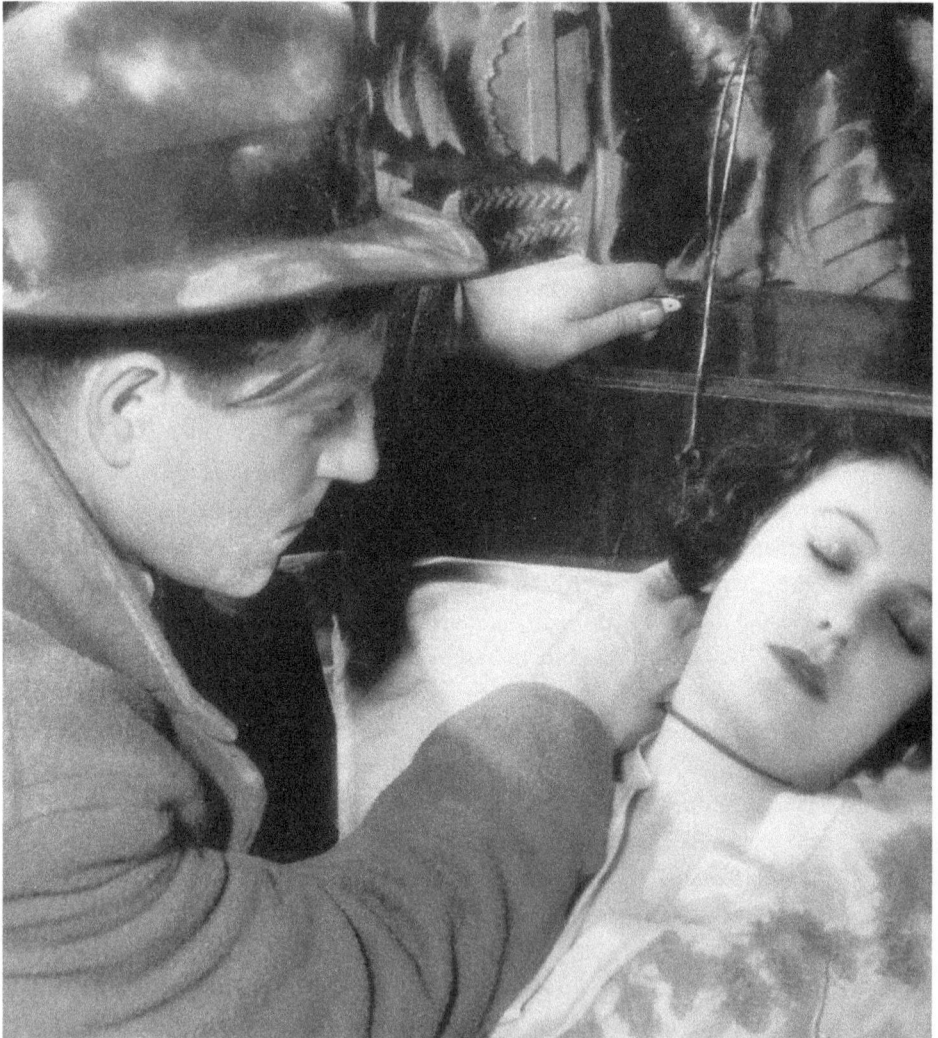

With Viviane Elder, in "Mephisto" (Film 2, right).

FILM 2

Mephisto

France, 1931

Directed by Henri Debain and Nick Winter. Produced by Adolphe Osso. Screenplay by Arthur Bernde, based upon his Novel, "Le Petit Parisien." Directors of Photography (black and white), Julien Ringel, Pierre Rene-Navarre, and Julien Charmant. Production Designer, Lucien Jaquelux. Music by Casimir Oberfeld and Charles-Louis Pothier. (GENRES: SUSPENSE/SERIAL) Running Time, 2 hours 44 minutes (Four Chapters of 41 minutes each, shown as a 'serial,' over four consecutive weeks.) An Osso Films and Gaumont-Petersen-Paulson Production. Released in France, in 1931. Never Released Theatrically in the United States.

"Fat women make me sweatier than a bicycle…"
— *A song sung by Jean Gabin's Detective Jacques Miral, in "Mephisto"*

Part of the treasured American moviegoing experience, back in the 1930s and 1940s, was always the exciting, pulse-pounding serial, or 'chapter play,' which preceded the main feature. (Eleven chapters of Bela Lugosi as *Chandu the Magnificent*; twelve chapters of *Buck Rogers* or *Flash Gordon* or *Dick Tracy*—each one, always, "to be continued next week.") But the French made some pretty outstanding movie serials, too, actually inventing the serial genre back in the silent days, just like they also invented operetta: One of the first French movie serials, *Judex*, which was made in 1916, is available on DVD, both in France and in the U.S., and, in its own right, it's a stone groove, and *Mephisto*, France's one and only sound serial, was made in 1931. This is *Mephisto*:

We know we're in *Bizarro World* right away because, over hand-scrawled beginning credits, we see a huge, monolithic black question mark ("?"), which indicates, right away, that this is a film where we, and Jacques Miral, the young singing Detective (!) who is played by twenty-seven-year-old Jean Gabin, are going to be truly stumped by the identity of the film's sadistic killer. A silhouette of playful hands mischievously glides over the film's opening titles, and it looks intentionally-cheesy, like a too-spirited school kid who's making hand-wolves in front of an unattended overhead projector. In the hands of lesser-talented filmmakers, the device may have come across as being silly, but *Mephisto's* two co-directors, Nick Winter (*né,*

George Vinter) and Henri Debain were skilled enough to make the cheapjack effect look *multo-sinisterio.*

Chapter One—the First of *Mephisto's* four, forty-one minute Chapters (each episode was presented, at a one-week interval, at a 'theater near you' [assuming that 'near you' equaled France])—is identified, on screen, as *"Le Petit Parisien"* ("The Little Parisian").

MEPHISTO, EPISODE ONE:
"LE PETIT PARISIEN" ("THE LITTLE PARISIAN")

A wealthy American industrialist, Willie Dixon (not to be confused with 'the real Willie Dixon'—the great, Mississippi blues musician who influenced Elvis, Led Zeppelin, and the Rolling Stones), who's played (of course) by a Frenchman, Jacques Maury (he's the spitting-image of the British thesp David Manners, who played the goofily-psychotic bug-muncher, Renfield, in Tod Browning's *Dracula*, which was made at the same time as *Mephisto,* on the other side of the Atlantic, carries his new bride, Fanoche (France Dhelia), over the threshold of his Gatsbyesque mansion and of course, it should go without saying that somebody's been following them. A pair of offscreen hands (the hands we saw during the beginning credits?) pops open a briefcase and, as the couple starts in with some pretty heavy-duty lip-lock, somebody cuts off the lights. ("Don't leave me alone," the scared bride quivers.)

The shadowy figure, whom we've already witnessed opening the briefcase, is now sneaking through the house with a flashlight, and his costume is hilarious: The guy's wearing a major panama hat, and his face is completely obfuscated by a scarf, *a la* the American pulp hero Lamont Cranston (better to known to you and me, as *The Shadow*). Willie lights a candle and looks around, trying to satisfy his new wife that there's nobody around except for the two of them and *their hot lips,* but she doesn't believe him and, as it turns out, she's the one who's right. Suddenly, the Mystery Intruder pops into frame and stabs Willie right through the heart. Directors Winter and Debain have chosen to film this beat of the story in fast-motion, and the effect, just like the effect of the shadowy hands which we saw over the beginning title sequence, is truly scary. Fanoche passes out, cold.

After the Mystery Guy makes sure that Willie's good-n'-dead, he kidnaps Fanoche, and physically hurls her into the back seat of the Dixon limo, but there's no immediate victory for our Mysterious Stranger: He's so out-of-breath-excited about the murder he's just committed, that he's unable to concentrate on the road, and he smashes his limo right into a tree. Next, right on cue, a second fancy auto zooms into frame: The driver of this second car discovers Fanoche in the back seat, her no-faced kidnapper slumped over the steering wheel, and seeing that she's breathing shallowly, he—this 'new guy'—transfers her into his own car, and screeches away, hopefully to safety, and not, say, to some secondary, *Texas Chainsaw Massacre*-styled nightmare, which will be even more terrifying than the nightmare which she's already just endured.

Next, we cut to a local bar, the kind of place where, to paraphrase Bob Hope in one of his old movies, "Men are men, and women are proud *of* it." Some surly types are busily gambling and carousing, and a good-natured-but-tough young Paris detective, Jacques Miral (Jean Gabin) doesn't look too busy at all; in fact, when we first meet him, he's *tying one on* with his other off-duty cop pals (You've heard of 'plaster of Paris?' Well, these lawmen are getting 'Plastered in Paris!'), telling them that, while he likes being a Detective, his ultimate goal will be to make Inspector. Anyway, we can already figure out that our hero will solve whatever big crime(s) this film has to offer, regardless of the job-title on his business card.

Holding court at one of the tavern's nearby tables, we now get to meet France's best-loved mystery author, 'Fortunae,' a big, happy lug who's played by Lucien Callamand, who clearly relishes his role as Gabin's Falstaffian sidekick in this picture. One Drunkard at the bar is excited, and he mentions to a fellow barfly that Fortunae, that great author whose stories are syndicated in most of France's great newspapers, is in their presence.

Fortunae confesses to Miral that he's been suffering from some pretty major writer's block lately and, meanwhile, while the two men are conversing, one of Miral's police brethren runs in, alerting Miral that he's needed down at headquarters, and *stat*. Comically, as Miral and the other cops leave through the bar's front door, a gaggle of old men sneak stealthily in through the kitchen: This bar is clearly a speakeasy, with a secret entrance.

When Miral arrives at police headquarters, the Chief (who's played by Jean-Marie L'Isle) asks him if he's ever heard of Willie Dixon before, which is a silly—and almost even redundant—question, considering that Dixon is one of Paris' richest men: "Dixon was just stabbed on his wedding night, and his wife's been kidnapped." To complicate matters ("Now it's personal," Clint Eastwood or Arnold Schwarzenegger would growl more than sixty years later in their own pictures, when discovering that their own cop-characters have 'personal connections' to the cases which they had been called-upon to solve), Jacques Miral, as we're going to be finding out shortly, is engaged to a girl named Monique (Viviane Elder), Dixon's cute-n'-sassy brunette secretary. Jean Gabin's movies, as you'll be seeing throughout this book, are always chock-a-block full of hot brunettes for our hero to romance, and Viviane Elder has the distinction of being the very first one.

Miral puts in an early-morning appearance at the Dixon place: Cops have been swarming around the huge library all night, interrogating members of the household staff about what each one may or may not have seen, and in primo Agatha Christie/'What-the-Butler-Saw' fashion, 'the law' is even questioning Dixon's dutiful old butler, Edward. ("You came in to open the window, and you found Mr. Dixon stabbed?") Dixon's good friends, Dr. Cornelius (Paul Clerget) and Professor Bergmann (he's played by the film's producer, Rene Navarre) are in attendance as well, and both men claim to have seen Dixon at one a.m.—but will Miral's investigation bear this out? (One of the Inspectors on-the-scene tells Bergmann and Dixon that it would have been impossible for them to have seen Dixon at that time, because he had already been butchered before 1:00.) Since everybody, at this point, is handing out so much conflicting information, we've now got a gaggle of possible suspects.

As the present parties continue to debate what happened the night before, we next cut to the hallway outside the library, where a comical, Keystone Kop-looking character replete with a huge, walrusy mustache, is stalking around, his cape draped goofily over his face, *a la* Bela Lugosi. (Is this the guy who cut off the lights and stabbed Dixon? Maybe. Anyway, whoever it is, he's played by an American nightclub comic of the time called Gil Lamb, a guy who would, in ten years time, star in his own series of American comedy shorts, all of which have been forgotten, today, for Columbia Pictures, and for the Three Stooges' usual producer, Jules White.) When Miral and the other cops file out of the library, the figure dashes behind a curtain, so as not to be seen. Next, it's time for news from a newly-arriving Cop: Dixon, it turns out, hasn't actually kicked *le bucket*—he's just been critically injured, and now, under a doctor's care, he's actually beginning to revive! Fanoche, who's somehow made her way back to the house (Who rescued her last night? Who's car was she in?) is now ministering to her husband, happy and relieved, to say the least, that her hubby is still among the living.

Miral interrogates the Good Samaritan who picked Fanoche up in his limo when she was out cold, and, as it's turning out, her rescuer is a real, live Count: 'Robert's' his handle, and he's played by the legendary screen lothario, Gilbert Roland who, in *Mephisto*, will be sharing screen-space with Jean Gabin for the one-and-only time in both of their long and illustrious movie careers. Robert tells Miral that, after he rescued Fanoche, he brought her home to his own castle, where she stayed and rested up for the night and, while Miral and Robert continue chatting, other cops on the scene are learning that the first car, the one which the Mysterious Stranger used to kidnap Fanoche, had been stolen earlier the same evening, from the garage of a local mechanic.

The cops are also interrogating Monique, who is both Detective Miral's fiancée as well as Dixon's Girl Friday-secretary, asking her if she saw anything out of the ordinary, and she replies, coolly, that yesterday was a normal day around the house—well, except for all of that pesky stabbing!—and that Mr. Dixon sent her home early, because there wasn't that much for her to do. Monique's a good girl, and she's also the only character in the film, so far, whom we don't suspect of being involved in any unsavoriness.

Dixon's manservant, Edward, is pleased to see Count Robert because, while he's butlering for Dixon now, he used to 'buttle' in the service of Count Robert. Miral asks Professor Bergmann, whose scientific work Dixon was subsidizing (Red Flag Alert to Moviegoers: Is Bergmann the murderer? Is he not just a scientist, but a disgruntled, and possibly even *mad*, scientist?!), if Dixon had any known enemies, and Dixon replies, "Somebody wanted to buy the invention that I've been working on. When Mr. Dixon and I wouldn't sell, [that person] tried to blow up the house, and I'm not sure, but I think the mystery-bomber might be Mephisto." This casual utterance reflects the first time in the film that we're hearing the character name of 'Mephisto,' the film's eponymous and elusive bad guy. Mephisto may or may not be one of the shadowy figures who we've already seen, lurking around stately Dixon Manor.

Mephisto, according to Bergmann, was once a magician, a guy who's well-known throughout Paris for the flashy magic shows which he used to perform in his devil costume, and a man who, several years ago, traded in his career in legerdemain, to become one of

Paris's most notorious criminals. Bergmann informs Miral that Mephisto wanted to work on his own version of what Bergmann was working on—a new super-bomb!—and that Mephisto wanted to get 'his' version out into the world first, so he could attain all the credit and glory for himself. "When I wouldn't stop working on my version," Bergmann tells Miral, "Mephisto sent me threatening letters." Bergmann hands Miral a stack of those letters, which he just so happens to have on-hand and, meanwhile, outside the library, our Keystone-esque Cop (Mephisto?) continues to lurk behind the curtains.

Jacques Miral feels uncomfortable at having to interrogate his own fiancée, Monique, but he does it, anyway. (His cop friends don't even know that the two of them are an item, because just like every other cagey character that Jean Gabin will play throughout his brilliant film career, Miral always keeps it on the D.L.) Monique tells Miral that, the previous night, Edward the Butler left the house at half-past-one, to gas up Dixon's car, which is about half-an-hour after the stabbing of Willie Dixon is supposed to have happened.

As Miral makes his egress from the room and enters the hallway, his super-sleuthing skills spy a pair of shoes behind the curtains, and he lifts them back (we saw this coming!) to reveal that there's nobody there—just a pair of shoes without anybody standing in them. Miral guesses that these are the killer's little shoesies, and he asks Monique if there's any place in the house where somebody who didn't want to be found, could hide. She refers him, immediately, to the basement, and they head down into its dank bowels, where they suddenly hear a disembodied sing-song voice, spookily/playfully warbling a mysterious children's song—and, obviously, for their benefit: (LYRICS: "The housemartin is running away! Catch me if you caaaaaan!") When Miral's eagle-eyes adjust to the lack of light, he sees an axe buried in a block of wood, under an archway. The unseen singer then spookily trills, "You can't catch meeeeeeeee!"

That night, Monique snoozes on the sofa in Dixon's house (she's a dutiful secretary, even when her employer is too out-of-it to know she's there), as Mrs. Dixon—a/k/a Fanoche—ministers to him. Dr. Bergmann tells Monique it's okay for her to go home. (Ooohh! Maybe Bergmann really *is* Mephisto, and maybe, he wants Monique and Fanoche out of the house, so that he can smother his Big Boss with a pillow and finish the job properly!)

In the next scene, a Mysterious Guy, his face completely obfuscated by a scarf (the 'Dixon-Stabber?'), sneaks stealthily into Dixon's office, hiding a sheet of note paper in a desk drawer (is it a clue to our mystery, or is it just some kind of a calling card?), and just when the guy is about to *amscray* out the window, the lights flick on, and it's Jacques Miral to the rescue! The two tangle like World Wrestling Federation Gone Amuck, and then 'Mystery Guy' breaks free from the Gabin Kung-Fu Grip, shimmying hastily out of the window. As soon as the guy has left, the mustachioed Keystone Cop, who's a completely different guy than the guy with whom Miral's just been fighting, not knowing Miral is in the room, enters: Miral yanks this guy's big fake mustache off, to reveal that it's none other than his goofball sidekick-buddy, Fortunae, and he next asks Fortunae what the hell he's doing there, dressed up so ridiculously. Fortunae answers that he's been trying to find inspiration for new stories, and that when since he heard about the presence of a 'Masked Stranger' around the Dixon place, he thought he'd disguise himself as a masked stranger himself, to see what would happen. (Fortunae came into the room just in time to see Mephisto, or whoever it was [probably, it was the Keystone Kop-looking guy], although the film never addresses who it was, exactly, that was escaping out of the window.)

Just as Miral looks like he's going to give his more-trouble-than-he's-worth pal the 'why-I-oughta'-ear-boxing of all time, suddenly, KABOOM!—a mighty explosion rocks the property, having come from somewhere outside. Fortunae, who fancies himself a superhero, yells out, "Don't be afraid! I'm here!" and he then, comically, faints dead away! Fortunae, like the comedy relief characters in any number of other French movies, both yesterday and today, has a whimsically-regional southern-French accent, the American equivalent being 'hillbilly' (as opposed to the sophisticated, 'northern-French' [read: Parisian] accent, which always gets employed by any movie's 'serious' characters).

The explosion has obviously been caused by The Masked Stranger, the guy who's just escaped from Miral's clutches: He's blown-up Professor Bergmann's new laboratory, for what we'll now learn is actually the second time. Miral, some other cops, and Fortunae charge outside, and they watch the conflagration in slack-jawed silence.

In his office at the police department, the next day, Miral types an entry into the police station's internal log, a few sentences relating to the impossibility of tracking down the cunning Mephisto, and we see him typing a new fact which he's just learned—namely, that Mephisto's accomplice, in many of his former crimes, and maybe even in this crime, is a lady-singer by the name of Fanny Palmarede, who's already spent five years in jail (for what exactly, the film will never tell us), but who is now free, and living in Marseilles.

Fortunae now enters Miral's office in his new 'costume-of-the-minute,' an enormous ten-gallon cowboy hat! "I came to apologize for last night," he sighs at his Gabinian-pal, in Texas-accented French! "You didn't want me to help you with your investigation, and I should have listened to you." He then asks Miral for a favor: "Listen, Jacques, I know you're heading to Marseilles to question Fanny Palmarede. And I've got something to share with you: She's one of my most avid readers! I've never met her in person, but I recognize the name, because she's written me dozens of fan letters from jail. So I'd love to help you investigate, and I can help you trap her, because I know exactly where in Marseilles she is. She sings in a sailor bar there, and I even know which one it is, because she wrote in one of her letters that if I'm ever down that way, that she'd love to have me go there, and see her perform." We can tell that Miral would rather not be burdened by his loutish friend, but since Fortunae might be a good entree into The World of Fanny Palmarede, he reluctantly agrees to take him along, for the ride. Miral buys himself and Fortunae plane tickets to Marseilles, and Fortunae next, and for the first of several thousand times, in this movie, utters his goofy catchphrase—"I like this kind of sport!" (Talk about 'catch-phrases that never caught on!')

The film's co-directors, Debain and Navarre, now split the screen into two equal sections, so that we can observe two simultaneously-occurring actions. In the first frame, which we're seeing on the left-hand side of the screen, Miral is telling Monique that she should meet him at a local Paris café, because he's going to be leaving town for a few days, and he wants to see her before his departure (obviously, just in case he gets in over his head and gets *offed*). On the right-hand side of the screen, in 'frame two,' Mephisto (we see his masked face, pressed against a phone receiver) is whispering to a Mystery Woman-accomplice—not to Fanny Palmarede, but to the shadowy *'Femme X'* (that's what her character's really called!), who's played by Helene Terpse—over the phone, tipping her off that that meddling Jacques Miral will soon be in the café. Mephisto, whoever he is, has been spying on Jacques, so he's well-acquainted with everywhere that our hero happens to be going.

In the next scene, *Femme X* is at the café, hiding in the background, and eavesdropping on Jacques, Monique, and Fortunae, who are taking up a table in the front. Jacques is telling Monique that he and Fortunae are going to Marseilles for a few days, to make some further investigations. When Jacques, Monique, and Fortunae leave the café, *Femme X* phones Mephisto, and tells him what Miral's destination will be and, moments later, after Jacques, Fortunae, and Monique have left the café, Mephisto, himself, enters, his face still hidden by a cape, and he hands *Femme X* two dope-filled cigarettes.

X must now high-tail it over to the airport. She finds the young pilot of the single-engine prop plane which will be carrying Jacques and Fortunae from Paris to Marseilles. His name is Laurent, and she asks him, seductively, if he wouldn't mind delivering a letter to a friend of hers there. As a present, she hands him the two 'special' cigarettes.

After X leaves, Laurent eagerly puffs one of the *ciggies*. He doesn't feel well afterwards, but doesn't say anything about it, deciding to 'continue, as planned,' flying Miral and Fortunae, and one other passenger, a lady who won't be figuring into the story-proper, to Marseilles. When Jacques and Fortunae board Laurent's single-engine plane, Fortunae flirts with the lady passenger, comically, but she shows no interest, and he's still smiling, even in the face of rejection: He loves to fly and, when the plane takes off, he excitedly blurts his catch-phrase out, to his two fellow-passengers: "I love such sport!"

Femme X watches the plane leave the ground, with a knowingly-evil look spread across her face, and we've now reached, according to the final credits, the "End of Part One."

MEPHISTO, EPISODE TWO:
"LE FURET DE LA TOUR POINTUE"
("THE FERRET FROM THE POINTED TOWER")

In American movie serials (the ones we're used to, anyway), each ensuing Chapter always begins with a montage of highlights from the previous episode (in case you missed it last week), leading up to the cliffhanger which begins the present episode. But *the French did it differently:* The second, third, and fourth episodes of *Mephisto* will all open with scenes of bystanders—'normal' Parisian working stiffs, who become, in effect, *Mephisto's* veritable Greek Chorus—standing around at their jobs, talking about what happened in the last episode, as if whatever happened, has already become gossip, all around Paris.

"Episode Two" opens at a newsstand, where a woman purchases the morning newspaper, and the headline makes direct reference to what we already know from Episode One. "How about this?" the Male Newsagent says to the woman, indicating the large headline ("INTERNATIONAL BANDIT MEPHISTO ON THE LOOSE! WILL THE POLICE CATCH HIM?"). "Can you believe it? An American, Willie Dixon, was stabbed on his wedding night!" He reads the article out loud, summarizing what we already know, and then a newspaper delivery truck pulls up, carrying another load of papers. "I've brought you extra copies," the Delivery Guy winks, smirkingly, at the Newsagent, "Because this story is hot stuff!"

And now, our film's co-directors, Debain and Winter, dissolve back to the story-proper, returning us to Jean Gabin's policeman, Miral, who's clearly the 'ferret' of this Chapter's subtitle (while the mysterious killer/magician, Mephisto, is 'the cat who's chasing the ferret,' and not *vice-versa*).

We're now back in the little single-engine plane which we saw at the end of the last episode: The pilot, Laurent, has passed out in the cockpit from the effects of the drugged cigarettes which had been proferred to him by *Femme X*. Since nobody's flying the plane (and Miral and Fortunae don't know that, yet), we now get the obligatory herky-jerky stock footage of an out-of-control/ready-to-crash plane, which bobs and weaves through *the not-so-friendly skies,* but not to worry—every serial has its brave hero: Jean Gabin's mild-mannered Detective Miral runs into the cockpit and, without breaking a sweat, successfully guides the plane to its safe landing, in Marseilles. (Yes, friends, besides being a great detective, he's also every good action movie's 'guy who can fly that plane!') The directors, next, rather weirdly, make an offbeat filmic choice: They now aim their camera out of one of the plane's passenger-side windows, and proceed to show us three full minutes of static clouds. It becomes tedious very quickly, but it's possible that the filmmakers included it because, back in 1931, when seeing aerial footage projected onto a movie screen was still a relatively-new experience, audiences were still thrilled by any footage that may have been shot from thousands of feet up in the sky. Remember: *Mephisto* was made only one year after Howard Hughes dazzled moviegoers with his legendary, World War I/planes-'n-dames epic, *Hell's Angels.*

Arriving at the Port of Marseilles, Miral and Fortunae now head to the sailor bar where Fanny told Fortunae she performs, and they know exactly how to find the place, too: They simply follow a bunch of drunken-looking sailors, whom they see wandering around the docks, looking for their evening's entertainment, and we know these young guys are drunken sailors immediately, because they're actually walking around, singing "We are drunken sailors!" The name of the establishment is *Café Beaux Arts des la Marine* or, in English, 'Navy Aces.'

In the bar, a gaggle of hookers reclines alongside an American sailor of the 'aw-shucks-variety,' who's chatting them all up in English, and he's played by a real, 'ex-pat' American actor. The Sailor loses a game of cards to the hookers, who win three francs off of him and, in the second game, he wins, and the whores give him his prize, although, sadly for him (and for us), it's not the prize which he thought they were going to give him: They just plop a white rabbit into his hands! And while all of this is going on, Miral and Fortunae sit down nearby to have a drink, and to orient themselves, and immediately (you can't go anywhere without this happening), a turbaned Turk tries to sell them a carpet! Miral and Fortunae start interrogating the whores to find out where Fanny might be, and one prostitute starts telling Miral her own life's story, just like women are going to be doing, in lots of Gabin pictures. She tells him that she's moved to Marseilles from Brugge and, incredulously—and he doesn't mean anything mean by what he's about to say, he just really wants to know—he asks her, "You mean, you came all the way from Brugge to be a whore?" (She doesn't get mad at him, at all, though. *Au contraire, mon frere:* She thinks he's cute!)

A guy starts playing the accordion (when *doesn't* accordion music happen in old, French movies?), and Miral, who's jovially lubricated by liquor, begins dancing around the barroom, cigarette hanging from his maw and now sporting a jaunty beret, which he's borrowed from another customer, as the American Sailor watches, looking jealous, because the hookers are paying more attention to Miral, than they are to him. Apparently, Miral's been to this bar before, because the Owner, who's played by Louis Zellas, knows him, and is now asking him to treat the customers to a song. (Jean Gabin, when this movie was made, was only two years out of the Parisian Music Hall and, obviously, the producers of the film felt that, because many people were coming to see this film because they knew Gabin's as a singer, that he'd disappoint them, if he didn't 'perform.')

Miral, who's as ready to belt out a tune, as he is to catch criminals, then takes to the joint's small stage and pleads shyly with the audience, and this is a great 'Jean Gabin: Early Charisma Moment:' "If I make some mistakes, don't be too mad at me, okay?" The hilarious song which Miral now sings, which was penned by the film's composers, Casimir Oberfeld and Charles-Louis Pothier, is actually called, "Hooray for Fat Women" (!) and, of all the barroom songs which have been warbled in the whole history of French Cinema, this one has got to be the best. (It definitely deserves to be covered by a rock or hip-hop outfit, today.) And here are the lyrics that prove it:

> "You can have thin women!
> I like women over 215 kilos!
> At some parties, men invite thin women and fat women.
> But I (always) only invite fat women.
> I always ask the fat ones to dance.
> Fat women make me sweatier than a bicycle.
> And fat women are good at making you slim!"

The audience, which consists, for the most part, of rotund women (whom we notice for the first time, as Miral is singing), applauds wildly and, after the song has finished, the ladies start grinning at him, just like he's *a great big plateful of fried mozzarella!* After the song, Miral takes the Owner into the back and asks him if Fanny Palmarade still works there. The guy replies that she hasn't been in for awhile, and that he doesn't know where she lives, but that he does know her aunt, an old lady who sells fish, down by the docks. Miral tries to collect Fortunae, so that the two of them can leave, and he then sees Fortunae, who is moronically hitting-on one of the hookers: "Your eyes are as clear and deep as the Mediterranean ocean," Big Daddy Fortunae rhapsodizes at her. (*Go, Stud!*)

In the next sequence, Miral and Fortunae are on the docks, where they're interrogating Fanny's grotesque-looking Aunt Hilda (Janine Rang), a fishmongeress. Luckily for them, she just so happens to be reading one of Fortunae's serialized adventure stories, which appear in newspapers all over France.

"I wrote that article you happen to be reading," Fortunae brags to the old lady, tickled that anybody at all likes his cheesy pulp 'literature;' but portly old Hilda doesn't believe that he's the author, bellowing out, "If you are Fortunae—I am Miss France!" (Fortunae's taking the lead in this part of the investigation, pretending that Gabin's Detective Miral is his secretary! While Jacques Miral sings about how much he likes fat women, it's clear that, in real life, he leaves the unattractive ones, to his friend!) "Have you seen Fanny?" Fortunae asks Hilda. She replies that her niece, Fanny, is in Paris with a magician. (*Merde!* They came all the way to Marseilles, for nothing!) But Hilda's totally digging on Fortunae, anyway, and she now presents him with a photograph of her niece, which she just so happens to have, handy. "And speaking of pictures," she asks him, suggestively, "why don't you send me a picture of yourself, big boy! I just *lovvve* your stories!" (Fortunae's not interested in Hilda, sexually, but he does buy some urchins from her, because lunchtime is on the way—*and nothing says lunch, like urchins!*) Hilda tells Fortunae and Miral that she sent Fanny a letter, addressed to her in Paris, only this morning and that, possibly, it hasn't even left the local post office, yet. ("I don't have her address with me, but it's on the letter I sent her. If you go to the post office, they might still have it.")

Miral and Fortunae next sally forth to the post office to intercept the missive, and to find out the address, in Paris, to which it's been addressed, and while the two guys are there, directors Debain and Winter really start *making with the local color:* An Old Man is complaining that he sent a telegram, which the recipient never received; a fat lady is asking the clerk if she can buy savings bonds; and Miral, who, as we already know, in modern parlance, is a 'chubby chaser,' is eyeing the fat lady, lasciviously. (Now, she's the mozzarella sticks!) He gives her a smile, which she returns.

Fortunae now lies to the Clerk, telling him that he's a cop, and he commands the Clerk to dig up that letter which was sent by Hilda to Fanny, but the Clerk informs Fortunae that he's come too late, and that the telegram has already been mailed. Fortunae, with passive-aggressive gusto, next, angrily, makes his response: He drops his recent urchin-purchase onto the post-office floor.

Back in Paris, some hands (no doubt, they're Mephisto's) are busily steaming open an envelope, and guess what: It's not the letter we think it is (the one traveling from Aunt

Hilda to Fanny), but a completely different letter, one which Jacques Miral has apparently sent to fiancée Monique, informing her that he and Fortunae will be returning to Paris today, *via* train, at 1:50 p.m. (Miral and Fortunae have definitely had enough of planes!) Now Mephisto can 'ice' Miral, or try to, anyway, before Miral can bring him to justice.

Monique, who continues to work at Willie Dixon's house (in spite of Dixon's condition, which isn't improving) receives the letter a bit later, and wonders aloud about who it was that steamed it open. Professor Bergmann opines that it's possible that Edward the Butler may have been 'The Opener.' (Here's definitely a clue that Professor Bergmann might be Mephisto, and that he wants to throw everybody off of his trail.)

At that moment, Edgar appears, and asks Monique and Bergmann to come to Willie Dixon's room, because Dixon is really depressed: Dixon thinks that whoever stabbed him might come back to finish the job, and Dixon's ever-dutiful wife, Fanoche, has been unable to calm her husband down. Monique tells her boss that he has nothing to fear, because a policeman has been stationed safely outside and, while it's true that there is a policeman outside the Dixon estate, the guy looks about as effective as a gone-to-fat rent-a-cop at the Mall of America. A shadowy figure sneaks up behind this 'cop,' in the dark, and—WHAP!— knocks him out, *sans problem.*

Cut to the Marseilles-to-Paris train: Miral's in his own sleeping car, taking a well-deserved nap, when suddenly, a masked figure approaches him. Is this the end for our hero? Tune in next week, to find out!

MEPHISTO, EPISODE THREE:
"LES FORAINS MYSTERIEUX." ("TRAVELING CARNIVAL PEOPLE.")

As Episode Three begins, Miral's napping, in his sleeping-car, on the way back to Paris and, suddenly, WHACK-O-RAMA: Mephisto (we don't see who it is, but it's got to be him... doesn't it?!) knocks Our Hero out-cold, and then *boot-scoots* off of *le tren,* very quickly, so as not to be discovered. Fortunae, who was probably in the dining car (and, no doubt, munching-out on some heavy-duty *croque messieur*-action) arrives at his friend's side, too late, and when he sees his little buddy Miral passed out, he pulls the cord which brings the train to a sudden halt— SCREEEEEEEEEEEEE!!!!!!!!!

Finally, the train arrives in Paris, and Miral, who's not too-worse-for-the-wear, reads a newspaper article to Fortunae, an article which serves dramatically to remind us of what happened in the previous episode of Mephisto ("Episode 2"), and he proceeds to get us all caught up, *via* some major 'out-loud article-reading,' about Mephisto's nefarious evil deeds, and when he reads, he sounds, for all the world, just like how it used to sound whenever FDR would read the Sunday Funnies, over the radio, to American *kidlets,* back in the '40s: "After he stabbed Willie Dixon, Mephisto took Dixon's wife, and blew up Professor Bergmann's laboratory." Miral's all pumped-up over the fact that he's been mentioned, by name, in the article. ("Hey! I'm in the newspaper, too!") Fortunae continues reading: "The Ferret [Miral is well-known in Paris, and is always identified by that nickname] is trying to catch him." When Fortuane finishes reading the article, he tells Miral that, when the two of them meet Fanny Palmarede, he hopes she's "good-looking."

Bergmann's now meeting with Miral again, in the living room of Dixon manor, and he's telling Miral that Fanoche, Willie Dixon's bride, discovered a love letter which was written to him by another woman. (Maybe Mephisto wrote the letter, knowing that Fanoche would find it, in the hopes of freaking her out.) As Miral tries to absorb this rather heady information, the film's directors now place him, strategically and expressionistically, in front of a large, steel art-deco spider web, which happens to be hanging on the wall. (He's in Mephisto's trap!)

Watching the movie, and trying to keep ahead of it, I, your esteemed author, now had a few key questions: (1.) Did Fanoche arrange her husband's being stabbed by Mephisto, which would mean that she somehow knows Mephisto (but how?!), in retaliation for his alleged cheating heart? *And/Or* (2.): Did she simply want to have her husband killed, so that she could get her lunchooks on his bread? *Or* (Possibility #3): Could Fanoche be 'Mephisto?' We, the audience, and our on-screen surrogate, Jacques Miral, are both trying to figure this out, at the same time.

We next cut to a big Parisian carnival, where Fanny Palmarede (Mathilde Alberti) works as stage-assistant to magician Nostrodamus (Alexander Mihalesco, an actor who is the spitting image of Ron Moody's Fagin, from Carol Reed's 1969 Dickens adaptation, *Oliver*). Miral and Fortunae head inside, and while Miral just wants to find Fanny (all men need 'fanny,' sometimes!) and get the hell out of Dodge, Fortunae is enthused about enjoying a fun carnival, and he's having one hell of a lot of fun, flirting with the ticket girl, who's totally oblivious to what passes for his 'charms.'

The Carnival Barker next appears on the makeshift staging area, and tells the assembled audience that he will now be making a lady in the audience vanish, and this is where we're going to be meeting Fanny Palmarede, who's played by Marthe Alberti, for the first time, in the picture. We know that Nostrodamus isn't Mephisto, because Mephisto himself is backstage, palling-around with the strong man, a guy who has a bandana stretched tightly across his face, so you can't see his nose and mouth, and he's even offering the not-too-swift Strong Man some easy dough, if the Strong Man will consent to interfere with one of Nostrodamus' magic tricks, Mephisto's point being, of course, to catch Jacques Miral and/or Fortunae, who he knows are in attendance. (Miral expects to find Fanny at the carnival, and he has no idea that Mephisto is there.)

A skeptical Old Codger in the audience is next placed into Nostrodamus' 'disappearing box.' (Nostrodamus jokes with the old guy, "Are you over 18? Have you done your military service?") The Old Man, who's been briefed on what to do once he's inside the box, opens the trap door and rolls down the chute, which empties out under the big top. The Strongman helps the cheery geezer out of the box, and the old guy reappears victoriously in the audience, only moments later.

Robert, Gilbert Roland's young Count, is now back in Dixon manor, consoling Fanoche, upon whom he clearly has designs. (Robert can't be Mephisto, for those who insist on keeping score, because Mephisto was—we think, anyway—just seen at the carnival.) Fanoche tells Robert that, when she found the letters from her husband's alleged mistress, she thought she would die, but she figured, also, that the letters might, possibly, be fakes.

But Willie Dixon's second chance at life doesn't last: He finally bites the dust, and Fanoche is devastated, and this is the scene in which she's learning, too, that her husband really was having an affair, and that the girl he was diddling, happened to have been his secretary, Monique, who is also Jacques Miral's trusted fiancée!

Monique, as it turns out, really *did* engage in a steamy affair with Willie Dixon, but it was before Dixon was married to Fanoche, and it was also before Monique was engaged to, or had even met, Jacques Miral. (So we still like her because, in the time she's known Jacques, she's never once cheated on him.)

During intermission, Nostrodamus, who, judging from his incredible *speed-drinking* acumen, should really be called 'Toastradamus,' sits with the barker, as well as with a cute girl assistant, and Fortunae. Fortunae's engaging in a spirited game of footsie with the ticket girl, under the table. Fortunae asks Nostrodamus, "How do you make people disappear? You know, I'd love to volunteer to be the guy in your disappearing box tonight. [Here comes the catch phrase again:] *I love this kind of sport!*"

Simultaneously, Miral's burning the midnight oil down at P.D. H.Q.: He heads into the Chief's office, and Chief Richard, who's played by Andre Marnay, asks Miral to brief him on the latest Mephisto skinny: "There's a girl, Fanny Palmarede, who used to work for Mephisto, when he was a magician. Now she's working for another magician, a guy named Nostrodamus." Miral also tells the Chief he's learned that Willie Dixon's butler, Edward, used to work for Count Robert, who's been hanging around the Dixon estate of late, and the Chief thinks it's a strange coincidence that the Count was on the scene to rescue the passed-out Fanoche, after she had fainted, post her husband's stabbing.

Fanoche (what a bitch!) next shows Miral the letter from Monique, the letter in which Monique had admitted to her affair with Fanoche's husband, Willie Dixon, but Miral doesn't get mad: He investigates the letter with a magnifying glass, and simply decides that it's a fake. (Maybe Count Robert and Fanoche have been conspiring together to get Willie Dixon's money, *a la Double Indemnity* or *The Postman Always Rings Twice?*) The Chief tells Jacques that, even though it's unpleasant to think about, he shouldn't rule out Monique as an accomplice in the Willie Dixon stabbing, as she was the only person who knew Jacques was flying to Marseilles, and the Chief also opines that it's possible that Monique is somehow linked to Mephisto, as well—in fact, he's even ready to haul her in: "I know she's your fiancée, Jacques. But unless you bring me some evidence that she's clean by tomorrow morning, I'm arresting her."

The next night at the circus, Fortunae himself is volunteering to be the guy in Nostrodamus' disappearing box: Underneath the tent, the Strongman, who's been paid-off by Mephisto, is getting ready to chloroform our hapless rube, at such time as he rolls down the chute, insuring that he won't reappear in the audience, just like how that old guy reappeared the night before. When Nostrodamus tells Fortunae, "Get ready to disappear," there's more truth to his words than Fortunae will ever know.

Miral, resolutely, doesn't believe that Monique was in on Willie Dixon's murder attempt (he idealizes her, in the way that all men sometimes idealize hot women who, when you get right down to it, aren't really all that great), and he waits outside of her window while she sleeps, to protect her. Suddenly, two guys on motorcycles jump him and knock him out (BOP! BOINK!) and when Gabin's young detective-character wakes up in front of the house, after taking a pregnant pause to rub his achin' noggin,' the two creeps ride back to where he's standing, and knock him out for a second time! During the commotion, Mephisto has now crept into Monique's room. He takes a cord to her neck and strangles her. It is precisely midnight, as Episode Three of *Mephisto* ends.

MEPHISTO, EPISODE FOUR:
"LA REVANCHE DE L'AMOUR." ("LOVE'S REVENGE.")

E pisode Four, the final chapter in the Mephisto saga, begins the same way that Episode Two began—that is to say, it begins with a Greek Chorus of French proletarians: In this case, it's a couple of chambermaids at Willie Dixon's mansion who are telling each other (and who are, by doing so, reminding us) what happened in the previous episode: "Mephisto may have been the one who tried to kill Monique," one Chambermaid tells the other, and we know that this is true, because we've already seen it happening.

Jacques Miral, having survived his double-head bonkings with great panache, listens to Professor Bergmann, who's telling him that Monique's strangling may have, in fact, been a suicide attempt. "But she's always happy," Miral points out to the scientist, questioningly. "Plus—how can you strangle yourself?" (This is decades before Larry Flynt and *Hustler* magazine would introduce the world to the simple and unblemished pleasures of auto-erotic asphyxiation.) Miral knows that Mephisto, whoever he will, ultimately, be revealed to be, is the one who strangled her.

Meanwhile, back at the circus, Fortunae is tied up on a table, unconscious, and looking, for all the world, like a gargantuan turkey waiting to be carved, while the burly Strong Man guards him. "Da boss wants me to kill you," the gruff, but, as it will turn out, amiable, and even sweet-natured, Strong Man warns Fortunae, as our portly pal awakens, "but if you give me some money—I'll let you live!" (The Strong Man's allegiance is not to Mephisto, but to 'The Almighty Franc.') "I hate this kind of sport," Fortunae whispers under his breath, scared out of his mind, but still able to come up with his un-catchy catch phrase. The Strong Man takes money from Fortunae and unties him. (Miral's sidekick is indeed very 'Fortunate:' *Per* his name, Fortune favors him, although he is decidedly not, *per* Alexander the great, who uttered that famous phrase, brave.)

Meanwhile a gaggle of cops, who include Miral, bust into a Paris bar, trying to find people who may or may not be in on Willie Dixon's death, as well as on Monique's strangulation, and we now get a big, rollicking Barroom Fight-Sequence, which plays out like a typical, cowboys-smashing-up-a-bar-scene, in any American B-western, replete with tables smashing and people flying over the bar, and all of it shot in the deeply canted angles of German expressionism. Nostrodamus is in the bar, and he's the main guy the cops are looking for, at this point, since they believe that he might work for Mephisto. Miral dukes it out with the old magician, *mano-a-mano* (or is that '*mano-a-Gabino?*') and, at that moment, a bunch of surly dudes (most probably Mephisto's henchmen) break into the bar and find Miral. They tell Miral that he had better come with them, if he wants to save his friend Fortunae's hide.

Next, Miral and his cop brethren arrive at the carnival with Nostrodamus and Fanny Palmarede, in tow. They descend into the tent, where Fortunae, while he's no longer bound in ropes, remains a prisoner of the Strongman. Miral intimidates the muscular Strongman quite easily, backing the guy, who's twice his size, against a wall, and asking him who paid him to tie-up Fortunae. The Strongman cops to the fact that it was Nostrodamus who paid him to kill Fortunae, but he's lying: It was Mephisto who paid him, not Nostrodamus—unless Mephisto and Nostrodamus are the same person?!

Back in Paris, Fanoche Dixon is now dating Count Robert, while still living in her deceased husband's pad. (That's just like how it is, in the Beverly Hills of today!) Fanoche has just received a letter from Willie's attorneys, stating that she is sole heir to the Dixon Millions and, of course, upon hearing the news, she and her new flame, Robert, start to rejoice. When Robert leaves for the night, Professor Bergmann invites Fanoche to come and live with him in his own mansion on a permanent basis because, no doubt, he, too, wants to get his mitts on his dead pal's bread. (If Professor Bergmann, as I have already opined, is Mephisto, then why would he have burned down his own lab?) The Professor grabs Fanoche in a sexy embrace and tells her, with as much Old Man/Pre-Cialis Vigor as he can muster up, "I love you! I don't want you to see that Count again. He wants your money." (Yeah, like Bergmann's not more mercenary than the Count is!)

At the hospital, Monique is recuperating from her *choke-a-thon*, and somebody dressed in medical scrubs, whose face we can't see, sneaks in and tries to give her a great big glass of poison, to drink. But, Surprise, Suckahhhhhh! It's not Monique who's in the hospital bed—it's Miral, who's hiding under the covers of Monique's bed, brandishing his gun! He tells the intruding '*faux* M.D.,' who happens to be another, money-grubbing, friend of Dixon's, by the name of Cornelius (Paul Clerget), to drink the glass of poison which Cornelius has prepared for Monique. (Could Cornelius be Mephisto? Will the Real Mephisto please stand up?) Miral now begins wondering aloud, about why Mephisto would want to kill Monique, but he is still unable to come up with a satisfactory answer.

Back at Dixon Manor, Fanoche is on the phone with Robert, and—look out, behind you, Fanoche!—The Real Mephisto's in the room, and he's hiding behind a great big potted plant. "Oh, Robert," she whimpers at her suitor, "You mustn't come here to see me again. I can't explain—but I will say, that I'm very afraid for you."

Meanwhile, down at police headquarters, Dr. Cornelius is now receiving the third degree at the hands of Miral and some other cops. ("You tried to kill Monique. Are you Mephisto?" [Cornelius' reply: "No!"]) Miral points an accusing finger: "I know you're Mephisto. And if you're not Mephisto, you're, at the very least, his accomplice, and you made-up those fake letters saying that Mrs. Dixon was having an affair with the Count, because you wanted Dixon to kill her, and you wanted his money. Admit it!" Cornelius admits that it was he who wrote the fake letters, because Willie Dixon had an affair with Monique and, just like every other guy in the movie, Dr. Cornelius is hot for Monique, too. (In this movie, everyone's hot for either Fanoche or Monique and, clearly, the characters in this movie don't subscribe to the 'Guy Code,' whereby you never make a move on your friend's girl.)

Count Robert now has a little sit-down with Fanoche: He's come to see her again, in spite of her stern admonishments to the contrary. Mephisto's still in the house, but he hasn't yet moved in for the attack (he's still positioned behind that big fern) and Fanoche is crying on Robert's shoulder, stream-of-consciousness style: "I'm so afraid, Robert. I feel death coming closer and closer. Oh, won't you set me free?! Come away with me, Robert! My husband loved me and now, so do you—and Mephisto wants me, and now he's going to kill me if he can't have me. And he's going to kill you, too!"

Robert, who's the Original Pussy of All Time, freaks-out now, and tries to leave by himself, and just as he's about to exit the house, Mephisto pops into the frame and tries to stab him. But (Surprise Again, Suckers!), Brave Jacques Miral is on the scene. He makes Mephisto remove his scarf, to reveal that he's really (drum roll!) Professor Bergmann!

Professor Bergmann, just like the bad guy on any episode of t.v.'s legendary "*Scooby-Doo*" cartoon series, must now explain his whole M.O., for his crimes: He loved Fanoche, but he couldn't have her, so he dressed-up in his 'Mephisto gear' and tried to kill everybody who loved her, in that standard, If-I-can't-have-her-nobody-can!-manner. He admits that it was he who made up those fake letters, the letters which stated that Fanoche was cheating on her husband.

Bergmann says that, years ago, there was a magician who is now deceased, named Mephisto, whose identity he assumed. (Did Professor Bergmann kill the original Mephisto who, as we're now learning, was dead long before the film began? The film's three directors don't tell us, but we can guess that he did.) Bergmann, as we'll also learn in this scene, is not even a for-real aging professor—he says he dyed his hair white to look professorial, and that he murdered Dixon, in order to get at Dixon's fortune. "I made the letters. I burned down my own factory. I even tried to kill you twice, Miral!"

Miral asks Bergmann who told him about Miral's departure to Marseilles, and Bergmann replies that, not only will he *not* provide him with that information, but that his name really isn't even Bergmann: "Of course, I'm not going to give you my real name. I pretended to be Bergmann, pretending to be Mephisto!" So: There *was* a real Bergmann, and he, like Mephisto, was probably dead before the film started (and he was, no doubt, killed by this fake Bergmann, whom we've now learned to have been The Real Mephisto]!)

So, now that we know the whole story (kind of), it's *Surprise Time:* Fanoche, in plain view of Miral and the other Cops, pulls a little handgun out of a desk drawer, and blows Bergmann/Mephisto, or whoever he really was (we'll never know, but it doesn't really matter) to Kingdom Come.

Our four-chapter serial has now run its course, and now, our directors give us, according to the title card which we're going to be seeing next, our serial's "EPILOGUE:"

Detective Jacques Miral and Monique have just gotten married (of course) and we now see the couple framed in the arched window of their honeymoon suite. Outside, a marching band serenades the pair, not only on their nuptials, but also to thank brave Detective Miral for finally capturing the elusive Mephisto (a/k/a, Bergmann, the guy who 'played' Mephisto, since the real Mephisto, as Bergmann has already told us, is pushing up daisies). Miral, who's not ashamed at all to be a winner, tips his hat to the crowd which has gathered outside of his window, and he triumphantly crows without any trace of modesty, "I'm the guy who got rid of Mephisto!" Fortunae, who happens to be outside on the street (he's standing with the band) yells up to Miral, something along the lines of how Miral should 'sing that Fat Lady Song again,' but now that he's married, Miral has re-evaluated the 'size' of the kind of girls he likes, and he ends the film by singing a different song to the crowd which has gathered outside of his window, the lyrics of which are more beautiful than any *haiku:*

> "I'm a married man and I'm happy!
> I used to like fat women!
> But now I like small women!"

Mephisto which, currently, at the time of this book's printing, exists in only one print in the entire world, at the Royal Cinematheque of Belgium, in Brussels, which is where I saw it for this book, is an incredible find, not just because it's little-known (even in France, the country in which it was made), but also because it's consistently entertaining at every turn. The picture is gobs of fun, offering way more humor (and song interludes!) than the often turgid serials which America had been churning out at the same time, even though some of its specific plot details are often a bit confusing. Co-director George Vinter (1879-1945) was a popular director and actor of French silent cinema (he often played a character called 'Nick Winter,' which is the name under which his directing is credited, in *Mephisto*. *Mephisto* was his only sound film).

What a Critic Says Today: "This French chapter-play, released in 1931, was the country's first—and last—sound serial…" (All Movie Guide [website]. Critic: Hans J. Wollstein. Year: 2006.)

Top: Marcel Levesque, Josseline Gael, and Gabin. Above: With Josseline Gael.

FILM 3

TOUT CA NE VAUT PAS L'AMOUR

France, 1931

(Approximate English Translation: "NOTHING'S WORTH AS MUCH AS LOVE") Directed by Jacques Tourneur. Produced by Bernard Natan. Written by Rene Pujol. Directors of Photography (black and white), Nicolas Bourgaroff, Charles Barrois, and Henri Barrere. Editor, Germain Fried. Music by Hugo Kirsch. Production Designer, Lucien Aguetta. (GENRE: COMEDY) A Production of Pathe-Natan Films. Running Time, 1 hour 27 minutes. Released in France by Pathe-Consortium, in 1931. Also Released in France as "UN VIEUX GARCON" (Literal English Translation: "THE OLD BOY" or "THE BACHELOR.") Never Released Theatrically in the United States.

"Everybody says you're too kind. They laugh at you—and they're right!"
— A nice-guy bachelor gets dressed-down by his own housekeeper, in "Tout ca ne vaut pas l'amour"

While Jean Gabin was the main star of his first two feature films, 1930's *Chacun sa chance* and 1931's *Mephisto*, in this film, *Tout ca ne vaut pas l'amour*, as in some of the other movies which the actor will make during this first cycle of his movie career (1930-1933), he plays a supporting role, appearing only in a handful of scenes, but he's the guy in the movie you're really looking at, even though the main star of the film, one of France's great actors of the silent screen, 54-year-old Marcel Levesque, who had successfully made the transition from silent films (especially, 1917's *Les Vampires* and 1916's *Judex*), is also very good, sympathetic, and likeable. While this film is known, historically, as *Tout ca ne vaut pas l'amour*, the on-screen title, in the actual surviving 35-millimeter film print, which the CNC (French Ministry of Culture) showed me in Paris, is *Un vieux garcon*. (*'Vieux garcon'* is a French expression which translates, literally, as 'old boy,' but it's actually slang, and it means, *'bachelor.'*) Whatever the title is, this film represents the one-and-only time we'll ever see Jean Gabin thesping in the service of director Jacques Tourneur, the French filmmaker who, like many other of his countrymen, would emigrate to the United States during World War II, when the Germans occupied his native France. (While in America, Jacques Tourneur would turn out some of his best known and most visually-atmospheric movies, including RKO's 1945 horror flick *Cat People*, as well as the legendary 1946 *film noir, Out of the Past.*)

While Tourneur has gained a reputation in recent decades of being a Master of Suspense, here, in this early film, we see that's he's just as 'at-home' directing a frothy comedy about bachelorhood, with all of bachelorhood's attendant joys and sorrows. (The screenplay for this picture was written by *Chacun sa chance's* director, Rene Pujol.)

As our film begins, a woman walks by the drug store which is owned and operated by Julien Renauldin (Marcel Levesque), while a syrupy movie-tune called "Love is Stronger," which is performed by a songstress of the day called Valies, who will appear 'in the flesh' at the film's ending, to reprise her song, wafts over the soundtrack. The unmarried Julien is a nerd of the highest order, replete with a huge, comical nose and an even bigger mustache, and when we first see him, he's doing what every unmarried, older guy does on a Saturday night while all of the cool people are out, tripping the light fantastic: He's sitting around his pharmacy, *futzing around* with his stamp collection! A little girl, who's played by Gilberte Savary, keeps comically opening the door, slamming it shut, and ringing the doorbell, to try and annoy him—but that's not the only reason she's shown up: She's actually on a mission to pick up a prescription for her ailing dad. ("One pill at noon, one at night," Julien lectures the girl, listlessly, obviously more involved in his postage collection, than he is in dispensing *les medicaments*.) Leonie (Jeanne Loury), Julien's *plus-sized* live-in cleaning lady is there, too, scrubbing the floor, and she can't stand that her boss is still single, and like all *yentas*, past and present, she's more-than-ready to offer him a clue as to why he remains so: "Everybody in town says you're too kind. They laugh at you—and they're right! You give everything to everybody!" Julien's so nice, he'll even put up with this gently scabrous dressing-down from his own washerwoman, and *he doesn't even try to give her any shit back,* because he knows she's right.

But he's saved by the bell (literally, the bell that rings when the pharmacy's front door opens), this time allowing-in not a little girl, but another plus-sized lady, the morbidly-obese Mrs. Triron (Delphine Abdala, a woman so huge, she makes hefty Jeanne Loury look, by comparison, like Twiggy), who charges in and makes an unwelcome announcement—an announcement which we can all just add into our own 'more-information-that-I-wanted-to-know' files: "I have something in my stomach," she bellows, half-expecting the whole world to stop whatever its doing, to figure out what's bothering her. She rubs her boobs sensuously (ick!), and when Julien asks her what she ate for lunch, which is what he does, next, she gloatingly replies, "Only fresh mashed potatoes, wine, cheese, salad... and a liter of wine!" "The treatment is simple," Julien prescribes, listening to her voluminous chest, like he's the most dedicated of general practitioners: "For your cure, I want you to take twenty pounds of baking soda!" (He's putting her on, of course, but she's much too dense—literally, and figuratively—to realize it.)

Julien has to beg Mrs. Triron's pardon for a moment, because his tenant, in the basement, happens to be playing his music much too loudly, and this is a regular occurrence, because this tenant, who we're about to meet, has converted the pharmacy's basement into a music store. Julien phones down to the music-loving tenant, good-naturedly goofy Jean-Cordier (Jean Gabin!) and he wimpily starts *chewing Cordier a new a-hole:* "I'm going to close your music shop down, if you keep playing your gramophone that loudly!" But cheerful Cordier, who is completely unafraid of Julien, whose bark, he understands, is worse than his bite, just doesn't care.

Julien's now ready for more *freaky-deaky* customers (they're not in short supply, in this movie) and, at this moment, right on cue, a crazy, bearded guy comes into the pharmacy (he's the spitting-image of R. Crumb's 1960s underground comic book star, Mr. Natural), and tells Julien that he needs some laxatives, and *stat*, and it's no end of amusing that all of the customers suffer from one form of constipation or another—but then again, so does Julien: He's 'all blocked up' with pent-up love, which he's never allowed to let out, because he can never find a woman who's up for receiving it!

But: You know how your mom used to tell you that "if you wait around long enough, something good might happen?" (Yeah, yeah, *it's bullshit*, but it's your mom, so you have to listen, right?) Well, it does: A beautiful woman, Claire (Josseline Gael) next enters the store—and immediately passes out cold! Julien telephones for a proper medic, but *he can't hear shit*, because that *freakin'* Jean Cordier downstairs, has just turned-up his gramophone music even louder, just to rankle his perpetually *tres-nervieux* landlord. Meanwhile, downstairs in the Cordier Music Shop, Cordier's Mom, who's played by the wonderful Mady Berry, a French Margaret Dumont/Ethel Barrymore clone, whose presence we'll be enjoying in lots of other Gabin pictures from the 1930s, tells her son that he should play all of the gramophones in their shop at the same exact time, just to screw with Julien! (Julien's one of those guys who was born for other people to mess with.)

Dissolve to a few days later: Julien, even though he's severely wimpy, is, at the same time, just courageous enough to bring flowers and medicine to Claire at her family's home, because even though he's only met her once—he's already obsessed. He proposes to her that she should come back to his shop with him, to look at his stamp collection, and he's such a Sad Sack/Un-Lothario, that that is really what he means! She's honestly grateful to him: "I spent so much time at your place that day, when I passed out, and you were even kind enough to give me your bed. [!] But, no, I can't come over." Julien checks Claire's forehead for fever, and she doesn't have any; and next, to let him off the hook, and to make him feel better about himself, she reveals to him the kind-of-true reason why she can't get involved with him, which also happens to be the reason why she's been feeling so sickly, lately: "I'm in a bad way, Julien. My boyfriend made me pregnant." (In the 1930s, even in sexually-progressive [seeming] France, admitting to be *preggers*, out of wedlock, was tantamount to saying that you killed someone, and that you ate their guts, with some fava beans and a nice Chianti.) He tries to console her: "Well, it seems like the only guilty party is the father of the guy who knocked you up, because your boyfriend's dad is probably a rich guy [Julien's smart enough to know that beautiful women go for money—and plenty *of* it!] and he wouldn't give you any money for an abortion, am I right?" Claire's ocular floodgates then open up, because once you start confessing, you just can't stop, and she now admits to him that she's had affairs with lots of different men and that, because of her behavior, her father has thrown her out, onto the streets.

When Julien returns home, and mentions to his cleaning lady, Leonie, what Claire has just confessed to him, Leonie tells him that if he wants to be a real man, and maybe even if he wants to win Claire's heart, that he should go and see the father of the guy who knocked Claire up, and insist that the guy should give Claire some abortion money, and *plus-vite*. (In an American movie, smart-mouthed Leonie might have been played by Eve Arden, Barbara Bel-Geddes, or Kathleen Freeman, or by any other 'endearingly-smart-mouthed frump.')

Julien next steels himself, and pays a visit to Claire's rich *daddy-o*, Mr. Amanecer (Anthony Gildes), and this is where director Tourneur will give us a quick preview of the famous 'spooky, *Tourneurian*-atmosphere' which he's going to be conjuring up a decade later, and to much more of a sinister effect, in some of his American suspense and horror pictures from the 1940s: Julien paces in the background, addressing an offscreen 'person'—a person who happens to be casting a *gynormous* shadow on the wall behind Julien, and, uncharacteristically, he's acting really bravely, too: "You know, sir, when your son does something wrong—like, for example, getting a young girl pregnant—I see it as your responsibility to make everything right." Tourneur hilariously, next, yanks his camera back, to reveal that Julien's not in Mr. Amenecer's office at all: He's in Amanecer's waiting room, practicing his speech on the object which, as we're now learning, was casting that human-looking shadow on the wall—a twelve-inch-high female statuette. Amanecer's secretary, who's been sitting there watching the whole thing, is giggling her ass off, and she informs Julien, in between chortles, that her boss will be unable to see him today.

The next day (persistence pays off), Julien finally gets his appointment with Amanecer, and he explains the *sitch* to the man, after which Amenecer calmly replies, "My son couldn't have impregnated the young lady you're talking about, because my son has been in Madagascar for the last five years. Anyway, who are you? And why are you disparaging my son?!"

Knowing that the guy is full of shit, Julien, very bravely, just keeps plugging away, no doubt impressed by his own rarely-evinced bravura: "It is you who are the grandfather, sir! The young mother is poor, and your job is to help her." Worn-down, Amenecer next cops to the fact that, perhaps, his son did visit Paris, recently, but he still can't figure out why it is that Julien, who has come to see him today instead of his own son, the guy who was the actual 'sperm donor.'

When Julien returns to his pharmacy, looking confident for the first time in the film (or, more correctly, for the second time, following his extremely confident talk with Mr. Amenecer), he informs Leonie that his meeting with the businessman has produced positive results: "Mr. Amenecer and I are very good friends now. He gave me five thousand francs!" Instead of congratulating Julien about the fact that Julien seems to have suddenly developed 'a pair,' Leonie just barks (women are never satisfied!), "Well, Claire is going to need ten times more money than that. As usual, you didn't get anything good." Julien has finally displayed some intestinal fortitude, and people are peeing all over him, anyway—just like how it always happens in the real world!

The next day, Claire shows up at the pharmacy, again, not because she wants to see

Julien, or because she needs his help, but because, as it's turning out, she likes listening to downstairs-neighbor Jean Cordier's music, as it drifts upwards into the pharmacy through the air vents, although she hasn't yet met the handsome, young 'Gabinian' gentleman who's playing the music. The film's co-screenwriters, Marcel Levesque, Julien Renauldin, and Rene Pujol will now turn the film's narrative into a kind of isosceles love triangle, in which the three participants (or, I guess, 'the three unequal angles') are Claire, Gabin's 'Jean Cordier,' and not Marcel, but a record player! (This is definitely a *'ménage-a-RCA!'*)

While Julien loathes popular music, he sprints downstairs, anyway, to the Cordier music shop, to buy a radio for Claire, so that, as he's now telling her, very mooningly, she'll be able to have music in her life, and, all of the time. Now, remember: The character of Jean Cordier is played by Jean Gabin, and Jean Gabin always knows (it's second-nature) when there's a pretty girl upstairs; he's seen her, and he, like Julien, has become so smitten with her, that he now even offers to come upstairs and set the radio up for her. He enters the store, wearing a tux (he's strictly working-class, and looks mega-uncomfortable in this outfit), and his first, soothing, words to Claire are, "Just listen to a little violin. You'll feel better." Cleaning lady Leonie adores the music so much, that she accidentally leaves a pot of food to boil over, unattended, and you can bet that some hilarity is going to arise, from her kitchen boo-boo!

As it turns out, the pharmacy's new radio happens to be having a salient effect on business: Julien is now getting truckloads of new customers, because people are intrigued by the beautiful sounds which are emanating from within the shop (according to the logic of this movie, there's only one record player in the whole world!), and the next day, Cordier's up in the pharmacy dancing with Claire who, now that she's met him, is making herself a regular, over at the pharmacy. Julien comes in, having finished making some deliveries, and he is horrified, when he sees the girl of his dreams dancing with Jean Cordier. Cordier tells Julien that he's just there, in the pharmacy, "to make sure the radio is working well," but Julien isn't that dumb. (He's naïve, but no way is he dumb. He knows that Cordier wants to adjust some knobs—and not on the radio!) Julien takes Cordier aside and, with a burst of his newly-found bravado, roughly tells him, "Look, there's nothing wrong with the radio—so get out of here and don't come back, okay?"

Julien, now that he's 'a tough guy' (!), enrolls in driving school and takes lessons, thinking that he'll be able to impress Claire on a date, if he knows how to drive a car and, of course, he winds up driving onto the sidewalk, becoming confused between the gas and brake pedals, and, finally, he even crashes into a wall! He tries to soothe his slow-burning driving teacher, asking the guy, "So… Ever been in love?"

Later that day (at least, one of Julien's wishes is coming true) he's finally showing a bored-looking Claire his stamp collection; no doubt, she came into the shop looking for Cordier, but he's not around. She tells Julien that he doesn't have to worry about her having an affair with Cordier, because she's blowing town: "I'm going to go somewhere else—to another town. All I think about lately, is going far away, and starting a new life."

Julien and Claire are next interrupted by the obese Mrs. Triron, *the lady who eats more than most continents,* who now enters the store, feeling her customary 'sick.' Julien can't wait to ask her what she ate today, and she tells him that, just this morning, she consumed all twenty pounds of the baking soda which he had prescribed to her. (She made a giant cake out of it!) When Mrs. Triron leaves, Julien asks Claire why she wants to leave town and, of course, all the while, Leonie is in the back room, eavesdropping on this conversation, as she shines her boss's shoes. Claire says that she's bored here, but before she leaves for good, she'll allow Julien to take her to the carnival. (He's asked her on a date, so that she can ride bumper cars with him, and as we've already figured out, this is all the 'bumping' Julien's going to be getting out of her.) He makes himself seem even more pathetic on this 'pity-date' (if that's even possible), when he tells her that he'd be the perfect husband for her and, as they talk, they're also watching a couple with noisy kids, who are shopping in a nearby store. (It's a nerve-jangling tableau, and one which definitely doesn't make marriage look too wonderful.) "Are you sure you want to marry me?" Claire stammers at Julien, wishing she could get the hell out of this part of the conversation, and he just shrugs, "Well, you have to choose someone, right? Don't you want to have a nice husband to fight with?" As he's saying this, a clown walks by the store, and it's a very funny visual, because Julien's present behavior is pretty clownish, even though he, himself, doesn't realize it.

The next morning, post-carnival, Julien 'goes into training,' thinking that if he gets himself into shape, Claire might stick around. He, very agonizingly, tries to pound out a couple of sit-ups in his underwear and, at the same time, he's got a veal chop covering his face, which he hopes will take away his wrinkles! At this point, a tailor arrives, to fit Julien for a snazzy new suit and, while *the pinning* is happening, Leonie is just laughing *her fat butt* off, at him. ("You are such an idiot!")

Julien lamely defends himself, telling Leonie that he feels like he's still twenty, even though he looks more like he's pushing fifty. Claire has agreed to one more date with Julien, and we're starting to dislike her—not that we ever liked her too much anyway (at best, we've been pretty neutral about her)—since she's so wishy-washy about what she wants and doesn't want, and because it's getting more and more clear to us, not that we didn't already know this from the beginning of the movie, because we did, that she's just using 'pushover Julien' to get free stuff.

In the next sequence, Julien takes Claire canoeing (it's probably the first time he's ever been on a boat), and he lies to her, telling her that he was on the rowing team, in college. Next, it's off to a fancy restaurant, where he orders expensive champagne, while the fancy eatery's resident lady singer, Valies, croons the song, "Love is Stronger" (we heard her, but did not see her, singing the same song before, over the film's beginning credits). Julien and Claire dance, and he clumsily steps on her dress. (If Julien was Curly from the Three Stooges, we'd be hearing a big ripping sound right about now, and she'd be standing there, covering herself up in open-mouthed shame, and wearing only her slip!)

And guess who's now coming along, to ruin the date for Julien: It's Julien's 'rival,' Jean Cordier and, of course, Claire is excited about her surprise visitor. ("Oh, hello, Jean. I didn't know you eat at this restaurant!") Jean lies, modestly: "Oh, I come here a lot!" At this point, the Waiter whispers to Julien—not that we didn't already know this—that Cordier has never actually been to this restaurant. The girl singer asks Julien to dance—we can guess that she's probably a friend of Jean's, and that she's trying to get Julien away from Claire, so that Claire will be free to hang with the younger man—and she's hot; but Julien declines her offer of a dance, anyway: "No, thank you. I only like that one [Claire]." Note that, as Jean Gabin plays Cordier, Cordier, like most of Jean Gabin's movie characters, is 'a nice guy,' and we can tell that, even though Cordier's kind of a *wisenheimer*, that he doesn't want to hurt Julien... it's just that he really likes Claire, too.

As Claire and Jean dance, Julien is now alone at a table getting drunk, and before long, he's running over to a door marked '*toilette*,' his hand covering his mouth. The next day, he's more than a little hung-over. Leonie knows he's way too old to be getting righteously drunk, and she tells him that his behavior is now really starting to get childish, and maybe even more so than ever. His unrequited obsession with Claire worsening by the day, Julien has now taken to playing the same sad song on his own gramophone, over and over again.

But director Tourneur can't end his light-hearted comedy on a down-note, even though the main character is totally pathetic, so we finally get some good news for our hapless pharmacist: We find out that there *is* a lady in town who's hot for Julien after all, and that it's aging Mrs. Cordier—Jean Cordier's mother! Mrs. Cordier breezes into Julien's shop, and confesses to him that she's been in love with him, for ages. (So, as it's turning out, Julien wasn't the only one in the movie who was harboring an unrequited crush.) Julien starts getting all moony over Mrs. Cordier, and he now, sweetly, asks her if she would please begin addressing him as "my little mutton chop." (!) Julien tells the rotund lady that he's always loved her, as well, whether or not this is true, so, not only is Jean Cordier getting a happy ending with Claire, but Julien's getting one, as well. When Mrs. Cordier arrives back downstairs to her music shop a few moments later, her son Jean tells her that he's already married Claire. (It happened off-screen, so we didn't get to see their wedding.)

Tout ca ne vaut pas l'amour is a sweetly-entertaining little comedy-confection about life's persistent loneliness and about how we're all forever grasping for things (and, especially, people) that are beyond our reach, and it's one of the best movies you'll ever see about the combined joy and sadness which marks all unrequited love. After *Tout ca ne vaut pas l'amour*, Marcel Levesque would appear in a number of other pictures, including Jean Renoir's great, 1935 melodrama, *Le Crime du Monsieur Lange*, before passing away in 1962.

What a Critic Says Today: In this charming confection, one of the great light comedies of the early 1930s, the French star of silent movies, Marcel Levesque, assays a nerdy scientist whose rival in love for Josseline Gael is Jean Gabin—and guess who wins? Everything about this movie is charming and wonderful, and it's a shame that today, it exists in only one print, at the CNC/Ministry of Culture, in France. (Critic: Chuck Leonard, Website: Films de France.com, September, 2007.)

With Colette Darfeuil.

FILM 4

Pour un soir..!

France, 1931 [Released in 1933]

(Literal English Translation: "FOR A NIGHT..!") Directed by Jean Godard. Produced by Dony Freres. Written by Robert de Lisle. Non-Original Music by Tchaikovsky and Mozart, Arranged by W.S. Morris. (GENRE: MELODRAMA) A Gaumont-Peterson-Paulsen Production. Released in France in 1933, by Victoria Cinema. Running Time, 1 hour 17 minutes. Never Released Theatrically in the United States.

> "'Love,' with a 'Big L,' is no more than a trap for naive people. There is only 'Desire,' and to be satisfied, and that's all there is."
> — *Angry lady with heart of stone offers her views on life, in "Pour un soir..!"*

Like Jean Gabin's previous three efforts, *Pour un soir..!* is a sweet (and lowdown) little jazz-age confection, which will never be confused with *Citizen Kane;* on the other hand, at the end of its brief running time, you'll be totally satisfied. (How many of today's movies can you say that about?)

Director Jean Godard (no relation to you-know-who; Jean-Luc Godard's 'pops,' was a doctor) opens the film as only a person named Godard can, with an experimental, time-lapse shot—a seriously undercranked (a/k/a, 'fast-motion') shot of the night sky, in which automobiles skid through nighttime Paris, and street lights blend together into what resembles electric eels. Fifty years later, in a bunch of 1980s movies, including Godfrey Reggio's *Koyannisqatsi* and Francis Coppola's *Rumble Fish*, this effect will become *de rigueur*, and it's very surprising to find such a filmically-advanced shot in such an early movie, especially in such a rice paper-thin, albeit very good, little melodrama.

After dazzling us thusly, Godard next cuts to his first interior, the giant dining room of Le Lido, Paris's swankiest jazz club (in this movie, anyway), and he tantalizes us further, by now introducing us to the *glitterati* of his city, fancily-appareled folks who sit around small, round tables, watching an extravagant, proto-Esther Williams-esque synchronized-swimming ballet which is taking place in the club's indoor swimming pool, and all while whacking little paddle balls at each other, from table to table, and making a giant mess of the club, in the process. (Oh, those crazy 'idle rich!') It's funny to see the well-heeled carrying on like a bunch of spoiled children, which Godard very clearly wants us to know, they are.

Two men—one, old (Georges Melchoir) and the other, young (Guy Ferrant)—are taking this all in from a table in the back, and the younger man's eyes are fairly popping out of his head, as a beautiful brunette crosses the room. "Is it Marie?" he asks his older dining companion. "Do you know her?" The older man is amazed that his young friend has heard of her: "Know her? Are you kidding? I come here every night, just to see Marie sing." The girl they're talking about isn't really named 'Marie,' but 'Stella-Marie,' and she's played by Colette Darfeuil—*nee* Emma Floquet—who's first-billed, in the film. Stella-Marie belts out a lusty little torcher called "*Pour un soir..!*" ("For a Night...!"), as the roomful of guys gawk at her, all of them looking like love-starved wolves out of some demented Tex Avery cartoon.

The older man now tells the younger man his 'Stella-Marie story:' "She really is marvelous—you're right! In fact, once, I knew another young man who fell for her, just like you seem to be doing right now. He was a sailor, and didn't know that her love wasn't forever. This young officer who loved her died of heartbreak. Let me tell you a story about 'The Sailor who Loved Stella-Marie,' and then you will understand..." Such is (or, was) our story's framing device and now, director Godard transports us into a small seaside tavern, and to a grotty, old sailor bar, in the southern French port town of Toulon, and the name of this bar is '*On paie en servant*'—or, in English, 'Pay the Waiter.' (Toulon is the port city in which French sailors, yesterday and today, have always spent their shore-leave, and it's a city which, six years after *Pour un soir..!*, in 1937, will also figure into Jean Gabin's most famously iconic movie of all, *Pepe Le Moko,* the picture in which Gabin will play a crafty con-artist who used to be a sailor from Toulon.) The first person we see in this bar is a gruff male singer who's belting one out for a bunch of young sailors whose heads are topped with little sailor-berets which have little cotton balls on their tops, and the song which he's singing, is about his own, now-long-past affair with the legendary Stella-Marie. (Lyrics: "I regret loving a young girl... I hope that wherever she is, she is drinking to my health.") This is where we'll get to meet not only innocent, wide-eyed young Sailor Matthew (Jean Gabin) for the first time, but also the decidedly un-innocent Stella-Marie, and it's clear, judging from her too-sultry appearance, that she does more than just sing for the bar's customers. She asks Matthew to dance, introducing herself to him with the regulation opener, "Do you come here often," and he tells her, shyly, that, while it's his first time in this particular boat bar, that he does enjoy the occasional '*femmes-deluxes*' ('*Femme-deluxe*' = French slang, for 'prostitute.') Matthew is instantly smitten with Stella-Marie, and it's possible, from the way that she's staring right back at him, that she might like him, as well, and possibly even a bit more than she likes other members of her clientele.

After a few dances, it's time for all good things to come to an end and, besides, it's time for Matthew to get back to his ship. When he boards, a sailor-buddy comically (and literally!) kicks his ass, and his C.O. tells him that, because he's been so diligent in returning on time, and because he's "a credit, to the Navy," that he's entitled to an extra ten days of shore leave, here in Toulon. Matthew thanks him, profusely, and we know where Matthew will be tonight, and probably, for every other night of the next ten nights.

As soon as night falls, Matthew's back in the sailor bar, chatting Stella up, and she tells Matthew that she's happy he's returned. Clearly, it's instant *mega-lust* for both of them, as she grabs him and holds him tightly, burying his face in her heaving bosoms. (Matthew looks like the luckiest little boy you've ever seen and, comically, we see only the back of his head, while 'the Gabin Visage' is buried deeply within her cleavage, and we can actually hear him making *frisky, snorting sounds!*) Young Jean Gabin, in a few of the movies which he made during this first cycle of his film career, including this one, always wears his emotions on his sleeve, unlike the famous 'Movie Gabin' of just a few years later who, in his best-known pictures, won't wear any emotions at all on his sleeves (his cuffs, his trouser-legs, or anywhere). Stella's clearly hotter for Matthew, than she is for the other sailors, although she does tell him that, in her belief system, there's no such thing as 'love'—only lust.

The next morning (Matthew has spent the night with Stella, at her place), Matthew goes to visit his aging Mother (Regine Dhally) who, when we meet her, is asking her son about why he doesn't want to spend his shore leave going fishing with his father! Toulon's a small town, and *mamma-san* already knows that her baby boy is falling in love with this locally-notorious man-eater/tramp who, in the parlance of 1970's rocker, Elvin Bishop, "Loves 'em and leaves 'em alone." Mom tells Matthew, "Don't spend too much time with that Stella-Marie. She'll mock you, like she does all of the others—she's a slut!" But Matthew keeps his cool, just as we'll see Jean Gabin doing in most of his other movies. He just smiles at his beloved matriarch, happy to be around her, even though she's bitterly running-down his choice of *fucktoy.*

Matthew spends that same afternoon walking Toulon's deserted streets (where'd everybody go?!), a tiny, lone figure weaving through archways, knapsack slung over his shoulder, and accompanied, on the film's soundtrack, by some weirdly out-of-place music—music which seems like it might be more appropriate to a staged ballet, than it is to a pulpy, little French melodrama—Tchaikovsky's "Dance of the Sugar Plum Fairies." (In fact, the whole movie is punctuated by weirdly-inappropriate classical music, the tone of which is inconsistent with that of the story. Probably, already-existing music is all that the filmmakers of this smallish-budget film could afford, but director Godard, in choosing to use pre-recorded music, happens to be in good company, since Stanley Kubrick and Woody Allen are two other directors who normally use non-original music, as well, and when they do it, just like when the little known Jean Godard did it, it's always extremely effective.)

Walking all morning has made Matthew *powerful-hungry,* and he hurries home and kisses his mother, surprising her, with some good news: He's going to be staying at home, and visiting with her and his dad, for ten days. (*Daddy-o's* still out fishing, though; we'll only see him in the film a couple of times, and both times only in extreme-longshot.) She brings him his favorite lunch, and he now lights up like a Christmas tree, when he sees what's being set in front of him, exclaiming, with all the genuine enthusiasm in the world (and this is a very sweet, and childlike, moment), "I like leek soup!"

After lunch, Matthew again wanders the streets of Toulon alone, but this time, he's 'wandering, with intent,' and trying to find Stella-Marie. Sure enough, he sees her, down by the docks, and, of course, she's down there, *cruising for bone,* but Matthew's young and naïve, and he hasn't figured that out, yet. She's happy to see him, too, and she asks him how long he thinks he's going to be in town, so he tells her his good news, about his ten days of freedom. "We'll see each other again," she promises, offering him up her services as Toulon Tourguide, and their meeting is punctuated, on the soundtrack, with Mozart's "A Little Night Music." As she leaves, promising to see him again soon, she 'accidentally' drops a handwritten letter, onto the ground. Matthew ("Mr. Curious") picks it up and reads it and, of course, it turns out to be a love letter, written to Stella by another man. We, the audience, are a bit ahead of Matthew, and we already know that she's dropped the letter on purpose, to passive-aggressively screw with Matthew's larval emotions.

Later that day, Matthew's on his dad's fishing boat, when he decides that he wants to return Stella's lost letter to her. That night, up in her room, Stella's *doing the hang* with her dowdy, older sister, Monique, who's played by Cillie Anderson. (What would movies be without the frumpy older sister who gives homespun advice to the young, hot sister?)

The doorbell rings—it's Matthew. Intrigued by the young man's surprising presence, she asks him why he's come, and he informs her that he's returning the letter which she had let 'fall,' earlier that day. (We can tell that he definitely wants to ask her about the man who wrote the letter, and that he's feeling jealous, over this mysterious Other Guy, but that he's way too shy.) Then, he notices that she's wearing gloves and, excitedly, he asks her if she might let him keep one. Excited by his boyish enthusiasm, she hands one over, and, when she does, he's instantly the happiest swabby since Popeye! ("Thank you! You're nice!" he emotes, innocently.) Then he gets tongue-tied—"Uh… Okay, well, so, goodbye mademoiselle!"—and he tells her that he's going off to hang with his friends: One 'trope' which we're going to start seeing in nearly all of Jean Gabin films, whether they're made in 1931 or in 1971, is that the friendship between the films' male characters will almost always be more important to Jean Gabin than the love of *fickle women.* (Read more chapters, and see if I'm kidding!) She asks him if he'll come to see her, tomorrow, and he nervously mumbles, "Yes, tomorrow," and then runs out of the room, shyly, and as fast as his legs can carry him. We get some pretty extreme close-ups of Jean Gabin in this film and, no doubt, this is a carry-over from silent cinema, which had recently run its course; in this picture, Gabin is actually wearing false eyebrows and makeup, and, of course, this is because the big, industrial movie lights of 1931 would only capture faces if they were sharply defined, and the only way to define them, was to slather on the makeup.

When Matthew leaves, Monique asks Stella-Marie, cynically, what she intends on doing with "that one," and Stella-Marie replies, casually, "It's very simple," and we know, by the cavalier way in which she's said that, that any time now, she's going to be letting him down, big-time, just like she always does with *all of the other Men of Planet Earth*, all of whom are putty in her neatly-manicured hands, but he doesn't expect it, because he's young and innocent, and he hasn't yet learned that all life is, is deceit piled upon deceit, piled upon even more deceit! If you want to know why the famous Jean Gabin Movie Characters, which he'll soon be playing from 1934 on, will rarely allow themselves to get too attached to the women for whom they've made their feelings known, you can get some back-story, just from watching Gabin's early, too-vulnerable characters, whom he played in these, his first bunch of movies which he made between 1930 and 1933, in which his characters *do* get attached to women, because many of them are young and naïve, and they still believe in 'love'—and then, because these characters believe in love, they wind up getting hurt. (The more mature Gabin characters will rarely put themselves 'in harm's way,' like that.)

Stella-Marie is now soliloquizing, once again, about how stupid love is, and she tells Monique, that "real love" with, what she calls, a "Big L," is no more than "a trap for naive people." In her own words, "There is only desire, and to be satisfied... and that's it." Monique tells Stella that she's too cynical, and Stella succinctly replies, "I'm not cynical. I'm realistic."

The next day, Stella-Marie and Matthew are canoodling under a tree. "Did time without me seem long?" she asks him, teasingly grinning at him, and reminding him that he's just a kid. She, next, interrupts their big make-out session, to tell him that her friends are waiting for her—which is exactly what he told her the night before, except, when he said it, he wasn't referencing acts of prostitution! This particular meeting between our two lovers proves to be a very short one, since she just wanted to meet-up with him to toy with him a little, or in other words, to buoy herself up from the attentions of this 'too-nice' guy, so that she can go off and get her jollies with those more ass-holishly-brutish bad-boys whom she really craves. Matthew asks her if he'll be able to see her again, and she replies, coquettishly, "Yes. If you're a nice boy." They kiss and now, he's more smitten with her than ever. (This can't end well! In fact, we know already that it won't end well, because that's what the old guy at the Lido told his younger dining companion-guy, at the beginning of the picture.)

That night, Matthew returns to Stella's apartment again, to the strains of "A Little Night Music," and because Matthew is young and impetuous (and energetic), he happily shimmies up the side of the building to surprise her. Monique and Stella, two of the *vainest Frenchie babes* you'll ever meet, are sitting by their make-up mirrors, which they'll do for a good deal of the film, since the characters of Monique and Stella are defined completely by their sexuality. When Monique goes off to sleep, and Stella-Marie takes to the couch to thumb through a magazine, Matthew sneaks into the room! At this point, director Godard fades out quickly, and we can assume that a little *huggin'-and-munchin'* was probably the order of the evening.

The next day, a happy and, very obviously, post-coital Matthew is wandering alone on the banks of the Toulon beach, looking very relaxed. He watches as carefree families play in the sand, and he's then shocked to see Stella Marie on the beach—and with another guy!

(He's shocked, but we're not; in fact, we've been checking our watches, and waiting for the scene in which Matthew will actually see her with *another dude*.) Matthew and Stella-Marie take a long look at each other, and Matthew looks like a tire with all the air deflating out of it—SSSSSSSSSSS!!!!!

Matthew wanders away, backpack slung over his shoulder, and director Godard now double-exposes the young sailor-man's walk-of-shame, with a series of quick flashbacks to his past meetings with Stella-Marie. His ten days of shore leave are over, and he now decides to return to his mom's house to say goodbye, before stopping off for a final drink at *On paie le servant.* When Matthew gets to the bar, a new bar girl, Nini (Jacqueline Ford), whom we're meeting now for the first time, sees how sad he looks, and she asks him if he's alone, but at this point, feeling a bit melancholy, he's more interested in just sipping a solitary glass of wine, than he is in hanging with a girl who isn't Stella-Marie, even if Nini *is* a little cutie-pie! He gulps his wine, alone in a corner of the bar, while absently playing with the glove which Stella gave him, but a surly sailor sees the glove, grabs it, and starts making fun of Matthew, who instantly becomes *bull-mad.* ("Give it back! It's my souvenir!") This is the one-and-only time in the whole movie in which Gabin's character will get mad (and, similarly, in many of the movies he'll make throughout his career, he will also only have one 'outburst'). Next, a bum enters the bar, and everybody stops making fun of Matthew for just long enough to make fun of this other guy—a guy who's in even worse shape than Matthew is.

Then, it's time for Nini to take her place on stage, and to sing, and, while she warbles, a guy whose five o' clock shadow looks like it overslept, until 7:15, is ogling her just like she's a fancy *brioche,* straight out of *la boulangerie.* The lyrics to her song are all about class relations, which as I've already said, in this book (and don't worry, I'll only say it about five or six thousand more times) is pretty typical for a French movie, because Old French Movies, just like Old France, always seemed to be dealing with issues pertaining to social-class:

> "People sometimes come in here from high society/They come here to try
> and come down to our [proletarian] level/ But we know they're not 'from
> here,' because they have all the wrong manners."

Nini, who comes up to Matthew's table to sing, tries playfully to wrest the glove from him (she has no idea about the glove's significance, and she wants to use it as a prop, for her singing performance), but he grabs it back, defensively. The guy with the '7:15 shadow'—a real 'Bluto' type—sees Matthew yanking the glove away from her, and thinks Matthew's trying to mess with her: ("Are you done hurting that girl?" he grunts.) Matthew and the Big Lug engage in a little '*mano-a-Gabino,*' while another guy in the bar (one of the bar's musicians) is underscoring the fight, by cheerfully playing his accordion.

Matthew's down! Then he's up! Then, he throws the Big Guy across the room, and the guy's head smashes against the bar! Is he dead? (No!) The other sailors in the bar, who have been raucously favoring Matthew over the big guy in the fight, are very protective of him, as people will be with Jean Gabin, in all of his movies, because, no matter what side of the law Gabin's movie characters are on, he's always the consummate man-of-the-people, and everybody always loves him. Concerned for his well-being, they all advise him to blow town, and *stat*. "If the cops come looking for you," one friendly Sailor warns Matthew, "we'll pretend like you weren't here, okay?"

Of course, the bar's Owner, who's not as nice as his customers, brings a cop down to the scene and, to his own future detriment, Matthew has amscrayed from the bar so fast, that he's actually left his duffel-bag behind, complete with his identification tag. He makes for his ship, so that he can hide out, but it's not in the port—it's in dry-dock, getting repaired. The Cops next interrogate Matthew's mom, who tells them truthfully that she hasn't seen him: "So, you haven't seen your son? And you don't know where he is?" She just asks, through her tears, "Why? Is he in some kind of trouble?" (*Pour un soir..!* is a totally melodramatic 'weepy,' just like Al Jolson's 1927 *yiddishkeit* music-and-melodrama-fest, *The Jazz Singer*. In fact, because *Pour un soir..!* was actually one of the earliest French 'talkies,' even though it was released two years after it was made, it's worth noting that much of the emotion in the film is carried, not by dialogue, but by exaggerated facial expressions, mostly, 'crying' expressions, and sorrowful music, all filmic devices which are, of course, holdovers from the recently-defunct world of silent cinema.)

Pour un soir..!, in the melodramatic way in which it portrays its mother-son relationship, bears striking similarities not only to director Alan Crosland's *The Jazz Singer*, but also to the numerous Yiddish-language features which would be directed in America in the 1930s and '40s, by filmmakers such as B-movie maven Edgar G. Ulmer. What *Pour un soir..!* shares in common with these Yiddish pictures, is that both the Gabin picture and the Yiddish pictures deal, in addition to romantic love, with everybody's favorite 'Jewish subject matter' (to which this author can relate!), the intertwined issues of 'family love' and 'family misery.'

After the cops leave Matthew's Mom's house, she breaks down and cries. She isn't covering up for Matthew, either—she genuinely doesn't know where he is, or even if he's okay. She stares at a photograph of her beloved little *boychik*, Matthew, and even begins talking to it: "My son! My poor little one!" (In what other film will you ever hear quiet tough-guy Jean Gabin referred to, as 'my poor little one?' Only in this bizarre curio, folks! As Al Jolson said, in *The Jazz Singer*, "You ain't seen nothin,' yet!")

Mom's washing some plates that night, when Matthew makes his appearance. He tells her—and she's already figured this out, anyway—that he's been hiding out somewhere in town, and she closes the window-shades, so that he can't be seen, asks him if he's hungry and, next, proceeds to quiz him about what's been going on with him lately: "There is a story that you beat someone up. Is it true?" Matthew, who hasn't shaven in days, and who looks like he's at the end of his rope, merely changes the subject, asking her if his dad is home. She tells her son that the police have been looking for him, and he responds that he already knows that, and far too well. She wants him to eat something, but he tells her that he's going to have to leave right now, but that he's not going back to his ship, and that he can't tell her where he's going. He runs out, not wanting to subject her to any more pain than that which she has already experienced.

Matthew, on the way to wherever he's going, first makes a stop-over at Stella-Marie's apartment to say goodbye to her, and when he does (and we saw this coming, but Matthew didn't [again!]), he finds her with yet another sailor! Monique stops a fight between the two men, even before it starts, by lyingly telling the other guy that Matthew has come to see her, and not Stella. Monique leads Matthew off into another room.

Matthew, who's now in the adjoining room with Monique, is crying! "I'm not crying about Stella-Marie," Matthew sniffles to Monique. "I'm crying, about what I believed. You can't understand…" Like any young man, Matthew still believes in true love, whereas Stella-Marie, as we know only too well, believes only in hot, wet, hard, sticky, moist, pulsating, jackhammer-waisted lust (with, maybe, a couple of silver-dollar pancakes the next morning, for good measure).

Director Godard now dissolves to a cliff, at dusk. Matthew's dramatic silhouette is seen and, as he stands perilously-close to the precipice, we know what he's going to do next, because it's the same exact thing which military man Bruce Dern will do, forty years later, in Hal Ashby's *Coming Home,* when Dern's wife, who's played by Jane Fonda, has jilted him for Jon Voight, while Voight has been away in 'the 'Nam.' And just like Dern in that other picture, Matthew, too, leaves his uniform and his shoes on the ground, and he then makes his giant leap into eternity. *Pour un soir..!* is the first movie of many, in which Jean Gabin's character will be fated to an undeservedly tragic ending.

Le Club Lido, present day (actually, present night): We're now back in the film's wraparound segment, and the old male diner (Georges Melchoir) has just finished telling his young companion (Guy Ferrant) the sad, tragic story of Stella-Marie and her young sailor Matthew; obviously, the older guy has recounted the story to the younger guy as a kind of *caveat,* to warn him against striking up any kind of a relationship with Stella-Marie, that woman with a heart of stone. The younger of the two guys asks the older, if Matthew's body was ever found, and the older guy replies that it was not.

Next, right here in the nightclub scene, director Jean Godard will now present us with an incredible topless dance, which features full-on (and 'well-nippled') naked breasts, while the other women in the elaborate stage show, are all falling decoratively, and one-by-one, into the club's big, fancy pool; since we've just seen Jean Gabin dive into the ocean, in the previous sequence, this scene makes us feel uneasy, in spite of the fact that this little dance performance, in itself, is joyful.

Made in 1931, but unreleased in France until 1933, *Pour un soir..!,* a film which was unavailable for people to see for more than seventy years, suddenly turned up, in 2004, as a bonus feature on the French-language-only DVD of another thought-lost-for-decades Gabin picture, 1939's *Le Recif de corail (The Coral Reef),* a picture which you'll be discovering later. Lobster Films, in France, has done a yeoman's job of restoring both *Pour un soir..!* and *Le Recif de corail* for the French DVD and, maybe, in the due course of time, both pictures will get American DVD releases, with *sous-titres en anglais*. (For the monolingual, that means: "Subtitles in English.")

What a Critic Says Today: "This is the only film [directed] by Jean Godard. Gabin's famous movie persona [of] 'the unfortunate good guy,' is busy being born here. The hero of such [upcoming] masterpieces as *La Bandera, Le Quai des brumes, Le Jour se leve,* and *La Bete humaine* is not far." (From: Internet Movie Database. Critic: D.B. DuMonteil, 1-31-2006.)

With Jean-Max.

FILM 5

PARIS-BEGUIN

France/Germany, 1931

(Literal English Translation: "PARIS-CRUSH") Directed by Augusto Genina. Written by Francis Carco. Produced by Maurice Orientier, Adolphe Osso, and Geoffroy. Music and Lyrics by Maurice Yvain, Francis Carco, Serge Veber, and Robert Tessiere. ("Mme. Jeanne Marnac Sings 'It is for You that I Have a Crush,' on Parlophone Records.") Directors of Photography (black and white), Friedl Behn-Grund, Louis Nee, and Paul Briquet. Editor, Germain Fried. (GENRES: MELODRAMA, OPERETTA) A Production of Societe des Films OSSO and Serge Pimenoff Pictures. Running Time, 1 hour 57 minutes. Released in France by Films Osso, on September 10, 1931. Released in the United States (French-only, no English subtitles) on December 30, 1932, by Protex Pictures Corp., as "THE DARLING OF PARIS."

"You'd better not threaten me! My gun is bigger than yours!"
— *Low-level gangster Gabin isn't afraid of his psychotic crime-king boss, in "Paris-Beguin"*

As this very impressive comedy-drama begins, a gramophone record spins a popular song of the day, as a cute little lapdog lazes across a daybed. Some clothes are strewn on the floor and, next to them, a handwritten note reminds the popular stage star, Jane Diamond, who's played in this film by the real-life French stage-star and operetta-singer Jeanne Marnac, who lives in this little apartment, that "rehearsal has been set back, to 4:30." We see her face, first, as she's slathering on her makeup, and comforting her little dog. ("My little girl, you're so beautiful!") Jane's maid, Simone, who is very attractive in her own right, and who's played by Violaine Barry, comes in to tell her that her gluttonous-looking and much-older husband, Hector (Saturnin Farbre), is on the phone for her. Jane instructs Simone to tell hubby that she's not home, and when Simone hangs up, she tells Jane that Hector didn't believe it, but Jane doesn't seem to care a whit about what her old benefactor believes or doesn't believe: The union between Jane and Hector will never be confused with any of the great screen marriages, in fact Hector, who's basically her sugar-daddy, doesn't even live with her; the out-of-shape older man is basically, we can tell, happy for whatever crumbs he gets, after his wife is done having sex with other men—men who are both younger and stronger than he is. Since Hector never hung up the phone on his end, Jane finally decides to take the call, and she comically yells into the receiver, "Didn't you hear Simone tell you that I'm not in! Don't you understand French?" From this speedy little interchange, we can immediately see that she's the one who really wears the pants in the family.

Cut to a local vaudeville house, where preparations are being made for an upcoming performance of a new operetta, which is called "*Paris-Beguin*" or, in English, "Paris-Crush:" Yes, the name of this movie is also the name of the play-within-the-movie. A group of male dancers who are rehearsing their act, lift up and place a reed-thin and constantly sneezing comic, by the name of Ficelle, into a wooden box. Ficelle is played by Fernandel, the great rubber-faced movie actor and comedian who, just like Jean Gabin, was about to become a big star in his own right, and Fernandel would, in fact, remain one of Jean Gabin's closest friends throughout both of their lives: In fact, thirty-three years after this film was made, in 1963, the two men would even start a production company together, and once in awhile, Fernandel would cook one of Gabin's favorite foods—beans—for him.

The producer of the stage show which is being rehearsed in our film, the bespectacled and completely myopic Charmant (Pierre Finaly)—in English, '*charmant*' means 'Charming,' a quality which is completely anathemic to this guy—now asks Ficelle why he can't stop sneezing, and Ficelle replies, in a completely deadpan manner, "I had a fly on my nose a few months ago, and when I think about it, it still makes me sneeze!" The male dancers have placed a ring of flowers around Ficelle's head, and it is these flowers which are really causing his nasal histrionics.

Charmant is one of those producers who loves blowing his stack—oh, yeah, we've still got 'em, today—and when we see him next, he's screaming at his cast and crew, and we can tell by their giggles that they are completely unafraid of him. "I've had enough of you people!" he bellows. "If any of you laugh at me, I'll turn you into statues!" Ficelle starts comically imitating his boss, right in front of him, but Charmant is so nearsighted, he can't see what they're all laughing at: "You idiots! What's so funny? You know I can't see!"

Paranoid Charmant has three yes-men/stooges who follow him around, kissing his ass, lighting his stogies, and telling him that every decision he makes is right up there with Alexander's subjugation of the Persian Empire. Charmant wants to know who it is, in the cast or crew, that keeps hiring crazy Ficelle back every time he fires him, but nobody's willing to own up to it. Ficelle likes being at the theatre because, in spite of the fact that his boss hates him, everybody else there likes him a lot: In movies, Fernandel, just like Jean Gabin, always plays 'everybody's pal.'

At that moment, the star of the show, Jane Diamond, enters and, from the second she arrives at the theater, she's already on-the-warpath, disapproving loudly of the song which Charmant has asked her to sing in the first act. He tries to placate her ("It's such a charming tune!"), but she yells back at him that she thinks the song is stupid, because it's all about money, and not love and that, to her, love is more important than money. (What a hypocrite: We've already seen that Jane's completely money-hungry, and that she, like Stella-Marie in *Pour un soir..!*, hates love.) While Jane's not too crazy about the song, she is interested in the comedy sketch which she's also going to be performing in the show, and she tells Charmant that she'd like to rehearse it right now, before she does anything else. Charmant tells her—and he's not the most diplomatic guy you'll ever meet—that she's "annoying" and "sticky," and Jane just ignores him, asking to see her stylist, the matriarchal-looking Suzanne. As Suzanne starts pinning her, Jane, additionally, requests the presence of the play's author and, almost instantaneously, the professorial-looking Writer, who's played by Charles Lamy, enters her dressing room; everybody walks on eggshells around volatile Jane, and nobody, but nobody, would ever dream of keeping her waiting.

"Hello, my dear interpreter," the Writer greets Jane, with his lips planted firmly—and sadly, only figuratively—on her hot, round derriere. Charmant is there, too, and he starts throwing-out more of his lame suggestions but, and this is a clue to how unimportant everybody in the theater company regards him to be, the Writer actually tells the Producer to pipe down! Jane asks the Writer if her new male co-star, the empty-headed Beausourire (Pierre Mayer) has arrived yet—the word '*beausourire*,' in English, means 'nice smile' and, basically, a nice smile is all that this empty-headed actor is—and when Beausourire arrives, he, too, begins sucking-up to her, immediately. ("Hello, my dear! You are so beautiful!") But Jane's a very savvy lady, and she totally knows when somebody's bullshitting her: She announces to the whole company that she's now feeling "a little warm," and insists that the entire theatre should be cooled-down for her own, personal comfort: "Bring the wind, here!" she booms in her most God(dess)-like timbre. The stagehands frenetically beat the curtains to simulate wind, and their effectiveness can be seen immediately, because the orchestra conductor's toupee blows right off of his head, landing right in the orchestra pit. What we're seeing here, is comic mayhem at its finest.

After Jane gets the wind which she's demanded—and why not; she's a huge windbag—she begins complaining about the show's script, and she does so in no uncertain terms: "The public is not so lame! They won't believe the story. It's more normal that I don't fall in love with king, and that he shouldn't give my jewels back." Even though Jane's an utter virago, we're now managing to like her a bit anyway, and for the very first time in the picture, because we're seeing that she trusts in the intelligence of the public: Just like one of today's 'creative executives' in the movie business, Jane is trying to rewrite certain scenes in order to make the show a more satisfactory experience for its audience, and this is one characteristic of hers which is entirely commendable.

It's time now for Jane to rehearse her sketch, and her performance is going to be underscored by the orchestra, although the tympani player just can't seem to get his cues right. When the Director calls for action, and the curtain is raised, we see that Jane's asleep on a bed, in the middle of the stage, for real, and that she's supposed to be 'waking up' in the middle of the night,' which she next does, standing atop the bed and dancing joyously to a song which is called, "The Big Life." At the end of the number, a paper moon is supposed to appear over the stage, but none of the stage-hands can remember where he's placed it. "Where's the moon?" Jane screams. "Bring me the moon, dammit! You idiots all go and look for it! What are you all doing? Sleeping?!" (But don't expect too many 'warm fuzzies' from this frosty *fraulein!*) Fortunately for his job, a prop man finds the moon, and the crew now breathes a collective sigh of relief, but the crew-members are sighing too soon, because, when she sees the moon, she starts impugning its veracity as a satellite: "It's ugly to me. I'm not doing this stupid show anymore. I want to go to sleep!" She then lies down on the stage bed and actually nods off again, right in front of everybody, and nobody is brave enough to wake her; indeed, it's a whole lot quieter now, with her passed out like that.

The Writer slouches in the front row with producer Charmant, and they both look relieved momentarily, because Jane's asleep, and is therefore docile. Beausourire, the leading man, begins rehearsing his big song (Lyrics: "Money and jewels, they will make you *diiiiie!*"), but he's a diva, just like Jane is, and he throws up his arms, alerting Charmant to the fact he is unable to do it: "I just don't feel this song." Jane, who has woken up during his off-key warbling—indeed, she woke up because of it—agrees with him wholeheartedly.

Beausourire, a typically-narcissistic actor, can't believe that nobody's paying attention to him, and he's both flabbergasted and insulted by Jane's rampant obnoxiousness. The Writer, having realized already that the rest of the day is going to be a lost cause, tells cast and crew that rehearsal will resume tomorrow; probably, he wants to go home and rework the whole scenario, but Jane, who outranks everybody, tells the crew, nonsensically, that not only will today's rehearsal continue, but that it will not be continuing with her! And then, right after she says it, the moon falls off it's cables and crashes into the stage, funny 'punctuation' which definitely serves to relieve the cast and crew's stress.

Next, we're at a local Paris train station and, at about, twenty-five minutes into the film, we're going to get to see 'everyman' Bob (Jean Gabin) for the very first time. He's standing on a corner alone, since 'Jean Gabin' and 'aloneness' go hand-in-hand. He's identified on screen, first, by his nice shoes—his spats—because the first thing that the film's director, Augusto Genina, wants us to understand about smooth-criminal Bob, is that even though he's just a common street hoodlum, he's also, like some of the gentleman-gangster-characters whom an older Gabin will begin playing in the 1950s, a man of taste, and his character will also have an omnipresent cigarette dangling from his lips for much of the movie. A woman, Jobette (Rachele Berendt), notices Bob as he walks from the train station into a local bar, and she follows him inside, just like in one of those Warner Bros. cartoons from the 1940s in which the hungry wolf follows the beckoning finger-of-smoke toward the meal, and it goes without saying that it's easy to get girls when you're Jean Gabin: Gabin seeks out female companionship very rarely in his films, but girls always just hit on him because, to paraphrase Charles Darwin in an extremely roundabout manner, *they're girls and he's Gabin.* Jobette already knows Bob, though, and she smiles at him, telling him that she's happy to see him, and she asks him to take a good whiff of her neck, because she's doused herself in a special perfume, just for him. (How do you say 'stalker' in French?) Uninterested—and as we all know, feigning disinterest in people always makes them more interested in you—he tells her that he can't really tell, because his nose is plugged. He pours her a glass of wine, while checking out another girl in the bar whose neck he'd probably rather be snorting, and he next hoists his glass to, and winks at, this second lady: "To your love life," he grins, toasting the other woman. Jobette, who is undeterred, asks Bob why he's only taken one sip of his wine, and he tells her that he's taking a break: He's had four drinks already this evening, and he's having a well-deserved 'breather,' before approaching No. 5.

Ficelle (Fernandel) happens to be in the bar as well, and this little rubber-faced guy seems to be doing much better in the lady-department than Gabin's Bob is doing, if that's even possible; he's even sitting right between two women, and he's impressing them mightily, with crazy show biz stories. Apparently, Charmant has definitively fired Ficelle from the theater company this time, after months, or maybe even years, of only firing him half-heartedly, and always taking him back: "A fly messed up my career," he moans, attracting the sympathy of the two ladies, who seem angry that Ficelle has gotten himself canned, and Bob, who knows a good thing when he sees it—Jean Gabin's always a good guy in his pictures, but he's never above the occasional cock-block—takes a seat alongside Ficelle and his 'wimminfolk,' and this is where we discover that Bob and Ficelle already know each other: They're old friends, although Bob doesn't exactly trust Ficelle, a guy who sometimes narcs on his own friends, whenever it means that he's going to be remunerated for it; Ficelle's not bad (Bob recognizes this, and it's why he still likes the guy), he's just weak, kind of like John Cazale's Fredo Corleone-character in the *Godfather* pictures: Ficelle's the kind of medium-toxic friend with whom you like to hang out, even though you don't really want to tell him too much personal information about yourself, because it'll just give him 'ammunition.' (This same exact kind of character—a friend, or a brother whom you like, even though you can't completely trust him, will turn up again in three more Gabin pictures—1942's *Moontide;* 1957's *Le Rouge est mis;* and 1972's *Le Tueur*.) Bob's already heard that Ficelle has just been downsized by the theater company, because Ficelle's a pretty popular vaudeville comic, and the story of his firing has already appeared in the evening's papers. Ficelle doesn't care a whit that he's been fired and, of course, a big part of Fernandel's movie persona, is that his characters are always happy, even when—or, especially when—things aren't going well. In *Paris-Beguin,* Fernandel's character of Ficelle is really happy and excited, because his firing has gotten him into the newspapers.

At that moment, a surly, smoking gangster—a guy who appears to be right out of any early-thirties' WB crime flick—enters the bar. He's scar-faced Dede, and he's played by Jean-Max. Jobette, knowing that she doesn't have a chance with the object of her affections (Bob), now sets her high-beams on the similarly-sturdy Dede, instead: "It's me: Jobette," she coos, pursing her lips at the guy, just like Betty Boop. Dede sits with Jobette and, in tones which are both hushed and conspiratorial, they now start talking about Bob.

Dede now swaggers over to where Bob, Ficelle, and Ficelle's two ladies continue to make small-talk, and Ficelle, who's totally *emborrachado,* begins hiccupping wildly, and not because he's tanked-up, but because he's deathly afraid of Dede who, as it is turning out, one of

Paris's most notorious gang-bosses. Ficelle gets up and leaves, and Dede sits down in his place, a bit too-close to Bob; and since Bob is played by the always-cool-under-pressure Jean Gabin, Bob doesn't back away or look threatened: He just stares right back at the guy, with that famously hard-to-read Jean Gabin scowl, a scowl which we'll be seeing at least once in every Gabin movie which will be made from this point, on. Dede reminds Bob that, recently, he (Dede) stood-in for Bob during a crime which Bob was supposed to perpetrate for him, and that now, it's Bob's turn, tonight, to pay the favor back, by committing a crime for him. While Bob is a part of Dede's gang, he's not-at-all intimidated by his boss: He just pulls his own gat on Dede and tells him, in very calm tones, "You'd better not threaten me. My gun is bigger than yours!" Anyway, once they get the whole phallic/alpha-male/mine's-bigger-than-yours-posturing out of their systems, Bob agrees to 'do the crime.'

The following evening at the theater, rehearsal has gone well for a change, and Jane looks so happy, that she even goes out dancing afterwards with an older man, dark-haired Richard (Taki Galano), a man whom, when we meet him, is trying to impress her with the fact that he's a many-times-decorated Colonel. (She was vibing on him pretty heavily until he brought up the issue of his rank, and now—and we can tell this from the sour look on her face—she probably thinks he's bragging, to make up for some paucity of phallus-size.) She turns away from him, sits, and begins entertaining a tableful of other men, and these guys look appreciative that she has deigned to light upon their table.

At the end of the evening, Jane arrives home, slinks-up to her boudoir, and asks her maid Simone to, as they say in England, 'draw her a bawth,' and while readying herself for imminent immersion into sensuous liquid, she dances alone to radio music and laughs, still a bit tipsy from earlier in the evening. As she begins removing her jewelry, she suddenly hears her little lapdog, who is barking from elsewhere in the house: The dog only barks when something's amiss and, sure enough, we notice that something's moving behind the living room curtains, and this film, which started off as a light comedy, is now, very suddenly, turning austere. Director Genina shoots this 'mystery intruder' sequence as though he's making a horror movie, even amping-up the scary music, on the soundtrack. Jane pulls the curtains back and, of course, there's nothing behind them: Just like in every horror movie ever made, it is only the wind which was blowing them. "I'm out of it," she mumbles, heading back into the bathroom and laughing drunkenly. For a second, we think somebody might burst in and try to drown her in her bathtub but, thankfully, this does not happen; *Paris-Beguin* was made forty years before such crassly manipulative plot 'surprises' would become all-too routine. A minute later, someone sneaks into her living room for real, while she's bathing, in fact it's two people—two silly burglars who are more amusing than they are frightening. When they hear the deep-voiced, English-speaking BBC Radio announcer, they think he's the man of the house, and instantly freak: "Let's get outta heeeerrrre!"

When the two burglars leave, a third guy, who we didn't know was there, now pops out, suddenly, from behind the curtains: It's suave old Bob, who's been in the house the entire time, completely independently of the two other intruders; Bob's robbery of Jane's house—

it's the 'crime' which Dede had commissioned Bob to commit earlier, when the two men were talking in the bar—is happening quite independently of those two other guys. Bob's holding a gun on Jane and, instead of being afraid of her intruder, she's instantly attracted! He smiles at her, checking out her legs, next tossing his gun onto the floor. "Don't be afraid, don't worry," he shrugs. (Leave it to Jean Gabin to be the happy, good-natured molester!) "I like your place," he says, referring just as much to her as is he is to her house, even adding, as he shoots a glance at her great ass, "Not that it's big—but I like the interior!" (That line calls to mind that very funny double-entendre in Billy Wilder's underappreciated 1964 comedy *Kiss Me, Stupid,* when Dean Martin carries Kim Novak over the threshold of his small apartment, and describes his pad to her, mischievously: "It's not big... but it's clean!") Jane tries to run out and escape, but she isn't trying hard enough, because she's simultaneously attracted and repelled to Bob—with the emphasis on the former. He asks her where she's going, and lets her know that she doesn't have to fear anything from him, because he's not bad ('he's just drawn that way!'), but she just starts frenetically pocketing all of her expensive jewelry all the same, because she thinks he's trying to steal it; the jewelry is what he's come for, but now that he's seen her, he's forgotten all about it! Bob, like other Gabin characters, takes what he wants: He grabs Jane and kisses her roughly and, at first, she's screaming for him to go away ("You bastard!"). But very quickly, and just as we expected, she gives in, and begins kissing him right back—she's very literally melting right into her rape, which insures that this movie won't be finding its way into the National Organization of Women's Netflix queue anytime soon. And as Bob and Jane continue 'rassling away' hotly, and now off-screen, the radio's presenter announces that "the BBC World Service is now closing-down for the evening." Bob and Jane, it seems, are closing-down for the evening, as well.

The next morning, we see that charismatic Bob has spent the night with Jane, burglar and *burglee,* body intertwined with body, and since she's still asleep, he sneaks down the stairs quietly, each step punctuated by silly Robert McKimson/Bugs Bunny-on-tiptoe-style score-music ("dum, dum, dum, dum, dum, dum") in the background. After Bob has taken his leave from the house, Simone wakes her mistress up: "Wake up, Madame Jane!" Jane wakes up, happy—and I'm being very loose when I say, 'wakes up,' because it's clear that she probably didn't get that much sleep the night before, to begin with...

That day at the theater, the vacuous leading-man, Beausourire, is costumed-up like a caliph. Standing erect in his giant turban, he looks every inch the giant dork, as he preens and vamps haughtily, right into the camera, a fifty-years-earlier precursor of the American borscht-belt comedian Shecky Greene's 'Victor Mature/Roman Gladiator' imitation in Mel Brooks' slaphappy 1981 comedy, *History of the World, Part One.* As the female chorus line and the shirtless male dancers wait behind Beausourire for the Director, who is played by Alex Bernard, to give them their marching orders, Charmant sighs relievedly, to the Writer, about how he's glad that Jane hasn't shown up yet.

Then, Jane shows up and, of course, after her night with Bob, she's positively shiny with afterglow. The previous night has really changed her attitude about love, and she's definitely less suspicious of it, now that she's been properly 'used and abused, tasted and wasted, rode-hard, and put-away-wet.' "Hello, My dear friend," Charmant greets her—while he's calling her "dear friend," we already know exactly where they stand with each other—and in the same moment, Charmant's three yes-men (Curly, Shemp, and Pierre?) accidentally bash their own heads together, when they all bend forward at the same time to kiss Jane's hand. (All that's missing from the scene, is Moe Howard yelling, "Why, I oughta!") Jane, reversing what she said during the last rehearsal, about love not really existing, now tells everybody

With Fernandel and Jeanne Marnac.

who is within earshot that "Love is the only thing that counts!" Clearly, however, she won't be sharing any of that love with her husband Hector—a man who's aptly named, because she's always hectoring him—whom we'll now see sitting in the front row at the rehearsal, holding onto his wife's little lapdog, while she 'pounds the boards' (or whatever they call it, in 'stagecraft'). The dog growls at Hector, obviously not liking him too much. (Dogs instinctively love everybody, but they don't like this homunculus.) Jane's in an atypically stellar mood, now that she's gotten a serious injection of Gabin-Appendage, and she compliments each cast member individually, as to how beautiful each one looks! She adds, too, that she's really starting to "feel her role," which she used to think was a moronic one. The Writer tells Jane that, based upon the changes which she had suggested to him the previous day, he's rewritten the play to be about a million times better than it was before, and Jane, who's now happily sexed-up, tells him she thinks that it was fine just the way it was! Meanwhile, Hector's trying to make a move on a hot chorine, but the girl just isn't interested in him.

Jane now asks the Director and the Writer if they think that Beausourire's sword, which he's supposed to point at her in the scene, can be replaced with a gun, and we know exactly why, too: A gun is what Bob used the previous night to get Jane griddle-hot (and that little freak loved every minute of it). She coos at Beausourire, excitedly paying attention to him for the first time ever ("Point that gun at me, now!"), and then treats him to a fetching glimpse of leg (Jeanne Marnac's gams go 'all the way up') and now, for the first time, she's delivering her silly dialogue with gusto: "I'm trembling! I'm all alone in this world, and I have only one desire: You!" The Writer is unhappy now because, even though Jane is much more into the scene than she was before, she's improvising all of her own dialogue, to suit her new, happy mood. The Writer, like all scribes (present company included!), thinks his less-than-perfect words come straight from On High, and he goofily lambastes Jane with a cry of, "You can't treat The Truth like that!"—but Jane just ignores him, and continues making up her own sex-charged dialogue: "I look at you with desire... and I want to scream for help!" She tells Beausourire that the scene would be better if he were to grab her and kiss her, and three fey male dancers, who are behind them on-stage playing eunuchs (!), find the whole thing to be terribly amusing, and they now start 'doing their job,' which is, to dance around Jane in a circle, grabbing her with lust, or with as much 'lust' as light-loafered male dancers can ever hope to muster.

Next, Jane and Beausourire rehearse a scene in which Jane croons Beausourire a song, a song which definitely resonates with what happened to her last night. (Remember those old "Saturday Night Live" episodes in which Dan Aykroyd's prissy Leonard Pinth-Garnell-character hosted "Bad Operetta?" Well, this masterwork's lyrics would definitely qualify! [JANE: "When spring is here, I would like to offer my heart... I fell in love with a thieeeeefff!" BEAUSOURIRE: "Come back to my paaaaaa-lace! Forgiiiiiiive meeeee!"]) Nelson Eddy and Jeanette MacDonald, they are not.

That same evening, the show makes its big debut before the general public, and according to the poster outside the theater, "Tonight: It's the Sublime Artist Jane Diamant in *Paris-*

Beguin,' and meanwhile, the evening's newspaper is just hitting the stands, and the headline calls our attention to the fact that the previous night at midnight, a security guard was killed in the Parisian suburb of St. Cloud, and that Bob has been arrested and charged with the murder.

Director Genina now cuts to the police station for Bob's interrogation scene. Just like in the interrogation sequences which we're going to be seeing in a number of other Jean Gabin movies to come—movies which he'll make throughout his forty-six-year film career—Gabin never even gets riled up during this interrogation, and he remains the soul of calm:

"So, you didn't kill the Guard?" the Inspector (Jacques Maury) asks Bob, and very relaxedly—in fact, verging on 'dozing-off!'—Bob answers, truthfully, "No, it wasn't me. It's not my style. I was with a woman last night at midnight," and we know this is true, because we know that last night, he was making love to Jane. The Inspector wants to know whom he was with, and Bob tells him calmly that he's forgotten, because he's a good guy, and because he doesn't want to cause Jane any bad press on her opening night. The Inspector reminds Bob that not being able to supply him with the name of the girl he was with doesn't make for a very good alibi, and the cop insists now that Bob must give him the girl's name: "I know you didn't spend the whole night with a woman without even asking her what her name was." Gabin gives the first of his four-and-a-half decades worth of easygoing on-screen 'Gabin-Shrugs'—he and his shoulders will make them in almost every movie—and his Bob-character smilingly answers, "It happens!"

The rest of the conversation is pretty great, too:

> INSPECTOR: Well, maybe you also fired the gun without thinking about it?
> BOB (calmly): Naaahhh, it wasn't me. I am innocent." [Completely unafraid of the Inspector:] So don't mess with me, okay?
> INSPECTOR: (shocked, not believing a guy could be so calm during an interrogation): Wait—You do realize you've been accused of murder, right?
> BOB: (shrugs, yawns): It's not my fault.
> INSPECTOR: You'll get the maximum sentence, you know!
> BOB: Look, I'll sign any confession you want me to. I'll say that I did it, or that I didn't do it—whatever you want! Just let me go home, okay? I'm tired!

Bob, who is a total Jean Gabin Fatalist, in the same vein as a lot of Jean Gabin's most famous movie characters whom we're going to be meeting starting in about 1934, has even agreed to sign a paper, admitting to this murder-most-foul which he didn't even commit, if only this guy will just let him go home and get some sleep! The Inspector has never seen a guy like this—somebody who looks almost lethargic, during an interrogation—and movie audiences, at that point in time, hadn't either, which is one of the reasons why French movie audiences, in particular, embraced Jean Gabin so completely. (Relatedly, Gabin will also be completely unthreatened when he's interrogated by police in seven other pictures—*Coeurs joyeux* [1933]; *Martin Roumagnac* [1946]; *Razzia sur la chnouf* [1955]; *Des Gens sans importance* [1956]; *Le Rouge est mis* [1955]; *La Horse* [1970]; and *L'Affaire Dominici* [1972]. In all eight of these pictures, including this one, Jean Gabin's characters, when they are suspected of murder, will usually walk out on their own interrogations, and they're always so cool, the cops will never even try to stop them! No other movie star in the world gets 'I'm-so-cool-I-can-walk-out-on-my-own-interrogation scenes,' except, that is, for Jean Gabin, and it's one of the defining characteristics which makes him so unique, and so badass cool; I mean, don't we all wish we could be calm and confident when people are accusing us of this or that?)

Five o'clock in the morning comes: Dede and Ficelle cross the still-darkened street, both wearing comically over-sized gangster hats. It's easy for us to figure out that it was Dede who killed the security guard, but the newspaper is still investigating Bob, whose full name, as we're now learning, is not 'Robert,' but actually 'Marcel Gignard.' According to the paper, Bob—or, 'Gignard'—has pleaded not-guilty to the murder, and meanwhile, at her home, Jane's poring over the paper herself, and telling her maid Simone, "If I don't tell the cops that Bob was here with me, they'll throw him in jail. But if I say he was here that night, it will cause me such a scandal." Simone tells Jane that there's a way she can get around it: "We can say that he was with me, here, and not with you!" Simone calls the cops, to tell them that very story, and it's believable, since Simone, like Jane, is a very attractive woman.

Within a few hours, Simone, Jane, and even Jane's husband, Hector, are pow-wowing with the Inspector who had interrogated Bob the previous night, and Simone is telling the guy that Bob didn't kill anybody, and that Bob was, in fact, with her, when the murder was supposed to have taken place. Hector's sitting there, knowing that his wife made love to Bob, but he's way too wimpy to do anything that a real man would do—like, for example, he's too wimpy to obtain a speedy Mexican divorce, He even joins in on his wife's charade, just so he can continue to have arm candy—arm candy that doesn't even respect him—by his side. (For this guy, like all of the 'rich,' especially the rich as they're going to be portrayed in forty-six years worth of Jean Gabin pictures, appearance is very important.) Jane validates what Simone has just said: "She's right: Bob was at my place, and he was with her. He's not guilty."

Now, director Genina takes us inside the barbershop, which is owned by—and this is really the character's name—the barber, Emile Lavatory! Ficelle is right in the middle of receiving a natty haircut, when Dede barges in and grabs Lavatory by the lapels: "Where is he? Where's Bob?! We've got to find him, or he'll tell the truth!" So basically, this is the scene in which it's being confirmed, for us, even though we already knew it anyway, that it really was Dede who murdered the security guard, and that Bob knows that Dede did it; and even though Dede is a tough guy, he's more nervous, at this juncture in time, than you can imagine: "Bob'll tell the cops that I did it, and if that happens, both you and Bob are in big trouble!" Amusingly, a sign on the wall of the barbershop reads, "We can't cut hair without friction."

Dede and Ficelle next head into the local bar, and Jobette, the prominently-nosed/Bob-appreciating-girl looks sad, because Bob, for whom she pines away in solitude, is still in trouble. The bartender asks Dede and Ficelle if they've read the latest newspaper, the headline of which proclaims that Bob is about to be released from jail, and that he's no longer considered to be the killer—which means, by extension, that soon, the cops will be coming for Dede. Dede probably thinks that Bob gave him up to the cops, although we know Bob would never do that, because one aspect of Jean Gabin's recurring movie persona, is that his characters are never, ever stool-pigeons. (Gabin never squawks.) So now, Dede knows that he's going to have to dispatch Bob quickly, and he tells Jobette, in a classic line which actually foreshadows a similar line which will be spoken by a character seventy-five years later in Quentin Tarantino's *Kill Bill* saga, "Tonight, there will be one less bastard in the neighborhood!" Jobette now pleads with Dede: "Don't kill him! I know he didn't give you up!" But Dede won't hear of it, and he just asks Jobette if she knows where he can find Bob.

She doesn't tell him anything.

Back at the theater, the first-half of "*Paris-Beguin's*" (the stage play's) opening night is over, and Jane's in her dressing room, at intermission, excitedly receiving flowers from well-wishers, and she's over-the-moon, too, because she's been told that Bob will be at the theater in just a few minutes: Simone has picked him up from the pokey in Jane's car, and the two of them are now high-tailing it over to the theater, for what they hope will be 'Jane and Bob's Big Reunion.' Simone tells Bob to wait outside the theater's front doors, and she also lets him know that, when the show is over, Jane will come outside and meet him. He kisses her on the cheek, thanking her for making the soon-to-be *rendezvous* happen, and Simone next runs back inside, leaving Bob alone to puff on his usual cigarette in front of the theater's gigantic, steel front doors.

No sooner is Bob alone, than he's approached by Dede and Ficelle, who seem to have materialized from out of nowhere. "I want to talk," Dede menacingly hisses at Bob, and Bob knows what's coming, but he doesn't try and run from it, nor does he look even remotely scared: "Is this urgent?" Bob asks, still managing to crack-wise, even during this serious moment. Dede and Ficelle haul Bob into the theater's back alley, and Dede gets right up in his face: "I knew it was you who blew the whistle on me, you bastard!" Bob stands up to the guy, very calmly: "Don't be an idiot, Dede. It wasn't me!" (He's telling the truth.) Then: BLAM! - Dede shoots Bob through the heart, after which Dede jumps into a waiting car and burns rubber outta there, while a frightened-looking Ficelle runs away into the darkness. As Bob lies on the sidewalk, his life ebbing slowly away, the omnipresent cigarette which has been jutting out of his maw for much of the film, drops out of his mouth, and onto the street.

Meanwhile, Jane remains in her dressing room, waiting for Bob, having no idea about what's just happened to him. With a couple more minutes left to go before the second half of the show begins, she runs outside, throws open the theater's doors, and is shocked, when the first things she sees is Bob dying, right beneath a large pictorial representation of herself which looms directly over him on the show's poster. ("You're shot," she cries. "Oh, my dearest!") She lifts him up, leans him up against the wall, and he smiles; clearly, he's happy that the last thing he's seeing, in his life, is her—and after looking at her for a few seconds, he then slumps down, dead. Ficelle, who was watching the whole thing from behind the building—it turns out that, after Dede sped away, Ficelle returned to the scene-of-the-crime—cries for his friend, and so does Jane. Even Bob himself manages to squeeze-out a few random tears, during his last moments here on this earth.

But the show must go on and, since we now know that Jane actually has feelings (feelings are the gift which Bob gave Jane in this life), and that she is mostly a pretty decent person, it doesn't make her seem too assholish, that she has to go back inside, to perform the second half. The audience expects to see the rest of the show, and attention-whore Jane isn't the kind of person who would ever disappoint her public.

During the second half of the show, the thief character, who is played by Beausourire, dies onstage, just like Bob has now passed on, in 'real life,' and Jane sings a song to the dead thief who is onstage. The lyrics to the song which she's now trilling are something to the effect of, "I know in my heart that you cannot last any longer, my love…"

The crowd loves Jane, having no idea that the pain with which she's singing is real, and as her sad number ends, an overcome-with-emotion, fur coat-wearing audience member-woman shouts out, "What realism! She's really crying!" ("Ahhh, It's just theater stuff," her too-cynical male companion retorts.) Back in her dressing room, a couple of moments later, while she's changing her costume, Jane now continues to bawl while, onstage, a big, brassy Busby Berkeley-style musical number is in effect, one in which tuxedoed men dance and women kick in the famous style of the Can-Can. Jane waits in the wings for her next song, for which she is now, uncomfortably, supporting a huge and weighty-looking Indian headdress, *a la* Jean Gabin's real-life stage-partner from the late 1920s, Mistinguett.

Jane has a smile on her face during her last song, and it's a genuine one: The audience is definitely loving her final show-stopping tune and, as Genina's film fades out, Jane sings the play's title song (also the title of our film) which, in French, is called *"Paris-Beguin"* and which, in English, is called "Paris-Crush." According to the lyrics, "It was for you only that I had a crush, my love. Only for you."

The film, which was very popular in France when it was first released, was the first Jean Gabin movie to be exhibited, and only very briefly, in the United States, at one art-house cinema in New York city, where it played without English subtitling. (The standard practice of subtitling foreign-language films into different languages wouldn't begin until 1934). The picture's director, Augusto Genina, whose career spanned both silent and talking pictures, would make eighty-seven films altogether, between 1912 and 1957, but he mostly remains an unknown commodity in the United States today—although in October of 2006, Genina's 1930 film, *Prix de beaute* [*Price of Beauty*], which he made immediately before *Paris-Beguin*, was screened at the Los Angeles County Museum of Art. *In Prix de beaute,* the legendary silent screen vamp Louise Brooks plays a typist who wins a beauty contest.

What a Critic Said at the Time: "Jean Gabon [sp], as the burglar, is pretty presentable, and may turn in some good work someday." (*Variety*, 1-17-33 issue, Critic: "Kauf. [Wolfe Kaufman.]" Reviewed in Paris.)

What Another Critic Said at the Time: "A well-acted and clearly photographed little drama of music hall life in Paris. Gabin and Fernandel are excellent as Paris gangsters." (New York *Times*, 12-31-32 issue. Critic, "H.T.S.")

Jean Gabin and Andre Luguet fly the friendly skies, in "Gloria" (Film 6, right).

FILM 6

GLORIA

France/Germany, 1931

Directed by Yvan Noe and Hans Berendt. Produced by Bernard Natan. Screenplay by Franz Schulz and Yvan Noe, Based Upon the Play by Georg C. Klaren and Hans Szekely. Director of Photography (black and white), Frederik Fuglslang. Music Composed by Hans J. Salter. (GENRE: MELODRAMA) Assistant Director, Brigitte Helm. A Production of Pathe-Natan (France) and Matador Film (Germany). Running Time, 1 hour 25 minutes. Released in France on September 17, 1931, by Pathe Consortium Cinema. Never Released Theatrically in the United States.

"Because of you, I can't have money or glory!"
— *A stunt-pilot gets mad at his wife for killing his dreams, in "Gloria"*

G loria is the first of four Jean Gabin movies (1931's *Gloria*; 1932's *Adieu les beaux jours* [*Goodbye, Beautiful Days*]; and 1933's double-header of *L'Etoile de Valencia* [*The Star of Valencia*] and *Du haut en bas* [*From Top to Bottom*]) that were made as co-productions between Germany and France. Subtitling films into foreign languages, so that films could be exhibited in different countries, wasn't yet widely practiced, if, indeed, it was practiced at all, and what producers would customarily do with their French-German co-productions, most of which, as with *Gloria*, were produced under the auspices of the German film company UFA (Universum Film AG), is that, first, they would film the French-language version (starring Jean Gabin and/or the other French actors and a French director. Then, the French team would leave the set, and a completely different *German* cast and director would shoot an identical version of the scene, for the film's German-language version. *Adieu les beaux jours* and *L'Etoile de Valencia* are two films of Jean Gabin's career which no longer exist today, although the German-language/*Gabinless* versions do exist, and when it comes time for me to talk about those films, in the relevant chapters, I will, instead, be substituting the reportedly identical German-language versions. The French version of *Gloria* starring Jean Gabin does exist, however, although only in one print in the entire world, at the CNC/French Ministry of Culture, in Paris, and that's where I saw it, for this book.

When the American pilot Charles Lindbergh landed his plane, the *Spirit of St. Louis,* in Paris, on May 21, 1927, and became the first person in the world to actually fly across the Atlantic, the entire world went appropriately berserk, and not only did 'Lucky Lindy' become the very first ever international superstar, beloved throughout the world, but he also inspired movie producers to go off on a wild 'airplane-movie jag' which, famously, included *Wings* (1927), the very first film to win Best Picture honors at the Academy Awards, and also Howard Hughes' spectacular, World War I aviator epic, *Hell's Angels* (1930).

Lesser-known than *Wings* and *Hell's Angels*, but equally as entertaining as both of them, is 1931's *Gloria*, another very-cool aviation picture from the same period. Like a lot of European movies which were made in the early 1930s, *Gloria* is a French-German co-production, in which Gabin and his mostly French castmates were directed by Yvan Noe, and Noe's dramatic scenes were intercut into the flying footage which director Hans Berendt had already shot for the film's completely separate German version, which starred the actor Fritz Kampers, replacing Gabin. *Gloria*, which was filmed in Germany, in both its German and French versions, is a 'France-centric' fictionalization of the Charles Lindbergh story, in which the hero is called not 'Lindbergh,' but 'Pierre Latour,' and because *Gloria* is a European picture, the hero who crosses the Atlantic is not 'an American who flies to France,' but, *naturellement*, a Frenchman who flies to America!

Pierre Latour (Andre Luguet) and his amiable sidekick, Robert 'Bob' Nourry (Jean Gabin, who is second billed in the film [but, again, *he's the one you're looking at*]), are mail carriers, just like the real-life, pre-fame Charles Lindbergh was, and, as the film opens, the guys are boldly navigating their way through a terrible storm (jet-black rain clouds, lightning, and the whole nine yards), in their small mail plane. Down below, the good citizens are busily slamming their windows shut to keep out the rain, and Pierre's five-year-old son, Felix, who's played by Jean Boulant, is staring out the window of his own home, worrying for his dad's safety.

Up in the plane, meanwhile, Pierre and Bob are carefree, in the best possible 'Butch-and-Sundance' manner, and are not-at-all worried that something shitty might happen to them—like, oh, say, a fatal crash—and the two guys spend much of their time playfully sniping at each other. (PIERRE: "Okay, I'm landing now." BOB: "Where, idiot? In the trees?")

Back on *terra-firma*, little Felix can see his dad's plane landing in the distance, as he continues to stare out the window. He looks really happy that his dad, Pierre, is back on earth, not so much because his dad has arrived home safely, but because he wants to show his dad the new, white mice which his mom has just bought for him. Bob and Pierre touch down on the post office's little landing strip, right next to Pierre's motorcycle, Pierre straddles his hog and, ever the dutiful sidekick, happy-go-lucky Bob now plops himself down in the sidecar: He knows his place in life, and is happily resigned to it.

The weekend-upcoming, the two guys plan on participating together in a big, important stunt show, in which an avalanche of prize money will be involved, but Bob can't convince his wife to let him take part in it, since, as she's now reminding him, in her wifeliest tones, "Sunday is Family Day." Bob, meanwhile, doesn't have to worry about reporting to a wife; he's 'swingin' bachelor Jean Gabin,' and he always stays single, making himself readily available to all of the women of the world. Pierre knows he's going to have to work carefully, to soften his wife up.

Pierre's wife, Vera, who is played by Brigitte Helm, one of Germany's all-time great stars (she's known in the United States, mostly for playing the pixilated-looking 'robot lady,' in Fritz Lang's landmark 1927 sci-fi silent, *Metropolis*), is ecstatic that her ever-lovin' husband-man has arrived home from a hard day's work, but he's in no mood to receive her hugging. I mean, Vera and Pierre really love each other (we can see it, in this scene, in the loving way in which they gaze into each other's eyes), but Pierre's a man and, after work—well, you can forget about all that lovey-dovey stuff—real men just want dinner! (It's no different than when American t.v.'s Archie Bunker used to come home from work, and the first thing he did, was to ask dutiful Edith for a beer. [Times, it seem, never change.]) The Latour family chows down and Pierre has hidden a present for little Felix, under Felix's napkin. (Pierre's monster-in-law is there, too, but she's not too big of a shrew, so Pierre manages to get his food down okay, and without too much residual choking.)

Pierre's trying to find the right time to tell Vera that he's going to be participating in Sunday's stunt show, whether he gets her blessings or not, but he's not going to have to waste too much breath, because she already knows about the show, since Pierre and Bob's participation in the upcoming event has already been reported in the day's newspaper, the newspaper with which she is now confronting him. (Busted!) She's really afraid of these death-defying adventures which Pierre often takes-on (little Felix just thinks his dad's stunt performances are way-cool), and he tries to explain to her that the money which he'll be taking home, should he and Bob win together, will really augment the small stipend which he already makes as a flying mailman, and he even tells little Felix, "If I win, you'll even be able to buy a cat to play with your mice!" Vera is a good wife, because she seems to love Pierre more than she loves money, and she tells him that, in her opinion, they already have enough money to live on, and that he shouldn't be worrying about trying to grab more, but it's obvious that Pierre's not doing it for the money, and that he really just loves stunt-flying. Finally, this normally-taciturn guy blows his stack at his wife, unable to hold his true feelings in (or, at least, unable to hold in his feelings which seem true, during this moment of anger) any longer: "Look, I just can't stand it! Because of you, I can't have money or glory!" All she can think to answer back, with, is: "Think of your son... and of me!"

Pierre's whip-smart, though, and knows that 'one catches more wives with honey,' so he next switches gears (he's a pilot, so the metaphor is apt), and begins a 'kinder, gentler' approach: He pads over to a shelf and retrieves the trophy which he won back in 1924, when he was the first person on earth to fly across the Atlantic, between Paris and New York. (The real Lindbergh didn't make the world's first-ever cross-Atlantic flight until 1927 so, in this fictitious version of the story, Pierre's victory is actually pre-dating Lindbergh's, by three whole years.) Pierre's a guy who's trying to re-capture his former glory, just like in those American football pictures from the 1980s which dealt with 'over-the-hill, drunken players who have been phased out of their professions, in place of younger guys' (Jeff Bridges in *Everybody's All American;* Kurt Russell in *The Best of Times*), and he holds the trophy right in front of her face: "See? Look! This is what I am famous for... for being an acrobat!" One thing that's really great about this movie, is that its director, Yvan Noe, has managed to make the Pierre-Vera marriage seem real, and even when the couple fights, we can tell that they really love each other, and more than anything in the world.

While Vera doesn't really want Pierre to fly, she *does* deign to let him out for a post-prandial/Guys-Night-Out drink at the local watering hole with his best-buddy Bob.

Down at the bar, Pierre tells Bob about the conversation which he's just had with his wife and, with some 'typically-Gabinian earthy wisdom,' which is something else that's going to be on display in most Jean Gabin pictures, Bob tells Pierre, "Listen: It's always easy to win, when a woman is arguing with you. You just have to shout louder!" Pierre immediately calls Bob on his dime-store psychology: "But Vera's the quiet type—it's more difficult when they're quiet. Anyway, this time, I won't accept her 'no.' I'll do what I want to do, and not what she wants me to do." When Pierre gets home from his booze-up, he sees that Vera has tossed his bedding out into the living room, but Pierre has a sense of humor about the whole thing, and since she's making him sleep on the floor, he gigglingly sneaks into her room; and, while she sleeps, he places one of his son's white mice under her pillow, to scare her!

Morning comes (we don't get to see the upshot of what happened with the hidden mouse), and Pierre and Bob now head over to the post office landing strip, to start making their daily mail delivery. Pierre pretends he's decided on his own against participating in the big stunt show, but Bob knows his friend too well, and gives him one of those looks—a look which says, "Face it, friend: You're whipped!" Pierre cops to it: "It's going to be impossible for me to perform with you on Sunday. She won't let me do it." Bob just shakes his head.

When Sunday comes, Bob and Pierre aren't in the big stunt show: Another pilot has taken their place, and he's a second character named Bob—Bob Deschamp (Andre Roanne), who's another legendary stunt pilot 'in these parts.' Our own Bob (Gabin's 'Bob Nourry') has shown up, and he's watching the show with a group of reporters; and, while he's watching it, he's even hitting on a hot lady-reporter ("I'm busy today, but not tomorrow. I live above the café!"), and adding that, with her permission, he'd like to add her name into his little black book. (When she sees the book, which he happens to have handy, it's as huge as any metropolitan Yellow Pages!) Pierre, then, arrives on the scene, and tells Bob, snarkily, that he's been off, "having an affair with 'another woman,' but Bob knows Pierre's just saying this because he feels wounded by Vera, and that Pierre would never really cheat on his wife, and it is to the credit of the fine actor Andre Luguet, who plays Pierre, that he makes Pierre seem macho, even when Pierre's wife is the one who clearly holds the strings, in their marriage.

That night, Pierre, Vera, and little Felix bring Bachelor Bob along to dinner, as a third-wheel, and Bob tells the cutie-pie waitress that if she'll agree to come home with him tonight, he'll give her anything she wants, and when Jean Gabin hits on chicks in this movie, and in other movies, too, he's so likable and charming that the women never take offense. Bob now tells little Felix, smilingly (giving him some life-lessons, for when he grows up),

"When I meet a woman, the first thing I always propose, is to take her up in the plane with me." Pierre and Vera think it's funny that Crazy Uncle Bob is teaching their six-or-seven-year-old son about the Mile High Club, and Felix admiringly shouts out, "When I grow up, I'm going to do exactly the same things that you do, Uncle Bob!" Pierre and Vera cringe, but it's hilarious.

About a week later, another acrobatic show is taking place in town. Pierre's still not participating, but Bob, who has less to lose, since he doesn't have a family of his own, *is*, and, in fact, he's co-piloting with The Other Bob—Bob Deschamps. Many small planes are seen on the runway, all huddling together at the line of departure, and when the show begins, Felix looks up into the heavens, excitedly screaming to everyone who can hear him, "That's my Uncle Bob!" He next turns to his dad, Pierre, and tells him (he doesn't mean anything by it, because he really loves his dad, and wouldn't want to hurt his feelings), "You should be up there, Daddy!" When the Two Bobs land, Pierre and 'our Bob' stand together, watching other pilots doing their own tricks. Vera's with them, and she's giving Bob the evil eye, because she hears him trying to convince Pierre that Pierre should be up there flying in the next show; Vera's kind of a hypocrite because, while she won't let her own husband fly, she's truly amazed by all of the other pilots who are actually up there, engaged in their amazing stunts. (Is *Gloria* a movie about flying, or is it a movie about unhappy marriages?)

That night, there's a full-dress ball for Bob Deschamps who, since his recent victory, has become even more of a local hero than he already is. Our own Bob (Bob Nourry/Jean Gabin) is at the party, too, but he's hanging back: The consummate working-class guy, Bob looks really out-of-place in his tux, which, we can tell, he's probably worn all of once, in his whole life—and that night is tonight! While Jean Gabin always portrays nothing but confidence in his pictures, he looks really embarrassed about the fact that he's having to hang around the *hoi polloi*, since he's definitely working-class and, like many of the other characters who will be played by Jean Gabin, he abhors pretense.

At this point, an attractive woman-party guest catches Bob's eye, but she looks like she's used to men with money, and from the sad, hangdog look on his face, and without his even having to say anything, we can tell that he feels like he's not sophisticated enough to go up and talk to her, so, instead, he just gives her an uncomfortable/forced, Snoopy-doing-the-Cheshire Cat grin. And then, it gets worse: Bob starts looking so uncomfortable, that everyone else at his table gets up and moves away from him, just like he's got B.O.! Remaining at the table, he comedically lines three champagne glasses up in a row, sloppily, pours bubbly into all of them, tastes one of the glasses, and proceeds to spit out its contents—right onto the table! It's easy for us to see that Bob's really just being passive-aggressive, and acting 'all rough-and-tumble,' because he thinks that these goings-on are too pretentious, and so, therefore, this is his inarticulate way of articulating the idea that, in his opinion, *rich people suck*. As if that's not enough, and to drive his scary 'point,' home, Bob, next, starts spooning way-too-much custard into a bowl, making a veritable mountain of custard, wish resembles Richard Dreyfuss' mashed potato-mountain, in Spielberg's *CE3K*.

Vera approaches Bob, hoping to lift her husband's best friend out of his doldrums by sitting with him, and he asks her if she'd like to dance, and she says that she'd love to, but that first, she has to okay it with Pierre. Pierre gives his best buddy and his wife permission to trip the light fantastic together, knowing that 'one-night-stand Bob' doesn't pose any kind of a threat to anybody's marriage: Jean Gabin, in his ninety-five feature films, will almost never hit-on his friends' women. His movie characters are good and trustworthy friends to all, whether the characters he happens to be playing are good guys or bad guys. (In Jean Gabin movies, as I've already mentioned, the friendship between two men is always stronger than the love between men and fickle women.)

While Vera and Bob dance, Pierre's hiding-out in a corner, as a reedy little *proto-Vincent Gallo* tries to tell him dirty jokes, but Pierre just looks far away; clearly, if he can't be up in his plane bodily, he can, at the very least, be flying the friendly skies, in his mind. As he watches his wife dancing with his best friend, we can tell, just by looking at his expressive (and mustachioed) face, that he wouldn't be too upset if Vera were to take-up with Bob, if only because then, he (Pierre) would be free to stunt-pilot, completely unencumbered by her guilt-tripping attitude toward the one thing in the entire world which he really loves to do.

Guests are now moving off of the dance floor and, at this point, the President of the local Flying Committee, who's played by Jean Dax, presents Bob Deschamps with a trophy, praising him to the skies (pun intended): "Let me remind you all that this man whom you now see before you, Bob Deschamps, is France's Icarus! When he flies, he is high above the ground, looking down at us mice." The obvious comparison between people and mice, like, for example, Pierre's son Felix's mice, is obviously too close to comfort, for Pierre. Bob Deschamps, who has a fun-loving personality, just like Bob Nourry does, now starts reading a speech, which he's written for the occasion, off of a crumpled-up piece of paper: The speech is all about horses, and he then makes the crowd laugh, by pretending that he's mixed up his 'horse speech' with his 'flying speech!' Pierre, who is unable to take any more of this bombast, now disappears by himself, heading for his mail plane and, when we next see him, he's zooming up into the night sky alone, getting a head-start on the next morning's mail deliveries. The sky, as I've already mentioned, is the only place where Pierre Latour ever truly feels free, even if he *is* surrounded by large, ungainly sacks of mail, while he's in the middle of enjoying this freedom.

Vera's freaking now, because her husband has left the party without her, but Bob tells her not to worry, and that he will soon be back. Bob invites Vera to accompany him to the local amusement park, and she agrees to it without hesitation, although, after a few spins with ol' *'Bob-a-kazoo'* on the ferris wheel, she's starting to feel guilty, and so she runs back home, as fast as her legs can carry her. Bob, who's not ready to end his evening, remains at the park, plopping himself down on a bench next to two soused teen-aged girls, and starts valiantly assisting them in drinking the dozens of bottles of wine which they've got sprawled-out in their midst; as the girls gab away with each other, paying no attention to him, Bob even 'lifts' a few of the bottles, placing them in his jacket, for safe-keeping.

Director Noe next match-cuts the spinning of the carnival's merry-go-round with the spinning of Pierre's propeller: Pierre's still flying alone, and dive-bombing heavy mail sacks over local post offices—*klunk, klunk, klunk.* The next day, Pierre's mail plane is back on the runway, but Pierre, himself, hasn't returned: Vera knows that her husband would never cheat on her, and she just figures that he's probably off somewhere, brooding in some café, or in some lonely bar.

In the next scene, Bob shows up at Pierre and Vera's house, and offers to take Vera up for a ride in the mail plane, since the aircraft is back, and just sitting there on the runway, ready to be put to good use. Knowing that she disappointed Bob at the fair the previous night by leaving too early, she tells him that she's not sure if she wants to go up with him or not, but with a couple of quick-n'-charismatic Gabin Smiles, it happens: Vera won't fly with her husband, but she *will* fly with her husband's best friend and, without the filmmakers having to say it, there's a very practical reason for this: If Vera and Pierre, husband and wife, were both up in the same plane together, and an accident transpired, little Felix would be left all alone; obviously, it's safer, to Vera's way of thinking, that only one family member should be airborne, at a time. Plus (and we can't discount this): She might even be starting to dig-on Bob, a little.

Lo and behold, Vera's totally wild about being up in the plane. Bob (that mad, impetuous fool!) even starts kissing her neck while he's flying, and while she doesn't kiss him, back or try to repel him, she *is* laughing at his goofy gestures, thinking that he's just being silly; in other words, she's not interpreting *his kissy-wissy shit* as a hit-on type of a situation, which might be attributable to some ineffable flaw in Bob's game. Next, we see Pierre, who reappears on the post office's landing strip, because he's already been back from his mail deliveries, for quite some time. He looks up and sees his mail plane up in the sky and, since the plane's not that high, he can just make out the sight of his wife, riding shotgun with Bob. Pierre knows that Vera would never cheat on him, and that Bob would never hit on her, either, but he's still a little freaked, because he knows that Vera doesn't like to go up in planes—at least, with him, anyway.

Pierre and Vera have a maid, Therese, who's played by that great, big-boned wisecracker, Mady Berry (who played Mrs. Triron, the lady who ate twenty pounds of baking soda in that same year's Marcel Levesque-Jean Gabin comedy, *Tout ca ne vaut pas l'amour*). Therese tiptoes into Vera's room to wake her, as she does every morning, but Vera's gone, because, as we already know, she's flying with Bob. Therese pads into the kitchen, to prepare breakfast for little Felix and, while she's in there, Vera arrives home and quietly sneaks back into her bedroom, thinking that, if she gets back into bed before Pierre returns home, he'll never suspect that she was gone. She has no idea that her husband has already seen her up in the sky, doing loop-de-loops (while *looped*), with Bob.

When Pierre arrives home, he immediately calls Vera on her shenanigans, and she spills the beans without a fight ("Okay. I will tell you everything"), and what makes the characters in this movie seem real and three-dimensional, is that Pierre's not really even mad at her.

(Well, okay, he's just *medium mad*.) In fact, Pierre tells Vera that he's happy that she finally did something that made her feel good, since she always seems so depressed: "You never look happy, Vera. And, you know, maybe it's my fault, because I'm not happy and carefree like Bob is: Bob is supposed to be attracted to waitresses—not to you! But I know he doesn't mean anything with his flirtations, so I'm not mad at you, and I'm not mad at him, either. The only thing that does trouble me, though, is that you told me not to fly so dangerously anymore, and yet now, you're friendly with Bob, just because he does that." She's powerless against his air-tight (another flying pun!) logic, and so she finally grants him his most devout wish: "Okay, fine. If you want to start stunt flying again, you can do it." Bob's right: Pierre *is* whipped! (Permission from another person to do something? Isn't he 'over 18?!')

Although Pierre says he's not mad at Bob, there is definitely a little anger which is bubbling just under the surface (I mean, how would you feel if your wife was hanging around in ultra-close quarters with your friend, even if it they *were* only doing a little light petting?!) Pierre still wants to talk to Bob about it, anyway, if only to ease his own conscience: "So, I know nothing happened between you and my wife, but…" Bob stops him in his tracks, replying, truthfully, that he did nothing but kiss Vera's cheek, and only in friendship (which is, more or less, true). Pierre believes his pal, and their friendship (kind of) endures.

This coming weekend, Pierre will try to top his Paris-to-New York record from 1924: According to the newspapers, he'll attempt to fly across the Atlantic, faster than he did seven years before, and he's going to be doing it in *Gloria*, the plane in which he won all of his 1924 honors. *Gloria* has been grounded ever since, a conversation piece for people who visit the tiny local air museum, but Pierre's trusty ground crew (one guy!) is working around the clock, making 'her' better, faster, and safer than ever, because, when Pierre flies on Sunday, he's going to be doing it alone, and without a co-pilot. (He still feels a bit uneasy about Bob, due to the whole Vera situation, even though he's pretending that he feels o.k.)

The big day arrives: Pierre rockets into the firmament, all by his lonesome, and he's still a mite worried about any potential sexual relationship that might be happening between his wife and Bob, but he's trying to put it out of his mind. Then, suddenly, he gets the surprise of six lifetimes: Bob's right there in the plane with him, passed out drunk, in the back. (Yes, he's been there the whole time!) The friends hug, best-of-buddies in spite of all of this recent wife-kissing business, and Pierre is ecstatic that Bob is alongside him again, in the co-pilot's seat. "Where are we going?" Bob asks Pierre, totally deadpan, even though he knows exactly where they're going, and that's why he's signed-on. "To America," Pierre cheers (and if it were eighty years later, he might instead blurt out, "to infinity and beyond," or maybe even, "I feel the need… the need for speed" [but, thank God, in 1931, *horseshit* hadn't been invented yet])! Of course, it's not just our characters' little French town that's interested in Pierre and Bob's newest crossing: Their flight is being broadcast over the radio, and it's getting live coverage all over the world.

An optical wipe-effect now brings us into a ship's radio room, where the French-language announcer is keeping us apprised of Gloria's coordinates and, simultaneously, other radio commentators from all over the world are giving out the same information, in German, Spanish, Italian, and English. Vera, at home, is listening to this ongoing, real-life soap opera with her son Felix, who's playing, excitedly, with his little toy train set.

Meanwhile, up in the plane, and somewhere over Nova Scotia, the weather is dreadful, and Pierre and Bob have to do a lot of jockeying around to do, so that their flight can proceed smoothly. (In real life, Charles Lindbergh encountered major weather issues over Nova Scotia, as well.) "Maybe," opines the French radio reporter, and this isn't doing Vera's stomach any good, whatsoever, "they won't make it. But we'll give you the news as soon as we have it!" A photographer, who's played by Andre Saint-Germain, now heads over to Pierre's house, to snap photographs of Vera and Felix, the wife and son of the great pilot, and Felix excitedly tells this Veelox-purveyor, "Make sure you put in a caption that says I am the son of a winner!" Meanwhile, 'the Other Bob,' Bob Deschamp (who also knows Vera, platonically), is sitting at her kitchen trying to console her but she's beyond consolation.

Up in *Gloria*, Pierre tells Bob that they should probably start thinking about heading back home to France, instead of continuing on to the U.S., because a huge storm is coming their way, but Bob, who's got his typical 'Jean Gabin Movie-Character Resigned Fatalism'-thing' (a/k/a: 'fatalism, tempered by bravado') going, makes the heroic decision for the both of them, which happens to be a resounding cry of, "No!" Not only does Bob not seem to care too much that the two of them might die, but he even picks this very moment to start snacking down on some handy treats which he just so happens to have brought along with him. Pierre asks Bob why he's eating at a time like this, when they happen to be navigating through the roughest, toughest, blackest clouds you've ever seen in any movie, ever, and with a resigned Gabin-Shrug, Bob casually replies, "Well, you know, you have to eat. It doesn't change anything!" Yes, friends, Jean Gabin is so cool—*danger just gives him the munchies!*

The next day, newspaper headlines all over France somberly announce that Pierre and Bob have disappeared somewhere over the Atlantic, and that there's been no news from *Gloria* at all, for quite some time, and so, naturally, we're just pleased as punch, when we cut to an exterior shot of our little plane, which is still flying proud, although it is acting a tad skittish, due to a major oil leakage. Bob, who happens to be a great mechanic, smilingly (even in hell, especially in—the face of danger) climbs out onto the wing, to rectify the problem: Will Bob fall off the wing and disappear into a cloudy abyss? No way, Jose! 'Super Gabin' has quickly rectified the problem, and he pops back down into his seat, his face and goggles now jet black with oil (or, as they say in Brooklyn, '*erl*'). In fact both guys' mugs are black with liquid crude, which, because the film was shot monochromatically, looks more than a little like dark, arterial blood. Back at the Latour residence, meanwhile, Vera continues sobbing at the kitchen table, as Bob Deschamps' silhouette (he's pacing back and forth, out of the camera's view) has spread itself out on the wall, behind her.

While we know that Bob and Pierre are a-ok, the other characters in the film are still in the dark about how they're doing. Various countries have sent their navies across the Atlantic to scout for the 'missing' plane and, meanwhile, back at Pierre and Vera's place, the usually-calm Vera is now in the midst of a rare (for her) freak-out, and she's yelling at Deschamps that it's his fault her husband has decided to take this flight because, when Pierre saw Deschamps flying in the stunt show a few weeks before, that's what re-sparked his interest in stunt-flying.

And then, good news! *Gloria's* been spotted over Canada! Our Bob's so happy that he and Pierre have successfully made it across the Atlantic, that he howls with delight, and we next dissolve to the requisite stock footage of the Statue of Liberty (France's gift to the U.S.), and we hear the French radio reporter announcing that Pierre and Bob have made it safely to New York. Since the entire film, even the New York scenes, have been shot in France we now get another lusty helping of stock footage—this time, of a Wall Street ticker tape parade: We see two figures in the car, waving, which we're supposed to interpret, as being 'Bob' and 'Pierre,' but the image is in extreme long-shot, so we can't see their faces, and it actually happens to be documentary footage of Charles Lindbergh's real-life NYC ticker tape *love-a-thon* of June 13, 1927, and the guys who are in the car waving, happen to be the real Lindbergh, as well as Lindberg's p.r.-guru, Grover Whalen. Next, it's another stock-shot—this one, of the Eiffel Tower—and we're now back in Paris, where the French-language radio reporter is speaking about 'the two courageous pilots who will soon be returning to France,' and of how the whole country will soon be partying-hearty, in celebration of their triumphant return.

When Gloria makes her descent at our small town's little airfield, the crowd looks positively orgasmic. Now reunited with his wife Vera, Pierre tells her that he hopes she's not too angry with him for being out of touch, while he was in the sky. The Mayor, who made his brown-nosing speech at Bob Deschamps' victory dinner, now makes a new one, on behalf of the victorious Pierre Latour and Bob Nourry, and little Felix, very sweetly, doesn't even care that his dad is being honored, and he just cries out, "I'm hungry!" Pierre carries little Felix on his shoulders, as he and Vera walk away with their favorite third-wheel, Bob, and as our story comes to a close.

The film's leading actress, Brigitte Helm, would also appear alongside Jean Gabin in director Andre Beucler's no-longer-existing *Adieu les beaux jours,* and here's an interesting 'fun-fact' about her involvement with this picture (*Gloria*): Not only was she the film's female lead, but she's also credited, in its production notes, as being its assistant director. Besides being a wonderful actress, Helm was also very interested in the craft of directing, so on *Gloria,* and on many of her other movies as well, she was either a credited, or uncredited, 'A.D.' In America, it would be another fifteen years before women would begin occupying prominent positions behind the camera (I'm thinking, particularly, of the directors Dorothy Arzner and Ida Lupino), but in Europe, even back in the 1920s and 1930s, a lot of women were already occupying creative positions: In Germany, Leni Reifenstahl directed the great documentary *Olympia,* in 1938 and, as you read through this book, you'll discover that, even back in the 1930s and 1940s, it is very often women who are credited with editing many of Jean Gabin's films.

'Your author' (me) was able to experience a beautiful 35-millimeter print of the French-language, Jean Gabin version of *Gloria* (the only copy in the world, and I'm happy to mention that it was in great shape), and while the Gabin version of *Gloria* remains unavailable on home video, at the time this book goes to press even in France, the German-language, 'Gabin-less' version (apparently, it's exactly the same as the French version, scene-for-scene and shot-for-shot, except that it's set in Germany instead of in France, the two pilots are meant to be German instead of French, and the character of 'Pierre' is, instead, called 'George Kohler') is available for your home-viewing pleasure, through International Historical Films (www. ihf.com). This German-language version stars Gustave Froelich and Fritz Kampers as the two pilots and, while 'Froelich and Kampers,' are no 'Gabin and Luguet,' they're very good actors, in their own right.

What a Critic Said at the Time: "ROMANCE AND FLYING: An excellent piece of work, both from the technical and the sentimental side. Particularly interesting are the scenes of the trans-ocean flight." (*Variety*, 10-28-32 issue. Critic: "H.T.S." Reviewed in Germany.)

FILM 7

LES GAIETES DE L'ESCADRON

France, 1932

(Literal English Translation: "FUN IN THE BARRACKS") Directed by Maurice Tourneur.
Produced by Bernard Natan. Screenplay by Georges Dolley, Edouard Nores, and Maurice Tourneur.
Based Upon the Novel and the Stage Play by Georges Courteline. Editor, Jacques Tourneur. Directors of
Photography (black and white, with two color sequences), Raymond Angel and Rene Colas. Production
Designer, Jacques Colombier. (GENRE: COMEDY) A Production of Pathe-Natan Films. Running
Time, 1 hour 21 minutes. Produced and Released in France on September 17, 1932, by Standing-Films.
Never Released Theatrically in the United States.

"I'll change you into a fruit tart! You look like an oyster!"
— *A superior officer disciplines lazy 'Private Gabin,' in "Les Gaietes de l'escadron"*

The World War I-set ensemble-comedy *Les Gaietes de l'escadron*, which is as great a farce as any movie made by the Marx Bros in the early '30s, is the fifth feature in which Jean Gabin would appear in 1931, and while he shows up only in a supporting role, he is, as usual, *the guy you're looking at*. The picture is directed by Maurice Tourneur, the father of Jacques Tourneur, who directed Gabin, earlier that year, in *Tout ca vas pas l'amour*, and who'll show up again, in this film, in support of his father, and not as a co-director, but as the film's editor. (When have you ever heard of an already-established director stepping back, just to cut a film? *Wow*, the French sure take their '*libertie, egalite, fraternite*'-business, seriously!) *Gaietes i*s one of moviedom's best, and least known, 'wartime ensemble comedies,' arriving twenty-one years before Billy Wilder's *Stalag 17* (1953), and thirty-eighty years before 1970's awesome double-header of Mike Nichols' *Catch-22* and *M*A*S*H*. *Gaietes* is also filmdom's very first ever 'Slob Comedy' (or, 'Slacker Comedy'), pre-dating all of the great, American-made ensemble-Slob/Slacker comedies by more than forty years, and here, I'm especially thinking of George Roy Hill's *Slapshot* ('slobs on the hockey rink,' 1977); John Landis' *Animal House* ('slobs in college,' 1978); Harold Ramis' *Caddyshack* ('slobs on a golf course,' 1980); and even Ramis' *Stripes* ('slobs in the military,' 1981), and *Gaietes*, also, has the distinction of being 'the *other* ensemble war movie' in which Gabin would appear, six years before he acted in his single most famous movie of all, director Jean Renoir's *La Grande illusion*. *Gaietes de l'escadron* translates, in English, as *Fun in the Barracks*, and the fun-loving, layabout, slacker-soldiers in this movie, which is based upon a vaudeville romp, by author Georges Courtelin, have nothing but fun!

The movie's biggest *slobbola* is Jean Gabin's charismatically-lazy Private Fricot, who acts as boss/straight-man to his 'little buddy,' Private La Plotte, who's played by an actor called Donnio, and for English-speaking readers, here's your French lesson for the day:' *'Fricot,'* in French, means *'slop;'* and *'la plotte'* is the slang word, for *'pussy!'* As this film will prove, the French could make lowbrow farces just as down-and-dirty as, or often better than, their American counterparts.

The main, first-billed star of the film is the man who, next to Jean Gabin, has always been recognized as being one of France's very greatest actors of all time, the burly Raimu (full name: Jules Raimu), whose portrayal of the barracks' slovenly Captain Hurluret is hilariously funny. (Raimu usually played funny roles on the stage, and serious roles in his films, and if you want to some of Raimu's finest work, and you're in the U.S., where Raimu movies, like Gabin movies, aren't too plentiful, you can check him out in Kino Home Video's beautiful boxed-set DVD release of writer/producer/director Marcel Pagnol's mind-blowingly fantastic, three film *Fanny Trilogy,* which was made, between 1930 and 1936.) Not only does Captain Hurluret run his camp with only the bare-minimum of effort, but he, like his men, is also incredibly messy-looking, and he's even got a bizarre, never-explained, shaving problem: One side of his mustache is long, and the other side is short, and he never corrects it, nor will anybody ever mention it to him. The junior-ranking officers under Hurluret are bored-out-of-their-skulls, because there's no war on (remember, it's 1932: There aren't any Panzer tanks on the horizon, yet [hell, at this stage of the game, the Germans were still co-producing movies with the French]), so they spend most of the movie running around, hilariously giving all of the low-ranking soldiers solitary confinement, for only the lamest of infractions: "You! You're singing like a crow: Four days in the hole!" OR: "You! You're shaving without looking in a mirror: Eight days in the hole!" OR: "You! Your hat is too small: Eight days in the hole!" Eventually, every character in this movie, whether he did anything wrong or not, will wind up spending, at the very least, four or five days down in the hole! (Or, per the 1938 Humphrey Bogart picture, *Angels with Dirty Faces*, and the 1972 Humble Pie tune which it inspired, "30 Days in the Hole!")

One of the lazy, Gomer Pyle-esque *soldats,* Private Venderague, is played by the great, and magnificently-sympathetic rubber-face (or, more specifically, horse-faced) Fernandel who, with *Gaietes,* is now appearing with Jean Gabin for the second time and, as we remember, in the previous year's *Paris-Beguin*, Fernandel played the goofy vaudeville star-*cum*-gangster, Ficelle. The various officers keep ordering Venderague to sweep the floor, and they continually hand him brooms, which they, just as quickly, take away, just to drive him up the wall! In fact, in one of the film's funniest sequences, a C.O. orders Venderague to sweep, thusly: "If you can't find a broomstick—do it with your nose." The Officers call Venderague *'bambote'* (idiot), and no matter how much or how vociferously they chew his ass out, the sweet-natured and always cheerful private likes them anyway, even commenting, right into the camera, and addressing us, the audience, in the same way in which Bob Hope and Bing Crosby used to do it, in their 'Road pictures,' although, this movie came first, "Aren't they nice guys?!" (Just like Jean Gabin's most known movie persona is 'the world-weary, stoic, ill-fated guy,' wispy-thin Fernandel's recurring movie-persona, in the one hundred and fifty movies in which he starred during his lifetime, can be defined as, 'the always-optimistic guy who loves everybody— even people who are peeing all over him.' Fernandel, France's most popular movie comedian of all time, is, basically, 'Jesus Christ's lessons of forgiveness, filtered through the rubbery-gawkiness of Jerry Lewis,' and the biggest reason that *Gaietes de l'escadron* is so endearingly funny, is that Fernandel, and all of the other characters in the picture, even the officers who antagonize the 'nice' soldiers, have been written, and played, so likeably. Sweetly, we can tell that the officers would love to be perceived as being mean, but that it's just not working out for 'em.)

The film's first-of-two plot complications—well, they're not really complications, *per se*—they're more like the most gossamer little spider webs upon which director Maurice Tourneur hangs the film's non-stop barrage of winningly-silly jokes and comic set-pieces— involves the fact that, during the movie's first reel, and off-camera, two soldiers, whom we'll never properly see in the film, have managed to escape, over the wall. Hilariously, Capitain Hurluret and his men are so lax, that nobody is really interested in finding the escaped men at all, although Hurluret does, very dutifully, note the fact that the two men escaped in his log book, thinking that such a notation will suffice, in case his superiors should ever make any kind of an inquiry. Of course, next, the camp will suddenly be visited by the aged, yet still-hearty, General, played by Henry Roussel, who shows up, quite unexpectedly, to make a surprise inspection. Hurluret is so freaked-out that the General will discover that two men have gone AWOL, and, therefore, that *he sucks, as a Captain*, that, on purpose, he spills ink all over the log book in which he had just documented that the men were missing. The General sees the book and tries to get to the bottom, not of who escaped, but of who spilled the ink!

Le General then inspects the barracks, and he is utterly horrified by what he sees: It's a barracksful of happily-lazy, carefree soldiers, all of whom are singing, smoking, and playing cards! There are even piles of horse manure all over the place, since horses often walk right into the garrison and crap right where they're standing, and the men, who include Gabin's always-unshaven Fricot, are too relaxed to clean it up. The General, with Captain Hurluret in tow, lines all of the men up, and instead of reprimanding them (this incredibly-elderly man is *shit-scared* [pun intended] of all of the vital young men, before him), asks them if there's anything they don't like about being under Hurluret's command, at which point, Venderague goofily raises his hand, and informs the General that he hates the soup which the men are always getting served: "The Chef doesn't care what we think of his soup, because he's of a higher rank. But we hate it!" All of the other men, next, begin vociferously denying that they, too, hate the soup and, afraid of getting sentenced to solitary confinement, they actually start defending it so Captain Hurluret, who's wanting to discipline a man in front of the General, to demonstrate that he's an able commander, sentences Venderague to five days in the hole. The General then, very meekly and tentatively, adds-on an additional eight days, to prove that he, too, is capable of issuing an order, and he next comments on all of the rampant drinking which he has been witnessing ever since he arrived for his visit. The General tells the men that they shouldn't booze too much, because, in his opinion, "… people who drink are inferior."

Then, Hurluret introduces the General to the extra-lazy, and sublimely-carefree, Private Fricot (Jean Gabin): "*Mon General,* here is Fricot: He is our pig-headed one." As in all of Jean Gabin's films, Gabin is, in *Gaietes de l'escadron,* a good guy who has zero patience for authority figures; whenever we see Gabin in this film, he's mostly lounging around on his bunk, smoking and reminiscing about all of the girls he's fucked. The General tells the slovenly Fricot to get a haircut, but Fricot is completely unafraid of the high-ranking guy, and he tells the General, casually, "I don't have time to go to a hairdresser. I'm always in solitary" (and, of course, Gabin will, very famously, get thrown into solitary again, in the 1937 film, *La Grande illusion*). Fricot hopes that the General won't be checking his bunk too carefully, because he's hiding a side of pork between the mattress and the springs, chunks of which he and his goofy sidekick, La Plotte, have been selling illegally, around the base. (This scene foreshadows the plot of another comedy which Gabin will make twenty-four-years-later, 1956's *La Traversee de Paris,* in which co-stars Jean Gabin and Antoine Bourvil, one of France's great movie comedians, will spend the entire movie lugging suitcases full of black market pork across WWII-torn Paris, with the Gestapo hot on their trail.)

As a capper to the General's visit, Hurluret, because he wants to present his men in a favorable light, now decides that his troops should put on an impromptu horse show, and the Privates all start looking at each other, as if they're thinking, "What?! Is he *nuckin' futs?!* I've never been on a horse, before. Have you?!"

Director Tourneur cuts to the next scene, and Fricot and La Plotte are now both atop horses, shaking like leaves, and looking all-kinds-of-uncomfortable, while dressed-up, in way-too-ostentatious parade clothes, *and/plus:* Both men have cigarettes jutting out from their (slack) jaws! Captain Hurluret, who's now pretending, in front of his own superior officer, that he disapproves of the two Privates' behavior, tells the General, "I always try to be understanding of those two, but they definitely belong in manacles." But the General tells the Captain that he's beginning to really like the free-wheeling (and free-mealing). Fricot's (Gabin's) refreshingly candid/no-bullshit personality.

Captain Hurluret's not-so-secret wish, which is no different than the wish of any other toadying martinet, in any job, is to be promoted, in his case, from 'Captain' to 'Commandant' (or, in English, 'Commander'), and so he decides to take this moment to remind the General of his qualifications, in a sweetly eloquent little speech: "Uh… You know, I hope you haven't forgotten, sir, that we started out together, all those decades ago, and, you know, I wouldn't mind a little promotion—that is, if you would see fit to promote me. And sir, I, also want you to know that I already have a lot of respect from my men, so if you don't see fit to promote me, that's fine—I understand. I know it's hard to get advanced, at my age." The General tells Hurluret that he has just spoken with eloquence, and he offers him the promotion instantaneously, which is a complete surprise to Hurluret: Hurluret thought the General was horrified by slovenly conditions of the base, but the surprise, is that the General is really enjoying all of the fun that Hurluret's men are having, and he attributes the men's "great morale" to Hurluret. The General really loves it here, surrounded by all of these funny, goofball soldiers and he even tells Hurluret, approvingly, "Very funny, this base!" Indicating Fricot and La Plotte he next makes with a thumb's-up sign: "They're funny guys! I like them!"

When the General leaves the camp, the first thing Captain Hurluret does, is to 'try on' his new rank, by issuing his first order, as Commandante: He makes Fricot and La Plotte pour him a glass of water, because he can't think of anything else to order them to do. Fricot pours out the H2O, but snarlingly mutters, "I wasn't born to do this. I stayed in school until I was *eight!*" At one point, some Commanding Officers emerge from their barracks, where they've been drinking, and they see Fricot and La Plotte lazing around, and smoking. Fricot, with the cigarette hanging right out of his gaping maw, actually challenges the Officers: "What do you mean, you think I'm smoking? I'm not smoking!" Hurluret now screams at Fricot and La Plotte, very nonsensically, "Next time I catch you men, smoking, I'll transform you into fruit tarts! You look like oysters!" Meanwhile, Fernandel's goofy Venderague is sitting outside of the barracks, smilingly sharing his ration of food, and having a good conversation with a horse, and the joke is, of course, that when you look at Fernandel's face and a horse's face, side-by-side—well, they could be brothers! (Lots of movies which Fernandel will make, throughout his own forty-plus year film career will recycle this same visual joke, and really, how could they not?)

In the film's third act (I mean, the story is so slight, that there's not really any 'act,' to speak of), a busload of fresh-faced new recruits enters the camp, and Hurluret has no earthly idea where to put them, since the camp is already overstuffed. "If you don't find me sixteen extra beds in fifteen minutes," he warns his already-existing troops, "that will be eight days in the hole, for every single one of you!" Cut to a *charcuterie* (a restaurant where the specialty is pork) near the base, in which we see nattily-dressed civilian men chowing-down, while they're chatting-up the place's uniformly *zaftig* waitresses. When we meet the place's Proprietress, who's played by an actress called Ketty Pierson (who, just like the women who work for her, is 'large, and in charge'), she's entertaining her masticating customers with a song, accompanied by her extraordinarily-frazzled-looking pianist, and her song happens to be about a beautiful new baby; the song is actually so touching, that it makes Fernandel's Venderague, who also happens to be on the premises, having escaped from the horrible soup, which he hates so much, cry! One of the waitresses is perching upon the lap of one of Venderague's pals from the base, enormous-girthed Private Poitron (he's played by Pierre

With Rene Donnio.

Labry [in English, the character would be called 'Private Pumpkin']), who's having one-hell-of-a-good-time squirting seltzer water at the pianist. Poitron, as it's turning out, is just as great at 'cutting-up, in public' as Rodney Dangerfield was, when the comedian famously broke wind at that high society party, in *Caddyshack*. "May God make your nose like a sausage, and your chin like a *butt!*" the Pianist yells, waving an angry fist, at Poitron.

Fricot and La Plotte happen to be standing right outside of the restaurant—they're too cash-poor to actually venture inside, so they just huddle around the window, savoring the mixed aromas, and staring jealously at the diners; and when a cook places a freshly-baked pork-pie on the windowsill to cool, naturally—it's Manna from Heaven: "Say! A piece of that pie would be better than a kick in the ass," Fricot proclaims, nudging his pal's arm, playfully. Needless to say, the two men abscond with the sumptuous pie.

That night, as the soldiers in our *barracks-o'-fun* sleep, Hurluret bursts into their quarters, accompanied by the restaurant's Proprietress, as well as with a couple of MP's: "I know that there are two of you in here who have stolen a pork pie from this good lady's restaurant, and I know exactly who the thieves are, too, but I want them to confess to it, themselves—and right now!" He stares accusingly at Fricot and La Plotte, who have very generously given up their bunks, to newly-arrived recruits. ('F' and 'L' have both been sleeping, and rather comfortably, on the floor.) Hurluret sternly issues Fricot and La Plotte a week in solitary confinement, and Fricot tells Hurluret that he "just doesn't feel like going." But this time, Hurluret, who's newly tough, now that he's been promoted to Commandant, is probably, for the first time in his whole life, firmly in charge, and he orders his MP's to take the two lovable slackers away. With a Gabin-Shrug, Fricot, with La Plotte at his side, moseys-off to solitary, as the film ends.

Not only did *Gaietes de l'escadron* really cement how likeable Jean Gabin could be, when he was playing a lovably-defiant guy (Steve McQueen isn't the only movie star who can do *that*, you know), but it's a consistently smart and amusing slobs-in-the-military comedy, and, maybe it is a whole bunch slighter than Altman's M*A*S*H, but, damn if it's not one heck of a lot of fun, in its own right. It's definitely worth discovering, for anybody who likes movies, or fun, or just, fun movies, plus any movie in which the characters are named Private Slop and Private Pussy, is just *swellsville,* in my book.

When the film was initially released in France, in 1932, it was a major hit, grossing the franc-equivalent of $5,000 U.S. on its opening weekend, at only one Paris theater, the Olympia, and remember, I'm talking $5,000, in 1932 dollars. (Today, that would be, like, *five zillion dollars!*) What probably got *the asses into the seats,* is that the initial 35-millimeter prints of the film featured two hand-colored sequences, in which the soldiers' uniforms were apparently tinted red (for the pants) and blue (for the shirts), frame by frame! This magical candy-colored print is currently unavailable, although it was unspooled in 1995, at UC Berkeley's Pacific Film Archives, seven years before I had the idea of writing this book, and with English subtitles. The Archive is no longer in possession of the print however, so for this book, I had to rely only on the French DVD, which has neither English subtitles, nor groovy colors. Before *Gaietes de l'escadron* was even made, its producer, Bernard Natan, correctly anticipated that it would please French moviegoers as much as it did, and so he gifted *Gaietes de l'escadron* with twice the budget of the usual French film of that time—$100,000 (U.S.), in lieu of the standard $50,000. Additionally, he paid his star, Raimu, the franc-equivalent of $12,000, instead of the actor's normal fee of $8,000.

What a Critic Said at the Time: "An exceptional smash in this country [France], but possibilities abroad are hard to predicate. There is no definite story in the film, but [the] treatment is clever enough to produce continuity of a snappy tempo... Jean Gabin and Donnio [play] a couple of permanent defaulters, whose gags keep the audience roaring from beginning to the end. The whole thing hangs on subtlety, showing how, despite petty annoyances and trivialities, there is something really great hidden in the military. [Pic] evokes pre-war soldiery [by showing us] distinctive red pants... [The movie is] a fun stag party, headed by Raimu, with good direction, sound, and photography." (*Variety*, 10-4-32 issue. Critic: "Maxi." [Edwin 'Maxwell' MacSweeney.] Reviewed in Paris.)

What Another Critic Said at the Time: Director Maurice Tourneur proves that collaboration between a scriptwriter and a director can have a great outcome. The film is more satire than slapstick, and it is always alive—maybe it's not very artistic, but it has soul and instinct. We laugh, not from the military mumbo-jumbo but, also, because the characters themselves are so alive. The film continually renews itself [by virtue of] its own comic nature." (*Vu* Magazine, *No. 236,* Paris, 9-21-32 issue. Critic: Maurice Bourdet.)

Top: Jean Gabin and Serjius, in the lost race car drama, "La Foule hurle."
Above: James Cagney in the existing U.S. version of the same film.

FILM 8

LA FOULE HURLE

The first of three lost Jean Gabin films (1932)

La Foule hurle *(The Crowd Roars),* Jean Gabin's race car picture, which was directed by Jean Daumery, is the first of the three feature films made by Jean Gabin out of his ninety-five, which is considered to be "lost." An estimated fifteen percent of films which were made between 1930 and 1950 no longer exist today, due to the fact that they were produced on brittle nitrate film stock, a celluloid product which was notorious for decomposing. Also, movie studios, very typically, used to throw away their old movies, negatives and all, not believing that anybody would ever be interested in watching "the old stuff." What they didn't anticipate, is that today, the 'new stuff' is so bad, that all people want to watch, is the 'old stuff!'

La Foule hurle does not exist in any archive, or in any movie studio vault, anywhere in the world. Families of the crew members who worked on this movie don't have copies, the film is not in the library of any French t.v. station, there are no bootleg videos of it popping up on eBay, and there are no film collectors who have copies in their closets or attics, although, hopefully, one day, a copy may very well turn up. Five years of trying to find the movie, for this book, bore no fruit. *La Foule hurle* is gone, and it's a shame, too, because it would have been *a stone groove,* to see Gabin as a race car driver. However, we are lucky, in one respect:

La Foule hurle was produced by Warner Bros.' French production unit, in 1932, as a scene-for-scene, and shot-for-shot, French version of Warner Bros.' American-made/ English-language production *The Crowd Roars,* starring James Cagney. Howard Hawks directed the American-Cagney version, and he then sent WB-France the completed racing footage which he had shot, as well as his script, fully translated into French, by the scribe Paul d'Estournelle de Constant. The U.S./James Cagney version *does* exist, however, and, indeed, it turns up, with some frequency, on the American cable television station, Turner Classic Movies (TCM). So, while the French-language/Jean Gabin version is no longer with us, I will now offer you, as a substitution, a complete synopsis of the reportedly identical American version, so that you can have a feel for what the French-Gabin version would have been like.

THE CROWD ROARS

United States, 1932
Starring James Cagney: The American version of Jean Gabin's missing film, "La foule hurle"

Directed by Howard Hawks. Produced by Raymond Griffith. Screenplay by John Bright, Niven Busch, Kubec Glasmon, and Seton I. Miller. Based Upon a Story by Howard Hawks. Music by Bernhard Kaun. Directors of Photography (black and white), Sidney Hicox and John Stumar. Racing Footage Supervised by Carl Akeley, Elmer Dyer and Ray Ramsey. Editor, Thomas Pratt. Production Designer, Jack Okey. Makeup by Perc Westmore. Stunts by Harvey Parry. (GENRES: MELODRAMA/ ACTION) Running Time, 1 hour 25 minutes. Released in the United States by Warner Bros., on April 16, 1932. (Most of the credits are the same in director Jean Daumery's French-language Gabin version, because most of the footage was cribbed from the Cagney version.)

In the early, Depression-era 1930s, Warner Bros. Studios had the lock on fast-paced, nail-biting action flicks, movies which introduced the public to the likes of Edward G. Robinson, Pat O' Brien, James Cagney and even, an up-and-coming supporting player by the name of *Humphrey Bogart*. WB also, at that time, maintained a working movie studio in France, which existed specifically for the creation of French-made versions of their popular American films, starring all-French casts. Such was the case with *The Crowd Roars* (1932): 'American Warner Bros.' made the flick in early 1932, teaming James Cagney up with director Howard Hawks, and after Hawks completed shooting his movie, its screenplay was translated into French, and a director called Jean Daumery then helmed the French-language version, which featured Jean Gabin in the James Cagney role, and in which Gabin's scenes were intercut with Hawks' U.S.-lensed racing footage. (Reportedly, more than half of the footage in the Gabin version, comes from the Cagney version.)

Hawks' version of the film, which is the only one which currently exists, opens with a pre-credit sequence, which was unusual, for the early 1930s, in which we get to see a lightning-paced car race, and one, by the way, which is more genuinely exciting than anything which *Jerry Bruckheimer can pull out of his ass,* today. As a car smashes into a wall, with the camera, seemingly, right inside of it, and as the crowd stands up, cheering with excited bloodlust, the opening credits begin to roll.

When we meet the three-time Indianapolis-500 champion, Joe Greer (Cagney in this version, Gabin in the French version), he's on a train, returning to his midwestern hometown, of Indianapolis, Indiana. (Even the French version of the film, although it was filmed on soundstages in Germany, is meant to take place in Indiana! [*Don't ask!*]) Aboard the train with Joe is his pit-crew, which includes his smart-aleck relief driver, Stubby (the hilarious Frank McHugh, who played James Cagney's Irish-American pal in lots of Cagney's movies). Joe's car and his girlfriend, Leigh (unfortunately for their relationship, in that order) are present as well, and Leigh's upset, because the excitement-chasing Joe won't commit to her.

Other passengers recognize Joe, and he's happy to shake hands and give autographs, because he's not at all conceited—he's 'a real guy,' although he loses a few points for actually telling Leigh that he can't get married to her, because his true love is *speed!*

Leigh tells Joe that, when she first met him she just wanted to have fun, too, but that now, she needs something more serious, and she adds that, in her opinion, he's not even risking his life for that much money, and that the audience, which he thinks loves him so much, doesn't really care about him at all, and that they just, as we already saw, during the pre-credit sequence, want to see blood. Brushing her off, gently, he just shrugs, "We'll take it up at the next meeting," then sipping from his omnipresent flask. Joe's not only a driver, but he's also an imbiber of some repute, and it looks like somebody in this movie is going to be crawling out of a bottle—and I'll give you one guess, who that somebody's gonna be!

Joe and Spud disembark from the train in Indianapolis, but Leigh stays aboard, continuing on to Los Angeles, where she keeps a small apartment. (In her daydreams, Joe has retired from racing, and he lives in bucolic—or, at least, in *colic*—L.A., with her, in peace and happiness.) As Joe climbs down from the train, he greets his Dad (Guy Kibbee), as well as his little brother, Eddie, who's played by Eric Linden, and this happens to be great casting, because Eddie looks a lot like Cagney, as though the two of them could be real-life brothers. Dad's a mechanic, and he and some of his own crew, comically, carry Joe's car, which has, of course, been detailed, with a large '#1,' off of the train.

At home, little brother Eddie (he's an 'aww shucks'/'apple pie'/'homespun' kid) takes Joe up to his bedroom, and shows him the shrine which he keeps to him: The walls are blanketed with newspaper articles which cover Joe's most notable racing victories all over the country. The brothers next head into the family garage, where another racecar, a Duisenberg, is hidden under a tarp, and Eddie starts gloating about the machine's virtues for his big brother's benefit, even revealing to Joe that he, too, has been racing lately (locally), and that his big dream is to follow in his big brother's footsteps: "I want you to be proud of me, Joe. And next time you go off to race, I want you to take me with you." Joe is protective of his little brother, and doesn't like the idea, nor does he welcome the competition! "You want to be a driver, Eddie? You want to be crippled, or killed? For what? You know, Eddie, I hate to break this to you, but most boys don't win." Then, he starts quoting his girlfriend, Leigh, even though, most probably, he can't remember that she's the one who said this to him: "When you race, they're not cheering for you, you know. They're cheering for blood. You could get crippled today and killed tomorrow! You can't take the roar of the crowd to the bank and cash in on it." Eddie asks Joe why he's 'in it' if it's so dangerous, and he (Eddie) then asserts himself: "I already *am* in it, Joe." So, as it turns out, Eddie's not as 'aww-shucks' and 'cornpone' as we originally thought he was: He's strong-willed in his own right, and can definitely hold his own against his big brother. Joe's come home to Indianapolis to participate in a big, local race, and this is where he finds out that, in fact, his little brother is going to be competing with him, in another car!

Director Howard Hawks next cuts to this big race, which has been shot very excitingly (even more so, perhaps, than any of the 'newer' race car pictures [James Garner, in John Frankenheimer's *Grand Prix*, from 1966; Tom Cruise, in Tony Scott's *Days of Thunder*, from 1989]), and much of this has to do with the fact that Hawks had the foresight to hire, as his second-unit directors of photography, three great documentary-film cinematographers who specialized in shooting racing footage—Carl Akeley, Elmer Dyer, and Ray Ramsey, and the lenses of these three camera wizards place us right into the action, in a way which is so far ahead of its time, we almost think we're looking at 3-D. Not only do Hawks and his cinematographers undercrank a good deal of the film's racing footage into fast-motion, but they also bolt their cameras directly to the hoods of the various cars, so that, throughout the movie, we get to see both 'the thrill of victory' and 'the agony of defeat' in blistering close-up, and right on the various actors' faces. Plus, back in 1932, the race-cars were all 'open'—there weren't any *shitty old windows* to get in the way of the fun—so it's also very cool that we get to see the wind, as it cakes the drivers' faces with black dirt, making vision next to impossible, as they all whiz around the tracks. (Prior to this movie, cameras had never before been this close to exciting race-car action.)

In this first race of the day, according to the announcer, Eddie is in the lead, and brother Joe is in second, right behind him, and there are several other cars in the race, as well: One spins out, and the audience cheers, and here, Hawks is again showing us that the crowd really goes for blood, in a big way, but he chooses, wisely, not to linger on the moment, because the movie isn't on any big soapbox, in the way in which a lot of new movies are, today.

Eddie wins the race! Proud of his little brother, in spite of the fact that the little fellow has beaten him, Joe now asks Eddie if he'd like to drive his (Joe's) car ("#1"), from now on, and Eddie instantly morphs into his phony, 'aww-shucks'-*shtick:* "Awww, that's your car, Joe! Gee whiz, I can't do that!" "It's yours now, kid," Joe tells him, proudly.

Meanwhile, back at Leigh's apartment in L.A., we see Leigh luxuriating around with her feisty/sexy roommate, Anne (Joan Blondell). Leigh has just received a letter from Joe, in which he's written that he won't be able to come and see her for another month, because he's going to be busy, "taking his brother out, and showing him the ropes." Both Leigh and Anne are suckers for racers, just like how the women characters in American movies are always going *apeshit* for athletes, as well (*Bull Durham, Top Gun, etc.*) Leigh and Anne love dating bad-boy drivers (Anne, too, has 'a driver, of her own'), although both women also complain, at the same time, about how terrible their badass men are, because the guys are always leaving them alone, and are never willing to commit to involving themselves in serious relationships. Anne's not waiting for her own (unseen in the film) racer-beau to show up this evening, though, because night's falling, and she's ready to go out and kick up her tootsies! ("If you can't be with the one you love," the song goes, "love the one you're with," and Joan Blondell's Anne is living proof of CSNY'S profound/turgid hippie maxim.) Annie tries to get Leigh to go out and party with her, but Leigh just wants to be alone tonight: For her, just thinking about her absent Joe, is better than being with any other man who would actually be physically 'present.'

A couple of days later, Leigh receives a telegram from Joe, in which he's letting her know that he'll be joining her in L.A., along with brother Eddie and his side-man Stubby in a few days, and when we see Joe next, his train is arriving at Los Angeles's marvelous Union Station, one of the City of Angels' magnificent, 1930s'-era, art-deco venues, which still exists today, and which still looks exactly the same today, as it did nearly eighty years ago, when the movie was made. Leigh has come to greet him, and so has Stubby's wife, who's brought-along their little boy, Mike. When Joe sees little Mike, he whispers to Leigh that professional drivers have no right to have children, since they probably won't be around to see their kids grow up, but Leigh just shrugs-off the remark, recognizing it for being what it is (just more of his lame 'commitment-phobia'), and you can totally see why Jean Gabin was chosen to play the Joe Greer-character in the French version: Gabin's movie characters, not to mention all real (and most movie) racecar drivers, always know that they're fated to bad ends, but they also enjoy *the heady rush* which they get to experience on the way to their unpleasant fates.

Whenever Joe visits Leigh, in L.A., he lives at her apartment with her, in 'pre-Hays Code sin,' but this time out, since little brother Eddie is in tow, Joe no longer thinks that these living conditions are appropriate: "My brother and I will take the vacant apartment down the hall from you," Joe tells Leigh, and Leigh takes the innocently-delivered remark personally, feeling like he's telling her that he thinks she's a whore (this isn't what he's trying to tell her, but he's not very articulate sometimes, so that's the way it came out), and she starts crying. Annie comes in, after the guys have left, sees her friend in tears, and consoles her, gently: "Boy, I'll tell ya: Those mugs break their bones… and, then, they break our hearts!"

A few days later, Leigh is telling Annie that, even though Joe has returned to L.A., she hasn't been able to see too much of him lately, because he spends his nights with his brother at the garage, and his days at the racetrack: "I think," she confides to Annie, "that he thinks I might be a bad influence on the kid." But really, what the problem is, is that Little Brother Eddie is *horny* for his big brother's girl, too! One night, when Joe's not around, Eddie pays Leigh a visit and, as we've already seen, he's even cockier than Joe is: Right off-the-bat, he demands a drink, wanting to show the girls that he's tougher than his big brother, and Annie pours one out for him, impressed by his show of manliness. Joe, of course, has picked this exact moment to come in, and he's horrified by what he's seeing: "You tramps are feeding my brother liquor? Why, you're all tricked out to ruin him!"

At this point, Joe tells Leigh, "Look, Leigh: We have to call it [that's how he characterizes their relationship—'*it!*'] quits for good, because of my brother," and Leigh, not expecting that he would say this, is horrified: "What does your kid brother have to do with me? You think I'm interested in him—but I'm not!" (She's telling Joe the truth.) "Be that as it may," Joe insists, "I'm going to keep Eddie off booze and women," and, after he says this, Leigh puts her foot down, asserting, in a very pre-woman's lib manner, "I'm not 'all women!'"

The next day at a local garage, Eddie is bodily underneath his, and formerly Joe's, car (#1), making some repairs, when Joan Blondell's Annie-character comes to visit him. He invites her to a big race that's going to be taking place that night, at L.A.'s Ascot Speedway, and she accepts, happily. Well, suffice it to say, it's not long before Eddie and Annie are having a fling, and, of course, over-protective Big Brother Joe means to put a stop to that, as well. Joe bolts into the girls' apartment, and tells Anne, that he doesn't want her to see his brother, anymore—and he's plenty mad: "I told you to lay off my kid brother. Give him the air! What do you want offa him, anyway? He don't have any money. [Plus], why would you want to hurt him? Haven't you told him that you've already got another fella, beside him?" Anne replies, "If you want your brother to know that I've got another guy—you tell him." At this moment, Eddie enters the girls' apartment, having overheard only the tail-end of the conversation: "Tell me what, Joe?"

Joe lyingly tells Eddie, right in front of Anne, "Annie likes you, just because you're coming up. But I've got news for ya, kiddo—she likes other drivers, too!" The two brothers now start beating the crap out of each other, right in front of a horrified Anne, and Joan Blondell plays Anne in the same vivacious way in which she plays all of the gum-chewing firecrackers whom she'd be assaying throughout her career: Her characters are always tough-cookies on the outside, but sticky-sweet marshmallows on the inside.

That night, it's time for the big race at Ascot, where Joe and Eddie, who are again going to be competing against each other, will be playing out their eternal/fraternal drama, before a huge crowd of racing fans. The racetrack's announcer, Reid Kilpatrick, who was one of the 1930s' most famous sports commentators, keeps the crowd apprised of the fact, that "… fourteen of the most famous drivers in the world are competing here, tonight!" Indeed, some of the top American drivers in the world, at the time this movie was made, play themselves, and participate in the on-screen races, including Harry Hartz, Billy Arnold, Fred Frame, Ralph Hepburn, Wilbur Shaw, Shorty Canlon, Mel Keneally, and Stubby Stubblefield.

Joe takes a big pull of booze from his flask, just before he climbs into his car, since booze, always (as we know) makes driving better! Eddie's not in the car Joe gave him (#1), but in another car—one, which is numbered #25, while Joe is in #18. Eddie's smart: He's not going to drive a car, which the brother with whom he's fighting gave him; after all, what if Joe somehow (intentionally) sabotaged the vehicle, so that Eddie would lose? Reid Kilpatrick, who's now sounding more like Macdonald Carey announcing the opening of "Days of Our Lives" than a race-announcer, tells the audience, "It seems like there's been some trouble in the Greer family, and that younger brother wants to snatch away older brother's laurels! Watch out, Joe!"

Only moments after the checkered flag has dropped, Eddie's car is *already up Joe's ass* and, while ten different vehicles are participating in the race, Hawks doesn't bother to show us any of the other drivers in close-up, except, of course, for Eddie and Joe. Eddie gets his car too close to Joe's and it looks, for all of the world, like he's trying to run his own brother off of the road! Spud, who's also participating in a car of his own (he's there as Joe's relief driver), shifts his own car in between the brothers' two cars, to protect them from each other: He knows, all too well, that with the anger which these two Fighting Greers feel toward each other, one of them might wind up dead.

Soon, just like in any other race-car movie, and like in any real-life race (and, also, in 'the race of life'), cars are dropping like flies (#69 spins out; #37 crashes into the wall). But Joe and Eddie Greer are still in the game and, according to Reid Kilpatrick, "The Greer Family Feud is sure raising Cain with the other drivers!" Joe's tires dig at his brother's tires, and the sparks begin to fly—literally.

And then, another casualty: Spud's car is on fire! He's screaming in agony, while his car is now burning up, all around him. Spud's wife is present, and has to be calmed down, and Joe, who has suddenly gone into shock, seeing that his buddy's car is on fire, accidentally smashes his own car into the wall. But the race keeps going, and the winner is Eddie Greer. The younger brother has triumphed over the older, but the moment isn't as triumphant for Eddie as it should be, because Spuds, who was a friend to Eddie, Joe, and all of the other drivers, didn't make it.

The requisite spinning newspaper headlines, which had been written subsequently to the race's conclusion, now proclaim that Eddie has achieved victories, not only at Ascot but also at other races which have been held lately at other large racetracks, including racetracks at Imperial Valley, Oakland, and Phoenix. Eddie's in the big time now, and the real-life car-maven Fred Duisenberg (he plays himself, in the movie), hands him the keys to one of his newest models.

Cut to several months later: Anne and Eddie are married now (she's given up 'her other fella,' for Eddie, '*the big champeen*'), but they haven't heard from Joe, who disappeared months ago, after the death of his good buddy and relief driver, Spuds. One newspaper columnist, in his "Whatever Happened to…?" column, opines that the now-reclusive Joe Greer has disappeared, probably having "lost his nerve" after the death of his friend. Leigh hasn't heard from Joe, either, outside of the few dribs and drabs which she's been able to get from local newspapers, one of which has proclaimed Joe to be "yellow." (In any early-1930s Warner Bros. drama, the worst thing in the world you can be called, is "yellow.' [In James Cagney's 1931 gangland epic, *Public Enemy,* people refer to his gangster-character, Jimmy Malone, as being "yellow," and he doesn't take it very well.]) Selfishly, Eddie doesn't know or care what happened to his big brother, Joe; he's definitely not the nice kid who we met at the beginning of the picture, and, probably, he never was.

In spite of all of Joe's frailties, however, Leigh still wants him back, and she tells Annie she knows that, if Joe came back to her, she'd be able to make him feel good about himself and proud of himself again, and this is a far cry from the Leigh whom we met at the beginning of the picture, who didn't want Joe to race at all. Even though she doesn't know for sure, she's worried that Joe's been off drinking somewhere, on a four month-bender, and we're about to find out that her prediction is pretty accurate.

Annie can't believe that Leigh's wasting her energy on defending a guy who's been so cruel to her. "Joe's not yellow," Leigh inveighs, responding to the newspaper's point-blank proclamation. "He's got more nerve than anyone I've ever met. If he can't drive, it's only because he's broken and sick." Annie tells Leigh that Joe hardly rates her, after how he's treated her, and Leigh just retorts that she lays awake, every night, knowing that Joe's probably in some flophouse somewhere, crying over Spud's death, and she continues, "I don't know if he still loves me, but I'll always love him." She guesses that he's probably back in his hometown of Indianapolis, and so she next decides to go and find him, herself, after borrowing some train fare from Annie (since Leigh is miserably broke).

Next, a superimposed title card tells us that we're in Indiana. Not only is Joe in Indiana (Leigh guessed right), but he's now a heavily-bearded drunken hobo (!) who lives in a trainyard with a bunch of other hobos. We see a shot of a train arriving, but director Hawks is tricking us: Initially, we thought we were getting a shot of Leigh, arriving in Indianapolis from L.A., but it's really a view of the train which Joe and his new unwashed friends are on.

The hobos, including Joe, are helping to unload vegetables from the *choo-choo,* a few of which fall onto the ground, and Joe is so hungry that he woofs them all down. Soon sated by his macrobiotic hobo meal, he lumbers over to the Indianapolis Speedway and approaches some of the real-life racers, who are playing themselves in the film. He first accosts Harry Hartz, and asks Hartz if he might happen to have a spot open for him, as a relief driver, but Hartz, whereupon seeing Joe's Delicate Condition, makes with a categorical cry of "no dice." Joe also asks the same question of both Fred Frame and Billy Arnold and, of course, their answers are the same as Hartz's.

Billy Arnold's relief man, not recognizing Joe, tells his boss that it would be great to have an extra pit-crew guy around, but Arnold puts things in perspective for him. "Don'tchya know who that is? That's Joe Greer, the greatest driver on earth! No matter what condition he's in now, I'm not asking him to go under a car." At this point, Joe lopes up to Tom Beale's Lunch Counter, where Beale, who was, famously, a real-life Indianapolis Speedway concession owner, serves the drivers *nice, healthy, all-beef hamburgers,* while also handicapping the races. (The sign on Beale's concession stand reads, 'Tom Beale's Dope.') Tom is happy to see Joe and, recognizing that he's broke, and way down on his luck, feeds him for free. Tom, next, heads into the kitchen, and tells his newly-hired waitress whom we're seeing, so far, only, from the back, "There's a guy here. He's broke. Give him whatever he wants. He used to be a great driver." She turns around and, of course, she's Leigh, and Leigh has taken a job as a racetrack waitress, to keep tabs on her man. (*Inside of every woman, there's a waitress waiting to get out!*) Joe is beyond-happy to see Leigh, but he feels so embarrassed about how he's treated her in the past, and he's so embarrassed that she should be seeing him right now, when he's in such terrible shape, that, at first, he can't even look her straight in the eye. "What brought you here, Leigh," he asks her, tentatively, and she exclaims, very tenderly, "You did, Joe."

That evening, Leigh brings Joe up to the little apartment which she's just taken near the Indianapolis Speedway. Joe tells her that he's been "bumming around the country" for a few months, and he tells her, also (and this is the truth) that he hasn't had a drink since Spuds died, and then he breaks down and cries, in her arms: Formerly a cocky man he's now as broken as broken gets. Leigh tells Joe that Eddie's still mad at him, and she adds, "The fight you had with your brother was all my fault. I pushed your brother toward Anne. I wanted you to have the feeling of what it's like to lose somebody that you've loved, just like I've always had that feeling, for you." Leigh tells Joe that if he puts his mind and body to it, that he could probably drive again, and better than ever, but he definitely doesn't have the same faith in her, which she has in him: "Drive? How could I do that? Everybody's turned me down. I'm yellow!" He thinks it's his fault that Spuds died, since Spuds was driving a separate car, instead of riding side-saddle with him, which is what he usually did. But soon, and thanks to the miracle of the time lapse dissolve, a few months have passed: The Indianapolis-500, the country's biggest race, at that time, is now upon us, and a very sober (not to mention, a very clean-shaven) Joe is now back racing again, and guess who's there to compete against him again? *Yup*, it's Eddie, all right, so get ready for *'Brother-vs.-Brother: Part Three!'* (The Indianapolis-500 was named so, because it was originally intended to be a five hundred-mile race, even though it's actually always been only 375 miles, or, 150 laps.)

After the festive parade, which opens the day's events, we finally get to see the race, itself: Eddie, who's now in a car which is marked '#2,' takes the lead from Billy Arnold, who's in '#4' Since director Howard Hawks is only showing us the best bits of the race in the montage sequence which he is now providing, we next see that lots of the drivers are spinning-out and/or crashing—including Joe! (But Joe doesn't get hurt.) By the time the final laps are at hand, there are only two drivers left, in the race—Eddie Greer and Billy Arnold.

But Eddie's been hurt! He's cut his arm, which is bloody, and so now, it's very easy for Arnold to take the lead. Eddie knows that a substitute driver can take over for him, but he doesn't want any part of it. Then, a relief-driver pulls up in another car, and hops into the car, with Eddie—yes, it's big brother Joe, who's arrived on the scene, just to help his brother win! The two Battling Greers are now together again and working, for the first time in both of their adult lives, as a team! Needless to say, Joe takes his brother to the win (Arnold spun-out) and, just as they cross the finish line—one of Eddie's tires explodes!

Of course, we get one of Hollywood's requisite happy endings. ("We won, Joe!" "No... you won, Eddie.") Joe lets his little brother enjoy the victory, not wanting to hog any of the credit for himself, because he's truly proud of his little brother. We won't see Leigh and Anne any more in the picture, but we can guess that the four of them (the two couples) will probably wind up happily, ever after, even in spite of all of their constant bickering. And, as a comical coda, and because Eddie's arm is continuing to bleed, he and Joe now hop into the back of an ambulance, and Joe, who's always up for a challenge, orders the ambulance driver to race to the hospital, directing him to speed past all of the other traffic ("You! Driver! Take the curb!"), as this fun film ends.

Seven years later, in 1939, Warner Bros. Pictures would churn out a second American version of the *Crowd Roars/Foule hurle* story, entitled *Indianapolis Speedway*, and that version is as good as the Cagney version: In the '39 version, Pat O'Brien, who happened to be James Cagney's real-life best friend, would assume the role of Joe Greer.

While it would be absolute nirvana to be able to see the French version of *The Crowd*

Roars, and to see Jean Gabin as a race-car driver, the James Cagney version is going to have to suffice, for now, at least until that magical day when somebody in France is rooting around his or her great-grandparents' attic, and accidentally discovers a thirty-five-millimeter print of this lost film. And while the Gabin version is gone, today, *Variety's* review of it does survive. And here it is, for your approval:

What a Critic at the Time Said (About the [No Longer-Existing] Jean Gabin Version): "Technically very poor, with production and acting, apart from Jean Gabin, also poor... The old trick of using [the] French actors for close-ups and inserting them between [the] American long-shots has [already] been done [in too many other pictures]. But the film is doing big business [in Paris], all the same." (*Variety*, 10-25-32 issue. Critic: "Wolfe. [Wolfe Kaufman.]" Reviewed in Paris.)

What a Critic at the Time Said (About the [Still-Existing] James Cagney Version): "A spectacular film, which ought to fit the public mold. Its mainspring is action, and that's what will see it through, spectacularly. Welcome audience fare which will likely shine at the box-office." (*Variety*, 3-22-32 issue. Critic: "Maxi. [Edward 'Maxwell' MacSweeney.]" Reviewed in New York City.)

Gabin projects a film for gangster Gabriel Gabrio, in "Coeurs joyeux" (Film 9, right).

FILM 9

Coeurs joyeux

France, 1932

(France, 1932) (Literal English Translation: "HAPPY HEARTS") Directed by Hans Schwartz with (uncredited) Max de Vaucorbeil. No Credited Producer. Written by Hermann Kosterlitz with Jean Guignebert. Director of Photography (black and white), Eugene Schufftan. Production Designer, Enrico Metzner. Music by Helmuth Wolfes. Songs by Paul Abraham. (GENRES: COMEDY/OPERETTA) Running Time, 1 hour 17 minutes. A Pathe-Consortium-Cinema Presentation. Released in France on February 11, 1932. Never Released Theatrically in the United States.

"It's okay if you want to kidnap me; I wasn't doing anything, anyway.
But… can we eat first?"
— A carefree Jean Gabin, to the gangsters who are forcing him into their car, in "Coeurs joyeux"

For the first several minutes of director Hans Schwartz's very winning *Coeurs joyeux*, a deliriously delightful screwball comedy with musical interludes which also happens to be the final of Gabin's three operetta movies—the previous two, of course, being *Chacun sa chance* and *Paris-Beguin*—we think we're watching a silent movie. But why would anybody be dim enough to have made a silent movie in 1932, when talkies had already been around for about five years? Was director Schwartz so artistic that he preferred the antiquated 'old ways?' As in all silent movies, the film's opening dialogue is written on very simplistic title cards, and the first image we're going to be seeing, is that of a woman who's peeking through a trellis and spying on a pair of young lovers who bill-and-coo at each other with the usual smarmy silent movie platitudes—"You are stupid!;" "I forgave you a long time ago;" *etc.*

But then, Schwartz pulls out to reveal that we're actually in a Paris movie theater, the Victoria Palace, and that the little interaction which we've just witnessed has been playing out only on the screen. And as we pan up to the projection booth, guess who the projectionist is—it's *Notre Jean,* and the film-within-a-film which we've been watching, according to the posters which line the walls outside of the theater, is called *Le Joli peche* or, in English, *The Pretty Peach.* In his movie career, Jean Gabin will play cops, criminals, drifters, and high-flying captains of industry, but *Coeurs joyeux* is a milestone, because it's the only film in which we'll ever see him playing a movie projectionist.

When we first see Gabin's 'Charlo' character ('Charlo' is the francophone version of the English-language nickname, 'Charlie') he's shutting down the booth for the night. His co-worker Jules (Marcel Delaitre), the theater's organist, is relieved that the work day is finally over, and because the night is still young, he asks Charlo if he feels like hanging out with him tonight at the local amusement park because, in his view, it's a fine place to pick up girls. Charlo, who is as easygoing as are most of Jean Gabin's characters, thinks it's a fine idea ("Sure! Okay!"), and these two guys-on-the-make next, goofily, put on identical jaunty berets and begin fantasizing-out-loud about all of the cuties they're going to be meeting.

As Charlo waits outside the theater for Jules to finish locking up, three thuggish characters in straw hats, who resemble a barbershop quartet, suddenly screech up in an intimidatingly-huge black sedan, and he asks them for a light for his cigarette, but they're in no mood. (Charlo [casually]: "If you guys can afford a nice car, you can afford some matches, too, right?") The thugs kidnap Charlo at gunpoint, and the joke, is that Charlo is so 'Gabin-Easygoing,' he doesn't even care, nor does he even put up a fight! He just climbs into the car with them, dispensing a resigned-to-his-fate-Gabin-Shrug, and telling them, "Hey, I don't care if you kidnap me, because I didn't have anything too important to do tonight, anyway. But, listen: Can we eat first?" After the car pulls away with Charlo in the back seat, a girl with whom he had made a temporary date for this evening, but whom he had forgotten all about, now sashays up to the theater looking for him, and she looks very disappointed—to say the least—that he's gone, and that he hasn't waited around for her.

The carful of roughs, with Charlo agreeably in-tow, now pulls up to a mansion, and one of them whistles a secret password so that they can get in. A fourth gangster, who answers the door, next takes their straw hats and shows them upstairs, to a room in which a movie projector has been set up. These gangsters have kidnapped Charlo so that he can project a movie for them, because they have no idea how to work the rickety, old machine which they own. Charlo tells them, laughingly, that he can't believe they're making him project a movie so late at night, but the head gangster, whose name is Olivier—he's played by the film's first-billed star Gabriel Gabrio (Gabin gets second-billing)—tells him he'll be well-paid for his efforts, and that if he knows what's good for him, he should just shut the hell up and start the movie. Charlo starts making fun of the ancient projector, and he then holds the celluloid up to the light, examining the frames and squinting, trying to make out the images: "Wow, this film looks really stupid! Anyway, pass me a screwdriver. If you want me to project your film, I'm going to have to fix this projector." Olivier doesn't like the insouciant Charlo from the get-go, however, and he tells Charlo that if he doesn't play ball, he'll see that Charlo is thrown in jail—but Charlo just 'Gabin-Shrugs' and tells them, matter-of-factly, that he doesn't "care for jail." The gangsters are livid, because Charlo is not properly intimidated by them: As we've seen already, in a few of Jean Gabin's prior movies, and as we'll be seeing in many more to come, Gabin is never intimidated by anybody; even when his antagonists are packing heat, he is always the absolute soul of calm.

With the projector soon fixed, Charlo projects the film for the gangsters, as instructed. In the film, we see a group of men, and one of them, an elderly gentleman in the middle of the frame, Hendrik Van-Hoolst (Paul Amiot), has a comically-pointed beard, and looks a great deal like Germany's beloved silver-screen swashbuckler, Baron Munchausen. As it turns out, Van-Hoolst is an Amsterdam diamond broker who is currently visiting Paris to buy jewels, and Olivier and his men are studying this film of him, because they mean to rip him off.

After Charlo has finished unspooling the film, Olivier remunerates him to the tune of five hundred francs, ordering him to "take a hike" and to forget everything that he's just seen, and as quickly as he can. Charlo asks Olivier, "So, what was that movie all about, anyway?" but Olivier's had more than enough of him: "Don't try to find out. Now get the hell out of here!" So our hero, Charlo, just tips his beret and leaves, genuinely happy that he was kidnapped, because he was able to pocket five hundred francs.

Just as Charlo leaves the mansion, he next, completely of his own free will and accord, returns: Even though Jean Gabin, in many of his movies, plays the ultimate 'guy who doesn't want any entanglements,' he decides to bring a police officer back up to the mansion with him, because while Gabin's movie characters are consummate loners, they're also consummate loners who can never abide wrongdoing of any kind.

Charlo lets fly with the 'secret whistle' which he saw the gangsters giving earlier, and the gangsters open the door. A beaming Charlo tells the cop whom he's brought along, "Okay! Here are the guys who kidnapped me. You can arrest them now!"—but Charlo's been set up: Not only does this crooked cop work with the gangsters, but he's also a very important part of their organization, because he keeps the good cops at bay. The cop points his gun at Charlo and drags him back into the house, and Olivier, next, commands Charlo to return the five hundred francs—you didn't think they were going to let him get away with that kind of scratch, were you? Charlo, who's still completely unafraid of the gangsters, smilingly deadpans to them that he doesn't have it ("I lost it, somewhere!"), even though they just gave him the money thirty seconds ago! One of the gangsters finds the money in Charlo's pocket, and Our Hero just grins widely, raising his shoulders in a 'Gabin-Shrug.'

Of course, the gangsters can't set Charlo free, since he knows too much. They're now just a few minutes from heading off to the Grand Hotel, where Van-Hoolst is staying, but before they leave the house, Olivier decides to lock Charlo up in an upstairs room so that he won't be able to escape, because he knows that if Charlo escapes, he'll 'sing' to the real cops.

Of course, it's fortuitous that Charlo's being held prisoner in the mansion, because Olivier's pretty, blonde sister has been ordered to stay and guard him. Her name is Lucette, and she's played by Josseline Gael, who played Claire, the object of nerdy pharmacist Jules Renauldin's love in *Tout ca ne vaut pas l'amour*. Lucette acts as a maid/serving-wench for her gangster-brother and his cronies, and not a great one, either: When she comes up to Charlo's room to deliver him a meal, with her psychotic brother right there beside her, she gets so flustered in front of Charlo—she really likes him!—that she spills the whole kit-and-kaboodle, all over the floor. "Wow! Your sister is really clumsy," Charlo grins at Olivier, and we can tell, by the huge grin on Charlo's face, that he's as smitten with her as she is with him. Olivier then tells his cohorts, "Okay, kids, it's time! *Allons-y!*" Olivier and his four henchmen—who are played by Rene Bergeron, Henri Vilbert, Georges Vitray, and *Mephisto's* own 'Fortunae,' Lucien Callamand—leave for their incipient rendezvous with some great diamonds, at the Grand Hotel.

At this point, Charlo has been locked up in the room for about an hour, and nobody's brought him another meal to make up for the one that spilled. "Come on, you bastards," he yells through the locked door, more amused than he is angry, and not realizing that the guys are no longer on the premises. "Open the door! Get me out of here! You're bullies... and I'm hungry! I want steak and french fries... and red wine... and beer... and that's all!" The only piece of furniture in the room with Charlo, is a two-foot statue of a naked woman and, still smilin'-through, Charlo cheekily gives it a little pat on the ass. Talk about Jean Gabin always being resigned to his characters' fates: Charlo certainly knows how to turn his own kidnapping into a fun adventure.

He tries to break down the door, using the naked statuette and, while he is unable to do this, he is able to make a small hole, and he gets a good eyeful of Lucette in the process. Lucette tells Charlo that she's been ordered, by her brother, to keep an eye on him, and he excitedly tells her that he thinks that's good; obviously, he hopes she'll be keeping more body parts than just her eye on him.

Charlo finally breaks the door down with his shoulder, and he tells Lucette not to worry, because he's just going to leave, "grab something to eat at a café, and be right back"—which we know is true, because he's hot for her. She tells him that if he leaves, and if Olivier returns and finds him AWOL, that he'll probably kill both of them, and this gives Charlo a whimsical idea: He positions Lucette in a chair and they began to rehearse something devious: He hands her a gun, and he then throws his hands up and melodramatically cries out, "Don't shoot." Now, they're covered! When her brother returns, she'll be able to tell him, truthfully, that she was just protecting herself against that big brute Charlo when he was escaping. Lucette returns Charlo's gun to him, and tells him that, if he'll agree to take the bullets out and not leave the house, she'll bring him something to eat.

Dissolve to a bit later: Charlo and Lucette are together in the house's modest dining room. She's cooked him a huge meal, and he's gulping it down hungrily, the gun positioned right beside him on his placemat just in case the gangsters should happen to come back earlier than expected, and this is really turning out to be a great first date; Lucette and Charlo are wolfing down sausage, ham, and salami and they're drinking wine, and the meal is accompanied by side-orders of suggestive smiling and hot, smoky-glances

Director Schwartz now cuts to a restaurant in the Grand Hotel, where a male singer is entertaining the customers with a typically-sappy, 1930s movie-song (LYRICS: "Beautiful flowers have a great smell... What an enchantment; our hearts full of joy for always... [*etc.*]"). Van-Hoolst is dining with a visiting Parisian diamond broker, and when Hoolst is interrupted, because he has to go and take a phone call, he is replaced by one of Olivier's henchmen, who is disguised as Van-Hoolst, and the clueless French broker consigns the diamonds to him, believing him to be the real V-H. Olivier and his gang now have what they came for.

Meanwhile, back at Gangster Manor, Charlo's enjoying a smoke, and he and Lucette are seriously discussing the possibility of running away together, but she tells him that this might not be the most stellar idea, since her brother and his cohorts would catch up to them, no matter where they'd go. Suddenly, the front door bursts open: The gangsters are back! Charlo, who's amped-up and ready for some good-natured fun, tells Lucette to aim the gun at him, just like how he showed her, and to shoot behind him.

When the guys enter, they hear the pistol's loud report, and they see Lucette holding the smoking gun on Charlo. Olivier is proud of his sister, because it looks like she was protecting herself, but when he notices Charlo's cigarette burning in the ashtray, he figures out that Lucette and Charlo were enjoying a meal together, and that Charlo wasn't really threatening her at all. Charlo tries to protect Lucette, telling the cons that he wanted to run away, but that she wouldn't let him, and he's so 'Gabin-sincere' when he says it, that Olivier actually believes him.

Impressed by Lucette's courage, Olivier now gives her a ring which he and his boys have just lifted from the Grand Hotel heist, as a medal of courage. Next, he orders her to bring him and his men a little post-crime snack; even though he's just given his littler sister an award, for her bravery under fire, he still wants her to know that he's the boss.

Lucette locks Charlo in another room, and tells him, loudly enough for the gangsters to hear, that she's going to double-lock the door this time, so that he won't be able to escape, and she's winking at him as she's saying it! While the gangsters hear the lock turning, and while they believe that she's locking him inside the room, she's really unlocking the door, which will make it easy for him to escape, at such time as the coast becomes clear. "I have to be careful with a guy like you," Lucette tells Charlo, also, very purposely, much-too-loudly. She next pads back downstairs, to serve the five gangsters their daily bread.

Olivier next alerts his cohorts about what's coming up next on their crime-docket: "Now that we've got the merchandise, tomorrow, at this time, we'll be in the middle of the ocean!" The gangsters plan on escaping from Paris with the purloined diamonds, which they will fence, for a very large profit, in America, and all of the gangsters now, hilariously, break out into song; and not only does this bizarrely-enchanting moment not break with the scene's dramatic flow—because, remember, this film is operetta, and in operetta, just like in today's Bollywood movies, things like that happen all the time—it's actually a very fun and charming moment, even though the lyrics to the song which the hoods begin to sing won't be winning a Tony Award, anytime soon. (SAMPLE LYRICS: "La, La, La! We can share between friends… We don't have to worry about tomorrow… Tomorrow we're leeeeeaving!") You've really got to love a movie where the criminals sing about the crimes which they are about to commit.

While the gangsters continue dancing around gaily, in their sweet little faerie-circle,

Charlo and Lucette escape through the back door, and they proceed to board a bus together. While riding, he serenades her with a whimsical little song called "*Mon bonheur est avec toi*" or, in English, "My Happiness is with You." (LYRICS: "1, 2, My happiness lies with you… 1,2,3, We add up perfectly…!") When Jean Gabin breaks into song in some of his earliest films from the 1930s—*Mephisto, Coeurs joyeux,* and a few more—the singing doesn't make him seem any less manly, in fact, Gabin's life-affirming caterwauling just makes him seem even more likable and more human than he already is. A mustached and drunken straphanger loves Charlo's free, impromptu concert so much, that he raises the beer, which he's taken along for the ride, to their health: "*A son gout, mes amis!*" ("To your health, my friends!")

Lucette and Charlo next arrive at Charlo's small, one-room apartment. ("When you don't work much, you can't have much more," Charlo Gabin-Shrugs at her, but he looks very proud of his place, anyway.) He's got a little stuffed animal hanging in the window ("My mascot!" he grins), and suggestively, he now winks at her and—God Bless the French—says, "You know, if you blow on him three times, his tail will wiggle." Lucette asks Charlo if the little toy has brought him happiness and, not-so-enigmatically, he replies, "Not yet."

Charlo next decides to be a gentleman (he knows he'll score faster, if he pretends to be disinterested), so he gives her his bed, invites her to sleep well, and shakes her hand, politely. And just as he's leaving the bedroom, she asks him where he's going, and he tells her that he'll be in the living room—and he's joking, of course, because there is only one room in the entire apartment. Charmingly, he pads outside onto the stairwell with a blanket, where he proceeds to fall right to sleep. Charlo's neighbor from the apartment which adjoins his own, his work pal Jules, awakens him, and asks him what he's doing, sleeping out in the hallway. Charlo tells him, winking slyly, that his house is currently being "… haunted by a ghost."

Of course, Charlo eventually heads back inside. Lucette's wide awake, and she tells Charlo that she can't sleep in his room, because "there's too much light." He takes her hand sensuously, removes the ring which her brother gave her from her finger, tosses it on the floor, and they kiss.

The next morning, when Lucette wakes up, Charlo's sleeping on the couch, but she's smiling widely, so it's not too hard to figure out that the two of them made love the previous night. When he looks over at her, she pretends, very cutely, to be sound-asleep. Violin music wafts over the soundtrack as Charlo lopes out onto the balcony and, for Lucette's benefit, because he knows she's watching, he starts exaggeratedly bending back and forth, stretching and washing his torso in a large basin, and this is a total proto-Tennessee Williams moment. Remaining shirtless, he now begins exaggeratedly grinding her some coffee, making sure to throw his whole body into the act. But there's one thing which he's forgotten all about—he's forgotten to buy actual food, for their breakfast! So he leaves to buy some comestibles for her, and for himself, and since Lucette now appears to have fallen asleep for real, he knows he'll be able to surprise her with a sumptuous feast, when she wakes up.

Charlo slides down the balcony happy as a clam, ripping his pants in the process, and even pinching his landlady's behind and pulling a cop's cap down over his face! Lucette, who awakens now and figures out that her man has probably gone out to hunt down some breakfast, starts setting the table and, as Charlo heads cheerfully back to his apartment, bearing food as well as a bouquet of flowers, he stops and spends about an hour on the street, talking with a man who is comically telling Charlo that he should definitely think about investing in "some better pants."

When Charlo finally returns to his apartment, after having been sidetracked for a while, it's now empty, because Lucette has gone out to buy him flowers, not knowing that he has also bought some flowers for her. He thinks that she must be at the gangsters' mansion, so he heads over there and gives 'the secret whistle.' Unbeknownst to him, the cops are hiding in the bushes, and because they see him on the premises, they immediately arrest him for being part of Olivier's gang! The cops arrest Charlo and bring him down to the station, and we next get a great 'Gabin Interrogation Sequence,' one which is strikingly similar to the one we already saw in the previous year's *Paris-Beguin,* and the kind of a scene that we'll be seeing again in countless other Gabin movies which will be made over the next forty-five years. It's a 'third-degree scene,' in which cops are trying to intimidate Gabin, but he's just not scared of them—in fact, he looks eminently bored by the whole situation, as if he just wants to go home! The Inspector asks Charlo how he knew Olivier's gang's secret whistle if he's not part of their organization, and he coolly shrugs, "Look: I'm just a projectionist. I have nothing to do with those guys. I live at 31, St. Marie Street. And that's all I'm going to tell you, because I don't know any more, okay?" When they go to his apartment and find Lucette's ring—the ring which Olivier gave his sister from the Van-Hoolst heist—it confirms for them, very erroneously, that Charlo is part of the gang. While the cops are at Charlo's house, they also talk to his Landlady, who defends him, because, in *Coeurs joyeux,* as in other Jean Gabin pictures, his neighbors always come to his defense: "He's so honest," the nice woman tells the cop. "I run an honest house here, and Charlo would never steal anything." And while this is happening, Olivier and his henchmen are already down by the docks, readying themselves to get the hell out of France, on a cruise ship called the Albert Ballin.

Back at Charlo's apartment, Jules and Lucette are now looking for Charlo, unaware that he is in jail. Jules asks Lucette if Charlo - and here, Jules is calling Charlo by his real name, 'Charles'—is still sleeping. "His name is Charles?" she asks, not knowing that Charlo is merely his nickname. (It's possible that Lucette just isn't that bright, since the nickname Charlo, in France, back in the day, was a common French diminutive for 'Charles.') She tells Jules that she doesn't know where Charlo is, and she has no idea that he's become the fall-guy for her brother's robbery. Jules consoles her, inviting her over to his own apartment next-door, to play piano for her, and his offer is without any hint of menace or menacing sexuality—he is merely acting nicely and 'brotherly' toward her: "We'll listen to music, until Charlo comes back. I always play this song during the love scenes, in the movie theater," he smiles at her, warmly. Of course, they will soon learn that Charlo is in jail.

In an ensuing scene, Lucette goes to the Grand Hotel and meets the real Van-Hoolst, explaining to him that it was her brother who stole the jewelry, and not her boyfriend Charlo who has been wrongly incarcerated, and that her brother and his men mean to escape to America with the cache. Jules, meanwhile, goes to the police station and explains the same thing to the Commissioner. The cops and Van-Hoolst will now go down to the docks with Lucette and Jules, to see if what they are saying checks out, but the police are not willing to set Charlo free until they can prove that it was the other men who were the actual thieves. And because he's in the pokey, Jean Gabin's Charlo character will not be participating in the movie's big, pumped-up 'wrap-up'-action sequence, which happens next:

Down at the docks, Olivier and his men are in the customs area, as pre-amble to their hightailing-it out of France to America. Customs officials have been notified that jewel thieves are in their midst, and the chief customs officer asks Olivier if he's got anything to declare. Olivier tells the guy, with a totally straight face, that he's got nothing with him but the clothes he's wearing, and the officer asks him to open his suitcase. Sure enough, there's nothing inside but toys and toiletries, and that's because his henchman Theo (Henri Vilbert) has the jewelry, a man whom nobody had ever thought about searching.

Theo heads into one of the ship's staterooms with the suitcase full of gems. Lucette enters, takes the gun out of his back pocket, and points it at him. Next, Olivier comes in with a gun of his own, which he proceeds to point at his own sister. Lucette tells her brother that she loves Charlo, and a really sweet surprise in this scene, is that Olivier is so touched by her story of love, he agrees to hand the jewelry over to her and give himself up to the police—at least, that's what he's telling her, at this particular moment.

Lucette disembarks from the ship with the merchandise, ready to hand it over to Van-Hoolst, and what ensues is a great screwball montage which might remind you of the suitcase-switcheroo business in Peter Bogdanovich's hilarious 1972 screwball-throwback comedy, *What's Up, Doc:* She accidentally hands the suitcase it to Olivier's henchman who is now, for the second time in the picture, disguised as Van-Hoolst. The fake Van-Hoolst hands it off to Theo, who is also off the ship now, and Theo tosses it to the real Van-Hoolst, believing him to be the fake Van-Hoolst—so now, quite by accident, the real Van-Hoolst has his gems back, and the bad guys have nothing. At that moment the Coast Guard speeds up on motorboats, arrests Olivier and his henchmen, and carts them off to jail.

Or course, Charlo is set free from jail, the newspapers report that the Grand Hotel robbery has been solved, and the film ends in a fun and unexpected way: Director Schwartz, who would only work with Jean Gabin this one time, now pulls out to reveal that the criminal gang's arrest has just been unspooling, on screen, at Charlo's movie theater, as the final story in the current week's newsreel. As the crowd pours out into the night air, Charlo stands at the front door, bidding all of the patrons goodnight, and guess what: Lucette now works at the movie theater, too, as the concessions girl. Charlo and Lucette smile at each other, as this smart light-entertainment ends.

Coeurs joyeux's director, Hans Schwartz, was aided and abetted, in this project, by the Belgian-born filmmaker Max de Vacourbeil, who is not listed in the film's credits. (In the '30s, '40s, and '50s, de Vacourbeil would also serve as assistant director on a number of

European films, including Federico Fellini's 1953 classic, *I Vitelloni.*) But the real behind-the-scenes star of *Coeurs joyeux* is its screenwriter, German-born Hermann Kosterlitz, who supplies the film with just as much punch and 'moxie' as you might find in any of the great comedies of Ernst Lubistch and Preston Sturges. After writing several French films in the early 1930s, Kosterlitz, at the invitation of Universal Pictures' head Joe Pasternak, will move to the United States, change his name to Henry Koster, and direct several notable American movies, including 1947's *The Bishop's Wife*, 1950's *Harvey*, 1953's *The Robe* (the very first Cinemascope movie), and 1961's *Flower Drum Song.*

Besides the great writing, another 'engine' which moves *Coeurs joyeux* along at a fast clip, is the jaunty/bouncy song, "*Ca n'sert a rien de penser au lendemain*" ("No Use in Thinking About Tomorrow"), composed by Paul Abraham, and this piece is heard in both diegetic and non-diegetic versions throughout the majority of the picture. Abraham also composed the songs for Jean Gabin's first movie, 1930's *Chacun sa chance.*

What a Critic Says Today: "Gabin is handsome, and the only reason you should watch this!" (From: ***Internet Movie Database***. Critic: D.B. DuMonteil. Date: 6-6-2006.)

FILM 10

LA BELLE MARINIERE

France, 1932

(Literal English Translation: "THE BEAUTIFUL SAILOR GIRL.") Directed by Harry Lachman. Screenplay by Marcel Achard, Based Upon His Article. Director of Photography (black and white), Rudolph Mate. Editor, Jean Delannoy. Production Designer, Henri Menessier. Music by Maurice Yvain. (GENRE: MELODRAMA) Running Time, 1 hour 20 minutes. A Paramount Picture. Released in France on December 3, 1932, by Paramount Pictures-France. Never Released Theatrically in the United States.

"I've never seen a harmonica like that before!"
— *Madeleine Renaud to Jean Gabin, after their first night of love, in "La Belle Mariniere"*

AUTHOR'S PREFACE TO THIS CHAPTER:
"I Found a Lost Film:"

When I was about one year away from finishing this book, I felt empty inside: *La Belle Mariniere* (*The Beautiful Sailor Girl*) was one of four—or, now, as you're about to see, only three—Jean Gabin feature films, out of the ninety-five he made, which has been long considered to be missing, on both sides of the Atlantic, one of those films which has been lost to decades of extreme disinterest, bordering on shameful neglect. Worse, Paramount Pictures made the movie and, today, even they don't even have a copy. In his 2000 book, *Missing Reels: Lost Films of American and European Cinema*, author Harry Waldman cites *La Belle Mariniere* as being one of the films which has been lost to the ravages of time.

During this book's roughly five year writing-and-researching processes, which spanned from 2002 through 2007, I had managed to uncover most of the hard-to-find Gabin movies, even the titles which true, dyed-in-the-wool Gabin fans, movie archivists, and video collectors, and even Gabin's family members, couldn't find.

Anyway: Just when I figured that *La Belle Mariniere* was gone forever...

... *it turned up.*

In January of 2006, I received a call from Mark Quigley, of UCLA's Film Archives in

Los Angeles. Mark told me that UCLA had just received a crate of old, nitrate-stock 35mm film prints from a private collector, in France, some of which were from the old 'Paramount-France' studios (Paramount made movies in France, in the very early 1930s), and that one of the titles was—that's right!—*La Belle Mariniere*. He even told me that he would be able to project it for me.

Then, a couple of days later, Mark gave me an earful of bad news, which canceled out the good news, when he called me again and told me that one of his dedicated archivists had tried to thread several reels of *La Belle Mariniere* through his projection equipment, but that it wouldn't 'feed through.' After fifty years of sitting in a crate, the celluloid had become heavily damaged, and so, sadly, I would not be able to see the movie, after all.

Another week went by, and I was now resigned to not being able to see the movie, when, very suddenly, Mark called me again, to give me some new *good* news which canceled-out the bad. He told me that a lot of what the UCLA archivists had initially believed to be water damage on the *La Belle Mariniere* print was really just half a century of dirt and that, after cleaning the film, that six of the film's nine reels, or, more than two-thirds of the film, could be projected for me, after all.

So: The screening was back on. I would actually get to see *La Belle Mariniere* (the surviving two-thirds of it, anyway), a movie which hadn't been seen, even in its native France, since its original release back in 1932, with my own eyes. (It's fun, *in a nerdy way*, to be the first person to watch a movie, since the 1930s.)

February 1, 2006: I'm at the UCLA's archival screening room in Hollywood, and I'm watching the two-thirds of *La Belle Mariniere* which *could* be projected. Even though the film was incomplete, it seemed like most of the important plot-advancing material was still present, and I'm happy to report that the film is just as great as are any of the other great Gabin movies which you're reading about in this book: It's a light, fun melodrama/comedy, which has, at its center, a great, and likable, performance by *You-Know-Who*, and it seemed very complete, even with those missing reels.

And now, I file this report on the still-existing hour of the eighty-minute feature:

I can't start off this synopsis of American-born (Illinois) director Harry Lachman's French film, *La Belle Mariniere* by saying "as the film opens," because Reel One of the film is *dust:* It no longer exists today. So: 'As Reel Two opens,' Pierre Braquet (Jean Gabin), captain of the fishing boat the *Cormorant*, which is moored in Paris, along the Seine, and a beautiful blonde waitress by the name of Marinette (Madeleine Renaud) have just slept together, down in the boat's galley. Apparently, they met only the night before, and quite by accident: Marinette fell into the Seine, and Pierre fished her out, dried her off, and gave her a place to 'sleep,' and he's also been cavalier enough to loan her his sister's dress to wear. He's now admiring how she looks in it, when, suddenly, their moment of bliss is broken, as a rat scampers across the floor.

Even though Pierre and Marinette have known each other only for one night, the rules of Movie Melodrama 101 insure that they're instantly in love with each other, and we can tell that Pierre, a bachelor, would like to make more out of their new relationship, because he's mentioning to her, already, that he doesn't *just* want to be a small-time boat captain, circumnavigating canals and rivers, but that his true goal in life, is to own a big fishing business and sail around the world. He's even studying, as he's now bragging to her, so that he can get his license to fish professionally—and not just in France, but internationally, as well.

At this point, Pierre's sister, Mique (Rosine Derean) arrives on the boat, and she's now meeting Marinette for the first time. Marinette's busy playing Pierre's harmonica (!), taking her mouth off of it for just long enough to exclaim that she's "... never seen a harmonica like this, before." (You gotta love the French; they 'do symbolism' like nobody else!) The two women become instant friends, and Pierre breaks up their new, *sisters-are-doing-it-for-themselves* camaraderie, temporarily, by taking Marinette out on land for a day of on-shore fun, all of which is depicted in a montage sequence: First, we see Marinette riding Pierre's horse, whose name is Timbuktu, as he walks alongside of her; next, she's sitting on the dock, watching Pierre as he paints his boat; and then later, finally, she's watching him smoke a pipe, with a dreamy expression, in her eyes.

At the end of the day, they're both back on the *Cormorant,* and even though they've only known each other for twenty-four hours, he's now ready to ask her a bit more directly, if she'd be *up for a little marryin,'* but he starts out cautiously, afraid, obviously, of being rejected:

> PIERRE: So... do you think you'd like this kind of life?
> MARINETTE: Why are you asking me that?
> PIERRE (a little nervous): I mean, do you think you'd like this life more than you like being a waitress? What I'm trying to say is: Do you think it would be possible for you to like my life so much that, maybe, you wouldn't want to leave it?
> MARINETTE: (pretending she doesn't know what he's talking about): What?
> PIERRE [more directly]: Do you want to be a part of my family? [long beat]: Aww, heck... *will you marry me?*
> MARINETTE: But we've just met!
> PIERRE: I'm so happy! You're exactly the kind of woman I want!

We know that she's said yes because, next, director Lachman cuts to, what is probably, a few days or weeks later: Pierre is painting a new name on his boat: Instead of the *Cormorant,* it's now called *La Belle Mariniere* ('The Beautiful Sailor Girl'), and he's decided to affix that name to it, because the word '*mariniere,*' which means 'sailor girl' in French, sounds just like her name, 'Marinette.'

Next, we get a quick series of 'Scenic Paris' shots which include the Seine, as well as Paris's belching smokestacks, and it's now Pierre and Marinette's wedding day: Our charming young couple is getting married at Notre Dame Cathedral, and it's a completely festive event. Paris's whole Seine-River-based boating community, which, in this film, is portrayed as being one, big happy family, especially, because captains and crews from other vessels have all shown up at the church, to celebrate the union; even Pierre's beloved horse Timbuktu is dressed-up for the occasion, wearing a fancy, flowered bridle! The couple says 'I do' on the docks of the Seine, with *La Belle Mariniere* (the boat, not the girl) bobbing up and down, right behind them.

While everybody-and-his-brother has been invited to the ceremony, the celebration meal which is about to take place down in the galley of the *Mariniere*, is a family-only affair. (While the crews from the other boats haven't been invited to the big dinner in Pierre and Marinette's honor, it's a tribute to how much they like Pierre, that they're now celebrating the couple's nuptials, on their own vessels.) Around the *Mariniere's* galley dinner table, we've got Pierre, Pierre's bald-pated and robust dad (Hubert Daix, who played hosiery-clerk Gabin's boss, in *Chacun sa chance*), Pierre's sister Mique, and of course, the blushing bride herself. Marinette is so happy, she's crying, and Pierre's dad tells his son, "She's crying, because she loves you."

Then, it's comedy relief time, aboard *La Mariniere*: A drunk-off-his-ass naval-officer-on-leave, Valentin (who's played by Jean Wall) is now front-and-center, and when we first meet him, he's weaving his way through the streets of Paris. He's overheard people all over town talking about the big wedding which just went down along the Seine, because news travels fast, throughout Paris, or, at least it does, in the world of this film. Looking to meet some fun people, he finds the *Mariniere* and descends down into 'her,' crashing Pierre and Marinette's wedding dinner, which is still in progress. Pierre and his kin are immediately enchanted by this newly-arrived stranger (Valentin's the kind of great movie-drunk/comedy relief-figure whose wobbly entrance, in American movies, is usually musically underscored with a few bars of "How Dry I Am"), and Pierre's dad now invites the guy to dine with them. Valentin picks up a bottle of wine and toasts the new couple, and he next, nonsensically, asks them if they have any cheese he can 'borrow,' before he finally drawls, "I have received special permission from the French Navy to attend your wedding!" He offers to sing the little family a song, in honor of this auspicious event, and he's so (in the *langua-Judaica*) *shikker*, that it takes him only about one minute to forget the offer of singing which he's just made.

Then, we see a second stranger who's wandering the streets of Paris, and this one is clasping a suitcase: This is the scene in which we're going to be meeting Pierre's best friend, Sylvestre, who's played by the picture's first-billed star, Pierre Blanchar. (Gabin was second-billed in the film's advertising and in its on-screen credits, even though he's the actual 'main star' of the film, which is to say that he's got twice as much screen time as Blanchar.) Sylvestre, as it's now turning out, works on another fishing boat, and one which is based in Marseilles, a vessel called *La Felicite*, and Pierre and Sylvestre are such good friends, that both men have always referred to each other as 'my brother.' When Sylvestre surprises Pierre during this never-ending family dinner scene, the two guys are very excited to see each other and, in fact, Sylvestre is so happy that his buddy's just gotten married, that he nudges Pierre's dad and guy-bondingly exclaims, "Wow! I leave this guy alone for five minutes, and he gets married. How 'bout that?!" He joins the family at the table, and drunken Valentin next attempts a magic trick: He covers a wine bottle with a cloth and tries to make it disappear, but when he whips the cloth off of the bottle, the *vino* spills all over Pierre's proud papa. Valentin apologizes for screwing up. ("This trick *used* to work!")

Pierre introduces Sylvestre to his new wife, and when Sylvestre and Marinette meet each other for the first time, get ready for Love Triangle Time, because (natch), it's love at first sight! Director Lachman, who would work with Gabin only this one time, now gives us a number of 'proto-Sergio Leone' extreme-close-ups of Marinette and Sylvestre, as the two of them begin boring holes through each other with their eyes, eyes which, of course, are watery with lust. We know, instantly, that Sylvestre will (and sooner, as opposed to later) be making his move on Marinette, and since we know that this is what's going to happen, part of the fun we're having in watching the film, is that we're waiting to see exactly when it's going to be happening, and we can tell from the hot glances which Marinette and Sylvestre are sending each other, that the two of them would probably start *doing each other* right now, if nobody else was around.

Jokingly, Pierre whispers to Valentin, "Maybe this wedding was a mistake," but he's a trusting guy, and he would never in a zillion years think that his friend would ever make a pass at his wife.

In fact, Pierre is so completely trusting of his best friend, that he even encourages his wife's flirtations with Sylvestre: "Do me a favor, Sylvestre. Tell my wife that you find her pretty. Kiss her! It's o.k., she's your sister now!" And meanwhile, Valentin, the inebriate, even while he's stoned out of his mind, is the only one among our present company who's already figured out that this introduction of Sylvestre to Marinette can't possibly be good, and he tells Pierre his feelings on the subject, but only in the most roundabout of ways, because he doesn't want to offend his new pal, who's been nice enough to offer him dinner, and even better, and more personal than dinner, *cheese*): "I had a friend, and we got pissed off at each other once," Valentin reports, to Pierre. (Pierre inquires, "Over a woman?" Valentine replies, sarcastically, "No! Over a bicycle… of course, over a woman.") But Pierre's still not putting 2+2 together, because it's his wedding day, and because he's lost (literally) in a sea of love.

At this point, Pierre's sister Mique, who has been in the city purchasing some more wine for the little dinner party, pokes her head down into the hatch, and she now, just like Marinette several minutes before, is meeting Sylvestre for the first time. (Even though she's heard her brother talking about Sylvestre a lot over the years, this is the first time where she's actually meeting him, in person.) Mique, like Marinette, is instantly smitten with Sylvestre (Strike what I said, before: This is a love quadrangle, not a love triangle), but Sylvestre can't be bothered with paying attention to Mique, because he's already smitten with his buddy Pierre's new bride, Marinette. Mique tells the assembled dinner-munchers that there's a big carnival and dance in progress along the Rue de Rivoli and the Rue St. Antoine, the Parisian streets which parallel the Seine, and she suggests that they should continue their party on dry land. Pierre doesn't feel like partying though, and he doesn't even have to say why not: He's played by Jean Gabin, whose characters, even in most of his earliest movies, were always intensely private, and so even though Pierre's just gotten married, we accept that he needs his 'Gabinian alone-time,' nor would we ever dare to question it. He next gives his new bride a suggestion: "Why don't you go up-top, and dance with Sylvestre? It's okay with me."

As they dance together, all of two seconds later, Marinette is now paying Sylvestre a sexually-charged compliment: "Pierre said that you do everything so perfectly, it's scary! I'll bet Pierre can't dance as well as you dance!" Meanwhile, Mique is tripping the light fantastic with Valentin, but she keeps looking over Valentin's shoulder at Sylvestre, since she'd rather be dancing with *him*. The carnival features a marionette show and, in it, a bride puppet and a groom puppet are dancing, but it's a violent dance, and it also looks, at the same time, like the two puppets could be fighting! Right after director Lachman treats us to a few moments of this puppet show, he then cuts to a different part of the Seine, where we see an elderly drunk, who's trying to walk on a tightrope, although he falls over, the second he starts. (The best way for filmmakers to portend future doom is to show a bunch of goofy carnival mishaps!)

I've just described Reels 2 and 3 of the film. Reel 4 is missing from the UCLA Archives' Print. So now, *it's on to Reel 5:*

The next day, Marinette and Mique are below-deck, and Mique mentions to Marinette that she likes Sylvestre. And even though Marinette likes Sylvestre as well, she doesn't want to be too out front regarding her feelings for him, because she's just married Pierre. She tells Mique that if she wants to start attracting men of Sylvester's ilk, that she's going to have to start wearing makeup. (Rosine Derean, who plays Mique, is *hot* with or without make-up, so we've definitely got some not-so-veiled jealousy rearing its head around here, between these two hot women who both crave Sylvestre.) Even though 'Mique doth protest,' Marinette now starts applying rouge to the other woman's mouth.

Even though Sylvestre thinks Mique is cute, Marinette, his best friend's wife, is the one he really wants, but he also knows that he shouldn't be encouraging Marinette, since *it's not too cricket* to fuck your best friend's betrothed… but Marinette is *so* hot that Sylvestre just can't help it. In the next scene, Sylvestre gets Marinette alone (she's a little shy around him, because she's married to Pierre), and he asks her, flirtatiously, if she's afraid of him. "I'm not afraid of you," she blushes, looking at him with shy lust. "I'm afraid of *me.*"

In the next scene, Pierre, Sylvestre, and the two women are below deck, and they're all just hanging out: Sylvestre's got both women to himself, and Pierre's all the way over on the opposite side of the movie frame, sitting by himself and playing happily on his pan flute. Pierre tells Sylvestre that he should take Mique dancing: "She likes you. She has a crush on you. Anyway, why should you just sit around down here, with boring old me? Take her, and bring Marinette, too." Pierre still can't figure out that, by doing this, he's pushing his wife into his buddy's arms, although maybe, on some subconscious level on which he, himself, is not even aware, that's exactly what he wants to do: When girls stick around too much, even if you're married to them, they wind up hurting you, and in the Gabin Universe—that's a big no-no! Meanwhile, it's Marinette who now wants to go dancing and, even though she's heavily into Sylvestre, she thinks that it's her husband, Pierre, who should be escorting her, since they're married, and she's a little weirded-out by the fact that he's not putting any effort into their new union at all. She tells him, gently, because she still loves him, even though she's also hot for his pal, that she's a city girl, and that she hates being cooped up in the boat, and as they're conversing, the sound of festive music echoes down to them from one of the innumerable bars which line the Seine.

Sylvestre takes the two women dancing up on the Rue de Rivoli, just like he had already done the previous evening. Marinette and Sylvestre talk about how they both love Paris, and she brings up her particular affinity for the artists' district of Monmartre, and she then starts complimenting him, just like she did the night before. ("Pierre describes you as being mythic.") Meanwhile, Pierre's still in the galley of his boat, and he's *Gabin-Happy*, just being by himself and listening to radio music. (To paraphrase the American author Charles Bukowski, "The only thing worse than loneliness, is *not* being lonely...")

As Sylvestre dances with Marinette, a guy hits-on her and calls her '*poule,*' which is French slang for 'chick,' although the more accurate English translation is 'whore,' and Sylvestre, very promptly, knocks the guy flat on his fat ass. A bit later, Sylvestre, Mique, and Marinette, all of whom are now completely partied-out, are headed back aboard the *Mariniere,* and the first thing they see is Pierre, who's putting on a nice evening jacket, and bounding up the boat's little staircase: He's decided to join them, but it's too late, because they're all now arriving back at the boat. That night, Pierre characterizes his only days-old marriage with Marinette, to Sylvestre: "I fight with her—but I love her." Ever since Marinette met Sylvestre, she's starting to feel a little angry toward the aloof Pierre, but Pierre's so wrapped-up in his own little world, he hasn't quite figured out yet, that it's because she wants Sylvestre more than she wants him.

That night, all four are sleeping in the galley, in pretty close quarters, and it's midsummer so, as you can imagine, it's stiflingly hot down there. Mique whispers to Sylvestre, so as not to wake Pierre and Marinette (who are, per Charles M. Shulz, 'ZZZZZ-ing,' nearby), that he should come and 'sleep' next to her, because, as she now puts it, "There's more cool air on my side" (!), but he declines. (If Marinette asked Sylvestre the same thing, he'd no doubt be over there *in two shakes.*)

———————

(Note: Reels Eight and Nine are Missing. Here's Reel Ten):

———————

Sylvestre and Pierre are now fighting with each other. Obviously, somewhere in the missing footage which comprises Reels 8 and 9, Pierre must have caught his wife Marinette kissing Pierre, and Pierre, instead of just sitting-back and playing his pan flute, is finally *showing some balls,* and he roundly castigates his 'friend:' "My sister isn't enough for you? Now you want my wife, too?!" Sylvestre fights back, though: "You'd better not fight with me, Pierre, or you'll say something you'll regret." Even though Pierre is upset with his friend, Pierre's also, like all Gabin characters, a nice guy at heart, and we can tell that it's really hard for him to say something mean to Sylvestre, so he has to dig around a lot inside of his soul to find something snarky to say to him, which, after a few seconds of fumfering, he actually does: "And, you know, also, you're not a good sailor, Sylvestre. You don't even know which way the wind is blowing. *And* you hurt my horse!" (Apparently, somewhere in *La Belle Mariniere's* missing footage, Sylvestre took Timbuktu out for a ride, and the horse injured a leg.) Pierre tells Sylvestre that the local veterinarian has just informed him that Timbuktu must be put down, and this is all too much for Pierre, Timbuktu's proud owner, to take in. Pierre wants Sylvestre to go and shoot the horse himself, but Sylvestre just doesn't want to do it.

Sylvestre doesn't mind being accused of being a philanderer (hell, 'partying-naked' with chicks is a big-ol' notch on any guy's belt!), but he can't abide the fact that Pierre has just impugned his sailing abilities: "Even though we've been friends for ten years, and even though our relationship is now over, Pierre, you'd better take back what you just said." Pierre, instead of recanting, punches Sylvestre out, and Sylvestre plunges ass-over-face into the Seine, causing Marinette to cry out in horror; when Sylvestre makes it back onto the boat, a few moments, later, a bit wet, but otherwise unharmed, Pierre continues acting like a schoolyard bully. ("Awwww, did I hurrrtt you?") Sylvestre tells Pierre, Marinette, and Mique, who are all together with him on deck, that he's now going to be leaving for good: He knows that he's just, in every sense of the word, 'rocked the boat,' and he doesn't want to cause any more problems with his once-friend, or with his once-friend's wife. Marinette is panicked that Sylvestre is leaving (now, she won't have anybody to flirt with, anymore), and in addition to that, she's also mad at her husband for forcing the other man away: "Look," she screams at Pierre, "your best friend is leaving Don't you want to do anything about it?" Pierre who, at this point, doesn't care if he ever sees Sylvestre again, just 'Gabin-Shrugs.'

Dissolve to Three Months Later:

Pierre's scrawling in his ship's log by night, and we get to see his hastily-scrawled entry: "Our trip is not going well. It's been three months since my friend Sylvestre left. I wrote to him and told him that he should come back, at least to please Mique, but I have received no reply." In Jean Gabin movies, of course, Gabin's male friends are always more important to him than are his female lovers and, over this relatively short period of three months, his anger at Sylvestre seems to have dissipated, and he's now feeling upset, because he's lost his best male friend in the whole, wide world; he doesn't even seem to care, like he used to, that his best friend was kissing his wife, and maybe more!

And it's not only Pierre who's scrawling away during this action-packed 'journal-writing montage:' Next, director Lachman shows us Mique, who's on deck, scribbling-away in her own diary: "I'm so happy! I learned, today, that my dear Sylvestre will be coming back, and that he and Pierre are friends again. I wonder if he's coming back to make me happy?!"

It's not long (in fact, it's the next scene) before Sylvestre returns to the *Mariniere*, and he and Pierre are both very happy to see each other, as if time has healed all wounds. Sylvestre shakes Marinette's hand, too, trying to look, at least, in front of Pierre, like he's got his whole 'lust-thing,' for her, under control. Pierre tells Sylvestre that they're going to be setting sail, and he asks him if he'd be interested in coming with them, instead of returning to his own boat; but Sylvestre tells Pierre that he has two more weeks left aboard the *Felicite*, and that, as far as 'after that' goes, he's going to have to play it by ear.

That night, Sylvestre strolls through the park with Marinette, and Marinette lets him know how it's been hard for her without him, over these last several weeks he's been absent. Sly's still trying to brush her off, though (in deference to his friend, whose wife she remains, whether she actually loves Pierre or not), and so he now changes the subject, telling her that he's going to surprise Pierre, by buying him a new horse, which will replace the currently resting-in-peace Timbuktu. Marinette confesses to Sylvestre that she's been thinking of him a lot lately and, finally, even though he wants to, he just can't control himself anymore, and he suddenly blurts out that he can't "just be friends" with her, because he loves her, and maybe even more than she loves him. Naturally, they both start cooing "I love you" at each other (lots of whispered *'je t'aimes'* and *'mon amours'*), and she then adds, not actually believing this, but trying to make it real by saying it, because even though she doesn't love her husband, Pierre, just the same, she doesn't want to hurt him, "Goodbye, my love. We will not see each other again." But their words are in direct opposition to how they really feel about each other because, as soon as she says this, they really start going at it, and we're now looking at total make-out madness, 1932-style. (Just when he was "out," to paraphrase Michael Corleone, *in Godfather III*, she's pulled him back in!) Sylvestre now offers-up a precise summary of everything that's just transpired in this sequence: "We simply cannot hide our feelings for each other from your husband any longer."

Later, in the middle of the night, Sylvestre and Marinette leave the *Mariniere* together, being extra-careful not to wake Pierre and Mique. Marinette has written her husband a note, informing him that she's leaving him to go off with Sylvestre, and when we next see the illicit couple, they're illuminated only by, *per* David Bowie, 'the serious moonlight,' as they're perched up on the dock, looking down at Pierre's boat, with their suitcases in hand. Obviously, they're both wondering if what they're doing, is the right thing.

Pierre, who's been awakened by the sound of Sylvestre and Marinette's footfalls, now leaps onto the *Mariniere's* deck. Sylvestre's boat, the *Felicite* is moored next to Pierre's boat and, obviously, Pierre doesn't want to stick around to watch his wife going off with another guy for any longer than he actually has to, so he simply unmoors the *Mariniere* from the dock, and takes off. As the two boats pass each other, each one venturing off in the opposite direction, the two men reach out to shake hands with one other, but both strategically miss. (It's like one of those 'high-fives' which you intentionally miss, when you want to *mess with somebody*.) Mique, who's on board the *Mariniere* with her brother Pierre, waves goodbye to Sylvestre, as the two ships pass in the night, just like... well, *just like two ships, passing in the night*.

This is one of the first movies of many, in which Jean Gabin will be betrayed by a woman and, instead of fighting back, he'll just let her go, his characters always understanding, instinctively, that the 'lot' of women, in this life, is to hurt men.

I'm glad that *La Belle Mariniere* turned up at UCLA, because, in spite of its downer ending, it's a very sweet, briskly-paced, and often very funny movie. The Paris-by-night cinematography comes courtesy of the legendary cinematographer, Rudolph Mate who a decade-and-a-half-later will contribute photographically, and without credit, to Orson Welles' *Lady from Shanghai* (1948), before turning director, himself, and churning out two of America's most highly-regarded film noirs, *D.O.A.* and *Union Station,* both of which were made in 1950. Another interesting name in *La Belle Mariniere's* credits, is that of the picture's young editor Jean Delannoy, a guy whom you're going to be reading about later in this book, because, starting in the 1950s, Delannoy will become one of France's really superb motion picture directors in his own right, and he'll be directing his good buddy, Jean Gabin, in six feature films.

Before *La Belle Mariniere* gets packed up in its UCLA crate for another fifty years, here's a brief bio of the film's director, Harry Lachman. How did Lachman, an American guy from Illinois, wind up in France, directing French-language movies, in the 1930s? I'm going to let a blogging film lover, Brian Raymond (who wrote this biography of Lachman, for the website imdb.com) tell us:

"A former magazine illustrator, [the Illinois-born] Harry Lachman traveled to Paris, in 1911, to begin an art career, and soon became recognized as a first-rate post-Impressionist painter. Decorated for his contributions to art by the French government, Lachman, afterwards, became a set designer at a film studio, in Nice. In 1925, the American director Rex Ingram hired him as an assistant director... and soon thereafter, Lachman gave up his painting career, and traveled to England, to begin a career as a film director. [Author's Note: The legendary British filmmaker of *The Red Shoes,* Michael Powell started off his film career as Lachman's assistant, on a number of British productions.] He [went] to France and made several films, then [returned] to the U.S., in 1933, and settled in Hollywood. Mainly given B-pictures, his best films were a Laurel and Hardy comedy, *Our Relations* and a Spencer Tracy/Claire Trevor picture called *Dante's Inferno,* (1935), where his painter[ly] eye was evident in the intense, ten-minute 'hell sequence.' Lachman ended his career with a Charlie Chan movie in the 1940s, and returned to painting. His artworks can be seen in such museums as Spain's Prado, and the Luxembourg Museum." (Brian Raymond, *Internet Movie Database.com,* 2006.)

FILM 11

Coeur de Lilas

France/U.S., 1932

(Literal English Translation: "HEART OF LILAC") Directed and Produced by Anatole Litvak. Screenplay by Dorothy Farnum, Anatole Litvak, Serge Veber and (uncredited) Maurice Barber. Based Upon the Play by Tristan Bernard and Charles Henry Hirsch. Director of Photography (black and white), Curt Courant. Music by Maurice Yvain. Production Designer, Serge Pimenoff. (GENRE: DRAMA) Running Time, 1 hour 37 minutes. Produced and Released in France on February 2, 1932, by Fifra. Released in the U.S. by United Artists (without English Subtitles) in 1932, as "LILAC."

"Oh, what a filthy whore! She's up, she's down—just like a rubber baaaaand..."
— *Bawdy song, sung by tavern-bouncer Gabin, in "Coeur de Lilas"*

If a couple of the behind-the-scenes names which are associated with the above-average *Coeur de Lilas,* (director Anatole Litvak; co-scenarist Dorothy Farnum) sound familiar to you, they should: Litvak, the film's Russian-born director, is mostly remembered today for his atmospheric American pictures, which included the landmark Barbara Stanwyck/Burt Lancaster *film noir,* from 1948, *Sorry Wrong Number,* 1956's Technicolor, Ingrid Bergman classic, *Anastasia,* and 1967's Peter O'Toole picture, *Night of the Generals.* Dorothy Farnum wrote dozens of important films in America and in Great Britain, both silent and sound, before and after she worked on this movie in France, including 1924's silent John Barrymore classic, *Beau Brummel,* and a controversial British movie which dealt with the nature of anti-Semitism—a film which is known in Britain, as *Jew Suss* (1935), and in America, as *Power.*

Taken from what was, at that time, one of France's most popular plays, this effort opens with a battalion of French soldiers marching valiantly through Paris, because World War I is in full-swing. Director Litvak next cuts to a group of young boys who are playing soldier, arching around in paper helmets and bossing each other around, just like they've seen the real soldiers doing. One scared little boy instinctively tells his friends, "I don't want to play soldier, anymore! *I don't like war,*" and as the kids continue to march, their fun comes to a frightening end, because they accidentally come upon the body of a man, an older businessman who's just committed suicide by throwing himself into the Seine. The police arrive at the scene,

Reunited with his "Gloria," co-star, Andre Luguet.

but they can't readily identify the 'floater,' because, as the Inspector involved (Andre Luguet, who starred in and flew over the Atlantic with Jean Gabin when he played Pierre in 1931's *Gloria*) says, after having made his ultra-quick diagnosis, "his cranium has been destroyed." Limonaire, the blind, bearded accordionist (Rene Maupre) is on the scene, too, playing his instrument, and, indeed, whether or not we'll be seeing Limonaire or not in each scene *bodily*, the tunes which he's playing will be underscoring a good deal of the film. The Inspector notifies Limonaire, solemnly, that it's inappropriate for him to be playing the accordion, in the presence of a dead body.

The next morning's newspaper alerts us to the fact that, at eight-o'clock the previous night, a man in his fifties, who happened to be the director of France's biggest fabric-and-novelty company, committed suicide by jumping into the river, and that "...a glove which was found next to the body reportedly belongs to a well-known prostitute by the name of Lilac Couchoux ('*Couchoux*' is meant to sound like '*chouchou*,' a French slang term which means 'darling' or 'honey.') Also, the company owner's wallet has disappeared, and this is a guy who was known for carrying a wad of cash that could choke another wad of cash!

According to the attached story, Miss Couchoux was not around when the body was found and, at this point in the narrative, the cops bring an American Sailor down to headquarters for questioning; like the goofy American sailor-character in *Mephisto*, this guy, too, is as American as apple pie, and he's played, with 'aw-shucks abandon,' by an uncredited American actor.

The Inspector now questions one of the fabric magnate's most loyal employees, good-natured punch-press operator Darny (Marcel Delaitre), a guy who's so frail-looking, he'd

With real-life vaudeville entertainer, Frehel.

probably turn to dust in a strong wind. "Mr. Darny, we know that this morning [the day after your boss's murder, and with his wallet missing], you bought your wife an expensive dress—a dress which is definitely out of line with your modest income. We've also just learned that you paid your rent on time this month which, as we've also discovered, is not typical for you." Darny, a genuinely-honest guy who, we can tell, would never steal a penny, says, "It's true, I did use cash to pay my rent, and to buy my wife the dress, but I did those things with my own money. It made me feel good to buy this dress for her." He tells the Inspector, also, that when he was walking home along the Seine, that he did see his boss consorting with a woman, but that it wasn't Lilac Couchoux, a woman whom everybody in Paris (it would seem) knows—at least, she's known by everybody with a surfeit of testosterone and fifty francs! Darny continues, "I saw the boss bump into a girl, on purpose. She seemed like she might be a street girl, and I saw her face very clearly, and it wasn't Lilac Couchoux." Darny, additionally, tells the Inspector that his boss, as 'everybody' knew, had no shortage of mistresses.

The Detective locks Darny up, and while Darny looks, and is, honest, he's also the most logical suspect in the businessman's death, based upon his behavior over the last several hours, and in France, a Judge can have a potential criminal locked-up for forty-eight hours, even if he only has a reasonable suspicion. Darny's wife, who's played by a singularly-monikered actress called Fordyce, decides to retain a Lawyer, the suave, and amiable Merlu, who's played by Paul Amiot (Jean Gabin's movie theater organist-pal, Julien, in director Max de Vaucorbeil's *Coeurs joyeux*), and in this picture, it is Amiot who has the leading role.

Merlu is pretty 'hands-on,' especially, when it comes to investigating crimes with hookers in them, and his hands-on (very literally, as we'll soon see) investigation soon takes him to a local hotel/bar/whorehouse, which is a recurring locale in lots of French movies (just as the Good Lord intended!), where the notorious Lilac pliantly plies her trade, and just as Merlu is arriving there, he sees an old john in a filthy coat, who's trying to get out of paying for the hooker whom he has just *strombolied*. The bar's proprietor, Charignoul (Pierre Labry), without even batting an eye, calls for his intimidating bouncer, 'Martousse,' to help out, and here, about twenty minutes into the movie, is where we'll finally get to meet the film's seventh-billed (seventh in billing but, as always, first in cool) Jean Gabin, who's decked out in a scarf and a floor-length leather coat, seventy years before Keanu Reeves made the whole 'floor-length leather coat-style' cool, in the *Matrix* pictures. Martousse, heroically, picks this non-payer up by the seat of his pants, and tosses him onto the street, but, of course, only after extracting the *gelt*, 'for services rendered,' from the guy's pants pocket.

Merlu doesn't want to let the clientele in on the fact that he's a lawyer who's working on the 'Lilac+Dead Businessman Case,' so he's dressed-down for the occasion, tossing his usual three-piece suit away, in favor of a more workingman-friendly turtleneck, and he alerts Charignoul that he's going to be requiring a room and a girl for a couple of hours, and he also gives a false name for himself. Charignoul asks Merlu if he's interested in any woman in particular, and Merlu replies, trying to be casual, "Uh… Isn't there a woman named Lilac working here, tonight? I've heard that she's very interesting!" Charignoul tells Merlu that she is, in fact, upstairs, but that she's busy with a client, and that he should make himself at home, while he waits for her.

The bar's working-class clientele likes the affable Merlu immediately, regarding him as one of them, and Gabin's bouncer, Martousse, suggests to Merlu that he should join them in the role-playing game which they were all just starting to play, right before he came in: Martousse, who has no idea that Merlu is actually the lawyer on the case, tells him that a rich man was found murdered last night, in the Seine, and that the guy's body was discovered, lying next to a woman's glove, and that now, and just for chuckles and grins, they're going to be re-creating the crime, based upon what they've all read about the story, in today's newspaper, to see if they can solve it. While the barflies are immersed in their silly re-enactment, Lilac herself, who is played by a stunning actress called Marcelle Romee, now wafts down the stairs.

Merlu makes a bee-line for Lilac's room and she immediately does her 'whore-ly duty,' and starts removing her blouse, and unfortunately we're just seeing her from the back! [*Shit!*] She tells him that she's never seen him here before, and that she knows he's not a local, and he then tries to change the subject, by telling her that he's come to this part of town for work, although he doesn't tell her exactly what line of work he's in, nor will she even ask him. Meanwhile, downstairs, at the same time, Gabin's Martousse is regaling the patrons with a bawdy song about what Lilac is probably doing upstairs with this newly-arrived stranger, and his lyrics are almost haiku-like, in their beautiful simplicity: ("Oh, she's a filthy whore! She's up and down—she stretches just like a rubber baaaand!") When Merlu returns downstairs, the patrons, who are suddenly more suspicious of this stranger than they had originally let on, ask him to see some identification, and he tells them that he's left it in his other jacket.

Of course, it's not long, before Lilac is swooning over Merlu, for-real, as opposed to 'for-whore,' and running away with him. He's supposed to be doing his job as Darny's lawyer, and trying to find out who really killed the businessman, in order to get his client, Darny, out of jail, but, instead, he's just thinking with his little lawyer and, at this point, director Litvak now cuts to Darny, who's sequestered away in a small, dank jail cell; he's sitting there, head in his hands, wondering aloud about just where it is that his lawyer has gone.

Merlu and Lilac now make their way over to a fancy garden-party wedding, which is being held at a country resort-inn, on a small island outside of France, *L'Ile d'Amour* (the 'Island of Love'), and the wedding singer, played by Fernandel who, in this film is making his third appearance in a Gabin picture in two years (although, this time out, he won't be sharing any scenes with Gabin), warbles a tune which is called, "When You Get Married, You're Everybody's Wife:" According to the lyrics, "Never choose a woman that's pretty, or she'll be somebody else's wife… Get one, instead, with a horrible snout!" (It's the 1930s' equivalent of Harry Belafonte's jaunty 1950s' hit, "Get an Ugly Girl to Marry You.") Lilac and Merlu decide to remain on the island, to enjoy a dirty weekend.

Meanwhile, Gabin's Martousse has been enlisted by the Proprietor, to bring Lilac back and, when he shows up at the island resort, she questions him: "What are you doing here? Who told you where I was?" Martousse informs Lilac, "Your new boyfriend, this lawyer—he works with the cops!" He drags her back to Paris, since any time she's not on her knees and back constitutes a bad business day for Charignoul, who makes a profit not just out of *booze* but also, out of *cooze.*

Dissolve to a few weeks later: Darny's trial, in his boss's murder, is in progress, but director Litvak shows us only the tail-end of it. Lilac has apparently been called to the stand already and, as it's turning out, she really *is* a hooker-with-a-heart-of-gold, and she admits that she was the murderer, because she's been feeling guilty, ever since she found out that the innocent Darny is taking the blame for her crime: "Your honor, I confess: I'm the one who killed the man—not Mr. Darny," and she now gives the Judge, who's played by Georges Paulais, her reason for committing that savage act:

"That businessman disgusted me: He was always grabbing me and calling me crude names, so I grabbed something and hit him." Merlu, by this point in the film, has truly come to love Lilac and, before the court can absorb the full weight of her confession, she suddenly freaks-out, hating herself for having just confessed, and she bolts out of the room. She next starts panic-running frantically down the street, even though, pre-Existentially (Existentialism, as a field of philosophical thought, wouldn't be invented yet, for another decade), she's aware that there's nowhere she can really run, and, filmically, this is a very surreal, Salvador Dali-esque moment, because Litvak has chosen to double-expose close-ups of a running Lilac, over nightmare images of drunkenly-laughing partygoers from the wedding which she and

Merlu attended together, on *L'Ile d'Amour*. The juxtaposition of this imagery makes it appear that the wedding guests are laughing, and not at Fernandel's funny song, which they're enjoying, but at her abject terror.

Of course, she can't run too far, and it's only a matter of minutes before the cops find her, and haul her ass in: Merlu, knowing that Lilac is the murderer, but still head-over-heels in love with her anyway, now lies to the police, and tells them that it's impossible that she committed the murder, in spite of her confession. "Well," an Inspector tells Merlu, "It is definitely true, and now we have the autopsy with Lila's fingerprints, to prove it." The next day's newspaper headline reads that the guilty party in the businessman's murder has been established as being Miss Lilas Couchoux."

The film ends as it began, with small boys again playing war in their paper helmets, and just like today, the kids are pretty savvy about what's going on in the world, and one of the boys, who is a little too wise for his own age, tells the others that, in his studied opinion, "A cop should never feel soft about a culprit. He should just get on with his job."

Jean Gabin appears in only a small, supporting role, in *Coeur de Lilas*, a movie which was filmed during the third-quarter of 1931, and released at the beginning of 1932, and in the film's opening credits, relatedly, he's seventh billed. But something great had already started happening for the actor: By the time the film was ready for its theatrical release, in the spring of 1932, Gabin had already started becoming more and more popular in France, and to capitalize on his burgeoning popularity, the producers decided to bill him first on the film's theatrical posters, marketing *Lilas*, misleadingly, as 'a Jean Gabin movie.' *Lilas* was, at the time it was made, the most costly movie which had ever been made in France, with a budget of $120,000 U.S., thirty-five-percent of which was put up by a Dutchman, Jan Hulswit, head of the film's French production company, Fifra. The other sixty-five percent of the film's budget came from the picture's North American distributor, United Artists—which means that, properly, *Coeur de lilas* can be classified as a 'French-U.S. co-production,' and Gabin clearly made the picture the box office success which it was, in France. The film is still remembered in France today, where it turns up occasionally on television, yet it hasn't been seen in the United States since its initial token release, *via* United Artists, at one U.S. art-house cinema in New York City, in 1932. Today, Warner Bros. which holds the catalog of most of United Artists' (and MGM's) old films no longer owns the U.S. rights to it; in fact, *nobody* owns the picture today, in America. ("Hint, hint!")

There is some sad news associated with *Coeur de Lilas:* The film's leading lady, Marcelle Romee, who played Lilac Couchoux, took her own life shortly after the movie had finished production, when she was only twenty-nine years old. A lifetime depressive, Romee drowned herself in the Seine, the same river into which her character pushed the unseen businessman in the movie. During her all-too-brief film career, she appeared in only four feature films, including *Coeur de Lilas* and, apparently, according to a 1938 magazine, Gabin was aggrieved by Romee's death, because the two of them had become such close friends on the set of the movie. The actor Paul Amiot, who plays Merlu, the lawyer, would appear with Jean Gabin the following year, in 1933, in director Serge de Poligny's Coast Guard epic, *L'Etoile de Valencia*. (In that film, Gabin and Amiot play two *Spanish* Coast Guardsmen.)

What a Critic Said at the Time: "So far, the best pic [about] the French underworld. Credit goes to two Americans, [screenwriters] Dorothy Farnum and Maurice Barber. Farnum's Hollywoodian continuity gives the film a fast tempo." (*Variety*, 2-9-32 issue. Critic: "Maxi. [Edward 'Maxwell' MacSweeney.]" Reviewed in Paris.)

Rallying the troops.

FILM 12

LE TUNNEL

France/Germany, 1933

Directed and Produced by Curtis Bernhardt (as 'Kurt Bernhardt'). Screenplay by Reinhart Steinbacker and Alexandre Arnoux. Based Upon the Novel "Der Tunnel", by Bernhard Kellermann. Director of Photography (black and white), Carl Hoffmann. Editor, Rudi Fehr. Music by Walter Gronostay. Production Designers, Karl Vollbrecht and Heinz Fenchel. (GENRES: SCIENCE-FICTION, DRAMA, ADVENTURE) A Tobis-Klangfilm-Vandorfilm Production. Running Time: 1 hour 12 minutes. Released in France on November 29, 1933, by Cinedis. Never Released Theatrically in the United States.

"Tunnel 9! It's going to BLOW!"
— A miner freaks out, in Curtis Bernhardt's "Le Tunnel"

A *Jean Gabin Sci-Fi Picture?!* Okay, well, not exactly... but, sure—almost! (Why not?!) While true movies fans might believe director David Butler's *Just Imagine* (1930) and William Cameron Menzies' *Things to Come* (1933) to be the greatest sci-fi flicks of the early 1930s, you can't really say that either of those pictures is really, to use the vernacular, *the shit*, until you've gotten yourself an eyeful of Curtis Bernhardt's amazing sci-fi drama, *Le Tunnel:* Like many of the other of Jean Gabin productions from the early '30s, it's a French/German co-production which was filmed simultaneously in both the French and German languages, the French version starring Jean Gabin, and the German version, featuring an actor called Paul Hartmann. Based on a popular novel of the time by Bernard Kellermann, the picture deals with what would happen if Europe and the United States joined forces to build an underground Transatlantic Tunnel between the two continents. Jean Gabin is the principal star of the picture (it's his face, on the film's poster), although he's still second-billed, to Madeleine Renaud, his co-star from the previous year's *La Belle Mariniere*, who in this film, just like in the other one, plays his wife.

The film starts off with a fake but very realistic-looking newsreel, which gives us some back-story about the underground tunnel's construction, and this is eight years before *Citizen Kane* would trot-out the exact same *'faux* newsreel' device. The newsreel's Narrator (Victor

Vina) informs us that the tunnel will, for the first time, link Europe to the United States and, as it ends, the film-proper gets underway, and we cut to a couple of years earlier, when the tunnel was no more than a twinkle in the eye of some proto-Trump-like developers.

Welcome to what is supposed to be New York City: The film was shot in Germany, but we immediately get the requisite stock shot of the Statute of Liberty: Naturally, the film's French co-producers chose Lady Liberty to represent America, because their ancestors gave it to us, and, in fact, on that same note, what's really fun about the movie, not to mention, what's also a bit off-putting about it at times, is that all of the film's French-speaking characters, including the lead, Jean Gabin, are meant to be American, but once you suspend your disbelief, you'll find yourself having a lot of fun with this picture.

A tuxedo-wearing 'swell' leaves his limo and makes his big entrance into the swank Waldorf-Astoria Hotel and, once inside, this chrome-domed dapper-dan, whose name is Woolf (Gustaf Grundgens), informs the desk clerk that he'd like "a room on the highest floor," and we know, right off the bat, that he's got to be some kind of a spy because, after securing himself a room, he heads up to the roof garden, where a fancy party's being set up. He plants a microphone in a flowerpot and *amscrays* quickly, just as a bunch of wealthy-looking guys and dolls start arriving.

Back in his hotel room, meanwhile, Woolf is radioing his unseen cohort that the meeting is going to start, and the meeting which he is referencing is a fancy party which is hosted by the wealthy venture capitalist George Lloyd (Andre Nox) who, when we first meet him, is thanking his well-heeled guests for accepting his invitation, and telling them that it's time for them to all start pooling their services (read: their cash) together, for a huge project. "My friends: I am about to start building the first Transatlantic Tunnel between the United States and Europe. I will personally be investing twenty-five million dollars of my own money on the project, but we need more—much more." Lloyd wants everybody present to become shareholders in his new company, which he intends to call *Le Tonnel Atlantique Fonde* and, as he continues his *spiel,* one of his guests finds the microphone which Woolf has hidden, and not too well, in the planter—but Woolf's nowhere to be seen: He, like Elvis, has already left the building.

Lloyd continues: "And now, since our principal engineer, Mr. MacAllan, knows about what the project will physically entail better than anybody else, he will now address you," And this is where we meet *Our Rugged Hero,* MacAllan (Gabin) who, very modestly, takes to the podium, as his dutiful wife Mary (Madeleine Renaud) beams up at him pridefully, from the cheap seats.

Mary MacAllan is sitting beside Mac's lifelong best friend, Frederick Robbins (William Burke), an effete scientist who's invented the ultra-futuristic radium drill which, as Mac is now telling us, the tunnel builders will be using, to drill through thousands of miles of underground rock. 'Freddie,' as the MacAllans both call him, is their 'not-too-sexually-threatening third-wheel pal,' which every committed couple needs. (Freddie is best friend and co-worker to Mac, and he's also a friendly confidante to Mary, whenever Mary confides in Freddie that she's afraid of what might happen to Mac, down in the tunnels: "I believe in him—but I'm afraid." In that sense, Mary's not too different than 'Vera Latour,' Andre Luguet's long-suffering stunt pilot-wife in Gabin's Charles Lindbergh-inspired flyboy epic, *Gloria*.

In the kitchen of the Waldorf, meanwhile, Woolf is now meeting up with his short/fat/goofy little partner/sidekick, Gordon, who's played by Andre Bertic, and the two of them together definitely resemble Abbott and Costello! We know, from *grokking* this skeevy duo, that they're probably going to be doing something underhanded the second tunnel construction gets underway, and, in fact, what they're going to do, or, what they plan to do, is to sabotage the tunnel's building, which (they think) will cause the stockholders in Lloyd's new Atlantic Tunnel Fund to pull out, at which time (this is their plan, anyway) they will buy back all of the shares themselves, put in their own workers, make the tunnel a great success, be beloved around the world for being the two visionaries who initiated the tunnel, and grow as fat as kings. For now, however, Woolf tells Gordon that he thinks the two of them shouldn't be seen together (just like Bush and Cheney, post 9-11): "I don't want anybody to know what we're planning. I will be President of the Tunnel, and you will be my Vice-President. This will be an important mission for the two of us—financially, spiritually, and artistically." (Yeah, right; like these cretins give two-shits about 'art!')

But Woolf and Gordon aren't the only ones spying on Lloyd's gathering: There's also a shitty yellow journalist-lady from the New York *Evening Post,* who's been planted at the rooftop ceremony by her editor, to whom she's now reporting, *via* phone. She tells him that, currently, she's watching fifteen people on the roof of the Waldorf-Astoria who are putting together a deal which will be worth fifteen million dollars, and keep in mind that this is fifteen million dollars in 1933 money.

Back "Up on the Roof," *per* that great, summery 1963 song by the Drifters, Gabin's MacAllan-character is now really impressing the crowd with his mega-lofty, and yet realistic, tunnel-building plans. He tells the attending guests that construction will begin simultaneously on both the American and the European sides of the tunnel, and that both teams of workers—the American team, which he's going to be heading-up, and the European team—will be burrowing toward each other from either side, and that, when the two teams reach the middle, the tunnel will be complete. Lloyd tells the crowd that the money earned from the completed-tunnel's ticket-buying commuters will more than double the return of all those who have invested in its construction.

Of course, *Le Tunnel* wouldn't be a proper French movie if MacAllan's wife didn't have some (sultry, young) competition in the Gabin-Seducing Department, and director Bernhardt serves her up hot, in the person of Lloyd's smoldering daughter, Ethel (a hot girl with an *un-hot* first name), who's played by Raymonde Allain. Very clearly, Ethel's *Betty Crocker-moist* for MacAllan because, while he was speechifying up on that rooftop podium, she's been boring holes through him with her eyes, like *she's the radium drill and he's the big, hard, underground rock.* "Good job, Mr. MacAllan," she whispers lasciviously, as he disembarks from the podium and walks by her, returning to his wife's side.

MacAllan, like all of Jean Gabin movie characters, is a smart and intuitive guy (at least, when he's not being lead around by his *schmeckle*), and Mac Gabin-Shrugs at his wife, Mary, *re:* the potential investors, "They're all sharks. They're not interested in the tunnel—only, in lining their own pockets!" Third-wheel Freddie Robbins looks a tad insecure about how Mac's presentation went, but MacAllan is quietly and supremely confident, about it. He shrugs and, in a very confident manner, proclaims very simply to his wife, regarding the tunnel's incipient construction, "It will start," and when he says this, it sounds like the last few seconds of Jesus' life, when the Savior apparently cried out, "*It is finished.*"

Now that the pledge-drive part of the afternoon is over, Freddie and Mac whack each other playfully in the shoulders, and Mac even jumps on top of Freddie, pinning him down like a *luchador,* while grinning at him. Meanwhile, *hottie* Ethel Lloyd is alerting her dad that she wants pictures of herself taken with handsome MacAllan and, as we all know, 'whatever Lola wants…'

Next, Bernhardt flashes forward, to several months later: The tunnel's construction is now already in progress, and it is going very smoothly. Mac's underground, on the American side of the tunnel, supervising a hearty crew of thousands of dutiful workers, while wife Mary is able to communicate with him *via* a large, wall-mounted t.v., in the tunnel's underground offices. (Remember, *Le Tunnel* was made in 1933, fifteen years before television came to pass for the masses, in real life.) Mary buoys Mac up with compliments, all of which he's too genuinely Gabin-Modest to acknowledge. ("You will be a success, Mac. I'm so proud of you!") Mac then goes into conference with his crack-team of engineers, as well as with his army of dedicated worker-bees.

With a quick dissolve, we see that the first three years of tunnel-building have now elapsed, and director Curtis Bernhardt now gifts us with a second *faux* newsreel, which is bringing us up-to-speed on what's already happened: The newsreel's Narrator tells us that, during Year One of construction, the tunnel workers ran into their first big problem, a major mine explosion in the segment of the tunnel, which MacAllan's 'American' crew dug beneath Long Island, about one hundred and eighty kilometers beneath the earth's crust; during Year Two, Mac's crew dug two-thousand meters under the ocean, followed by an additional three-thousand kilometers, in Year Three. When the newsreel is over, we now see *Mac and his Merry Men* underground, three years after we saw them the last time, and they're all shirtless, covered in muck, and looking a whole lot like those big, muscle-bound galley slaves, in *Ben-Hur.* One concerned worker even sets up explosive charges, and tells the others to run for cover, because the earth through which they're digging is about to blow, *and blow it does*—very spectacularly: The explosion blasts one guy through the air, but he's lucky, because he hasn't been hurt.

Next, we're in the Foreman's shack, above ground, near one of the tunnel sites. A gnarled-looking 'Out-of-Work-Guy' (who's played by Henri Vaibel), who probably hasn't had *three-square* in quite some time, enters, and asks the Foreman (Edmond van Daele) if he can talk to 'Mr. MacAllan, the Chief.' The Foreman, who's a good gatekeeper, informs the miscreant that Mr. MacAllan is "too busy to talk to all of the people who want to talk to him," but, by a stroke of sheer luck, guess who walks in, right that second: It's Mac, himself! Since MacAllan, like all of Jean Gabin's movie characters of the 1930s, is always sensitive to the problems of the working man (*shit,* he's a working man, himself!), he's very friendly toward the guy, and asks what he can do to help him. The guy tells MacAllan his hard-luck story. (Remember, even though the actors are French, the characters are supposed to be American, and this movie takes place in the years which immediately followed the Depression). "I started as a boss," the poor soul mumbles. "I even had a white horse!" Mac takes pity on the clearly delusional guy and pats him on the back, with a fraternal cry of, "So! Are we going to work together? Well, let's start now!" and the guy looks so suddenly ebullient, that you can tell Mac's made not just his day, but probably, also, his whole life.

Next, we dissolve to another fancy-dress social-do, given by Mr. Lloyd: This one takes place at his gargantuan estate, where the tunnel investors have gathered to celebrate the first three years of its construction. Rugged Mac seems to be the big star of the evening, and he arrives in a limo with wife Mary, as guests surround the vehicle, cheering him. (It's definitely a 'Fanfare for the Common Man.')

As the party spills outside onto the mansion's grounds, we see that a pretty-sizable makeshift carnival has been set up, replete with a merry-go-round and other fun rides. Mac and Mary hop on the swings and the merry-go-round and woof down some hot dogs.

Mac and Mary steal into a carnival tent, which is the only place where they can have a little private time, together: "I have such little time to be with you," he tells her, soothingly, "because I'm leaving again for the tunnels... tonight." One of Mac's underlings now telephones him from down in the tunnels, with some news which is not very promising: "I'm sorry to bother you during your party, Mr. MacAllan, but it's an emergency! We're on the verge of a cave-in. Tunnel Station Nine has touched an underwater lake. We're trying to preserve the area, so we've built a dam, but the dam is fifteen meters under the sea, and it's not gonna hold for long!" Mac bounds into the john, just like Clark Kent, tears off his tux, and emerges only moments later, in his overalls and miner's hat. (Gabin is always more comfortable in work attire, anyway, than he is in stuffy tuxes.) Mary is saddened, because she had originally planned a three-day vacation for just the two of them, which she hoped would be starting right after the party: In fact, she was all packed-up and ready to go. And just when she looks like she's about to burst into tears, Freddie Robbins, who's always popping up just at the right time, shows up, to console her.

Back down in the hole, Mac and his men try to dam the underwater lake with sandbags, but the bags are failing, and filmmaker Bernhardt shoots this sequence hand-held, which gives it a very urgent and documentary-like flavor, as though what we're seeing is really happening, in real-time. A frightened worker lets his boss, MacAllan, know that he has children, and Mac is genuinely sympathetic to the guy, even though Mac doesn't have any *cracker-munchers* of his own. Mac knows that his men are scared, so he puts on a brave face for them, heroically shouting, "Anybody who wants to, can follow me!" As we've already seen in his other movies, Jean Gabin almost always remains calm in every situation, his zen-like inner-quietude always making everybody around him feel a whole lot better.

Meanwhile, the two conspirators, Woolf and Gordon (they're like the two grotesque baddies in 1959's *Tom Thumb,* who were played by Peter Sellers and Terry-Thomas) are now hand-wringingly continuing to conspire together: They've heard that the tunnel is failing, and they've now got a new idea: They want to invest in the company that makes the building equipment which MacAllan and his men are using: "We'll buy stock in the equipment company," Woolf strategizes out loud, "and then, when we push the company's stock prices up, it will be too expensive for the Tunnel Fund to buy mining equipment, and the workers will strike. And then, we'll take over the tunnel company!" Woolf and Gordon are so ready to have the tunnel all for themselves, they can taste it.

Not only does Mac have these two clowns to contend with, but he's also got problems brewing from within his own organization: Unbeknownst to him, at least, thus far, his workers have decided, very quietly, to unionize, and in one of the underground tunnels, we see a meeting at which thousands of Mac's workers are in attendance, and they're not happy, as we originally thought them to be. One at a time, disgruntled workers stand up on a makeshift stage, voicing their complaints and their fears: "They want us to be heroes," one disgruntled tunneler orates. "We've just celebrated our five thousandth kilometer, and our bosses are partying up-top, while we're down here, waist-deep in mud!" Another disgruntled guy agrees: "Let's not go back to work! Bosses are bastards!" After the usual cries of "Hear! Hear!" a third guy now gets his turn at the Torah: "Mr. MacAllan wants to be a celebrity, and we're all dying for him! We're dying for a company that's been paying us one dollar per hour. Well, we want one thousand dollars per hour... or four thousand! The tunnel syndicate wants our skin... but they won't get it!" Now, of course, this guy is joking, regarding the crazy amounts which he thinks they should all be asking for, but the sentiment is true, and there are more cries of "Hear! Hear!" and "You said it!" *etc.*

Then, suddenly, a voice that is rich with calm *gravitas* interrupts them, from somewhere in the shadows: "It's easy to scream in a tunnel," the familiar voice tells them, and a few of the miners who are in attendance (the minority, who are happy about the present conditions) tell the disembodied voice not to listen to the complainers. The disembodied voice belongs to MacAllan, who then enters dramatically, because he's been there the whole time, listening to his men's complaints, only they didn't know it. Mac steps up to the podium, and the third guy who was complaining (he's a real badass, when the boss isn't around) backs away surprised, now suddenly becoming deferential, as Mac beings making his searing speech: "You think there's a difference between you and me? I am working *with* you, not above you!" This is a stirring reminder that Jean Gabin is a working-man, just like they are.

"Two hundred men just died in Tunnel Nine," a worker cries out, pointing an accusing finger at Mac, as though Mac's the one who personally made it happen. Mac is saddened by the news, but he realizes that, in spite of it, they must all continue on with the project: "So, you think we should just stop working? We have to keep going! There are risks everywhere, in life. Do you guys want to end up in the streets? We didn't ask for these problems, but we have to deal with them. Follow me—and trust me!" Bowled over by the much-vaunted 'Gabin Sincerity' (which gets 'em, every time), the men suddenly love and respect Mac more than ever, realizing that that he truly is just like they are. Within seconds of Mac's speech's coming to its conclusion, the men begin singing raucous work songs together, as they all march happily away, ready to combat any problems which *Le Tunnel* may have in store for them.

While Mac has vowed to stay down in the tunnels with his *hombres*, we have to assume that some time has passed because, in the next scene, he's back home visiting his wife Mary, and we can tell he's in the dog-house with her, because he's all dressed up in a nice suit, to placate her, and Jean Gabin never dresses up, in his 1930's pictures, unless he absolutely has to. Mary's in bed, crying about how alone she feels, and he promises her that, in a week's time, he'll take a few days off, to be with her. We can tell by the way that Mac is looking at Mary, that he really does love his wife, and that he'd absolutely choose staying at home with her, over returning to work, were it only possible, and this scene represents the film's solitary lapse into melodrama.

This is the part of the film in which we're going to be finding out, expressly, although we've known it all along, anyway, that arch-villain Woolf is the one guy who's been causing all of the tunnel disasters, including all of the explosions, and all of the flooding; in fact, he's been sabotaging the tunnel, using a cadre of carefully-placed 'shill' worker/'mad bombers' of his own employ! Mac's learning this because there are workers down in the tunnel whom he doesn't recognize, men whom he's never personally hired, and he even backs one unfamiliar guy up against the wall, and makes with the standard, "Who do you work for?"- bit. Mac tells Freddie Robbins, who's down in the tunnels with him, that he and his men are going to have to fight against these acts of terrorism, and he actually uses the word 'terrorism,' which makes the movie very relevant in today's world.

Mac makes his next trip 'up-top,' to visit George Lloyd's estate, intending to finesse the zillionaire out of some completion funds for the tunnel, and when he gets there, he's in for an unexpected shock, and so are we: Woolf's in Lloyd's study with him, and he's trying to finagle Lloyd into turning over the Tunnel Company to him—in fact, from the shocked look on Lloyd's face, we can tell that Woolf's just been threatening him. But when Woolf sees Mac, he suddenly caves, *just like a sniveling, little bitch.* Mac tells Woolf, right in front of Lloyd, that he knows Woolf is the one who's been causing all of the damage in the mines—three million dollars worth of damage—and that he knows this, because some of the shill workers whom he's questioned have already admitted to Mac to having being sent into the tunnels by Woolf. Woolf, who's now realizing that 'the jig is up,' looks like a deer who's caught in the headlights, and Mac tells him that if he doesn't give him the three million *smack-a-roonies, plus vite,* and if he doesn't pay for all of the damage which he's caused in the tunnels, that he's going to have Woolf arrested; and right after Mac *kicks Woolf a new ass,* Woolf evinces a rare and genuine moment of vulnerability: Suddenly embarrassed about what he's done, Woolf apologizes to Mr. Lloyd, and then retreats into the hallway by himself, where he cowers in a chair, in the corner, wiping his brow with a handkerchief.

When Woolf returns to his own office, shaking like a leaf, Gordon tells him that the cops are already looking for him. ("You're being investigated as a criminal, you know!") But Gordon isn't 'all-bad,' like his partner is—in fact, he now decides to help his friend out of his predicament: He heads over to the secret hideout of a bizarre, greasy-looking moneylender, Brooce, who's played by one of France's most intense, and most tormented (in real-life) actors, Robert Le Vigan, and tells him his problem, which is that he and Woolf need three million dollars, and *stat*. Brooce tells Gordon, pointedly, that if the money is for the tunnel, that he's just not interested. Gordon, a guy whom we've regarded, thus far, as being no more than a comical sidekick to Woolf, suddenly becomes, for the first and only time in the movie, completely menacing: "Listen, Brooce, I can force you to help us." *Meaning:* Gordon will probably narc to the cops that he knows where the notorious moneylender lives, if Brooce doesn't cough up some *cash-ola*. Since Gordon has just 'out-crazied' Brooce, Brooce now caves, and promises that he will lend the two guys the three million clams they need, and right away, and then Gordon adds a 'P.S.,' to his request: "Oh, and by the way: I'm going to be needing that whole three million in three days, or else the cops are going to arrest my partner, and he'll go to jail." It's funny that Gordon is so protective of his partner, because we know, just by looking at Woolf, that he'd sell Gordon down the river in a second. And while we're on the subject of Gordon, there's an inconsistency in the way in which the film's screenwriters, Reinhart Steinbacker and Alexandre Arnoux, have designed his character: Watching this movie, we're starting to wonder: If Gordon is smart enough to finesse three million crackers out of Brooce, wouldn't he also be smart enough not to need Woolf in the first place? Maybe Woolf is the 'big-picture/idea man,' and Gordon is the 'business' brain— but the film never answers that question.

Back in the tunnel, in 'Section #9,' at the same time, MacAllan is telling his workers not to worry, and that, somehow, they'll have the money they need, in three days. And meanwhile, in another section of the tunnel, a few hundred miles away, an army of Woolf's terrorists is now swarming through the tunnels, savagely gunning-down Mac's workers. MacAllan, who is as Gabin-Calm as usual, orders his men to seal off all of the exits, so that the bad guys can't escape. Mac finds one of the terrorists, and grabs the guy by his grease-stained lapels: "You'd better tell me who you work for, by the time I count to three, or I'll kill you." The panicked guy confesses that he works not for Woolf, but for Woolf's associate, Gordon! That's right: Not only is Gordon tougher than we originally thought he was, but he's actually trying to double-cross Woolf. (Wow! *Who knew?* Yes, it's a 'reverse double-cross!')

Up-top, on *terra firma*, Freddie Robbins is dining with Mary MacAllan, and they're both gushing proudly about their hero, Mac, and Freddie even brags, "Fifteen minutes of Mac are worth six hours of anybody else." Well, Mac does make an appearance up-top, but he's not going home: He's making for Lloyd's estate again, because he wants to make sure that Woolf hasn't come back to try and influence Lloyd again, unduly. Of course, Woolf (who, apparently, is just as stupid as he is STUPID), happens to be in the study with Lloyd, again, and he's doing just that! Lloyds's fetching daughter, Ethel, happens to be on the premises, too, and she's excited to see Mac: "Hope everything is okay," she coos at him. Mac looks incredibly overwhelmed by everything that's been going down in his tunnels lately, and he tells her and her dad that he's resigning from the tunnel, effective immediately: "I'm leaving the project, and without sadness. The tunnel needs money, and since you can't give it to us, Mr. Lloyd, well—I'm just quitting. I don't want this to damage our friendship, but I can completely understand it, if it will."

Outside the Lloyd estate, meanwhile, a gaggle of cops are now barreling up the stairway to arrest Woolf, and we can guess that Gordon tipped the law off about Woolf's presence, to take any possible 'legal investigation focus' off of himself. Hearing the cops running toward him, Woolf (as every good German knows, sometimes in life, 'the jig is up!') picks a carnation out of a bowl, places it in his jacket pocket, and then whips a gun out of his jacket, and blows himself clean to Hell!

Now, it's Tunnel-Time again: Down in the dank, steaming bowels of *le tunnel,* Mac and one of his top engineers, Hobby (Pierre Nay), are burrowing through layers of hard rock, in a very sleek-looking, futuristic mining car. (The movie is a triumph of stunning production design, and Karl Vollbrecht and Heinz Fenchel are the guys to thank for it; their work, in this relatively little-known [in the United States, anyway] picture, absolutely rivals any of the most expensive *CGI-bullshit* we're getting, today.) Even though Mac has just announced that he's going to quit, when he sees that his men are in trouble, *he forgets that shit* and, within seconds, he is once again ready to take charge. Hobby tells him that many of the men are out, looking for a bomb which one of Woolf's terrorists, whom they've just apprehended, has already planted, in Section Nine. The Bombers, as we're now finding out, have also cut off all communications between many of Mac's underground teams, as well as all communications between the American section of the tunnel and the world up-top.

Mac and Hobby make haste to Section Nine, but they arrive too late, because the bomb explodes, seconds before they arrive. Mac thinks he's been unable to save his men, and we next find out, much to his relief, and also to our own, that most of the guys who are working in #9 are still alive, but the bad news, is that they've been caved-in. The filmmakers next give us a very sad and unexpected twist: An avalanche of rocks hit the men who survived the bomb, and now, the majority of them really *are* dead.

Back in Civilian Land, meanwhile, Freddie Robbins is driving Mary MacAllan home, after the two of them have, for the millionth time, dined-out, together. She starts wondering out loud about what her husband is "doing right now," when, suddenly, a trio of Red Cross ambulances zooms by Freddie's car, cutting them off. Freddie pulls alongside one of the meat-wagons, and asks the driver what's going on, and the EMT Guy tells him that there's been a catastrophe, down in the tunnels. Mary, who's not thinking straight (in fact, she's been a raw nerve, ever since her husband took the job) jumps out of the car, freaked, and starts yelling, "I need to find my husband!" She starts frantically panic-running, not even knowing where she's going, and Freddie starts chasing her on foot, but (look out!) she doesn't see the huge train that's barreling right toward her, and SMACK—*MacAllan is now a widower.*

Sous la terre (under the ground), Mac and his men are struggling to free Tunnel #9's few remaining survivors, and Hobby even announces that they're not leaving until "we find all of our friends." Then, suddenly, a really shocking 'unexpected:' Somebody (obviously, it's one of Woolf's and/or Gordon's terrorists) shoots Hobby dead, right where he stands. Mac and his workers jump into one of their monorail-looking mining cars, turning-tail right outta there.

Slow dissolve to a graveyard: Big, looming crucifix. Many graves (the resting place of the scores of workers who've sacrificed their lives, in all of the tunnel's various construction disasters). Mac's been vacillating on whether to quit the project for good, or whether to stay on, until the bloody end. (The building of one of America's great wonders, the Hoover Dam, in 1931, apparently inspired author Bernard Kellerman to write his 1932 novel *Der Tunnel,* upon which this 1933 film was based; the Hoover Dam's construction, of course, was just like the construction of the Transatlantic Tunnel in this movie, fraught with danger.) Freddie tells Mac that he (Mac) isn't responsible for the things that have gone south with the project and that he can't just give up, when they're this close to finishing the project, and Mac, who's not mad at his friend, but who is just at the end of his nerves, now Gabin-Outbursts, "I told you: I'm done with the tunnel! I quit! If you want to keep going, you can—but I'm done. Now, leave me alone!"

That night, Mac stands before his wife Mary's grave, and talks to her: "What did you get from life?" he asks her, and then, of course, *on account of how she's dead,* he has to answer the question, himself: "Nothing. I gave you nothing. I want to die, like all of the other ones." Mac, who is the ultimate 'good man,' feels personally responsible for the deaths of his men, even though those deaths were caused by the terrorists, and not by him.

Director Bernhardt dissolves, next, to what must either be days, or else weeks, later: Tunnel construction continues apace, and we're discovering now that Freddie's pep-talk must have really worked, because Mac's back, leading his crews, and he's better and stronger than ever before. Obviously, he's returned to work, as a way of honoring the memories of his workers and his wife—and besides, there are only fifty kilometers left to go, until Mac and his American digging teams will be getting to the middle of the tunnel, where they'll be meeting, at their under-the-Atlantic midpoint, halfway between the U.S. and Europe, the European crew, for the first time.

Now, finally, the big day arrives: The American and European teams (we haven't seen the European team yet, but only Gabin's 'American' side) have reached the exact center of the tunnel: Both teams are directly in the middle of the Atlantic Ocean, and it's now time to blast that final earthen wall, and to forever unite the two continents. Mac valiantly instructs his men, "Tell those Europeans on the other side to move out of the way. We're ready to blast!" One of Mac's men starts beating out Morse Code with a hammer, on the final, standing dirt wall which divides the tunnel, instructing the *Eurodiggers* on the other side, that they should seriously consider 'moving it or losing it.'

Then: BOOM! It happens. The final barricade crumbles to the ground, and working men from the two continents, America and Europe, run toward one another, hugging, and greeting each other, like brothers—"Hi, America!" "Hi, Europe!" (It's a very funny, and extremely giddy, celebration scene.) The Europeans are excited that they are finally getting to meet the project's chief American engineer, MacAllan, whom none of them has ever met before, in person.

At the tunnel dedication ceremony, MacAllan, relieved that the work is finally complete, makes a speech, which is broadcast to the entire world over the radio: "Now that I've made it to the end of the tunnel, I'm very happy. But I also know that my life will now probably be more complicated." What he means, most likely, is that now that his job is done, and he's going to be having quite a bit of spare time on his hands, he'll have to start dealing, in a direct manner, with his demons which means, that he'll have to battle the images of the ghosts of the men who gave their lives to the tunnel, not to mention, the 'ghost' of his wife Mary, who also sacrificed herself, although unwittingly, in front of that fast-moving train. He finishes-off his speech by thanking all of his workers, all of whom now love him-to-death (they've forgotten all about all of their 'unionizing' bullshit), and who are all shouting out, "Viva MacAllan!" The last shot we're going to be seeing in the movie, is that of a drill-bit which is digging its way through hard rock, and this image seems to be telling us: You can't mess with progress! The wheels just keep on a-rollin'!

Curtis Bernhardt's *Le Tunnel* is one of the great, undiscovered (in the U.S., anyway) movie-gems of the 1930s, and it's a great example of what we would today, in our Extreme-Sports-loving world, refer to as being a white-knuckle pulse-pounder. Two years after director Bernhardt shot both the usual French-language/Jean Gabin and German-language/ Paul Hartmann versions of the film, the Americans and British joined forces in 1935, for their very own English-language remake, which happens to be a very fun movie, in its own right, and which stars the American cowboy actor, Richard Dix. (This R. Dix version *is* available on home video in the U.S.)

What a Critic Said at the Time: "This picture is a splendid thriller. Jean Gabin does a convincing portrait of an intense worker. [Director] Kurt Bernhardt gives his best, assisted by excellent technicians." (*Variety*, 12-12-33 issue, Reviewer: "Maxi. [Edward 'Maxwell' MacSweeney.]" Reviewed in Paris.)

With Brigitte Helm, in "L'Etoile de Valencia."

FILM 13

L'Etoile de Valencia

The second of three lost Jean Gabin films (1933)

"L'ETOILE DE VALENCIA" (France/Germany, 1933) (Literal English Translation: "THE STAR OF VALENCIA") Directed by Serge de Poligny. Screenplay by Jean Galtier-Boissiere. Based Upon the Novel by Otto Eis and Rudolf Katscher. Directors of Photography (black and white), Werner Brandes and Karl Puth. Production Designer, Otto Hunte. Music by Richard Stauch and Hans-Otto Borgmann. (GENRE: ROMANTIC MELODRAMA.) A Production of/Released by UFA. Running Time, 1 hour 31 minutes. Released in France on April 14, 1933. Never Released Theatrically in the United States.

Director Serge de Poligny's 1933 *L'Etoile de Valencia* is the second of the three Jean Gabin films (the first, was the previous year's Gabin race car picture, *La Foule hurle*), which doesn't exist today. A German/French co-production, Jean Gabin filmed *L'Etoile de Valencia* in Germany for the UFA Film Company, and when Hitler's propaganda minister Joseph Goebbels took control of UFA in the late 1930s, he demanded that all of the 'French' movies which UFA made be destroyed. (The company filmed completely different French and German versions of their films, as part of a co-production agreement under which the two countries operated in the early 1930s.) Thankfully, however, at the same time during which UFA was making the French version, starring Gabin, they were also making the allegedly identical German-language version, starring Paul Westermeier, a German movie star of the time who was chosen for his incredible physical similarity to Jean Gabin, and the German version does exist in its entirety, although it is very rare; I was able to screen the world's only surviving print of this Gabinless version at the Bundesfilmarchiv in Berlin...

Der Stern von Valencia

Germany, 1933
German-language Alternative Version' of Jean Gabin's Missing Film, "L'Etoile de Valencia"

(Literal English Translation: "THE STAR OF VALENCIA") Directed by Alfred Ziegler. Screenplay by Friedrich Zeckendorf. Based Upon the Novel by Otto Eis and Rudolf Katscher. Directors of Photography,

Werner Brandes and Karl Puth. Production Designer, Otto Hunte. Music by Richard Stauch and Hans-Otto Borgmann. A Production of/Released by UFA. Running Time, 1 hour 31 minutes. Released in Germany, on September 2, 1933. Never Released Theatrically in the United States.

"You: Wear something skimpy!"
— *Oily theater impresario, to one of his dancing girls, in "Der Stern von Valencia"*

We're somewhere off of the coast of Valencia, eastern Spain's third-largest port city, and we're also aboard the *Leone*, a Spanish Coast guard vessel, where Captain Pedro Savedra (Paul Westermeier) and his good friend, Diego (Friedrich Gnab)—that's right, two big, blonde German actors, playing swarthy Spaniards!—are staring out to sea, searching the blue ocean for any potential monkey business. (Paul Amiot, who played the lawyer, Merlu, in 1932's *Coeur de lilas*, plays Diego, in the French-language version.)

Pedro's happy, because he and all of the other guys aboard the *Leone* have earned shore-leave for tonight, and he's finally going to be able to *do the hang* with his wife, Marion (who's played by Liane Haid in this German-language version, and by Brigitte Helm in the missing French-language/Jean Gabin version), a gal who works aboard a traveling party ship called *La Estrella de Valencia* (*The Star of Valencia*) which, as it just so happens, is going to be moored in Valencia this very evening. Marion performs in her ship's huge theater, the Paradise Club, along with her friend Rita (Ossi Oswalda) and several other lithesome honeys. Pedro understands all too well that most of the other women aboard the *Valencia* do more than just dance with the clients, but he and Marion have a solid marriage, in spite of the fact that they don't get to see each other too often and, in the past, she's promised him that she *only* dances on the boat, and nothing more. When we finally meet her, we'll immediately see that she's a good person, so we believe her.

The film's director, Alfred Zeisler, then takes us aboard the *Valencia:* Marion and the other dancers are up on deck, receiving their marching orders for the evening from their boss, Patesco (Oskar Sima), the Paradise Club's oily/seedy impresario, a guy who's definitely cut from the same cloth as actor Alan Rachins' seedy strip club owner in director Paul Verhoeven's 62-years-later, 1995 camp-classic, *Showgirls*. Patesco tells the ladies that, tonight, aside from the usual townies who come aboard for hijinks, that some big businessmen are going to be visiting their fun-boat, and that these heavy-hitters are going to be bringing along a surfeit of *cashola*. (PATESCO: "Look smart, you girls! The fish salesmen are coming aboard tonight, with *their centipede hands,* and you gals are going to be selling them a lot of champagne—get me?" RITA: "Forget the centipede hands! Let's talk about their big, fat wallets!") Patesco then informs Marion that, even though she's the most conservative member of the whole dance team that, tonight, she's going to have to wear something skimpy; but since she's a strong woman, she stands up to him, telling him that it's not in her contract to run around naked. So he then caves, telling her, instead, to just go ahead and put on her nicest dress.

The women descend down into the bowels of the *Estrella* and, at this point, everybody's favorite Coast Guard vessel, the *Leone,* pulls up beside it, and Pedro and Diego hop aboard. Patesco and the *Valencia's* equally-seedy-looking captain, Mendoza (Peter Erkelenz), greet them, and they're not too happy about receiving Coast Guardsmen aboard their boat, because these meddlesome Guardies are always checking into things. Pedro asks Patesco permission to head down into the bowels of the ship to say hi to his wife, but Patesco tells him that he's going to have to wait until tonight, and he adds that, if he wants to see his wife so badly, he can pay to see her, just like everybody else. (Patesco's referring to the fact that Marion's appearing in the show, but the comment gets Pedro steamed, because it sounds like he's made a prostitution reference.) Pedro knows all too well that, in addition to putting on burlesque shows, Patesco and Mendoza occasionally take the *Valencia* to South America, where they 'rent' their ladies, temporarily, to *the local horndogs,* and Pedro's a little worried, because Marion is relatively new to the *Valencia,* and hasn't worked on it long enough to be selling her body to anybody, yet—here, in Spain, *or* in South America— and, naturally, he doesn't want her to. So he tells Patesco and Mendoza that, just maybe, if he can't see his wife right now, that he and his partner, Pedro, are going to be heading down, below-deck, anyway. Unafraid of Pedro, Mendoza summons Paul, a big, balding, Tor Johnson-esque-brute-of-a-guy up to the deck, to threaten our hero. Paul says something dirty to Pedro about Marion, and Pedro, without even thinking about it, knocks the big lummox out cold. Unfortunately, since the *Leone* is side-by-side with the *Valencia,* Pedro's superior officer, Lt.-Colonel Diaz (Eduard Wesener) has just witnessed *the big punch-out,* and he bolts aboard the *Valencia,* apologizing to Patesco and Mendoza for Pedro's non-professional behavior. Diaz orders Pedro back to the *Leone,* where he'll be receiving his punishment.

Lt.-Col. Diaz is a nice guy, however, and he really likes Pedro, whom he considers to be one of his best men. Still, as he's now telling Pedro, Pedro can't just be going around, punching people out—even if they deserve it! Diaz now informs Pedro that tonight, while all of the other Coast Guardsmen of the mighty *Leone* are taking their shore-leaves in Valencia (in the town of Valencia, as well as on the boat, the *Valencia*), Pedro's going to have to stay alone, on the *Leone,* pulling nighttime sentry-duty. Pedro makes with a dutiful cry of, "Yes, sir," and pretends like it doesn't bother him, but it definitely does.

That night, Marion and Rita are readying themselves for the evening's (*per* Ed Sullivan) '*rilly big shooow*' in the tiny, cramped dressing room which they both share. They've heard, from Patesco and Mendoza, that Pedro won't be coming aboard the *Valencia* tonight, because he beat-up the bald guy, and Marion feels awful, because she's really been looking forward to seeing her husband, although, at the same time, she's not 100% downhearted; she also feels all warm and toasty inside, because she knows the reason Pedro is in trouble, is because he had been defending her honor earlier that day, when he punched out *that big freak* who was *talking shit* about her.

Simultaneously, in the town of Valencia, two other Coast Guardsmen from the *Leone,* Beppo (Willi Schur) and another sailor, are wandering through the local marketplace, and some of the *Valencia* (the boat's) male crew-members are there, too, strolling back-and-forth, and wearing sandwich boards which advertise the fact that their vessel's in town, and that tonight, the Paradise Club's dancers are going to be putting on their biggest and hottest show ever. Pedro's two colleagues are discussing how upset Pedro is, because he's been unable to come-with.

It's not long before the party aboard the *Valencia* is in progress, and the dancers are all assembled on stage, twirling around in the skimpiest of costumes, and performing their big, show-stopping number. (LYRICS: "You shouldn't look women deeply in the eyes, because their love will get you, every time.") Beppo and his sailor pal are seated at a table in the front, and at the end of the number, they're both clapping like seals; Beppo even nudges his friend, wolfishly referencing one of the girls— "I like the one who did the cartwheels"—to which his friend's *equally-horned-up* comeback, is a haiku-like rendition of that great, time-honored horny-male sound-effect: "Heh-heh-heh!" (!)

Meanwhile, Pedro's all alone aboard the *Leone*, pulling sentry-duty. He's bored-as-all-hell, and really wants to sneak off of his own tub and hop aboard the *Valencia*, which continues to be moored close to the *Leone*, but he knows, too well, that if he leaves his post, he'll be in even more trouble than he's already in. But because he wants to be with his wife (love is stronger than court-martial), he decides to chance it.

Pedro sneaks aboard the *Valencia*, and is able to catch the tail-end (pun intended) of the show. Marion's bestest gal-pal Rita has never met Pedro before, but Marion's shown her photographs of her beau, and she's excited that he's shown up. Rita brings Pedro back to Marion's dressing room, to see her.

Marion tells Pedro that even though she's excited he's come to see her, she's also scared, because she knows that Pedro's C.O., Diaz, will punish him when he finds out that Pedro has deserted his post. He asks her why she can't just break her contract with Patesco, and she tells him that if she does, it's written into her contract that she'll be required to pay Patesco two thousand pesetas—money which she just doesn't have. This gives Pedro an idea: He tells Marion that there's a club in town called the Trocadero, which happens to be the hangout of a rather swarthy former Coast Guardsman, who's now descended into a life of iniquity, Sgt. Jose (Hans Dieppe), a guy who just so happens to owe Pedro two thousand pesetas, which Jose lost to him in an ancient gambling incident. Pedro tells Marion that he's going to go and see Jose right now, to collect the money, and that as soon as he does this, he'll come right back to the *Valencia*, settle-up with Patesco, and free her from her *indentured sex-i-tude*.

Genuinely jazzed about her husband's bold, new idea, Marion next reaches into her closet, and hands her man a civilian's suit to wear into town, telling him that he probably shouldn't be seen around town in his Coast Guard get-up. When he asks her how she happens to have come upon a man's suit, she tells him that it belongs to 'the engine man,' and he doesn't question her about it, because he knows that she'd never cheat on him. Meanwhile, in the ship's lounge, the girlie-show continues: Two businessman-types, who are seated at a table out in the front, have just gifted Rita with a stuffed toy animal, and she excuses herself from their (musky) presences, because it's now her turn up on stage, and we now get to see her performing her own song, solo. (LYRICS: "Women are loved, because they know what love begat/One smile from me, has lain many men flat...") [!]

When Pedro arrives at the smoky, back-alley, Trocadero Club, Sgt. Jose, the guy who owes him the two-thousand, is enmeshed in a hot card game with a tableful of surly-looking gangster-types. Unafraid of the hoods, Pedro asks Jose for the two thousand pesetas that he's owed, and Jose, who's a total smartass, shrugs, tells Jose, with a completely straight face, that he won't be able to pay him tonight, because someone has stolen his wallet; well, really, Jose's just taking the piss out of Pedro, because, as we're now seeing with our own eyes, Jose, now, as he's playing cards, is surrounded by hundreds of thousands of pesetas, which he's just won from the gangsters. (In other words, Jose's completely flush with cash.) Pedro's a guy who gives as good as he gets, however, in the world of intimidation, and, rather mischievously, he holds-up one of the cards the guys are playing with, cards which have apparently been supplied, for this game, by Jose. ("Say, Jose... aren't these marked cards? For three years, I worked vice in Madrid as a beat cop, so I've definitely seen a few marked cards in my time.") Pedro's afraid to press the point with Jose, any more than he's already had to, though, because the gangsters are now shooting Pedro an assortment of steely, 'get lost'-glances. Pedro amscrays from the joint, tail between his legs, while Jose and the rest of Jose's shifty-looking pals now begin laughing at him.

Pedro boards the *Valencia* again, greets Marion, and is embarrassed to tell her that he wasn't able to procure the money, but that he's now (Plan B!) going to try to make a deal with Patesco, anyway: Pedro tells Patesco that he'd love to get his wife released from her contract, but that he wasn't able to come up with the required two thousand pesetas, and then Patesco, placing an arm around Pedro's shoulder in oily mock-friendship, presents him with a counter-offer: "Tell you what I'm going to do, my friend: You Coast Guard boys can fix engines, right? Well, we're having a problem with one of our main engines, and if you can get it working, I'll release your wife from her contract, okay?" Patesco walks Pedro down into the engine room, and then (yeah, like we couldn't see this coming!), pushes Pedro down the stairs, locking him inside. And worse: Guess who else is down there? It's Paul, the big, chrome-domed behemoth whom Pedro laid-out, at the beginning of the flick.

Marion, meanwhile, is now up in the club's showroom, slow-dancing with a civilian-dressed guy whom she believes to be a rich businessman, and, as they dance, she's telling him all about her husband, 'Pedro Savedra,' and about how Pedro left his 'beat,' aboard the *Leone*, to try and get some money to release her from her contract. Then, she gets a surprise: The guy with whom she's dancing (she had no idea) is Pedro's superior officer, Lt.-Col Diaz, himself. As we've seen already, he's a pretty nice fellow, though, and he tells her, "I like your husband a great deal, but he's not supposed to be away from his post. So if I have to punish him, please don't be mad at me."

Now, the film's director, Hans Zeisler, cuts to Captain Mendoza's shipboard office, and Patesco runs in, joining him: "Got it all worked out, Captain! That nosy Coast Guard Captain won't be giving us any more trouble." As it turns out, tonight after the show, Patesco and Mendoza will be taking all of their women, including Marion, for a fun-filled (maybe not for the girls!) trip, to South America. The two baddies are having a whale of a lot of fun, hatching their nefarious plan, but what they haven't counted on, is that Mendoza's second-in-command, Captain Rustan (Fritz Odemar), who's been positioned outside of Mendoza's office door, the whole time (!), has overheard the entire conversation. Rustan, a good man, is relatively new to the *Valencia,* and has no idea that his boat is ever used for anything at all, except for good, old fashioned, and only slightly-naughty, burlesque entertainment—he's probably not even aware that his dancers are prostituting themselves, post-performance. Mendoza opens the door, and Rustan (a/k/a, 'the man who knew too much') now looks like a deer who's just been caught in the headlights.

Next, we're in the *Valencia's* engine room. Pedro's been unable to fix the engine, but he *has* made a great new friend: Paul, the guy whom he had earlier knocked-out, is so impressed with the fact that Pedro was man enough to knock him out, that he's now become Pedro's best buddy in the whole world: In fact, this gentle giant even lets Pedro knock him out again, and for the second time, in one day (and this time, with a wrench) so that Pedro will be able to escape from the engine room, rescue Marion, and then make like a banana, and split! Paul actually 'comes-to,' after he knocks himself out, and then knocks himself out again with the wrench, and when he does, this not-too-bright, but well-meaning guy is out-cold for the third time in the picture, wanting to make sure that he stays out, so that, just in case Mendoza and Patesco should happen to come into the engine room to check up on Pedro, they won't get the idea that he (Paul) let Pedro escape.

Just as Pedro's about to grab Marion and escape to freedom, an offscreen gunshot is heard: Beppo and his sailor friend see Pedro standing outside of Captain Mendoza's office door and think he's the killer, so they haul him down to the town's local precinct house. Marion tells the cops that her husband was with her when the gunshot was fired (he was not), but they don't believe her, and, in fact, she's such a good wife, that, to protect her cherished husband, whom she knows has never been anything less than a good and upstanding man, she lies to the police on his behalf, telling them that it was she, herself, who murdered Mendoza, even though she didn't! They don't believe her, and they lock Pedro up.

Meanwhile, the *Valencia,* with snaky Patesco at the helm, is now about to escape into international waters, as it begins its voyage to South America. 'Nice' Captain Rustan makes a bee-line into the police station, and confesses to the cops that he's the one who shot Mendoza, not Pedro (it's the unvarnished truth), and that he murdered his own first-in-command, to stop the guy from smuggling the women. The police are so happy with Rustan for having committed this small(-ish, depending on your conception of things) crime, to prevent bigger crimes from happening, that they now set Pedro free.

In only a few minutes time, Pedro and Rustan are back aboard the *Leone,* and they're now bringing Lt.-Col. Diaz up-to-speed on what's been happening, and letting him know that, right now, as they're speaking, the *Valencia* has already begun its escape. Diaz knows that, once the *Valencia* gets twelve miles out into international waters, that the Coast Guard will be powerless to stop it from 'its evil mission,' so he, Pedro, and Diego now rev-up the Leone's engines, and the Leone begins it's action-packed boat-chase, with the *Valencia*. The *Leone* catches up to the *Valencia* quickly (remember: the *Valencia* had that engine problem which couldn't be fixed, so it's tortoise-slow), and hordes of gun-toting Coast Guardsmen, who are headed-up by the ultra-brave Pedro, now storm the ship, arresting Patesco, and freeing all of the girls.

Ultimately, only Patesco is arrested (for being complicit in the smuggling operation with Mendoza, who's now serving a long sentence of his own—in hell!), and Marion is happy, because, by default, she's now free of her contract with the seagoing Paradise Club. Pedro takes Marion aboard the *Leone* with him, and it's not long before creepy Sgt. Jose, who's had a change of heart, shows up with the two thousand pesetas which he owes Pedro. So, on top of being back together with his wife now, Pedro has some unexpected *shekels* in his pocket. It's time for Pedro and the mighty crew of the Coast Guard ship *Leone* to return to duty, and Pedro tells Marion that he'll be with her again soon, and that, in the mean time, she should "… keep [her] head held high." As the movie fades out, director Alfred Zeisler treats us to a view of a family of dolphins, which plays happily in the surf.

Der Stern von Valencia, the today, just barely existing Jean Gabin-less, German-language version of the completely non-existent French-language/Gabin picture, *L'Etoile de Valencia,* is an enjoyable little melodrama, and one which really whet my whistle to see more of UFA's German-made genre pictures from the 1930s. There are hundreds of them (comedies, dramas, romances) and, basically, very few of them have ever been released in North America: U.S. DVD distributors continue to release innumerable French and Italian genre movies from the 1930s and 1940s, stateside, but very few old German features ever turn up, no doubt (I'm just guessing) due to the old hostilities…'

Paul Westermeier, who plays the German version's lead character, Coast Guard Captain Pedro Savedra, is the spitting image of Jean Gabin and, while you're watching the movie, you can absolutely tell that the producers brought Westermeier aboard to 'replicate the Gabin Experience' for the film's non-French-speaking, German audiences, since Gabin was already in the early stages of becoming very popular in France, and I'm sure the producers thought, "Maybe Paul Westermeier could be a new Gabin." (Well, that never happened but, if it's what they thought, then I guess it was a pretty good idea.)

While the French, Jean Gabin version of *L'Etoile de Valencia* was never released in the United States, this German version, starring Paul Westermeier, *did* pop up in the U.S., at the 79th Street Theater, in New York—in German only, and without any English subtitles. The New York *Times* even reviewed it, and the critic, 'H.T.S.,' mentioned in his review, which is dated April 21st, 1934, that "the acting is excellent." (I'll bet it was doubly-excellent, in the Jean Gabin version.)

Top: With Janine Crispin. Above: With Margo Lion and Janine Crispin.

FILM 14

Du haut en bas

France/Germany, 1933

(Literal English Translation: "FROM TOP TO BOTTOM") Directed by George Wilhelm Pabst.
Produced by Georges Root. Screenplay by Anna Gmeyner, Georges Dolley, and Jean Oser. Based Upon
the Stage Play by Ladislaus Bus Fekette (as Leslie Bush-Fekete). Music by Marcel Lattes. Lyrics to the
Song, "Chaque semaine a sept jours," by Herbert [Gerbert] Rappaport. Director of Photography (black
and white), Eugene Schufftan. Editor, Jean Oser. Production Designer, Erno Metzner. (GENRE:
COMEDY) A Tobis/ Filmkundst Production. Running Time, 1 hour 19 minutes. Released in France
by Tobis-Klangfilm, on December 15, 1933. Never Released Theatrically in the United States.

"I can't take off my trousers in front of you! I'm delicate!"
— *Soccer champion Jean Gabin, to his new inamorata, in "Du haut en bas"*

W hen I talked about Jean Gabin's first movie, the comic-operetta *Chacun sa chance,*
we mentioned that French movies, from the lightest, frothiest comedies to the
darkest dramas, often deal with issues of class, and of how hard it is for 'rich and poor' to
get together. Well, just as it was in *Chacun sa chance,* and in *Gloria* (in which *pilot Gabin*
was uncomfortable, at the party with the rich people), so it is, too, in 1933's *Du haut en bas:*
Think: A Socialist-Utopian *Melrose Place,* in which the lower, middle, and upper classes live
together in peace, all in one U-shaped Parisian apartment building. That's the premise of the
great, and mostly unknown comedy, *Du haut en bas,* which is the only movie which will ever
team Jean Gabin up not only with one of the great masters of silent cinema, *Pandora's Box's*
immortal G.W. Pabst (this film shows that Pabst was just as great a filmmaker, when it came
to making talkies), but also, even though the two actors won't be sharing any scenes together,
with Peter Lorre, a couple of years before Lorre would emigrate to Hollywood, to make his
mark in all of those wonderful Warner Bros. gangster pictures. (*Du haut en bas* was made
only one year after Lorre had already become well-known, in his native Germany, for having
played the notorious child-killer Hans Beckert, in Fritz Lang's one-of-a-kind classic, *M.*)

In *Haut,* the poor people live on the top floor and the rich people live—and *love*—on the
bottom. And of course, the 'poor' aren't really poor, and the 'rich' aren't really rich, and the

whole thing is based upon a stage play (by Ladislaus Bus Fekette), which explains the fact that most of the film's action takes place in a very stagey-looking apartment building, which features a large courtyard in the front, so that, in the exterior scenes, we can see everything that's happening in every part of the building, at the same time.

The building's best-loved resident straddles both classes: He's France's own world's-famous champion soccer player, Charles Boulla (Jean Gabin), a working-class guy who's become newly-wealthy through his staggeringly-frequent victories. The film opens with Boulla winning, for his team, a soccer match against Spain, while hordes of women attendees cheer him on, as though *they're witnessing the* Second Coming—which he (kind of) is. (Charles Boulla is the mega-charismatic 'David Beckham of 1932.') As the President of France is, in his nationally-broadcast radio announcement, personally congratulating Charles, neighbors from Charles' building are listening-in on their radios, from their respective apartments, and we can see that each and every one of them is excited about his famous friend's good fortune. Rotund Miss Poldi (Milly Mathis), housekeeper for the pretentiously-wealthy (maybe) Mr. and Mrs. Henry Binder, is listening to the radio as well, as she's being dressed for a date by the other maid who works alongside her in the Binder household, the way-more-*svelte*, Nelli (Christiane Delyne). Once *gussied-up*, Poldi decides to send a personally-prepared fish-dinner upstairs, to a crazy (or is he?) neighbor, the wild-haired Maximilian Podoretz, who's played by Michel Simon, a guy who, alongside Jean Gabin and Raimu, is considered to be one of France's all-time great movie stars. Podoretz doesn't really venture into his own apartment that much: He mostly spends his days sitting out on his balcony-veranda (with his legs poking through the slats, it looks like he's sitting in a baby carriage), telling neighbors, as they wander around in the courtyard below, all kinds of crazy fabrications about himself, the most unbelievable one, being that he's a lawyer, and that he'll soon be receiving the money which he has just won, on his most recent jaunt to Monte Carlo. (He carries an omnipresent bag of beans, which he thinks are money!) Little neighborhood kids cheer Podoretz, whenever they see him: They have no idea he's crazy, and they just respond to him favorably, because, with their childish instinct, they know that he's nice, and that he has a good heart.

The next resident whom we'll be meeting, is Paula (Ariane Borg, who is credited in the film, under a different name, 'Olga Muriel'), a woman who is in love with Gabin's Charles secretly, even though he never gives her the time of day, but Charles isn't an insensitive asshole: Gabin plays him as being a really nice guy who's just super-busy and extremely pre-occupied with his sports career, as well as also being pre-occupied with *other girls who aren't Paula*, even though Paula's definitely the hottest babe in the movie. Paula's most fervent wish is that she and Charles might marry one day, even though committed bachelor Charles, as we can see, from the astounding numbers of women who hang around him, in this movie, has no interest in settling down at all, ever.

When next we check-in on the Binders' maid, Miss Poldi, her date is in progress, and it's a real hoot: She's actually jumping up and down, fully-clothed, on her bed, with her equally-stout boyfriend, Teddy, who's played by Jacques Lerner, and the two of them together look just like two gleeful kids who are having a whale-of-a-time (pun intended) at a slumber party. For them, sexual congress is obviously out of the question, due to their combined and individual, girths, and so jumping up and down is the only thing they can do together which, for them, can ever simulate any form of intimacy. Hilariously, Poldi's employers (Mr. and Mrs. Binder's) little lap dog, Apollo, happens to be bouncing around on the bed with them, too, and he's yapping with unbridled glee.

As Charles is arriving home that night, Paula's checking him out with lust, and she's about to approach him when, suddenly, another chick, Pola (Catherine Hesling) *cock-blocks her,* inviting Charles out with her to catch a show: Everybody in the building kisses Charles' ass, because Charles is a celebrity and, in this way, *Du haut en bas* pre-dates our 21st-century obsession with celebrity-culture by more than seventy years. Pola is sitting around the courtyard with Charles, watching him munch-out on the tasty snack which she's just brought him, and offering to wash his muddy, *postgame nastypants* for him, and he tells her, flirtatiously, that he can't remove his trousers in front of her, because he's so "delicate!"

Meanwhile, Mr. Binder (husband Henry is played by one of those French actors, who's *too cool to use his first name,* so he's just billed as 'Mauricet') and his wife, who's known in the film only as Mrs. Binder (she's played by Margo Lion, the French-born/German-living actress who was a good friend and, by all written accounts, *a whole lot more,* in real-life, to Marlene Dietrich), are returning home from an evening of operetta, and Miss Poldi, hearing them enter, tries to hide her porcine boyfriend in the closet, in the standard manner in which all bedroom farces (*and* French operettas, *and* American television sit-coms) operate. Of course, the Binders see Teddy right away, since he's too hefty to fit in the small closet, properly, and they instantaneously threaten to fire Poldi for bringing a guy home, even though Poldi looks to be at least two decades past the age of consent. They're also *majorly freaked-out,* because Apollo, their innocent and unsullied little doggie, was in the room with them during *their almost-concupisance:* "This is a mansion," Mrs. Binder yells at her maid, hysterically (even though this tiny apartment has absolutely nothing to do with a mansion)! "You can't do that here!" (They can't bounce on a bed? Is she serious?) Teddy tries to explain to the Binders that he's just shown up tonight, to 'bring Poldi something' (yeah: *cock!*), but they toss the big fella out on his *keister,* anyway. Meanwhile, upstairs, crazy Mr. Podoretz is getting hungry, and he starts wailing, helplessly, for anybody in the building who might be able to hear his voice, to come and bring him some food: "My stomach says it's 11:45! Lunch time! Somebody feed me!" Miss Poldi, who's in no mood for hijinks, after this dressing-down, by her bitchy mistress, offers to cook that bag of beans which he's always lugging around, but he tells her *no way,* since he doesn't want anybody cooking his 'money!' Not getting anywhere with Miss Poldi, he throws his jacket down to the other maid, Nelli, as she's walking by, and he then asks her if she can pawn it for him.

And just when we thought that everything was complicated enough, a beautiful blonde stranger, Maria Kruschina (Janine Crispin), enters the office of the apartment's scatterbrained-looking manager-slash-medical doctor, Dr. Fersteis. (The slang-word, *'fersteis'* is Yiddish, and it means, *'fucked,'* as in, *"you're so fucked!"*) She tells him that she'd love to have a job in a Doctor's Office: "I'm a history and geography teacher by profession, but jobs like that are hard to come by, and I really need any work I can get, and as soon as possible." When she starts crying, we know, suddenly, that there's going to be a lot more to her, and to her situation, than meets the eye. She looks like she hasn't eaten in weeks, so Fersteis brings her some food, which she politely declines, demurring, "I barely eat in midmornings… or in the afternoon… *or at night.*" (She's just like 'The Women of Today,' who don't eat when they're trying to land guys but who then proceed to *chunk-up*—and chop off all of their hair!—as soon as they've got the men under wraps.) He tells her that, while he doesn't need an assistant, he *is* aware that his upstairs neighbors, Mr. and Mrs. Binder, have been looking for a third maid to work alongside Poldi and Nelli. Maria tells the Doctor she'd love the job, if the Binders would consider hiring her on, but that she's got this one very pressing problem: She's going to need a fake I.D. to work because, as she tells Fersteis, her family is rich, and she doesn't want them to know that she's 'slumming it' (to get back at them?), by engaging in common labor, under her true identity. Like everybody else in the movie, Marie's not what she first appears to be and, as we've already figured out, each character in *Du haut en bas* is either 'poor, and pretending to be rich,' or else, 'rich, and pretending to be poor.' Director Pabst is (more than) implying that none of us is really who we seem to be, and that there's always more (and, most of the time, less) to all of us, than initially meets the eye. (As such, *Du haut en bas* is a great example of an expression which would become popular, some forty years after this movie was made, "You've got to fake it, 'til you make it.") While all of this 'pretending' is going on, Nelli, the Binders' other, and thinner, maid, has pawned Podoretz's shoes, in order to buy him some lunch, and what's very sweet about this movie, and what makes it so likeable and memorable, is that all of the people who live in this building, no matter how *loco en la cabeza* each one happens to be, really look out for each other, and while we're watching this picture, we're wishing that our own neighbors would look out for us, like this, too.

While Gabin's Charles Boulla doesn't pay too much attention to Paula, who continues to pine away for him from afar (and, much more often, from *anear*), he *does* take an immediate liking to Maria Krushcina, the building's hot newbie, and when he meets Maria, for the first time, he turns the Gabin-Charm 'up to eleven'—in fact, when Charles learns that Maria's just been hired-on as one of the Binders new housekeepers, he gallantly, and without her even having asked, begins hefting her suitcases upstairs to her new home. He next tries bragging to her about some of his recent soccer victories and, as he's doing this, it is to Jean Gabin's credit, as the fine actor he is, that he's not making the 'Charles' character come across as being sleazy or conceited: Charles is just really excited, because he's made himself a success in this life. (In fact, in ninety-five movies, which he'll make over forty-six years, you'll never, ever see Jean Gabin act sleazy.) He now I.D.'s himself to Maria, thusly: "I'm Charles Boulla, the *great* soccer player," and her response is classic: She's not interested in soccer, and only shrugs at him. We can tell from the way that his mouth drops when she does this, that he's definitely not used to this kind of non-response from a woman.

Poldi, meanwhile, tells her new charge, Maria, that she, herself, has been working for the Binders, for two years. Mrs. Binder, who's a classic bitch-on-toast, informs her new, young maid, Maria, that one of her duties in the household will be the care and feeding of Apollo, her little doggy; clearly, the Binders don't want Poldi taking care of Apollo, since she might be traumatizing the little nipper, by bouncing in front of it with fat guys!

Now: Enter a bumbling, violin-carrying, vagabond—who's played by Peter Lorre! Still identified with his child molester-character he played in Fritz Lang's haunting 1931 classic, *M*, Lorre was unable to score too many more starring roles in movies, and apparently strung-out on morphine in real life, he was forced to take whatever small movie roles he could get. This charming, no-named character doesn't utter a single syllable in the whole movie, but his hangdog expression and torn clothing cause even the building's poorest residents to start bestowing both money and food upon him. Maria sees him, and helps him pick up his violin when he drops it—and then, right after she hands it to him, he goofily drops it for a second time, on purpose. (This is a guy who really loves sympathy!)

Mrs. Binder, who we can tell right off the bat, doesn't have the most loving relationship in the world with her husband, is starved for somebody to talk to, and she takes delight in showing her new maid, Maria, the paintings of all of her *many* dead husbands, artworks which trail the complete length of her living room wall. All of her ex-husbands, just like the present one, were named 'Henry' and, presumably, the current Henry will one day (at least, if she has anything to say about it) be joining all of 'those Other Henries!' "All of them sent me chocolates and champagne," Mrs. B. yawns, as if the highest honor any man can attain in this life, is to make an appearance on her 'P-*Whipped* Wall-of-Fame.' Mrs. Binder can't be bothered *only* with chatting with 'the help,' though, and when late afternoon brings tea-time around, it's soon time for her to be sitting around her living room, blabbing-away with other rich—or, 'pretending to be rich'—*yenta-hausfraus* from the neighborhood, while they all munch-out on little cucumber sandwiches.

During today's particular *tea-stravaganza*, Charles stops over to the Binders apartment to say hi, and just as he's expected (he's shown up, for an ego-boost!), all of the old ladies immediately start going ga-ga, over him. "Here's our football star," gushes starfucker (she wishes!) Mrs. Binder. "He is a natural champion!" "How strong you are," one of the women, Helene (Olga Muriel) gloats, rubbing Charles' arms and chest, as though she's bidding-on a well-torsoed slave, at an Antebellum auction. "In football," Mrs. Binder tells her friends, "you need more legs, than arms!" Charles laughs, believing the whole thing to be funny, and he tells the women that he can't stay, because he's off on a hunting trip. The ladies, who are interested, ask what he's killed in the past, and he replies, acting extra surly, "Two rabbits… and *two policemen!*" Helene offers Charles a drink, and he tells her that he'd love to take it, but that his trainer wouldn't approve; and meanwhile, while all of this is going on, Peter Lorre's silent vagabond has been invited to the apartment of the building's plain-jane seamstress, Miss Kreuzbein (she's played by Pauline Carton), who's offering to sew up the sixteen-thousand holes in his pants, if only he'll take them off and stand behind her dressing-curtain, and, hilariously, while she's sewing up his *pantaloons,* he's behind the curtain, cutting holes into his *jacket,* because he needs holes in his clothing in order to garner sympathy, not to mention sympathy's red-headed stepchild—cash-flow.

But it's not just shrewish Mrs. Binder who's ogling people, today: When night falls, she's off to the opera, and her husband, the current Henry, doesn't want to go: Obviously, he means to stay home, so he can hit on his hot new maid, Maria, whom he's been smacking his lips over, ever since she first arrived.

Alone with Maria, and this is within about three seconds of his wife going out the door, 'the Lascivious Mr. B.' (*sounds like an Agatha Christie novel*) does the first thing which you should always do when you're trying to impress a new girl: He takes off his pants! "You seem to be afraid of me," he grins, stepping out of one 'leg' (which is, then, followed, by the other). "Is it because—I'm getting undressed?!" Henry asks her to bring him some wine, and she does it while looking away from him, because his flabby old physique is grossing her out, big-time. He tries to make her ladyloins quiver, by telling her about his own, successful hunting trips, and about how, on one such jaunt, he sustained a head injury which, as he's now bragging to her, he wears like a badge of honor. (Most of the people in this movie are definitely brain-damaged, but you've got to respect Henry Binder, because he's the only character who ever actually comes out and admits it!)

Henry, who is fascinated by his own stories (just like, for example, *every single person who lives in Los Angeles, today*), then looks away from Maria, for a moment, which is just long enough a period of time for her to dilute his wine with water, so that he won't get totally *faced* and jump her; but when she tries to leave the room, after serving him his 'near-wine,' he blocks the door with *his gnarly old bod.* Today, seventy-five-some years after the movie was made, this type of action is usually referred to as 'attempted rape,' and/or 'stalking,' or 'holding somebody against her will,' but in the innocent sex farces of the 1930s, it's all in good fun! (Remember the good old days before that crazy word, '*inappropriate*' came along, and put the kybosh on everything that's fun?)

"Why are you trying to leave?" he asks her, drunk-off-his-ass (it's 'the Placebo-effect,' in action!) on his *mineral water.* She tells him that she has to return to work, and he impotently whines, "But you're so cuuuuuuute!" "Don't worry about my being cute," she smiles uncomfortably, right before she pushes him away, amscraying to safety.

At night, while the building's old janitor, Mr. Berger (Vladimir Sokoloff) is sweeping out the courtyard (the guy moves at a snail's pace, but the tenants keep him around anyway, because they love him), Charles is sitting around, paying no attention to Paula, his secret-admirer, who's gotten all dolled-up for his benefit. And while he's cordial to her, and even semi-friendly, he's just not noticing her sexually, because he's still trying to impress the *buxotic* building-newbie, Maria, who happens, at this very moment, to be out-and-about in the courtyard as well, walking Mr. and Mrs. Binder's '*l'il ruff-ruff.*' Charles tries to impress Marie, goofily, after Paula storms off, by showing her a newspaper clipping about himself, which he keeps folded-up in his pocket for just such eventualities, in which he's winning that big game against Spain. "I've been everywhere," he brags to her, but she's now more unimpressed, than ever: "Where's 'everywhere?'" she retorts. "*Les Invalides?* [Paris's war memorial to dead soldiers!] The *Louvre?*" He asks her if he can kiss her (she says yes), and Mr. Binder is looking out the window the whole time, fascinated by the fact that, at least someone in the building is getting some nooky off of that hot little minx, Maria, even if it isn't him. Mr. Binder yells down to Charles, asking him what he's doing there, and Charles just Gabin-Shrugs, replying, stoically, that he's teaching her judo! Meanwhile, Michel Simon's goofy Podoretz, who never ever goes inside of his own apartment, even at night (Why does he even have an apartment, since he doesn't use it? [It's a very funny part of this movie.]), cools Charles and Maria's romantic ardor, by taking this moment to hit Charles up for ten francs, and when Charles turns him down flat, Podoretz is sublimely undeterred: "Well, okay! How about *five* francs?" Charles declines again, and he then starts playing soccer with neighborhood kids to impress Maria, although he's wasting his energy, since she's already, very clearly, pretty impressed by him.

While Charles is out, kicking the ball around with the kids, Podoretz (he's nuts, but he's still a guy, right?) is trying to make a move on Maria, as well: He tells her he can ascertain, just by looking at her hands, that she's not a real maid, and he now continues, with a totally-straight face, "I'm not a real poor guy, either! Did you know that *I am a prophet?*" Maria feels sorry for this bizarre curio-of-a-person, a guy who, most definitely, did *not* 'have her, at hello.' She's genuinely nice, though, and does feel sorry for old Podoretz so, very thoughtfully, she offers to sneak him one of her boss, Mr. Binder's, good jackets, so that he can stay warm out on his favored balcony, on cold nights.

While the Binders' maid, Miss Poldi, is continuing to date, or more accurately, just, 'to jump up and down on the bed with', Teddy, her big bear-of-a boyfriend, she, just like Paula, has an unrequited secret crush—but her crush isn't on Charles: It's on no other than crazy, old Maximilian Podoretz! Simultaneously, as Poldi's staring out of the Binder's kitchen window at Podoretz, who's out on his balcony as usual, and at the same time, as Paula is down in the courtyard, trying to impress Charles, the soundtrack now mists over with a typically 'movie-maudlin' song-of-longing, called "*Chaque semaine tiene sept jours*" or, in English, "Each Week Has Seven Days." Meanwhile, a busybody neighbor-lady who lives in another unit can't wait to share some gossip with Mrs. Binder: "So, I just saw that new maid of yours, downstairs… with Charles Boulla!"

Still down in the courtyard, Maria is now offering to teach Charles, post his soccer game with the kids, how to sing some songs from France's big, musical stage hit of the time, "*Arsene Lupin, le banquier*" (in English, "*Arsene Lupin, Banker*") and, in addition, she gives him some 'cultured' books to read, including *Madame Bovary*, but he tells her that he doesn't like to read, and that he can't sing, which is an in-joke, because, as all of France already knew, three years before *Du haut en bas* was made, back in 1930, and right before he starred in his first feature film, *Chacun sa chance,* Jean Gabin sang and performed on-stage in that very musical play.

Henry Binder, meanwhile, is growing more and more jealous of Charles' luck with white-hot Marie, and he even comes right out and asks the rugged footballer if he knows "… how many 'l's' there are, in [the word] jealous." When Mrs. Binder leaves the house for a second night of opera-going *sans* her hubby (and maybe, these frequent opera-jaunts suggest that she's really out with another man, although there's nothing in the movie which proves this), Mr. Binder takes the opportunity to hit on his lithesome chambermaid, again asking her if she'd like to go for a ride with him in his jaunty jalopy. He even offers, goofily, to become her boyfriend, and it's an offer which she most definitely can refuse.

Meanwhile, Miss Poldi has brought her dreamlover, Podoretz, a brand-spankin' new suit, which brings his new suit-total, to *two* new suits, counting that one, which Maria already gave him. And while all of the people in the building are always lamely hitting-on each other, the only one who's not trying to get into too many people's pants, surprisingly, is Charles Boulla, whom we'll next see in his apartment alone, hilariously reading the copy of *Madame Bovary* which Maria had given to him, and, even more hilariously, trying to make sense out of all them big words.

Later that same evening, cops show up in the building's courtyard, inquiring of the residents as to Maximilian Podoretz's whereabouts (he's disappeared for the very first time, from his usual perch, on his balcony), since Podortez, as we're now finding out, has committed some crimes, although the film will never tell us exactly what kind. (Doesn't sound like these crimes would be too big; he's crazy, but he doesn't come across as being 'bad,' and so, maybe, he just stole some shoelaces, or something.). Miss Poldi warns Podoretz, who's actually inside of the Binders' apartment, of the law's presence, inviting him to hide out in her own bedroom, since her employers, the Binders, have already gone to sleep, and when the cops finally burst into Podoretz's apartment, they're shocked, when they discover a figure which is hanging by the neck from a rope; upon further examination, it turns out that the hanging figure is only Podoretz's new suit jacket, hanging from a noose, some very clever subterfuge, which Podoretz has meant to misdirect the cops. (So Podoretz isn't a total idiot, after all.) Podoretz, meanwhile, feels shitty, because he has nowhere to go, and Poldi offers him a good hide-out, at her family's farm in Spitz, Germany.

That night, Charles and Marie are dining in a fancy restaurant, and she's continuing to give him culture lessons, which he's playing along with, very good-naturedly. She gently reprimands him about how he makes too much noise when he drinks, and how she can always hear him sipping his coffee, "in the mornings." (Aha! So they've made love already! She's around, when '*Le Yuban*' is percolating!) She tries to get Charles to remove his elbows from the table while he's eating, and he's getting riled, but only slightly, since Jean Gabin rarely gets too worked-up about anything. ("How can I eat, if my elbows aren't on the table," he wonders.) She tells him, too, that his napkin belongs in his lap, and not across his chest like a baby's bib, which is exactly how he's wearing it. Charles is frustrated, because he really wants to impress Marie, but he just doesn't know the first thing about Emily Post, at all; like a lot of Jean Gabin's working-class characters, he's charmingly out of his element, when it comes to life's pretentious fineries (which is a good thing)!

Next, to illustrate to Maria that he *is* possessed of *some* culture, he starts quoting some half-remembered passages to her from *Madame Bovary*, and she thinks that the effort he's putting into trying to recite the story's lines correctly, is very cute. When these two (*Beauty and the Beast*) leave the restaurant, the first thing they come upon is a baby carriage with water leaking out of the bottom, and she gasps, thinking that she's watching an abandoned baby urinate, but it's really a baby carriage full of leaky fruit! This carriage is a surprise gift from Charles to Maria, and it's his inarticulately-roundabout way of asking her if she'd like to get married and have a baby with him, without his actually having to say those wimpy words, himself, because Jean Gabin's quiet movie characters always know, instinctively, that 'words are for losers.' She's impressed by his bizarre, but sweet, gesture and, instead of showing her true feelings for him, she now looks like she's about to start weeping, out of sheer joy. She sublimates her feelings into, as our British brothers and sisters often say, taking the piss out of him, and asking him if he's the person who stole the baby cart.

Up at the Binders' place, meanwhile, and under cover of the night, Miss Poldi has packed her suitcases, and is readying herself to join Podoretz at her farm, in Spitz. As she's leaving, she gives rail-thin maid Nelli some sage advice, telling her not to resist Mr. Binder's gross advances. Poldi probably has an idea that, after Mr. Binder dumps Mrs. Binder, that Nelli could use the situation to her advantage, marrying him and, thereby, squeezing some bread out of the weird old freak!

Come the weekend, we find that the residents of our U-shaped building are all busy, sprucing the place up: After all, the building is part of all of their identities and, just like they all want to put their own personal, best 'human' faces forward, so, too, do they also want to do the same thing, *vis-a-vis* their building's fascia. Charles whistles away, from high atop a ladder, where, currently, he's involved in some heavy-duty re-shingling action, and there's some good news to be had, as well: Dr. Fersteis has found Maria a proper teaching position in Austria, because, apparently, there's a 'morality class' (!) in Salzburg which needs a teacher, and Maria's going to be leaving our little cuckoo's nest, to start this new job, effective immediately. Charles looks forlorn, when Maria tells him that she's leaving, but she tries to make it up to him by giving him something new to read, a dog-eared paperback copy of *Anna Karenina*. He tries to turn the lemon which he's just been handed (loneliness) into '*limonade*,' telling her he'd like to go to Salzburg with her, because he's truthfully (there is no lying, in Jean Gabin) in love with her, and he even admits to her now, very sweetly, that she's the only real friend he's ever had, and this is true: She's the only character in the entire film who doesn't care about his soccer career, and who likes him, 'just for him.' She tells him, though, that she has to go it alone, and so he starts grasping at anything he can think of, which might make her stay: "You know, you might not know this, but women can't live without men!" She nips his progressive, new ideas in the bud, however, just leaving him with a dispassionate cry of, "think of me," before running away from him quickly, not wanting him to see her face, which, at the present moment, happens to be squirting out major tears. Charles is crushed, and if you want to know why, in many of the films which will follow this one, Jean Gabin's characters will seldom open-up to the women whom he truly loves, the seeds of his movie persona's future famed closed-offedness can be seen in early pictures like this one, or like *Pour un soir..!,* films in which, as soon as Gabin's characters open-up to women, they get their hearts trampled on.

But the real thing that's wounding Charles is as much of a surprise to him as it is to us: He has no idea that Maria's going away to teach, believing erroneously that Mr. Binder is leaving Mrs. Binder, and that Maria's going off to be with *him!* Mrs. Binder knows that her present Henry has cheated on her, and not with Maria, but in the past, with other women, and that's got to be one of the main reasons that she's such a shrew.

That night, Maria's preparing to leave, and she's going from apartment to apartment, bidding goodbye to the nice neighbors, whom, in her short time in the building, she has come to know, and love. At that moment, a surly Cop makes an appearance at the Binders' place, and he gives Mr. and Mrs. B. 'the skinny,' on Maria: "Folks, I hate to tell you this, but your maid, Ms. Maria Krushcina, has spent two months in jail, for theft and prostitution!" The Binders are shocked, and the Cop now starts using Maria's absence from the apartment, to start rooting through her packed belongings. At this point, Maria and Dr. Fersteis enter the Binders' apartment together, and Fersteis explains to the cops, truthfully, that Maria was never in jail, that she's not really 'Maria Kruschina' at all, and that she's merely another woman who's using Maria Kruschina's identity papers—papers which he, himself, gave to her. Mrs. Binder doesn't believe what Fersteis is telling them, and he sends the Good Doctor a little dollop of sarcasm. ("Thank you for sending us a prostitute to be our maid!")

At this point, Podoretz enters the apartment, as well. (He was too scared of leaving the building to attempt a trip to Spitz, as Poldi had invited him to do.) Hearing that Maria's in trouble, he again starts claiming to be a lawyer but, before he gets too far, Mr. Binder starts chewing him a new one: "You *can't* be a lawyer. Those aren't even your pants! Those are my pants!" The Cop-on-the-scene, still believing that our Maria is 'the other Maria' (a/k/a/, the 'whore/thief'-Maria), tries to handcuff her, but just then heroic Charles arrives on the scene, and just in the nick of time! He doesn't *exactly* come to her rescue, although he definitely means well, with the announcement which he is now making, to all-assembled: "Even if Maria is those things that you've just accused her of, I love her anyway!"

So now, we're wondering about 'our' Maria's true identity, and here it is (hold on to your berets): She's Dr. Fersteis' own daughter—Maria Fersteis! (But even she didn't know her true identity, because Dr. Fersteis gave her up for adoption, when she was young.) Now, Mrs. Binder, whose feelings toward people change as often as most people change their underpants, instantly starts adoring Maria, again: "Are you really a school teacher? Can't you stay-on here and tutor the neighborhood kids?" And as all of this is going on, Poldi is skipping off-screen with Podoretz (literally, the two of them are *skipping*)! She really does own a farm in Spitz, and they really *are* going there together, to live in peace, happiness, and undoubtedly, three square meals per day.

Early the next morning, Charles is bidding goodbye to Maria, but he doesn't look unhappy about her incipient departure, because he's optimistic that he'll be seeing her again. She's embarrassed about not being able to get her valise shut, and predating the wit and wisdom of Gloria Steinem by more than forty years, she frustratedly shouts out, "I'm an emancipated woman, and yet I can't even close my own suitcase!" Mr. Berger, the building's slow-moving old janitor, asks her what the word 'emancipation' means, and the newly-cultured Charles tells everybody, confidently, that emancipation is "a kind of football." And just like everybody else in the building, Janitor Berger has a secret, too, and, amusingly, he has picked right now, to reveal what that secret is, telling the amassed crowd that, while he *does* happen to be a custodian at the present time, he used to, before his retirement, and when he was younger, be a medical doctor! Charles tells Maria, excitedly, that he and his team will be playing football in Salzburg the following week, and that, because she's moving to Salzburg, that he hopes they'll be able to meet-up there.

Dissolve to a few days later: All of the families who live in our crazy but love-filled apartment complex, are reading their newspapers and, according to the sports section, Charles has not only just won his latest soccer game in Salzburg, but now, additionally, he's engaged to Maria. "She will teach him many things," one old biddy in the apartment building winks at another.

Just like at the end of *Mephisto*, *Du haut en bas*, too, ends with a scene in which a band is serenading a newly-married couple: In this picture, the band is *oom-pah-pahing* away, outside of Charles and Maria's honeymoon hotel window, in Salzburg. The couple was married days ago, and the band is serenading not them, but—surprise!—Maximilian Podoretz and Miss Poldi, who were also married, only today, and who happen to be standing on the street, outside of The Boullas' window, chatting with Charles and Maria, and listening to the band. As Charles and Maria wish them well, Podoretz and 'his new missus,' after they listen to the band for a few moments, walk away together, with their two umbrellas sweetly intertwined.

While one can make arguments, one way or another, about why so many of Jean Gabin's movies were never released in the U.S., the fact that *Du haut en bas* never made it to American shores is nothing short of cultural robbery. Not only is it a fun, laugh-packed, ensemble flick, but it's also got a great message, which is that we're all the same, irrespective of social class, or by extension, color or creed. The one flaw in the movie is that poor Paula, who's played by Ariane Borg (the girl whom we met near the beginning of the movie, who had a crush on Gabin's character) just kind of disappears about three-quarters of the way through the movie. We want to see her get some happiness, and so the fact that there is no resolution to her thread of the story kind of sucks, but, in a way, it's also okay, too; I mean, in real-life, how many of us ever really get to be with the people we really want? (True Answer: None of us.)

Currently, as this book goes to print, there is only one surviving thirty-five millimeter print of *Du haut en bas* in existence, and I was able to view it at the archives of the Royal Cinematheque of Belgium, in Brussels (and the print, by the way, is in pristine condition). It's too bad that the world is completely ignorant of a wonderful Jean Gabin/Peter Lorre/G.W. Pabst comedy, because *Du haut en bas* is definitely "*Du haut* to handle," and yet, at the same time (to misquote some 'old school rap lyrics'), not "too cold to hold!" The French critic from whom I'm about to quote, who reviewed the movie in 1933, didn't like the film as much as I did, but keep in mind that he was writing his review of the movie seventy-five years ago.

What a Critic Said at the Time: "Is it a bad film? I think not. Certain passages are well brought out and it is, above all, not important enough to merit serious reproach. There remain a few scenes sprinkled throughout the film that have good humor and a few good actors that we watch willingly." (Magazine: *Les Annales Politiques et Litteraires*, 12-22-33 issue. Critic: Pierre Bost. Reviewed in Paris.)

FILM 15

Adieu les beaux jours

The third of three lost Jean Gabin films (1933)

Like *La Foule hurle* and *L'Etoile de Valencia*, *Adieu les beaux jours (Goodbye, Beautiful Days)* is a missing Jean Gabin movie. Just like *L'Etoile de Valencia*, *Adieu les beaux jours*, too, is a German/French co-production which was filmed in Germany, by the production company UFA, and which Goebbels destroyed during World War II. Fortunately, just like with *L'Etoile de Valencia*, the producers also filmed a second, simultaneous, 'alternate' German-language version of the picture, *Die Schonen tage von Aranjuez*, with German actors, standing in for Jean Gabin and the rest of the French cast, and this version *does* exist today. It stars Wolfgang Liebeneiner, in the role which Jean Gabin played in the French version and, as a substitution, here is my report on the 'Gabinless' German-language version, which I screened at the Bundesfilmarchiv, in Berlin.

Die Schoenen Tage von Aranjuez

Germany, 1933
German-Language, Alternative Version of Jean Gabin's missing film, "Adieu les beaux jours"

(Literal English Translation: "BEAUTIFUL DAYS IN ARANJUEZ") Directed by Johannes Meyer. Produced by Max Pfeiffer. Screenplay by Peter Francke and Gerd Karlick. Based Upon the Play by Robert A. Stemmle and Hans Szekely. Director of Photography (black and white), Friedl Behn-Grund. Production Designers, Erich Kettelhut and Max Mellin. (GENRE: COMEDY) A Production of UFA. Running Time, 1 hour 41 minutes. Released in Germany on September 22, 1933. Never Released Theatrically in the United States.

Die Schonen tage von Aranjuez (*Beautiful Days in Aranjuez*) begins with a shot of the mountains of southern Spain, and it's accompanied by a theme song which features the usual, sappy/1930s movie-music lyrics. (Sample: "How I like it, in the grand world!") We next cut to an office in Paris, where we see a handsome young man, Pierre Duval, who's played by the actor Wolfgang Liebeneiner, the actor who's taken over the role which Jean Gabin played in the lost French version (in the Gabin version, weirdly, the character is called 'Pierre Lavernay,' instead of 'Pierre Duval,' but in both the French and German versions, *weirdly*, both of those surnames are French!), sitting at his desk, cheerfully working on a crossword puzzle; so, at once, we're getting both the idea that he's a total innocent, and also, that somebody in the movie is going to be trying to *screw him over, big-time*. Pierre's a salesman for a big Paris car company called 'Diavolo 8,' and he's excited, because these are his last few minutes of work before he leaves for a week's vacation: He's going to be driving south to Spain, to frolic in the sun in a brand new Diavolo 8, which his company will be loaning him.

Director Johannes Meyer, who took over, in the German-language version, for the great screenwriter/novelist Andre Beucler, who helmed the French version, then cuts to the fancy jewelry store which belongs to Charles Dergan (Jakob Tiedtke). A very high-toned-looking lady who, from her patrician looks, has got to be royalty of some sort, enters the store, and her eyes are immediately drawn to the most opulent pearl necklace you've ever seen. She calls herself the 'Baronness Olga,' and she's played by Brigitte Helm, who will also appear with Jean Gabin in the French-language version of this picture. (Helm, of course, also played Andre Luguet's wife in *Gloria* and Gabin's wife in *L'Etoile de Valencia*). She tells jeweler-Dergan that she notices a flaw in the piece, and he congratulates her on her savvy, adding that he'll be happy to sell her the necklace for the ultra-low price of only eight hundred and fifty thousand francs. She tells him she's definitely interested, although, because of the flaw, she'd like him to knock fifty thousand off of his price. Obviously, because *she's hot*, he does so, and without even batting an eye.

Olga tells Jeweler Dergan that she's not in the habit of carrying cash around, and that he should send the bill to her husband, Dr. Rommay, a very prominent Paris neurologist. (The movie takes place in Paris, but like all of UFA's German/French co-productions, the interiors were shot entirely in Germany.) Dergan tells Olga that he'll go and see her husband tonight, personally.

And now, *the con is on:* After leaving Dergan's jewelry store, Olga high-tails it over to Dr. Rommay's office (Rommay's played by Max Gulstorff), and not only is she not married to Rommay, but Rommay's never seen her before in his entire life! Olga tells Rommay that she's married to Dergan, the jeweler (!), and that she doesn't know what to do about her husband, because he's afflicted with a strange mania: He often visits prominent people in their offices, and presents them with bills for expensive jewelry, which the people-in-question have neither bought nor received. She tells Rommay that her delusional jeweler-husband will be visiting him tonight, and that Rommay should just ignore the fake bill and immediately remand him into the care of a mental institution. What's particularly funny, in this scene, is that Dr. Rommay's office is located on '7 *rue Maligon*,' which translates, into English, roughly, as 'Number 7, Sickly Street,' which is a very funny address for a psychiatrist's office.

That night, right on cue, Jeweler Dergan arrives at Dr. Rommay's office and presents him with the invoice for the 850,000 francs. ("Here is the bill for the necklace that your wife bought, today.") Rommay, who has no idea that 'griftress' Olga is playing him against

With Brigitte Helm.

Dergan, now tries to set him straight: "You're giving me a bill for a necklace which my wife bought, today? My friend, may it interest you to know that I don't have a wife, and that I have never authorized anybody to buy any necklace. This is all a fantasy you're having, right?" Believing Dergan to be insane, Rommay buzzes a buzzer under his desk, and two men with white coats come in, dragging the poor jeweler away.

Olga makes it home safely to her Paris flat, and the first thing she sees, is a goon who's switching her car's license plates for her, and this is something which this particular guy probably does, a lot. Heading upstairs, she's now face-to-face with her chrome-domed grifting partner and boyfriend, Alexandre, who's played by Gustaf Grundgens (the guy who played the *uber*-bad guy, Woolf, opposite Jean Gabin, in *Le Tunnel*). Whenever they grift together, Olga pretends to be a Baroness and Alexandre is always a Baron and, as it will soon become clear, the two of them, like all of movie history's other, great grifting teams, have lots of identities, which they change as often as you and I change our underwear.

Alexandre informs Olga that she's going to have to drive south to Biarritz, which is eleven miles north of the Spanish border, to deposit the necklace with their chosen fence, a guy by the name of Sebastian, and right after we see this, the picture's director, Johannes Meyer now cuts to a courtroom: Jeweler-Dergan and Dr. Rommay are both standing before a Judge (Rommay's taken Dergan before the Judge, for permission to have Dergan remanded into his care), and hizzoner is reaming both of them out for being the rubes which he knows, very clearly, that both of them are: "All of Paris is laughing at you two clowns, because this woman duped both of you. In my opinion, instead of working against each other, it would behoove the two of you to work together, to help us find this Olga." This scene is kind of a loose-thread, because neither Dergan nor Rommay will, during the course of this movie, be looking for Olga themselves, but the police will.

The next day, Olga's driving south. Police throughout southern France have been notified that she's on the loose with the expensive necklace, and they've also been notified that it shouldn't be too tough to track her down, because, even though her cohort changed her license plates, he didn't change the large decorative horseshoe which her car happens to have mounted on its back. At one point, two motorcycle cops see Olga whizzing by, and they start chasing her through some scarily-twisty mountainous roads, and when one cop blows-out a tire, the second cop stops to help him. Free, at least for awhile, Olga gets to an overpass where nobody can see her, pulls her car up to the edge of a precipice, and pushes the vehicle off of it; naturally, the vehicle explodes, rolling down a mountain, and its charred remains land in a cave.

Now that filmmaker Meyer has given us some 'action,' it's time (*ooh-la-la!*) for 'romance:' The now-vacationing young car exec, Pierre (a/k/a/, 'Crossword Puzzle Boy') happens to be driving by the precipice from which Olga's just dumped her car. (Pierre's such an innocent that, whenever he's in the movie, he's always accompanied, on the film's soundtrack, by his own 'happy-go-lucky' musical-theme, which sounds like outtakes from the opening of American television's popular 1960s' sit-com, "The Andy Griffith Show.") He sees Olga standing by the side of the cliff, and he stops, unable to believe his good fortune.

Pierre tells Olga that he's on his way to Pau, in the south of France (yes, it's the place where berets—and some of this author's own French cousins—come from), and that he'd be happy to give her a lift. She tells him that she's on her way to Biarritz, which is further south than Pau is—in fact, Biarritz, which borders Spain, is about as far south as you can get, in France, without actually falling off. He tells her he'll be happy to take her "all the way." (!)

The two really seem to like each other (he asks her, shyly, "Aren't you happy that I'm your chauffeur?"), and he drives her all the way to Biarritz, dropping her off at the fancy beachside hotel where she's already booked a room. She invites him to join her the following day for a sailboat ride, and he's happy to accept the offer.

Meanwhile, back at the site where Olga had dumped her car off of the cliff, director Meyer next cuts to the cave, where a gaggle of cops are checking out the remaining detritus of the destroyed vehicle, and the cops have even got a secretary/stenographer down in the cave with them, a woman who's actually sitting on a rock, typing away. When the lawmen start foraging through what's left of the car's trunk, they find Olga's suitcase: It's pretty burned-up, and when they rub some ashes off of it, they notice a brass tag, and this is how they learn that the suitcase was made personally, for 'the Baroness Olga,' by the luggage-maker Jose Rosas, who's based in San Sebastian. The French cops radio-over to some Spanish cops who, now taking the lead, head into Rosas' shop, to have a few words with the guy. Rosas informs them that he's only made three suitcases like the one which he made for 'the Baroness,' in his entire life, and that all he knows about her, as he's now telling them, is that she lives "… somewhere in France."

The next day, Olga takes Alexander out for the sailboat ride which she had promised him, and she continues, very sweetly, to refer to him, as "my chauffeur," although, at the same time, she's also flirting with Gaston (Paul Fromet), the boat's elderly owner, whom she has hired to take her and Pierre out onto the ocean, for 'their special day.' Clearly, Olga and Gaston know each other already and, conspiratorially, Gaston now tells her that, for an additional hundred francs (beyond the hundred francs, which she's already paying him), he'll take them out of French/Spanish waters, and into international waters—a/k/a, the Mediterranean—where, of course, she'll be free from the police. When a French Coast Guard boat happens by, the officer on deck asks Gaston where he's going with the young couple, and Gaston tells the guy, with an innocent, smiling shrug, that he's just taking them toward the Mediterranean, as part of their romantic date. Gaston next starts waxing poetically to the cop, spewing out mega-corny platitudes, like, "There are no frontiers, for love!" and "Love is not subject to duties!"

When the Coast Guard boat leaves, Gaston docks his boat off of the coast of San Sebastian, and Pierre, who's still blissfully ignorant that his new fantasy woman is a wanted jewel-thief, and Olga arrive at the city's majestic Continental Palace Hotel. When the two of them enter the teeming venue, Pierre is amazed and impressed, because everybody there seems to know her—as a Baroness, no less!—and everybody is genuinely excited to see her. The manager tells her that her usual room is all ready for her and, for appearance's sake, she orders up a second room for Pierre.

When Olga gets up to her room, she gets a surprise which we expected, but which she didn't: Her chrome-domed crime partner, Alexandre (a/k/a, 'the Baron') is already there, and he's waiting for her. He congratulates her on getting out of France with the necklace, and demands that she hand it over to him, and *stat!* Clearly, she's afraid that, once Alexandre fences the necklace himself, that he'll try to welsh on giving her, her 'cut', so she tells him that, in lieu of going through Sebastian (the 'fence-guy,' not the city), that she's going to try and sell the piece, herself, and maybe, to one of the wealthier hotel guests. But he tells her not to be stupid: "You can't sell that necklace, here. It has a defect. And since it's one of a kind, if you try to sell it, you'll go to jail."

Olga and Alexandre continue their business conversation in the teeming hotel lobby, where an opera performance happens to be taking place, and this is the moment where she confesses to Alexandre that she's recently just met a young man, Pierre, with whom she's falling in love, and that, for the first time in her whole life, she's thinking about leaving crime, going straight, and settling down; when Olga gushes to Alexandre about Pierre, there's genuine love in her eyes, and we get the feeling that this is the first time in her life in which she's ever actually felt real, heartfelt feelings for a man, instead of just feeling what's in his wallet! Alexandre hates hearing this, because, as he's telling her now, he thinks that the two of them should get married to each other, and buy a poultry farm! He warns her that, in his opinion, she's making two huge mistakes (in falling in love with Pierre instead of with him, and in wanting to fence the necklace, on her own), and that she'd better get her ass in gear, because, after they finish this caper, he's already booked a new con for them to pull: After they get rid of the necklace together, he tells her that, for their next crime, they're going to be heisting the Bank of Madrid, and that after they do that, he's going to take her for a few weeks of R&R in southern Spain's resort town of Aranjuez, which is about thirty miles south of Madrid. She tells him, in no uncertain terms, that she wants no part of his future plans and, now pissed, he starts threatening her that she'd better hand the necklace over, and right now. Fate intercedes on her behalf, though, and because she's truly falling in love, for the first time in her life, Fate is kind: Suddenly, the lobby, which was already crowded to begin with (with opera-watching guests), now starts filling up with French and Spanish cops, who descend upon the hotel, in great numbers. When Alexandre sees the cops, he ducks into a phone booth, and Olga hides behind a column. Pierre, who's been in the lobby the whole time, checking out the opera performance, grabs her by the shoulders, and this is the scene in which we're learning that he's not as dopey as he looks because, for the first time, it's now dawning on him that she has something—and, probably, everything—to do with why the cops are there:

> PIERRE: Look, I don't know what it is that you've done, Olga, but whatever it is—I don't care! Come with me, and I'll help you. I'll make sure nobody ever gets to you.
> OLGA: You don't really know who I am, Pierre. It's too dangerous for you to be with me. Please, just let me go!

Even though Olga's probably never been honest with anybody for even a single day of her whole life, she's genuinely into Pierre, as we can now see by the smoldering glances which they're sending each other in this scene, and she doesn't want to hurt him.

Pierre, who truly doesn't want to know what Olga's done (like most men, he likes his women to be possessed of a little mystery) helps her to make her getaway and, when we see the two of them next, they're back in Pierre's Diavolo-8, and she's instructed him to take her to Seville. Obviously, she wants to fence the necklace there, before Alexandre gets to her and, as the Diavolo-8 careens through a mountainous overpass, Olga finally tells Pierre her whole story over his protestations, including the fact she's a jewel thief, and that, besides being chased by the police, she's also on the run from that bald guy who was lurking around the hotel lobby—her psychotic partner, Alexandre. Pierre, who recognizes Olga's essential goodness, tells her that he loves her, and that, as long as she promises him she'll go straight (and she makes that promise, in the very next sentence) and 'give the necklace' back to the jeweler, as soon as they arrive back in France, that he'll even let her hide the necklace in one of his hubcaps, for safekeeping. Amusingly, as the Diavolo zooms out of frame, a couple of comedy-relief farmers who are standing on the side of the road, recognize her, and one nudges the other: "There's Olga again. Guess she found herself another sucker!" And of course, they're more than comedy-relief: They're two of Alexandre's carefully-placed henchmen, and they now report to Alexandre about where they think Olga may be going.

The cops are currently unable to trace Olga, since she and Pierre are now whizzing through southern Spain's back roads, and as they do, director Meyer starts superimposing teletyped-written messages over them, messages which are being typed-out, in real-time between law enforcement offices in many of Europe's various capitals: The first teletype, which is meant to be issuing from the Spanish police, reads, "Beaumont [Olga's last name; yes, as we're finding out now, she's British, not French] has escaped from San Sebastian with her cheeky tricks!" Since she's British, and because she's wanted in the U.K. (she's also considered to be a public enemy, for other crimes which she has committed, in the past, both in France and in Spain), Scotland Yard is now in on the action, as well, and the British crime-fighting organization next responds with a teletyped-message of its own, which reads: "Olga Beaumont… still in business with John Link," and 'John Link,' as we're now discovering, is Alexandre's real name, and the same teletype message mentions that he, like Olga, is also wanted, in other parts of Europe, for other crimes which he, too, has committed—many of them, under yet another alias: 'Reginald Parker.'

Next, we see Pierre and Olga arriving in beautiful Seville, and a bunch of small children immediately swarm around the Diavolo-8, fascinated by the ultra-cool car. Of course, what Pierre and Olga didn't count on, but we did, because we already saw those henchmen, is that Alexandre has followed them to Seville, and since Olga and Pierre are spotting him before he can see them, they now make an ultra-quick decision to just keep driving. Soon arriving at a crossroads, where they can choose between two small southern towns, Cadiz and Ronda, Olga and Pierre choose Ronda. (*Fun Fact:* The town of Ronda, today, just like back then, is where the world's lost souls go, to enlist in the Spanish Foreign Legion.)

In Ronda, Olga and Pierre make 'love, sweet love' (*per* Burt Bacharach), up in Olga's hotel room, and they then head downstairs into the courtyard, where a huge garden party is in progress. The people who run the hotel have invited Olga to this fancy-do, because it's a feather in their caps to have a real (they think) 'Baroness' present, but it's difficult for Olga to enjoy the proceedings all that much, because this fenced-in garden party happens to be papered with wanted posters, posters which have her and Alexandre's faces on them, and which state that a fifty thousand-peseta reward will be awarded to whoever finds the two of them and brings 'em back, alive. Alexandre is now circulating through the party as well, because he was tipped-off, by his henchmen, that Olga would be there, and he's noticing the posters now, too, at about the same time that she's noticing them. Both Alexandre and Olga have figured out that the jig is up, and fatalistically, they are both too tired now to run, after all (because, as the saying goes: "You can't run away, from yourself!") Cops swarm toward the party, and Olga, who realizes that she's only got a few seconds of freedom left, tells Pierre that she's going away and, most probably, for good, and that she really does love him. The two kiss tenderly, and she instructs him to get a move-on, since he's not involved with her criminal life, nor does she want him to be considered an accessory to her crimes. The crowd parts, as the Spanish *policias* swarm in, arresting Alexandre and Olga, who don't even put up a fight. Pierre watches this happen (sadly) from a distance, after which he walks away alone and, for what is probably the very first time, in his entire life, he doesn't look so ' happy-go-lucky.' It's still, *per* the film's title, a 'beautiful day in Aranjuez,' but now it's a bit less-so, because our story's true lovers are fated never to be together. (Even though the Jean Gabin version of the film doesn't exist anymore, the whole walking away alone-conceit is a total Gabin ending, which means that the lost Jean Gabin movie, *Adieu les beaux jours,* should properly be considered the first of many movies, in which Gabin's character, who is almost always Fated for Eternal Sadness, will walk away all alone, at the end of the picture.)

In 1935, the Robert Stemmle/Hans Szekely play, "*Die Schonen tage von Aranjuez,*" upon which the two 1933 (French and German) UFA-produced films, *Die Schonen tage von Aranjuez* and *Adieu les beaux jours,* were both based, would be re-made in America by Paramount Pictures, this time under the title, *Desire,* and starring Marlene Dietrich as the lady grifter and Gary Cooper as her happy-go-lucky car-exec/loverboy. The American movie is basically the same as the French and German ones, with a few, key alterations: In the American/Dietrich-Cooper version, the young car exec and the lady-grifter's oily male crime partner are actively competing with each other for her attentions, using all kinds of one-upsmanship on each other, and we don't get to see this in the French and German film versions, and the American version also features a portly cop-character, played by the great Akim (remember in *For Whom the Bell Tolls,* when he hissed, "*I don't provoke*") Tamiroff, who's forever on Dietrich's tail. The biggest difference between the twin European versions which were made in 1933, and the American version, which was produced in 1935, however, is that, in the American one, we naturally get the happy ending which the European versions denied us, an ending in which Dietrich's lady-jewel-thief serves her time in jail, is released, goes straight, and then marries the young car exec; and not only that, but *also* in the American version, the jeweler from whom she had stolen the necklace is even present at the wedding ceremony, to give her away! Since the Jean Gabin version of this story no longer exists today, and because the German one, which I've just unpacked for you, exists only as one 35mm-print in the entire world, in Berlin, Germany's Bundsesfilmarchiv, you won't be slumming it if you can only see the easily-available (on U.S. DVD) American/Dietrich-Cooper version. In its own right, *Desire,* just like *Die Schnonen tage von Aranjuez,* and probably also, like *Adieu les beaux jours,* is one of the 1930s' best, and most fun, movie comedies.

While director Andre Beucler's French-language, Jean Gabin version of *Adieu les beaux jours* does not exist today, it did open in New York, at the 65th Street Playhouse, on April 21, 1934 (not with English subtitles, but with occasional English-language title cards, which were flashed every few minutes to advance the film's major plot-points), and *Variety's* critic,

'Wolfe' (Wolfe Kaufman), filed this review of the film, in the May 8, 1934 issue:

"[*Adieu les beaux jours*] is a fast action yarn. [Jean] Gabin is one of the younger French juveniles who seems to have a future. With some adroit handling, he can develop into a big star. For some reason, producers of this film are hiding its German identity, and presenting it as [being] completely, French, afraid that its German origins may hurt it's box-office potentialities."

At the outset of this book project, I wrote a letter to the Andre Beucler Society in Paris, asking them if they knew anybody who had a print of the Gabin version of the film, and I received a very short/curt letter back from them: "Dear Mr. Zigman: If you are writing a book about Jean Gabin, please learn to speak French." (Wow! Not everybody can be supportive of a creative project!)

✤

THE FILMS
CYCLE TWO

Gabin as The Ultimate Pre-War Tragic Drifter
#1 Star in France and Famous Throughout the World
His French Films from this Period Make Him
Famous in The United States, as Well

FILM Nos. 16 to 31, 1934 — 1941

OF JEAN GABIN'S NINETY-FIVE FILMS, ONLY EIGHT ARE KNOWN TODAY IN THE United States, and five of those eight films were made during this period, the actor's 'Second Cycle' of films. During this cycle, Gabin will begin playing the famous doomed, tragic drifter character for which he remains the most known today throughout most of the world. In many of these films, Gabin's character has committed a crime (or has been accused of committing a crime, or has deserted his military post) before the movie began. His characters know that they are fated for imprisonment or death, so they'll usually engage in action-packed adventures, while romancing scads of hot brunettes along the way. 1935's *La Bandera*, 1937's *Pepe Le Moko*, 1938's *Le Quai des brumes*, and 1939's *Le Jour se leve* are the most significant examples of this trope.

The movies which Jean Gabin made during this period are part of a cinematic style known as Poetic Realism, which was particular to France during the mid-to-late 1930s. They deal with the frustrating lives of regular, working-class people, but in a poetic and very often highly-stylized manner, and the filmmakers who directed Gabin in these pictures included Jean Renoir, Marcel Carne, Julien Duvivier, and Jean Gremillon. Stylistically, Poetic Realist films are very dark and claustrophobic, because in the mid-to-late '30s, the French people, who were on the verge of being conquered by Germany, often felt helpless, tense, and pulled by outside forces, and the films of Poetic Realism crystallized this feeling, emotionally. 1938's *Le Quai des brumes* and 1939's *Le Jour se leve*, both of which were directed by Marcel Carne and star Gabin, are considered to be two of the darkest Poetic Realist films ever made, and not just stylistically (lots of shadows, fog, and night-time), but emotionally, as well.

Josephine Baker, Jean Gabin.

FILM 16

Zou Zou

France, 1934

Directed by Marc Allegret. Produced by Arys Nissotti. Screenplay by Carlo Rim and Albert Willemetz. Based Upon a Novella by Pepito G. Abatino. Music by Alain Romans, Georges Van Parys, Roger Bernstein, Vincent Scotto, and Georges Koger. Directors of Photography (black and white), Boris Kaufman, Michel Kelber, Jacques Mercanton, and Louis Nee. Editor, Denise Batcheff. Production Designers, Lazare Meerson and Alexandre Trauner. Choreography by Floyd Du Pont. (GENRES: MUSICAL/COMEDY-DRAMA) Running Time, 1 hour 32 minutes. A Production of Arys-Nissotti Films/Les Films H. Rousillon. Released in France on December 13, 1934, by Corona Films. Released Theatrically in the United States with English Subtitles in September 1989, by Bernard E. Kellerman and Kino International Pictures.

A Sailor Friend (to Gabin): "You have many women, my friend."
Jean (Jean Gabin): "Yeah... I know. I find them in my travels."
— *From "Zou Zou"*

In director Marc Allegret's *Zou Zou* (a/k/a, '*Zou-Zou*' and '*Zouzou*') a successful French attempt at aping Hollywood's flashy Busby Berkeley musicals of the same time, Gabin is second-billed to the striking African-American entertainer Josephine Baker who, just like Paul Robeson before her, had to go to Europe in order to achieve her initial successes. The film begins with a twenty years earlier pre-amble, in which eight-year-old singing protégés Jean (he's white) and Zou Zou (she's black) put on their magnificently showstopping singing-duo performance in the main tent of the Romarin Circus. Young Zou Zou and Jean, as we're going to be finding out at the beginning of the picture, were adopted at birth by Papa Mele (Pierre Larquey), the circus's owner, who has billed the obviously unrelated Zou Zou and Jean as a brother-and-sister act. Romarin has even made up a crazy back-story for Zou Zou and Jean, and he captures the crowd's imagination, by regaling it with stories pursuant to how Zou Zou and Jean were the progeny of "a Chinese man and an Indian girl, who met in Polynesia." Papa Mele loves Zou Zou and Jean as his own children, even referring to them, endearingly, as 'his little freaks' (!), and people congregate from miles around, to catch a glimpse of these two kids who have such magnificent singing voices. (At the age of eight, Zou Zou and Jean are played by Irene Ascoula and Serge Grave.)

Twenty years later, Jean and Zou Zou are *all growed-up:* Zou Zou is now played by Baker, and Jean, appropriately, by Jean Gabin. Zou Zou has a massive unrequited crush on her adopted brother, and she becomes devastated when he sets off to join the Merchant Marines. (When a fellow sailor, who sees Jean scoring babes effortlessly in a local tavern, appreciatively remarks to Jean, "You have many women, my friend," Jean shrugs, nonchalantly, a cigarette dangling from his hand, and replies, "Yeah. You know, I find them in my travels…" While Jean is 'in the Service' (serving his country, while being served by hot, sailor-lovin' babes), tragedy strikes on the homefront: Papa Mele lays dying, having fallen from a scaffold, and the Circus Romarin must now shut its doors. Jean returns home from the sea and, for the first time in their lives, Zou Zou and Jean are forced to find employment, independently.

The two take subsistence-level jobs at (where else?) a local vaudeville house, Jean as an electrician (all of the chorus girls pine for his swarthy affections), and Zou Zou as one of the theater's many laundreses, in fact, in a poignant sequence, a small group of starstruck, young show-laundresses fold the clothing of the show's bold-n'-brassy blonde diva, Miss Barbara (Illa Meery), while wondering aloud about how fantastic her life must be, off-stage.

Zou Zou's luck quickly sours, though, when Miss Barbara impulsively leaves the show, only minutes before the evening's performance, to be with her nameless Brazilian lover, a man to whom she refers in the film only as 'the Jaguar,' and who is played by a heavily-mustached and wild-haired young actor named Emile Barrara. Needless to say, Miss Barbara's sugar-daddy, the theater's rotund impresario Saint-Levy (Pierre Palau, who plays the role in the same grossly-Semitic stereotype which you'll notice in a lot of older French films) is miffed because now, his very popular musical show is without a star, and showtime is only minutes away. (For a minute, a jealous Zou Zou believes that Jean is in love with Miss Barbara, since Zou Zou caught Jean in Barbara's dressing room when he was helping her to escape from the theater. [He had her climb out of the window on his back!]) Well-liked Jean successfully convinces Saint-Levy to let the unknown Zou Zou replace Barbara, and when we next see Zou Zou, she's performing onstage that night in the Busby-Berkeley-styled production number for which the film is mostly known, in which she trills a song called "Haiti" (and when she does, she's perched almost naked in a giant bird cage, her bosom covered by some strategic feathers). Thanks to Zou Zou's performance, the show becomes more popular than ever.

While Fate has now turned sweet for Zou Zou, *alas,* the same cannot be said for Jean: After watching Zou Zou perform, he leaves the theater to score some cigarettes (nicotine is The French Oxygen!) and, wouldn't you know it, while he's out walking, he witnesses a murder. Since Jean is the only person on the scene, the arriving police believe him to be the killer and, in very short order, they drag him off to the gray-bar hotel. In prime/fatalistic Gabin style, though, Jean doesn't even resist his arrest, just like Gabin's 'Bob' didn't resist getting shot in the alleyway, in *Paris-Beguin* (even though, in both pictures, he didn't actually commit the crime for which he has been arrested). He just Gabin-Shrugs, and the cops take him away without a fight: Jean's not a passive guy, especially when it comes to scoring with the babes, but he also realizes, in *Zou Zou* and in most of his other pictures, that *'Whatever happens, happens…'*

Zou Zou risks her newly-acquired fame, by taking a powder from the following evening's performance to bail Jean out of jail but, as it turns out, her sacrifice will have been all for naught, because after she's gone to the trouble of rescuing Jean, he tramples off with Zou Zou's blonde laundress friend, Claire (Yvette Lebon), leaving Zou Zou to another performance of the melancholy and yet showstopping song, "Haiti," which she again performs in that giant bird cage, and when you listen to the song's lyrics, you see that they're really referring, not-so-obliquely, to Jean: "I love him, but he gives his love to others…"

Zou Zou is a great movie, which features some pretty spectacular musical numbers performed by the chorus of Saint-Levy's theater, a handful of impressively-gargantuan showstoppers which definitely give the American Busby Berkeley musicals of the time a run for their money, including one number in which a group of the show's ingénues, not including Baker, perform on, and are also dwarfed by, a massive bed. Another production number has an underwater theme, and manages to better similar sequences which you might find in any of the Hollywood-lensed Esther Williams movies.

We all know what happened to Jean Gabin after he made *Zou Zou*—forty-two more years of making movies. (Plus, because at this stage, Gabin was still singing, in addition to making movies, and he'd continue to sing for a few more years in the '30s before he mostly gave it up, this picture would give him yet another hit record in France, *"Viens Fifine"* [*"Come Here, Fifi"*], which Gabin sings in the movie, and which you can find today on various CD-compilations of French music.) But what about Gabin's luminous co-star, the legendary Josephine B.? Well, after making three popular movies in a row, in her adoptive country of France, *La Sirene des tropiques* (1927), *Zou Zou* (1934), and *Princess Tam-Tam* (1935), Hollywood invited Josephine Baker back: She arrived in Los Angeles in 1935, but none of the jobs which were promised to her actually came to fruition, and so in 1936, according to author William Robert Faith in his book *Bob Hope: A Life in Comedy*, Baker headed east to New York, where she appeared on Broadway in the Ziegfeld Follies, alongside Hope and Jimmy Durante. The show in which they appeared ran so long in its previews (almost four hours), that its producers, the Schubert Organization, decided to trim a few of the acts which they felt weren't working with audiences, and one of the performers whom they decided to cut was Josephine Baker, their reason being that, to them, she was "too *chic* for American audiences" and "too French" (even though she was an American)! So Baker returned to France, where she remained a popular nightclub-draw for the rest of her life, also appearing in occasional Italian and German movies up through 1955, and guesting on various t.v. shows, throughout 1966.

Zou Zou wasn't released in the United States in any form until fifty-five years after it was made, in 1989, and this is due to the film's brief glimpses of upper-torso female nudity, as supplied by Illa Meery and an uncredited black dancer, which would have been unacceptable to the rigorously censorious Hays Code of the time. Today, *Zou Zou* continues to be one of Kino Home Video's most popular DVD releases, and the film represents a rare opportunity for Americans to see a movie which was directed by the imaginative Marc Allegret, a man who made more than fifty feature films between 1927 and 1970, but who worked with Gabin only on this one film.

What a Critic Said at the Time: "This musiker is proving to be the big French film grosser of the season, thus giving a double-click to the American colored-girl [Josephine Baker]. Miss Baker is finely supported by Jean Gabin, who is one of the half-dozen best male leads in France today, and worth-watching. He is one of those lads with the tough type of femme appeal—not handsome, but strong. Can sing a little..." (*Variety*, 1-18-35, issue. Critic: "Stein. [Jerry Stein.]" Reviewed in Paris.)

With Madeleine Renaud (Film 17, right).

FILM 17

MARIA CHAPDELAINE

France, 1934

Directed by Julien Duvivier. Produced by Maurice Juven. Screenplay by Gabriel Boissy and Julien Duvivier. Based Upon the Novel by Louis Hemon. Director of Photography (black and white), Georges Perinal. Music by Jean Wiener. Directors of Photography (black and white), Jules Kruger and Georges Perinal. Editors, Marthe Poncin and Claude Iberia. (GENRE: MELODRAMA) A Production of Societe Nouvelle de Cinematographie (SNC). Running Time, 1 hour 15 minutes. Released in France in 1934, by SNC. Released in U.S. with English Subtitles by France Films, on September 24, 1935.

"I will not be tethered like a cow!"
— *Jean Gabin's character Francois Paradis, explaining that he needs lots of women, in "Maria Chapdelaine"*

Maria Chapdelaine, a film which is based upon a 1913 novel by Louis Hemon, a novel which is extremely beloved in France, is the 17th feature film in which Jean Gabin would appear, and it's an important movie (besides the fact that it's really great) because it's the first movie which Gabin would make as France's #1 Box-Office Star: After his last picture, *Zou Zou*, France, which had been taking Gabin to heart since his film debut, in 1930's *Chacun sa chance*, was suddenly more than just *enjoying* him: Suddenly, the whole country had gone Jean Gabin-nutty, and *Maria Chapdelaine* was actually the first movie in which people were lining up in droves, very specifically to see a Jean Gabin movie (just like how today, people line up for Tom Cruise or Brad Pitt), although he was still second-billed, to Madeleine Renaud, with whom he had already co-starred twice, in 1932's *La Belle Mariniere* and 1933's *Le Tunnel*.

In his first fifteen pictures, the ones in which he acted between 1930 and 1933, Gabin's young characters were often happy-go-lucky, and sometimes, as I've already mentioned in previous chapters, they were *so* optimistic, that they'd break right into song! But now, suddenly, and starting with this picture, Gabin's recurring on-screen character would become somber, world-weary, and usually fated for ill.

Maria Chapdelaine was the first of seven films in which Jean Gabin would star over a period of twenty years, for Poetic Realism's great visual stylist, Julien Duvivier (Poetic Realism = 'stories of the common man, filmed in a stylized manner'), and the picture was shot on location, in French-speaking Quebec, Canada. The film's background and vistas are peopled with genuine, Iroquois Indians, who strut their native stuff in the film's genuine Native-American dance sequences.

Madeleine Renaud's eponymous title character, Maria Chapdelaine, is the daughter of a family of trappers, and all of the strapping male trappers in the cozy little *Quebecois* encampment of Peribonka are actively competing for her affections, especially since Maria's the only woman in the camp under the age of ninety. Maria's most ardent suitors are Eutrope Gagnon (Alexandre Rignault), a big and good-hearted but 'Mongo-dumb' man-mountain, as well as Lorenzo Suprenant (Jean-Pierre Aumont, one of France's greatest leading men), a smooth French banker who's traveled from Paris to Quebec, in order to purchase some of Canada's big, unspoiled land.

The only guy who isn't actively competing for Maria's love, though, is the quietly-proud Francois Paradis (Gabin) and, of course, Francois is the only guy in the flick whom she wants, simply because he's not paying attention to her. 'Gabin's Lesson in Landing Babes,' which we'll be observing repeatedly, in many of the movies which he'll make throughout his career (and this is a lesson which all men might do well to observe) is: "Show little interest. Make the doll come to you!"

Maria, like Zou Zou before her, is destroyed when Francois announces to her that he's leaving Peribonka for the winter, to work in a lumber camp a hundred miles away, and understand: Francois digs Maria as much as she digs him, but, in a Jean Gabin movie, whenever Our Hero starts falling for a woman, his first instinct will usually be to flee, obviously wanting to avoid getting hurt. Francois screams at Maria that he doesn't need to be "tethered, like a cow" (Gabin will utter a similar line, twenty years later, in another picture, director Jean Renoir's *French Cancan*), but the audience knows, from the way in which he's looking at her, that he genuinely loves her, and so he promises her that he'll be back at winter's end.

With Francois gone, Maria counts the days, weeks, and months, until his return, something which she usually does in the company of her slow-witted or, what we would today call 'challenged' teen-aged brother, Tit-Be (Emile Genevois), a twentysomething manchild who spends most of his time smoking a huge pipe, while staring out the window, grinning like a freakin' chucklehead.

Meanwhile, back at the lumber camp, Francois' testicular hankering for Maria is growing stronger by the day, and he decides that he can't wait until spring to see her again, so he now attempts to return to his lady-love, in spite of the deadly blizzard which is blanketing the Great White North with cold, white goo. Ready to trek all the way across Canada on foot, Francois snaps-on a set of giant, tennis-racket-looking snowshoes, and it is here that director Duvivier will begin cross-cutting between Gabin's Francois, a man alone in wobbly, rear-projection nature, as he's rushing to get back to Maria, and shots of Maria, in her bedroom, as she's fondling rosary beads, and praying for his speedy return. Maria's mother, Laura (she's played by Suzanne Despres) has told her daughter, with (to misquote 'Mayor' David Huddleston, from Mel Brooks' comedy classic, *Blazing Saddles*) 'good, sound prairie logic,' that, if she prays all night, she'll get whatever she wishes for. (And we know, of course, *exactly* what's she's wishing for: A big, hunky 'French-Canadian' dude, called Jean Gabin!)

After a night of frenetic bead-pulling, Maria awakens and looks out of the window, where she sees a figure way off in the distance, riding toward the Chapdelaine family's log cabin, on what we, the audience, first believe to be a dog-driven sled. She runs outside, excited that her industrious Francois has found a way to return to her, and is then horrified to learn that it's another guy riding the sled (it's not Francois)—and to make matters worse, the 'human sled' upon which this other guy is standing is Francois himself, since Francois had died from frostbite, while making the trip back to her. (Maria's mother will pass away before the end of the film, as well.) After Francois dies, both Lorenzo and Eutrope propose to Maria, but she chooses to remain alone, preferring her memories of Francois over real-life relationships with either of the two other men.

While Jean Gabin's character dies in director Julien Duvivier's 1935 classic *Maria Chapdelaine* (the film would be re-made twice in France, first in 1950, by *Zou Zou's* director Marc Allegret, but without Gabin, and then for a second time, in 1983) Gabin's career was definitely *very alive*, and he would have many, many more films (79, to be exact) to come. This particular picture won France's Best Picture of the Year Award (the '*Grand Prix du Cinema*').

What a Critic Said at the Time: "Jean Gabin makes a fine, two-fisted trapper, [and] this film seems to be a sure, 100% draw for the French, and [for] French-Canadians. In addition, it might have value for the U.S. *arties* [art-houses]." (*Variety*, 1-8-35 issue. Critic: "Stein. [Jerry Stein.]" Reviewed in Paris.)

What Another Critic Said at the Time: "One of the best pictures to come out of France. A fine achievement, properly paced. Picture was awarded the *Grand Prix du Cinema* in France, and deserves it. The novel [upon which it is based] was popular in France, in the 1920s, as well as in its English translation." (*Variety*, 10-9-35 issue. Critic: "Wolfe. [Wolfe Kaufman.]" Reviewed in NYC.)

What a Third Critic Said at the Time: "It should be tribute enough to say that *Maria Chapdelaine* survives the naked spotlight of having won the *Grand Prix du Cinema Francaise*. There are excellent performances [all around], especially by Jean Gabin. [*Maria Chapdelaine*] is a stirring, full-bodied, and tremendously beautiful screen edition of Louis Hemon's novel. It presents the Gallic cinema at the height of its achievement, and the film has all the nobility of an epic poem." (New York *Times*, 9-30-35 issue. Critic: Andre Sennewald.)

Top: The Real Pontius Pilate. Above: With Edwige Feuillere.

FILM 18

GOLGOTHA

France, 1935

Directed by Julien Duvivier. Written by Julien Duvivier and Joseph Reymond. Produced by Philippe Bouteron and Lucien Pinoteau. Directors of photography (black and white), Marc Fossard, Robert Juillard, Jules Kruger, and Rene Ribault. Editor, Marthe Poncin. Music by Jacques Ibert. Production designers, Jean Perrier and Andre Roux. (GENRE: BIBLICAL/HISTORICAL DRAMA) A Production of Ichtys Films, Gray Films, and Transat Films. Running Time, 1 hour 35 minutes. Released in France by Sirius, on April 12, 1935. Released in United States in 1935 in an English-Dubbed Version, by Admiral George McLeod Baynes.

"One of thou who dippest with me shall betray me!"
— *Jesus, to his Apostles, during The Last Supper, in "Golgotha"*

The whole point of this book, is that most Jean Gabin movies are great, and Julien Duvivier's 1935 picture *Golgotha*, the film in which he'd reunite with Jean Gabin for the second time after *Maria Chapdelaine*, is no exception. *Golgotha* was the very first *sound* movie to be made about Jesus, in any language (the one before it, Cecil B. DeMille's 1927 *King of Kings*, was silent), and France's current (at the time) shining-new mega-star, Gabin, was added to the cast by Duvivier to bolster the film's box-office appeal. Gabin is second-billed in the film's opening credit sequence to Harry Baur, the actor who plays King Herod in only a couple of the film's scenes, and he's also billed above the star of the movie, Robert Le Vigan (who appeared as 'Brooce' the cave-dwelling moneylender in *Le Tunnel,* and as Inspector Fernando Lucas in *La Bandera*), who plays Jesus, and this is amazing, because Gabin's part in *Golgotha* (he plays a sympathetic/laid-back Pontius Pilate!) is, just like Harry Baur's part, no more than an extended cameo which lasts only a few scenes; in fact, Gabin is also the only member of the cast who appears on the film's poster, and just from looking at the poster, you might think you're going to be seeing a movie starring Jean Gabin... and that's exactly what the producers wanted you to think.

While *Golgotha* remains a stirringly-powerful movie, it's also a highly problematic work, in the same exact way in which Mel Gibson's 2003-tempest-in-a-multiplex, *The Passion of the Christ*, was problematic: In both Duvivier's and Gibson's films, the Jewish characters are portrayed with massively-hooked noses and nasty attitudes, and they're painted as being solely responsible for the death of Jesus, whereas in the more balanced and historically-accurate Jesus movies (De Mille's and Nicholas Ray's two separate versions of *King of Kings*, which were made in 1927 and 1961, respectively, and George Stevens' 1965 *The Greatest Story Ever Told*), we see *the plain, simple, and-unvarnished truth,* which is that *only* the Romans were responsible for the death of Jesus, just as they were also *solely* responsible for the deaths of many of their other 'uppity' Jewish slaves, whom they tortured routinely and then crucified, for their own, sickly-decadent amusement. (As the great historians have all borne out, it is only the Romans who would have ever been threatened by Jesus' teachings, since, in Jesus' famous Sermon on the Mount, he announced that man cannot serve both 'earthly masters' [the Caesars] and a 'Heavenly Master' [God] at the same time, and that's exactly what the Romans were doing, and they took exception to what he was saying.)

Here's author Weddig Fricke, in his 1990 book, *The Court-Martial of Jesus Christ:*

"Despite all the efforts to make the Jews look responsible [for the death of Jesus], and to cast the Roman procurator in the role of an unwitting instrument, . . . the biblical accounts make it quite clear that Pontius Pilate alone pronounced the death sentence . . . which was carried out by his [Roman] Legionnaires."

In spite of the fact that the central conceit in *Golgotha* is based upon the same wild misinterpretations of the New Testament which have caused anti-Semitism, Inquisitions, Pogroms, and Holocausts, the film merits a viewing anyway for Jean Gabin completists, simply because, in spite of the film's basic narrative problem, it is, inarguably, a breathtakingly-visual and superbly-entertaining piece of work, and one which can be appreciated aesthetically, even if one can't exactly get behind its rather dubious re-writing of history. As *Golgotha* begins, the film's unseen voice-over Narrator sets us up for, and gives context to, the people whom we're about to meet and the places we're about to see: "It is a memorable day. Ancient Israel is glorious in its splendor. Jerusalem is the seat of the Roman Empire, run by Governor Pontius Pilate, who represents the Caesar, Emperor Tiberius. But this film will speak of one who is greater than all of the Herods and Caesars, one who speaks of the Kingdom of Heaven. Even his disciples will not fully understand him. So how will the Priests and tribunal understand him?"

Jerusalem, as we first see it, is in an uproar (not the people, but the city's rulers). Jesus of Nazareth will soon be 'in town' and, as part of his traveling ministry (his last stop was Galilee), he's going to be preaching his new/special 'magic words' to the common clay of Jerusalem's capital city, Judea. King Herod (Harry Baur), the earthly King of the Jews, whose seat of power is in Jerusalem, is incredulous: "He would hardly dare come right into our city." But dare, he will!

While the Jewish High Priests aren't too happy about Jesus' incipient arrival, since they feel, quite unsubstantiatedly, that he might be challenging their teachings, the cripples are ecstatic, since wherever Jesus goes, he's been known to cure the blind and *the infirm*. ("He'll cure me! He'll cure me!" one excited peasant yells out, in the marketplace.) The Jewish high-priest Caiphas, who's played by Charles Granval (Caiphas was benign in real-life, but was portrayed in this film, just as he was also portrayed in Mel Gibson's film, as being an angry psychopath) declares that Jesus must be arrested as soon as he arrives, because he is a direct threat to the town's Jewish elders: "Rome would enjoy taking from us what few liberties we have left. Those who choose to follow this Jesus will pay dearly for his folly."

The city of Jerusalem is overseen by the tender, violence-hating (!) Roman Governor, Pontius Pilate (handsome Jean Gabin who, when we first see him in the film, is stroking his pet dog), who's been dispatched to the area by Emperor Tiberius, his wife's father, to act as a peacemaker between the city's constantly-warring Roman and Jewish citizenries. In Pilate's palace, the women servants (all hot!) are wondering aloud about whether 'this new guy' who's coming to town (*J.C.*) really is a prophet, and if can really resurrect the dead and cure the sick, as they've heard he can. Even some of the underpaid and unappreciated Roman Centurions whom we're now seeing are excited about Jesus' arrival, and one is even heard to exclaim, "We'll be repaid a hundredfold... anyway, that's what he says!"

Outside of Pilate's dwellings, as Jesus approaches, the sellers in the marketplace are all busy, 'cleaning up their acts.' While the Jesus character in the film is always a super-nice guy (Robert Le Vigan plays 'the Christ' like a Hallmark Card Jesus, his eyes turned eternally Heavenward), when he first arrives in Jerusalem, he starts *kicking-ass and taking names*, in fact, in a wildly-frenetic sequence, he tears into the marketplace, and starts *whipping the shit* out of the merchants, setting their caged sacrificial goats and sheep free, as an incredibly fluid moving camera spins around and around the circumference of the action on a dolly track, giving us a panoramic '*360 Degrees of Jesus*'-effect, an effect which will be re-used, fifty years later, by pictorially-inventive American directors like Spike Lee and the Coen Brothers. Jesus now points a finger at the shocked vendors: "My house is the house of prayer, and you've turned it into a den of thieves." He makes one of the merchants hold a coin up, and then asks the guy to tell him whose face he sees on the obverse, and the guy replies that it's the face of Caesar, and it is this admission which gives Jesus wide berth to utter one of *His Supercool Catch Phrases:* "Render unto Caesar which is Caesar's, and render unto God the things which are God's!" Caiphas sees this, as he peers out of the Temple window, and he looks more than a little jealous, because everybody looks more afraid of Jesus than they are of him: "If he keeps this up," he opines to his cohorts, we shall not be masters for long."

The Priests start trying to figure out how to get rid of Jesus, and Caiphas has an idea: "Let's get his friend Judas to do it for us." Judas Iscariot, as Caiphas reminds his followers, still loves his good buddy, Jesus, but he harbors some residual resentment toward him anyway, because he's devoted his life to Jesus, and wanted to be part of Jesus' inner circle, but in spite of all of his incessant brown-nosing, it just didn't work out for him, because, when it comes to Judas, Jesus is, as we say, today, 'friendly, but not friends:' "Judas thought he would be important in Jesus' realm, but he is not," Caiphas tells the temple's elders of Judas and, to utilize a *Godfather*-analogy, Judas is 'Fredo Corleone' to Jesus' 'Michael:' Judas is weak and would dishonor his friend in a New York Minute (or: 'in a Judea Minute'), but Jesus recognizes his weakness, and so he likes him, in spite of his frailties.

Now we get to actually meet Judas, and he's played by the actor Lucas Gridoux. Caiphas meets with Judas and, to continue the *Godfather* analogy, makes him 'an offer he can't refuse:' "Deliver your friend Jesus into my custody, and I'll give you thirty pieces of silver." While Judas is mad at Jesus, he is, at the same time (at least as Gridoux is playing him) genuinely kind-hearted, and in *Golgotha*, Judas is a bit more reticent to give his friend up to the enemy than the Judas character usually is, in other Jesus movies. (Still, that thirty pieces of silver looks pretty inviting!) Caiphas has basically told Judas to 'take it home and think about it,' and while Judas is doing just that, we can hear Jesus' voice echoing in his head: "Love thine enemies! Do good to those who might hate thee! Those who will crucify me will be ashamed," *etc.* After a soul-searching midnight walk, Judas agrees to The Big Sell-Out, and tells Caiphas that he will deliver Jesus to him, and *stat.*

What's really interesting about *Golgotha*, is that it does something very cool, not to mention something which no other Jesus movie has ever done, before or since: This film doesn't show Jesus' suffering, at all. Instead, director Duvivier makes the character of Judas into his film's one, lone sufferer, and he gives us not one, but two separate sequences, in which Judas wanders alone in the forest, his troubled, agonized visage (which is photographed in extreme close-up) telling us what words just can't: He hates himself for what he knows he has to do, and is really wrestling with his conscience. Jesus' other disciples are just background characters in this movie; they don't say or do too much as they do in other Jesus movies, although even in this movie, they all (as most of us do) show up for dinner.

Jesus alerts his disciples that he won't be perishing (like month-old milk) until he's enjoyed a final Passover meal ('the Last Supper') with them, and he even gathers all of them around the table, and makes with his patented, *'One of you will betray me'-shtick:* "One of thou who dippest with me shall betray me!" (*Damn! Don't dippest with this homeboy!*) After he makes this proclamation, Judas, who's present at *El Grande Din-Din*, and who is heavily involved in munching-out on some tasty flatbread (this is some two thousand years before they started calling it 'foccacia'), feels super-guilty about what he knows he's going to have to do soon, and so he gets up and leaves and, when he does, none of the others, including Jesus, does anything at all. (Each disciple just keeps on passing the potatoes.) Duvivier now cross-cuts between the dinner sequence, with another sequence in which Judas is wandering through the forest, racked with guilt. After dinner (presumably, the waiter already brought the check), the other eleven disciples, who are still present, tell Jesus they will all gladly die with, and for, him. Judas is seen, next, at the Temple, giving Caiphas 'Jesus' coordinates' for the evening: He alerts Caiphas that Jesus will soon be *truckin'* through the Garden of Gethsemane.

One of the lower Priests now elucidates to Caiphas on the subject of how their scheme will play out legally: "We can arrest Jesus, and we can also judge him. But only Pilate can give the orders to execute." So now, Caiphas has to go and meet with Pilate, whom Jean Gabin portrays, in the film, as being a carefree and peace-loving guy, just as Pilate is also portrayed in the Mel Gibson version. Pilate, who's a lover, not a fighter, isn't interested in Jesus at all: "If he's as dangerous as you claim, I will issue the orders, and send Centurions with you, to arrest him. I suppose I can even have him executed. But, myself, I have no problem with this Jesus. I've never even heard of him. And if he's a magician, as you say he is, then so what? Who cares?" When Caiphas leaves, Pilate sits on the edge of the bed with his beautiful wife, Claudia, the daughter of Emperor Tiberius, who's played by Edwige Feuillere. (Of course, Gabin is going to get a hot, on-screen love interest, even if he's only in a movie for a handful of scenes.) Claudia knows that her husband, Pilate, is a good man (in the world of this movie anyway), and she tries to convince him not to issue the orders to have Jesus killed: "I know you can have this Jesus of Nazareth executed, but are you sure you would want to? This man has cured the sick, and we have proof. So prove your authority. Give Jesus a second chance!" (Historic Note: In real life, the Roman Governor, Pilate, was not beholden to the demands of the Temple Elders; he, alone, governed Judea, and would have never done what a minority of his population had told him to do.)

Later that evening, Judas comes upon Jesus in the Garden of Gethsemane and bounds up to him, pretending to still be 'on his side.' ("Hail, Master!" he exclaims, very insincerely kissing Jesus full-thrush on the mouth.) But you can't fool Jesus, and Jesus (or 'Jeezy,' as a slow-witted hospital orderly referred to the Savior in Thomas Harris' second Hannibal Lecter novel, *Hannibal*) 'calls' Judas on what he already knows, instinctively: "Friend, is it with a kiss that you betray me?" (Yes, it's true. The Big Jesus/Judas Smoochfest is where the Mafia Kiss of Death, which signifies 'betrayal from a friend,' comes from. Vito Corleone, it would seem, is only one Kevin Baconian 'degree' away from Mister Jesus Christ, himself!) Roman Centurions, next, charge into the garden, and one Centurion gets right up in the Lord's face: "We seek Jesus of Nazareth! Is that you?" Jesus is ready to go quietly. ("If it be I who you seek, then you may do your will.") When the Centurions arrest Jesus, they can't believe that he's as impassively-accommodating as Martin Sheen protesting in front of a nuclear reactor. ("Don't you have anything to say?") Worse, right in front of Jesus' face, one of the soldiers asks Judas if he's a friend of the man whom they're about to cart away, and Judas mutters, as he stares at his fair-weather friend, something along the lines of "Never seen him before in my life"—and with enemies like that, who needs friends?

The Centurions bring Jesus into the atrium-looking courthouse for his trial in front of the Sanhedrin, the seventy-one man Jewish tribunal of law, over which Caiphas presides: "We have heard that you have been preaching a new religion. Is it true?" Jesus says he's only been going around saying nice, loving things, most of which seem to have been falling on deaf ears. Caiphas calls witnesses to take the floor, to talk about how Satanic they feel Jesus is, although, clearly, these false witnesses have been coached, and probably bribed, by the temple's elders, to spew-out all of this patently-untrue horseshit about him. One stoolie-witness, the shifty-looking Gerson (Edmond van Daele), actually tells the court, "I heard

Jesus say that he would destroy the temple and build another one in three days!" Invited members of the public, of course, believe all of the various witnesses untruths and, within seconds, the whole room is chanting for Jesus' death, and what Julien Duvivier is saying here, is that the masses are blood-thirsty, and more than that—they're dumb as shit! Caiphas asks Jesus if it's true that he's the Son of God, and Jesus replies that, no matter what answer he makes, nobody's going to believe him anyway and that, ultimately, it really doesn't matter. Caiphas now asks him the same question for a second time, and this time out, Jesus' response is short and sweet, and not proud, but truthful: "I am." Of course, the crowd won't hear of it, and audience members start shouting out cries of, "Blasphemy!" and "This is not Galilee!" and "You can't say those things here!" Caiphas orders the Centurions to bind Jesus up, in ropes. (Interestingly, in *King of Kings*, Nicholas Ray's 1961 version, there are no Jews present at Jesus' trial, at all; in Ray's excellent film, only the Romans try Jesus.)

Gabin's Pilate is present at the trial, and he honestly can't see that Jesus is doing anything more than preaching Love so, on the way out of the atrium, he passes the buck to Caiphas: "Try him according to your own laws, Caiphas. I'm washing my hands of this" (and he washes them literally, too, pouring calm, cool H20 over his own meathooks). Then, Pilate utters that notorious, completely fabricated/apocryphal/it-was-never-really-said line, which was created by the authors of the Gospel, a line which has been quoted by Jew-hating zealots throughout history: Indicating the Jews who are present, he decrees, "Let it be on your hands, and on those of your children," and this same line is also spoken, in the Aramaic tongue, in the 2004 Mel Gibson movie. Pilate, next, has a moment alone with Jesus, before the King of Kings is led away (and Willem Defoe's Jesus gets the same exact moment alone with David Bowie's Pilate, in Scorsese's 1986 film, *Last Temptation of Christ*). Pilate asks Jesus if he's really 'King of the Jews,' and Jesus replies, "I am king…but not of this world."

Before meeting the Fate which we all know he'll shortly be meeting, King Herod wants to have a little sit-down with Jesus as well, since the two men have never been properly introduced. ("Bring me the Prophet!" he screams.) Centurions escort Jesus to Herod's palace, and Herod really, as they used to say two thousand years ago, 'lays unto him:' "The Senate has accused you of provoking the masses. For a long time, I have wished to know you. I hear you are a magician. Well, abandon your modesty and show me a miracle. Cure the crippled son of my major-domo! Make a fountain spin! Stop the sun! If you're such a wonderworker—do one of these things!"

Later, outside of Pontius Pilate's dwellings, a large and rambunctious crowd of Jews is chanting for Jesus' death. Pilate, who's still vacillating on the whole issue of whether he should condemn Jesus or not, informs the crowd, "It is custom that I kill one man." Do you want Jesus or Barrabas?" Barrabas is the Jewish rebel who tried to lead a violent uproar against Rome and (for those of us who fell asleep in Sunday School) the Romans 'lumped Jesus in' with Barrabas, even though Barrabas was a man of violence, and Jesus was 'The Original Mr. Love.' The crowd starts vociferously demanding the death of Jesus, even though Jesus is the more benign of the two men.

As pre-amble to The Big Crucifixion, Centurions now start flogging Jesus, and Pilate, who's watching, is starting to get a little squeamish about the whole thing. We don't see the actual whipping, but we can hear it happening off-screen, because Julien Duvivier, unlike Mel Gibson, felt that it was inappropriate to show the Son of God getting tenderized (although, hypocritically, Gibson did feel it was okay to present Jews as being Satanic), and we 'see' it only through the eyes of one hysterical woman, a lady who, very promptly, faints—and, right where she's standing! One Centurion, who has just finished whipping Jesus, laughs and nudges a buddy of his: "So, that's the son of God? Muahahahahaha!"

That night, Pilate's wife, Claudia, is chewing him a new a-hole, because Pilate has decided to honor the wishes of the temple elders, by crucifying Jesus: "You promised me that you wouldn't let him be executed!" Pilate tells her that, ultimately, he has no choice, because, as he's now letting her know, the decisions of the Jewish elders override his own. (Per Mike Myers, in *Wayne's World*, "Not!"): "If I don't execute him, I'll be exiled. The High Priest will accuse me to Tiberius." Apparently, Governor Pilate's jonesing to be 'Emperor' Pilate, on such a day in the future when Tiberius is no longer able to serve, and he doesn't want to incur Tiberius' wrath.

The next day, it's Crucifixion Time: A Centurion places that Uber-itchy crown of thorns atop Jesus' head, and starts laughing, menacingly. ("The king is crowned!") A Jewish guy in the crowd, who's feeling his oats, even stamps right up to the placid Jesus and slaps him right in the face! Then, Jesus is forced to endure His death-march up the Via Dolorosa with his cross. As he passes the peasants, whom he's cured, they are all in tears, because most of them really love him, and it's hard for them to grasp what's happening to their cool, new Magical Buddy. ("But what has he done? It is he, who gave me back my sight!") As Jesus continues his Walk of Shame, Romans and Jews alike scream out for his crucifixion, and Jewish children even throw rocks at him (and at least, they're not the fanged, afro-haired, Jewish vampire-kids, as depicted in the Mel Gibson movie)! A few handicapables whom Jesus passes along the way even ask him for some last minute, 'Stop-'n-Shop Miracles.' ("Give me back my sight!" "Make me walk!") Jesus stops in his tracks, points to the Jews who line the street, and urges them to "… weep not for me, but for yourselves, and for your children." (Whoops, another burst of anti-Semitism! Thanks, Duvivier… [and, Thanks, Gospels]!) As the Romans and Jews drag Jesus up Mount Golgotha, Duvivier cuts away to the Garden of Gethsemane where, at the same time, Judas is now seen, as he's trying to hang himself from a tree.

The Centurions, next, hoist Jesus up the cross, along with two of his disciples (one on either side to keep him company) and in a matter of minutes, his mother Mary (Juliette Verneuil) is escorted up to him. He looks down at her and utters his two oft-repeated, but never-bettered lines, "Forgive them, for they know not what they do" and "Mother, behold thy son!" The bloodthirsty Jews, who are crowded around the base of the hill watching the crucifixion really seem to love watching Jesus getting tortured, and one wisenheimer even calls out, "If he is the Son of God, let him descend from the cross!" (These Jews who surround Jesus' cross are just like any annoying hecklers you might run across at any Raiders game.) Anyway, day turns into night, Jesus is now resigned to die, and he shouts out his obligatory, "It is finished"-line. He then looks over at his two 'also-hanging' new pals and assures them that today, they will be joining him in Paradise. Jesus next shuffles off this mortal coil, agonizingly screaming-out his last word—"Faaaaaatherrrrrrrrrr!!!!!"

Then: Cue the Special Effects! Only moments after Jesus' head drops to his chest, a huge rainstorm blankets the horizon, replete with dark, eerie clouds, courtesy of some seriously cheesy-looking back-projection and stock-footage of lightning bolts (which looks like it may have been borrowed from one of Universal's 1930s'-made Frankenstein movies). Frightened Judeans, Romans and Jews alike, run away from the mount, as birds fly away in panic. "Truly, this man was the Son of God," one Centurion, who has remained stationary throughout the entire storm, remarks. (In *The Greatest Story Ever Told*, it is John Wayne himself who plays this Converted Centurion, and who utters that same exact line. [You really haven't lived until you've heard the Duke say it!]) After Jesus' spirit has finally ascended, we now see a cheap but kind-of-cool-looking matte painting of the sky, as well as bridge of clouds which stretches from the Earth, all the way across to Heaven.

Now, it's time for those wily Jews to get what's coming to them! Massive winds blast through the Jewish Temple, destroying it instantly and, at the same time, all the Big Jews in town start running around like chickens with their heads cut off, screaming-out that God is abandoning them and their Temple. Caiphas himself is even acting all freaky-deaky, because he knows that, in demanding Jesus' death, he's done the wrong thing: "It is the Messiah whom we have crucified!"

Jesus' body is buried, and his earthly father Joseph (Marcel Chabrier) alerts local authorities that they had better seal the body up, so that nobody can steal it, *a la* what would happen more than two thousand years later, with rocker Gram Parsons. The hermetic-sealing is done, per Joseph's wishes, and the following day, Jesus' body has disappeared. Freaked-out Centurions, who had spent the night guarding the tomb (in fact, they were sitting right in front of it) run to Caiphas, telling him that there is no way that the body could have been removed under their watch—and yet, it did! Caiphas, who's hot-under-the-collar, gives them an alibi: "You'd better say that somebody stole the body while you were sleeping!"

It's a great day for Jesus' disciples, though: Matthew (Paul Asselin), Peter (Hubert Perlier) and Simon (Jean Forest) all run through Judea, each of them having caught a glimpse of a 'V.I.V.' ('Very Important Vision.') Matthew cries out, to anyone within earshot, that the Savior has just appeared to His followers: "We saw him. His shadow appeared over ours! He broke bread with us!" Then, we actually get to see Jesus, who's now back among them in the flesh, since he's just risen like so much Fleischman's Yeast. He shows his disciples his hand-wounds from the cross's nails, after which he starts piling on the aphorisms and flowery words: "Peace be unto you... See: It is me!... I will stay here below, a little more time." Peter is ecstatic, and he cries out, "We shall meet again in Galilee, Jesus!" Simon sits on the beach next to Jesus, who's giving him some important instructions: "Tend my flock! Loveth me! Feedeth my sheep!" He then asks of all of his disciples, "Go ye, and teach all the nations that I am with you always, even unto the end of the world." The film ends with a sweeping panorama of thousands of crosses dotting the horizon, as Jesus' disembodied voice echoes, over the soundtrack. ("I remain here a little time...") We then get some nice, majestic, 'outro' music, to help us walk out of the movie theater feeling either good or bad about ourselves, depending upon which religion we profess to.

In spite of its horrible anti-Semitism, *Golgotha* is a film which you might just want to experience for yourself, if for no other reason than because you've probably already seen all of the American-made Jesus movies (*Last Temptation of Christ, Passion of the Christ, King of Kings, Greatest Story Ever Told*), and you want to see 'how the French did it.'

The most interesting thing about this movie, for this author, has to do with what director Julien Duvivier chose to show, as opposed to what he chose *not* to show: For example, Duvivier felt like he could portray Jews as being evil, monster-faced Christ-killers, in some of the most unflatteringly stereotyped, big-nose close-ups imaginable, but at the same time, he is very respectful about how he physically portrays Jesus: Duvivier, apparently, felt that no filmmaker, including himself, could appropriately present the physical 'face' of Jesus Christ, which is why, when you watch *Golgotha,* you'll notice that Jesus' face (or: Bob Le Vigan's face) is never seen in close-up. Film directors are, by nature of their chosen profession, 'all about the choices they make' (even more than the rest of us), and Duvivier will definitely make better choices in the other pictures which he'll make throughout his career, most of which will be very good.

At the time *Golgotha* was made, it featured the largest budget of any movie which had yet been made in France, a reported $350,000 (U.S.D.). It continues to be a staple on French television today, although also today, it is 100%-unknown in the United States, even though it was released in the U.S. (very briefly) at one theater (in *Brooklyn)* back in the '30s. And while Gabin himself would never play Jesus, he would, thirty years after *Golgotha,* play a Christ-like character, in a Jesus parable-picture, a contemporary comedy from 1965 called *Le Tonnerre de Dieu* (*The Thunder of God*), in which sixty-one-year-old Gabin played a retired country veterinarian with an understanding wife named Mary (they've been married for decades, and she's more of a mother to him, than she is a wife), and in that film, Gabin and his wife spend their time 'saving' some very Mary-Magdalene-like prostitutes. (I'll talk about that film in Chapter 80.)

While there would be good things ahead for both Jean Gabin and Julien Duvivier, the same, alas, could not be said for *Golgotha's* first-billed star, Harry Baur ('King Herod'). In 1942, Baur was arrested by the Gestapo and tortured, denounced for being Jewish, even though his parents were actually Catholic. (Conversely, Robert Le Vigan, who played the loving Jesus in *Golgotha,* was reportedly, in real-life, a rabid anti-Semite who collaborated with the Nazis during World War II.)

Besides being the first talking picture about Jesus, *Golgotha* also has the distinction of being the very first non-English-language movie ever, to have been dubbed completely into English: In the years immediately preceding *Golgotha,* filmmakers could film two and three versions of their movies from beginning to end, in different languages, and with different casts of actors (as with *L'Etoile de Valencia, Gloria,* and *Adieu les beaux jours*) but it would have been impossible to film *Golgotha,* the most expensive movie ever made, over again, from beginning to end. The film's dubbing and American release were taken on by Admiral George McLeod Baynes, an early American pioneer of silent cinema, who also happened to be extremely pious, and when Baynes finished dubbing the film, he presented its North American run exclusively, as an event at the Brooklyn Academy of Music, screening it at two shows per day.

> In 1938's one-off, French magazine, *Jean Gabin: Sa Vie/Ses Films,* which hit French newsstands in November, 1938 (*with a full-color cover)* this is what Edwige Feuillere ('Mrs. Pilate!') said about her experience, working with Gabin on *Golgotha:* "Jean is a man without pretension, and he's very nice, cordial, and spontaneous, never hiding what he thinks, even though what he thinks, he says very abruptly. He is full of intensity, truth and life. We shot for four days together, and whenever he would see me on set, he'd call me 'Mrs. Pilate.' Even though I would say that Jean and I don't exactly know each other well, I do like him very much…"

What a Critic Said at the Time: "This is the Passion of Jesus Christ made into a moving picture. Everybody said it couldn't be done. Paris had been shaking its head and [director] Duvivier predicted disaster. Headshakers can now go and bury their heads: *Golgotha* is a great picture. It is an accomplishment that should bring worldwide prestige… There is nothing which should offend Jewish susceptibilities." (*Variety,* 4-24-35 issue. Critic: "Stein. [Jerry Stein.]" Reviewed in Paris.)
What Another Critic Said at the Time: "… [better than] Cecil B. DeMille, at his best… Another whose performance is startlingly well-done is Jean Gabin, as Pilate. He plays the part with excellent restraint and poise." (*Variety,* 2-17-37 issue. Critic: "Char. [Roy Chartier.]" Reviewed in New York.)

FILM 19

LA BANDERA

France, 1935

(Literal English Translation: "THE FLAG") Directed by Julien Duvivier. Produced by A. Garbour. Screenplay by Julien Duvivier and Charles Spaak. Based Upon the Novel by Pierre Dumarchais (writing as 'Pierre MacOrlan') Music by Roland Manuel and Jean Weiner. Director of Photography (black and white), Jules Kruger, Editor, Marthe Poncin. Production Designer, Jacques Kraus. (GENRES: DRAMA, ADVENTURE) A Production of Societe Nouvelle de Cinematographie (SNC). Running Time, 1 hour 40 minutes. Released in France on September 21, 1935, by Gray Films. Released in United States with English Subtitles as "ESCAPE FROM YESTERDAY, by Hoffberg Productions, Inc., on May 2, 1939.

"Death arrives without pain, and is not so terrible as it seems.
The most horrible thing, is to live as a coward."
— *Captain Wells (Pierre Renoir) to Gabin and his other new Foreign Legion
recruits, in "La Bandera"*

Some of the most lauded American movies have always trafficked in one particular kind of stock character, 'the man alone, against society,' and this archetype is typically personified by the Cowboy or the Sheriff—usually, Gary Cooper in *High Noon*, most of Clint Eastwood's Supercops, and all of Charles Bronson's Supervigilantes. But in France, starting in about 1934, the drifter-loner was always just played by one man—Jean Gabin. Usually, as in this movie, his characters know that their Fates are going to be bad ones, so on the way to their unpleasant dooms—and usually, in the case of Jean Gabin's 1930s and 1940s movies, this means either jail or death—they]' are going to make sure they get a lifetime of living packed in to a very short time, drifting from town to town and country to country, in search of adventures, and adventuresome women. It is no surprise, then, that a couple of Jean Gabin's most outstanding movies from the 1930s will be brilliantly-entertaining Foreign Legion pictures, the first being director Julien (*Maria Chapdelaine, Golgotha*) Duvivier's 1935 *La Bandera* (literally, it means the *The Flag*, but it can also mean *The Batallion*), and the second being Jean Gremillon's *Gueule d'amour*, which will come in 1937. *La Bandera* is a

Top: With Annabella and Robert Le Vigan. Above: With Raymond Aimos.

crackerjack Legion entry penned by the prolific Charles Spaak, a man who would wind up writing a number of wonderful Jean Gabin movies, and it's based upon the novel by the legendary Pierre MacOrlan (real name, Pierre Dumarchais) who will also write one of the actor's best known movies of the 1930s, director Marcel Carne's *Le Quai des brumes* (1938).

La Bandera is also the first of many movies which traffic in the whole 'Gabin-Movie: Tragic Drifter'-trope in which, before the movie has started, his character has either killed someone, gone AWOL, or both. As the film opens, the year is 1921. A very nervous-looking Pierre Gilieth (Gabin) exits a Paris bar on the rue St. Vincent, and immediately runs into a drunken couple, weaving happily down the street. Pierre, has just stabbed an older man, who will later be identified as being a Mr. Morin, and he realizes—and this is unspoken, but we can tell—that he'll eventually be apprehended by the authorities for this crime, so he high-tails it out of France, making a bee-line for Spain.

Arriving in Spain, Pierre is alone and broke, with nowhere to go, so he heads into the local outdoor plaza-watering hole which is peopled by topless female dancers and transvestites. Instantly, as we will also be seeing in others of Gabin's Matinée Idol/Tragic Drifter Pictures in which he will star during this period of his career, these women (and, in the case of this film, 'pseudo-women') are attracted to Pierre, offering him succor in the form of food, shelter, and even affection, which he turns down. He eats and drinks with a tableful of surly men, one of whom pilfers his wallet, so that he is unable to pay for his meal. Worse, because he has no money, the boarding house in which Pierre has been staying tosses him out, and the proprietor tells him that he will keep his extra clothes until he gets the money which he is due.

With the Spanish police hot on his tail, Pierre now does the only thing he can: He heads to the recruitment office of the Third Battalion (*El Tercero*) of the Spanish Foreign Legion. As casual viewers of any foreign legion picture, from *Beau Geste* on up, are already aware, the Legion—whether it's the French Foreign Legion or the Spanish Foreign Legion—is the ideal hideout for accused criminals, because Legionnaires are customarily issued new identities, and are always safe from the police. Gabin's Pierre, however, is such a fatalist, that when he signs up for service, he does so under his real name, knowing that his ultimate destiny will be to get caught and executed anyway—because no man can ever escape from his Fate.

"My men deserve to be forgotten," the *Tercero's* surly Captain Weller (Pierre Renoir, director Jean Renoir's brother) intones, and Weller is the kind of classic, no-nonsense movie commander who could definitely go head-to-head with Lee Ermey's I-eat-nails-for-breakfast Gunnery Sergeant Hartman from Kubrick's *Full Metal Jacket,* and he even happens to be based upon a real-life personality, the Spanish army officer Lt. Colonel Jose Millan-Astray, who started the Spanish Foreign Legion, and whose motto was "*Viva la Muerte!*" ("Long Live Death!") In *La Bandera,* Pierre Renoir copies Millan-Astray perfectly, even down to Millan-Astray's famous shaven head and prominent eyepatch; in fact, 'the Millan-Astray look' would eventually be co-opted by another of history's famous military leaders, the great Israeli General Moshe Dayan, the man who brought Egypt, Jordan, and Syria to their knees during Israel's heroic Six Day War of 1967. Weller will even deliver a speech in this movie, which is word-for-word of what the real-life Milan-Astray—who was best friend, in real life, to General Francisco Franco, to whom this film was originally dedicated (an on-screen dedication to Franco appeared in the film's original prints)—told the troops of his *Tercero:*

"You have lifted yourselves from among the dead. For don't forget, that you were dead, that your lives were over [before you joined the *Tercero*]. You have come here to live a new life, for which you must pay, with death. You have come here to die. Since you [joined], you have no mother, no girlfriend, no family. From today, all of that will be provided by the Legion. Death in combat is the greatest honor. You die only once. Death arrives without pain, and is not so terrible as it seems. The most horrible thing, is to live as a coward."

While Legion service has freed Pierre from being pursued by the police—for a time, anyway—he continues to remain a prisoner of his own guilty conscience: While snoozing in-barracks on his first night after enlistment, frightening nightmares of the murder which he had committed in Paris are back-projected behind his head. (Director Julien Duvivier, the filmmaker who's widely recognized as being one of Poetic Realism's great master-stylists, always loves back-projecting surreal images behind his actors, in each of his films, and we'll see him doing it in all seven of the movies which he will make with his good friend, Jean Gabin.) Cruel Fate soon, inevitably, unleashes a vengeful cop, seemingly out of nowhere, to make Pierre's life hell for the Paris murder which the newspapers are now referring to, quite sensationally, as "The Murder in the rue St. Vincent." The 'Crooked-Cop-who-has-a-Vendetta-Against-Gabin'-trope, which we're going to be seeing in a number of Jean Gabin's movies—particularly in 1937's *Pepe Le Moko* and 1958's *Les Miserables*— begins in *La Bandera,* arriving in the person of Inspector Fernando Lucas, who's played by Robert Le Vigan, an actor whom we have already seen as the underground-residing moneylender 'Le Brooce' in 1933's *Le Tunnel* and as a healer in 1934's *Maria Chapdelaine.* (Le Vigan will also appear opposite Jean Gabin in three later pictures—1935's *Golgotha,* 1936's *Les Bas-fonds,* and 1938's *Le Quai des brumes.*) Lucas joins up with the *Tercero* under an assumed name and a phony occupation, so that his true identity as a policeman won't be revealed, and while viewers of the film know that Lucas has joined up in order to apprehend Pierre, and to get the fifty thousand franc reward which has been offered for Pierre's capture, Pierre remains ignorant of this fact—for awhile, anyway. While serving in the *Tercero,* Pierre will make a number of great friends, other men who, like him, have joined the Legion to make fresh starts, and principally, this includes the affable Mulot (Raymond Aimos, who will also play Gabin's friend in another Duvivier picture, 1936's *La Belle equipe*). *La Bandera,* in fact, is the first of many films in which the sturdy Gabin will have a sidekick, the others being Jean Renoir's 1937 *La Grande illusion,* as well as an American picture which Gabin and Julien Duvivier will make together in the 1940s, *The Impostor.* While Gabin's movie characters are tight-lipped and rarely open up to anybody, in each of these three films, his characters always open up to their nice, non-threatening 'little buddies,' and in *La Bandera*, Pierre tries to confess to Mulot that he murdered a man in Paris, and Mulot is such a good-hearted person, he doesn't even care—he just stands up, halfway through Pierre's confession, and ambles away to relieve himself! Another friend in Pierre's unit is the hot-headed Muller, a man with a chip on his shoulder for all of the authority figures in the world—especially Captain Weller—and Muller is played by France's square-jawed 1930s' movie favorite Gaston Modot, an actor who will be seen in four more Jean Gabin movies—1937's *La Grande illusion* and *Pepe Le Moko*, 1939's *Le Recif de corail*, and 1951's *Victor*.

The gallant men of the *Tercero* sail for Morocco, where they will be staying at the Legion's desert barracks in Rifien. While in Morocco, waiting for assignment, Pierre and friends frequent a brothel in the coastal town of Birdjibir, a place which is owned by a blonde German woman named Planche-a-Pain (or in English, according to the subtitled DVD, "Flat Chest"), and Flat Chest is portrayed by Margo Lion, who played the housewife, Mrs. Binder, in G. W. Pabst's 1933 Gabin effort, *Du haut en bas*. (Lion will also play Gabin's sister, in a 1946 melodrama called *Martin Roumagnac*.) There are a number of "dancers" at this establishment, but Pierre is instantly smitten with a beautiful Bedouin woman, Aischa, who is played by the popular—and, in real life, reportedly, bisexual—French siren, Annabella, a woman who also, in real life, happened to be the wife of the major American star, Tyrone Power. (Annabella will also co-star in another film with Jean Gabin later that year, the circus melodrama, *Varietes*.) From the second Aischa lays eyes on Pierre, she renounces the regular spate of male visitors who pay top-*peseta* for her exotic *après*-show affections, and the two immediately declare their all-consuming love for each other in a frenetic, voodoo-like marriage ceremony, a ceremony which seems to have emerged wholecloth, right out of Bela Lugosi's 1932 Haitian head-trip, *White Zombie*. In an amazingly-surreal wedding sequence which takes place in the brothel, we see the lovers only minutes after one of Pierre's comrades-in-arms has tattooed Pierre's chest with Aischa's name and Aischa's forearm with Pierre's, and the lovers next lap blood out of each other's arms, to solidify their pact. "You have mixed your blood," a swarthy middle-eastern priest informs the two. "You are now man and wife." The prostitutes, and Pierre's friends from his platoon, all look on approvingly, and in a moment of love, shortly after the wedding, Pierre even tells Aischa that he plans on borrowing some Arab garb to wear, so that the two of them can run away to her birthplace of Rabat, to be together.

Pierre is beginning to suspect that Lucas might be a cop, based on Lucas's increasingly squirrelly behavior, so he asks Aischa to pretend to love Lucas, who also likes her, so that he can attain information about Lucas's true identity. Of course, when Lucas is alone with Aischa, he tells her he loves her. Pierre warns Lucas, "If you confess who I am [to military authorities], one bullet will be for me, and the other will be for you."

As in all war pictures, it's soon time for *la bataille:* Captain Weller informs his troops that twenty-four men are needed immediately, and that they will accompany him to a mountain outpost, where they will reinforce another battalion, against a tribe of 'Riffians'—and of course, the Riffians are actually Berbers, the earliest settlers of Morocco, whose presence in this part of the world pre-dated the Arabs; in the Riffian War of 1921 to 1926, which is the war depicted in this film, the Riffians revolted, in defiance of Spanish occupation.

In the ensuing sequence, Pierre, Lucas, Weller, and a group of other men from their outfit are now holed up in a haphazard fort in the blazing sun. The men—most of Pierre's cohorts whom we have already met through the course of the movie—die one by one, because the Riffians have poisoned the fort's water supply, and each time a man tries to crawl out of the fort to obtain a drink of water, he is immediately shot down. (Riffians are an 'unseen' enemy in this film; we see the bullets they fire at the Legionnaires, but we never get to see them in the flesh, save for a couple of dead ones who are splayed-out on the ground.) Sadly, kindly Mulot even dies, after he, too, crawls out of the trench to get a drink. Pierre tries to remain 'Gabin Level-Headed,' but under these circumstances, it is impossible.

Eventually, Lucas and Pierre are the last men alive in the fort, and it's not long before Jean Gabin's Pierre gets picked-off by enemy bullets, dying instantly, and Lucas feels miserable: Ironically, the sole survivor of the trench will be Lucas, a man who joined the regiment for dishonest reasons. Pierre, the man whom Lucas had originally intended to betray—a man who unexpectedly became Pierre's true friend only in the last moments of Pierre's life—is now gone.

A newly-modest Lucas now returns to Birdjibir, where he informs Aischa of her husband's fate. "Pierre died thinking of you," Lucas divulges to her, and director Duvivier ends *La Bandera* with a haunted-looking close-up on Aischa's darkly-beautiful face.

Filmed in France, Spain, and the Spanish Sahara, *La Bandera* is a very impressive film to watch, not only because of its gripping war story, but also because it is the first of more than forty years worth of pictures which will portray Jean Gabin as 'the quiet-but-tough drifter/loner who is fated for a bad end,' the hallmark trait of his world-renowned movie persona. It's also worth pointing out that the notion of 'Soldiers-as-Fun-Loving Cohorts,' a trope which director Duvivier is presenting in *La Bandera,* will become popular in scores of military pictures which will follow it, in years to come: We saw this trope already in Gabin's *Les Gaietes de l'escadron* (1932), and we're gong to be seeing it again in pictures such as *La Grande illusion* (also starring Gabin,1937), Billy Wilder's *Stalag 17* (1953), Robert Aldrich's *The Dirty Dozen* (1967), and Robert Altman's *M*A*S*H* (1970).

What a Critic Said at the Time: "The acting is excellent. The Frenchman Jean Gabin is a first-rate tough guy. It's a picturesque and sometimes gripping tale of soldiers in North Africa." (*Variety*, 10-9-35 issue. Critic: "Stein. [Jerry Stein]. Reviewed in Paris.)

What Another Critic Said at the Time: "A picturesque and interesting adventure film about hunted men. Jean Gabin's performance of 'the wanted man' dominates the others, inevitably." (New York *Times*, 5-4-39 issue. Critic: Frank S. Nugent.)

FILM 20

VARIETES

France/Germany, 1935

(Literal English Translation: "VARIETY") Directed by Nicolas Farkas. Produced by Ernest Franzos. Written by Nicolas Farkas, Andre-Paul Antoine, and Rolf E. Vanloo. Based Upon a Novel by Friedrich Hollander. Director of Photography (black and white), Victor Armenise. Editor, Roger Spiri-Mercanton. Music by Hans Carste. Production Designer, Serge Pimenoff. (GENRE: MELODRAMA) A Production of Bavaria Films (Germany), Les Films EF (France) and Vandor Films (France). Running Time, 1 hour 40 minutes. Released in France by Pathe-Consortium Cinema on October 5, 1935. Never Released Theatrically in the United States.

"Drive a car over the Mighty Hercules, and win this great wristwatch!"
— *Circus ringmaster asking for an audience volunteer to drive over*
performer Gabin's prone body, in "Varietes"

After stepping-back to play a cameo role in *Golgotha*, Gabin's "right back on the edge, where he needs to be" (to paraphrase Al Pacino, from Michael Mann's insufferable non-classic, *Heat*), as the star of director Nicolas Farkas' spry comedy/drama *Varietes*, a great comedy/melodrama, which sets its scene within the confines of a traveling circus.

The *Cirque Maxime* (Circus Maximus) arrives in a small southern town, and its members spend the daylight hours circulating through its streets, perpetrating handstands and flips, rat-a-tat-tatting on the drums, just generally showing-off, and drumming up business for the upcoming evening's (*per* Ed Sullivan) *'rilly big shoo.'* The circus' biggest star is the rugged Georges (Jean Gabin), trapeze artist extraordinaire, who performs under the name of—what else?—*Hercules!* Georges' main interest in the circus isn't the trapeze, but the company's beautiful, brunette trapeze girl (trapezix? trapezatrix? *trapezoid?*), Anna, who's played by Annabella, the actress who, earlier that same year, had given Gabin a run for his money, when she played the exotic Aischa, in director Julien Duvivier's *La Bandera*. Anna's so beguiling, that not just Georges, but all of the men in the circus, take to her instinctively, like moths to an oh-so-seductive flame. As the circus members circulate through town, one aging townswoman dips out of her apartment window, to stare daggers at Anna; apparently, the

Circus Maximus has come through her town on more than one occasion, and *this koo-koo-ka-joo lady* thinks that Anna's been *making it with her husband,* and when we see the actual husband, who pokes his estimable frame outside the window, as he stands beside his wife, we know she's got to be dreaming, because he's a septugenarian *nebbish* in a massive bathrobe. She even calls out for the cops, but they ignore her, knowing full well that she's *full of shit.* This lady *does* have a more legitimate claim, too, about seeing to it that the circus should be getting 86'd from their town: She doesn't much like their noise.

The impresario of our little shoestring circus, the gruff but amiable Max (Jean Sinoel), keeps his troops in a perpetual state of *near-orgasm,* by reminding them, continually, that he might have an opportunity coming up, in which they'll be able to perform in Paris, which, to the members of this low-rent operation, might be tantamount to an invitation to Mecca. Jean Gabin's 'Georges,' Annabella's 'Anna,' and Fernand Gravey's 'Pierre' make up the circus's tripartite trapeze act: They call themselves *Les Trois Maximes* ('The Three Maximes'), and if you're guessing that there's going to be some kind of a love triangle between this tumbling triumvirate, in which feelings (and bottoms) are about to get hurt, you are oh-so-right. (Nicolas Farkas' *Varietes* is, according to the film's original, 1935 press materials, "Love, at 40-Feet Above the Ground!") Pierre and Georges both have an unrequited *thang* for lithesome Anna (the three are best friends, but both guys, even though they're appropriately tough and manly, are shy when it comes to trying to make anything happen sexually with her), although, at the same time, they *are* guys so, while they're waiting for Anna to capitulate to their special needs, they're also hitting on everything else in skirts. Pierre's probably got a better chance of getting into Anna's Danskins than Gabin's Georges does because, even though Jean Gabin is way more charismatic than Fernand Garvey, Garvey's 'Pierre' character is better at expressing his feelings to Anna, while Georges (at least, this is how Silent Gabin plays him, in this picture) never really tells her his true feelings, at all. (He's Jean Gabin, and so he expects the babes to come to him!) Really, *Varietes* is not about the 'variety' of acts in a circus show, and it is, instead, about the varieties of combinations of circus folk in the movie who love each other and, mostly, unrequitedly.

George and Pierre are bunkmates and, when they wake up the next day, Pierre's got Coffee Duty. Anna joins them in their tent, and the three immediately start in on a little callisthenic exercise. While Anna practices a dance routine, a bunch of clowns sneak in under the tent's flap and start hitting on her playfully, thus giving new meaning to the phrase 'scary clowns.' She really likes all of the guys in the circus, though, because they're all very brotherly and protective of her, and she recognizes that their 'awww-shucks' style of flirting is, more-or-less, just a little innocent fun, meant to help pass the time. One of the clowns even promises her, very paternally, "Don't worry. We will find a nice husband for you. You will marry a rich guy!" (What?! They're going to find her a rich clown with an MBA degree?!)

Night falls and, as Roy Scheider told us so presciently in Bob Fosse's *All That Jazz,* "It's showtime, folks!" It seems like the entire town has shown up for opening night, and not so much because they love circuses, but because there's nothing else to do, here in Lilliput.

Top: Gabin, Annabella, Fernand Gravey. Above: With Nicolas Koline.

Backstage, big-boss Max peppers his pre-show pep-talk with a little gently-paternal finger-shaking: "You guys did a good job getting people in here, but [and, here, he's indicating Anna] *you* kind of screwed up, because you were flirting with a married guy." (Aha! So the crazy Neighbor Lady was right: Anna really *has* been boffing that old crone's hubby!) Others in the crowd have shown up, because they're fascinated with the idea of getting a glimpse of this homewrecking harlot who's dared to screw around with a married man. The working-class people in this movie aren't too swift, and because Jean Gabin, in his other movies (and in his real life) was all about the working class, and about portraying working-class people heroically, it's no wonder that *Varietes* represents the only time Jean Gabin would ever work under director Nicolas Farkas, even though, at the same time, Gabin and the other leading players are all very well-served by the director, who seems to really know his way around drama, pacing, and suspense.

Max tells Georges and Pierre that he hopes they're ready for The Evening's Big Stunt: Not only will they perform their usual trapeze act but, tonight, in addition, they'll also perform a 'bit,' in which Pierre will drive a car over George's prone physique! During the show, Max pretends that the whole stunt hasn't even been invented yet, and he makes a rather generous offer to the audience: "Ladies and gentlemen: Who among you will let my friend Pierre drive his car over him? The man who does, will win this great *wristwatch!*" Since nobody lines up for a chance at pocketing the chintzy treat (the crowd is actually disgusted, even at hearing that this stunt-driving debacle will be part of the show), Georges lopes out onto the stage, and dutifully lays down, waiting for the chance to become *pavement pizza*. One audience member is really freaked about how dangerous the stunt might be, and yells up to Max, "Listen, why can't that girl drive over the big guy? She's lighter than that Pierre guy!" This line is another dig at 'the peccadilloes of the working class.' The crowd wants to see blood, but it's also kind of embarrassed about the way it feels, and it expects the blood to be 'let' as carefully as possible.

One reason the gang will be doing this stunt, a stunt which they extricate from the mothballs only rarely, is because tonight, the head of Paris's Apollo Theater is coming to see their little show, and Max has been informed that, if his performers do a great job, the Apollo's big muckimuck, Mr. Felix (Camille Berte), will invite them all to the big city, to participate in his theatre's big twenty-fifth-anniversary party. Felix shows up, right on cue, in his big fancy auto, and our troupe is righteously amped that the guy has deigned to join them.

The evening's show opens with Anna, who's dancing with a clumsy, lumbering bear. The crowd yawns through this act, though, and audience members even start throwing candy and popcorn at the bear, but they've definitely made a mistake, because—GRRRRR!!!!—it's Jean Gabin in the bear suit! Majorly pissed-off about getting booed, he yanks off his bear head and shakes a violent fist at the crowd: "Hey! You can't talk like that! How the hell would *you* like to be up here in this stupid get-up?" (You haven't lived until you've seen *Pepe Le Moko* dressed like a bear!) Georges' actions precipitate a big brawl between cast and audience, a brawl which seems to be matched, in its sheer intensity, only by those Who concerts in the '70s, in which all of those people got trampled. Georges, who's mad-as-hell, four decades before Peter Finch in *Network*, now stage-dives into the fighting crowd (it's Mosh Pit, 1935!), and the sequence ends with a bang: The performers-*vs.*-audience fight is so big, and so unruly, that the whole tent collapses!

But all is not lost: While the backstage crew is cleaning up at the end of the night, Max bolts over to his performers excitedly, to give them the good news, which is that Mr. Felix *loved* the whole show (he even enjoyed that interactive brawl, with the audience) and that, because of it, the whole Circus Maximus cast-n'-crew has now, officially, been invited to perform at the Apollo. Of course, since the next scene will take place in Paris, as will the rest of the picture, director Farkas next cuts-in the obligatory establishing 'stock shot' of the Eiffel Tower, just to confirm for us that we're not in, say, *Tokyo* or *Pyongyang*.

At the *Apollo-palooza*, Georges, Pierre, and Anna decide to perpetrate their daring flying trapeze act without a net, and all of the trapeze sequences in the movie are filmed in long-shot, because Annabella, Garvey and Gabin's stunts were all actually performed by a popular real-life trapeze act of the time, Madame Alexime and the Two Marces Brothers. The three are a little worried about the whole 'no-net situation' at first, but are immediately calmed by one of the most unlikely members of their troupe, Violet (Nicolas Koline), a funny old geezer who always follows the Three Maximes with the comedy act which he performs with his beloved *duck,* a duck whom he's actually named *Suzanne!* The old codger talks like a loving stage-mother to Suzanne the Duck, his best friend in this life, preparing the small fowl for the evening's performance. ("Do you remember what you have to do, Suzanne? *Eh, bien, Suzanne, c'est bon!*") The duck quacks-out its response in the affirmative, and the bemused stagehands proceed to play with it.

Tonight's Apollo-set performance of the Circus Maximus is just a preview for a handful of Paris' *hoi polloi*. Max meets with Mr. Felix, who wants to make sure that the whole Maximus Gang will be ready, and not just for tonight, but also for the following evening, which is when the paying public is going to be getting its chance to 'dig in' for the first time. Felix also alerts Max that tonight, after the show which they're going to be putting on for the 'swells,' a big, fancy party will be held in their collective honor.

While making final preparations for opening night, Pierre sees and starts flirting incessantly with a local girl, Valentina (she's played by a Spanish actress called Lena Dartes, a dead-ringer for Maggie Gyllenhaal), and Anna, of course, becomes jealous: She clearly likes Pierre as 'more than just a friend,' just as he likes her that way too, although the two of them remain strictly platonic, at this point, and she's jealous that this other girl is speaking to him. Georges, who's no slouch in the lovemaking-department himself, is using some of his prime down-time, wisely, to hit-on a similarly-pulchritudinous *buxotic,* a pert young Circes by the name of Jeanne (Germaine Reuver), and he tries to sell himself to her, thusly: "I know you're waiting to meet a rich guy with money, but I'm better!" Actually, Georges and Jeanne already know each other: They're platonic friends, although Georges would love to be able to change that scenario for the (naked) better, if only he could, and he's very aware that the sexual situation between them would probably change, in a flash, if only he had some money. So, for your records: Jean Gabin's Georges has two platonic loves in this picture, Jeanne and Anne.)

The Maximus Gang's first night of performing for the Paris swells goes off without a hitch and, after the show is over, it's time for the promised after-party, which takes place in a swanky mansion. Anna enters, dressed-to-the-nines in a fancy gown, and Pierre and Georges gawk at her like a pair of lovestruck wolves, right out of a Tex Avery cartoon. While guests and performers mix and mingle, Max, who's always promoting 24/7, is busy, regaling the fancy partygoers with stories about how his little circus has recently completed its whoppingly successful tour of Australia. (Like all producers worth their salt: He's lying his ass off!)

Georges has more plans in life than just being 'Circus Boy,' though: His ultimate goal is to marry Anna, and to get the hell out of Dodge, but he's never even told her how much he loves her, because he's afraid of opening himself up to her, especially when he sees that she pays more attention to Pierre than she does to him. (Nobody likes rejection, especially not Jean Gabin.) Still, he knows he's going to have to lay it on the line for his own sanity (although, very sweetly, he's too scared to tell Anna how much he loves her in-person, and so instead, he asks Pierre to do it for him, and he says it just like this: "Hey, Pierre: Would you mind telling Anna that I'm in love with her?") Of course, Pierre wants Anna, too, and so he tries to quell his eager friend's stirrings, by responding with a little bargain-basement pychology: "You know, Georges, life isn't easy. But we three are friends. Isn't that great? And isn't that enough? I already know that you'd like to marry Anna. And if that's what you want, well, you're just going to have to ask her yourself." Georges stares down at his shoes, shyly and uncomfortably, and Pierre next tells him the real reason he can't help him out (we already knew it, anyway, but we've been waiting for Pierre to say it with his own mouth): "I can't ask for you, Georges… because I love Anna, too. In fact, one of these days, I want Anna to marry *me*." The three have always been like brothers-and-sister, but now, things are beginning to get a bit more complicated.

In the next scene, Pierre surprises us, and quite happily so: He truly *is* a good friend to Georges and, as we're now seeing, his friendship with Georges even overrides his strong feelings for Anna:

> PIERRE: Would you like to get married?
> ANNA [shyly]: I… I thought you'd never ask!
> PIERRE: I'm not asking for myself. I'm asking for Georges.
> ANNA: [deflates; she likes both guys but, of the two, Pierre's the one she's vibing-on more]
> PIERRE: We'll all die single, if you don't marry Georges.
> ANNA: Oh…

Later that night, Georges and Pierre, who are both smoking huge cigars (because they've got to sublimate their feelings for Anna, somehow) see her as she's walking toward them. Suddenly confronted by both men, she immediately starts crying because, in the end, she's just realized that she really *is* in love with both of them equally, and that she's just as afraid of her feelings as they are. Summoning his courage, Georges finally asks her, directly to her face (when Pierre steps out of the room) if she'll marry him, but she's too weepy to make any kind of reply at all.

Before bed that night, we can tell that Pierre hates himself for having 'talked Georges-up,' instead of trying to help himself, so he tries to reverse the damage he's done to his own, potential future with Anna, by giving Georges a little bad news, about her—false news which, we can tell, he's probably making up, right on the spot: "Anna doesn't want you, Georges. I'm not trying to hurt your feelings, I'm just telling you the truth." Georges now stares Pierre down: He's a smart guy, and knows that Pierre is cock-blocking him... so he just walks away.

Night Three of Circus Maximus, in Paris, finds cast and crew chowing-down together, while a band, which has been hired for the occasion by Mr. Felix, is playing in their honor. Blonde Jeanne, the other girl whom Georges likes besides Anna, is crying now, because she's just looked within herself to discover that, while she's always been hot for Georges, that she, just like Anna, happens to like Pierre a little bit more she likes George; and, more than that, she's too shy to admit her feelings to Pierre, just as Georges is too shy to admit his true feelings to Anna. Pierre doesn't really understand what Jeanne's so upset about. ("Don't cry," he tells her, gently, "You need to be pretty for the show!") Just like in the fancy party scenes from other Jean Gabin movies, especially *Gloria*, loner Georges, who's looking uncomfortable in his tux (which he's probably worn all of twice in his whole life) eventually winds up sitting by himself at the fancy dinner, absently playing with the silverware, while Pierre, Jeanne, Anne, and Max all natter away happily, at another table. Just like in *Gloria*, working-class Gabin is mega-uncomfortable at trendy parties, and looks like he can't wait to get outside into the fresh air, to enjoy a relaxing smoke.

The following evening's show, which is the first one which the Circus Maximus is putting on for Paris's *publique generale*, is a heady admixture of fun and frolic, and the circus' singers and plate-spinners all seem to be in fine form-and-fettle. Backstage, while our trio of trapeze-artists gets into makeup, Jeanne waves to Pierre, and Anna, who sees this happening, doesn't like it one bit. Jeanne leans on Pierre, playfully placing her head on his shoulder, and this 'move' absolutely gets the result she wanted: Anna looks jealous, as if she's about to erupt like *Krakatoa, East of Java!* Pierre, who doesn't see Anna in the wings, gets in on the Jeanne-flirtation, too, tousling the young woman's hair, which she then makes him brush, luxuriantly.

Simultaneously, Georges, who's been stumbling around backstage, drunk-off-his-ass, which is not the best position to be in (for a person who's about to participate in a trapeze act) is peering into each dressing room, and noticing that everybody in the company has somebody to love—everybody, that is, except for him. (Why, even that crazy old Violet has his duck!) Indeed, Georges is *so* liquored-up, that the next thing he does, is to start looking for a fight with anybody and, as the saying goes, "Sometimes, when you don't know who to fight with—just start with whoever's closest!" When Pierre comes over to Georges to check up on him, Georges takes a swing at his unsuspecting friend. The crowd of performers and stagehands part like the Red Sea, and the two men start going at it, *mano-a-mano*, 'duking it out on the eternal plains,' and Georges is so soused, that Pierre and a bunch of other co-workers grab him and lock him in a room to cool off. Max has had to call-in a doctor for Pierre, whose arm was sliced-up pretty badly by Georges during their fight, and Jeanne's with Pierre, too, bandaging-up his arm. Pierre would love to talk to his buddy Georges, to find a solution to their problems, since he really values Georges' friendship, but now that they've had this big fight, he knows that this may never happen.

While the human characters in the film seem to be having a hard time finding love, it seems like all the ducks in the movie are getting laid right and left because, in the next sequence, Suzanne the Duck is actually escaping through the window, looking for other ducks to screw! When Suzanne's owner, Violet, returns from an all-night bender, and learns that Suzanne is missing, he (I know, I know, it's a bad pun, but I have to do it:) 'goes quackers.' The next morning, Georges wakes up, hung over, and has no idea what happened the night before; in fact, he is completely unable to remember his fight with Pierre.

Lunchtime comes, and Georges is sitting around with Violet, munching-out on some rather tasty mystery meat. He tells Violet that tonight, after the show, he'll help him to track down his beloved *canard perdu* ('lost duck'). But guess what (or, should I say, 'guess whom') they're eating? Needless to say, this scene is, at once, both hilarious and tragic—not to mention, I might wager, tasty, and maybe even slightly crispy and pungent. Nothing, it seems, goes down better than a big plate of crunchy '*Suzanne a l'orange!*'

The first part of that evening's performance consists of two women who are playing the *William Tell Overture* on xylophones. Georges perambulates backstage, calm, cool, and collected. He can't remember fighting with Pierre the night before and, when he sees Pierre, he greets his friend cheerfully, telling him that tonight, they should work without nets, just like they did on that first, big, preview night. Jeanne overhears the conversation, and is just as shocked by it as anybody else. She takes Pierre aside, and tells him that they're going to have to cancel the trapeze act for tonight, because it will definitely be too dangerous for Georges to participate in, especially since Georges is dealing with a lot of bad feelings, and is feeling prodigiously unloved. (Jeanne knows, as we all do, that you just don't want a hung-over guy monkeying around on a trapeze.) Everyone tries to talk Georges out of working that night, even (especially) impresario Max, but Georges has a more forceful personality than even his own boss, just like how Jean Gabin is always more forceful, in his pictures, than all of those shitty old authority figures who are always trying to tell him what to do.

Now, everybody in the cast and crew is freaking-out: What if Georges tries to kill himself, up on the trapeze? *Or:* What if Pierre swings toward Georges, and Georges doesn't catch him, on purpose? While buzz of this nature continues to circulate through the cast and crew, Pierre and Jeanne are now deciding that, ultimately, they are meant for each other, and Jeanne is now pleading with him: "Look, Pierre, if you love me, let's leave the circus now, forever—before the trapeze act starts. Before somebody gets hurt. We can leave right now, and be happy, and *not* do the show tonight. This isn't the life we want."

Even though Pierre knows Jeanne's right, and that it would be wrong for him to take advantage of his diminished capacity-buddy Georges, by sending Georges up the trapeze rope tonight, Pierre is also a consummate showman who knows the age-old maxim (it's great that, in the Circus *Maxime*, people actually observe '*maxims*'), that "the show must go on." Pierre informs a horrified Max that the trapeze act will be proceeding tonight, as planned, and with all three of the Flying Maximes taking part: "But just in case something happens to me," he tells Georges, "promise me that you'll take care of Jeanne."

Some unpleasant news which is about to rattle 'the company grapevine,' is that Georges has overheard Pierre and Jeanne talking about how much in love they are with each other, and now Georges looks more depressed than ever. Now, not only has he no chance for Jeanne, but he's also just heard Anna telling *her clown friends* that she doesn't love him (Georges) either, and that now that she's had the chance to think about it a bit more, she realizes that she loves him only as a friend. So now there are two women who love Pierre, instead of him. (*Shit!*)

Georges sits alone, silently staring into his make-up mirror, as Jeanne tries to console him: "I didn't know that my not being interested in you would be so painful for you." But—*Go, Gabin!*—when she sees how lachrymose he is, she now, instantaneously, begins changing her mind, because Jean Gabin demonstrates overt, outward sadness so rarely in his films, that when he actually does open up, it always works in his favor.

But now the question in every smart (or even kind-of-smart) moviegoer's mind, should be: Is Jeanne just pretending to love Georges, so that Georges will be gentle with Pierre (and with himself, and with Anna) during the trapeze act? Max brings Georges and Pierre together, and the two friends shake hands, putting on a façade and pretending that all of their problems are behind them. "Next time," Georges tells his pal Pierre, smilingly (remembering, only now, that he fought with him the previous night), "I'll only drink water, okay?" The two friends hug, and both men (at least) *look* happy. As the show begins, Jeanne's waiting near the exit, suitcases packed, because she knows she's going to be leaving the circus with Pierre, at the end of the show. Meanwhile, 'up on the flying trapeze,' we've got Anna and Pierre on one side, and Georges (all alone, as Jean Gabin always seems to be) on the other side. Since we, the film's audience, are now well-invested in the characters, and are accepting them as real people, we're now very eager to see how the act will turn out. Anna swings over to Georges, who catches her safely. (Whew! We were wondering about that!) Then, she swings back to Pierre, and Georges sits on his little trapeze swing, alone.

Then, a big surprise for us: As it turns out, it's not Pierre or Georges who starts going through a mental disorder up on the bar that night, but *Anna*, who loves both men. Suddenly, she gets dizzy and passes out, right atop her swing, and forty feet above solid ground. Pierre takes her in his *mighty French arms* (I know, I know: 'Mighty' and 'French arms' is oxymoronic, but just go with it), and then carries her safely offstage, but Georges remains perched in his swing, a boss alpha-monkey at the top of his tree, not at all ready to relinquish his power. Nobody dares to go up there with him; he looks volatile and angry about how Pierre's just taken her away from him.

Backstage, a doctor checks Anna out, revealing that there's nothing wrong with her, and that her fainting has resulted only from nerves. Since Anna knows that it was Pierre who rescued her, she's now more in love with him than ever before, and this isn't good news for Jeanne: She's still waiting by the exit, for Pierre, with both of their suitcases packed. Back on the trapeze swing, meanwhile, Georges remains alone, in close-up, not sure whether, in the parlance of the 1992 American action movie *Speed*, to "Stay on or get off."

The crowd really has loved the trapeze act tonight, even in spite of the fact that Anna passed out right in the middle of it, and Georges is now alone in the wings, consoling old, duckless Violet (well, you might say that Violet still has Suzanne... *in his colon!*), and both men, young and old alike, are in the same boat, both vowing out loud now that they are finished with the circus. Meanwhile, Pierre and Anna are back onstage, taking their bows without Georges. Anna sees Georges in the wings, and tells him to come up and join them, but he just doesn't want to. He waves to the crowd from the wings, silently forcing a smile.

Director Farkas cuts to a few days later: Georges has left the trapeze act, which as Big Boss Max is informing his players, will now be called The *Two* Maximes instead of The Three Maximes. Pierre has decided to stay with the circus, having chosen Anna over Jeanne, and Jeanne has already run away from the circus, by herself. As per usual, in a lot of Jean Gabin movies, and especially, in the ones which he'll make during this stage of his career, Georges, our Gabinian hero, walks away alone, into the night.

Varietes was made during the period of Jean Gabin's biggest international fame (1935-1941), but it's one of the few films he made during that period which is not discussed all that much by the world's film critics, probably because they feel that it's just a melodrama, and they're probably also not talking about it, because it's so rare: At the time of this book's printing, there's only one (gorgeous) 35mm print of *Varietes* in the world, and it's sitting in a vault, at the Paris archives of the French Ministry of Culture (the CNC). It's a great movie, though, and it also happens to be one the best movies ever made, in any country, on the subject of shyness, and of the loneliness which shyness often brings. It's a movie about how sometimes (okay, okay: most of the time) we sabotage ourselves, and it's also about how we never really get the things or people we want, just because we're too timid to ask for them (because we, just like all three of the main characters in this picture, are afraid of risking rejection, and of getting hurt). Georges, Anna, and Pierre are three very confident and attractive people and, just like lots of attractive and confident people in real-life, they don't go after what they really want, and I'm not just talking about romantic involvement, here: I'm also talking about being afraid to go for that flashy career you want, or even that fancy, exotic vacation you've always dreamed of taking. Thematically, another movie which is close to *Varietes*, is a great movie which would be made fifty-eight years after it, in 1993, the excellent Merchant-Ivory adaptation of Japanese author Kazuo Ishiguro's somber novel, *Remains of the Day*, in which two *veddy-proper* members of a London household staff, butler Anthony Hopkins and chambermaid Emma Thompson, both really love each other, but are both way too shy to admit it, the result being that nothing ever happens between them and, at the end of the picture, they're both left miserable and alone. Both *Varietes* and *Remains of the Day* are compelling pictures, because all of us have felt (and feel, and will continue to feel) what the characters in them are feeling; in other words, all of us are Georges, Anna, and Pierre, whether we're French trapeze artists, or butlers, or none of the above.

While *Varietes* was never released theatrically in the United States, or in any other English-speaking territories, it was a big box-office hit in France, and in the following year of 1936, the British director Herbert Wilcox would remake the picture in English as *The Three Maxims*, and the three love-trianglers in Wilcox's picture, were played by Tulio Carminati, Anna Neagle, and Leslie Banks. Nicolas Koline, who played Violet, the old Duck Guy, in the French version, is the only actor from the French Gabin/Farkas movie, who would return for this British remake.

What a Critic Said at the Time: "This film stands high as a French production. A good job of film producing, it hangs together, sustains its interest throughout, and hits them hard at the climax. [The film's leading actress] Annabella was knocked down by a 'tame' bear on the set, and it was doubtful it the picture could be finished. [Director] Farkas wouldn't have troubles, if he was working for a good American company!" (*Variety*, 11-6-35 issue. Critic: "Stein. [Jerry Stein.]" Reviewed in Paris.)

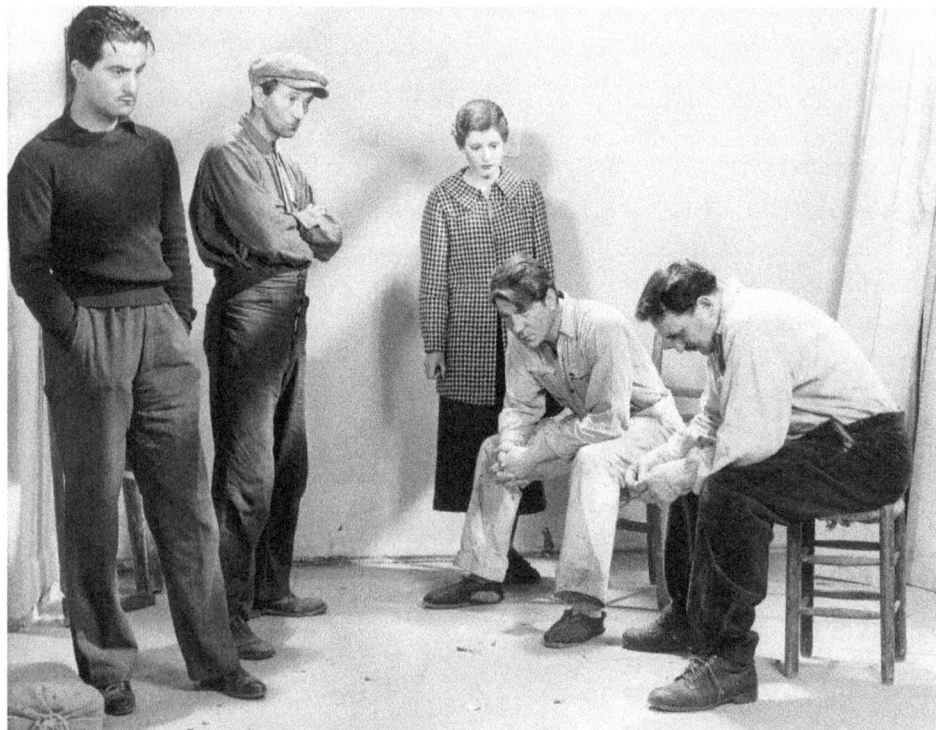

Top: Rafael Medina, Raymond Aimos, Micheline Cheirel, Jean Gabin, and Charles Vanel.
Above: With Viviane Romance.

FILM 21

LA BELLE EQUIPE

France, 1936

(Literal English Translation, "THE GOOD TEAM") Directed by Julien Duvivier. Produced by Rays Biscotti. Written by Julien Duvivier and Charles Spaak. Music by Maurice Yvain. Directors of Photography (black and white), Marc Fossard and Jules Kruger. Editor, Marthe Poncin. Production Designer, Jacques Kraus. (GENRE: ENSEMBLE COMEDY) Running Time, 1 hour 41 minutes. Produced and Distributed by Cine-Arys. Released in France on September 17, 1936. Released Theatrically in the U.S. by Lenauer International Films, Inc., on May 31, 1938 with English subtitles, as "THEY WERE FIVE." Re-Released in the United States on January 1, 1952, (NYC) by Lenauer, as "FIVE MEN AND A WOMAN."

"I've been deported from Spain, Germany, and France. So, what?
They're going to deport me again? Who cares!"
— *Gabin holds forth to his friends, on 'the nature of his drifting ways,' in "La Belle equipe"*

Winning the Lottery. Picking Some Numbers. Easy Street.
The lottery isn't just something we all wish we could win, today. Julien Duvivier realized it, and directed a great ensemble comedy-drama about that very subject, seventy-two years ago, in 1936.

As the film begins, the cops, including a surly Inspector who's played by Fernand Charpin—a great French actor who'll play another surly Inspector two years after this film, in one of Gabin's most famous movies of all time, *Pepe Le Moko* (which was also helmed by Duvivier)—are on the lookout for the swarthily-mustached young card, Mario (Rafael Medina), a Frenchman of Portuguese descent. Mario wants one of his four good-naturedly goofy and perennially out-of-work friends to hide him out. One of his pals is Jean (Jean Gabin) who, when we first meet him, is in the tiny room he lives in at a filthy hotel which, quite hilariously, is called, 'The King of England.' And just as Mario is arriving at Jean's, the hotel owner, Mr. Jubette (Jacques Baumer), shows up as well, and he means to toss Jean out, because Jean hasn't been paying for the room. Jean, who's never afraid of anybody—as per usual with Gabin's movie characters—noisily informs Jubette that he'll gladly pay his rent, at such time as Jubette should begin taking care of his room. ("Unplug my sink! Sweep! Bring me some clean towels! Then, I'll pay, okay?") Nobody really wins the argument—it's a draw, slightly weighted toward the angry Jean—and Jubette skulks away.

Exit Jubette and enter Mario, who now tells Jean that he's being chased by the law, and could Jean possibly hide him out until the cops make themselves scarce. "It's not the best time to ask me for a favor," Jean tells his upset-looking pal, "I just chewed-out my landlord!" Next, Mario and Jean's other ne'er-do-well pal, a sad-sack called Charles (Charles Vanel), arrives. Charles' wife, Gina, has just left him for—Heaven forefend!—a man who is actually able to earn a living, and naturally, this makes Charles feel more horribly about himself than he already does.

As in all of Jean Gabin movies, the bond of friendship between male friends is stronger and more enduring than the sexual love between men and women can ever be. Jean consoles Charles by telling him, "You didn't need her, anyway. Listen to me: Women are good for an hour. Just give them compliments. They come and they go." In another Gabin picture which will be made three years later, 1939's *Le Recif de corail* (*The Coral Reef*), Gabin will tender a similar opinion, when he tells another character that "women are just perfume, hair, and a name." (Ahh, the good old days, when men were men!)

Mario doesn't want to get arrested but, on the other hand, he's a fatalist, and just like many of the roles which had always been played by Rafael Medina's co-star Jean Gabin, he knows that 'getting caught' is all mankind's true lot in life, so he isn't too worried about it; their fourth friend, Jacques (Charles Dorat), now logs an appearance at Jean's place, too, and now Charles, Jean, Jacques, Mario, and a fifth pal, Raymond (Raymond Aimos)—a man whom they affectionately call 'Tintin,' after the cartoonist Herge's famous cartoon adventurer—all of them being bored-out-of-their-skulls and out of work, head over to a local bar, very sweetly, to try and win Mario's girlfriend Huguette (Micheline Cheirel) some presents. They try their hands at that machine where the metal claw makes failing attempts to grab a stuffed animal, but they lose all of their coinage in the process; undeterred, Jean tilts the machine over until it delivers a sweet little stuffed animal for his pal's girl, and they also win her a razor. Mario even wins Huguette a powder-puff, the gift for which she had most hoped. This pack of funny, youngish bachelors-on-the-prowl isn't deterred by anything: These guys observe the practically Masonic 'Guy Code,' in which men throughout the ages have always helped each other out. In a cold and unforgiving world, these five friends—in fact, in the U.S., the movie was released as *They Were Five*—have formed a family, a family in which level-headed Jean is, very clearly, the voice-of-reason—the father-figure.

That night, Charles, Jacques, Mario, and Raymond play poker in Jean's hotel, and Jean tells them that they'd better stop, since they're out of work: "When you're stuck like we are," he lectures his pals, "you play marbles, not poker." At that moment, the Inspector, whom we have already seen, knocks at the door, and Mario hides under the bed. They assure the Inspector that Mario is not there, and he leaves.

So we've got five good-natured, down-on-their luck-guys—men who are real enough for anybody to identify with—and then, suddenly, and without warning, Fate—a/k/a, Duvivier and his *La Bandera* screenwriter, Charles Spaak—changes their collective situation, for the better: The guys suddenly find out that they've won the lottery on a ticket which they have bought together, and this collectively makes them one hundred thousand francs, or twenty thousand francs per man, richer. "It's not very much," Jean tells them, "but in this poverty-stricken world, it means a lot." The guys immediately throw themselves a party at Jean's, and then, just like the itinerant farm workers George and Lenny in Steinbeck's *Of Mice and Men*, they spend the following sequence sitting around, daydreaming out loud about what they'll be able to liberate from local shops with their newfound windfall: Jean, very sweetly, mentions that he has always wished to have a nice grandfather clock; and Jacques, who is secretly in love with Mario's girlfriend, Huguette, tells them that maybe he'll buy a plane ticket to Canada, since Canadians speak French. (Obviously, if he's far away, in another country, it will be hard for him to pine away for his friend's girl.)

The guys have practical things which they would like to do with their new income, too: In the ensuing sequence, the five decide to go out and buy some natty new shoes, and Duvivier will next present us with a comically-inventive dissolve, in which the guys' old, torn-up shoes magically 'become' new shoes, and all of these new shoes, by the way, happen to be much too tight: They all walk down the street together, each man constantly tripping over his own heel in the ill-fitting shoes which he has just wrangled.

Back up at Jean's apartment, in the next scene, the men all sit with their feet aching miserably, and Jean now proclaims, "The only way the five of us will ever truly be able to find freedom, is if we can be together for always. So instead of wasting all of our money on stupid things, I've got an incredible idea: Let's all buy a farm together!" Mario replies that, in his opinion, most farms are too close to police stations, and that, besides, when people own property together, they always fight—but Jean assures them that they will not. "We'll have a farm with a little house in the middle. A house for all of us."

When Saturday comes, all five men begin looking for an old farm which they can fix up. Sailing down the Marne River—the 525-mile tributary of the Seine, between the towns of Nogent and Joinville—they come upon a decayed washhouse which all of them instantly love. It's hidden among messy canals which are overgrown with trees, and there's even a great branch, overhanging the river, which replicates a beautiful, Venice-like archway. The romantic side of Jean now comes out, as he announces that they are going to fix the place up and turn it into a paradise for sportsmen and fishermen: "And we're going to bring our lovers here, too! Lots of them!"

Duvivier dissolves to the next sequence, in which the five guys have, in a relatively short period of time, posted a sign which one of them has written in chicken scrawl, and it reads, "Coming Soon: A Bar!" (Sounds romantic enough to them!) Since making the little sign—it probably took all of about ten seconds—has been enough work for one day, and drinking time is near (because "it's always five-o'-clock somewhere"—especially, in France), the five next sit around, lushing-it-up and scraping their noggins together, trying to come up with a name for their new '*guinguette*' (the name given to France's combination bar/hotel/dance-halls, which were very popular in the 1920s and 1930s); the best they can think of, however, under the dual and pernicious influences of too-much-liquor and hot sun, are, 'The Green Pig;' 'The Beef Stew;' and perhaps the most haiku-like of all, 'The Floor of Water.' Jean doesn't much like that last suggestion, though. ("Floor of Water? Naaah, that's no good. People will think that this is a place where you come to drown!") Finally, when all five are completely blotto, they come up with the best name of all, 'The Goose's Ass.' Anyway, after busting themselves up over it, they come to their senses, finally settling on the more tourist-friendly name, '*Chez nous*' ('Our House.') The five men sign the deed, shake hands with the now-former owner (he's played by Robert Moor), and the place belongs to them.

Of course, it's not long before Charles' estranged *femme-fatale* girlfriend, Gina shows up, and she's played by Viviane Romance, an actress was seen briefly in 1934's *Zou Zou*, during the scene in the bar in which Gabin is singing "*Viens, Fifine.*" When the scrotumless Charles sees Gina, he hides, but not before sending Jean as his emissary to try and scare her away. Gina finds Charles—because he's not the best hider in the world—and it's clear that she still wears the pants in their relationship, even though their relationship is over, and they're no longer together. "You won the lottery," Gina reminds Charles. "I'm your wife. And I want my cut!" He tries to be the boss: "But we're separated! You're the one who left! Nobody chased you out. You walked out on me!" While this is happening, the other four guys are hiding, just out of eyeshot: They're checking her out because she's gorgeous, and even though she's screwed-over their friend, it's still a lot of fun for them to hang out and ogle her. Then, Jean tells her to get lost.

Once the guys get rid of Gina, without having had to pay her any money, it's time for our five friends to weather another storm, and this time, it's a literal one: A huge, wind-driven rainstorm drenches the hotel, only hours after the guys have re-roofed. The five climb the roof, struggling against the wind and, in a great sight gag which is definitely worthy of Blake Edwards or Jacques Tati at their best, each man now tries, completely unsuccessfully, to catch the shingles—and each other—before the shingles can sail off, onto the ground. After the storm, Jacques leaves France, for Canada, and so now, there are only four.

The rainstorm has put the guys behind on their work so much, that they now have to use some of their emergency cash reserves, so they'll be able to re-re-roof. When Jean pops open the cashbox, he discovers that it's a bit light, because somebody has pilfered some of their not-so-petty cash. Jean asks his friends who they think may have stolen it, and—this is no surprise—weak-willed Charles now admits that he gave his share of their lottery winnings to Gina, when she had last visited. (The three glare at him as he wimpily explains, "But... she told me that the money was her right!") Because Charles is their friend, though, and because they all love him even in spite of his thick-headedness, they are unable to get too mad at him, and this moment, in the film, is very sweet and real. Of course, Jean tells Charles that Charles is going to have to go and retrieve the money from Gina right away, but Charles replies that he can't go to her place, because he's afraid of her! "Well, then, I'll go myself," Jean replies, resolutely.

When Jean arrives at Gina's apartment—the apartment she used to share with Charles—she's happy to see him (since no woman can resist Jean Gabin's charms), and Jean tells Gina, in so many words, why he's there: "We need our money back for our *guinguette,* and you've got to give it back right now!" When she refuses, Jean starts pushing her around, and she really seems to enjoy it! Next, director Duvivier and screenwriter Spaak weave a not-so-unexpected plot twist: Jean and Gina make love, and it is a tribute to Jean Gabin that his 'Jean' character, in this film, is so charismatic, we'll still like him, even when we find out that he's just had sexual relations with his friend's lady: We know Jean would never intentionally hurt any of his friends, and that, well—a man just has his needs. (This, by the way, is the only one of Jean Gabin's ninety-five feature films in which one of his characters will ever sleep with a friend's woman.)

As Jean leaves Gina's place with the money, he is confronted by Charles, who knows that Gina and Charles were sleeping together, and the fact that Charles is now arriving at Gina's doesn't bode well for Charles either, because Charles has come to Gina's house to try and sleep with her, as well—and this, after he has already made a promise to his friends that he will never see her again. Jean is so embarrassed that Charles has caught him with Gina that he stares down at his shoes and mutters, very meekly and quietly, "I guess the wife of a friend is always interesting…"

When Jean is back among his friends, he tells them that Gina only had five hundred of the two thousand francs which Charles had originally given her and, in a way, even though Jean is a nice guy, he's kind of passive-aggressively getting back at Charles here, for having given her his share of their lottery winnings, when he now says, "You screwed-up by letting her have your money. But I guess I screwed up, too, by sleeping with her." Charles still thinks highly of Jean, however, and the really nice thing about this film, as I have already mentioned, is that the friendship between the main characters always overrides the occasional flare-ups.

Next, we get another problem over at the King of England hotel, and hopefully one which won't be insurmountable: The police show up, led by Fernand Charpin's Inspector, because the authorities are still hot on Mario's trail. And why, exactly, have the cops been looking for Mario since the beginning of the picture? It's because Mario is a foreigner, from Portugal, and while he's been in France, he has possibly been involved in some illegal political activities. Mario, who decides to give himself up, now enters the room, even though his friends have told him to hide under a bed, and the Inspector tells him that he will be deported from France within the next forty-eight hours. As long as the cops are here, Jean smilingly asks them for a favor: "Listen, before you take our friend away, could you guys help us move this cabinet?" The Inspector and his men, very sweetly, help the guys out, while they all hum "Volga Boatmen" together!

Easter Sunday: While grand-opening day at our quaint *guinguette* is still a few months away, today our friends are going to have a little preview for the townspeople—in fact, they are going to be having a major party—and the police have been nice enough to allow Mario to stay in France a bit longer, just so that he can attend this event. The French 'worker's flag' has been placed atop the now re-re-tiled roof, and tons of locals show up for their first look at the now beautifully-restored former washhouse. Gabin, as he does in a number of his 1930s films, now interrupts the crowd, to sing a buoyant song, "*Quand on se promene au bord de l'eau*," ("*When One Walks Near the Water*"), the lyrics of which are as follows: "Every Sunday is beautiful when you have a farm… If you find a little land where you feel comfy, there is no need to look anywhere else… Everything in nature is drowned-out in greens and blues…" (After the film was released, the song, as sung by Jean Gabin in the film, became a hit record, and you can still find it today on any number of French music CD-compilations.) The fun which the crowd is having at this big party is marred only when Raymond ('Tintin'), who's been up on the roof checking it to make sure the new tiles are in place, slips off, dying, instantly.

A Few Months Later:

Mario's now in Portugal with Huguette, who's just officially become his fiancée, and Jacques had, of course, already left France for Canada earlier in the film—since he can't pine away for Huguette if he's in a completely different country than she is. Plus, as Raymond has now died, only two of the original five are left—Jean and Charles, the two men who had both dated Gina—and Jean tells Charles that the best night of his life, was that rainy night they all spent together on the roof, when they were catching the falling shingles. Gina is still hanging around Jean and Charles, and she's beginning to panic, because neither of the two remaining men seems to have any need for her. She tells Jean how alone she feels, and Jean puts her in her place right away, doing his patented, 'I'm Jean Gabin: My Male Friends are More Important than My Female Lovers'-routine: "I don't care too much for complainers. My friends are better than you, and they're worth a whole lot more than you are."

The hotel's previous owner now appears, because he's interested in seeing what the guys have done with his former place. He sees the hotel's sign, with its evocative pair of shaking hands, and tells the guys, "Forget the hands. Put a phone number on the sign, instead. It's more commercial." Now that the guys have fixed the property up so nicely, it's natural that the old owner wants it back. And guess what: He can take possession of it if he wants to, because he is a majority shareholder in the place, having bought-out Raymond's, Mario's, and Jacques' shares.

Jean solves the problem by letting-fly with a powerful Gabin-Outburst, in which he gives the old owner nearly the same *spiel* which he gave the manager of the cruddy hotel at the beginning of the film: "Us, give the hotel back to you? Are you kidding?! The toilets need fixing! A lot of stuff here needs work. Are you going to get down on your hands and knees and work with us, and fix everything that needs to be fixed? I thought not! So if you're not willing to work, just get the hell away from us!" The guy is so frightened by Jean, he changes his mind about taking the place back, and scampers away like a frightened puppy. (Being on the receiving end of a 'Gabin-Outburst' is something you'd never want to wish, even on your worst enemies.)

Before long, the *guinguette's* official opening day is finally at hand: Raymond's brother, Rene (Robert Lynen) shows up, and he presents Jean and Charles with an antique grandfather clock—so now, Jean finally has the clock which he had wished for at the beginning of the film. (Rene knew that Jean wanted a clock, because Raymond had mentioned that fact to him, a long time ago.)

Wealthy vacationers are now pouring in, and everybody's dressed-to-the-nines. Huguette's grandmother, who's played by Marcelle Geniat, comes, too, bringing good tidings from Mario and Huguette in Portugal: "I have news from the kids! They've found work and happiness, and they said that they are here with you in spirit."

That same day, Gina shows up at the hotel's restaurant with a new beau, hoping to make Jean and Charles jealous, but they don't care, because they're both already way past her. A Waiter (Marcel Maupi) brings Jean a big stack of fresh, clean towels, and we're happy for him, because Jean has finally received the clean towels for which he asked Jubette at the beginning of the film. (Jean Gabin is always a man of modest goals and simple tastes: All he needs are good friends, the occasional brunette, a clock, and some clean towels!) Gina takes leave of her new boyfriend's side, for just long enough to whisper in Jean's ear that she still loves him, but he just smiles widely, telling her, "Don't fall in the water!" Since she hasn't been able to win Jean back, she next makes a furtive, half-hearted attempt at seducing her wimpy 'ex,' Charles—if she can't have Jean, then she wants, at the very least, to be with someone who, by association, reminds her of Jean. She thinks Charles will fall for her again, but Charles is now much stronger than he used to be, and he doesn't buy her "I still love you"-nonsense at all, so she stomps off in defeat. As the film ends, Jean dances up a storm with a woman who is a lot nicer than Gina—Huguette's cute old grandmother.

While the ending of this film is pretty buoyant and happy, this is not the actual ending which Julien Duvivier had shot—the tragic ending which he and screenwriter Charles Spaak preferred: In Duvivier and Spaak's completely different ending, Gina causes Jean to kill Charles in a fit of anger, Jean is arrested, and as the police lead Jean away, he softly mutters, "But it was a good idea," referring to the sheer hopelessness of trying to do something positive—in this case, starting a fun country *guinguette* where all people can be together in peace—in such a crazy world. Thirty-five millimeter prints of *La Belle equipe* which featured the original tragic ending dropped out of circulation for decades, until an original print turned up just a few years ago. Today, when *La Belle equipe* is shown on French television on the channel France 3, as it was on June 7th, 2006, it is the version of the film with the happy ending which is screened, and after the film is over, the channel typically broadcasts Duvivier's recently-re discovered 'downcast ending,' separately. The false 'happy ending' was cobbled together by the film's producers, who rearranged some footage and added one shot of Gabin reading Charles a letter which he has received from Jacques, in which Jacques is wishing them success in their new *guinguette* endeavor. And since Viviane Romance ('Gina') wasn't available for re-shooting the happy ending, her exit, in that version of the film, is approximated by a shot of the men slowly turning their heads as 'her' footsteps subside, suggesting that she has slunk off in defeat. Interestingly, French movie audiences in 1936, although they enjoyed the film, didn't really take to either of the two endings.

The most important thing in the world, according to this energetic and bittersweet 1936 movie-confection, is the hand of friendship, which no man—and, especially, no woman—can ever hope to tear asunder. Like many of the films in this book, while *La Belle equipe* is considered a very important film in France, it has rarely been screened in the United States a handful of times, since its brief theatrical release in a few arthouse cinemas, in May of 1938.

What a Critic Said at the Time: "While [Jean] Gabin carries the entire pic, [Charles] Vanel portrays a slow-thinking workman to high degree of perfection. This film will appeal to the lower layers, because what takes place could happen to anyone." (*Variety*, 10-7-36 issue. Critic: "Hugo." Reviewed in Paris.)

What Another Critic Said at the Time: "The film has been agreeably played by a modest French cast, in which Jean Gabin is perhaps the best known, and the best. Having no extreme emotional highs to present, the film's lows become more interesting to consider. Having no illusions about the lives it studies, it gives its characters just such dignity as they deserve. An interesting little picture, eminently practical in its attitude[s], moderate in its dramatic achievement[s]. A good mixture of humor, burlesque, and tragedy." (New York *Times*, 6-3-38 issue. Critic: Frank S. Nugent.)

What a Critic Said More Recently: "This warm, lyrical 1936 film consolidated Jean Gabin's position as France's Everyman, on the screen.. it is an affirmation of brotherhood, in the shadow of the Depression." (Los Angeles *Times*, 8-4-1982 issue. Critic: Kevin Thomas.)

FILM 22

LES BAS-FONDS

France, 1936

(Literal English Translation: "THE LOWER DEPTHS") Directed by Jean Renoir. Produced by Alexandre Kamenka. Screenplay by Eugene Zamiatine, Jacques Companeez, Jean Renoir, and Charles Spaak. Based Upon the Stage Play by Maxim Gorky. Music by Jean Weiner. Directors of Photography (black and white), Fedote Bourgasoff and Jean Bachelet. Editor, Marguerite Houlle-Renoir. Assistant Director, Jacques Becker. (GENRE: DRAMA) Running Time, 1 hour 35 minutes. Produced and Released in France by Films Albatros, on December 5, 1936. Released in United States with English Subtitles as "UNDERGROUND," on September 10, 1937, by The Arthur Mayer and Joseph Burstyn Company, Inc.

"Somehow, the job that'll put you on easy street never pans out."
— *Gabin accepts that he will always be poor, in* "Les Bas-fonds"

Gabin was back in action, in 1936, in *Les Bas-fonds*, a film which would be released in the United States under its literal title, *The Lower Depths*. It's an adaptation of Maxim Gorky's 19th-Century Russian novel, as adapted by Charles Spaak (*La Bandera* and *La Belle equipe*), although the picture is only nominally Russian, since the actors in it speak only French, and there's never any indication of anything even remotely Russian, outside of the word '*ruble*.' Clearly, the great Jean Renoir (son of the painter Pierre Auguste Renoir), who is here directing Gabin in the first of the four films which they would make together (1937's *La Grande illusion*, 1938's *La Bete humaine*, and 1955's *French Cancan* will follow), really means to show us the post-Depression/pre-World War II France of the 1930s, more than he's trying to show us Russia, fifty years earlier.

Most of the film sets its scene in the decrepit flophouse which is owned by the elderly criminal Kostyev (Vladimir Sokoloff) and Kostyev's selfish, blonde trophy-wife Vassilsa (Suzy Prim), and this is definitely a couple that takes the whole concept of 'abusive relationships' to exciting new highs (or lows): Kostyev tells Vassilsa that she'd be nothing without him, and she flaunts her relationship with one of the place's tenants, a handsome young thief by the name of Pepel (Jean Gabin), in front of him, this in spite of the fact that Pepel, very sensibly,

Top: With Louis Jouvet. Above: With Junie Astor.

broke up with Vassilsa before the movie began (because her maliciousness outweighs her hotness)! Vassilsa is preternaturally threatened by the attentions which Pepel pays to her much nicer little sister, Natacha (Junie Astor, no relation to *The Maltese Falcon's* Mary Astor), whom Kostyev and Vassilsa keep in perpetually indentured servitude, like a bargain-basement Cinderella. Vassilsa still holds a torch for Pepel, even though he's no longer interested in her, and when she's 100% sure that he won't reciprocate her feelings, she alerts him that if he doesn't kill her husband for her and run away with her, she'll have him arrested for some crimes he committed which she knows about, but which she's been keeping under-wraps. The 'Gabin-Cool' Pepel doesn't feel threatened by her, though, letting her know that he's not interested in killing anybody, because for him, as he says life is problematic enough without adding extra unnecessary complications into the mix. (In 1938, two years after *Les Bas-fonds*, Gabin and director Jean Renoir would again team up, this time on an adaptation of Emile Zola's 1890 novel *La Bete humaine*, another film in which, similarly to this one, a *femme-fatale* asks Gabin to kill her husband and run away with her, and he expresses reticentness about the whole situation.) Pepel resignedly Gabin-Shrugs, telling Vassilsa, "What's the use of killing? I'll go to prison… and you'll come, too!"

Besides the Pepel-Natacha-Vassilsa-Kostyev love quadrangle, director Renoir also supplies us with the tale of a long-penniless, and perpetually in debt, Baron, who is played by another of France's great stars of the stage and screen, Louis Jouvet. (Jouvet would play one of the coolest movie cops ever, in Henri Georges-Cluzot's amazing 1947-*noir*, *Quai des orfevres*, and when he wasn't acting, Jouvet even presided over his own popular Paris playhouse.) The Baron lives in an old, decaying (think: *House of Usher*) mansion, and his loyal butler Felix, who's played by Leon Larive, continues to labor for him for free, one hundred percent-loyal to his charming master, in spite of the fact that said master hasn't been able to pay him since forever.

One night, Pepel enters the Baron's mansion to rob him, and the Baron, instead of feeling intimidated, is endlessly amused by his *shabby-chic* intruder, and he informs Pepel that he, just like Pepel, is completely broke, and that while he has no money to speak of, he'll be happy to let Pepel help himself to any of the (ratty old) furniture he wants! These two men of different backgrounds, but equally-easygoing dispositions, discovering that they share something in common (poverty), quickly become fast friends, and director Renoir next dissolves to the following morning: The Baron and Pepel have been up all night, drinking and laughing their asses off together, and now they're even playing cards! The Baron is fascinated by Pepel who, unlike him, is worry-free, not to mention completely without debt. He's delighted by Pepel's stories of sleeping out on the grass on starry nights, in the public square (shades of wealthy Peter Sellers, who slummed-it in the park with homeless transient Ringo Starr, in director Joseph McGrath's weird/great 1969 film adaptation of Terry Southern's hypnotic 1959 novel, *The Magic Christian*), and he even insists that Pepel should help himself to a pair of bronze racehorses which are prominently displayed on his mantelpiece. After the police seize the Baron's property (everything except for one chair), the Baron cheerfully heads off to

With Louis Jouvet.

live with Pepel in Kostyev and Vassilsa's flophouse, where he becomes extremely impressed by how simply the 'other half' lives.

In *La-Bas fonds*, just like in real life, everyone wants what he or she can't have: Nastia (Jany Holt), a sad-but-eternally optimistic girl from the neighborhood can be observed, throughout the film, toting around a romance novel called *Unrequited Love*; the Baron pines away for Pepel's 'simple' life; and Pepel is jealous of what he (at first, anyway) has believed to be the Baron's comfortable, moneyed existence. Yes, everyone in this flick is perennially unsatisfied, especially the film's Greek chorus of lower-class street people who populate the film's background (street people are a staple of France's Poetic-Realistic cinema of the 1930s), who include an alcoholic, down-and-out actor, played by Robert Le Vigan (*Le Tunnel, Maria Chapdelaine, La Bandera, Golgotha*). At one point, the wild-haired Le Vigan (in this film, he looks amazingly like Sean Penn), even ventures into foreground, and begins inebriatedly chanting, "*My organism is completely intoxicated!*"

When a good-naturedly porcine police inspector (Andre Gabriello) visits the flophouse and informs Kostyev that he might have to take him to jail for some recent crimes which he's committed, Kostyev and Vassilsa basically sell him Vassilsa's kindly little sister Natacha, who (naturally) can't abide the chubby lawman. Of course it's not long before Pepel, Natacha's admirer, rescues her from the Inspector, and when Kostyev and Vassilsa find out about this, they both become so livid, that they beat Natacha within an inch of her life. When Pepel is

With Junie Astor.

informed of this beating by the Greek Chorus of street people (who in this movie, just as in most of Gabin's other films which would be made throughout the decades, love him), he—a guy who previously stated that he would not kill Kostyev—slays the old man offscreen, defending Natacha, the woman he loves. (Yes, friends, Gabin can kill! [*Like the rest of us, he just needs a reason!*])

Vassilsa, who's still angry at Pepel because Pepel prefers her sister over her, calls the cops on him ("He killed my husband!") and the townspeople love Pepel so much, they all start pretending that they, too, were instrumental in the old man's murder (nobody, but *nobody,* liked Kostyev), turning themselves into a human barricade (the French love those things!) to prevent *les flics* from carrying their Natacha-saving hero off. In *Les Bas-fonds,* as in most of Gabin's pictures from the mid-to-late 1930s, Jean Gabin's perpetual drifter-character is resigned to his unpleasant fate, and is carted away to jail, but eventually, *per* David Mamet, "things change," and within the space of a few scenes, the cops eventually set him free. In the film's penultimate sequence, Pepel and a knapsack-wielding Natacha walk away happily, just like Charlie Chaplin and Paulette Goddard in 1936's *Modern Times,* poor as dirt, but ready to begin a new life together, and Louis Jouvet's Baron gets a little reprieve from life's disappointments, as well: He winds up with Nastia, the romance novel-*connoisseur* who will now get to experience romance firsthand, as opposed to simply reading about it.

1936's *Les Bas-fonds,* which garnered the *Prix Louis Delluc* award in France, in 1937, is spirited entertainment, and Maxim Gorky's play, upon which it was based, would be raided once again in 1955, which is the year when Akira Kurosawa decided to lens his own version of the story, setting it in 18th century Japan.

In 1937, director Jean Renoir would even repeat one of *La Bas-fond's* main themes, "the friendship which all men can aspire to, in spite of their class differences" (exemplified by the friendship between Gabin's working-class man and Jouvet's Baron) in yet another movie which he would make with Jean Gabin, 1937's *La Grande illusion,* which is perhaps the best known film that both Gabin and Renoir ever made: In *Illusion,* Gabin's World War I fighter-pilot is again working-class, and his best friend, an aristocratic pilot, is played by another wonderful French actor, Pierre Fresnay.

————————

In the one-off French fan magazine *Jean Gabin: Sa Vie/Ses Films,* which hit Parisian newsstands at the end of 1938, this is what Gabin's co-star, Junie Astor said about working with him on this movie: "I admire Jean as a great actor and as a colleague, but he's also a great star who never tries to steal the scene from his partner. At first, I was insecure about acting with him, because he was so famous. But his calmness gave me confidence. When you're acting with him, he's great to watch, because he's giving you a lesson in acting without making you think that's what he's doing. In person, Jean Gabin doesn't have a 'nice side,' just a 'human side:' When he came into the studio each morning, and greeted the crew, he was always nice to everybody, asking if the food was good, how was the weather, and if everybody had a good sleep. When the weather was bad outside the studio and people were in a bad mood, he was always very positive, and [his positivity] spread to the whole crew. Jean always had great stories to tell about the food he ate, too: He's a man who appreciates great cuisine—he's a gourmand!—and he really loved telling us about all of the parties he was going to..."

What a Critic Said at the Time: "This is the first of Maxim Gorky's pictures made with the approval of the author (he ok'd it before he died). Pic won best French film of the year prize and its director, Jean Renoir, was made a Knight of the Legion of Honor. Notable, are Jean Gabin and Junie Astor as the fallible hero and heroine. [The film has] an ironic humor which evens out the grim incidents, and lends a tang to the drama." (*Variety*, 9-15-37 issue. Critic: "Hugo." Reviewed in Paris.)

What Another Critic Said at the Time: "[*Les Bas-fonds*] is a mature, impressive, and extraordinarily fascinating production. [Playwright] Maxim Gorky advised Renoir not to [make the film], telling him that audiences would 'break their teeth' on it. The film explores the slimy recesses of the minds of hovel-made men. If Hollywood could do nothing half so well, we should be content." (New York *Times*, 9-13-37 issue. Critic: Frank S. Nugent.)

FILM 23

Pepe Le Moko

France, 1937

(Approximate English Translation: "PEPE, THE SAILOR FROM TOULON") Directed by Julien Duvivier. Produced by Raymond and Robert Hakim. Screenplay by Jacques Constant, Julien Duvivier, and Henri Jeanson. Based Upon the Novel by 'Detective Ashelbe' (a pseudonym for Henri La Barthe). Directors of Photography (black and white), Marc Fossard and Jules Kruger. Editor, Marguerite Beauge. Production Designer, Jacques Kraus. Music by Vincent Scotto and Mohamed Ygerbuchen. Production Designer, Jacques Krauss. (GENRES: ROMANTIC DRAMA/ POLICIER/ ACTION) Running Time, 1 hour 30 minutes. Produced and Released in France on January 28, 1937, by Paris Films. Released in United States with English Subtitles on March 3, 1941, by The Arthur Mayer and Joseph Burstyn Company.

"Oh, that Pepe! He's got a smile for his friends… and a knife for his enemies!"
— *From "Pepe Le Moko"*

Jean Gabin's previous twenty-three feature films had placed him squarely on the map as a shining new star all across Europe, but his next two films, which were completed in succession, one right after another in 1937, Julien Duvivier's *Pepe Le Moko* and Jean Renoir's *La Grande illusion*, would skyrocket him into the movie star stratosphere internationally, including, for a brief and shining moment, in the United States.

As all serious film buffs know, Julien Duvivier's tart slice of Poetic Realism, *Pepe Le Moko* (or, on some of the original French posters, *Pepe-Le-Moko,* complete with the hyphens), was so popular on both sides of the Atlantic, that it would even spawn a practically scene-for-scene and shot-for-shot American remake one year later, director John Cromwell's *Algiers,* which starred another famous Frenchman, Charles Boyer.

As director Duvivier's yarn begins, lovable rogue Pepe Le Moko, one of France's most notorious gentleman criminals, is sequestered away in Algiers, in French North Africa, a fugitive from his native France, because he's 'lifted' two million francs from the Bank of Toulon; in fact, the word '*Moko*' or '*Moco,*' according to a 1933-edition *Larousse's Dictionary,* is slang, meaning, 'a sailor from Toulon,' Toulon being France's big port town in the south,

With Mireille Balin and Lucas Gridoux.

on the Mediterranean (hence, '*Pepe le Moko*' really means, '*Pepe, the Toulon-ian*'). Legendary as being 'The Prince of the Underworld,' Pepe is one of the few Caucasians whom the dark-and-swarthy Algerians love, and they all consider the dashing and enigmatic criminal to be a mythic figure, a man who, as one character tells us, has "… a smile for his friends, and a knife for his enemies." And a life of crime has definitely been much more lucrative to Pepe than his former trade, that of a cabinet-maker, ever was!

Prince-of-the-Underworld-Pepe feels especially at-home in a section of Algiers, which is known as the Casbah, a surreal/dangerous/'Tim Burton-*via*-Dr. Seuss World' of strange archways and paths, which functions in the picture as a safe haven for those who are in hiding from international police, and especially, for those who are in hiding from crafty Inspector Janvier (Philippe Richard), who pines-away for the notoriety which he knows will come his way, when he apprehends that notorious playboy-thief, Pepe Le Moko.

While the real-life Casbah is just a series of dark, dingy alleys (let's call it, 'the bowery of Algiers'), this movie-Algiers, which was constructed on the set at Pathe Studios in Joinville (although the panoramic shots of the city of Algiers happen to be the real deal) is a triumph of early production design, an amazing honeycomb consisting of vast stairways, winding streets, underground hideaways (home for crooks like Pepe), ornate archways and, as some wonderfully-gravitasy voice-over narration informs us at the beginning of the film, "… home to some forty thousand-plus Chinese, Gypsies, Slavs, "Negroes," [!] and Maltese."

With Line Noro.

(Yes, the Casbah is so progressive, it will even admit those often-marginalized Maltese!) The interlocked roofs of the Casbah's hundreds of houses give the city the appearance of a maze which extends down into the sea, and the Casbah, as we're also going to be noticing in this scene, is separated from the rest of Algiers by huge gates, which hover between the Casbah and the harbor.

Director Duvivier will at first depict the police only in long-shot, as policemen run around the circumference of the Casbah, and these policemen look, for all the world, like tiny, insignificant ants. Every-once-in-awhile, when crazy-brave cops are stupid enough to penetrate the gangster-infested world, Pepe, who spends a lot of his time peeking up at them through a slat in the ceiling of his underground dwellings, shoots upwards, his omnipresent gun purposely hitting them in the kneecaps, a treatment which, as he comically remarks, is "good for their varicose veins."

Much of the always-impeccably dressed Pepe's (black shirt, black tie, black jacket, a style which is still *en vogue* today, and which was actually created specifically for this film, more than seventy years ago, by costume designer Cecil Beaton) time is spent in masterminding imaginatively-plotted robberies which happen outside of the Casbah, daily, crimes in which he can't physically participate, but from which, nevertheless, he still manages to extract sizable takes: He spends the remainder of his time making love to the all of the Casbah's darkly-sensuous women who adore him like crazy, especially Ines, who's played by Line

Noro. ("Pepe's home," one worshipful Casbah-residing lady tells another, breathlessly, "is wherever a woman is!")

Pepe's slimy 'frenemy' (half-friend, half-enemy) Inspector Slimaine (Lucas Gridoux who, two years earlier, played 'The Ultimate Slimy Friend,' Judas Iscariot, in Duvivier's *Golgotha*), a crooked cop-on-the-take, spends most of his time in the Casbah, too (he's the only cop who the bad guys will allow in there, since he helps Pepe to plan his crimes), although Slimaine, unlike Pepe, is free to leave whenever he feels like it. Like Robert Le Vigan's backstabbing Inspector Lucas-character, in *La Bandera*, Slimaine is genuinely Pepe's good friend, but is still not completely adverse to the idea of someday putting Pepe away in the klink, and achieving the notoriety which he knows will surely come from such a major bust. Pepe likes his goofy cop friend, even though he knows that Slimaine's ultimate dream is his arrest. (Wouldn't it be great if we could overlook our own friends' foibles like this? Well, we don't have to, because Jean Gabin, our surrogate on the sixty-foot movie screen, gets to be 'the idealized us,' for us!)

Meanwhile, outside of the Casbah, in the city of Algiers-proper, director Duvivier introduces us to a chubby, skeevy, sweat-on-the-back-of-the-neck/Akim Tamiroff-looking informer-guy, Regis (Fernand Charpin, who played the Inspector who was gunning for one of Gabin's lottery-winning friends, in *La Belle equipe*). Regis, like Slimaine, is hatching a plan to capture Pepe, and his favorite thing on earth, seems to be spending all of this time filling the heads of the Algerian police force with his grandiose ideas about how to do it. When we meet Regis first, he's telling the assembled French *federales*, who've come to see him in his office, about Pepe's young protégé, Pierrot (Gilbert Gil). Pepe and Pierrot have a father-son/mentor relationship, in which Pepe teaches Pierrot all about the ins-and-outs of the crime world. (Lots of Gabin movies will feature 'Our Hero's' mentoring of a younger man, not only this movie, and the same year's upcoming film, *Le Messager*, but also in the 1950s and 1960s, which is when producers would often team an older Gabin up with young, up-and-coming movie stars, such as Jean Paul-Belmondo and Alain Delon.) Regis thinks that the best way to catch Pepe will be to send erroneous word, down into the Casbah, that Pierrot's beloved mother has taken ill, so that when Pierrot leaves to go to his mom's bedside, the cops can kidnap the young man. Regis knows full-well that Pepe will come out of the Casbah to look for his young friend, and that when he does, the fuzz will be able to nab him, as well. But swarthy Pepe is onto Regis' plan, thanks to an incredible, and Pepe-supporting, grapevine of Algerian rogues, who whisper the daily news to each other through the Casbah's solid stone walls, forming a surly chain-of-protection for their beloved rogue. Knowing that Regis means to have him arrested, and maybe even worse, Pepe takes the pre-emptive strike, and has some of his henchmen bring Regis down into the Casbah. When Pepe confronts Regis, face-to-face ("So, I hear you're trying to kill me!"), Regis starts to sweat (even more than he does normally, which is a lot!), as Pepe and his men surround him. Regis' big death scene is an incredible set-piece, which you can tell inspired Orson Welles, when Welles would eventually direct his own *noir*, *Touch of Evil*, in 1957. Regis' killing is underscored by the music which surges-forth from a jaunty player piano, music that grows louder and more buoyant, as Pepe and his men move closer to Regis, sending him on a one-way trip to Kingdom Come.

At roughly the same time during which this is happening, a Parisian champagne czar, Maxime (Charles Granval, another holdover from *La Belle equipe*) and his hot young mistress, Gaby Gould (Mireille Balin, who will show up later that same year, playing Gabin's love-interest in another picture, *Gueule d'amour*), who are visiting Algiers, are enjoying dinner with their old friend, Inspector Slimaine. Gaby has heard of the legendary Pepe Le Moko, and she's interested in meeting him. Even though Slimaine's telling Gaby that it will be dangerous for her to enter the seedy Casbah, she's got *that special itch that dilettante chicks sometimes get*—an itch which she knows can only be scratched by lower-class (a/k/a, 'rough-trade') guys, as opposed to the usual 'Biffs' and 'Chips,' over at Exeter and Choate. She insists on going down there, and Maxime looks jealous, but he lets her go, anyway. (*'Abie gezin'* as we say in Yiddish. ["Go in good health."]) Maxime is old, and Gaby is young, and he's obviously afraid that if he doesn't let her go off sometimes, *to get her freak on with younger cock,* that she'll leave him, forever.

When Gaby meets Pepe, they shoot each other long, smoky glances, and Duvivier cuts back and forth, Sergio-Leone-style, between their two faces, a device which manages to avoid cliché, just because the Pepe-Gaby chemistry is simply so *gol-durned hot.* After Pepe and Gaby's first night together, Duvivier resorts to some of his trippy/Poetic Realism-magic tricks, when he next shows us a sequence which is basically a bizarre proto-music video that's shot on weird, canted angles which seem to be right out of an episode of t.v.'s campy, candy-colored 1960s' "Batman" t.v. series, which this movie pre-dated by thirty years: In this bizarro-world montage sequence, all of the Casbah residents are seen to be dancing around happily, as Pepe sings (Gabin gets to test out his pipes with a song, in this picture) about how happy he is. (Damn! Outside of Clint Eastwood and Lee Marvin in *Paint Your Wagon*, what other movie tough guy can sing a song while he's also kicking your ass up and down the block, until you cry for your mama? *Seulment Gabin, mes amis!* [Only Gabin, my friends!])

As the film concludes, Gaby, who's used to being pampered, knows she won't be able to stay in the dangerous Casbah forever, and that her ultimate destiny is going to be to return to Paris. Pepe is so eager to follow her, because he's fallen in love with her (in spite of the fact that Jean Gabin's movie-characters almost always try to avoid long-term commitments), that he finally takes a decision to leave the Casbah. He knows he's going to be risking his life by leaving his protective sanctuary (go back to the chapter in which I talked about *La Bandera,* and see what happened when Gabin escaped from the Spanish Foreign Legion), but he's willing to risk it all for love, which is why this movie has always been a big favorite with women, because it actually plays to their naive, fairy tale-like beliefs that men will actually do anything for them.

In one of the saddest and most memorable endings of any Jean Gabin film, Pepe makes it out of the Casbah and he starts running like a bat-out-of-hell over to the gigantic and

With Mireille Balin.

tightly-locked gates which separate the Casbah from the harbor where, from his vantage point (Noooo!!!), he can see Gaby boarding her steamship back to Paris. She has no idea that he's come to see her, and he tries to yell over to her, but she can't hear him, over the din of the ship's smokestack. And just as Slimaine and the other cops run up behind Pepe to take him away (Jean Gabin ain't going out like that, *mon frere*), Pepe slits his wrists, dying instantly. ("Women will be your undoing," Slimaine told Pepe, prophetically, in an earlier scene, and how right he was.)

Pepe Le Moko, which was released in France in 1937, would become a major art-house hit for Jean Gabin in the United States, when it finally made it to North American shores in 1941 and, at this point, Gabin was already well-known in the U.S. for the movie which he would make directly after *Pepe Le Moko*, director Jean Renoir's anti-war classic, *La Grande illusion*, which had already become a huge North American art-house hit, in 1938.

When *Pepe Le Moko* became a hit in France in 1937, the very famous American producer, Walter Wanger, took notice. (Wanger [you pronounce his name like '*ranger*'] began his producing career in 1929, with the Marx Bros.' first movie, *The Cocoanuts*, and finished-up [literally!] with 20ᵗʰ Century-Fox's 1963 mega-bomb, *Cleopatra*.) Wanger decided that American audiences would love the story of *Pepe Le Moko* as much as he and the French people did, but he believed, also, that 'middle-America'—the people in 'the fly-over' (read: everybody who doesn't live in New York, or L.A.)—would never go and see a French-language

With Saturnin Fabre, Gabriel Gabrio, Gilbert Gil, and Gaston Modot.

movie with subtitles. So he bought the American distribution rights to Julien Duvivier's film and, instead of releasing it stateside, as he promised Duvivier he would, he remade it from scratch as an American/English-language production: In 1938, Wanger recruited screenwriter John Howard Lawson, as well as an uncredited James M. Cain (*Postman Always Rings Twice*) and, as a result, Americans first became aware of adventures of Pepe Le Moko, not from the original Jean Gabin/Julien Duvivier version, but through Wanger's practically scene-for-scene and shot-for-shot remake, known as *Algiers*, in which Charles Boyer played Pepe and Hedy Lamarr played Gaby Gould; Wanger had approached Gabin to reprise his role as Pepe for this American remake but, at this point in Gabin's career, he wasn't yet interested in working in America. (That wouldn't happen for another three years, when the Nazis invaded France and took over the French film industry, forcing Gabin and many other European film denizens to relocate temporarily to America, so that they could continue toiling in front of cameras.)

In spite of the fact that Jean Gabin's *Pepe Le Moko* and Charles Boyer's *Algiers* are almost identical (many of the scenes, shots, and even editing are the same, in both of the films), the Jean Gabin original is fast-paced and energetic, while the Charles Boyer version, which nevertheless was a huge hit in America anyway, is wan, listless, and slack-paced, 'losing something in the translation,' and existing, basically, as a paint-by-numbers remake of the original; the biggest difference between the French/Gabin version and the otherwise identical American/Boyer version, is that, in the Boyer version, Pepe doesn't slit his own wrists: Instead, the cops shoot him down as he runs to the gates, because, back in the '30s and '40s, Hollywood's Production Code, very explicitly, did not approve scenes which depicted on-screen suicide.

Weirdly, however, even though Walter Wanger's *Algiers* is dishwater-dull, Americans at the time loved it so much when it was released in the U.S. on June 28, 1938, that not only did it become a huge box-office hit, but Wanger decided to capitalize on his own, American film's success, by then, subsequently, releasing Gabin's original 1937 *Pepe Le Moko* into American theaters three years later, on March 3, 1941. And guess what: The original, French-language, 'Gabin/Duvivier' version then became a huge hit in America, as well. (Several biographies of Jean Gabin state that, when Gabin arrived in America, in 1941, the first thing he saw, when he got off the boat from France, was a movie theater which was showing *Pepe Le Moko,* but this oft-repeated story is patently false, because Gabin arrived on American shores in February of 1941, and *Pepe Le Moko* wouldn't be released in the U.S. until March of 1941, one month later.)

I can't put enough emphasis on how huge a hit Gabin's original version of *Pepe Le Moko* was, when it was released in the United States, where it spread beyond the typical (for a foreign-language film) art-house cinemas, and played in the 'real' theaters, where teeming audiences were usually lining up to see big American movie stars, like Bogart and Cagney. America was so wrapped up in *Pepe Le Moko-Fever* (a whole decade's worth of *Pepe-Fever*, in fact) that in 1948, Universal Pictures even churned out a truly horrible musical remake, *Casbah,* in which the great, and yet mostly forgotten today movie-crooner Tony Martin played Pepe. (In spite of Yvonne DeCarlo's presence as Ines, and Peter Lorre's as Slimaine, this musical version of Henri la Barthe's novel is a snoozer, full of some of the most unmemorable showtunes you'll ever hear.)

The most famous *Le Moko* offshoot, however, which is known even to American children, today (even though they don't know it) is Warner Bros.' perennially-famous Looney Tunes cartoon skunk, Pepe Le Pew, whose signature catch-phrase, "Come with me to the Casbah. We will make ze beautiful mu-zeek togeh-zaire," was mimicked, in the '30s and '40s, by every popular movie comedian of the time, from Abbott and Costello to the Three Stooges, in spite of the fact that Jean Gabin never actually uttered that line in the movie. In 1949, the Italians, who were also wrapped-up in *Pepe Le Moko*-mania, would even release their own comedy 'sequel' to Pepe Le Moko, director Carlo Ludovico Bragaglia's 1949 effort, *Toto Le Moko,* in which Pepe's bumbling cousin, who's played by the extremely popular Italian movie comedian, Toto (who starred in 107 films), a Naples street musician, assumes his famous Cousin Pepe's position in the Algerian crime-world, shortly after Pepe's death. If you're an American, and you think you've never seen Toto (his real name was Antonio de Curtis Gagliardi Griffo Focas Comneno), whose movies have never been released in the United States, with the exception of director Mario Monicelli's 1958 art-house caper hit,

I Solti Ignoti [Big Deal on Madonna Street], guess again: In director Guiseppe Tornatore's internationally-popular 1988 film, *Cinema Paradiso,* the elderly movie projectionist, who's played by Phillipe Noiret, projects a movie on the side of a building, in the Palermo town square, and Toto is the star of that movie.

Pepe Le Moko remains popular today on both sides of the Atlantic, aided immeasurably by the Criterion Collection's masterful 2004 restoration, and the company's subsequent North American DVD release. People love it not just because it's a great movie, but also because this great Poetic Realist film from 1937 is considered to be one of international movie history's earliest and best examples of *film noir:* In the 1940s and 1950s, American studios were making all-manner of hard-charging B-movies, movies which usually starred guys like Lawrence Tierney, Charles McGraw, and Aldo Ray, in which the main characters, whether they were corrupt cops or corrupt bad guys, have committed some crimes at the beginning of the movies, and even though they try to run away from their cruel fates, they just can't. And if that trope sounds familiar to you, it's because it's a direct lift from the French Poetic Realism of the 1930s: All of your favorite American *film noir* movies, from *Double Indemnity* to *The Postman Always Rings Twice,* to *Laura,* to *Kiss Me Deadly,* to *Touch of Evil,* would never have existed without Jean Gabin's Poetic Realism/tragic drifter-pictures, like *La Bandera* and *Pepe Le Moko.*

While *Pepe Le Moko* became one of the most known and beloved Jean Gabin films in the world, its female star, Mireille Balin, who was one of France's most popular pre-War actresses, would not enjoy such a propitious fate: During World War II, Balin, like a lot of other French women whose boyfriends were away fighting on other shores, fell in love with a German officer, and by doing so, she disgraced herself in front of her own people. Because of what was perceived as being her affront to her own nation, she worked only sporadically, before passing away in 1960 at the age of fifty-nine. Notorious for being a very frail personality, Balin apparently died penniless.

What a Critic Said at the Time: "One of the best films produced this year. The role [of Pepe] is Jean Gabin's meat, and he masticates it well... Gabin neatly molds the character of a hardened criminal who holds both his white and native enemies at bay with brutality and harshness, mixed with the proper amount of kindness." (*Variety,* 3-24-37 issue. Critic: "Hugo." Reviewed in Paris.)

What Another Critic Said at the Time: "The most distinguished new French film [of the year]. A raw-edged, realistic, and utterly frank exposition of a basically evil story. All the filthiness and vice of the Casbah are impressively shown in this film. Jean Gabin's tough, unsentimental performance of the title role is credible and revealing." (New York *Times,* 3-7-41 issue. Critic: Bosley Crowther.)

What a Critic Says Today: "*Pepe Le Moko* is the stuff that dreams are made of!" (Kenneth Turan, Los Angeles *Times,* 4-19-2002.)

Left to right, Erich von Stroheim, Jean Gabin, Pierre Fresnay.

FILM 24

LA GRANDE ILLUSION

France, 1937

(France, 1937) (Literal English Translation: "THE GREAT ILLUSION") Directed by Jean Renoir. Produced by Albert Pinkovitch and Frank Rollmer. Written by Jean Renoir and Charles Spaak. Director of Photography (black and white), Christian Matras. Editors, Marthe Huguet and Marguerite Renoir. Production Designer, Eugene Lourie. Music by Joseph Kosma. (GENRES: DRAMA/COMEDY) Running Time, 1 hour 54 minutes. Produced and Released in France by RAC (Realisation D'Art Cinematographie) on June 8, 1937. Released in United States with English Subtitles as "GRAND ILLUSION" by World Pictures Corporation, on September 12, 1938.

"I just want to hear spoken French!"
— Captured French WWI pilot Gabin's words while in solitary confinement in a German prison camp, in "La Grande illusion"

Jean Renoir's 1937 masterpiece, *La Grande illusion*, is the one Jean Gabin picture which even the most casual 'old movie-fans' know about, both in Europe and in the United States, and maybe even more so than they know *Pepe Le Moko*, because *Illusion* is on almost every important movie critic's 'Top 100 Films of All Time' list. Alongside Lewis Milestone's 1930 adaptation of Erich Maria Remarque's novel *All Quiet on the Western Front*, which also portrayed the First World War, *Illusion* is considered to be the finest anti-war film of all time—in fact, it's so 'anti-war,' that there's not a single battle scene in the whole picture: It's a human interest story about the camaraderie of soliders from different European countries, who've been captured and incarcerated together as prisoners-of-war. One of the few Gabin titles to have become a major hit in the United States, *La Grande illusion* played sold-out theatrical engagements in New York City for six solid months, and it continued its successful North American run throughout 1939, which is when it spread its celluloid 'wings' to other cities, many of which had never before shown a 'foreign-language film,' with English subtitles.

While *La Grande illusion* has always been known, in the U.S., as *Grand Illusion*, a literal translation of its title is actually *The Great Illusion*, and it's an ensemble picture. Director Jean Renoir who, a year earlier, had put Jean Gabin through his paces, in *La-Bas fonds* (and who, by the way, before he was a film director, was a *potter*) was, in this picture, more interested in allocating an equal amount of time to *all* of the film's dozens of great actors, the result being that no single actor in *La Grande illusion* outshines any of the others, and this was not an accident: *La Grande illusion* is a film about captured war prisoners who represent a cross-section of 20th-century Europe's social classes—the rich, the poor, the middle-class—and by not making any one character any more significant than any other, Renoir, who has always been considered to be one of international cinema's most humanistic of directors, is saying that, in his opinion anyway, we all have equal value. *Illusion* is a film about World War I which was made when World War II was right around the corner: Renoir saw fascism emerging, both from within France as well as from *without* (from the Nazis), and so he decided to make a film which would be so powerful that it would (he hoped, anyway) show the futility of war, thereby stopping countries from fighting with each other, forever. (It was a noble effort, but, of course—*World War II happened, anyway.*)

France, 1916: We're now two years into WWI. Gabin's sturdy, working-class French Lieutenant, who is named 'Marechal,' is seen first on a French air force base, and in the picture, Gabin is actually wearing the actual uniform which was worn by Jean Renoir, when 'the director, as a young man' was as a second lieutenant and a pilot. Marechal is listening to a gramophone record, and singing along with Lucile Paris' 1908 recording of a bawdy French song, called "*Frou Frou,*" which is an ode to *women who wear tight pants while riding bicycles,* and remember, this song became famous in France, seventy-five years before *lycra* and *spandex* made their joint appearance onto the bicycle-fashion scene. Check out the English-translation of this French tune's charming lyrics:

> A woman sometimes wears pants at home —
> it's an established fact, I think, within the marital life.
> But when she goes cycling in pants,
> this fact becomes more worrying,
> and I worry, myself, at that sight.
> Frou-frou
> Frou-frou
> By her petticoats, a woman troubles a man's soul.
> For surely, a woman entices, above all, with her gentle "frou-frou."
> A woman with a masculine aspect is never that attractive —
> it's her petticoat's "frou-frou" which makes her so exciting!
> When a man hears "frou-frou," what he dares to do, is astonishing:
> He sees, at once, "the life in pink," gets electrified, and then—
> *he becomes crazy!*
> Frou-frou
> Frou-frou
> "In pants," you are going to tell me, "cycling is more comfortable."

But I say that, without "frou-frou," a woman is not complete!
When you see her lifting up her skirt, you are bewitched,
you are enchanted!
Her "frou-frou" is like the sound of a wing,
which comes and caresses you.
Frou-frou
Frou-frou...

But Gabin is going to have to get his mind off of *thinking about girls' frou-frous*, because, within moments, his commanding officer shows up to issue him his marching orders: Marechal's C.O. informs him that he's going to need him to fly a mission over the town of Epernay, in the Champagne region of northeastern France, and here, he introduces Marechal to Captain de Boeldieu, who's played by the great French movie star, Pierre Fresnay; in the movie, Marechal and Boeldieu will become the best of friends, in spite of the fact that Marechal is 'working-class' and Boeldieu is a born aristocrat..

———————

Pierre Fresnay (*ne,* Pierre Jules Louis Laudenbach [1897-1975]) was, at the time *La Grande illusion* was made, a major French movie star in his own right, most notably, as far as Americans are concerned today, for having starred in director/writer Marcel Pagnol's amazing three-film "Fanny Trilogy" (1931, 1932, and 1936). Fresnay, who was Alec Guinness' favorite actor (according to Guinness' 1996 autobiography, *My Name Escapes Me*), enjoyed an illustrious movie career which spanned the years between 1915 to 1973 (he made 76 movies), and he would even appear alongside Jean Gabin one more time, twenty-three years after *La Grande illusion,* in a 1959 comedy called *La Vieux de la vieille*—a film which even featured a couple of inside-jokes about *Illusion.* Fresnay, unlike Jean Gabin, remained in France during the Second World War, continuing to make movies for the French studios during the German occupation including, very famously, H.G. Clouzot's suspense picture, *Le Corbeau (The Raven).* Importantly, Fresnay was not director Jean Renoir's first choice to play Boeldieu, in *Grande illusion:* 'First choice' was Louis Jouvet, who played the Baron opposite Jean Gabin, in the previous Renoir-Gabin collaboration, *Les Bas-fonds,* and it's worth mentioning, here, that both Fresnay and Jouvet were members of France's prestigious *Comedie Francaise* theatrical organization.

———————

Needless to say, Marechal and Boeldieu's plane gets shot down over a German-occupied sector of France (we won't see this happening, since director Renoir was unable, financially, to secure any planes for the film), and the German officer who shot them down, Captain von Rauffenstein, feels badly about what he's just had to do: Rauffenstein, who's played by the movies' legendary actor and film director, Erich von Stroheim—that's right: Gloria Swanson's bald-pated butler, from *Sunset Blvd.*—tells his own aide that if anybody in the plane has survived, and if they are fellow officers, that his aide should invite them to dine

With Pierre Fresnay.

with him in the German squadron's mess hall. (Erich von Stroheim [1885-1957] was Jean Renoir's favorite filmmaker, and Renoir, by his own admission, 'learned filmmaking' by watching the silent films which Stroheim directed in America—especially, 1922's *Foolish Wives* and 1924's *Greed*— and apparently, Renoir and Stroheim fought like cats-and-dogs on the set of *La Grande Illusion*, because they were both extremely opinionated men.) While Rauffenstein looks mean, he's really 'a nice guy, at heart.

Erich von Stroheim's 'Rauffenstein' is one of the most recognizable characters in movie history (the characters of 'Blofeld,' from the James Bond flick *You Only Live Twice* and 'Dr. Evil' from the *Austin Powers* movies are direct tributes [the bald head, the officer's tunic with the standing-collar, the monocle, the scarred-cheek] to Stroheim's character, in *La Grande illusion*), and Rauffenstein is considered, also, to be one of the *best* movie characters of all time, as well: In other war movies, the 'evil German *Commandant*-character' is usually portrayed as being a total, raving psychotic, but *La Grande illusion*'s director, Jean Renoir (who, in this film, wants to show us 'the inherent goodness of all mankind') paints him as being *a nice guy who's just a little bit lonely,* and who dearly wishes that he could have *some nice, cool friends, to hang-out with,* even if they're friends from an enemy country with which

With Pierre Fresnay, Sylvain Itkine, and Erich von Stroheim.

his own country happens to be at war.

———————

Rauffenstein is now dining with the two French officers whom he's just shot down, Gabin's Marechal, whose arm was injured in the crash, and Fresnay's Boeldieu, and as the three men eat together, they're listening to a Strauss waltz, and sharing some of Rauffenstein's very expensive bottles of Moselle. (You can't hate your enemies too much, when they're sharing their stashes with you!) Marechal and Boeldieu take an immediate liking to their kind captor, and their meal together is very quickly turning into a meeting of the French/German Mutual Appreciation Society: Rauffenstein makes an eloquently-heartfelt toast to all of the valiant fighting men, both Germans and French, who are continuing to give their lives for… for—*well, what for?*—and after the meal, Rauffenstein discloses the fact to Marechal and Boeldicu that, even though he genuinely likes the two of them, still, because he's shot them down (and because they are, after all, his prisoners), as a matter of course, he is going to have them sent to a prison camp. Marechal and Boeldieu who, so far, have been charmed (and not harmed) by their gracious host, readily agree to Rauffenstein's insistence that they should be placed in a P.O.W. camp. (If this prison camp which Rauffenstein is trying to sell them is anything like this fine meal which they've just enjoyed, *it should be a stone groove…*)

Sixteen years after the release of *La Grande illusion,* in 1953, Billy Wilder very famously directed his own classic prisoner-of-war picture, *Stalag 17,* a film which opens with some rather cornball voice-over narration, supplied by one of the ensemble film's many characters, Sergeant Clarence Henry 'Cookie' Cook,' who's played by Gil Stratton. Cookie tells us, the film's audience, "I don't know about you, but it always makes me sore when I see those war pictures all about flying leathernecks, and submarine patrols, and frogmen, and guerrillas in the Philippines. What gets me, is that there was never a movie about P.O.W.'s—about Prisoners of War." *Whoops!* It seems that when Billy Wilder and his co-scenarist Edwin Blum wrote *Stalag 17,* they had conveniently forgotten all about *La Grande illusion!*

When Marechal and Boeldieu arrive at the German P.O.W. camp, they now become wards of camp guard Sgt. Arthur Kantz (Werner Florian) a guy who, like Rauffenstein himself, is very nice to them: Kantz even tells them that, because they are officers, they will be treated with all due respect to their rank, although he also makes it clear that this 'respect' will be tempered with German discipline, just by nature of the fact that this is a prison camp. He reminds them also that, because they are prisoners, they must always remember to follow all of the orders which they are given, and in particular, he instructs them that they are always to salute all German officers whenever they see them, and that they must also never speak against Germany. ("The Camp's Minor Housekeeping Note:" Kantz also lets them know, in no uncertain terms, that if they try to escape, they will be shot dead, right on the spot.)

Marechal and Boeldieu's new cellmates in the cavernous quarters into which Arthur has escorted them, the camp's previously-arrived prisoners, are all, just like Marechal and Boeldieu, officers who've been captured by the Germans, and they're not just French, but also British and Russian, and the French prisoners greet the new arrivals with a funny song of warning. ("LYRICS: "Hide your gold! They're going to be searching us! Hide your valuables...")

One of the first men whom Marechal and Boeldieu meet, is Lieutenant Rosenthal (Marcel Dalio), a French-Jewish inmate whose wealthy family sends him care-packages full of sumptuous comestibles, which he takes great pleasure in sharing with all of his roommates, and the guards let Rosenthal keep the gustables, because he shares with them, as well. ("Ahh, the stupid honesty of the guards, who let us have this," Rosenthal smiles, examining this particular day's tasty spoils.)

Born 'Israel Moshe Blauschild,' the great actor Marcel Dalio (1900-1983), a Frenchman of Romanian-Jewish descent, would appear in a lot of great French movies, even appearing in some classic American ones, as well: Dalio is on view as a croupier in 1942's *Casablanca,* and you can see him also in comedies, such as 1959's *Some Like It Hot* and 1964's Doris Day/ Rock Hudson confection, *Pillow Talk. La Grande illusion* was not the first time that Gabin and Dalio would appear in a movie together (Dalio played an underground tough who gives Gabin *tsurris* in the same year's *Pepe Le Moko,* and he would play Gabin's *boss,* eighteen years after *Grande illusion,* in a 1955 film noir masterpiece, called *Razzia sur la chnouf.*)

Soon, Marechal and Boeldieu are settled into their new living quarters, and they and all of their fellow P.O.W.'s are discussing how beneficial it would be for 'the group morale' if they were to put on some kind of a show, but Jean Gabin's Lt. Marechal is *all-man,* and he shrugs them off with a wave of his hand: "Ahhh, I don't like theater. I like bicycles!" For that matter, Marechal doesn't like tacky designer food either, and now, slyly (and directly referencing Rosenthal's fancy, canned gift-meats), he also snorts, "I don't like Maxim's. [Here, he's referring to famously-ritzy restaurant, which remains in existence, today.] I like a good, cheap place!" After Marechal has finished with his twin anti-show biz and *anti-yummy food diatribes,* one of his fellow inmates, a character who is known only as 'The Engineer' (Gaston Modot), actually washes Marechal's feet, for him. (Friends, if you need proof that Jean Gabin is Jesus—here it is! [In spite of this 'joke' which I've just made, there's no religious significance to the scene; the Engineer is just washing Marechal's feet for him, because Marechal's arm was injured when his plane was shot down, and so he has been unable to do it for himself.])

No sooner have Marechal and Boeldieu settled into the barracks, than the other officers are all crowing to them that they've been planning an elaborate 'group escape,' for as long as they can remember. Rosenthal next lets Marechal and Boeldieu in on the plan, as it currently exists: "We will escape after roll-call!" The prisoners who've already been in the barracks for awhile, have actually been digging a deep hole in the room's stone floor for quite some time, completely unafraid that, at any minute, guards might come in and discover this infraction. (Whenever the guards storm into the prisoners' quarters unannounced, the prisoners just nonchalantly, and without becoming worried, cover the hole up, and the guards are so laid-back and exhausted looking, none of them ever even thinks to question them about it!) Marechal asks some of the men who have been digging the hole what they do with all of the dirt that they're pulling up and, in the next sequence, we actually get to see what they do with it: They go outside onto the yard, and nonchalantly turn their pockets out, emptying only a little dirt at a time onto the ground, a trick which will be copied from *La Grande illusion,* in decades-worth of prison movies, from John Sturges' *The Great Escape* (1960), to Clint Eastwood's *Escape from Alcatraz* (1979), to Frank Darabont's *The Shawshank Redemption* (1995).

The prisoners in the camp do lots of other stuff to keep themselves busy as well, and 'camp' is definitely the operative word: One day, the men receive a package of ladies' dresses which they've ordered, because they've decided to put on a drag show for their own amusement, and the P.O.W. whose idea this whole 'proto-*La cage aux folles*-gambit' is, is Cartier, who is played by Julien Carette.

Julien Carette (1897-1966), another of France's great stage and screen actors, made 121 films between 1931 and 1964, including a handful with his friend, Jean Gabin. His on-screen 'stock-in-trade,' for those who don't yet know him, is that he typically played what *the small-*

minded non-Frenchmen of decades ago used to consider to be 'the stereotype of the typical Frenchman'—the 'fast-talking, madly-gesticulating, moon-faced, happy-go-lucky, *que sera sera,* aphorism-spouting guy-with-the-horizontal-striped-gondolier-shirt-red-beret-five-'o-clock-shadow-and-cigarette-always-hanging-out-of-his-mouth.' Carette, in other words, is very likeable.

When the evening of The Big Drag Show finally comes around, the British prisoners are all prancing-around on stage, singing "It's a Long Way to Tipperary," at the tops of their lungs, to a roomful of P.O.W.'s and German guards, while Gabin's Lt. Marechal just stands off in the wings, wearing the *butchest* of black turtlenecks, stage-managing (obviously, under extreme duress), and looking like he wishes he could be anywhere else in the entire world, but here. And while Marechal looks super-uncomfortable with having to manage these *ladyboys*, it's clear that he's going along with this whole spectacle, because he realizes that it's a great way to raise the prisoner's morale, and perhaps he's also doing it, to deflect any of the suspicions which the guards might be harboring, pertaining to some of the prisoners' potential ideas for a break-out.

Cartier is now seen in a tux, for just long enough to warble a 1913 song by Vincent Telly and Albert Valsien called, "*Si tu veux… Marguerite*" ("If You Want… Marguerite"), and Marechal interrupts the show to hold up a French newspaper which he displays proudly for the German guards: The headline proclaims that, as part of the Battle of Verdun, the French have re-captured Fort Douaumont, in northeastern France (a real event, which took place on October 24, 1916), and the cast is so thrilled, that its members cease dancing, and begin reverently singing the French national anthem, "*La Marseillaise.*" (Director Michael Curtiz loved this moment in *La Grande illusion,* and this is why he continually plays bits of "*La Marseillaise,*" in his own film, 1942's *Casablanca.*) The German guards look very uncomfortable, at being bombarded with the national song of their prisoners, and many of them start nervously making their way out of the makeshift theater. (As Jimmy Durante once malapropped to Buster Keaton in *The Passionate Plumber,* an American-made sound comedy from 1930, which was set in France but filmed in Hollywood, "I always stand up and salute, whenever they play "The Mayonnaise!")

Other non-transvestite activities in which the prisoners engage, to pass the time, include 1.) forcing one of their group dress as a clown, because he's a cuckold and 2.) making fun of Rosenthal, for being Jewish. Yes, this movie does feature *a dollop of good-natured, French, anti-Semitism,* but the funny thing about Rosenthal, is that he's so nice, he doesn't even mind the other guys, who he knows are his friends, making fun of his religious background: In fact, he thinks it's *good fun* that the men are talking about him, even if it's not exactly in the best of terms since, at the very least, they're talking about him, and he knows that if they didn't like him, they wouldn't be talking about him at all; Rosenthal's no Rhodes Scholar, but he *is* smart enough to realize that 'any publicity is good publicity.' (In one of Jean Renoir's earliest outlines for the film, the character wasn't called 'Rosenthal' at all; he was called 'Dolette,' and

With Julien Carrette and Pierre Fresnay.

he wasn't even Jewish.)

As a result of his jumping on the stage and provoking the singing of "La Marsellaise," Gabin's Marechal is punished and sentenced to solitary confinement. Going a bit stir crazy, he goofily tries to hack through a wall to freedom— in broad daylight, and using only a dull teaspoon! The guards ask Marechal what the hell he thinks he's doing, and with the crazy-bravery of Burt Reynolds circa 1974, only without the much-vaunted Reynoldsian gum-chewing, he tartly replies, completely unafraid of them (and with a mischievous glint in his eye), "I'm busting out!" This is one of the few moments in *La Grande illusion,* in which director Renoir is giving us a glimpse of one of Gabin's most famous Movie Traits—'the guy who's not afraid of authority-figures'—and while he's in solitary, Jean Gabin bellows-out one of his most well-known lines from the movie: "*I just want to hear spoken French!*" Needless to say, when the personable Marechal returns to his quarters, his fellow officers are excited to have him back.

As a stroke of bad luck, just as the P.O.W.'s are in the final stages of planning their escape, the French prisoners, including Marechal, are suddenly given orders that they will now be transferred to another prison camp. As they are leaving, a new group of English officers is brought into the camp (we can tell they're British from the tennis rackets which are sticking out of their luggage), and Marechal breaks rank just for long enough to run over to a British officer; he tries to explain to the Brit that there's a completed tunnel in their room that they're free to use, but the British officer doesn't speak a word of French, and so the two men are unable to communicate. (One of the newly-arrived British officers is played by Jacques Becker, Jean Renoir's first assistant director on this film, a man who will become a pretty fantastic film director in his own right only a few years after *La Grande illusion;* in fact, Becker, who also happened to be Jean Renoir's platonic male roommate between 1932 and 1939, would direct one of Jean Gabin's finest films of the 1950s, 1954's amazing crime picture, *Touchez pas au grisbi.*)

The new camp to which our P.O.W.'s are transported is meant to be in Bavaria, although the location of its filming was actually in France. (It's the imposing 12th-century castle, Chateau du Haut-Koenigsbourg, in Alsace.) This place definitely looks every inch the medieval torture trap, a proto-Alcatraz from which (as we can tell, immediately) no man has ever escaped. Marechal and the other P.O.W.'s freak when they enter the foreboding-looking place but, shortly thereafter, they are relieved, when they find (surprise!) that it's being run by their good-hearted old buddy, Von Rauffenstein! Marechal, Boeldieu, and their third buddy, Lieutenant Demolder (Sylvain Itkine), a professor of Greek literature, are immediately taken before Rauffenstein, who tells his new charges not to be upset, because he intends on applying the rules of French military discipline (as opposed to what he mockingly calls the 'barbarism' of German discipline). Rauffenstein gives his three pals 'the big studio tour,' taking them up to the top of the castle's highest tower, showing them that it's a long drop to the bottom, and as he's bragging to them, he looks just like an excited little kid who wants to show the other kids his cool, new treehouse. (Again, Rauffenstein is a nice guy; he's not, in other words, threatening them.)

That night, in their new quarters (which, as usual, they're sharing with a number of other captured P.O.W.'s, including their old friend, Rosenthal), Marechal, Boeldieu, Demolder, and Rosenthal are now planning their escape which, if it works out according to their plans, will take them into 'neutral' Switzerland. Right before the men slip off to sleep, Rauffenstein enters the room, under the guise of performing an inspection, but what he really wants, is to bid goodnight to his fellow aristocrat, Boeldieu: Rauffenstein feels more of an affinity toward Boeldieu than he feels toward the other three guys, because Boeldieu, like Rauffenstein himself, is a born-aristocrat—in other words, Boeldieu and Rauffenstein are both men of the professional military caste, while the other men are of somewhat lower social standing. Rauffenstein, knowing that Marechal, Boeldieu, and the two other guys have an innate, built-in love of escape, gently asks Boeldieu to give him his word that they won't try to escape, and the reason that he's asking Boeldieu to make this promise to him, instead of asking the other guys to do it, is because he feels, since Boeldieu is a fellow 'swell,' that his word will somehow be better than theirs. (Even though Rauffenstein likes Marechal, Rosenthal, and Demolder, he does tell Boeldieu that the fact these men have been able to become officers, is no more than what he terms to be, a "gift of the [French] Revolution.") Rauffenstein invites

Breakout in Cellblock Gabin!

Boeldieu for a private chat in his quarters, and when we next see the two men, they're both wearing white gloves. When the two men are alone together, they occasionally speak to each other in English (which is considered to be a sign of fine breeding), and in this particular scene, Rauffenstein confides to Boeldieu that his having been newly placed in command of this P.O.W. camp, having previously been a dashing fighter pilot, is a direct result of his having been badly wounded in air-combat, and that he has now been reduced to being what he considers to be no more than a useless and undignified policeman.

Meanwhile, back in their quarters, Marechal is also having a class-related conversation: He whispers to Rosenthal, conspiratorially, "I want to escape with you, but not with Boeldieu: He's educated, and we're common. Plus, you've always shared your food with me, so it's only fair of me that I take you along." Rosenthal is pleased to have been asked and, feeling victorious, he now tells Marechal, "We Jews are always accused of avarice—but we are just as often generous!" Marechal, the consummate 'Gabinian-Everyman' who doesn't care what religion people are (as long as they are, in his own specific words, "a good guy") doesn't give a hoot-in-hell whether Rosenthal is Jewish or Chinese, and he even Gabin-Shrugs, "Aww! I don't care about that stuff. You're just a good pal," and as we already know, 'friends,' in any Jean Gabin movie, are the most important thing in the world.

The next morning, a Russian officer bursts excitedly into the prisoners' room, to tell the sleepy-eyed P.O.W.'s that the Czar's wife has just sent them all some gifts. The prisoners all tear-ass over to the huge crate which they've just received from her, and are very quickly disappointed, when they learn that the crate doesn't contain the fine Russian vodka which they thought it would be, but merely, *a bunch of crappy books!* The Russian officers are so disappointed, that in a fit of 'Mad-Russian' rage, they set the books on fire!

Boeldieu, who is being treated extra-well by Rauffenstein due to their shared class-status, tells Marechal that he won't be escaping with him and Rosenthal, but that he *will* help them to escape, if they would like him to. Marechal genuinely likes Boeldieu, but tells him they have little in common: "I should have known, Boeldieu! We've been imprisoned together at one place or another for eighteen months, and in that entire time, you've never stopped calling me '*vous*' [the French polite word for 'you,' which is meant to be used between people who are only casual acquaintances]. Anyway: Your white gloves, your English tobacco—everything comes between us." Boeldieu tries to make Marechal feel better, by telling him that he shouldn't feel too badly about his choice of language, because he refers to his own wife, and his mother, as '*vous*,' as well!

As part of their current escape plan, the captured officers have all obtained flutes, which they will use to create enough of a disturbance to distract the guards while Marechal and Rosenthal make their escape. After the guards have taken the flutes away from the captured soldiers, the P.O.W.'s continue making a racket, banging-out discordant 'music' on pots and pans.

After all of the flutes have been confiscated, the cacophony of one flute remains, and the beam of a guard's searchlight reveals that is Boeldieu who is playing it, from atop one of the castle walls, and while Rauffenstein is paying attention to Boeldieu, Marechal and Rosenthal are able to successfully escape over the castle walls, to freedom.

While Rauffenstein hasn't seen Marechal and Rosenthal escaping, he *does* scream out into the night, in English, to his friend Boeldieu, that if Boeldieu tries to escape, he will have no choice but to shoot him, even though, very genuinely, we see that doing this would pain him greatly. But Boeldieu just keeps goofing around, up on the ramparts; like other characters in French cinema of the late '30s, maybe he just feels that ultimately, he's fated to die anyway, no matter what he does, and so he's just inviting 'fate,' in the form of Rauffenstein, to hasten 'the inevitable.' Rauffenstein next shoots Boeldieu (he's just trying to 'wing' him) as he promised he would, and Boeldieu is mortally wounded, but remains alive. In the camp's infirmary, hours later, as Boeldieu is near death, Rauffenstein apologizes to him for his having had to shoot him, and he even asks for his French friend's forgiveness, telling him that he was just aiming at his leg, which is true.

A slow dissolve:

Marechal and Rosenthal have, of course, escaped from the camp, and have been traveling through the countryside for days. They're heading for Switzerland, and for freedom, both of which are still a few days away. And like any two people who are stuck together for any length of time without a break, even the best of friends, they soon begin bickering and pushing each other's buttons. At one point during their long hike, Rosenthal, who had sprained his foot during their Big Escape, tells Marechal that it's going to be difficult for him to keep walking, and this prompts a noisy 'Gabin-Outburst:' "Ahhhh! You're just a ball and chain! I can't stand you Jews, anyway!" (We know that Marechal doesn't really mean the ethnic slur which he's just made, and that 'it's just his starvation talking.') Rosenthal shakes a fist at Marechal and starts walking away, but then, as both men start heading-off in their own, separate directions, they find that, quite independently of each other, they both happen to be singing the same song. "Come on, friend," Marechal smiles warmly at Rosenthal, patting his friend on the back, and the two men now continue together, on what will, very literally, be 'their road to freedom.'

As night falls, the two men come upon a barn, and decide that this is where they will be spending the night, and the barn is part of a farm which belongs to a single-mother/German *hausfrau*, Elsa (the German-born actress, Dita Parlo) whose husband, a German officer, was recently killed at the Battle of Verdun. Elsa is a very friendly (and obviously, also, a terribly lonely) woman, who lives with her small daughter Lotte. Elsa tells the two men that they are welcome to spend the night in her home, and both she and her little girl are instantly fascinated by the strapping Marechal. (Elsa's eyes say it all: *"You're all man, Jean Gabin!"*) Marechal and Rosenthal confess to Elsa that they are escaped P.O.W.'s, and after they've told her that, she takes pity on them and tells them they can stay with her for as long as they want—especially, Marechal!

Christmas Eve: Marechal, who's now dressed-up in one of Elsa's deceased-husband's suits, makes a small, edible manger for Lotte, and the first thing the little girl tries to do, is to eat the little Baby Jesus! (At the beginning of the film, a soldier washed Jean Gabin's feet, and now, near the end of the movie, a girl is attempting to eat Jesus!) Marechal tells the little girl, with total Gabin-Charm (which provides some great, and greatly-comedic, punctuation to the scene), "Don't eat Jesus. Just eat Joseph!" At the end of the evening, when Rosenthal and the little girl have both turned-in for the evening, Marechal accompanies Elsa into her room, and closes the door. They kiss…

The next day, Marechal has to tell Elsa that today is the day when he and Rosenthal are going to have to leave and, not too surprisingly, she knew this would happen, although she *does* cry regardless, telling him that the last few days which he's spent with her have been among the happiest of her and her little daughter's lives. Marechal tells her that after the War, he hopes that she and her daughter can come to live with him in France, and Marechal hugs little Lotte goodbye (trying to speak German, he clumsily stammers, *"Lotte hat blaue Augen"* ["Lotte has blue eyes"]), and the two men leave. Marechal tells Rosenthal that, when he walks out the door, he's not going to be looking back at Elsa because if he does, he'll never be able to leave.

During the past night, the snow has spread a fresh, white blanket across the land, and Marechal and Rosenthal now continue 'their hike to freedom:' As they are about to make

With Dita Parlo.

the final dash across the Swiss frontier, Marechal reminds his little buddy, very soberly, "It's time that you go your way, and I go mine." They toss a couple of epithets at each other ("Goodbye, Dirty Jew;" "Goodbye, old nut"), but they do it with firm friendship, and just as they're about to go their own, separate ways for good, some German soldiers now start firing upon them from atop a hill. Marechal and Rosenthal run in the same direction (fate is forcing them together, again), and they successfully make it over the border to Switzerland as our film ends, and as Marechal and Rosenthal disappear into the horizon. We don't see what will happen to them next, but we can guess that it will probably be a happy ending for both of them.

––––––––––

According to the film historian Peter Cowie, who delivers spoken commentary on the Criterion Collection's 1998 DVD release of *La Grande illusion,* an early version of Jean Renoir and Charles Spaak's screenplay for the picture presented an alternate, 'sad' ending, which Renoir never filmed: In the early draft of the script, Marechal and Rosenthal decide to 'go-it-alone' at the end of the picture, agreeing that they will meet each other at Maxim's restaurant, at the end of the War; in this unfilmed final sequence, we would have seen a crowded restaurant full of French soldiers, all of whom are cheerfully celebrating Christmas on December 25, 1918, and we would have also seen an empty table with two vacant chairs, signifying that Marechal and Rosenthal have died or, more specifically, that both men have been killed. Thankfully, this version was never photographed, because at the end of the movie as it now exists, and has it has always existed, we feel hopeful, and not just for Marechal and Rosenthal's future, but also, for the future of all of Europe.

Any sentient life-form who still hasn't rented *La Grande illusion* on DVD, because he or she has heard that it's 'heavy' (or, as we used to say in film school, that it's 'good for you'), is missing out on a great, irreverent, anti-establishment war comedy which pre-dates other anti-war comedies like Billy Wilder's *Stalag 17* and Robert Altman's *M*A*S*H*, by twenty and thirty years, respectively. While the ultimate message of *La Grande illusion* is a painful one (that, even though we're all flesh and blood, we're all doomed to be separated anyway, due to our differing classes and national heritages), the picture, nevertheless, remains energetic and fun. Just like Jean Gabin's previous films in which he had also played soldiers (*La Bandera* and *Les Gaietes de l'escadron*), *La Grande illusion* is a French film from the 1930s which hands us over to a gaggle of offbeat misfits, men who are able to survive their less-than-savory conditions, through their use of humor, irreverent behavior, and (most importantly of all), friendship.

Not-so-weirdly, *La Grande illusion* continues to inspire pop-culture's greatest artists, all around the world:

—Director Jean Renoir was well-known for shooting his films in long, 'theatrical,' master shots, in which we can see can see all of the characters in each scene at the same time as well as the entire room which the characters occupy (which is meant to replicate 'how our eyes see things' both in real life, and in stage-plays). Master shots relax the narrative, 'letting it breathe,' and making us feel as though we're experiencing movie scenes in real time, and the Swedish director Ingmar Bergman would eventually borrow this visual idea from Renoir in the '40s, when he began making his own films. (And of course, Woody Allen, in turn, borrowed his 'own' style, in which scenes are filmed almost exclusively in long master shots of the entire room, from his hero, Bergman;)

— Besides shooting his scenes in 'master shot,' Renoir was also partial to spinning his camera around his cast members, whenever he had them seated together around tables, and today's filmmakers who have 'cribbed' this tracking shot from Renoir, include Spike Lee, the Coen Brothers, and all other filmmakers whose budgets are large enough to incorporate camera tracks;

— Pop-diva Madonna is such a big fan of *La Grande illusion* that, when she issued her notorious 'dirty' photo book, *Sex*, in 1990, she named her (all-nude) alter-ego, in its pages, 'Dita,' after the actress Dita Parlo, who played Elsa in the Renoir/Gabin picture;

— Rocker Marilyn Manson was married, through 2006, to the burlesque performer Heather Sweet, who rechristened herself as 'Dita Von Tease,' also, after Dita Parlo;

— And of course, as any aficionado of American 'classic rock radio' will attest, this film even inspired the 1970s rock-and-roll band Styx to create its own tribute-song to the film

"Grand Illusion," a piece of music which has been a steady staple of American classic rock FM radio, since it made its bow in 1977.

We should count ourselves lucky that we can see *La Grande illusion* today, in its pristine and uncut state, because for many years, it was not possible to do so. In 1940, the controversial film's original negative was 'borrowed,' in the sense that, when the Germans occupied France in 1940, the Nazis seized it; the Nazis referred to the movie as 'Cinematic Public Enemy #1,' because they felt that it was both anti-war and pro-Jewish, and relatedly, in his book-length 2001 examination of Hitler's conquest of France, *Strange Victory,* the historian Ernest R. May wrote that it was France's anti-war cinema of the mid-to-late 1930s, including (and especially) *La Grande illusion,* which gave Hitler the idea that it would be easy to conquer France, because in his opinion, the movie represented the pacifistic national mood in France, at that time. At any rate, the Nazis shipped the film's original negative to Berlin, where it remained until 1945, which is when the Soviet Army found it, seized it, and carried it with them, back to Moscow. Then, *the story becomes even stranger:* Due to a post-War film exchange program between the Russians and the French, the Cinematheque of Toulouse acquired the film's original negative in the 1960s, which means that, over a period of twenty years, *La Grande illusion's* original negative traveled from France, to Germany, to Russia, and then, back to France, again! (This 'little film-that-could' was more well-traveled than most people!) The original camera-negative sat unnoticed in the Toulouse Archives for another three decades, until the U.S.-based Criterion Collection DVD company, working in tandem with France's Canal+, restored *La Grande illusion* to its original luster, for a 1998 theatrical, and a subsequent DVD, re-release. (Everyone, including Jean Renoir, had always considered the original negative to have been destroyed, and all of the thirty-five millimeter prints of *Illusion* which had been minted between the 1940s and the 1990s, prior to the Criterion/Canal + restoration, had always been duplicated from second and third-generation prints.)

According to the American filmmaker and film historian Peter Bogdanovich, who introduced a 2005 broadcast of *La Grande illusion* on the U.S. cable channel Turner Classic Movies, the legendary director John Ford had actually entertained thoughts of producing an American remake of *La Grande illusion* for Twentieth-Century Fox, but Fox's chief muckimuck, Daryl F. Zanuck (and very sagely, so) put the kybosh on the idea: "Forget it. You can't touch it." (It's too bad that the remake-happy American movie studios of today don't think in those same, intelligent terms.)

In 1979, director Jean Renoir passed away in Beverly Hills, where he had spent the last years of his life, and his body was flown back to France, for burial. Interviewed on a 1970 edition of American Television's "The Dick Cavett Show," Renoir's friend, Orson Welles, who was a great admirer of Renoir's films (Welles even wanted to star *Illusion's* Dita Parlo in his never-made film version of Joseph Conrad's *Heart of Darkness*), even said that if he could 'save' only one movie ever made for future generations, that he would save *La Grande illusion.*

How popular was *La Grande illusion* during its North American release, in 1938 and 1939? The movie industry trade magazine, *Box Office*, kept up on the trends:
• At the Savoia theater in Philadelphia, as a publicity stunt, a local radio station played half-an-hour of the film's dialogue over a local radio station (2-25-39 issue);
• Because the film dealt with anti-Semitism, special screenings were held around the U.S. for Rabbis, who were directed to give their congregation-members sermons about why it was important for them to see the film. American Rabbis were aided by *La Grande illusion's* producer, Albert Pinkovitch who, before he became a producer, went to school to become a Rabbi (3-11-39 issue);
• Erich von Stroheim would become so popular in the U.S. (for awhile), based upon the success of this film, he announced to the press that he would be dropping the 'von' from his name, to make it sound more 'American!' [Note: He never did this!] (9-23-39 issue);
• Eleanor Roosevelt chose *La Grande illusion*, to be the film which was screened on her 47th birthday, on October 11, 1938.

What a Critic Said at the Time: "An artistically masterful feature. Jean Renoir displays imaginative direction. Jean Gabin, who recently starred in *Pepe Le Moko*, recalls Victor McLaglen with his rugged personality. He is tremendously effective. This film looks like the leader of the new productions from France." (*Variety*, 9-14-38 issue. Critic: "Wear." [Mike Wear.] Reviewed in New York.)
What Another Critic Said At the Time: "This film warns the British that they no longer have a monopoly upon that valuable dramatic device known as understatement..." (New York *Times*, 9-17-38 issue. Critic: Frank S. Nugent.)

In the one-off, French fan magazine, *Jean Gabin: Sa Vie/Ses Flms*, which was published in 1938, the great actor Marcel Dalio, who played Lt. Rosenthal, practically bubbled over, when it came to talking about his good buddy, Jean Gabin:
MARCEL DALIO: "[Jean] is an honest man. The biggest actor in movies—not just in French movies, but in movies, period! He is the most honest friend you could have, and he always gives his friends good advice. He always helps me a lot, with his intelligence and his experience. I hear people say that the reason Jean Gabin is so successful, is because he's 'playing himself.' Well, I say: There's no miracle to his success, because he's working very hard. When you watch him, you notice that he's paying his dues, shot by shot; Jean Gabin does nothing by chance." (<u>Author's Note</u>: For an actor whose movie characters are usually 'ruled by fate,' it's interesting that, when it comes to acting, Gabin doesn't let fate make his 'on-camera choices,' for him. Cinema history's greatest actor of all time, Jean Gabin, makes his acting choices—not *'fate!'*)

Top: Gabin goes native. Above: 'La Princesse Kandou,' Gabin and Jean-Pierre Aumont in "Le Messager."

FILM 25

LE MESSAGER

France, 1937

(Literal English Translation: "THE MESSENGER") Directed by Raymond Rouleau. Produced by Vladimir Zederbaum. Screenplay by Maurice Achard. Based Upon a Story Idea by Henri Bernstein. Director of Photography (black and white), Sam Levin. Editors, Henriette Caire and Maurice Sereine. Production Designers, Eugene Lourie and Jean Lafitte. Music by Georges Auric. (GENRE: MELODRAMA) A Production of Films Alabtros. Running Time: 1 hour 38 minutes. Released in France on September 3, 1937, by Pathe Consortium Cinema. Never Released Theatrically in the United States.

"J'en ai marre!" ("I've had enough!")
— *Jean Gabin cries out to the heavens, after suffering a major loss, in "Le Messager"*

A young and successful executive of a profitable French company which specializes in international trade (mostly with Africa), and is based in the southern port city of Marseilles, Gabin's character, Nicolas Dange (or in English, Nick Danger—it's a great, pulpy name for a character who's going to turn out to be a grand adventurer!) has divorced his shrewish wife, Florence (Betty Rowe) and, as our film begins, she's reaming him out over the phone, demanding the remaining one hundred and eighty-thousand of the three-hundred-thousand franc settlement which she is claiming now that he owes her, and she wants it, *stat!* "No way!" Dange yells into the phone. "You're not getting my money!"

Florence's brother Jack (Henri Guisol) happens to be Dange's partner, and Dange next tells him that if he doesn't resign from his position, he'll go crazy: "I quit! I've had enough of your sister and of this company! You're the [sole] director now. I'm out!" Nick is no longer interested in working in a place where he can be manipulated by his ex-wife's family.

But just as Nick is about to tender his resignation officially, he's forced to rethink his position, when something a little more 'tender' than his resignation enters: It's Marie (Gaby Morlay), a hot brunette with giant, penciled-on eyebrows (which are more than reminiscent of McDonald's Golden Arches), who enters Nick's office, seeking secretarial work. The two are immediately falling in love and, within nanoseconds, he (hilariously) both hires and fires her in the same breath, so that they can be free to date each other. Then, right after he fires her (she's had the job for less than one second), *he* quits, as well! (In *Le Messager*, as in other Gabin pictures from the 1930s, the 'harbinger of cruel fate' is embodied in the form of a breathtaking brunette.)

Nick and Marie quickly marry, off-screen, and soon they're at home, making out on the couch. As a hobby, Marie builds toy monkeys and she's bought one for her new husband as a wedding gift and, as we're going to be finding out very soon, this movie's real 'toy monkey' is Nick himself, and it is Marie who is, very deftly, going to be pulling all of the strings in their relationship. Nick swooningly tells her that he's dreamed of meeting somebody like her, for his whole life ("You build toys: You are my life."), and when the two of them resume their hot, steamy make-out session, he accidentally leaves a cigarette burning on the tablecloth. She gently chastises him, as they continue to kiss.

Neither Nick nor Marie has a job right now though, and even in the movies, man (and woman) can't live on love alone, so Nick needs another occupation, and fast. He hits up an old friend, a prominent builder played by Lucien Coedel, who heads-up the French subsidiary of a British construction company. The guy tells Nick that he doesn't have any managerial positions available for which Nick would be suited: "I mean, there *is* a job that's opening up—a one-year [gig]—but it would be a step down for you: We need a good construction foreman in Uganda, but the climate is incredibly humid there, and it's definitely not a place where your wife would be happy." On the plus side, though, Nick would be paid one hundred thousand francs. Nick's friend gives him two days to think it over, and we know already that he'll say yes, and not just because Nick's last name means 'danger,' but also because most of Jean Gabin's movie characters, whether they're rich or poor, are always salt-of-the-earth/working-class types, at heart.

As we already know from watching other 1930s-made movies in which the eternally-peripatetic drifter/traveler Jean Gabin starred, Nick Dange would probably love to leave Marseilles and head off to Uganda, but boy, does he have a problem: He really loves his new wife, and doesn't want to leave her. On the other side of the coin, though, the money which he's being offered in connection with this new position is pretty awesome and, as we're also going to be finding out in this scene, one point in favor of Nick's taking the job overseas is that, if he leaves the country, he'll get a reprieve from having to pay alimony to his ex-wife, Florence.

Dange heads home that night, all keyed-up to tell Marie about his new, faraway job opportunity, but first, like any 'good' husband, he has to listen to her drone-on, *ad nauseam*, about her new purchases: Marie loves to buy a lot of expensive stuff, just like Florence did, but at least Marie, unlike Florence, is always very nice and supportive of her husband, so he minds... but he doesn't mind too much: "I went out and bought fancy things today. I got a leather jacket ...and a Holstein cow couch!" (She's not kidding, either; we're staring right at this white and black eyesore-of-a-sofa right now, as she speaks.) Next, it's time for Nick to break his own news to her—"I was offered a new job, today!"—and she's excited when he tells her about it, although he hasn't told her yet that the job will be taking him far away, and that she's not going to be going with him. He takes her dancing at the Cape of Good Hope bar, their favorite haunt, and gives her the full brunt of the news on the dance floor, as they're tripping the light *fantastique:* "I accepted a new job. The money is great... but it's in Africa." Excitedly, she asks him when they're going to be leaving, and he tells her that he's decided not to bring her along, because she'd be the only woman in the whole place, and that she'd probably just be bored-stiff there. She deflates like a tire, and he feels awful about what he's just had to tell her: Unlike other husbands, who use out-of-town work gigs as an excuse to fuck anyone and anything, Nick really loves Marie and, as they continue dancing, they try to 'keep on smilin' through,' while the band is playing a song which comments, not so obliquely, on the action in this scene: According to the song's 'a little-bit-too-on-the-nose' lyrics, "She is Like She Is... He is Like He Is...," and in every single one of his movies, Jean Gabin is always "like he is:" His characters are always resolute, and once they make up their minds about doing something, they never change it. He won't take her along with him 'for her own good,' even though he truly wishes that he could.

He tells her that he'll be in Uganda for eighteen months and that, when the job is done, he'll return home, and with lots of money for them to live on. We think, from the subtly-conspiratorial way in which she's arching her huge eyebrows when he says 'money,' that she's going to be doing something underhanded, like stealing the bread out from under his nose as soon as he brings it home, but it is to the credit of the filmmakers that the film never falls for such overt clichés: Marie, throughout the film, remains nice and sweet at all times.

Nick leaves for Uganda, absently leaving his cigarette to burn on the club's tablecloth (this guy really needs to learn about ashtrays!), a foreshadowing, for the audience, that something's definitely going to be 'burning-out' at the end of the film, and that 'that something' will probably be either the Nick-Marie marriage, or maybe even Nick, himself.

Uganda, probably a few days or weeks later:

When we next see Nick, natives are carrying him on a decorative sedan-chair, festively beating jungle drums with alligator-bone drumsticks, in celebration of the arrival of their new '*jefe blanco*.' Nick next makes the acquaintance of the guy whom he'll be replacing, Geo (Maurice Escande), a, bearded Bluto like character, who, when we first meet him, is in the middle of watching a topless native girl, who's dancing for him. (The film features scads of upper-torso female nudity, which is probably what kept it from being released theatrically, in 1937's puritanical, Hays Code-ruled U.S.A.)

Nick takes over Geo's hut, and is amused, instantly, by the pictures of naked chicks which the guy's got strung-up all over the place, and so he takes them down: Jean Gabin, in every picture, is never any less than one hundred-percent classy; his characters are also always very hard workers, and having pictures of sexy, barely-clothed women around would definitely interfere with all of that good work he has to do.

Nick, then, *steps out onto the steppe,* to check on the progress of the workers, and they're not toiling away that hard; in fact, many of them are just laying around, drunk-off-their-asses, just like Gabin and his fellow soldiers did in *Gaietes de l'escadron.* He introduces himself, tells the guys he's the new man in charge, and then assures them very gently, and with a smile, that their lazy days are over.

Director Raymond Rouleau, who'll only work with Jean Gabin on this one film (Rouleau was a handsome and popular movie actor, who also directed several films), next crosscuts between shots of Nick, in Uganda (in which Nick is acclimating himself to his new surroundings) with other shots of Marie, who remains in Marseilles, and who is getting used to her new husband's absence. More specifically, in Uganda, an Architect is showing Nick a scale-model of the hospital facility which their company is building for the locals while, back in Marseilles, Marie is sketching a picture of a lonely soldier. (But who's the 'lonely soldier?' Does this cartoon figure represent Nick, Marie—or both of them?)

While Nick has, at least for the time being, lost his wife's companionship, he has gained a protégé, young, twentysomething Gilbert, who's played by Jean Pierre-Aumont, the actor who two years earlier had portrayed Eutrope Gagnon, Gabin's rival-in-love for Madeleine Renaud, in Duvivier's *Maria Chapdelaine.* Gilbert tells his new boss, Nick, that he too has a girl back in Marseilles, and that just like Nick's woman, his own lady's name happens to be Marie. (Don't worry: These are two different Maries. This is a very well-made film, so it never falls for easy clichés, like, for example, having both men realize that they're with the same woman.) Gilbert's own Marie writes her man a letter, which he reads out loud to a laughing Nick: "I hope your new boss, Mr. Dange, isn't too ugly and too vulgar, and that you'll be home soon. I can't bear this loneliness!" Nick asks Gilbert if the bosses in Marseilles have sent him to Uganda to spy on him, and Gilbert remarks truthfully that they have not, and that he's just been sent there to assist Nick in whatever way he can.

Gilbert tells Nick that his own Marie is married to another man, but that she'll soon be getting a divorce, and that she'll be able to be with him on a full-time basis, when he returns to France. He shows Nick the picture of his own Marie. Nick thinks she's *a real cutie,* and Gilbert is very amused: "Isn't it funny, Nick, that we've found ourselves in the same part of the world, and all because of two Maries?!" Nick asks Gilbert if he can take one more look at his (Gilbert's) Marie again, and it's obvious that he likes his new associate's Marie, just as much as he also likes his own. When Nick's alone in his tent, later that evening, he sings the song which he and Marie danced to earlier in the film, at Marseilles' Cape of Good Hope Club:

Director Rouleau now dissolves to two months later: Nick and Gilbert are panning for gold together in a stream, and Nick's rhapsodizing out loud to Gilbert about how light his own Marie always feels when they dance. Gilbert laughs: "You've been talking about her for two months straight, boss," and Nick now sighs, with a completely-moony look plastered across his face, "Well, that's because she can't do anything wrong!" (While Jean Gabin would sometimes let this vulnerable side of himself show in his earliest, pre-fame pictures which he made between 1930 and 1933, *Le Messager* is one of the few pictures he'll make during his big, international stardom-period of the late thirties and early forties, in which he'll open himself up so rawly, and we know that nothing good will come of it.) "I am loved!" Nick cries out, just as joyously as Julie Andrews on a mountaintop, "and more important[ly] than anything else—my woman is nice!"

Now, it's time for the film's big action set-piece: The Company needs to raze a mountain for the hospital construction, so Nick, Gilbert, and a native aide climb up to the top, set the charge and haul-ass down. But (whoops!) Nick's left his wallet up there, and it's got his only picture of Marie in it, so he's got to go back up and retrieve it, before it's too late. Yes, Nick actually risks death in order to save a little 2 x 2 glossy of his wife; this bit is definitely a little hokey, but because of Gabin's amazing *gravitas*, we're really rooting for him, because we can see that he genuinely and unreservedly loves his wife enough to risk his life, and not even to save his wife, but to rescue a tiny, veeloxed representation of her. Needless to say, our heroic Nick Danger gets that old wallet back after all and, naturally, he's made it down the mountain safely, with the wallet and the prized picture, only seconds before the big explosion.

A few days later, Nick's Marie sends him a recording, a personally-recorded phonograph album of her voice, which she hopes will keep him company. Gilbert, who happens to be walking by the boss's hut, hearing a woman's voice, peeks into Nick's hut, and sees his boss drunkenly swooning over Marie's recorded message. "You have my love," Marie tells Nick soothingly, over the scratchy vinyl, "and you are adored." Nick is so lonely (and drunk, and overcome by emotion), that he covers his eyes, throws himself on his knees and, in an amazing, pre-Stanley Kowalski-Primal Scream, lets go with a mighty-river Gabin-Outburst of "*J'en ai marre*" which, in English means, "I've had enough!" and "*J'en ai marre*" is the #1 catch-phrase which Gabin will utter in a lot of his movies, whenever his characters are at the end of their tethers: He really owns "*J'en ai marre*," even to the point where we should probably start referring to the phrase as, "*Jean ai marre!*" "*J'en ai marre*," in any Gabin picture, is always a great pressure-reliever for Our Hero and, after he says it, he always becomes nice and calm again. (In many other movies, if you listen closely, you'll also hear the actor sarcastically spouting-out "*sans blague!*"—or, in English, "no kidding!"—and "*sans blague*" might be considered to be his '#2 catch-phrase.' [It's the first thing he says in *Zou Zou*, after he gets arrested.)

It won't be too long, before Nick is racked with malaria. 'The Movie Jean Gabin' rarely gets too emotional, so we're now figuring out that, just maybe, the vulnerability which he's been displaying throughout the last few scenes has really just been 'the disease talking.' He whines feverishly about how much he loves his Marie, whose eyes, as we now hear him saying, "shine in the dark," and who, he says, is "more beautiful than happiness;" within a couple of scenes, suffice it say, Gilbert, too, has developed malaria, the ailment which seems to be catching around these parts faster than Disco Fever, and when Gilbert catches the malaria, and Nick has already recovered from it, Nick ministers to him sweetly, just like a father who's taking care of his son. Gilbert is freaked, because he hasn't yet heard from his own Marie, and, as he's now reminding Nick, he's been in Uganda for one hundred and thirty-four days. Nick tells Gilbert, dreamily, "When I see my Marie again, the doors to my soul will open, and my heart will truly beat!"

Back in Marseilles, Nick's Marie is lazing by the country club pool with her girlfriend, Pierrette (Mona Goya), and she's admitting to Pierrette that, while she hates this forced-separation from her charming husband, that now, she herself is at the end of her own, 'j'en ai marre-tether.' Pierrette, a 'frenemy' who means well, but who likes to 'bring you down to her own level' by making you feel as badly as she does, and who's trying to cheer Marie up, now eyes a hot young guy who happens to be playing tennis nearby. "I think he likes you," Pierrette nudges her. The ladies watch the young man batting his little ball around, and both of them look like they're eyeing a big, fat, juicy steak.

Gilbert's job in Uganda finishes-up before Nick's does, so Gilbert gets to return to Marseilles before Nick. Dressed-up in a natty suit, Gilbert sallies forth to see Marie, and it's not his own Marie whom he plans on seeing, either. (Anyway, don't worry too much, because he's just come to Nick and Marie's house to deliver her a message to her, from her still-away-in-Uganda husband. [Gilbert is 'The Messenger' of the film's title.] "I'm Gilbert Rollin, your husband's friend," Gilbert tells Nick's Marie politely, and he's happily surprised to learn that she's already heard of him: "It is so nice to meet you, Gilbert. My husband is always talking about you in his letters. So: How is your girl, the one who has the same first name as me?" Getting nervous around such a hot lady, Gilbert now changes the subject: "Your husband told me to deliver this letter to you. (Gilbert is Nick's carrier pigeon and, in French, the word 'pigeon,' which is the same in French as it is in English, also has a secondary, slang meaning: Besides being a bird, a 'pigeon' is also a cuckold: Somebody in our story is about to be cuckolded, and we can guess that the 'cuckoldee' is somebody who's still in Uganda.)

Gilbert leaves Nick's Marie and heads off on his own, to the Cape of Good Hope Club, where he takes-in a sexy can-can performance. A hot blonde cigarette girl, who looks a lot like Jean Harlow, is immediately attracted to Gilbert, but he's not paying any attention to her. We can just see that he's really thinking about Nick's Marie whom, of course, he's just met.

Back in Uganda at the same time, Nick just can't wait until the day he'll be able to return to Marseilles to be with his wife and, when we next see him, he's listening to her recorded voice, for what must be the umpteen-thousandth time: "You have the strength of the absent," her voice reassures him, over the scratchy vinyl disk.

And meanwhile, back in Marseilles, Gilbert, who's now growing strong himself, from strong drink, heads back to Nick and Marie's place, and makes a confession to her: "From the second Nick showed me your picture, I was in love with you, too!" Marie's flattered by this younger man's attention, but tells him that she'd never think of cheating on Nick. So Gilbert now starts whining (okay, so he's not that strong) just like the kid he still is: "But… I came back from Uganda just for you! I wanted to tell you how I felt about you earlier this evening when we first met, but I couldn't." Feeling sorry for Gilbert, and since she's bored out of her (pretty) skull from sitting at home, she agrees to go back to the Cape of Good Hope with him, for a nightcap.

And then, surprise! (Or, maybe it's not such a big surprise): Nick has also returned to Marseilles already (just today, on the spur of the moment), months earlier than he had initially planned. Even before going to his own home, his first stop is the Cape of Good Hope Bar, since it's the place where he danced with Marie the night before he left for Uganda, and because he knows that it's her favorite place to go. When he arrives at the club, wearing a tux, he finds her sitting at the table with Gilbert, and he's not shocked at all, because he knew the whole time that this is the tableau that he'd be walking in on; in fact, Nick has probably pushed Gilbert into Marie's hands intentionally, because on some subconscious level of which he's not even aware, it's the only way he can get rid of her: Nick really does love Marie, and more than anybody he's ever met before in his entire life, it's true; but he's also Jean Gabin and, ultimately, Jean Gabin needs to be free. For Nick's first few moments in the club, he hangs back, behind a planter, where he can see 'the illicit couple' before they can see him.

When Marie and Gilbert get up from their table to dance, Nick mischievously *parks his carcass* at their table and, when they arrive back, their throats both parched from *la danse*, they look like two illicit deer caught in his headlights. Before she even sees Nick, Marie first sees his trademark cigarette, burning a hole in the tablecloth (as per usual), and she next sees Nick, himself. As we say so eloquently today: "She is soooo busted!"

"Am I scaring you so much?" Nick asks Gilbert and Marie and, as Nick confronts them, he's being, and this is typical for Jean Gabin's movie characters, one-hundred-percent level-headed and calm. "That's right: It really *is* me! I'm not a ghost!" He sees that Marie suddenly looks very dizzy, and he then asks her, with just a hint of malice in his voice, "Are you going to pass out?"

The three sit down together, and Nick keeps his cool, now segueing into a speech which sounds like it could be right out of Humphrey Bogart's mouth in *Casablanca*, even though 1937's *Le Messager* was made six years before the famous Michael Curtiz picture: "Gilbert, I went to the hotel where you told me you'd be staying, and you weren't there. Of course, I knew you'd be at my house with [my] Marie. In my mind, I pictured myself breaking down her door and heroically fighting her for you. But anyway, forget about it. Neither of you is worth it. So, good luck to the both of you."

At this point, Nick smoothly removes a gun from his tux pocket and points it right at the both of them and, weirdly, nobody in this packed-to-the-rafters nightclub seems to notice that Nick is brandishing a loaded weapon in public. He continues his rant: "I came here to kill you, Marie, but I just don't feel like doing it anymore. So now, we're going to separate again, and this time, for good. Let's just say that I'm 'giving you two back to love.' The two of you look perfect together. And, anyway, my contract to work in Uganda has been extended by three years, and I've decided to go back. Well, goodbye, all." Nick quietly places the gun back into his jacket pocket, without having killed anybody, and then walks out of the club, silently. (Wow! What a speech! He said everything except for Bogey's poetically-famous line from *Casablanca*, "Maybe not today, maybe not tomorrow, but soon, and for the rest of your life.")

The next morning, Nick's at the train station, again leaving Marseilles, and for points that are so far west, they're not even in France. Marie has come to talk to him, and to apologize for cheating on him, although it's a weird beat in the story, because we're not even sure that Gilbert and Marie have slept together, since everything between them, including their initial meeting, happened in only one night. "I look at myself and I can't stand it," she tells her husband. "I feel like I'm my own enemy. The entire time you were in Africa, you were in all my thoughts. Even when I went to the store to buy a hat, I always thought about you. Please come back home and be with me. Please!"

Nick is expressionless, and is no longer letting himself get overcome by emotion, as he had done in earlier scenes. (He's much stronger at the end of the film than he was at the beginning.) "Are you done?" he asks her dismissively, and he then lets her know, matter-of-factly, that there's nothing he can do for her now: "You're not the same girl I used to love. You've given your love, and your kisses, to another—to a kid. He's the one you chose. You're low. So you'd better go away, and quick!" (Again: Nick's just guessing that Marie and Gilbert have fucked, because the only time the two of them have ever been together, is this very evening.) Instead of leaving, Marie just follows Nick onto the train, but he keeps pushing her away and shushing her: "No more words! Stop talking!"

And now, director Rouleau will give us a new surprise, and not a very happy one, at that: "Nick," she tells him, welling up with tears, "It's about Gilbert: He killed himself last night, at 4:00 a.m. He felt so badly about what he did to you. His friendship with you meant everything. So he wrote this letter to both of us." She produces a handwritten letter, and hands it to him.

Gabin is teary-eyed, as he reads the letter from Gilbert, feeling his strongest emotions not for a woman, but for a male friend. Now that he's just learned Gilbert is dead, Nick suddenly reassesses his feelings about his young protégé. All of the anger which he had been feeling toward the kid, only moments before, has suddenly dissipated, and now suddenly, not only is Nick no longer angry with Gilbert, but he's actually defending him: "He was my friend, Marie! Not yours! He was nothing to you! He came to visit you, to bring you my passion! He completed his mission—and then he died." Talk about 'rewriting history:' Suddenly, Nick is telling Marie that Gilbert was doing exactly what Nick wanted him to do, by falling in love with her!

Marie pleads with Nick, because she wants to return to Africa with him—"You can't keep all this sorrow to yourself!"—and after thinking it over for a few moments, he agrees to take her along. Gilbert's unexpected suicide has given Nick and Marie permission to start over and, as she boards the train with her husband, Gilbert's suicide letter blows out of the train's window, carried upon the wind, and the last image we see in this extremely-haunting film, is Gilbert's handwritten note fluttering away into the air, and getting stuck in the train tracks. ("Don't blame the messenger for the message," this extremely worthwhile film seems to be telling us.)

Le Messager is another great Jean Gabin movie which American audiences would have loved, if only they would have had the chance to see it, which they didn't, because the picture was never exhibited in North America at all. The reason that the film didn't attain theatrical release in the U.S., has little to do with the fact that distribution for foreign-language films has always been spotty in America, and probably also not so much to do with the fact that the movie (mercifully!) shows us the occasional *naked boob:* Psychologically, the movie may have been too murky for American audiences who, at the time, were used to characters who were either 'all good' or 'all bad:' In this movie, we get a guy, played by Gabin, who really loves a woman, and yet at the same time, on some subconscious level, he feels like he's not good enough to have her, so he forces her into the hands of another man, even though, if you ever had the chance to ask him about it, he'd probably swear up-and-down that he did no such thing. (Of course, this kind of stuff happens all the time in real life: Lots of times, we don't know just what the hell our psychological reasons are for doing half of the shit we do, and it takes expensive shrinks to dredge it up out of us!) Just based on the fact that we've already seen other Gabin Movies which were made during this, his 'matinee idol-period,' we know that he's pushed his friend into his woman's arms because he knows that, even if she isn't hurting him now, she'll eventually be hurting him at some point in the near future, so he takes the pre-eminent strike, and dumps the woman before she can dump him. Anyway, whatever the reason is that it was never shown in the U.S., *Le Messager,* like most of the movies in this book, is a very good Jean Gabin movie which deserves to be remembered, and not just in France, but all over the world. The movie's female lead, Gaby Morlay, who was eleven years Gabin's senior, was just as big a star as Gabin was in the France of the late 1930s, and this is the only movie which Gabin made during this, the period of his biggest pre-War fame, in which he accepted second-billing to his leading lady. (Morlay will appear again with Gabin one more time, twenty-seven years later, as a crotchety old *grandmother,* in a 1964 comedy called *Monsieur.*)

What a Critic Said at the Time: "This will undoubtedly go down as one of the better films produced in France this year, and it deserves applause. Jean Gabin, again, [plays] a hardboiled guy, who takes what he loves, and leaves what he does not… Gabin and Morlay handle the difficult closing scenes with conviction." (*Variety,* 10-6-37 issue. Critic: "Hugo." Reviewed in Paris.)

The Original Ladykiller.

FILM 26

GUEULE D'AMOUR

France, 1937

(Approximate English Title: "IRRESISTIBLE SEDUCER") Directed and Edited by Jean Gremillon. Produced by Raoul Plouqin. Screenplay by Charles Spaak. Based Upon the Novel by Andre Beucler. Director of Photography (black and white), Gunther Rittau. Music by Lothar Bruhne. Production Designer, Jean Gremillon. (GENRE: MELODRAMA) A Production of L'Alliance Francaise Europeene. Running Time, 1 hour 34 minutes. Released in France, on September 15, 1937, by La Societe de Films Sirius and L'Alliance Francaise Europeene. Released in Great Britain with English Subtitles as "LADYKILLER," in 1938. Never Released Theatrically in the United States.

"You are going to shut up! You are going to shut up! I've heard you enough!
You are going to shut up!"
—Gabin, to the love of his life, before he strangles her to death, in
"Gueule d'amour"

D irector Jean Gremillon's top-notch 1937 melodrama *Gueule d'amour* was written for the screen by Gabin's frequent movie scenarist Charles Spaak (*La Bandera, Les Bas-fonds*) from the novel by Andre Beucler (*Adieu les beaux jours*), and it was filmed on location in France and Germany. Gremillon, like Julien Duvivier and Jean Renoir, was another of France's great Poetic Realist directors of the 1930s, and in his *Gueule d'amour*, Gabin is the free-wheeling Lucien, an officer of the SPAHI, an elite branch of the French cavalry. When his regiment arrives in Orange, in southern France, we immediately see how popular he is with women, which is why he has the slang nickname '*gueule d'amour*' or, in English, 'irresistible seducer.'

Lucien receives a short leave to go to Cannes, where he is going to be collecting a small inheritance, and this is where he meets the beautiful Madeleine (Mireille Balin, from *Pepe Le Moko*). If, on Lucien's end, it's love-at-first-sight, Madeleine's feelings are more ambivalent and complex. She is, of course, physically attracted to Lucien, but it is difficult to tell, at this stage of the story, what her real feelings are. Lucien and Madeleine spend a few hours together: They walk on the dam, they talk, and they dance in a casino's night-club. At the casino, Madeleine gambles away Lucien's small inheritance, but Lucien is so smitten with her, he doesn't care.

In the morning, Lucien takes Madeleine home, hoping to sleep with her, but while he's paying the taxi driver, she enters the house and locks the door behind her, without a word, to Lucien's complete surprise. Obsessed by this woman, who is so different from all of the other women he has known, he decides to resign from the Army, and he moves to Paris where Madeleine lives, and he confides that he will be doing this to his best friend, Doctor Rene (Rene Lefevre). Rene tries to warn his friend not to, and he reminds Lucien that since Madeleine has left all of Lucien's letters unanswered, she probably doesn't care. He also tells Lucien that it's foolish to fall for a woman with whom he has only spent a few hours, and of whom he knows nothing, but Lucien doesn't listen.

In Paris, Lucien finds work as a typist, and after months, he and Madeleine are re-acquainted, and become lovers. One day, he invites Madeleine to dinner but she sends him a cancellation note, telling him that she has to leave for three days, and that they will meet when she returns. On the day of her return, she tries to phone Lucien at his workplace, but his boss refuses to put her call through.

After the day's work, Lucien goes to Madeleine's apartment, but Madeleine is not there, so he decides to wait for her. Madeleine's mother (Marguerite Deval) comes to her daughter's apartment for dinner and is informed by the butler (Jean Ayme) that Lucien is there. The mother is determined to preserve her daughter's 'upwardly mobile' status and she is annoyed by Lucien's presence, so she informs him—and this is true—that Madeleine has a wealthy boyfriend in Deauville. Lucien, hurt, leaves, but the good news, is that when he returns to his small apartment, Madeleine is waiting for him. Lucien is happy to see her, but he's also mad at her, because she's constantly manipulating his feelings. He tells her that he will soon have two weeks' leave and that he would like to take her on holiday. She says that she would like to go, but that it won't be possible, because she has to go to Deauville again.

The day before Madeleine is to leave again for Deauville, Lucien arrives, unexpectedly, at Madeleine's apartment. He first asks her to dismiss the butler, who looks down on him, and he also asks her to put her mother out (she's there, at the time, having lunch), saying that he can't stand her. Madeleine, noticing Lucien's irritation, agrees. The mother calls Jean-Pierre Moreau (Robert Casa), Madeleine's rich lover, and tells him that her daughter doesn't feel well, and that it would behoove him to come to Paris, immediately. By asking him to come, she knows that he will find Madeleine and Lucien together, and that is exactly what happens. Madeleine is surprised to see Moreau, and tells him that she wasn't expecting his visit. Lucien tells Moreau to go home, and Madeleine is upset, because she understands that this could put an end to her 'easy' life, so she apologizes to Moreau. Lucien asks Madeleine to throw Jean-Pierre Moreau out, but it is exactly the opposite that happens: Madeleine tells Lucien that he has gone too far, and she orders *him* to leave, which he does.

Lucien returns to Orange, and this is where he realizes that, without his elegantSPAHI

With Mireille Balin.

uniform, and with his tired look, he is no longer '*gueule d'amour*'—or the focus of attraction—anymore, and he opens a small bar. One day, his friend Rene learns that he's back, and goes to the bar to pay him a visit. As they talk, Rene says that he's in love with a woman whom he's just met fifteen days before, here in Orange, and as they go on chatting, Lucien understands that the woman in question is Madeleine, but he says nothing to his friend. Rene invites Lucien to have dinner with him and Madeleine the day after, and Lucien accepts, and in the next scene, we understand why Madeleine is in Orange: She has actually come to locate Lucien! Rene meets Madeleine and tells her that he is glad because he has found an old friend again, and as the conversation continues, he tells her that his friend's nickname was '*gueule d'amour*,' and that he has opened a small bar. Madeleine, who knows Lucien's nickname, acts as if nothing has happened, but she knows now that Lucien is indeed in the neighborhood and she also knows that her search is over. Rene asks Madeleine if she will dinner with them the day after and she says yes.

The following evening, Lucien arrives at Rene's home for dinner, but Madeleine is not present; she has, however, sent a note, in which she writes that she won't be able to attend, because she feels sick. Rene calls Madeleine's hotel to talk to her, but Lucien says it's not worth the trouble. Lucien decides to tell everything to his friend (his misfortunes, what kind of woman Madeleine is, the fact that he assumes Madeleine is in Orange to see him again), and Rene takes this quite badly. He says that he has all his chances of success with Madeleine, and he also says that he doesn't believe Madeleine is still thinking of Lucien, also declaring that what Madeleine has done in the past is not important to him. Lucien is very sad at his pal's reaction, as their friendship is very important to him. He leaves in a depressive state and goes back to his bar.

When he arrives, he sees that Madeleine is waiting for him there. He puts the two customers who happened to be there out, and he also sends the waitress away, so that he can be alone with Madeleine. Madeleine explains that she has never forgotten him, that she wants to be good to him and that she's there to take him back with her to Paris. He asks her about Moreau and she answers, "You will never meet him, you won't even realize that he exists," implying that she still sees Moreau, and that what she wants, is to pursue a relationship with Moreau and Lucien at the same time, which is exactly what she was doing before. Lucien next asks her about her relationship with Rene. Madeleine says that she doesn't care about Rene and that she considers him to be just one of the dozens of men who are interested in her. Lucien tells her that Rene is really drawn to her, and Madeleine replies that she finds Rene to be bland and foolish, and she asks Lucien what he wants her to do. Lucien answers that he wants her to leave immediately, as his friend Rene could rightly blame him for her presence. Madeleine next asks Lucien if he wants her to phone Rene, and an incredulous Lucien answers, "Would you dare to do that?" Madeleine answers that she will. Lucien begs her not to do so and tells her that it will break Rene's heart, as he in love with her, but Madeleine is resolute. Despite Lucien's repeated pleas, Madeleine phones Rene and tells him coldly that there will no longer be anything between them. As she hangs up, Madeleine asks Lucien, "Do you believe me now?" A stunned Lucien replies, "Do you realize what you just did?" Madeleine says, "Ask me anything, I'll do it," but Lucien just tells her to get out. He adds, "Now, why don't you phone Moreau just the way you've done with Rene? Of course, you won't, because Moreau is too rich to get rid of. It's much easier with a man like Rene." Madeleine turns to Lucien, trying to embrace him, and she affirms, "You still love me, Lucien!" Lucien pushes her aside and answers, "Yeah, but that's my business. I want to stay alone to be able to cry, even if I die from it. I want to stay alone. I've had enough!" Then, Madeleine turns cold and viperish towards Lucien, and he's so angry at her manipulations, he does the most unexpected thing in the world—he strangles her to death.

A shattered Lucien next heads to Rene's place to tell him what happened, telling Rene that Madeleine is dead and sobbing, "I loved her!" He asks for his friend's help, as he is at a loss what to do—should he give himself up, or should he flee? Rene helps Lucien to take the train to Marseilles where, hopefully, he will be able to embark for Africa.

Today, *Gueule d'amour* remains an immensely popular film in France, and hopefully one day, and sooner than later, it will also be known in the United States. It is a primo example of the kind of (great) films which Gabin made during this Cycle of his career and features every important characteristic—'tragic drifter,' 'manipulated by a woman,' 'friendship of his male friend ultimately stronger than the love of a woman,' *etc.*—that we will see in most of Jean Gabin's movies._

What a Critic Said at the Time: "This one was made for Jean Gabin, and he's pivoted himself higher in the star firmament by hanging up the best piece of acting he's ever done. [*Gueule d'amour*] furnishes another reason why the standard in France is climbing to a higher level. [Screenwriter Charles] Spaak's adaptation of Andre Beucler's story has been excellently done, and [Gabin packs a] virile punch... Gabin never wavers or falters [as a] tough, colonial cavalryman who 'finds 'em, feeds 'em, loves 'em, and forgets 'em...' This film is so excellently executed that it really can't be forgotten." (*Variety*, 10-27-37 issue. Critic: "Hugo." Reviewed in Paris.)

What Another Critic Said at the Time: "Gabin again plays a toy in the arms of a woman. There is good cinematography and the rhythm is right. Jean Gremillon has directed the film like the intelligent artist he is. Gabin is full of spontaneity—he has found a great role, one which sets him apart from other stars who are only capable of focusing on their own characters." (*Pour Vous Magazine*, 9-2-37 issue. Critic: "Lucien.")

With Michele Morgan.

FILM 27

LE QUAI DES BRUMES

France, 1938

(France, 1938) (Literal English Translation: "THE PORT OF SHADOWS") Directed by Marcel Carne. Produced by Gregor Rabinovitch. Screenplay by Marcel Carne and Jacques Prevert. Based Upon the Novel by Pierre Dumarchais (as Pierre MacOrlan). Director of Photography (black and white), Eugen Schufftan. Editor, Rene Le Henaf. Music by Maurice Jaubert. (GENRE: DRAMA) A Production of Cine-Alliance. Running Time, 1 hour 31 minutes. Released in France on May 18, 1938, by Les Films Osso and Mondial. Released in United States with English Subtitles on October 29, 1939, by Film Alliance of the United States, Inc.

"The fog is in here!"
— Angst-ridden Gabin indicates his own forehead, in "Le Quai des brumes"

1 938's *Le Quai des brumes (The Port of Shadows)* is another of Jean Gabin's supremely-powerful Poetic Realist pictures, and it's very important, because it represents the first of Gabin's two late 1930s collaborations to have been presented by the visionary creative duo of Marcel Carne (a former cabinet maker) and Carne's preferred screenwriter-of-choice, Jacques Prevert. (The second Gabin/Carne/Prevert team-up, which would be made during the following year of 1939, was *Le Jour se leve*, or in English, *Daybreak*.) *Le Quai des brumes* and *Le Jour se leve* were the two darkest and most tragic films, not just of Jean Gabin's 'Poetic Realist period' of the 1930s, but also the two 'darkest' films, both visually as well as thematically, which Jean Gabin would ever make in his entire career. *Le Quai des brumes* and *Le Jour se leve* are the two most primary examples of French Poetic Realism's main theme, in which "Helpless characters are trapped in claustrophobic worlds, from which they can never hope to escape."

WHENEVER A COUNTRY IS GOING THROUGH DARK TIMES, IT'S CINEMA BECOMES DARK: As I mentioned in the introduction to this book, the Poetic Realist movement was France's filmic response to the 'darkness' which had been plaguing

France throughout the '30s (widespread unemployment, encroaching Fascism, and a general feeling of helplessness among the populace) and, as such, French Poetic Realism can be viewed as being a direct offshoot of, and a a pre-cursor to, other international film styles, all of which seem to have come to pass whenever various countries were similarly faced with trying times: After Germany lost World War I, the citizenry was in panic, the currency depreciated to practically nothing, everybody was out of work, and the result, on movie screens, was a forerunner of 1930s French Poetic Realism, the Expressionistic Cinema movement of the 1920s, which was personified by directors such as Fritz Lang [*Metropolis*] and F.W. Murnau [*Nosferatu*]. French Poetic Realism also pre-dated two other 'Cinemas of Dark Fatalism' which arose out of other countries' tragic times—Italy's Neo-Realistic cinema of the late 1940s and early 1950s (films like De Sica's *Bicycle Thieves* and Rossellini's *Rome, Open City*, in which, similarly to Poetic Realism, working-class characters were responding to 'post-War [in the case of these particular films, World War II] uncertainty'), and America's *Film Noir* pictures, which were made during the same time period as the Italian Neo-Realistic pictures (*Postman Always Rings Twice, Kiss Me Deadly, Night of the Hunter*, etc.), in which trapped characters always seemed to be stuck in dark, night-time worlds, worlds which were meant to be emblematic of the 'Cold War paranoia' which Americans felt, post-World War II, as a reaction to the threat of possible nuclear annihilation from the Russians.

German Expressionist, French Poetic Realist, and American *Film Noir* pictures, were all heavily-stylized (shot on sound stages, incorporating weird and distorted camera angles and weirdly-poetic dialogue), to show how trapped their characters were, while the Italian Neo-Realist pictures were more documentary-like, in the sense that they were photographed on 'real' locations, often made use of natural lighting, and starred 'real people,' as opposed to professional actors.

Le Quai des brumes won't stray from the tried-and-true Gabin/'Tragic Myth' Formula, and it's based upon a novel by the great French novelist, Pierre MacOrlan (real name: Pierre Dumarchais) who, in addition to *Le Quai des brumes*, also wrote the novel upon which Gabin's 1935 Spanish Foreign Legion picture, *La Bandera*, was based.

The film opens at night, on a dark road, twelve miles from France's northernmost port city of Le Havre. A Truckdriver (Marcel Peres) picks up Gabin's aptly-monikered 'Jean,' who's just deserted the military, because he's sick of fighting. Jean hits the guy up for a ride to Le Havre, and reluctantly, he begins regaling the driver with stories of his recent combat adventures in French Indochina ("It's nothing to shoot," Jean tells the driver, nonchalantly. "The man you shoot holds his stomach like a kid who's eaten too much food, and then his hands turn red.") when he suddenly grabs the steering wheel away from the driver, to avoid hitting a dog. At first, the driver is upset with Jean, but when he calms down, he sees that Jean was just saving the four-legged-friend, and the two men part on a friendly note.

When the Driver drops Jean off in Le Havre, guess who's following him—it's the dog whose life he's just saved. At first, Jean repeatedly tells the "dog" to beat it (Gabin rues

With Raymond Aimos.

attachments to animals, just like he does to people), but gradually, he begins to like the little thing; after all, the dog is a stray just as he is—a four-legged tragic drifter...

Meanwhile, at a swank local bar called The Little Joker, a trio of dapper young gangsters led by a man whom director Renoir wants to present to us as being 'The Ultimate Little Joker,' Lucien Legardier (Pierre Brasseur), are interrogating a merchant called Zabel (he's played by the Charles Laughton-looking French actor Michel Simon, a master of celluloid slovenliness), a bearded/stoop-shouldered old Rasputin/Bluebird-clone who's probably never seen the inside of a gin-joint in his entire life. Lucien has invited Zabel for this *tete-a-tete*, because one of his gang-members, Maurice, is missing, and not only is Lucien certain that Zabel has killed him, but Lucien even knows what Zabel's motive may have been: Zabel is guardian to Nelly, a seventeen-year-old heartbreaker whom he's been raising since her mother ran away when she was a girl. Zabel has grown fond of Nelly, beyond the normal level of fondness which a 'godfather' should be feeling for his goddaughter, and relatedly, he always becomes jealous when Nelly dates *anybody*, including her current suitor, the 'missing' Maurice. Zabel won't own up to anything, and Lucien tells him words to the effect of "you can run, but you can't hide," but Zabel isn't afraid of Lucien for the same reason that we aren't afraid of him, either—Zabel knows that Lucien is a "trust-fund gangster," a kid from a good family (the 1930s equivalent of a 'wigger') who's dressing up as a hood, but who isn't all that threatening. (Baby-faced Lucien is afraid of his own shadow and, to quote from any good cowboy movie, he's "all hat and no cattle.")

Perambulating through Le Havre, meanwhile, Jean, who's broke and hungry, runs across a gaggle of military police (every deserter's worst nightmare), and here, he's aided by Half-Pint (Raymond Aimos), a kindly drunk who offers to hide him out. Half-Pint escorts him to a seaside bar called Panama's where, just like "Rick's Café Americain" in *Casablanca* (only without the 'flash' [and the 'happiness!']), all of life's displaced drifters are welcome, no questions asked. Of course, Jean's new dog follows him into the place.

The bar's eponymous owner, Panama (Edouard Delmont), is an amiable guy who sees that Jean is hungry, and so he immediately fixes Jean up with bread, cheese, and sausage. One customer, a depressive painter called Michel Krauss (Robert Le Vigan), tries to chat Jean up, but like all of Jean Gabin's other cagey 1930s' movie characters, Jean would prefer to be left in peace, while he shares his comestibles with his new canine. (While Krauss is a depressive, he's definitely got a good heart: Ascertaining that Jean is a deserter who is in need of a new identity, Krauss sweetly offers him his own, moaning that he's already in possession of "one identity too many." [We know, when he says this, that Krauss won't be long for this earth.]) Anyway, Jean's need for solitude is quickly forgotten, when Nelly, Zabel's lithesome charge, enters, and she's played by Michele Morgan, one of France's most enduring stars. Jean is immediately attracted to Nelly and *vice-versa,* and we can tell not only that she's a girl who's used to a lot of unwarranted male attention, but also that the reason she's reacting to him so favorably is that, unlike other guys, he's not "all over her." And why has Nelly shown up at Panama's? She doesn't say it directly, but she'll admit, later in the film, that she likes to "run away" and "hide out," because it's a much more acceptable alternative than going home and getting hit-on by her lecherous, old godfather.

With this film, seventeen-year-old Michele Morgan (she was born during a leap year, on February 29, 1920, as Simone Roussel), who had recently vaulted to French stardom with her role in her fifth film, director Marc Allegret's 1937 murder mystery, *Gribouille,* was now appearing with thirty-four year-old Gabin in the first of the five pictures which they would be making together, and Morgan and Gabin would even have 'an on-again off-again' romantic relationship throughout the late '30s and early '40s, even when both of them were married to their respective spouses; some people at the time balked at the seventeen year age gap between Gabin and Morgan, but only six years later, in 1944, on the American set of Howard Hawks film *To Have and Have Not,* Humphrey Bogart, age forty-five, would very famously begin romancing nineteen-year-old Lauren Bacall, and their twenty-six year age gap definitely made Gabin and Morgan's paltry seventeen-year age difference seem insignificant, by comparison. In the 1930s, Michele Morgan (she was cinema's first 'M.M.,' more than a decade before Marilyn Monroe) was considered to be one of France's most famous film actresses.

At dawn, Nelly and Jean leave Panama's together (with Jean's dog), and we see that during the course of the night, their attraction to each other has blossomed rather quickly, no doubt because like Jean himself, she, too, due to her unpleasant circumstances at home, must sometimes 'drift.' ("NELLY: Where are you headed?" JEAN: "I don't know." NELLY: "Me, too.") As they stroll along the docks, she slips money into his pocket surreptitiously, since he has been too proud to accept it directly, and most importantly during this scene, Lucien and his two henchmen screech up in their sedan. Lucien begins coming-on to Nelly, grotesquely ("You shake your fanny at Maurice and every other guy… but you don't give me anything."), and when Jean tells Lucien to leave her alone, and he refuses, Jean slaps him in the face, right in front of his two thugs. Lucien almost starts crying, telling Jean words to the effect that 'he hasn't seen the last of him,' and Nelly is impressed that Jean has protected her honor, so gallantly. The two make plans to see each other again.

After wandering along the docks and checking out civilian-wear in a shop, Jean, who's excited about his upcoming date with Nelly, heads into a gift shop, because he's enamored of a jewel-encrusted box which he sees in the window, and he decides that he'd like to buy it for her. What Jean didn't know when he entered, is that this shop is owned by Zabel, to whom Jean hasn't yet been introduced, and Jean is surprised (in a good way) to see Nelly emerge from the apartment behind the store. He tells Zabel to inscribe the box "to Nelly," and, amused, Zabel pleasantly hands Nelly the trinket directly, telling Jean, "Your gift to Nelly is my gift to you." (Nelly has apparently already regaled Zabel with the story about how Jean slapped Lucien, and this was probably music to Zabel's ears, because Lucien is another 'lowlife thug,' besides Maurice, whom Zabel hates, since Zabel considers Lucien, just like Maurice, another competitor for Nelly's affections this, in spite of the fact that frumpy Zabel has never been in on the competition, in the first place)! Zabel invites Jean to stay and have a cognac, and while Jean isn't too eager to hang around with this guy, whom he's already pegged as being incredibly enervating, he says yes anyway, because it's an excuse to see a bit more of Nelly before their upcoming date. Zabel instructs Nelly to go into the basement and procure a bottle of cognac, and while she's down there, she's stunned, when she discovers Maurice's cufflinks on the floor—while, in her mind, she already knew that it was Zabel who killed Maurice, now she's got irrefutable proof; horrified, she faints.

Jean is left on screen alone (feeding his omnipresent pooch) while Zabel is off screen ministering to Nelly, and when Zabel returns, he tells Jean that he's seen Jean's serial number (3416) on his uniform, realizes that he's a deserter, and reminds him that 'one hand washes another:' "If you push that Lucien into the ocean for me, I won't [report your absence to the military.]" Jean, who loathes getting in on other people's murderous schemes (witness *Les Bas-fonds* and *La Bete humaine*) grabs Zabel around the neck and tells him that the old shopkeeper reminds him of a centipede which he once saw, washed up on Tonkin Beach. ("Every time in my life something goes well, somebody like you shows up to make trouble!") When Jean leaves the store, not wanting to get caught up in this other man's (unsavory) business, Nelly runs out to him, and tells him that she'll hope she'll see him, later that evening.

Meanwhile, back at Panama's, sad *artiste* Michele Krauss has finally drowned himself, and Panama hands Jean the painter's clothes and I.D.; in effect, Jean can now cast off the uniform of a deserter quite literally, becoming an entirely new (and free) person. Jean puts on Krauss' clothes, leaves his military uniform with Panama ("If I don't come back for them, throw

them away."), and leaves the bar.

Next, walking along the docks, Jean comes upon a steamship, the *Louisiana*, and a pleasant looking man, Dr. Molene (Rene Genin), introduces himself to Jean as being the the ship's surgeon. Molene informs Jean that the *Louisiana* will be leaving for Venezuela, very soon ("Why don't you come along? An ocean voyage can be restorative to [somebody with] an artistic soul.), and Jean knows he's going to have to leave town anyway, what with these new problems he's facing (Zabel and Lucien), so don't think that he isn't actually considering this man's kind offer...

That night, at a local carnival, Nelly and Jean are on the bumper cars, and accidentally (although in the fate-driven world of Poetic Realism, there are no accidents), they bump into Lucien, who happens to have been in the car behind him. Lucien makes one of his usually suggestive comments to Nelly, and Jean again slaps him, now humiliating Lucien for the second time in the picture (and this time, in front of "paying customers"). Lucien once again threatens to "take care" of Jean, but Jean blows the threat off, just as he did earlier, when Lucien had earlier threatened him, down by the docks.

Outside the carnival, Nelly and Jean talk about life, as they stare deeply into each other's

eyes. Nelly tells Jean that she never really loved Maurice ("Nobody really loves each other…
nobody has the time."), and that Maurice just 'scored points' with her because he was nice,
and she also admits to Jean that, even though she's only known him for a short while, that
he is probably the only man she's ever really loved.

> NELLY: Don't leave me.
> JEAN: Who said I was going to leave you?
> NELLY: You're in civilian clothes. If you leave, take me with you.
> JEAN: When people see a beautiful woman, it's like when they see a man
> who wants to be free. They gang up on her, like a pack of wild dogs.

That night, Jean and Nelly sleep together at the dockside motel, and it's already 'the next
morning:' He's already taken the decision to head for Venezuela, but he didn't want to tell
her the night before, because he wanted their last night together to be a blissful one. The
bellboy brings them a newspaper, the headline of which causes immediate panic in Nelly:
Apparently, last night, police officers discovered the "horribly mutilated" body of Maurice
washed up on the shore, and in close proximity, they also discovered an officer's uniform
(clearly, it's Jean's uniform, which he had left behind at Panama's). While it's unspoken in
the film, there is little doubt that Zabel buried Maurice and the uniform in the same area,
in an effort to have Jean arrested for the murder which he (Zabel) himself committed— yes,
to Zabel, Jean is no more than just another of Nelly's boyfriends, whose sole purpose, in this
life, is to be 'gotten rid of.' Not wanting to be a part of the fomenting danger any longer,
Jean bids Nelly a tender goodbye, and boards the boat to Venezuela with his dog, but
he quickly feels guilty because, *Pepe Le Moko*-like, he wants to see Nelly again one more
time, before he leaves. He, therefore, disembarks from the Louisiana (leaving his dog on
the ship, tied to a post in Dr. Molene's cabin) and runs to Zabel's house, to bid Nelly one
final goodbye.

Of course, Jean couldn't have picked a better (or worse) time to get to Zabel's digs because,
when he arrives, Zabel has just confessed to Nelly that he really *did* kill Maurice, because he
was jealous of him. (It's this movie's classy, Jacques Prevert-penned version of the usual, "If
I can't have her, nobody can" speech.) Zabel happens to be copping a little post-confession
'feel,' when Jean comes in and orders him to move away from her. Zabel picks up a knife to
kill Jean, and Jean, without even thinking about it too much, beats the old man to death, with
a brick. While Jean has returned to Nelly to see her one more time, she knows that because
of the murder which he's just committed, now he's *really* going to have to leave Le Havre,
and as fast as he can. The two share a tender goodbye, make a promise to meet each other
again soon, and as Jean heads out into the street, ready to return to the ship, fate, in the form
of Lucien, drives up in the middle of the street in his car, and shoots Jean dead, right where
he's standing. Nelly runs out to Jean, cradles his head, and kisses him, just as he's breathing
his terminal breath; in *Le Quai des brumes*, just as in *Pepe Le Moko*, Jean Gabin's decision to

stay with the woman he loves will have wound up being a fatal one for him.

Pierre MacOrlans's original novel of *Le Quai des brumes* was originally intended to be a German production for UFA, but Hitler's Minister of Propaganda, Joseph Goebbels, believed that presenting a military man as being a deserter was a demoralizing message to send to his countrymen. The French producer Gregor Rabinovitch subsequently purchased

With Michel Simon.

the rights from UFA, hired director Marcel Carne and screenwriter Jacques Prevert to adapt it, and the three of them together turned Pierre MacOrlan's novel it into this incredible film which still retains every bit of its power, today, and *Le Quai des brumes* remains one of the most powerful, haunting, and legendary films in all of French movie history.

Lawrence Peck, a Los Angeles-based film historian, is a huge fan of this movie, and here's what he had to say pursuant to why the bar in the film, and the bar's owner, are both named 'Panama:'

"Why is the bar [in *Le Quai des brumes*] named the Panama? Well the name 'Panama'—the country, and the site of today's Panama Canal—had its own special connotations to Frenchmen at the first half of the twentieth century: Because [the architect] Ferdinand de Lesseps' failed French attempt to build a canal in Panama in the 1880s, more than twenty years before the Americans [built it, successfully, in 1914] was a huge scandal, both financially (some say it was the biggest scandal of the Third Republic) and in terms of lives lost (at least 20,000), the very word 'Panama,' to a Frenchman of the first half of the last century, conjured-up connotations of failure, doom, or a total mess. That is why the Panama bar has such a sense of ill-foreboding or impending disaster about it, especially when you think about the suicide of the artist there. The Panama bar is also, of course, the place where Gabin's character first meets Michele Morgan's character, and this, as we'll learn later in the film, will turn out to be a doomed relationship… John Le Carre wrote a great article [New York *Times,* October 20, 1980] in which he recounted that, during the first half of the twentieth century, the French even had a very popular expression - "*Quel Panama!*" - which they used for many years, whenever they wanted to describe any kind of hopeless mess, or tragic situation."

What a Critic Said at the Time: "[*Le Quai des brumes*] is raw from beginning to end [and shows us] some of life's most despicable characters. A winner, with some excellent acting." (*Variety,* 6-15-38 issue. Critic: "Hugo." Reviewed in Paris.)

What Another Critic Said at the Time: "This film—all mood and atmosphere—is nothing more than a lament for the living, expressed somberly by a camera [which is] greedy for shots of rain and fog. One of the most engrossing and provocative films of the season, *Le Quai des brumes* is a film that shrugs its shoulders at gloom and murder. Such is life. It is a thoroughgoing study, in blacks and grays, without a free laugh in it. It is a remarkably beautiful motion picture." (New York *Times,* 11-4-39 issue. Critic: Frank S. Nugent.)

Top: A man alone. Above: With Simone-Simon.

FILM 28

LA BETE HUMAINE

France, 1938

(France, 1938) (Literal English Translation: "THE HUMAN BEAST") Directed by Jean Renoir.
Screenplay by Renoir, Based Upon the Novel by Emile Zola. Produced by Raymond and Robert Hakim.
Director of Photography (black and white), Curt Courant. Editors, Marguerite Renoir and Suzanne
Detroeye. Production Designer, Eugene Lozure. Music by Joseph Kosma. (GENRE: DRAMA) A
Production of MM Hakim/Paris Film. Running Time: 1 hour 40 minutes. Released in France on
December 9, 1938, by Lux Films. Released in the United States with English Subtitles on February 19,
1940, by Juno Pictures.

"I apologize for my impulsiveness. It's not me: It's my blood…"
— *Gabin apologizes to his godsister for choking her, in "La Bete humaine"*

Gabin's next 'tragic drifter epic' will share 1939's *Prix Melies Award* (the French film award which was named for the director, Georges Melies, the legendary cinema-innovator, who gave the world 1909's famous *Journey to the Moon*), with that other big Gabin film which had already been released earlier that same year, *Le Quai des brumes,* and it is a film which would also reunite the actor, for the third time in his career, with Jean Renoir, the great humanist director who had already put Gabin through his paces twice before, in *Les Bas-fonds* and *La Grande illusion.* The screenplay for *La Bete humaine* was adapted by Renoir, from the seventeenth novel in Emile Zola's seventeen-novel saga of the Rougon-Macquart family, a French family whose generations have been hereditarily pre-conditioned (poisoned, made violent, and given-over to suffering from 'whopping super-headaches'), by the alcoholism of previous generations. (Anyone who reads Zola's novels, in which characters have been corrupted by their own body chemistry, might more accurately want to re-christen the legendary author, as 'Emile *Zoloft.*') While the book sets its scene in 1890, which is the year in which it was written, Renoir has set his film in the year in which he made it—1938.

Gabin's character, Jacques Lantier, is a cheerful, but frequently agitated-looking Le Havre train engineer who's never too long for one place or for one woman, and he even refers to his train, '*Lison*,' as his 'girl,' telling his engineer-buddy Pecqueux (Julien Carette, who played fun-loving Cartier, the P.O.W. who sang the "Marguerite" song in *La Grande illusion*) that he's married to 'her'—and why not? 'Real women,' in Jean Gabin pictures, are always way more trouble than they're worth. The drifter-life of a train engineer, in which *a train is your only piece of ass,* is a whole lot easier to deal with.

Stopping in Le Havre to mend a broken axle, Jacques pays a visit to his godmother, Phasie Misard (Charlotte Clasis) and Phasie's daughter Flore (Blanchette Brunoy), a girl who, in the best possible silver-screen tradition, has *grown up hot.* As Jacques and Flore are not actually related, they share a kiss, and then suddenly, his familial 'disease' takes him over, and he begins *choking* her, stopping only when a train screeches by and brings him back to his senses; he apologizes to her, and while she's shaken, she's not angry with him, because she knows that he didn't attack her of his own volition, and that "it was just the disease talking." (FLORE: "Was that part of your illness?" JACQUES: "Yes.") Not only is she not appropriately angry with him, but she even, in the space of just a few moments, expresses a desire to marry him, to which he replies that, while he loves her, he simply cannot. ("Me and women…" he sighs, and while his thoughts have trailed off into the ether, we know exactly what he means by them: It's another riff on that whole trope that Jacques, like all of Gabin's peripatetic characters from those 1930s' movies, is a man who *doesn't hang around…*)

Parallel to this, director Jean Renoir also presents us with the story of Severine, who's played by the alluring actress, Simone-Simon. (Simon had previously appeared alongside Jean Gabin in 1933's 'missing' UFA production, *L'Etoile de Valencia,* and she, like Gabin, was one of France's biggest stars of the 1930s [although today, she is best known to Americans for having starred in RKO's haunting 1945 horror classic, *Cat People,* which was helmed by Jean Gabin's *Tout ca ne vaut pas l'amour* director, Jacques Tourneur].) Severine is a bewitchingly raven-haired twentysomething, who is controlled by her manipulative older husband, the fortysomething stationmaster Roubaud (Fernand Ledoux), a man who, pimp-like, is alternately loving toward her and cruel to her. Roubaud is the definition of the classic cuckold, which is to say that he is an insecure man who encourages, and becomes excited by, his wife's familiarity with other men (*because he's got her, and they don't*), while at the same time, he always freaks out whenever she actually deigns to sleep with those same, exact men.

When we first meet Roubaud, he's on the train tracks, having very confidently upbraided a wealthy customer for his having brought a dog along on the train (this is class-conscious France, and work is the one place where working-class Roubaud gets to boss around a rich guy!), and when said wealthy man, the sugar tycoon Turlot, threatens to complain to railroad's upper management, Roubaud (besides being 'the classic cuckold,' he's also 'the classic functionary,' a king of his own world who rules over his customers and his underlings with a heavy hand, while at the same time, being completely terrified of his own superiors) heads home, now a bit shaken, and asks Severine if she wouldn't mind taking a day-trip to Paris, in order to ask her godfather, an elderly man called Grandmorin who happens to be one of the railway company's most powerful directors, if he might be able to talk to his

(Roubaud's) immediate superiors, thus making his 'Turlot problem' vanish. As a little girl, Severine lived in Grandmorin's mansion where her mother was a chambermaid, and the priapic Grandmorin apparently engaged himself in affairs not only with Severine's mother, but with Severine as well, when Severine was a teen-ager (not to mention, with innumerable other women on his household staff). "Why don't you go see him," Roubaud asks her. "While you're there, you can shop, and I'll come up and visit you. Anyway, he's got money, so it would be good for both of us if you could go and spend some time with him, [and really act like] a daughter." So while Roubaud wants Severine to suck up to Grandmorin, when the day comes, and it turns out that she's stayed a few too many hours in Paris, Roubaud worries that Severine has just made love to Grandmorin (which, in fact, she has), and so he next berates her for giving him 'an old man's leavings.' (Roubaud pushed Severine back into Grandmorin's arms, but didn't like it when she stayed there!)

As punishment for the cuckoldry which he himself has encouraged, Roubaud now decides to kill Grandmorin (Roubaud has no more use for Grandmorin anyway, now that he's used the old man in order to save his own job), and so he forces Severine to write a letter to Grandmorin, in which she invites him to meet her on the 6:20 p.m. train, at the St. Lazare station in Paris. Of course, the seductive tone of the missive is meant to suggest to Grandmorin that, when he arrives at the train, he and Severine will be sharing more than just a train ride.

When 6:20 comes, Roubaud's sinister plan goes through, perfectly: He and Severine enter Grandmorin's car, the shades are pulled, the film's composer Joseph Kosma ratchets-up the film's haunting theme, and Roubaud stabs Grandmorin with a knife which Severine had just brought her husband as a gift, during her day trip to Paris (we don't see the murder, but we know it's happening). When Severine and Roubaud emerge from Grandmorin's car, they find themselves face to face with Jean Gabin's engineer-character, Jacques, who's been hanging around an open window in the passageway, trying to clean a speck of dirt from his eye. Now, suddenly, this gentle drifter, a man who rues most attachments to others, finds himself fatalistically thrust into the destiny of this corrupt couple, and more than that, as we can tell from the hot way in which Severine and Jacques are now checking each other out, he doesn't mind it all that much! (Gabin's tragic drifter-characters always have fun, on their way to their *unpleasant dooms…*)

Roubaud believes that Jacques saw the murder, so he encourages Severine to take a pastoral walk with Jacques (there he goes again, with the cuckoldry!), and to flirt with him, just enough to throw Jacques off of their murderous scent. ("I didn't kill anybody," Severine smiles. "Don't you believe me?") Jacques says that he saw her and her husband emerging from Grandmorin's compartment, but that he won't tell the police anything about what he saw, or didn't see.

Meanwhile, down at the local police station, a very suspicious Inspector (Alain Tavernier) is in the midst of interrogating a fellow whom he believes to be the prime suspect in Grandmorin's *filleting*, a man who we, the film's audience, already know to be (*per* the name of a great, overlooked Alfred Hitchcock picture from 1956) *The Wrong Man:* It's another of Jacques' engineer buddies, the rotund (and always-unshaven) Cabuche, who is played by the picture's director, Jean Renoir, himself; Cabuche, like Jacques, was aboard the train when Roubaud murdered Grandmorin, and the Inspector even believes that Cabuche has had a motive for the murder: It comes out, during this scene, that Cabuche once dated a different young woman who worked on Grandmorin's household staff, a woman whom Grandmorin, apparently, raped. And while the fact that Cabuche dated a girl isn't a crime, it *is* problematic to the Inspector that Cabuche once served five years in prison, for killing a man in a fight where he used—*yeah, you guessed it*—a knife...

The Inspector next interrogates Jacques (with Severine and Roubaud waiting in the wings), and when Roubaud leaves the room, leaving Severine with Jacques, Jacques tells Severine that he would be angry as hell with her if Cabuche had to take the heat for the crime, because of her intransigence about owning up to her and her husband's involvement in it. ("If you know that my friend Cabuche was not the murderer, and you didn't tell the police, I think I would have to do something about it," he tells her, not being too angry with her, though, because he genuinely likes her.) Obviously, she won't confess her and her husband's guilt, not just for the obvious reason (she doesn't want to go to jail), but because she always protects her husband, in spite of how horribly he very often treats her: Severine doesn't really love Roubaud that much, but as she'll admit later in the film, she knows that her own particular fate is to stay with him, and maybe even, one day, to die by his hands! (It's easy to figure out that she brought Roubaud the gift-knife from Paris, not so that he'd snuff Grandmorin out with it, but so that he would kill *her* with it, thus ending the lifetime of suffering which she's frequently venting about throughout the picture.) Severine is the female equivalent of all of Jean Gabin's 1930s characters who know that they are fated for bad endings, and this is the one thing, besides the obvious physical attractiveness which they feel toward each other, that is definitely beginning to band Jacques and Severine together.) Delusional Roubaud believes that now that Grandmorin is out of the way, Severine will be only with him, but he hasn't counted on Severine's *falling-in-lust* with Jacques, even though Roubaud has pushed Jacques into his wife's hands, just like Roubaud had earlier pushed her into Grandmorin's. (Roubaud to Jacques, when the three of them are together in Roubaud and Severine's home: "You should visit us and have dinner sometime, Lantier!... And please, you needn't be so formal with my wife!")

When Roubaud, who's still jumpy from the murder and the subsequent police inquiries, leaves his house, Jacques admits to Severine, for the first time, that he actually *loves* her (even in spite of the fact that she is uninterested in 'setting the facts straight' about his friend), and that night, he takes her on a moonlit walking tour of his train, *Lison.* ("She eats coal!" he brags, proudly.) He's ready for intimacy with her, and as much as we can see from the hungry way in which they're boring holes through each other with their eyes, that she likes him just as much, she tells him that, at this point, she'd rather just have a good platonic male friend, since people have been known to disappoint her. (Here, she's audibly throwing

'Movie-Gabin's' own 'Tragic Drifter Ethos' back into his face, and he conspiratorially tells her, "I could tell you some stories, too...") Of course, on a second, rainy, nighttime date in the train-yards, Severine and Jacques finally *do* make love, and when Severine steps inside a shed with Jacques, the two lovebirds embrace, and this is the moment in which director Renoir now cuts (Symbolism Award of 1938) to a drainpipe, which happens to be expelling huge torrents of rain water! Renoir next dissolves to later that same evening after the rain has stopped, and we see that Jacques and Severine are peacefully post-coital. She returns home in the middle of the night, and so does Roubaud, who has been out playing cards with some of his underlings. ("[Playing cards] is what they do... so I guess I should do it, too.") Roubaud confronts her, knowing that she was with Jacques (Jacques is the last person whom Roubaud encouraged Severine not to be so formal with) and this time, not only does he berate her, but he also thrashes her within an inch of her life.

During a subsequent assignation, Severine tells Jacques that her husband just beat her again ("... he dug his heel into my face..."), and we know—or, we think we know—exactly what's coming: Even though Jacques Lantier, like most of the characters whom Jean Gabin will play during his forty-six-year movie career, abhors violence, there's no doubt that he might be able to commit a violent act, in order to defend a woman with whom he's in love (and in fact, we saw this happening already, in a previous Jean Gabin-Jean Renoir collaboration, 1936's *Les Bas-fonds*).

That night in the trainyard, an especially-haunted/end-of-his-rope-looking Roubaud (he's as beaten down by life as Severine and Jacques, and we can tell that he also feels incredibly guilty about having iced Grandmorin) is making his nightly inspection of the trains, and Jacques and Severine are there too, hiding. Jacques wields a thin lead pipe, clearly ready to strike, but at the last minute, he is unable to 'brain' Roubaud, and Severine becomes enraged at him, because the idea that Jacques was going to kill another man to protect her honor (such as it is), has actually increased her libidinous feelings for him, tenfold.

The following evening, we're director Renoir's privileged guests a fancy-dress Railroad Engineer's Ball. Severine has left Jacques, because she has no use for him (since he was unable to 'man-up' and kill her husband) and he angrily stares at her as she dances with Dauvergne (Gerard Landry), a resident of her apartment who also happens to be yet *another* man whom Roubaud has pushed into his wife's arms! Jacques pulls Severine aside and dances with her, and they both look stiff and uncomfortable. Trying to win her back, he tells her that he thinks he could really kill Roubaud this time, and while she tells him that it's " too late" for that, she decides now that it's not too late in the evening for Jacques to escort her (to her) home, for a bit of late-night lovemaking.

Post "their tumble," Severine changes her mind, and decides that she'll give Jacques a second chance in the Husband-Killing Department; but instead, director Renoir supplies us with a great twist ending: Jacques kills *Severine*, instead of killing Roubaud (he begins strangling her, as he had done with Flore, and he then grabs a knife and finishes her off)! The ending isn't completely out of left-field, however, because we know that he's killed her

1.) due to her constant manipulation of his feelings, 2.) because she won't exonerate his friend Cabuche, and 3.) because of that impulsive family 'disease' which grabs hold of him at any given moment. (Basically, right now, *Severine is in the wrong place, at the wrong time.*) At this juncture, Renoir cuts back and forth, end of *Godfather I*-style, between the Railroad Engineer's dance, which is still in progress, where a tuxedoed male singer (Marcel Veyran) is trilling a haunting song called "Ninette," the lyrics of which resonate with the film's main story, because it's a piece of music about a woman who can give her love to nobody. Back in Severine's bed, meanwhile, we see her deceased body and the (sham of a) wedding ring on her hand, and we also get as an eerie shot of Lantier's haunted eyes, as he stares down at her. Jacques, having left before Lantier's return, walks all night along the train tracks, with the same haunted/end-of-his-rope look that we've already seen on Roubaud. (Severine, a true succubus, turns all men with whom she comes into contact into hollow-eyed living-corpses.)

As *La Bete humaine* winds down, Jacques is back at the trainyard with his friend Pecquex by his side. He confesses to Pecquex that he has just murdered Severine, and Pecquex tells him to turn himself in, but Jacques just isn't interested in that. Next, when the two men are on the train, Jacques begins wigging out (it's his biggest hereditary freak-out of the movie), and he suddenly jumps off the train, to his death. Pecquex, seeing his friend's inert body a few moments later, remarks how peaceful (how 'non-agitated') Jacques looks, for the very first time: Such is fate, in many of Jean Gabin's Poetic Realist classics of the 1930s and early 1940s that, even when Gabin's characters are in positions in which they *can* escape from Cruel Fate (I mean, Jacques Lantier *could* have skipped France, like Gabin's character did in *La Bandera*, but *he just didn't want to!*)

Not only in *La Bete humaine,* but also thirteen years later in another Gabin picture, 1951's *La Nuit est mon royaume,* we'll see locomotives being used as a metaphor for 'cruel fate, which seems to always be barreling out-of-control, toward the *inevitable conclusion*—death.'

What a Critic Said at the Time: "*La Bete humaine* is French production at its best. Throughout, Gabin never misses. His simple, ordinary, man-of-the-street [character] gives force to the incidents which carry the story to its unexpected ending. There is no lag [in the story] at any time." (*Variety,* 2-15-39 issue. Critic: "Hugo." Reviewed in Paris.)

What Another Critic Said at the Time: "[*La Bete humaine*] marches like an automaton to the beat of its own steam-driven metronome. A film that is shrouded in the grayness of madness and grief it is, by turns, macabre, grim, and oddly-fascinating." (New York *Times,* 2-19-40 issue. Critic: Frank S. Nugent.)

───────────

Sixteen years after Jean Renoir made *La Bete humaine,* the Los Angeles-living/German ex-pat film director, Fritz Lang, who would co-direct one of Jean Gabin's only two American features, 1942's *Moontide* (even though he would not receive screen credit for it) turned Emile Zola's story into savagely entertaining *film noir,* helming Columbia Pictures' 1954

American remake of *La Bete humaine,* called *Human Desire,* in which Lang re-teamed a sizzling star duo whom he had already put through its paces earlier that same year in another great film noir, *The Big Heat*—Glenn Ford and Gloria Grahame.

In Lang's noir-ish American remake of *La Bete humaine,* Glenn Ford's train engineer-character, Jeff Warren, has just returned home to Philadelphia from serving his 'stint' in the Korean War, and immediately comes into contact with Grahame's sultry trainyard vixen, Vicky (the 'Severine' of the film), as well as with Vicky's bulldog-faced stationmaster husband, Carl Buckley (the great Broderick Crawford who, here, plays a mega-tough Americanization of Fernand Ledoux's 'Roubaud'-character). Unluckily for Jeff, however, when Jeff runs into Buckley, Buckley just happens to be right in the middle of murdering his wife's lover, 'Mr. Owens,' who is this version's 'Grandmorin.'

Gone in this American version are Zola's heady references to hereditary alcoholism and craziness, but Fritz Lang makes up for it by adding his own cool alterations, especially his fast-and-furious use of sleek, 1950s-style bullet trains. The film's score, by Daniela Amphitheatros, is appropriately epic, and the exciting climax of the film, much different to the ending of the Gabin/Renoir picture, is one in which Jeff kills neither Vicky nor Jeff, but *somebody else:* In Fritz Lang's *Human Desire,* Glenn Ford's 'Jeff' is happily guiding his train out of town, not knowing that three cars back, Broderick Crawford's Buckley is strangling his own sluttish wife, Vicky, to death!

P.S. The final thing that needs to be said about *Human Desire,* is that it contains one of *film noir's* greatest lines, courtesy of screenwriter Alfred Hayes: Even though Broderick Crawford's Buckley-character is angry at his wife Vicky, for sleeping with both Mr. Owens and Jeff, he's got (unlike the Roubaud character, in the other picture) a (hot) mistress of his own on-the-side, and as they're dressing after their usual afternoon tryst, he tells her, "All women are alike. They just have different faces, so men can tell them apart!"

Top: With Gina Manes. Above: With Michele Morgan.

FILM 29

LE RECIF DE CORAIL

France/Germany, 1939

(Literal English Translation: "THE CORAL REEF") Directed by Maurice Gleize. Produced by Georges Lampin. Screenplay by Charles Spaak. Based Upon the Novel by Jean Martet. Director of Photography (black and white), Jules Kruger. Production Designer, Anton Weber. Editor, Victor de Fast. Music by Henri Tomasi. (GENRE: MELODRAMA) A Production of UFA/ACE. Running Time, 1 hour 31 minutes. Released Theatrically in France on February 17, 1939, by Alliance Europeene Cinematographique. Never Released Theatrically in the United States.

"Do I look like somebody who would read a Bible?"
— Jean Gabin turns down an offer of free reading materials, in "Le Recif de corail"

L ike *La Belle Mariniere, Le Recif de corail* is another Gabin film which, while considered lost for decades, has recently been found:

This amazing 'tropical' 1939 Gabin film, which was made during the period of his biggest international stardom, was considered to be lost for more than sixty years. When I started writing the book, back in 2002, it didn't exist at all, even in France, the country in which it was produced. But then:

Dateline, Belgrade: 2003.

Esteemed French film critic/theoretician Lenny Borger visits the Kinoteka Film Archives of Serbia, searching for some non-Gabin-related films and, accidentally, while he's in the process for looking for something else, comes across a beautiful, pristine, uncut print of *Le Recif de corail! Recif de corail i*s an integral part of Gabin's Tragic Drifter Cycle of (roughly) 1934 to 1941, and the only reason you've never heard of it is that, for sixty years, it just didn't exist, and hopefully soon, cinephiles all over the world will begin to know and treasure this great movie, just like how they've recently started to love it in France: In 2003, *Recif de corail* was restored, and in 2004, it was issued on a French-language DVD in France, as part of a three movie boxed-set, which also includes similarly-restored versions of two other very cool Gabin movies, 1931's *Pour un soir..!* and 1941's *Remorques.*

While *Le Recif de corail* is a French movie, and while it stars French-speaking actors, it's meant to take place in Australia, and Gabin's character, Ted 'Trott' Lennard is supposed to be *Australian!* Gabin's great in this movie as usual, but (sarcasm alert) he's just as much an 'Aussie' in this picture as he was an 'American' in *Le Tunnel*. (Forget 'throwing a shrimp on the barbie'—let's *throw an escargot on there!*) And, P.S.: To add to the confusion even more, the film was shot in Germany!

The picture opens on a hot August day in 1918, and director Maurice Gleize, who would work with Jean Gabin only on this one movie, presents us, right away with a tableau of half-naked little street urchins who are romping-away through garden hoses, before his camera zooms-up into an apartment window, where we first see Gabin's 'Ted,' whose back is facing the street. He's smashed the window open with his shoulder, in an effort to get a little air into the stuffy room.

He plops down on his bed alone, and not just alone, but 'Gabin-Alone,' which is the best and most brooding kind of Alone in the entire world. But, as we already know, Gabin's never by himself for long, especially when there are women in the world!

Cue a loud series of knocks on the door:

BOOMBOOMBOOMBOOMBOOM!

"Open up! It's me: Anna!"

When this fetching lassie comes in ('Anna' is played by Jenny Burnay), director Gleize widens out, so that we're seeing the entirety of Ted's room for the first time: As it's now turning out, Ted hasn't really been 100%-alone in there, because there's *a dead guy* on the floor. Ted, apparently, has just killed this guy, and probably, he did it right before the movie started, just like in *La Bandera* and *Pepe Le Moko:* The dead guy's name is (or more accurately was) Brooks, and we can tell that there was a struggle between the two men, because Ted's nursing a nasty-looking cut over his eye. He asks Anna, calmly, if she's going to be calling the cops on him, but it's eminently clear to us, from the sultry way in which she's looking at him, that she loves him, and that she's going to be protecting him, instead of ratting him out to the police. He tells her that he killed Brooks because he couldn't stand the fact that Anna was seeing Brooks, at the same time that she was also seeing him. (When it comes to women, Jean Gabin does not share!) Anna's worried for Ted's safety, and she doesn't seem to care at all about the fact that Brooks, her other lover, is dead: Of the two guys with whom she was sharing chromosomes, she (naturally) liked Ted better, and she tells him that if he doesn't get the hell out of Dodge (Brisbane), and soon, that he'll be caught.

That night, we see Ted's lonely silhouette as he skulks alone through the night-time streets of Brisbane (really, it's a movie studio in Deutschland, but don't tell anybody!), accompanied by nothing on the film's soundtrack, except for a brooding undercurrent of harmonica music. He heads down to the docks, and enters a sad sailor-bar (this is the kind of place that 'lost souls' always seem to frequent in old movies), where he comes across a boat captain, Nikolah Jolife (Louis Florencie), a man whose vessel, the *Portland*, happens to be moored down by the pier. Ted jokes around with Nikolah for a spell, and then asks the guy if he might happen to have any job-openings for new ship-hands. Needless to say, he's able to sell himself to

Captain Nikolah, who makes his living shipping (among other forms of contraband) guns to Mexico and probably, more specifically, shipping guns to Pancho Villa, who was leading his country's Revolution between 1911 and 1920 (although the film won't mention this flat-out), by telling him truthfully that, while he's never labored on a ship before, he's a very hard worker. Nikolah instantly likes Ted (Gabin—'Everybody's Pal,' a/k/a, 'the Universal Buddy to all working people, everywhere'), thinking that he's really funny, and he even ribs Ted about his funniness: "Maybe I do have some work for you, Mr. Lennard. Maybe you can organize the jokes!" Ted tells Nikolah that, since he needs to leave town, he'll do just about anything, and Nikolah knows that whenever somebody wants a seagoing job (or by extension, probably, a traveling carnival job) this badly, that the person has probably done something unlawful. Nikolah tries to pry Ted's secret out of him—"Did someone tell you that you need fresh air?"—and Ted's answer is cagey, but, at the same time, it is also instantly understandable: He simply leans in close to Nikolah, and whispers, "Do you know what horror is?" Nikolah asks Ted if he's a guy who can "hold it together, under any circumstances" which, of course, is cluing us in to the fact that Nikolah's ship might hold a few dangerous surprises of her own. Nikolah informs Ted that the *Portland* will be sailing from Brisbane to Mexico tonight, and that he'd be willing to drop him off there, if that, indeed, is what he wants. The two men shake hands, and Nikolah confirms with Ted that he'll give him passage, but only one condition: "I'll take you with me, friend. But if I need your skin, I can have it anytime, okay?" ("I need your skin" is a French expression which means, "I'll be glad to help you, but in return, one day, you'll owe me a favor," and it's a sentiment with which all of us who have ever seen *The Godfather* are already intimately familiar.) Nikolah next lightens the mood a bit, because he genuinely likes his new, Gabinian-pal: "Anyway, while I might need a favor from you one day, Ted, I wouldn't spend too much time worrying about it, because there's a sixty percent chance that I'll never ask you for anything." Ted replies, "Look: As long as we're talking about percentages, I only have a ten percent chance of remaining alive if I stay here in Brisbane, as compared to a sixty percent chance of living, if I go with you on your boat. So this is a very easy choice for me to make." (Damn! These guys have totally missed their true calling in life—as math professors!) Nikolah, instantly recognizing leadership qualities in his newfound friend, even takes this moment to measure Ted's head for a first-mate's cap.

Nikolah next walks Ted over to the *Portland*, and guess who's lying-in-wait, like a cobra: It's an extremely nebbishy cop, Abboye (Pierre Renoir, who played the stern Captain Weller, in *La Bandera*). Abboye, who's looking for Ted, is decked-out in a long, black leather jacket, seventy years pre-*Matrix*, and he understands instinctively that when a guy commits a murder, the first thing he's going to do will always be to look for the first boat out of town. Nikolah and Ted, however, are both able to board the boat, without Abboye's taking any notice.

Nikolah cheerfully escorts Ted to his cabin, and Ted instantaneously starts doing what comes naturally for Jean Gabin: He instinctively plops down on his bunk alone and starts brooding, just like Gabin does in lots of other movies. At this point, a nice little Chinese cook, Black (Ky Duyen, a Vietnamese actor) knocks gently on Ted's door, welcoming him aboard with a cheerful cry of "Bonjour, Commandante!" When Black leaves, Ted stares at his own reflection in a porthole, through which he can also see Abboye, who happens to be lingering around outside the cabin. Meanwhile, up on deck, Nikolah's standing around with his current First Mate, Springbett (Guillaume de Sax), who happens to be a very skeevy-looking guy. Nikolah, who's angry at Springbett, is telling the guy to *watch his ass,* and we don't see what started their little *contretemps,* but we can guess that Jim's probably feeling a little jealous about Nikolah's brand-new friendship with Ted, and doesn't want Ted to replace him as 'Nikolah's New, #1 Pal!'

The next day, the *Portland* has sailed, and its crew is hard at work. "Move it, slowpokes," Nikolah barks out to his crew (he's not that gruff, but he tries to be), and he then heads back into his own cabin, followed, in not-so-short order, by Ted. Since Nikolah hasn't given Ted any chores to do on the boat yet, Ted asks him what he can do to help out. ("I asked Mr. Springbett what I could do, but he just walked away from me.") Nikolah is pleased to have a new friend along, a 'smart' guy whom he can just talk to, and so he tells Ted to forget about work: "Just go and enjoy the day. I'll tell you when lunch is ready!" But Jean Gabin is a Working Man, and so his Ted-character now starts protesting that he has to do some work: ("Otherwise, the other guys won't like me!") Nikolah asks him if he's already had his breakfast: "The cook doesn't know how to make very good meals, but they're not terrible, either. Just go and have your coffee, and wait for lunch. And if you get bored, you can read my Bible." Ted replies, mischievously, "Do I look like someone who would read a Bible?"

Later, Ted's walking by Nikolah's cabin, and Nikolah invites him in, and Nikolah then proceeds, just like lots of characters in lots of Gabin movies, both male and female, to tell Ted his life's story. (Since Gabin is usually so quiet, people automatically misinterpret his quietness for 'being a good listener,' when, very often, he'd rather just be left alone!) Nikolah tells Ted (not that Ted asked, because he didn't) that he has a wife and five kids, and he next asks Ted if Ted has a woman of his own, to which Ted, who suddenly looks uncomfortable, cagily replies, "… there could have been one—but there's not." Nikolah then offers Ted *his Andrew Dice Clay-sounding theory,* on 'man-woman relationships:' "You're lucky. It's not good to worry about women, too much. All a woman is, is a tint of hair, perfume, and a name. My wife spends too much money—you're lucky you don't have to deal with that." Ted pours himself *a cuppa joe,* and Nikolah keeps right on pontificating.

Later that day, Ted, who now looks decidedly unproletarian in a dapper white suit, jaunty suspenders, and a panama hat, costuming which was probably a concession to Gabin's female audience who had, over the last few years, made the actor France's #1 Star (because there's no way this boat has a boutique on it which sells fancy, new glad-rags), checks into the wheel room. He asks Springbett why the boat seems to be moving so slowly, and wonders aloud if it's possible that they'll be able to reach Mexico at such a leisurely pace. Springbett, who is irritated, informs him that they won't be getting arriving in Mexico for three weeks, and that temporarily, they're going to be docking on the mythical Polynesian island of Tobugu.

(Shades of *Mutiny on the Bounty*. This author fully expects to see 'Gabin + Exotic Tropical Women' in Ted Lennard's future.) Ted walks around the ship, slowly (there's even an old French-Corsican expression which very accurately summarizes the whole, perennially-laid-back 'Gabin Attitude:' "*Ralentissez en matin, plus lent l'apres-midi*" ["Slow in the morning, not too fast in the afternoon"]), and he is now officially so bored, that he checks into the galley and starts peeling potatoes, just so he'll have something to do. The cook, Havelock (Julien Carette, who played the musical P.O.W., Cartier, in *La Grande illusion* [he's the guy who sang the "Marguerite" song]), who also happens to be the ship's surgeon (!), asks Ted what he's doing, and Ted smilingly holds-up a potato. Havelock tells Ted, in hushed and conspiratorial tones, that there's presently a good bit of, as he puts it, "unhappiness" on the boat, involving Black the Chinese, who is not only ill but who is also, in point of fact *dying*. Ted asks Havelock if somebody will be available to replace the frail Black, should he become unable to continue executing his shipboard duties, and Havelock answers in the negative: "Black told me he's going to keep working. Everybody knows he's not too well, but he's afraid to tell Captain Jolife how sick he really is, because he's afraid of losing his job. But of course, that's our secret."

Ted goes to see his new 'little buddy' Black, who's sweating profusely while, at the same time, he valiantly tries to shovel coal into the furnace. Ted buoys him up with a big dose of Earthy Gabin-Friendship and, before long, the *Portland* arrives on the beautiful tropical island of Tobugu. Of course, needless to say, the place is Heaven-on-Earth, just like how Polynesian Islands are always portrayed as being Heaven-on-Earth in every other movie, and the first thing we see on the island, when the *Portland* docks, are hot native girls who are all, of course, lolling-around and bathing in the surf, and none of them is wearing too much in the way of clothing at all. Ted's marveling at these ladies from the porthole window of his cabin, as he combs his hair, slicking it into *wavy Gabin-readiness*. (Let me note, here, that this movie was produced during a time when Margaret Mead was living with Samoans, and writing books and essays about 'the importance of physical perfection,' an idea which, ten years later, would transmogrify itself into Fascistic art, not to mention into still photography's big 20th-century conceit of 'the body beautiful.') As we've seen already, Springbett doesn't like Ted, and his most fervent hope, is that Ted will disembark from the boat, here in Tobugu, and not get back on: "I know you helped us out a great deal, and I thank you for it," Springbett tells Ted rather snidely, "but now, I want you to stay here on this island and live like a man, okay? Captain Jolife and I aren't going to be staying here for too long, but you should stay. I mean, the Captain and I would stay here if they had any petrol, but there isn't any, so we have no reason to." (*Holy shit!* This guy just said that there's no reason for the *Portland* to remain on Tobugu, because there's no oil there! [Remind you of anything from today's headlines?!])

Nikolah wants Ted off the boat too, and not because he doesn't want him around, because he does, and more than anything; it's just that he'd rather Ted should go off and have some fun with the tropical ladies, so that he (Nikolah, a married man) can live vicariously through Ted's adventures. He tells Ted, "I'll come back and visit you, and you can tell me what you're doing. The natives here sing and dance all day, you know." Nikolah then points out a happily-Hemingwayesque bearded-guy who, when we first meet him in this scene, is running up the gangplank to greet them. Hobson (Saturnin Fabre, who played Jane Marnac's henpecked husband in *Paris-Beguin,* and an underworld jeweler called 'Grandpa,' in *Pepe Le Moko*) is an Englishman who lives on the island. He's an old free-spirit, who is also an even older friend of Nikolah's.

Ted asks Nikolah why Hobson looks so excited, and Nikolah replies that Hobson's happy because they're bringing him the only thing from civilization which he just can't get on the island—flypaper! ("You and Hobson have a lot in common," Nikolah tells Ted, referencing Gabin's 'perennial drifterhood' [not to mention, the flypaper]: "He's like you: He doesn't stick.") Hobson hugs Nikolah, and asks him for the latest news from the 'civilized' world: "Who's winning the war, the workers or the capitalists? Has all of the wheat burned? Have you thrown the coffee overboard?" Hobson likes living on Tobugu because, unlike Europe, it's classless—it's just thousands of beautiful women and him! He's obviously tipsy on whatever the local grog happens to be, and leeringly refers to the Tobugans as being 'savages,' even though he really loves them. Hobson's a benign version of Marlon Brando's Colonel Kurtz character from *Apocalypse Now,* and he's also a contemporary of another interesting 1930s' movie character, a guy who was played by Walter Huston in a 1933 Warner Bros. jungle-potboiler called *Kongo,* 'Deadlegs Flint,' a white, wheelchair-bound drug dealer who lived among the black natives, keeping them hopped-up on drugs, while he was *getting laid* by the hot native women. Nikolah hands Hobson the flypaper which Hobson has asked for, and Hobson then crows ecstatically that, "… flypaper is the best invention in the world!" (Listen, it's no dumber a sentiment than that similar line from the movie *Gilda,* in which zillionaire George Macready alerted Glenn Ford, "The man who controls tungsten, controls the world!") Hobson tells Nikolai and Ted that, before he moved to the island, he was just 'surviving,' but he wasn't really 'living:' "I didn't know what life was before. But now, I do…"

Nikolah and Ted sit around the galley with Hobson, drinking, playing cards, and listening to Hobson prattle-on, relentlessly: "What we're doing now reminds me of those evenings back in England, where we used to sit around, debating Freud and [Freud's concept of the] Ego." As the three men continue their card game, some very lush, tropical-sounding guitar music wafts-up over the soundtrack, and Hobson tells Ted the story of how exactly it is that he wound up in Tobugu, more than a decade ago: "When I lived back in the civilized world, my brain was becoming a mechanical thing. I wondered if such a place as this could exist: A place without lawyers and scientists—just people!" Hobson cuts Ted and the Captain some delicious slices of pineapple, and Ted now asks him how the locals received him when he first arrived, to which Hobson replies, very simply, "Nicely, because I brought them something they loved—a radio! They were amazed by it… and afraid of it." (Author's Note: They were probably listening to Rush Limbaugh!) Hobson admits, however, that it hasn't been all *kiwis and screwing* since he's been on the island: "About a year ago, we had a big hurricane, and everything was in disarray. But soon food grew, and then it was paradise again!" Once more,

Nikolah tries to convince Ted that he should stay on the island with Hobson: "We're pulling out, tonight. But why don't you stay here? You and old Hobson are both carefree guys, and it really seems like you belong together—two kings together, ruling their own island." Hobson tries to convince him, as well. ("So, you're a drifter, huh? Well, why drift? Why not stay here with me, and be happy forever? Unhappiness is a disease, my friend!")

Hobson likes talking to Ted just as much as Nikolah does, so he accompanies Ted to his cabin, apologizing to our Gabinian anti-hero for "bothering you, in your solitude." He asks Ted if he's ever 'studied,' and Ted now gives him, and us, a little more backstory about himself: "I'm not exactly what you would call a 'college man.' I have no family. Then, the war came [he's referencing Indochina], so I was there."

Now, in other movies which take place in Polynesia, the handsome main character is always off the boat within seconds, and frolicking with the hot native babes (and here, I'm especially thinking about John Ford's *The Hurricane,* from 1937 [as well as that film's 1979 Mia Farrow remake], and Somerset Maugham's 1932 *Rain,* which featured Joan Crawford [and *that* film's 1953 remake, *Miss Sadie Thompson,* which starred Rita Hayworth].) But this picture is different: Ted's decided not to get off the boat and experience freedom for himself, and Nikolah's getting even more concerned than ever about Ted's weird behavior: "Look, we set sail in two hours. Don't you at least want to get off and look around? Just for a little while?" Well, of course not: See, Ted is Jean Gabin, and in Jean Gabin movies, especially the ones from the mid-to-late 1930s, the 'formula' dictates that his movie characters' negative fates have already been pre-determined—*so, what's the point, right?* In some of the other pictures in which Gabin appeared in the 1930s, his characters would always surmise, correctly, that they weren't 'fated for good' and, in a number of those pictures, they would almost always grab some *brunette gusto* anyway, realizing that, since their lives were about to end, that they'd better (to paraphrase Rita Hayworth also from *Gilda*) "Make hay, while the sun shines." But in *Le Recif de corail,* Jean Gabin's character is so depressed about the murder which he had committed before the movie began (in this movie, unlike in others in which he starred in the 1930s, Gabin didn't kill the guy in self-defense: He was just mad, because that other guy, Brooks, was *boinking* Anna), that he's not even looking for *the temporary band-aid of sex:* He's too wrapped-up in brooding about the horrible fate which he knows is probably lying in wait for him right around the next corner, and so he is unable to properly enjoy himself. Anyway, night falls (as is night's wont) and the *Portland* sets sail again. And poor Ted never got off (in more ways than one)!

It's now several days later, and the *Portland* is nosing closer to Mexico: In the middle of the night, Captain Nikolah aims his binoculars out, and stares at the ocean, and when he does, he just so happens to see a scary-looking ship, and it's heading right for them! It's a Mexican vessel, and this vessel's Mexican Captain, who is also played by a Frenchman (Gaston Modot, the engineer who washed Gabin's feet in *La Grande illusion*), has been waiting for the *Portland* to show up. Apparently, as Nikolah is now revealing to Ted, the Mexican Captain has an old score to settle with him; the movie doesn't tell us what it is, but we can guess that this Captain, if he's not dealing arms to Pancho Villa, must instead be an enemy of Pancho Villa (maybe he works for President Huerta?), and that he doesn't want the *Portland* to be supplying arms to the enemy troops anymore. Nikolah knows that his own fate, just like Ted's, will probably be death (in Nikolah's case, very specifically, at the hands of this Mexican Captain), and so he's kind-of-sado-masochistically returned to Mexico to take his punishment, walking (as it were) right into it, since, as I've already said two zillion times in this book, and as I'll only say three zillion more times—there's no fighting fate!

But as the Mexican ship draws closer to the *Portland*, Nikolah who, very suddenly, has gotten cold-feet when it comes to his heroic (in an abstract way) idea of 'meeting his enemy and accepting his fate,' decides to call-in that favor for which, as he warned Ted earlier in the picture, he might be asking him: "Listen, Ted, do you remember how I said that there's a sixty percent chance that I might be asking you to do me a favor? Well, the percentage just went up—to a hundred! I'm calling it in right now!" Nikolah removes his captain's cap, places it on Ted's head and, very cowardly, runs below deck to hide: Even though Nikolah knows that his 'Fate' is probably to be murdered by his old enemy, now that he's actually faced with his own potential death, all of his *ersatz* bravery has instantly dissipated. In fact, in the same moment in which he's now running below deck, he barks his very first-ever order at Ted: "You're going to pretend to be the Captain now, Ted. Remember, I have a wife and five children! Well [with a salute], so-long!" and he bolts, just as gunshots begin ringing-out from the Mexican vessel. Ted stays-put, on deck, and since he's played by Jean Gabin, he's very blasé about the attack. Springbett, like Nikolah, is also freaked out, and Ted calmly jokes with him, "So: Do you think those Mexicans are good at launching torpedoes?" Springbett asks Nikolah if he'd like to borrow his Bible (again, with 'The Good Book!'), and Ted just stares at him and smiles: "Naah... It's too late for me to be saved." When push-comes-to-shove, Nikolah is afraid of meeting Cruel Fate head-on... but Ted welcomes it.

Even though the Mexican ship has already fired a few warning-shots at the *Portland* (no doubt, just to scare Nikolah away), ultimately, it sails away without any large-scale attack having happened and, hilariously, the idea that something terrible could have happened between the two vessels has made Ted not scared but hungry, so he now retreats into the galley, and the cook, Havelock, shows him how to flip an omelet. Ted next makes a gift (of himself!) to the guy, in Havelock's other capacity, as the ship's surgeon. (He's not making a sexual offer!) "Look, after I'm dead, you have my full permission to open me up and [to] learn what I'm all about!" (What an amazing remark: As if you can really learn about people's souls by slicing them open bodily. In Woody Allen's extremely underrated 1992 comedy, *Shadows and Fog*, Donald Pleasance's superbly-sinister coroner-character opines to Woody's character that, in his own studied opinion, and through the gutting of dead bodies, he hopes to one day be able to "learn something about the nature of the soul.") Ted then changes the subject completely, telling Havelock that he approves of Havelock's homemade (or, I guess, 'ship-made') crisp-breads: "They're good, like my mother's... but, yeah, I guess I have to admit that hers were better." Willing to take any compliment he can get (he's no Wolfgang

Puck), amiable Havelock just grins, "Awww! You're a good guy too, Mr. Lennard!"

Now that the Mexicans have sailed away (*adios, amigos!*) without having killed any of our French *faux*-Australians, Nikolah tries unsuccessfully to grab his Captain's cap from off of Ted's head. ("You can give me back my cap now, Ted! They're gone!") Ted, who has no desire to ever truly be a captain of *anything*, now starts joking-around with Nikolah, and only good-naturedly, just to freak him-out a little bit: "It's not your ship anymore, Nikolah. It's mine, now. Anyway, you have to be sure you really want me to take my hat off, because I don't do that very often." Shifty old Springbett, meanwhile, is elsewhere on the boat, instructing (more like: *threatening*) the crew members that they should quiet the ship's engines, just in case any more swarthy, brown-skinned enemies should happen to be nosing around.

Soon, the *Portland* docks on Mexican soil, in a safe port, far from the bad guys who were attacking them, and we know we're in Mexico, because the film's director, Maurice Gleize, now makes with the stock footage (cacti, donkeys, mustachioed-guys with giant sombreros, *etc.*). When the *Portland* docks, and a Customs official asks Nikolah if he can check the ship's cargo, Nikolah tells him that his vessel is only carrying alcohol, game—and women's underthings! Ted, meanwhile, is now gussied-up in a *stylin,'* dark trenchcoat (it's Gabin's second snazzy outfit-change since he arrived on the boat, which is funny because, just like on t.v.'s "Gilligan's Island," he didn't even bring a change-of-clothes, with him). He's finally ready to 'jump ship, and explore the new world' by himself. Nikolah, who's sad to see his friend leave (even though in Tobugu he *wanted* Ted to leave) hands Ted some traveling money, and asks him what he's going to do next.

TED (with a 'Gabin-Shrug' [Typical Gabin-answer]:) I don't know…

And just as Ted is about to disembark from the boat, Springbett's cruel streak now manifests itself, and in a completely sadistic manner: Not realizing that Ted and Captain Nikolah are nearby, he starts beating the crust out of frail Black, a guy who he knows, full-well, is too sick to fight-back. (You have to be *a real asshole* to beat-up a wan, sick guy!) Ted and Captain Nikolah both come to Black's rescue and, just when Ted's about to punch Springbett's lights out, Springbett takes a pre-emptive strike against Ted, by lying to the Captain, and falsely accusing Ted of stealing money from the ship. ("Captain Nikolah: Your friend, Mr. Lennard, has opened the ship's safe. He and that Chinaman stole the ship's money!") Nikolah sneers at Springbett, a guy whom even he doesn't like that much: "I don't keep any money in the safe. I keep it right here in my Bible!" (Springbett is *'Busted, with a Capital B!'*)

Then, some bad news for the crew of the *Portland:* Mexican Customs officials won't let the boat remain in their country, and they order Nikolah's vessel to return home. (Yes, the 'Gabin-ian Circle of Cruel Fate' will now bring Ted back to Brisbane again, and—to paraphrase Al Jolson—"right back where he started from!") Even though Ted has always known that his fate will be for his life to end badly, he now (and this is against his character's nature, but I won't harp on it) begins complaining vociferously: "I wanted my life to end in Mexico, not in Australia!"

Soon, the *Portland* is back in Brisbane.

Ted wanders the streets by night, knocking on windows and searching for Anna, who has no fixed address at all, figuring that she'll probably be able to hide him out, but he is unable to find her. He decides to leave Brisbane again, and now makes for the train station, telling the railway clerk that he'd like a one-way ticket to anywhere his three pence will take him, as long as it's to a place where, in prime John Steinbeck-fashion, there's some work to be had. The clerk sells Ted a one-way-ticket to Knoxville, which is a small, logging-and-mining community.

When Ted arrives in Knoxville, he works in a factory for a few days. After he gets paid for his first week's work, it's time for an evening out, and he winds up, on this particular Friday night, in an amazing split-level (bizarre/fancy/movie-cool) Chinese-Aborigine nightclub/casino. This place, which is totally proto-*Blade Runner*, has a barbershop on its top level, and the first thing Ted does, when he gets to this crazy place, is to get himself a natty new haircut.

Post-haircut, Ted's now all decked-out in black (yet another costume change), and he's just won a lot of money in a craps game, to boot. A hooker, played by Gina Manes, asks him if he wants some company but he's not encouraging the flirtation, instead, he's making her do all of the work: "You don't like to talk too much, do you, mister. So tell me: What did you do to get here? I know that most guys who wind up in our town, working in our plant, are here because they've made some kind of stupid mistake somewhere else. Did you make a stupid mistake?" Ted's not too forthcoming with his reply and, of course, she finds his mysteriousness to be so sexy, that she now asks him, even though she's only known him for exactly one minute, if he'd like to come and live with her! She's mostly putting him on, though, and her suggestion has just made our notoriously tight-lipped anti-hero laugh; so finally, he opens up to her, on the subject of his life of drifting: "I move here, I move there—I travel." She tells him that his eyes remind her of "someone else I once knew," and because he doesn't feel like talking, he asks her to dance, instead. And suddenly, just as the two are about to start tripping the light fantastic, Abboye (Pierre Renoir's cop character, whom we haven't seen since the beginning of the film) enters the bar, wearing his trademark black leather jacket: He's followed Ted from Brisbane to Knoxville, although the movie never tells us how he found out that Ted was there. Trying to avoid Abboye, Ted now asks the hooker to invite him up to her room—and naturally, she's only too happy to oblige. And as soon as they get there:

KNOCKKNOCKKNOCK!

Abboye's found his way up to the hooker's fuckpad and, as Ted hides out on the balcony, the courtesan asks Abboye, flirtatiously, if he's 'looking for someone special,' but Abboye makes no reply: He just comes in, looks around a little bit, can't find Ted, and leaves. The coast, at least for now, is clear.

Director Gleize now cuts to Australia's mighty Blue Mountains, and it's probably a few days later: Ted is wandering alone in the woods, a man in nature (A *Gabin* in Nature), when suddenly, he comes across a cabin which is perched high atop a mountain, and not only that, but it's a cabin which happens to have smoke belching out of its chimney. He enters the cabin quite uninvited, and the first thing he sees is *ass*—and not just any *garden-variety ass,* either, but the ass of a woman who's trying to light an ancient induction stove. Meet Lilian White who, just like Gabin's Ted Lennard, is a runaway from society, and she's played by the luminous French movie star Michele Morgan who, here, is making her entrance two-thirds of the way into the picture, just when we thought it was almost over! *Recif de corail* is the second of the five pictures, in which (a now) eighteen-year-old Morgan would appear with Gabin, the previous one, of course, being *Le Quai des brumes,* and for one brief, shining moment, fate is looking up: Ted instantly *has the hots* for Lilian, and he asks her what she's doing in a desolate cabin all by herself (because he can tell, right away, from her delicate, refined manner, that she's a city girl). She doesn't know who this strange intruder who's asking her all of these impertinent questions is, but she is as instantly fascinated with him, as he is with her and, like all women in all Gabin movies right after they've just met him, she too starts telling him her whole life's story: "I left my home in Brisbane. My family wanted to marry me off to this guy, but I wasn't interested in him." As it turns out, the reason that Lilian was bending over the stove when Ted showed up, is because she was about to start preparing dinner. ("Whatchya makin? Soup?" he asks her, licking his chops. "Are you going to invite me?") He asks her if she's suspicious of people (it's a good question, since he's mega-suspicious of everybody on earth), and the only answer she makes, which isn't really, when you think about it, a direct answer to the question which he's just asked her, is simply that she's "not afraid of loneliness." Ted then tells her—and this part probably isn't true, but he's just looking to gain a little common ground, with her—that his own parents wanted to marry him off to somebody as well, but that he wasn't interested, either; and next, in typical Gabin Loner-Mode, he adds that he's "not happy with people in general," and that he doesn't have "too much use for the civilized world." As she continues stirring the soup, she tells him, demurely, that she "only has one soup bowl," and Man-of-Simple-Pleasures-Gabin just tells her not to worry about it: "That's okay, I'll eat from the pot." She giggles, smiling for the first time, which makes him smile, as well. ("See! You're not afraid of me!") Wordlessly, he walks out onto the porch to have a smoke and, when he does, she looks suddenly petrified that this enticing new stranger might leave her, even though he's just shown up. Just like that Knoxville hooker who proposed the exact-same arrangement only seconds after meeting Ted, Lilian now does the same: "Maybe we could help each other, and we can both live here. If I can trust you, you can stay here, in the attic." So far, Ted's not hitting on Lilian, which she likes. (We can tell she's not used to a man who acts like a gentleman.) He tells her he's tired, and she hands him a lamp so that he'll be able to see his way up to the attic, and when we see the two of them, next—Ted in his attic cot, and Lilian down below, in her bed—they are both lying awake, each one obviously thinking about the other, as director Gleize fades out.

The next morning, Lilian wakes up, and she thinks Ted is gone, but he's really just out by the river, washing his clothes. She scampers out to him in a fetching straw hat, and tells him that she's cooked them a delicious rabbit breakfast. They've very clearly *fucked* the previous night, based on the new, heightened level of their familiarity, and she's definitely over-the-moon about the fact that Ted has shown-up at the cabin. As she helps him in the wringing-out of his wet togs, he begins staring at her super-intensely, in that way in which hungry lions always seem to be checking out zebras on the Serengeti, and it kind of freaks her out a little, and not in a bad way, either. She tells him that she doesn't like being looked at "in that manner," but we can see by her eyes that *she does, does, does!*

Ted likes Lilian just as much as she likes him, and he clearly wants to open up to her, but it's always hard for Jean Gabin's movie characters to lay it on the line and talk about themselves, so the best that he can summon up, at this juncture, is a very vague and meekly-delivered explanation of his past, which is really just the tiniest elaboration on what we already heard him telling Nikolah and Hobson: "I used to live in the city, but I just didn't know what to do there." She tells him that, when she lived in the city, she didn't like to cook, but that now, since she's been out in the country, she's learned to love it. Ted does make one favorable concession to The City though, admitting, "Well, even though you can't really have any kind of a life in a city, I guess it is kind of fun there, sometimes. If we had met in the city, I would have taken you to a movie and dancing. But of course, this is much better. You have to acknowledge that the city really makes you stupid!" Lilian tells Ted that, before she found the isolated cabin, she stayed in a local Knoxville hotel for a few weeks, and she now asks him if he'd "be a dear" and go and pick-up some of the things which she left behind there, and also, while he's at it, if he wouldn't mind stopping off at the town's general store to pick up a candleholder and a couple of extra rabbit traps, so that they can trap their dinner!

Ted next sets-off from the cabin, clip-clopping across a lonely bridge, and finally arriving back in Knoxville, where he walks past a long shanty-town-looking row of tents which look like they're being used as some kind of a temporary hospital—in fact, these tents are surrounded by a bunch of harried-looking doctors, nurses, and Red Cross trucks. (*Recif de corail* takes place during the world's true-life influenza epidemic of 1917-1918 [in real life, even Walt Disney was touched by it, according to author Neal Gabler, in his 2006 biography of the famous cartoonist], and the flu is exactly the problem that which this ad hoc hospital is currently addressing.) He heads, first, into the small local hotel where Lilian told him that she had stayed, and tells the pre-occupied-looking Manager that he hasn't come to rent a room, but only to pick up Lillian White's personal belongings. ("I'm a friend.") An inquisitive Ted asks the guy what all of the hospital tents are for, and the guy tells him that everybody in town is sick: "The city fathers want me to tell outsiders that people are just dying coincidentally, but it's really influenza."

After picking up Lilian's stuff, Ted's next errand is Knoxville's general store, While he's there buying the rabbit-traps, he splurges on buying a bunch of other stuff for Lillian—several gaudy trinkets, as well as a kettle, a music box (this is the second film in which

Gabin buys Michele Morgan a music box [the first one being the previous year's *Le Quai des brumes*]), and a beautiful dress which, very fashionably, happens to have been 'Made in Sydney;' in fact, he's bought everything except for the candle-holder which Lilian had asked him for, expressly. (Whoops! *Guys suck at shopping!*) The store's Clerk, Jim Tecira, who's played by an actor called Rene Bergeron, tells Ted that the dress which he's just purchased is the last of its kind in this part of the country, and he next asks Ted, out of curiosity, what kind of a lady Lilian is, and Ted, with a huge, sly smile on his face, simply responds by forming the internationally-recognized 'sign-of-the-hourglass' with his two hands!

When Ted arrives back at Lilian's cabin he's walked all night (and he's Gabin, so he can do it!), she's still asleep. When she awakens at dawn, the first thing she sees is the beautiful music box, and she looks incredibly touched by the fact that he's spent what must have been all of his money on her. Very sweetly, when he presents her with the dress which he's bought for her, it's all dirty and mud-caked from his long walk back, and he tells her that he'd love her to wear it if they ever go into town. He tells her, also, that he'd love to take her to Tobugu, that magical place from whence he's recently just come. ("My English friend is there. You'd really like him!") Lilian loves her new music box, and she starts insouciantly dancing around to its tune. Then: It's a knock on the door. Ted answers it…

Of course, it's Abboye, the cop, and Ted steps out onto the front porch to speak with him. Very calmly, and realizing that Cruel Fate would have found him no matter where he had traveled, Ted sticks out his hands, in a handcuff-ready position, mumbling, "You're here to arrest me? Okay. I'll go. Just let me get my stuff." But Abboye has a surprise for Ted: "I'm not arresting you! You're the second guy who's pretended to have killed Brooks because, for some reason or another, you want to go to jail for a crime which you didn't commit!" Abboye's theory, which we already know is pure conjecture, is that it was Anna herself who killed Brooks, because Brooks was rich, and because she wanted to get her hands on his money: "It's a girl named Anna that I'm looking for—not you. I know that you know her, and the reason I've been trying to find you, is because I want to know if you know where I can find her." (Now it's very possible that Anna did kill Brooks, because remember: When the movie opened, Brooks was already dead. It looked like Ted killed him, but it could have been Anna who came into the room [or: came back into the room, for a second time], when Brooks' body was already splayed out on the floor.)

Now, we get a plot twist, and one which is genuinely very weird: Abboye tells Ted that he's come to the cabin, not just because he needs Ted to tell him where Anna is, but also for a second and completely unrelated reason which has nothing to do with anything which we've already heard about in the movie: Abboye now shocks Ted, and us, by telling him that Michele Morgan's Lilian is a murderess as well, of a completely separate and different murder, which has nothing to do with Anna, Ted, or Brooks! According to Abboye, Lilian killed a woman and buried her somewhere up in the mountains, near the cabin, which is the real reason that she's been hiding out there. When Ted and Abboye re-enter the cabin, Lilian is gone and, most probably, she snuck-out through the back window. Abboye informs Ted that Lilian's real name is not 'Lilian,' but that it is actually 'Mary,' and that the woman whom Mary is reported to have killed was a lady judge, and that Mary's parents sent the judge to look for her, when Mary skipped-town.

Even though he's only known Lilian, or Mary, for a couple of days, Ted knows, instinctively, that she's a good person, and so he now automatically starts defending her to Abboye, without even knowing any of the facts: "Well, if Lilian killed somebody, which I don't think she did, she must have been absolutely exasperated to have done it. Anyway, don't look for her! She's not here, and she's apparently inflicted a punishment on herself, by going away into hiding." Abboye apologizes for disturbing Ted (cops always apologize to Jean Gabin after having interrogated him in his films), and leaves. Ted runs outside and calls out for Lilian, using both of her 'handles,' Lilian and Mary, but she's nowhere to be seen, and his voice echoes impotently through the mountains.

Days pass. Lilian's been gone from the cabin for quite some time, and Ted, who has remained there, is missing her mightily. He looks for her at the temporary influenza clinic, and also at other places in town as well, but she's nowhere to be seen. Finally, he makes his way back to the local hotel. The Manager remembers Ted, and tells him that Lilian is, in fact, here—that she's upstairs in one of the rooms—but that she, like just about everybody else in town, is dying from the flu. He warns Ted against going upstairs to her room, but Ted goes, anyway. *Jean Gabin ain't afraid of no stinkin' deadly-virus!*

When a bedridden Lilian sees Ted she brightens, but tells him that he shouldn't have come, and she also admits to him now, without his even having asked her about it, that she murdered the lady judge, but Ted tells her truthfully that he doesn't care about that (he's not exactly 'a sterling personality,' either), and that all he wants, is for her to get better, so that they can go off to Tobugu together.

Ted is so freaked-out by how sickly Lilian looks, *and is,* that he now runs over to the hospital, fully intent on asking one of the doctors there, if he will come back to the hotel with him, to help her. When Ted arrives at the clinic, the first thing he sees is a morose-looking hospital official, who's reading a list of the latest flu victims who have succumbed during the previous night, to a group of assembled relatives. (One lady, who is related to one of the deceased, even screams out in agony, as the body of her loved one is carried out on a gurney.) Ted finds the main Doctor who runs the place (he's played by Pierre Magnier), and begs the Doctor to please accompany him to the hotel, but the Doctor tells him that he will be unable to accommodate such a request, since his hands are full as it is, with the hundreds of other flu patients whom he's already looking after. But Ted won't take no for an answer and, that night while the Doctor is asleep in his temporary offices at the hospital, Ted barges in, waking him: "You've got to come to the hotel, Doctor! You've got to take care of my woman." The Doctor asks Ted if Lilian is his wife, admitting here that he'd be more predisposed toward helping her if he knew that the two of them were married; and when the extremely irreligious Ted hears that bullshit, he lays down a Biblical Commandment of his own: "You just come and look at her, right now!" When the Doctor shrugs impotently, and tells Ted that he truly can't leave his other patients, Ted, instead, switches over to a 'kinder, gentler' begging-track. Of course, the Doctor responds to this show of niceness better, and tells Ted that he'll try to come and help Lilian, as soon as he has a free moment.

The next morning, guess who else shows up at the hospital to talk to the Doctor? Of course, it's Abboye, who's remained in the area, still steadfast in his search for Lilian. The Doctor tells Abboye that Lilian's at the local hotel and, a few hours later, when Ted goes up to the Lilian's hotel room to check on her, he sees Abboye emerging from her room. Abboye's nice to Ted, and tells Ted that while he was there, she was calling out his (Ted's) name. When Ted enters her room, he finds that a second Doctor is there, as well (he's played by Marcel Duhamel), and he also sees Lilian, who's screaming out, in the midst of what must be some very vivid hallucinations: "I didn't steal! I'm not waiting for you! Give me the dress—I want to put it on! The house is on fire!" Ted asks Abboye why he brought this second doctor to see her: "Is it because you want her to heal, so that you can convict her and arrest her?!" Abboye makes no reply.

We now dissolve to what is probably several weeks later: The flu epidemic has largely subsided, and the hospital tents are being folded-up. Former patients, who are now healthy, are boarding trains, which carry them back to their own towns, in other parts of Australia. Ted walks through Knoxville's town square, where members of the happy, and now flu-free, citizenry are singing and partying. Ted's wearing overalls and clutching two one-way boat tickets to Tobugu, one for himself, and the other for Lilian, who's healed completely. (Obviously, Ted means to sneak Lilian out of Australia, before Abboye can catch up with her.) Lilian looks great, too, and she even chirps, "How pretty everything is! It's wonderful to be alive!"

The next day, Ted and Lilian are back in Brisbane, and they're walking by the docks. The *Portland* is moored there, and Ted is introducing Lilian to his good friend, Captain Nikolah, who will be taking them away to start their new life in—where else?—Tobugu! Of course, *shitty old Springbett* has already been fired. (We won't be seeing any more of that crackpot! [Good riddance, to bad rubbish!]) And just as the happy couple is about to board the boat, guess who's decided to put in an appearance: It's Abboye, who's making his way up the gangplank. He still wants to arrest Lilian, but now he's also looking for Ted, because he's decided that he wants to charge Ted with harboring a known criminal (Lilian). When Lilian sees Abboye coming, Ted tells her that there's nothing to worry about: "No matter what the police do to us, nobody can ever stop us from being in love." And just when Abboye is about to arrest Ted and Lilian, he suddenly (and this is probably a surprise, even to him) decides, at the last minute, to let them both go. Obviously, this cop, who's more sensitive than we originally thought he was, is touched by the true love which he's now witnessing between Ted and Lilian, and he now tells the couple that he's going to let them get off the boat and remain free, "here in Brisbane." He doesn't offer a reason, but—who knows?—maybe we don't even need one: Ted is a Working Guy, Abboye is a Working Guy, and maybe—just maybe—these two men have recognized a soupçon of ineffable goodness in each other. For once, in one of Jean Gabin's Poetic Realist pictures, the lone figure who's walking away alone at the end isn't Jean Gabin (this time, fate will be kind to him, for a change), but Pierre Renoir's 'Abboye'-character: Gabin's Ted Lennard does walk away, but it's with his lady love, and we can only presume that they'll live happily, ever after.

While *Le Recif de corail* is a very entertaining movie, it was not a hit in France when it was first released in February of 1939, and was forgotten very quickly, after a few cursory theatrical runs in Denmark, Finland, and Portugal. It was never released at all, in any English-speaking countries.

Even though the film was made during the period of Jean Gabin's biggest international fame (*La Grande illusion, Pepe Le Moko, Le Quai des brumes, etc.*), it is the only picture from that period, besides *Le Messager*, which isn't that well-known today, even in France, not just because it was lost for six decades, but also because of the ultra-strange way in which it tells its story: At about one hour into the movie, just when we're ready for the final, 'third act,' which is the act in which movies usually resolve their stories, Ted finally meets Michele Morgan's Lilian, for the first time; in other words, just when we think the movie is going to start wrapping itself up, this brand new story begins. In spite of the weird way in which it spins its tale, however, *Recif de corail* is (almost) right up there with all of Gabin's other great 1930s' classics, and since it's just become available on DVD in France (finally!), I can only hope that sooner, rather than later, we'll get our own *Recif de corail* release in the English-speaking world, with English subtitles.

In 2003, after the film critic Lenny Borger re-discovered a print of the lost *Recif de corail* at the Kinoteka Film Archives, in Serbia, Paris's Lobster Films, and Lobster's chief curators, Serge Bromberg and Eric Lange, restored it to its full luster (apparently, there was a lot of sound damage, but the picture was still crisp and clear), and on May 17, 2004, on the occasion of what would have been Jean Gabin's 100th birthday, the film re-premiered in Paris, a full sixty-five years after it was made. In attendance, were such luminaries as Michele Morgan and Alain Delon, as well as family and friends of the cast and crew. Almost everybody in attendance was seeing the film for the very first time.

What a Critic Said at the Time: "Despite the draw names, *Recif de corail* has no crack exploitation possibilities, and is destined for the home market only. A big fault of this picture lies not in the acting, but in the story. The French idea of a rough Australian town and Mexican rebels is far from reality. Some cutting would help, but it wouldn't take the pic out of its ordinary[ness]." (*Variety*, 5-10-39 issue. Critic, "Hugo." Reviewed in Paris.)

FILM 30

LE JOUR SE LEVE

France, 1939

(Literal English Translation: "DAYBREAK") Directed by Marcel Carne. Produced by Albert Brachet and Paul Madeux. Written by Jacques Prevert and Jacques Viot. Directors of Photography (black and white), Philippe Agostini, Andre Bac, Albert Viguier, and Curt Courant. Editor, Rene Le Henaff. Production Designer, Alexandre Trauner. Music by Maurice Jaubert. (GENRE: DRAMA) Running Time, 1 hour 26 minutes. Produced and Released in France by Sigma/Vauban Productions, on June 9, 1939. Released in the U.S. with English Subtitles as "DAYBREAK" on July 29, 1940, by AFE.

"Everybody get the hell out of here! Leave me alone! So I'm a murderer! Big deal!
A lot of people get murdered! Leave me in peace! I'm through with life!"
— *A murderous Gabin hides out in his attic apartment and yells down at the crowd
which has congregated outside of his window, in "Le Jour se leve"*

D irector Marcel Carne's and co-writer Jacques Prevert's second fantastic Jean Gabin Collaboration, *Le Jour se leve*, is just as dark and fatalistic as was their first one, *Le Quai des brumes*—so much so, in fact, that it was initially banned by French military censors as being 'demoralizing,' although today, the film is considered (all over the world, including in North America) to be one of the greatest movies of the 1930s. *Le Jour se leve* follows the tried-and-true formula, not only of the last Gabin/Carne picture, *Le Quai des brumes*, but also of lots of other of Gabin's movies from the late '30s and '40s, as well. *You know the drill:* 'Gabin is on the run for a crime which he committed before the movie started, and he must find solace with a woman—and usually, an understanding and maternal brunette—before his inevitable demise.' Unmistakably the saddest picture in the entire Jean Gabin canon, it opens with this credit crawl.

"*Un homme a tue... enferme, assiege dans une chambre, il evoque les circonstances qui ont fait de lui un meurtrier.*" ("A man has killed... Sick, he sits in a room, evoking the circumstances which have made him a murderer.")

Then—BANG!—before the audience can catch its collective breath, Gabin's 'Francois' character shoots a man to death and, locked in his dingy, attic apartment, he waits for the

With Arletty.

inevitable—for the authorities to come and cart him away to jail. While he waits for them all night (in France, at the time the movie was made, it was illegal for the police to make an arrest in the middle of the night, and they had to wait until *daybreak,* which is the English-language translation of the film's title, to do it), he sits on the edge of his bed and smokes in dramatic half light (and importantly, each time director Carne cuts back to the attic, he and his director of photography Philippe Agostini illuminate a different part of Gabin's face), and we flash backwards to the events which got him up a tree, in the first place:

The Recent Past—A Factory:

Francois, who's decked-out in a futuristic, *proto-H.R. Geiger* welding suit (it's covered with surreal, octopus-like hoses) is spot-welding, when an achingly-beautiful brunette enters, bearing a bouquet of achingly-beautiful flowers. She is 'Francoise,' with an 'e' on the end, to his 'Francois,' which is co-screenwriters Jacques Prevert's and Jacques Viot's clever way of intertwining the two characters' fates through the use of the masculine and feminine versions of the same name, and she's played by the equine Jacqueline Laurent. Francoise has come to the plant to look for her friend Madame Legardier, the wife of the place's owner, and in the few moments in which she's there, Gabin turns on his 'indifferent charisma,' which, as usual, works like a charm.

After a slow dissolve, we'll see, next, that Francois and Francoise have been courting for quite a while, but that they have not yet consummated their aching passion for each other,

With Jacqueline Laurent.

although Francois has been lobbying for it, with his coyly-constant requests for her to "stay over." She tells him that she wants to make love to him, just like he does to her, but that she has already made plans for this particular evening, plans which involve another man. (She made the plans before she ever met Francois.) Francois looks really dour when she admits this to him, so she then tries to make him feel a bit better, by telling him, truthfully, that she likes him better than she does 'the other guy' (the guy with whom she has to keep her date), and that, of the two guys, Francois is the one with whom she would most like to "… pluck lilacs, at Easter." Francois, as Gabin will do in many of his other films, doesn't react at all when she's telling him this stuff, and he seems to be okay with it, although we can also tell that he's definitely jealous. Francoise leaves Francois with her favorite one-eared toy teddy bear, something to play with while she's out on her date with The Other Man (and this moment is very reminiscent of that scene in 1933's *Coeurs joyeux,* in which Gabin and Josseline Gael bonded over the little stuffed animal which, very similarly, Gabin's character kept in his apartment).

But Francois isn't content to just stay home and fondle a one-eared teddy bear, no matter how furry and warm it is, so he follows Francoise to a local burlesque house, where he observes her with her other suitor, Valentin, who's played by Jules Berry (a great French actor who looks a great deal like the American thesp, Clifton Webb), an older fop who happens to be the star of the show; Valentin has one of those stupid 'poodle-jumping-through-a-hoop' acts, which lulls the insipid-entertainment-loving crowd into a gleeful stupor.

While Francois is spying on Valentin and Francoise from the bar (they can't see him, but he can see them), he now meets a second woman, Clara, a striking *femme-fatale* who happens to be Valentin's stage assistant, and who also happens to have recently—just the night before, in fact—terminated her own romantic relationship with Valentin. (Clara is played by the incredibly vixenish Arletty, who was considered to be France's 'second-biggest star' of the 1930s, after Jean Gabin.)

Sharp-featured Clara tries to 'pick up-on' Francois, telling him that she's just broken up with the guy on stage, but Francois tells her, in his indifferent (and yet coolly-seductive) Gabin Manner, "You're charming. But I don't know you well-enough to hear about your personal life." Clara, however, isn't dissuaded easily by his indifference (as Frank Sinatra sang in the 1962 hit which he also co-wrote, *Hidden Persuasion,* "Your charming indifference is but a disguise"), and when he tells her that he thinks she's wearing too much makeup, she turns her *sex-o-meter* 'up to eleven,' lasciviously replying, "I always remove my makeup… before I go to bed!" Clara's mega-hot for Francois, and she adds, "You have a soothing influence. And even better—you don't talk much!"

When Francoise leaves with Valentin, Francois now saves face, by going home to engage in steamy love-making with the always ready-to-rumble-looking Clara and, after a few weeks, Francois is now alternating between Francoise and Clara. Soon, needless to say, each woman is growing jealous of Francois' attentions toward the other.

Shortly thereafter, Francois and Francoise are making plans to marry. (Rabid Gabin Fans can already sense that such a union won't work out, not from anything in this particular film, but because we know already that Gabin's recurring role, especially in the movies which he would make from 1934 through 1941, is to be 'the perennial drifter,' and he'd better not disappoint us!) At this point, the two lovers are visited by Valentin, who takes Francois out for a pow-wow at a local watering hole, and Valentin tells Francois that he wants him to stop seeing Francoise, not because he wants her for himself, but actually because, as he's now telling her, he's her father—he, in other words, is the deadbeat dad who, by his own proclamation, left her in an orphanage when she was a little girl, and he doesn't want her to be hurt by Francois, whom he sees, correctly, as being a penniless roué, who leapfrogs from one woman to another. Of course, Francois knows that Valentin is lying: Francois doesn't say anything about it in the scene (that's the great thing about Gabin) but we can see it in his face, through the accusing way in which he's staring at the older man, that Francois knows Valentin is just making the story up, because Valentin wants to keep Francoise all to himself.

Francois next confronts Françoise about the strange *tete-a-tete* which he's just had with Valentin, and she tells him that Valentin has lied to him about being her father, and that he's just made the whole story up, so that Francois would get lost. She tells Francois also, that he shouldn't be so hard on Valentin. ("Apart from you, he's the only person who's ever really bothered about me.")

Soon, Clara and Francoise are both putting pressure on Francois to pick one or the other of them. Francois decides that the demure Francoise is the one he wants, and so he breaks it off with Clara. Director Marcel Carne now dissolves back to Francois' apartment, in the 'Present Day,' and to the film's tragic climax which, circularly, takes place only moments after the shooting which we saw at the beginning of the picture:

Valentin, gun in hand, has come to kill Francois, but now that he's with Francois, face to face, he tells him that he can't go through with it. He drops his gun on the bed, the two men go at it *mano-a-mano,* and it is next that Valentin makes his fatal mistake: He insults Francois so vigorously for what he perceives to be Francois' working-class lack of refinement, that the normally-taciturn Francois now Gabin-Outbursts, "Stop talking slush! You're nothing but a dirty rat," a sentiment which he punctuates with a war-cry so raw, and so animalistic, that it seems to have issued-forth from several thousand wounded coyotes who've been glued together in a madly-chunking Cuisinart—"*YAAAAAGHHHHHH!*" Valentin admits (Francois, and we, already knew this, anyway) that he's not Francoise's dad, but that he is her lover, and by way of a response, Francois then picks up Valentin's gun, and blows Valentin to Kingdom Come. "You deserved that," Francois tells Valentin nonchalantly as the man lies dying, and it is here that director Carne now depicts Gabin once again in heroic half-light, as Francois, coolly, lights a refreshing '*après-murder*' cigarette (Murder + Menthol = Nirvana!), up in his dark attic apartment room.

The last several minutes of *Le Jour se leve* may remind the viewer of the whole of Sidney Lumet's classic 1974 Al Pacino-starring bank robbery-epic, *Dog Day Afternoon:* Francois stares out of his attic apartment window, as the crowd gathers below to see the spectacle of a murderer who is trapped alone and as surly cops swarm, S.W.A.T-like, out of the ass-ends of large vehicles. Parallel to this, Francois' two women, Francoise and Clara, are huddling-together in another apartment nearby, consoling one another, two rivals-in-love who have been brought together by the fact that the brutish but tender manchild whom they both love is about to die, in a *Bon-Jovian* blaze of glory.

In order to stave-off the freezing night air, Francois has donned a leather jacket and, in this scene, Jean Gabin actually pre-dates the whole 'Marlon Brando-James Dean leather jacket phenomenon' by more than a decade. He hates that the crowd is staring up at him like he's some kind of a buffoonish, trapped, King Kong/zoo-animal/freak, and he resignedly yells down at everybody (and here comes what is perhaps the most famous Gabin-Outburst of the actor's entire career) that everybody should just go away and leave him alone. ("Clear off! So, I'm a murderer! Big deal! A lot of people get murdered! Leave me in peace! I'm through with life!")

Francoise runs over to Francois' building, stopping directly under his window, but 'our boy' is so amped up from yelling down at the crowd, that his lady-love's appearance hasn't even registered with him. The cops decide to tear-gas Francois out of the room and, just as they begin rolling-in the canisters, Francois, who is emotionlessly resigned to his *shitty fate,* now shoots himself, firing a shot right into his own, already-wounded-by-life heart. Now, sadly, no lilacs will ever be plucked at Easter or, for that matter, at any other time, either.

Le Jour se leve's enduring power lies in its deafening silences, not to mention, in its blindingly luminous darkness(es). Many of the film's most intense moments feature Jean Gabin alone, walking around his cramped flat, smoking. He's always photographed in shadow, in these wraparound segments, and he's also always separated by, and set-off in stark relief from, his encumbering environment, which is of course director Carne and co-scenarist Prevert's clever visual shorthand of letting us know that Francois won't be around for too much longer.

In *Le Jour se leve,* as in other Gabin pictures made in the 1930s, the Gabin character, Francois, is a true 'man of the people' who is beloved by everybody in town, in spite of the fact that he has committed a criminal act: When Francois' kindhearted Landlady (Mady Berry) asserts to a Neighbor-Lady (Annie Cariel) that "Francois is a good fellow," and the Neighbor-Lady replies, "One of the best," it's just like the scene in *Les Bas-fonds,* in which Gabin's working-class man-of-the-streets, Vlaska Pepel, was defended by his neighbors who loved him, even in spite of the fact that he had murdered the old man.

Jean Gabin, Arletty, Marcel Carne and Jacques Prevert re-teamed, one more time after *Le Jour se leve,* fifteen years later, in a 1954 film called *L'Air de Paris,* in which Gabin played an over-the-hill boxing trainer, and Arletty played 'Mrs. Over-the-Hill-Boxing-Trainer.' Arletty, a great beauty who was, back in the 1930s, one of France's most durable female stars, suffered career-wise, because she was one of the French actors and filmmakers who remained in France during World War II, a period when many French actors and directors, including Jean Gabin, would temporarily relocate to America to find succor, solace and, most of all, wartime movie employment.

The free-spirited Arletty, who was as well known for her many real-life love affairs as she was for her movies, once famously quipped (and this is quoted in Geoffrey Nowell Smith's *Oxford History of World Cinema*), "My heart is French… but my ass is international," and in another famous interview, she notoriously defended her propensity for sleeping with Nazi soldiers: "I like German officers! They're handsome… and they make me come!"

In 1945, six years after *Le Jour se leve's* French theatrical release, France's Hakim Brothers, the producers of *Pepe Le Moko* (who, like Gabin, had relocated to Los Angeles during the Second World War), headed-up RKO Pictures' American remake of *Le Jour se leve,* which was called *The Long Night,* and they hired Anatole Litvak to direct it. (Litvak, of course, directed Jean Gabin fourteen years earlier, in one of Gabin's earliest pictures, 1931's *Coeur de lilas.*) *Night* features Henry Fonda as 'Joe,' a murderer who is holed-up in his attic-apartment for having killed the dog-show impresario, Maximilian the Magnificent (Vincent Price!), his rival for the sweet affection of young JoAnne (Barbara Bel Geddes). The principal difference between Marcel Carne's *Le Jour se leve* and Anatole Litvak's *noir*-ish American remake, is that the original film was haunting because, like most Gabin movies, it is mostly very quiet, while the remake features copious, and very often even redundant, snatches of dialogue, as if RKO had no idea how to better the previous version, except by adding a bunch of long and unnecessary speeches.

While, in Marcel Carne's version, Jean Gabin ventilates Jules Berry's Valentin with Valentin's gun, in Litvak's remake, Fonda has his own gun, so that the act of killing Maximilian in the American film, doesn't seem like self-defense, which is how it came across in the other film, and it just makes Fonda's character seem *uber*-creepy, in an 'If-I-can't-have-her-nobody-can'-manner, right out of any cheesy horror movie.

Even though *The Long Night* features way too much unnecessary dialogue, it's still very entertaining, and is definitely worth checking-out (it's available on DVD, in the U.S.) so that you can marvel at the once-in-a-lifetime team-up of earthy, low-key Henry Fonda, with over-the-top Vincent Price, and I'm happy to report that, in *The Long Night,* Price is as gloriously hammy as ever. *The Long Night* even betters *Le Jour se leve* in one sequence, but in one sequence only: When the cops shoot into Fonda's room, they blow the one-eared toy teddy bear, which had remained intact in the original, Gabin/Carne film, straight to Hell.

In *Le Jour se leve,* Jean Gabin's character has committed a murder, and he spends most of the film sitting in his room waiting to get caught, and if this reminds you of the plot of Dostoevsky's *Crime and Punishment,* it surely should, because even though *Le Jour se leve* is not an official film version of that novel, that's exactly what it plays like. (In fact, at one point in *Le Jour se leve,* Valentin even confesses to Jean that he's obsessed with very young women, which is a line right out of the Dostoevsky novel.) In 1956, seventeen years after starring in *Le Jour se leve,* an older Jean Gabin would additionally star in an official adaptation of Doestoevsky's *Crime and Punishment,* called *Crime et chatiment,* in which he played the investigating cop, and not the killer. Marcel Carne and Jacques Prevert's *Le Jour se leve,* however, is a better 'Gabin-*Crime and Punishment* film' than Gabin's actual *Crime and Punishment* film would turn out to be.

What a Critic Said at the Time: "The action of the film is slow and serves to emphasize Gabin's slow comprehension of the situation. *Le Jour se leve* is another in a series of psychological studies in which French directors specialize. The story is excellently conceived and planned. For once, Jean Gabin commits a crime which is morally acceptable. There is no fault to find with him, except that he is too much the Gabin of every [other] pic to date." (*Variety,* 7-26-39 issue. Critic: "Ravo." Reviewed in Paris.)

What Another Critic Said: "Mr. Gabin has previously [in other pictures] been the victim, but he has never, in our recollection, been more completely and mercilessly placed on the rack [as he has been, in this film]. Gabin is superb, as a tough, self-reliant, and generally hard-luck guy. The morbid preoccupation of certain French productions with characters who go crazy and do violent things is again being played out." (New York *Times,* 7-3-40 issue. Critic: Bosley Crowther.)

Top: With Michele Morgan and Fernand Ledoux. Above: With Madeleine Renaud.

FILM 31

REMORQUES

France, 1939/1941

(Literal English Translation: "TUGBOATS") Directed by Jean Gremillon. Produced by Roland Tual and (uncredited) 'Lucachevitch.' Screenplay by Jacques Prevert, Andre Cayatte, and Charles Spaak (uncredited). Based Upon the Novel by Roger Vercel. Directors of Photography (black and white), Louis Nee and Armand Thiard. Editor, Yvonne Martin. Production Designer, Alexandre Trauner. Music by Roland Manuel. (GENRE: MELODRAMA) A Production of MAIC and SEDIF, S.A. Running Time, 1 hour 31 minutes. Released in France on November 27, 1941, by Tobis Films. Released in the United States with English Subtitles by MGM on June 15, 1946, as "STORMY WATERS" at 1 hour 16 minutes, and released in Great Britain, as "MISTY WHARVES."

"You are a brute! How I hate you!"
— *Michele Morgan says this to Gabin, only seconds before she jumps his bones, in "Remorques"*

Jean Gremillon, the brilliantly-visual director of Gabin's 1937 picture, *Gueule d'amour*, dragged the actor into the 1940s with *Remorques* (literally, *Tugboats*), another powerfully-moody Poetic Realist epic, and one which is based upon author Roger Vercel's Concourt Prize-winning novel of the same name. (Vercel's book was issued in the U.S., as *Salvage*.) The picture opens at a local boat bar/restaurant in Brest, in northwestern France, one of France's most important port cities, which also happens to be the seat of the French Naval Academy—and also, as it happens, author Roger Vercel's hometown. It's a rainy night at the drinkery/eatery called *Le Petit minou* ('The Little Minnow'), and co-scenarists Jacques Prevert, Andre Cayatte, and Charles Spaak, first hook us into the story with a bit of comedy involving a few minor characters, before we arrive at the story-proper: The place's chefs are tossing a drunk, Roger (Henri Pons) out of a party which is taking place there, and the drunk is screaming at the cooks, accusing them of "cooking for Dutchmen," and even referring to the cooks as being 'potatoes'—which must be a really bad French epithet for Dutch people. This movie has some definite anti-Dutch bias going throughout, and it's no wonder: In Brest, when the picture was being made, Dutch fishing boats were taking business away from the French ones.

As the camera tracks, Hitchcock-like, into the restaurant, we see that it's actually raining inside (instead of '*Le Petit minou,*' they should really call this place 'The Leaky Roof'), and we get to eavesdrop on a fun, blue-collar wedding celebration which is happily in progress: Jean Gabin's Andre Laurent, who is the captain of Brest's mightiest rescue tugboat, the *Cyclone,* is a guest at the marriage of one of his crew members, Poubennec (Marcel Duhamel), and Andre has dispensed with the usual 'Gabin Quietude' for a few moments, in order that he may render a beautifully-evocative speech: "Here's to Mr. and Mrs. Poubennec, and also to my crew, the finest crew in Brest. And tonight, while we're here, let's not forget to think about our friends who are gone forever." Presumably, the *Cyclone* has lost a few men on some of its rescue missions and, no doubt, the deaths have been weather-related, since the seas, in this movie, are as black and as rough as they come. Post-Andre's toast, the hearty men of the *Cyclone* dance with their wives. Andre's own, dutiful wife, Yvonne (Madeleine Renaud, the lead from 1932's *La Belle Mariniere* and 1934's *Maria Chapdelaine*), with whom he's tripping the light French-tastic, is a raw-nerve, as well as being a frail, 'slip of a thing,' and as they're dancing, she's telling him how much she loves him (a lot), and when she does, he's very noticeably not saying it back to her, which clues us in instantly to the state of their marriage: I mean, it is possible that Andre's not telling his wife, "I love you, too" because Jean Gabin doesn't talk that much, but probably, that's not what's going on; here's a marriage which, at least on Andre's side, has definitely, just like a rescue tugboat at the end of a mission, run its course. As the seafaring couples continue dancing, Laurent's right-hand-man and 'little buddy,' Gabriel Tanguy (Charles Blavette), dances with his own wife Renee (Nane German), and their relationship is mostly the same as Andre and Yvonne's, only in reverse, which is to say that Tanguy loves Renee, but she thinks that he's a stupid rube, and she also happens to be cheating on him with other cocksmiths, whenever he's away at sea.

At that moment, a motorcycle messenger pulls up to the place, and the messenger informs Andre that he's sorry to bother him, but that he's needed ASAP, because a small passenger vessel, the *Mirva XV*—or, in English, the *Minerva XV*—is sinking, and Andre and his heroic 'Team *Cyclone*' are needed to save the day. Andre and his men excuse themselves from the party, leaving their desperate housewives alone, as the rain continues skittering down through the ceiling and right onto their heads, and this is definitely an image which manages to be both funny and sorrowful at the same time. (Talk about "raining on one's parade!")

The newly-betrothed Marie Poubennec (Anne Laurens) accompanies Yvonne back to Yvonne and Andre's house, and the two women now start commiserating over their sad existences. Yvonne confesses something personal/private to Marie which she has been unable to get across to her husband Andre, mostly because Andre's not around too much (like any true sailor, he's 'married to the sea'), which is that she's terminally ill. She tells Marie that, "… while Andre has the sea, I only have him." And while Yvonne's always upset because Andre's frequently absent, she also, at the same time, defends his right to be away from her ("I guess I have no right to keep him all to myself. One shouldn't keep things - one should live"), but it's very clear to us, that she really wishes that he could be home with her a lot more than he presently is, and also, that he would just forget about the seas once in a while. French movies, in particular, seem to be pretty enamored with that whole 'my-real-woman-is-the-sea'-trope.

Next, we join Andre and his men aboard the *Cyclone*. While they're heading over to the *Mirva*, which is about twelve hours out at sea (they won't get there until morning), Andre descends down into the galley, where his crew members are killing time, as well as whatever's left of their livers and brain cells, by indulging in a little good, old-fashioned woman-bashing, each man even offering-up his own thoughts on The Nature of Monogamy: The Cook tells the gathered crew members, "I know there are faithful women in the world. There are also three-headed snakes and two-headed sheep!"

The *Cyclone* finally reaches the *Mirva*, right on time, and the *Mirva's* distress signal actually sounds like a human scream! (This was intentional, of course, on the part of the film's style-and-atmosphere-obsessed director, Jean Gremillon, because the sounds of the signal resonate with 'the dying man-woman relationships' which this film is taking great pleasure in showing us. (Most of the ships that are in trouble, in this movie, are *relation-ships*.) Andre announces, over his megaphone, and to the *Mirva's* crew, that help has arrived, and that the *Mirva's* crew should worry no more, because the *Cyclone* will presently be attaching a big cable to them, to 'tug' them back to land. Andre's a nice guy, and he makes sure to congratulate one of his best men, the handsome young Hellegourach (Marcel Melrac), because well-muscled Hellegourach seems to be doing most of the 'heavy-lifting:' "You've got a fine Breton head," Andre smiles, complimenting Hellegourach on the toughness and resilience which is famously shared by the residents of Brittany. In *Remorques,* as in all Gabin pictures, the company of other men, in a completely heterosexual way, is much more fun than the company of a bunch of whiny wimminfolk!

Meanwhile, down in the bowels of the *Mirva,* that ship's captain, Marc, who's played by the actor Jean Marchat, is worrying, but not about his boat, and not about his own personal safety: He's actually down in the galley, having what the Brits refer to as a 'row,' with his wife Kathryn (Michele Morgan who, with this film, is making her third of four appearances in Jean Gabin movies). Kathryn tells her husband, a guy who, by the way, looks a bit unbalanced, that she's never really loved him, and that she fully intends on leaving him at such time as they'll be arriving back on shore: Kathryn and her husband have been married for two years and, very clearly, they've hated each other, on a cellular level, since the get-go.

Andre and Tanguy leap onto the deck of the *Mirva* to meet the fine folks whom they're going to be rescuing, and Andre and Tanguy first come upon Kathryn, who's husband has ventured off alone to another part of the boat, no doubt to try and recover from their argument, but Kathryn's already over it: She's instantly hot for her new, Gabinian savior, and when she asks him who he is, he tells her, with a cautious smile, "I'm catastrophe's errand boy!" When she asks him if he's the guy who's going to be towing them back to shore, and he answers in the affirmative, her reply is, *"c'est dommage"* ("too bad"): Clearly, she'd love to be stuck at sea with this brave-looking new acquaintance, and when Andre leaves the

Mirva's galley, and when he leaves Kathryn alone with Tanguy, she waxes approvingly about of Gabin's Andre character—"That That man is *frank!*"—Tanguy, who is ever a good wing-man in the Game of Love, now seconds her judgment: "He's a man, all right!" (As if we didn't already know that.)

Since it's going to take a few more hours for the *Cyclone* and the *Mirva* to return to land, and also since Kathryn's starting to get bored, she leaps from the *Mirva's* deck, up onto the *Cyclone's,* in an attempt to get to know Andre a little better. We can figure out already that Andre, like most other Jean Gabin Movie Characters from the 1930s and 1940s, will probably end up getting involved with her, at least for awhile, but that ultimately, he won't want to get too involved, because he's a man of the sea, he's married to Yvonne, and also because, ultimately, Gabin never wants to get hurt by somebody with whom he's (probably) fated not to be. At first, Andre acts disinterested, just like Gabin's Francois character did with Arletty's character in *Le Jour se leve,* and he tells Kathryn that she should return to her own boat, but she's just not interested in that. So Andre and Tanguy walk her back to the *Mirva,* and right over to her not-so-loving husband, who didn't know where she was, and who now starts berating her for her absence, even though he doesn't even like her, to begin with. (Ain't marriage grand?)

This is the scene in which Andre is meeting Kathyrn's husband, *Mirva* captain Marc in-person, for the first time, and Andre's not too happy with the guy, because he's just witnessed this clown in the act of trying to slice the tow-rope, so that he can take his own boat the rest-of-the-way back to shore, without having to pay the *Cyclone* for its towing services. Andre informs Marc that, according to 'Lloyd's Boating Regulations,' a damaged boat at sea can only be towed-in by another vessel. Marc, not knowing with whom he's dealing, starts getting a bit pugilistic, and even tries baiting Andre into a fight. (Marc even has a great line, during this scene: "A bastard is a bastard, even at sea!") Why, this half-wit even tries to punch Andre in the face, but Andre gets in the pre-emptive first blow, knocking the guy flat on his behind.

The next morning, after a hard night of both boat-rescuing and creep-punching, Andre arrives home at dawn, and his too-adoring wife, Yvonne, is excited beyond belief to see him, smothering him with hugs and kisses, to which he responds only by disinterestedly sighing, "You women just want to see us men at home, sitting by the fire!" (For a consummate, Gabinian-working-man like Andre, being at home, instead of being off at work doing something 'useful,' equals emasculation.) She kisses him and he just yawns, and next, by way of apology, he tells her that he's only "yawning from hunger," but she's not buying it. He plops down at the breakfast table, and she tells him that she wishes he'd 'love her like he used to' and, by way of a reply, he doesn't tell her that he loves her—only, that he's happy with her.

Ever dutiful, in spite of her husband's rather flagrant uncaringness, Yvonne now cooks Andre a nice breakfast, and just as he's about to dig in, his always-skittish-looking little buddy Tanguy shows up, and asks Andre if he'd mind taking a quick walk with him, because he needs to tell him something important. Tanguy and Andre head into a local bar and, when they get there, Tanguy, who's been putting a lot of effort into 'holding it in' on the way over, now freaks, telling Andre that, while he and Andre were away rescuing the *Mirva*, his wife, Renee, had left him, and not for the first time, either. Andre tells Tanguy that he shouldn't worry about it, because, in his own opinion, 'sleazy' Renee just isn't worth it, and he mentions to Tanguy also that not only he, but the whole crew as well, already know that Renee has been cuckolding Tanguy every chance she gets, and that in his opinion, Tanguy should just get the hell out of his sham-of-a marriage, and as quickly as he can. Renee then enters the bar—in-person, and right on cue—knowing that this is the place into which her husband always repairs when he's not working. She pretends to be happy to see him and, with a completely straight face, tells him that she's been away, visiting a girlfriend: "Oh, my dearest! I'm so sorry that I haven't been around! My friend was sick, and I've just been away at her house, taking care of her." Andre, who's been hanging-back during this ridiculous husband and wife confrontation, just rolls his eyes. (World-weary Jean Gabin, even though he was only thirty-six when this movie was made, has already seen everything!) At this point, a messenger boy arrives at the bar as well, and informs Andre that Kathryn has taken a room at the local hotel, and that she's waiting for him, there - and right now.

Andre's not too keen on running around on his wife, even though the love is gone from his marriage, just like the love is also gone in two other marriages—Tanguy and Renee's marriage and Kathryn and Marc's marriage—but because Kathryn is being played by Michele Morgan, naturally, he makes a bee-line for her hotel, anyway. When he arrives at Kathryn's room, she throws her arms around him (he doesn't 'hug back'), and immediately thanks him for saving her from her husband whom, as she's also letting him know, she hasn't seen since the *Mirva* arrived back on land. Andre tells Kathryn that he doesn't want to take the credit for having saved her, because his crew did most of the hard work, and he also tries to nip her flirtation with him in the bud, by telling her that the Maritime Commission has just fined him three thousand francs, because the *Cyclone* returned to shore with a sliced-up tow-line. (Andre hasn't come to the hotel to have sex with Kathryn; he's just come to tell her that her husband owes him three thousand francs.) When she doesn't offer him the money, he leaves the room without ever making a move on her.

Next up for Andre, it's a brief stop at the dockside offices of the *Cyclone's* Owner (Henri Cremieux), who's well-aware that Andre is getting tired of being a tugboat Captain. He doesn't want to lose Andre as an employee though, and so he tells him, "If you leave, I'll sell the *Cyclone* to the Dutch!" (A fate worse than death! Here's another crack about the Dutch, again!) The two men are now interrupted by a call from Andre's wife: Yvonne's physician, Dr. Maulette (Henri Poupon), is now informing Andre, and Andre didn't know this at all, that he's just been over at Yvonne and Andre's house, because Yvonne has suddenly become sick, and that, while her condition isn't too serious at this moment, that Andre should definitely be keeping an eye on her. Needing a break from all of the headaches which everybody he knows seems to be giving him, he now re-assesses his feelings for Michele Morgan's very-sexy Kathryn, inviting her for a stroll along the beach. The two walk together in silence (which is, of course, Jean Gabin's normal state), and Andre smilingly tells her that he can't imagine what possible fun she might be having with him since, by his own admission, he doesn't talk too much. ("So," he asks her, "you like to walk with a silent man?") The answer she gives him seems to be, as far as answers go, just right: "I adore silent men. I love to find out what they're thinking." She mentions also that she still doesn't know his first name, nor, as we find out, does he know hers, and he now tells her that it's Andre; she immediately begins swooning, as though 'Andre' is the greatest name that was ever invented, and to her, it's certainly, right up there with 'Hercules,' or 'Romeo.' As the two continue traipsing along the beach, he indicates a small deserted house, up on a nearby hill, and while he lopes up the hill to see if the place is available for their use, she crouches down in the sand, and writes his name in the sand with her finger.

A few minutes later, Andre and Kathryn enter the hilltop fuckhut which is dark, dank, and dusty, and clearly, nobody's been there for a long time. As it's getting later in the day, the winds can now be heard whistling outside, and she tells him that this hut reminds her of a horror movie which she once saw: "Everybody in the theater was laughing—but I was scared."

They head up into the small house's bedroom, and Kathryn starts batting her eyelashes at Andre, in the sexiest way imaginable. She lunges at him, but he backs off, and she clearly doesn't like the mixed-signals which she perceives he's been giving her. (He walked her into this boudoir, and yet he's not making a move on her.) Even though, only a few moments ago, she told him that she likes his silent-act, she's clearly changing her mind fast, and she now tells him that his non-communication is growing tiresome. She calls him a brute and, just as we expected, her derision works like a charm: Instantaneously, he's all over her, like white on rice, as director Gremillon fades to black.

The next morning, one of Andre's men arrives at the hut to advise Andre that he's needed at the docks and right now, because another boat is in trouble. Andre rushes through town to get to the docks, but when he arrives at the *Cyclone,* Tanguy tells him it's too late: A Dutch tug has already beaten Andre to the rescue. Instead of returning to the hut to be with Kathryn, he stops-off at his own house: It's breakfast time, anyway, and sometimes, all men are more hungry than they are horny. Yvonne's now in bed, looking very ill and, for the first time—and it's probably the illness which is probably making her talk like this—she lets it all out to him about how, while she'll always love him (even though he doesn't seem to care for her), that she absolutely hates everything relating to boats and boating, and that she's been wanting to tell him this for years. She tells him also that she's aware, because word travels fast among the local Boat Wives, that he's been spending a lot of time, of late, hanging-around with Kathryn, and she's jealous, because she's heard that Kathryn's a strong woman, while she herself, and this is something she knows about herself, is, of course, weak and sickly: "You only like strong things, Andre—strong things, like yourself. I remember when you first began working on the *Cyclone.* You caressed it!" Yvonne knows that Andre responds best,

With Madeleine Renaud.

not to real women, who often, like she always does herself and like she's doing right now, make demands on him, but to the quiet and respectful femininity of boats, and this is very similar to how, in *La Bete humaine,* Gabin's character, Jacques Lantier, responded best to the quiet, docile femininity of his train, *Lison.* Of course, Yvonne's outburst spurns Andre on, into this film's one, big Gabin-Outburst, and based upon what he's now saying, we can see that Andre is in total denial about his wife's condition: "Stop this nonsense! You're not ill!" (Is he kidding? She's so gaunt, she looks like she's only seconds away from death.) We can figure out, fairly easily, that he's just yelling at her out of anger, and that he really knows how ill she is. We know also that he's not really mad at her, but at himself, because he's afraid of her death, and he's also embarrassed, even though he can't, or won't, yet admit it to himself, about how he's been treating her, or precisely, how he *hasn't* been treating her, for years. She then throws him out of the house, acting tough toward him for what is probably the very first time in her entire life, and we can tell that he respects her for doing that very much.

In the next scene, Andre heads onto the *Cyclone,* where his crew has been discussing him in his absence, and he just so happens to have come in during their discussion of him, so he's heard the tail-end of it: "Andre is fed up. And you can't do anything for somebody who's fed up." He bypasses his friends and, not even saying hello to any of them, enters his cabin and plops himself down on his bunk, where he remains totally inert and coiled up like a cobra, for what, as we'll soon learn, is two solid days.

After two days of silent soul-searching, Andre wanders back to the hilltop beach- house, his "stabbin'-cabin" where he last saw—and did a whole lot more with—Kathryn. She happens to be there already, and she's been waiting for him, and probably, she never left: Since she's not with her husband anymore, presumably, she's been unable to return to her own home. A storm begins pounding-down outside of the hut and they begin to kiss and, as they do, she starts making-with some great, poetic Jacques Prevert-penned dialogue—"I love lightning. It strips you naked without hurting you. So can you, Andre..."—which is followed, of course, by a bout of frenetic off-screen sex. Kathryn is about as secretive, and as quiet, as Andre is and, post-coitally, she's now telling him that she has a secret nickname—one which she invented for herself when she was a child, 'Aimee.' Andre finally opens-up to Kathryn, telling her that, at this present moment, he's very happy, and that he never wants to leave her, and he adds, also, that for the entire two days in which he was sitting alone in his cabin aboard the *Cyclone,* he was thinking about nothing but her. Since he's happy right now—at least, he is happy at this very moment—we know that it won't be long before Fate, just like in lots of other Gabin flicks, is going to be throwing him a major curveball and, in fact, that curveball is going to be coming right now, because 'post-'their sex,' Kathryn now tells Andre that she's going to be going away, in order to think her life out, and she doesn't know if she'll ever return to Brest. She hands him a starfish and tells him that if he ever finds happiness in his life, that he should, as a 'sign' to her, chuck it into the sea. (See! That's why Gabin's movie-characters never open themselves up to women too much: Whenever his characters allow themselves to experience feelings toward women, they always wind up getting hurt. *Damn feelings!*) And right after she gives him this bad news, the couple gets visited by one of Andre's men, who informs Andre that he's needed at home right away, because Yvonne, his sick wife, is very close to death. He leaves Kathryn, without a word.

When Andre arrives home, Dr. Maulette is in the room with Yvonne. She's now, very obviously, only seconds away from her appointment with the Grim Reaper, and Andre is suddenly heartsick, feeling horrible about having ignored her for most of the years of their marriage; and as she lays there dying, he's now realizing, for the very first time in years, that he really does love his wife, after all. He apologizes to Yvonne profusely, telling her that he's sorry for the way he's always ignored her, and he adds that the only reason he never paid too much attention to her, is because he didn't realize just how sick she really was. She tells him that she forgives him, and that she's always known, deep inside, that he loves her just as much as she loves him, and that any words that he may have spoken to her in anger "don't count." She tells him that she's going to be able to die happily now, because she knows that he's always been faithful to her; in this, the final stage of her illness, it appears that she has forgotten what she already knew all too well, which is that he has been cheating on her with Kathryn. Andre suddenly looks like the guiltiest guy on earth; in fact, he looks like he wants to hurl himself out of the window, and fast.

Kathryn dies. And while Andre is just as taciturn as are any other Jean Gabin Movie Characters, Andre now bursts into tears, and he next primal-screams that same pre-human cry which we have already heard him unleash at the end of *La Bete humaine,* during that moment in which he threw himself from his own train; it's a howl of piercing anguish, a scream which seems to indict the whole misbegotten world with its sheer ferocity and magnitude. The *Mirva's* doctor and Andre's friend, Kerlo (Fernand Ledoux, Roubaud from *La Bete humaine*), next interrupts his boss's mighty angst-spill to inform Andre that the *Cyclone's* just received an S.O.S, and that there is another boat which must be saved— ironically, it's a Dutch vessel, called *The Hollander*—and right now. But forget that noise: Right now, we're looking at 'a human S.O.S.' and his name is Andre, and from where we're sitting, he's the only lost ship which needs any real saving.

As Andre runs through the storm by night, as fast as his legs can carry him, on his way toward the *Cyclone,* we can hear the distress signal of the lost boat which the *Cyclone* has just been enlisted to save, and it sounds a whole-hell-of-a-lot more like the scream which we've just heard emanating from Jean Gabin's mouth, than it sounds like the clarion-call of a seagoing vessel. Director Gremillon combines this haunting tableau, which he has chosen to film completely in long-shot, with a totally bizarro-world sound collage: As Andre runs, he's accompanied, on the film's soundtrack, by the moaning incantations of an unseen church congregation, a congregation which scream-chants—just like in all of those 1970s horror-flicks like *The Omen*—"I render you unto him, who formed you from clay! Free Us Lord! FREE US LORD!" When Andre finally boards the *Cyclone* and looks around, it's empty. There's nobody on board but him, all alone in the night, and in the thick evening mist. (In fact, the movie was released in Great Britain, as *Misty Wharves*.) He looks like he's might start crying again but, instead, he just heads back to work. While Fate has decided to let one of Gabin's movie characters live for a change, this might not be such a great thing, because his soul has died—Yvonne took it with her, when she passed on. While, usually, Jean Gabin is a hell of a man, at the end of *Remorques,* he's a shell of a man, because right before our eyes, in this scene, he has become a hollow-eyed, living corpse. In the film's very last shot, the *Cylcone* sails away into the dark and foreboding mist. In this movie, all of the star-crossed lovers are tugboats, each one trying to grasp the bigger ships which are just out of their reach.

Remorques is another fantastic Jean Gabin movie from his matinee idol/tragic drifter period, and it's a film in which all of the greatest elements of Poetic Realism really come together very beautifully, from Gremillon's haunting pictorial sense of doom, to co-author Jacques Prevert's simple, yet profound, dialogue. But the first time I saw the film I was unimpressed, because the version which is presently available on American DVD, Mad Hat Video's DVD re-release of Nostalgia Home Video's 1990's VHS release, is MGM's seventy-six minute American-release version, which had been shortened by sixteen minutes and poorly dubbed into English (which way over-simplifies the dialogue, situations, and characters). Further, MGM's truncated version of *Remorques* eliminates most of Jean Gabin's sense of contriteness about how he treated his wife, and it also makes his character seem like a real jerk, which the character, very clearly, is not. In 2005, however, there was a bit of good news to be had for this author, because the Los Angeles County Museum of Art presented a restored/ digitally re-mastered 35mm print of the uncut, ninety-one-minute French print of *Remorques,* with English subtitles, and there at LACMA, for the first time, I was able to see the film in its pristine, uncut state, and it is this restored ten extra minutes of film which makes *Remorques* into an entirely different, and fantastic, viewing experience, a film which is, finally, just as powerful, moving, and entertaining as were Gabin's previous Poetic Realism/Tragic Drifter classics which, of course, include, *La Bete humaine, Le Jour se leve,* and *Le Quai des brumes.* In the uncut French print of *Remorques,* we truly feel Jean Gabin's pain, as well as his soul-consuming guilt about the fact that he feels that his wife's death has been 100%-his own fault, and it's strange that MGM decided to cut-out much of the movie's essential, character-explaining material. While the uncut version of *Remorques* is not available on home video in the United States, it is available in Europe, in French-only and with no English subtitles or dubbing, either separately or as part of a three-movie boxed-set which also includes two other restored Gabin classics, 1931's *Pour un soir..!,* and 1939's *Le Recif de corail.* Until the day that *Remorques* gets a good, uncut DVD release in the US, it's such a great movie, that it might almost be worth it for you to learn French, just so you can see it.

Jean Gremillon filmed most of *Remorques* in 1939, completing principal photography on August 28, 1939, but the picture was not ready for release in France until 1941, for two very specific reasons: First, Gabin had a bit of re-shooting to do, but he suddenly became unavailable to the perfectionist Gremillon because, on the first of September of '39, Hitler, of course, invaded Poland, and the French, believing that they would be invaded as well—and how right they were—initiated the draft, and Gabin was suddenly conscripted into the Navy, for a period of six months. (Of course, Gabin had already served in the Navy for one year, back in 1924, when he was twenty years old.) And even after Gabin was released from his patriotic duties in the early spring of 1940, and was therefore able to participate in the needed re-takes, Gremillon also hadn't yet filmed the rainswept rescue of the *Mirva* which we see in the picture's first third, because he was waiting for 'just the right storm.' Since the terrifying deluge which he desired never presented himself, the director finally just filmed what is, very obviously, two toy boats, floating in a storm-tossed bathtub, and it is to the filmmaker's credit, as a master film-stylist, and also as a master of dark and foreboding movie atmosphere, that he actually made the scene work.

The following very humorous nugget comes from MGM's pressbook for its American release of *Remorques,* which the studio re-titled as *Stormy Waters:*

"The famous Gallic star Jean Gabin has a failing that is little known off studio lots: He likes his eyes to photograph blue. While he was filming MGM's latest French release, *Stormy*

Waters, Gabin would look, daily, at the shots which had just been taken and he was very worried that his eyes would not 'photograph blue.' [Author's Note: The film is in black and white.] One day he made his anxiety known to the cameraman, a tough boy of the old school. 'You want me to make your eyes blue?' the cameraman said, to Gabin. 'That was your father's concern!'"

What a Critic Said at the Time: "A true story of human motives and emotions due to French genius for honest realism." (Los Angeles *Times*, 7-21-46 issue.)

What Another Critic Said at the Time: "Jean Gabin turns up in a familiar waterfront part... [His wife] gives him up because he's a niggardly oaf... Might be worth your while, just for the fine views of the Breton beaches." (*New Yorker* Magazine, 7-6-46 issue.)

What Yet Another Critic Said at the Time: "[*Stormy Waters*] is a French film, deftly acted and directed. Jean Gabin gives his man strength, covered by gentle humility. The volcanic emotional force of Michele Morgan is held in effective restraint." (New York *Times*, 7-8-46 issue.)

❧

THE FILMS
CYCLE THREE

Gabin Goes to America and Makes Two Films.
Hates the Experience. (But the Films are Good.)

FILM Nos. 32 AND 33, 1942 — 1944.

JEAN GABIN ALWAYS SWORE THAT HE WOULD NEVER LEAVE FRANCE AND MAKE movies in America. (Why would he leave, when he was France's #1 star of the mid-to-late '30s?) But when Hitler invaded France in 1940, Gabin and many of his fellow filmmakers left their country, to work in the United States. Jean Gabin would star in only two American-made/English language features in his entire career,1942's *Moontide* and 1944's *The Impostor*, and both of these pictures were made during this cycle. In these films, the American producers copied the formula which made his French films so successful: In these American pictures, Gabin is a tragic drifter, ruled by fate, who has committed a crime before the movie started and is who fated for the customary bad end. While *Moontide* and *Impostor* are both very good movies, they were not hits when they were first released, and are both unknown today in the United States, even though they're both American movies. Gabin wasn't happy working on these productions, mostly because the American screenwriters gave him more dialogue than the normally quiet actor was used to, and after *The Impostor*, he returned to France, never to return to America again (not even for a vacation...).

With Ida Lupino.

FILM 32

MOONTIDE

USA, 1942

(USA, 1942) Directed by Archie Mayo and (uncredited) Fritz Lang. Produced by Mark Hellinger. Screenplay by John O'Hara and (uncredited) Nunnally Johnson. Based Upon the Novel by Willard Robertson. Produced by Mark Hellinger. Directors of Photography (black and white), Charles G. Clarke and (uncredited) Lucien Ballard. Editor, William Reynolds. Music by David Buttolph and Cyril J. Mockridge. "Remember" (Song) Composed by Irving Berlin. Production Designers, Thomas Little and James Bassevi. (GENRES: DRAMA/ROMANCE/FILM NOIR) AN AMERICAN FILM, IN ENGLISH. Running Time, 1 hour 34 minutes. Produced and Released in the United States by the 20^(th)-Century Fox Film Corporation, on May 29, 1942, Released in France by Fox as "PENICHE DE L'AMOUR" ("TIDE OF LOVE)" in 1946.

"When you find a girl like that you hold on tight, my friend, because
you may never find another."
—Jean Gabin offers this advice to another character, but should really take it himself,
in "Moontide"

The first of Jean Gabin's two American-made pictures, which are two of only three films in which the actor would ever speak his dialogue in English (the other two being 1944's *Impostor* and the English-language version of 1969's *Le Clan des Siciliens*, which was filmed twice, in both French and English) is producer Mark Hellinger's mesmerizing production of character actor/writer Willard Robertson's best-selling 1940 novel *Moontide*, which was made for 20^(th) Century-Fox in 1942. *Moontide*, an amazing picture, is credited to Fox's house-director Archie Mayo, although several of the best sequences were, in all actuality, helmed by an uncredited Fritz Lang, who quit about three weeks into the film's production, because he felt that the mood on the set was too dour, owing—among other things—to the fact that two weeks into production, the Japanese attacked Pearl Harbor; and Lang, of course, was the incredible, visionary German filmmaker behind both *Metropolis* and *The Testament of Dr. Mabuse* and he, like many Europeans uprooted by Nazism, including Jean Gabin, re-located to Hollywood during the Second World War.

In *Moontide*, Gabin's charismatic French sailor, Bobo (in the original novel, the character is an American, and his name is Swede) has, as the film begins, run away from his native France, and is drifting around the mythical Southern California port-town of San Pablo, a place which exists only in this film, and which is clearly meant to replicate the port town of San Pedro. (The studio originally intended to film much of the movie in Los Angeles Harbor, but after the Japanese invaded Pearl Harbor a few weeks into the film's production, studio head Daryl Zanuck moved shooting onto the set, at Fox's Los Angeles Studios.) The filmmakers don't say it, but Bobo has very clearly committed a crime in France prior to the beginning of the film, since that's what usually leads a person to flee his home country in favor of finding a safe haven somewhere else; of course, screenwriter John O'Hara, aided by an uncredited Nunally Johnson, recognized this trope as being one of the most important parts of the already-successful, tried-and-true Jean Gabin Movie Formula from Gabin's great, French-made Poetic Realist classics of the mid-to-late thirties.

We're at the Red Dot, a local boat bar, where salty seamen mix-it-up with zany barflies, including a Panama-hatted Brit called Nutsy, played by Claude Rains in the one of the films which he'd make right before his legendary turn as Captain Renault, opposite Bogart and Bacall, in *Casablanca.* Nutsy is a man who will serve as our film's *veddy well-spoken* voice-of-reason, a poet—at least he claims to be one—who's fallen on hard times and who, like Bobo, has washed-up, very literally, on the beaches of California. (The Second World War displaced a lot of people, and turned many more into drifters, especially in movies from the 1940s, like Humphrey Bogart's 'Rick' character in *Casbalanca:* Rick is the ultimate drifter, an American who, as you already know, bummed-around the world, before settling in Morocco and opening his storied barroom.)

Bobo enters the Red Dot with his rucksack, which holds all of his worldly possessions, placed squarely over his square shoulders, his faithful bulldog Gus by his side. Bobo instantly catches the eye of a red dress-garbed bar-babe Mildred (Robin Raymond) and, just as in some of the other pictures which Jean Gabin had made recently in France, he now interests her by feigning disinterest. ("You like me, huh?" he asks her, coyly.) The only person who isn't pleased-as-punch by this interchange is Mildred's surly boyfriend Mac (John Kelly), who lingers in the background watching the seduction, getting pissed-off at seeing this Frenchman moving-in on his lady-love. ("You know, we can make a plan to get rid of your Mr. Mac," Bobo whispers to Mildred, conspiratorially.) Mac, who is unable to stand it any longer, takes a swing at Bobo, and peace-loving Bobo, in self-defense, and just like Gabin did in some of the pictures which he made prior to *Moontide,* beats the stuffing out of Mac, then feeling instantly remorseful about the pummeling which he's just doled-out: Jean Gabin always manages to behave like a complete gentleman in all of his pictures, even when his characters are drunk out of their gourds, and his Bobo-character now apologizes, profusely and sincerely, to the other man, for having just decked him. This moment is very similar to the one when Gabin's character felt guilty for decking Pierre Brasseur's gangster Lucien in

Le Quai des brumes, in fact, much of *Moontide* seems to have been copied from *Le Quai des brumes,* especially its whole dark, foggy, *noir*-ish atmosphere.

Mildred next leaves the bar with Mac, and Bobo spends the rest of the evening getting spectacularly *faced*, in an eye-popping, proto-David Lynchian-drunk montage, which was inspired, but not directed, by the great surrealist painter Salvador Dali, who was initially hired to helm this sequence, but who quit because some of his images would have been too expensive to reproduce on film. In this 'Daliesque' montage, Bobo sits and drunkenly eyeballs Mildred and, from Bobo's tanked-up POV, Mildred's head keeps bizarrely popping on and off her torso, a torso which remains seated atop the stool, while its owner continues—without a head, no less—spouting a stream of nonsense ("The guy told me to leave... the guy told me to stay... the guy told me to leave... the guy told me to stay..."), all of which is interspersed with shots of a clock's spinning hands that are fashioned out of liquor bottles, and other shots in which a Chinese sea-merchant named Takeo (Victor Sen Yung) chants, "Drink! Drink! Drink! Drink!" over and over again. At this point in the action, we fade to black and, needless to say, so does Bobo.

The next morning, a deeply hung-over Bobo awakens in the hull of the bait-barge which belongs to another Chinese, the good-natured Henry (Chester Gan). Henry apparently brought the passed-out Bobo back to his barge the night before, and Bobo's first news from Henry, when he wakes up, is that, apparently, somebody killed the Red Dot's favorite old barfly, Pop Kelly (Arthur Aylesworth) the previous night, and relatedly, that the police are now searching for the killer: During Bobo's 'drunk montage,' we saw a fist punching an old man's lights out, but it happened so fast, we didn't see who belonged to the fist, nor, for that matter, did we see who the old man was. Bobo can't remember a single thing about the previous evening and, as he's now opining to Henry, the killer could very well be his (Bobo's) likable but unstable traveling buddy, Tiny, whom we'll be meeting very shortly. (Tiny's played by the great American character-actor Thomas Mitchell, a stocky, 'Hoss-like' guy who was equally adept at playing both scheming heavies and sub-moronic goofballs. Mitchell combines both of these traits into the volatile character he plays in *Moontide,* and he's really great in the picture, in spite of the fact that Gabin was initially opposed to his hiring.)

The Bobo/Tiny friendship is often fun, but sometimes terrifying: Tiny, a lumbering oaf who's not very 'good with people,' follows Bobo from port to port, using his charismatic French pal to help him secure the occasional dock-jobs upon which both men subsist. Bobo and Tiny—basically, they're Laurel and Hardy, without the laughs—genuinely like each other, but we're going to be finding out, also, that Bobo can't get rid of Tiny, who's not as 'duh/aw-shucks-oafish' as he first appears to be: Tiny is 'Bobo's Conscience,' a guy who's holding something over on Bobo, and harboring some of Bobo's darkest secrets, secrets which Bobo doesn't even know about himself, because they all pertain to things which Bobo did and then forgot about, when he was drunk. Tiny makes it eminently clear to Bobo, in more than once scene in this movie, that if Bobo stops taking him along for the ride, he'll be turning Bobo in, for some of those crimes. The Bobo-Tiny relationship is one of those parasitic-friendships which we've already seen in *Pepe Le Moko* and *La Bandera*, those earlier pictures in which, although Jean Gabin's buddy genuinely likes him, it's very clear that the same buddy would have no compunction about turning his Gabinian pal in, to the authorities, in exchange for gaining the cool notoriety which such a bust would inevitably bring; Tiny is what we, today, refer to as being a 'toxic friend,' or per t.v.'s "*Seinfeld*" a 'frenemy'—one of those people who's 'part friend, and part enemy.'

Later that same morning, Bobo pays a visit to Tiny, who's been staying in a nearby flophouse, and he's immediately treated to the wacky tableau of Tiny, who happens to be towel-whipping Claude Raines' Nutsy, and when this happening, both Tiny and Nutsy are in their underwear! Nutsy is clearly grateful to Bobo for rescuing him from the sting of the towel. (This is a scene which contemporary critics always cite as depicting 'repressed homosexuality,' but it does not. It's just a weird/offbeat/funny scene that kind of hits you sideways—as does most of the movie.)

Night falls again, and soon, Nutsy's on Henry's barge with Bobo, and the two of them are getting properly pissed on gin. Suddenly, they spot a lone figure as it's dropping into the Pacific: It's Anna, and she's played by the British actress Ida Lupino who, at the time this movie was made, was already one of Hollywood's biggest stars, based a few of her previous pictures which were very popular, including *The Light that Failed*, *They Drive by Night*, *High Sierra*, and *The Sea Wolf*. Anna is a troubled young woman who's trying to drown herself and Bobo, without even thinking about it (mostly because Jean Gabin is always a man of instinct) runs out into the tide to rescue her; and when an Irish Cop, who's played by Forrest Dillon, shows up to arrest Anna—he's charging her with 'attempted suicide'—Bobo charms them: "She wasn't trying to commit suicide. She was just wading!" The Cop buys Bobo's story whole-cloth, and takes off without arresting Anna, and apparently, according to the film's production notes, Lupino had gashed her leg very badly on a sharp boulder while shooting this sequence.

Bobo and Nutsy take Anna back to Henry's barge to recuperate. Obviously, Anna's attracted to Bobo right away, but she's already been hurt in love—and numerous times, as she'll reveal—and she tells him, defensively, that she doesn't "…want anything from you—or from other man in this world, for that matter." Bobo plays it cool, as per usual for Gabin, telling Anna that she doesn't have to worry, because he doesn't plan on getting personal with her, either. And of course, like all women characters in Gabin movies right after they've first met him, she immediately, and in spite of what she's just said to the contrary, begins telling him her whole life's story.

The following morning, to thank him for saving her, Anna cooks Bobo breakfast. She's in a much better mood than the night before, so it's pretty easy to figure out what happened between the two after the previous scene faded out: Gabin and Lupino share some pretty heavy lip-lock throughout *Moontide*, and apparently, their chemistry impressed studio head Daryl Zanuck so much that—at least according to 20th Century-Fox's pressbook for the movie—when Zanuck saw the rushes, he approved an extra $100,000 and an extra fifteen shooting days, solely for the shooting of additional love scenes; according to Fox's official pressbook, Gabin enjoyed playing these steamy scenes, however he drew the line when director Archie Mayo asked him to kiss Lupino's hand. "There'll be no hand-kissing in my pictures," Gabin wrote in a letter to Zanuck, and the letter continues, "This idea of 'a Frenchman making love' exists only in Hollywood. The French detest the gigolo type of Romeo, as much as do the Americans!"

Playfully, Anna tells Bobo that he should try and take a guess about why she tried to kill herself. Jean Gabin's not a big game-player though, and Bobo just Gabin-Shrugs, telling her that he doesn't care, although we already know that, in spite of his 'loner façade,' which is calculated to keep him from getting hurt, he really does: "Listen, you're a nice girl. You made me ham and eggs. That's enough." Smiling, he even re-christens her with a cute little nickname, 'Sunny-Side,' based upon the way in which she's prepared his eggs. Since we've already seen *La Bandera* and *Le Quai des brumes,* we know that Bobo's falling head-over-heels in love with Anna, against his better judgment and that, as usual, it will soon be time for to leave, before he falls in love and gets hurt. Bobo now tells Anna, in the umpteenth rendition of the speech which Gabin has already made in lots of his movies:

> "All my life, people attach themselves to me. But I don't attach myself to anybody. I'm free. I am not a man who can stay long in one place. I am a gypsy!"

But Bobo is falling for Anna, and hard, in spite of his strong, Jean Gabinian isolationist policy, and he admits as much to Nutsy later that day, when Anna's not around: "All my life, I knocked around the world. Then I met Anna." Nutsy, quite easily, talks Bobo into remaining in San Pablo—at least for awhile—and one way we can tell that Bobo and Anna are in love because many times in the film, when we see them in their bait-barge love nest, their scenes together are underscored by a piece of diegetic film music which plays over the bait-barge's radio, the lilting "Remember," by Irving Berlin.

Goofy Tiny soon lopes up onto the barge, asking Bobo when he thinks the two of them will be leaving for a highly paid—three dollars a day!—dock job, in San Diego. Bobo, who would now rather hang around with his newfound lover Anna, tells Tiny (and politely, since he doesn't want Tiny to start any problems with him), to get lost, and Tiny, who's jealous of Bobo's newfound relationship with Anna, suddenly shifts, on a dime, from his 'aww, shucks/cartoon bear-mode,' into his' psycho-mode,' reminding Bobo, "One word from me..." Devious and over-dramatic, Tiny, in this sequence, does everything except draw his finger beneath his own throat and make a slicing sound.

The days pass, and Anna—she's a drifter just like Gabin's characters usually are—is now staying with Bobo on Henry's barge, while Henry's off working somewhere, and the two new lovers now tart prettifying the barge, which Henry has told them they can live on for as long as they want to, with pretty curtains—and yes, the two have even agreed to marry.

That night, while Bobo's out drinking at the Red Dot, Toxic Tiny barges onto the barge once again and tells Anna—and we don't yet know if this is true—that it was Bobo who killed Pop Kelly the previous night. Anna doesn't believe Tiny, and she instructs him to get lost. Tiny's rejoinder: "If you don't leave Bobo, and let me and him go down to San Diego together, I'm going to tell the authorities that Bobo killed Pop Kelly!"

A bit later, when Bobo returns home from 'tying one on' (Tiny has already left the barge), Anna tells him about the confrontation she's just had with Tiny, and Bobo gets plenty mad about it but changes the subject, because he wants to tell her something new about himself: He tells her that, even though he was drunk the night Pop Kelly was killed, and even though he knows that he sometimes forgets things when he's tanked, he's absolutely sure that he didn't kill Pop Kelly, although he also admits to Anna, in the same breath, that he has taken human life in the past, but only in self-defense, or only in the defense of other people, and this is probably why he had to leave France and find a new host country, just like Gabin's characters in *La Bandera* and *Le Quai des brumes*. He confesses to Anna that, when he was a young man, he choked his own boy-cousin to death, because said cousin made fun of his father. ("My father: He was a criminal, but he was still my father. I had strong hands, when I was young. They brought me jobs and money—but they also brought trouble.") But Anna, and we the audience, already understand Bobo's essential goodness, and this confession of his makes her more intent on marrying him than ever before. She tells Bobo that they should pay Tiny to go away, so that they can be alone and, surprisingly, Bobo, albeit only very half-heartedly, now defends Tiny, even though weak-willed Tiny would definitely screw Bobo over in a New York-Minute: "Ahhh, Tiny isn't bad." Bobo reassures Anna. "He's just weak."

Meanwhile, back at the Red Dot, a local radio broadcast lets us know that Pop Kelly's strangler is still at large; amiable Charlie the Bartender (William Halligan) and the bar's usual crew of lushed-up customers know that the killer couldn't possibly have been good-old Bobo and that, even if Bobo was the killer, which they all doubt, that it doesn't matter anyway, because they all know, instinctively, that he's a good person. (A flaw in *Moontide's* screenplay, is that these same exact patrons were at the bar when Pop Kelly was killed, so you would think that at least one of them would know whom the murderer was, unless they were all so drunk, that they just weren't paying attention.) Charlie tells his gathering of chess-playing lushes, "I like Bobo, whether he's good or bad. Heck, we're all bad!" At that moment, Tiny lumbers into the bar and discovers, from eavesdropping on what Charlie's just been telling his patrons (because he's caught the tail-end of it) that Bobo and Anna will be marrying the following day. Tiny feels jilted, just like a spurned lover, and he now morphs into his cartoony, 'Droopy-the-Dog- mode,' groaning, "Awww, nobody asked me to come to the wedding. Geeee, I'm Bobo's best friend;" all that's missing from his pathetic statement, is a plaintive cry of, "Gawrsh, Mickey!"

Finally, Bobo and Anna's wedding day arrives, and all of the normally-slovenly barflies, whom we've already met, arrive at Henry's barge, all dressed-to-the-nines, and all ready for a classic Hollywood Movie-Wedding, and interestingly, for fans of pop-culture, the Reverend who marries Bobo and Anna is played by none other than Ralph Byrd—*Dick Tracy* from the Republic serials. (Yes, it's true: In *Moontide,* we've got Pepe Le Moko and Dick Tracy together, in the same scene!) Only moments after the nuptials have ended, Bobo tells his guests that he has to leave for awhile, because he wants to help a good-natured local M.D./ *bon-vivant,* Dr. Brothers (the Broadway stage actor Jerome Cowan), repair the engine of his clunky old motorboat. While Bobo's away, and after all the guests have gone home, Tiny bursts onto the barge, and thrashes Anna within an inch of her life, which places her in the hospital, only millimeters away from death.

Angered for the first and only time in the picture, Bobo now meets Tiny on the pier, getting the large man there, most probably under the guise that the two men will soon be leaving for the San Diego job, and it's a dark and stormy night, right out of the most frightening of German-Expressionist thrillers. "Come here, Tiny," Bobo angrily chants, over and over, staggering toward Tiny, his hands nine times more clenched and outstretched than Boris Karloff when Karloff played Frankenstein's Monster; even though Tiny's easily got a hundred pounds on Bobo, Tiny's still deathly afraid of him (Hell has no fury like Jean Gabin scorned), because Bobo looks positively demonic, and as Bobo continues inching toward Tiny, Tiny accidentally backs off of the wave-engorged pier and drowns himself, and his body instantly gets swept away by the unforgiving moon-tides. This sequence was pretty obviously directed by Fritz Lang, which means that it was filmed near the beginning of the picture's production schedule: Unlike the rest of the picture, which was shot pretty traditionally, with the exception of the brief Salvador Dali-inspired montage, this scene is Total German Expressionism: Bobo chases Tiny over the pier, which is dotted with weirdly-placed giant anchors, and the scene has been photographed at weirdly-distorted, not to mention extremely disorienting, angles.

Since Hollywood movies pre the 1960s, unlike French movies, always needed to have happy endings, Anna, of course, pulls through her ordeal with a clean bill of health (although the 'Anna' character dies in Willard Robertson's original novel upon which the film was based), and while she and Bobo will live happily ever after, their movie would not: After it's brief, and not too successful North American theatrical release in 1942 (a few great reviews [see below] but mostly lukewarm ones and small audiences) the film mostly disappeared for more than fifty years; I, myself, had a hard time tracking down a print when I began writing this book in 2002, but ultimately, this story has a happy ending: In 2006, the film was digitally restored and 're-premiered' on the U.S., on Fox Movie Channel, and in 2008, its reputation beginning to grow, it was issued on DVD for the first time, accompanied by insightful commentaries which are provided by *noir* authorities Eddie Muller, Foster Hirsch, and Alan K. Rode. Thanks to the Fox Movie Channel, the DVD, and a few recent, 35-milimeter screenings at the Los Angeles Museum of Art and the American Cinematheque in Los Angeles, *Moontide* is now being re-discovered as one of the great 'lost classics' of the 1940s, and viewers are finally able to get an eyeful of Charles G. Clark's (and an uncredited Lucien

'*The Wild Bunch*' Ballard's) gorgeous black and white cinematography, in fact, at the 1943 Academy Awards, Ballard's cinematography for *Moontide* was even nominated in the category of 'Best Cinematography, Black and White,' but Ballard lost out to Joseph Ruttenberg, who shot director William Wyler's mega-popular Blitzkrieg-set classic, *Mrs. Miniver.*

After *Moontide* wrapped production in February of 1942, 20th Century-Fox felt that it was about to have a big hit on its hands—ultimately, of course, it didn't—and the studio immediately announced that its second Jean Gabin production would be screenwriter Talbot Jenning's re-imagination of a 1923 silent film, director W. W. Hodkison's *Down to the Sea in Ships*, a nineteenth-century whaling story set in New England. Gabin didn't care for that script, nor did he have much use for any of the other ones which the studio presented him, including *The Night the World Shook*, an adaptation of French author Steven Wendt's novel, *Eight Hundred Convicts Marched on Caraibo.* Adapted by *Moontide's* uncredited co-screenwriter, Nunnally Johnson, *World Shook* would have dealt, according to a studio press release, with "convicts who sacrificed their own chance for escape, to rescue people in an earthquake-stricken city." Ultimately, however, Daryl Zanuck grew so impatient with watching Gabin turn down one script after another, that he released Gabin from his contract, leaving the actor free to make his second and final American film, *The Impostor*, for Universal Pictures.

MOONTIDE FUN-FACT #1: *Moontide* wasn't the first 1942 movie in which 20th Century-Fox would replace superstar-director Fritz Lang with it's house director Archie Mayo: According to the autobiography *A Third Face*, which was written by the legendary American B-movie director Samuel Fuller, Fritz Lang was also hired by Fox to direct one of Fuller's early screenplays, *Confirm or Deny*, just a few months earlier, but he was replaced by Mayo on that picture, as well.

MOONTIDE FUN-FACT #2: Who was Jean Gabin's first choice to direct him in *Moontide?* According to author Todd McCarthy's 1997 book, *Howard Hawks: the Grey Fox of Hollywood*, it was Howard Hawks, who wasn't actually available when the film was made. Fox's president, Daryl Zanuck agreed with the Hawks idea, because he wanted Hawks to mold Gabin into 'a new Spencer Tracy' or 'a new Clark Gable.'

MOONTIDE FUN-FACT #3: Nearly three years after *Moontide's* theatrical release, the film was given a second life, when it was adapted as a radio drama, featuring a big American star: On April 12, 1945, CBS Radio's very popular Lux Theater Program presented a one-hour re-creation of *Moontide*, featuring Humphrey Bogart as the sailor (in the radio version, the main character is American instead of French) and Virginia Bruce as Anna. The radio program is available on an out-of-print LP, issued in the 1980s on Sandpiper Records in the U.S., and it's pretty amusing, not only because it gives us an opportunity to hear a different take on the *Moontide* story, but also because the broadcast is narrated by Mark Hellinger, who produced both the film and the radio program. The radio version is just as worth checking-out as the film is, not just because it's good, but also because, at the end of the story, Bogart and Bruce both step out of their *Moontide* characters to *shtick-it-up*, playing heightened versions of 'themselves,' as follows: VIRGINIA BRUCE [joking about how, off the set, Bogart was an avid sailor]: "Glad you could get off that boat long enough to join us here in the studio, Bogey!"

What a Critic Said at the Time: "Not since [John Ford's] *The Informer* has a motion picture looked so deeply into the consciousness of the world's peoples. Jean Gabin is a strong dramatic star who dominates the film, and you can *make book* that he will be the rave of woman patrons, and men will not resent the idolatry of a shock-haired, barrel chested, he-man. The occasional acting tricks in which Jean Gabin engages have the eloquence of Gallic expressiveness and never appear studied. Producer Marc Hellinger provides [the picture] with memorable atmosphere and sincerity. It is not rubber-stamp movie making. Archie Mayo's direction is an accomplishment of first water, masterful [and] expert, in its timing." (*Hollywood Reporter*, 4-17-42 issue. Critic: A. May.)

What Another Critic Said at the Time: "William Robertson's best-selling novel of eighteen months ago has been brought to the screen by Fox as an American introduction vehicle for the French actor Jean Gabin. It serves that purpose admirably. Gabin, known as an 'earthy player' in France, is given just that type of role in *Moontide*. Much of the success of the film hinges on reaction to Gabin [and he] is a pleasing and able player. His English is good. It's easily understandable and with just enough accent to be quite pleasant. Director Mayo has cinematographer Charles C. Clark have given the film A-1 production trappings." (*Variety*, 4-22-42 issue. Critic: "Herb." Reviewed in New York.)

What A Third Critic Said at the Time: "The strapping masculine charm of tough Jean Gabin, [a man who is] often called the "Saint of French Pictures," is now being wholesaled to American audiences by 20th Century-Fox in this, the actor's first Hollywood venture... and you might get the impression that the film was made, mainly, to show him off. He has a lot of masculine 'oomph,' and is obviously one of the best 'slap 'em and kiss 'em' actors in the game. Seldom has an actor's frank allure been quite as deliberately dished-up. You might think the lights and camera were working on a glamorous female star, from the way [the filmmakers] are concentrating on Mr. Gabin's roughly-handsome phiz [physiognomy]... Again, Mr. Gabin is playing a tough guy, a social misfit, a chip on the stream of life as it swirls and eddies through the lower depths. His use of the English language is intriguing to the ear. Jean Gabin is Charles Boyer from the other side of the tracks." (New York *Times*, 4-28-42 and 5-8-42 issues [combined]. Critic: Bosley Crowther.)

With Ellen Drew.

FILM 33

THE IMPOSTOR

USA, 1942 [Released, 1944]

(USA, 1942) Directed by Archie Mayo and (uncredited) Fritz Lang, Produced by Mark Hellinger. Screenplay by John O' Hara and (uncredited) Nunnally Johnson. Based Upon the Novel by Willard Robertson. Produced by Mark Hellinger. Directors of Photography (black and white), Charles G. Clarke and (uncredited) Lucien Ballard. Editor, William Reynolds. Music by David Buttolph and Cyril J. Mockridge. "Remember" (Song) Composed by Irving Berlin. Production Designers, Thomas Little and James Bassevi. (GENRES: DRAMA/ROMANCE/FILM NOIR) AN AMERICAN FILM, IN ENGLISH. Running Time, 1 hour 34 minutes. Produced and Released in the United States by the 20th-Century Fox Film Corporation, on May 29, 1942, Released in France by Fox as "PENICHE DE L'AMOUR" ("TIDE OF LOVE)" in 1946.

"I have no memories. I live, just the same."
—*Typically-Gabinian Fatalism, in "The Impostor"*

Julien Duvivier's *The Impostor* is the sixth of seven films which the great, stylistic filmmaker would direct with Jean Gabin, after *Maria Chapdelaine, La Bandera, Golgotha, La Belle equipe*, and *Pepe Le Moko*, and it also happens to be the second of Jean Gabin's two, back-to-back, English-language/American films which the actor would make in the U.S., for an American studio in this case, the film was made for Universal Pictures—and it's also one of the first movies, made anywhere in the world, which depicted the up-to-the-minute exploits of General Charles de Gaulle's Free French Army. Filmed under the title *Passport to Dakar, Impostor* is an entertaining war story, and one which is made even more compelling by one of Gabin's great, tragic-drifter performances, although admittedly, the film's story and dialogue tend to be a bit pulpy, corny, and bordering on soap opera—something which you'll never find in Gabin's French pictures over which, even during the earliest years of his career, he had always exerted quite a bit of control.

The first several minutes of the film are going to disorient you, because the characters, who are all meant to be French, are played, with the exception of Gabin, by American actors, and all of them speak their lines in typically-American, regional accents, which include

'Midwestern' and 'Brooklyn,' and they speak in that peculiarly American, 1940s slang. But once you suspend your disbelief a bit, you're going to have a fine time with this one: *The Impostor* is just as good as *Le Tunnel*, that other picture in which Gabin and the other French actors were supposed to be Americans, or *Le Recif de corail*, in which Gabin and the other French actors were supposed to be Australians. In other words: It's a bit weird but, for the most part, it works.

The film opens during the German invasion of France on June 14th, 1940 (France surrendered to the Germans, in real life, about a week later). In many of the films which Gabin made prior to this one, his character is usually a man who has committed a crime before the movie started, one who knows that his time on earth is limited; in this film, we've got pretty much the same formula; but in *The Impostor*, he won't be having the usual Gabinian fun-with-a-brunette before his inevitable demise, although the film's advertising materials, which find him embracing the film's beautiful dark-haired supporting player Ellen Drew, give the erroneous impression that it will.

As the film begins, Gabin's character, a civilian by the name of Clement, is in a lonely jail cell in Tours, France, awaiting his execution for having killed a policeman outside of the factory in which he works. He is roused from sleep and taken, by guards and by a Priest (Fritz Lieber), to the guillotine. The Priest tells him that he "must have courage," and he is informed that he has not received his requested stay-of-execution, however Clement, in the typically-resigned Jean Gabin fashion, doesn't even care—in fact, he just Gabin-Shrugs. The Priest asks Clement if he thinks he's lived a good life, and the world-weary guy just mutters something along the lines of not being afraid to die, because he has never really lived.

"God is in all men," the Priest continues, as the guards ready themselves to move Clement toward the beheading machine, and just after the prelate has told Clement some poetic happy-crappy about how "the earth is sweet," and right before he is executed, Fate—and it's Kind Fate this time out, as opposed to the Horrible Fate which usually befalls Gabin's movie characters—intervenes, and in a much showier way than it usually does in the French Gabin pictures: In the very millisecond before he is killed, unseen German bombers, which we can hear overhead, begin bombing the prison, and almost everybody present at the execution site—all of the guards, and even the Priest—is instantly killed… all except for Clement, who climbs out of the rubble, completely unharmed. The only other blast-survivor, a policeman, sees Clement emerging from the rubble, and is about to 'take him out' with his pistol when, suddenly, part of the wall comes crashing down on the cop's head, killing him, as well. Clement, who narrowly escapes danger at every turn, is, it would seem, incredibly reminiscent of another Frenchman from an American movie, Peter Sellers' inimitable Inspector Jacques Clouseau—except, without the bumbling and the levity.

As Clement wanders over a long stretch of highway, we see fancy automobiles full of French and Belgian citizens fleeing *en masse*, because they are trying to avoid being killed by the Krauts, and we also see a sea of pricey cars, many of them Rolls-Royces and Bentleys— which is eminently strange because, during the War, those brands of automobiles simply did not exist in France. Clement flags down a military truck full of French soldiers—they're New York-accented and speaking in English—who have recently lost the other members of their units in various skirmishes, and he asks them how far the Germans have progressed into France. They reply that the Teutonic invaders have already arrived in Bordeaux, in the country's southwest.

And then—and you're not going to believe this, but it really happens—a German plane suddenly bombs the French truck! All of the French soldiers die instantly (at least, we think they do), but Clement survives. Yes, in fewer than ten minutes of screen time, Jean Gabin's character has actually survived three bombing incidents. Gabin's French films never trade in such cheap plot devices, and the natural reaction of any viewer of this film—even a viewer who, like this author, really happens to enjoy the picture—is along the lines of, "Ummm...I don't think so..."

Clement, fearing that he'll be apprehended, now decides to assume the identity of one of the French soldiers who was just killed in the current explosion, a fellow named Sergeant Maurice Lafarge. Thinking quickly, Clement strips the deceased Sgt. Lafarge of his I.D., and switches clothing with him, *Le Quai des brumes*-style, so that anyone who comes upon the vehicle and reads the dead man's dog-tags will believe that Clement is dead and, because of that—he thinks—nobody will be looking for him. (Philippe Bardet, one of this author's researchers on this book, laughed at the name 'Maurice Lafarge,' explaining that 'Maurice Lafarge' is an American screenwriter's cliché of a French name: According to Bardet, naming a French character 'Maurice Lafarge' might be tantamount to calling an American character something really generic, like 'John Smith.')

Now that Clement has a new identity, he's also got a new lease on life, so he heads down to the port city of St. Jean de Luz in the southwest, on the Spanish border, the place from which he intends to leave France. He plans on sailing for somewhere he thinks he will be able to be free to start a new life.

Arriving at the port finally, in a different truck upon which he has managed to hitch another ride, Clement sees a bustle of French soldiers, the last remnants of the newly-quashed French army, who are departing on troop-transport ships, and he asks one of the men where everybody's going, and one of the men he meets tells him that all present are headed for Africa. Now that Marshal Petain's new government has asked the Germans for an armistice, and the French army is therefore about to surrender to the Germans, these men are heading for France's African colonies, where they intend on joining up with Charles de Gaulle's all-new Free French Army of freedom fighters, a crack team which won't be surrendering to the Germans anytime soon. Since Clement's new identity is that of a Sergeant (of course, he is currently wearing the real Lafarge's stripes), all of the men immediately begin looking to him for guidance, especially the milquetoast Monge, who's played by John Qualen, from whom Clement bums a cigarette. If you've ever seen John Ford's *The Grapes of Wrath*, you're already familiar with Qualen, because in that movie, he plays the emaciated Muley Graves, the squatter who stands up to the company tractors. ("This land is our'n... and no piece a' paper with no writin' on it is gonner make it any different!") In this picture, Monge becomes Clement's good-naturedly sentimental sidekick, and when you see the scenes of Gabin and Qualen together in *The Impostor*, you'll notice that the screenwriters were probably trying to recapture the easy camaraderie which was shared by Gabin's sturdy 'Marechal' and Marcel Dalio's wispy little buddy 'Rosenthal,' in Renoir's *La Grande illusion.*

As the men wait to get shipped-off to Africa, they—including Clement—are gathered in a bar, listening to Marshal Petain's real-life speech in which he famously instructed the French people to lay down their arms, and give up to the Germans—"We must stop fighting!" (This speech, which is delivered in the film in English by an American voice-actor, is word-for-word-accurate of Petain's actual French-language speech.) The soldiers in the bar are smart enough not to believe a word of Petain's Tokyo Rose-like propaganda, however. "It's a trick!" one shouts, and another concurs, "Tomorrow, we'll all be in prison, if we lay down like that!"

Clement and the other guys now board the troop transport ship: Their original destination was Dakar, the capital of today's Senegal, but apparently, Petain's collaborationist (Vichy-French) forces control that region, so instead, these soon-to-be freedom fighters are going to change course and join other Free French formations in the Congo. One of the officers on board, Second-Lieutenant Varenne (Richard Whorf), shoots Clement a suspicious look: Does he suspect that Clement really isn't 'Sgt. Maurice Lafarge?' Probably not—probably, he's just looking at him in a funny way because he's not certain that Clement is fully committed to the Free French cause. Another soldier, the effeminate Cochery, who's played by Eddie Quillan (this American actor's character is supposed to be from Lyon, and Eddie Quillan, just like John Qualen, appeared in *Grapes of Wrath*, Quillan having played the role of Rosasharn's husband, Connie), is regaling his friend Bouteau (Allyn Joslyn) with his post-War plans, which include returning to his bank job as a loan officer, in order to help returning soliders purchase homes. (Similarly, in William Wyler's Oscar-winning 1946 drama *The Best Years of Our Lives*, which will be filmed two years after *The Impostor's* release, Frederic March's returning American WWII vet-character, Al Stephenson, is also a loan officer, resuming the same job which he had held before the War.) Cochery tells Bouteau that, as a loan officer, he won't be making loans to show-business people since, as he puts it, "they're the worst possible risks," and he's just saying it to rankle Bouteau, a perpetual schemer who also happens to be, in civilian life, as he's always bragging, some type of a cog in the entertainment world. Cochery and Bouteau serve as the film's comedy-relief, a not-too-masculine version of Abbott and Costello.

2nd-Lieutenant Varenne accosts Clement again, and it turns out that he really has heard of him—or more accurately, he's heard of the man who he thinks Clement is, the real Lafarge, who was a hero of a battle in the Champagne region, during the fighting in France: "I've heard of you! You're Sergeant Maurice Lafarge! You were in the 33rd Battalion! Weren't you guys in Africa?" Thinking fast, in case anyone should happen to wonder why he's not familiar with the terrain when they get to Africa, Clement replies, "Yes, I was in the 33rd, but I wasn't

Left to right, Milburn Stone, Jean Gabin, Richard Whorf.

with them there. But when I was young, I was in Morocco."

Arriving in Pointe-Noir, the port town on the extreme southwestern tip of the Congo in French Equatorial Africa, our hale-and-hearty supertroopers are now standing before the recruiting station of the Free French Army. Some of the other soldiers who've traveled on the boat with Clement ask him if he's going to be staying on with them and joining up with de Gaulle, and while Clement doesn't seem too interested in fighting (he's not a wimp, he's just 'World-Weary Gabin,' and he's tired), he finally agrees to join up, just because, as Richard Gere cried out to the Heavens—or, more precisely, to Louis Gossett, Jr., in *An Officer and a Gentleman*—he has "nowhere else to go." Also, Clement's new friend, Monge, really wants him to come along, and Clement smiles and grins, "Okay. I can't let you down, buddy!" Clement recognizes Monge as being a working-class guy just like he is, and this is why the two get along so well, even in spite of Clement's natural resistance to opening himself up to strangers, including the other men. And while the men are at the recruiting office, signing on the dotted line, Bouteau is trying to convince Cochery to forget about the world of home loans, and to enter the cosmetics business with him when the War is over, since women in Africa haven't yet been introduced to the all-important world of perfumes and face creams. Meanwhile, Monge, who happens to be a farmer in Normandy during peacetime, tastes the earth and proclaims it to be "sweet," an utterance which surprises Clement, because that's exactly the same thing which the Priest told him, right before he was almost executed. (Talk about 'being guided by Fate:' If you're hearing something that specific twice, it's just got to be Fate talking to you, and telling you, "*Monsieur*, this is where you are supposed to be, *n'est-ce pas?*")

Lt. Varenne tells the men that they have an afternoon of liberty, and that they shouldn't wander too far off. A local drunk/ex-pat Frenchman, Joseph Mortemart (John Philiber) introduces himself to Clement and the others, telling the guys that he's been at Pointe-Noir for forty-five years, and that he'd be happy to show them all around, and he's a man who gets paid, as he's now making all of the men understand, in booze. Clement, who's still thinking about escaping, asks Mortemarte if it's possible to escape across the river, but Mortemart tells him that for Clement to set himself up with a plantation, it would take six months of army pay; and this, for the time being, is what convinces Clement to stay, and to fight alongside these newfound acquaintances. While, at first, Clement was interested in purchasing civilian clothes, he's now decided to buy some 'sergeant-appropriate-attire.'

Not only do the men believe Clement to be a real Sergeant, but they all really like him, too, because his effortlessly-easygoing Gabin Personality is keeping the company-morale flying high—they like him in spite of the fact that he's still kind of quiet with most of them, with the exception of Monge. Varenne even announces to Lafarge that, based upon what he's read about the real Lafarge, the man whom he believes Clement to be, who happens to have been a War hero, that he will now promote 'our Lafarge' (Clement) from the rank of Sergeant, to that of Adjutant. (Clement appears to be the 1944 version of *Forrest Gump*, in the sense that things just keep happening to him, things which push him, willy-nilly, all around the globe.)

The new recruits spend the next several days moving inland, arriving finally in the town of Brazzaville (*The Impostor* was actually filmed in Palm Springs and Toluca Lake, California), and as they trek through the jungle, they see the sun bursting through the trees, an elephant, and monkeys hanging from limbs. "We're going to turn this jungle into an airfield," notes Varenne. "We have ten days to set it up. We will have the natives help us to build it, and we'll call it 'DeGaulleville!'" One of the men, a giant, square-jawed Alsatian from Strasbourg, Hafner (Peter van Eyck, a German actor who's playing a Frenchman in the film), is a little pissed-off that he has to be in a jungle, doing construction and operating the outfit's radio, when he'd rather be firmly ensconced in the thick of the battle, killing *boche,* and Hafner is an early prototype of the behemothian Private Posey-character whom Clint Walker would play in Robert Aldrich's 1967 pop-culture WWII classic, *The Dirty Dozen*. Hafner explains to the others that Germans killed not only his grandfather, in the War of 1870, but also his father, in 1916's Battle of Verdun, and that now, because of it, he wants to take his revenge on every single German he can find. "You'll fight, in time," Varenne tells the sometimes-gentle giant, calming him.

In no time, Clement and the other men in Varenne's unit have filled the jungle with a beautiful landing strip, some huts, and even a makeshift hospital, and in spite of the fact that he's a loner-at-heart, Clement is the consummate delegator: He's the one who's issuing the orders, just because the men are expecting him to, and they all do bang-up jobs; he's a calming, level-headed, father-figure to all of the men in the unit—even to the men who are his own age.

Monge knows that Clement, whom he, of course, knows as 'Lafarge,' prefers, like most of Jean Gabin's movie characters, to be alone a lot, so he tries to make Clement feel comfortable, by inviting him into his hut and showing him pictures of his own family, and even pointing out a copy of his income tax return, which he's posted in his tent to nostalgically remind of him of "back home." (It's a very funny joke on the part of the film's screenwriters: "I must be alive... I pay taxes!")

One evening, Cochery, Bouteau, Hafner, and Clement are sitting around a large hut which they've built, as torrential rains pour outside, and this entire scene is played-out against the off-screen rhythm of jungle drums, and the weirdest thing about this drumming, is that it happens to be rock-and-roll drumming. (It's that familiar '4/4-time' backbeat which we thought was invented in the 1950s and '60s, and it is actually showing up here, in a movie from the early 1940s—which proves, incontrovertibly, that Jean Gabin movies invented rock-and-roll!) Referencing the drums, Cochery opines, "It's not Mozart—but it is savage... and beautiful," and Bouteau interjects that he wishes the natives would "change the record." Clement begins pacing around the hut, while the other guys begin reminiscing about their lives back home, and he then, very brusquely and unapologetically, when they ask him to recount some of his own experiences, tells them that he has absolutely no memories of his entire life, and this is a very telling line for a perennial drifter played by Jean Gabin. Very calmly, Monge begins painting a verbal picture of how great Christmas day always has always been on his farm in Normandy, and he next begins describing the torrents of hot chocolate, presents, and children which always make the day so memorable. Bouteau opines that he likes Christmas better in the city. ("Forget the country! The best thing about Christmas, is being in the city, in a smoky dance-hall, the band giving out best tunes [and you've got your best girl by your side!]") This outpouring of what Clement feels is, most assuredly, advanced cretinism, sends the up-until-now pretty-quiet Clement into a Total Gabin-Outburst: "Cut it out, all of you! I'm tired of your stupid memories! Why don't you turn off your own records?"

Clement storms back off into his own hut and lies down on his cot, when Monge enters. Monge wants Clement to enjoy himself, so he shows Clement a small photograph of his wife's sister, whose name, as he's now telling him, is Jeanne-Marie. Clement likes the dog-eared little photo, so Monge makes him a gift of it, placing it up on the wall of Clement's hut for him. (Monge, who's basically a well-meaning simpleton, tells Clement, sweetly, "Now, you can pretend that you two know each other!") That night, Clement tries to get some sleep, but Lt. Varenne, who looked to be a bit ill in the previous scene, is becoming delirious from malaria, and he begins hallucinating that Germans are attacking him. Varenne gets up, runs outside the tent and, in the middle of a fever-dream, begins shooting wildly at his own men, believing them to be Teutonic, and he even shoots Monge in the leg. Coming to Monge's rescue, Clement knocks Varenne out, before the out-of-his-mind guy gets the chance to fire upon anybody else.

"Adjutant Lafarge, we appreciate your services," Varenne crows the morning after, when his sickness has subsided, not remembering that he previously shot Monge. In fact, all of the men like Clement, whom they believe to be Sgt. Maurice Lafarge, so much, that they all bestow beautiful, handmade upon him—after all, it's Christmas Eve. Cochery gives Clement some bedroom slippers; Bouteau presents him with a tie; Monge, the farmer, gifts him with large, red apples; and the big-galoot Hafner—by-golly, his heart is as large as his over-sized body!—even gives Clement a pendant with a little good-luck four leaf clover inside of it. The men are finally breaking through Clement's stoically-steely resistance, and he's genuinely touched by their kindness, and he picks this moment to smilingly admit, "Nobody ever gave me anything!" In fact, he's so moved by the guys' generosity, that he is now enjoying the company of others for what must be the first time in his life, and he even decides to give them something nice in return: He joins the others in setting up, a re-creation of one of the Normandy Christmases which Monge had so eloquently described, replete with a makeshift fireplace and gifts.

Within days, Clement is promoted again, for having successfully completed construction on the landing strip, and this time, he's being promoted from the rank of Adjutant to that of Second-Lieutenant, which makes him equal, in rank, to Varenne. Varenne tells Clement (a/k/a, 'Lafarge'), that he's delighted in the change which has come over him in the four months since Clement's been serving with them, and Varenne next proceeds to speechify (the speech is overwritten by the screenwriters, but it's definitely well-meaning): "You used to be 'for yourself,' Lafarge. But you've fallen in love—in love with France, although, right now, we're thousands of miles away from her. France is a beautiful woman, and if you give her an even break, she'll never let you down." Clement is so inspired by this speech, a speech which is inexplicably peppered with American slang, that he hustles over to Monge, and throws an arm around his shoulder, sentimentally telling Monge that he is his "best friend."

Five weeks later, Clement, Hafner, Varenne, Cochery, and Bouteau—all of the men except for Monge—are issued orders by another officer, Second-Lieutenant Menessier (he's played by that foremost film noir tough guy, Charles McGraw) to head three thousand miles north, to Fort-Lamy in Chad, where they will be bivouacked, en route to fighting in Libya at the true-to-life Battle of Koufra (1941), in which they'll be serving under General Philippe Leclerc. In the Battle of Koufra, the Free French Army defeated the Italian army in its very first victory, and in our film, something sad will come out of it: Good old Hafner will be killed. On Clement's return to DeGaulleville, Lt. Varenne promotes Clement, yet again, for his battle-courage—still, of course, believing him to be Lafarge—this time, to the position of First-Lieutenant, so that now, he actually outranks Varenne. In the ensuing sequence, the

Free French soldiers at DeGaulleville all drink a toast to the Americans, for, as Bouteau says, "giving us plenty of what we need." (*The Impostor is* an American movie, so naturally, America is depicted as being the primary supplier of the Free French Army, when actually, at the time when this scene would have taken place, in the spring of 1941, it was the British who were the primary source of assistance to the Free French. Relatedly, in the same speech, Bouteau also toasts another ally, Russia, and this is another historical revision on the part of the screenwriters, because Russia, in the spring of 1941, was not only *not* an ally of the Free French, but it was still allied with France's Nazi enemies, and would continue to be, until Hitler's invasion of Russia, on June 22, 1941.)

At this point in the narrative, a visiting Free French Colonel, de Boivin (Ralph Morgan), issues Clement the Croix de Guerre medal for the real Lafarge's earlier heroism in France, and even though Clement has been genuinely quite heroic in Koufra, he feels guilty when he learns that the decoration is not for his heroism, but for that of another man. And it won't be long before Clement, who is riddled by guilt, finally confesses his true identity to the one person whom he trusts the most, Monge, because, on a not-so-subconscious level, Clement wants Monge to tell the other men that he is an impostor, and he wants to be punished for pretending to be another man. He tells Monge, "I'm not the real Lafarge, you know. The real Lafarge is dead. A German bomb killed him. I stole his name. I'm a fugitive from justice. I killed a man, but I saw my chance to be free." Clement believes that it's time to pay for his masquerade, but the thing is, he doesn't really have to: He's already gotten away with his charade, scot-free. Like other Gabin Movie Characters—or, more accurately, like the ones we've been seeing since around 1935—Clement wants to get caught because, from his French, pre-existentialistic point-of-view, Lady Fate is supposed to deal all of us hard blows and, if she doesn't—well, then, she's just not doing her job.

The next morning, all of the soldiers wake up in their huts—in fact, the two effeminate guys, Bouteau and Cochery sleep right next to each other in a little tent of their own—when suddenly, they see a beautiful and impeccably dressed Frenchwoman, and she's walking right toward their hut! (How come she's dressed-to-the-nines and sporting a perfect Hollywood hairstyle and perfect, Max Factor makeup in the jungle humidity?) They are so excited to see a real woman (inasmuch as they can be; Bouteau and Cochery are masculine only in the sense that, say, Clifton Webb was masculine), that they begin frenetically combing their hair and grooming themselves like apes, and Bouteau gets so excited, he even cries out that he is excited because this new arrival is a white woman, and not a black woman—which is rare in the Congo. (You'd never hear a line like that in a movie made today.)

This newly-arrived woman is Yvonne (Ellen Drew, a very good Hollywood studio actress who passed away in 2004), and she tells Bouteau and Cochery that she's come to Brazzaville to see her fiancé, Lieutenant Maurice Lafarge, because she heard that "he" was heroic at Koufra, and she had lost track of him before. The two guys take her over to Clement, whom they, of course, continue to believe to be the real Lafarge. Clement has just awakened, and when Yvonne sees him, she is appalled, knowing immediately that this man is impersonating her lover. Clement first pretends that it's just a coincidence, and that just accidentally does he share the same moniker as her boyfriend, but she's not buying it: She knows he's an impostor, and she now alerts him that she's going to be notifying military authorities about him. When she storms out of Clement's hut in a huff, Monge pleads with her not to report Clement, telling her that even though what Clement did is wrong, that Clement is truly a great man, a true friend and a natural leader to all of them, without whom they would have been killed. Monge even tells Yvonne that Clement has "taken their burdens and made them light," which sounds like something Jesus might have done. (It's similar to that bit in *La Grande illusion,* in which Gaston Modot's engineer-character is washing Gabin's feet.)

Dissolve to later that day: Clement heads into the infirmary to get some healing quinine, and when the infirmary's newly-hired nurse turns around, she, of course, turns out to be Yvonne—in one day, she's magically shown up in the jungle and taken a job! He now tells her the complete and unvarnished truth, in yet another of the movie's great, and overly-florid but truly poignant, speeches: "I won't apologize for taking your fiance's identity because, when I did, my life started. I never had a life before I became Maurice Lafarge. I grew up, alone. Hungry. In orphanages. No friends. Always wandering. No place to go. Nowhere to call my own. [When I took your fiancé's papers and 'became him,' suddenly, I had a purpose in life.] For the first time, I had friends. And now, for the first time, I even have memories. So you can turn me in, if you want to—I don't care." Yvonne is touched by Clement's heartfelt 'whatever happens, happens' speech, a soliloquy which encapsulates that whole Jean Gabin Drifter-Persona we've come to know and love, all into one neat—although, admittedly, way too verbose—monologue.

Within days, there's celebration at an officer's club in Fort-Lamy, honoring the various units of victorious Free French soldiers—both the men from our own little group, as well as other men from companies which we haven't seen. Two men from other companies are presented with medals for their victories at Damascus and Tobruk and Clement is honored for his bravery at Koufra. And now, here's a bit of a rub: One soldier in attendance, a guy named Clauzel (Milburn Stone), happens to have been a good friend of the real Maurice Lafarge, and he knows that this man, who's receiving Maurice Lafarge's medals, bears no resemblance to his friend. Clauzel seeks out Varenne in Varenne's office and tells him that Clement isn't really Lafarge, and Varenne tells him that he's already figured that out, but that he's not interested in hearing it, because Clement, the man whom he knows as Lafarge, is the most valiant and brave soul he's ever met. At that moment, Clement himself walks into the office and confesses to being an impostor, himself.

Clement, very contritely, will also confess his true identity to the sympathetic Colonel de Boivin, the man who awarded him the Croix de Guerre. He tells de Boivin that he didn't want to receive honors which were made out in the name of another man, but that he had to, because otherwise, his cover would have been blown.

The next scene is a military tribunal, headed up by de Boivin. Varenne, who is defending Clement, stands up and makes a heartfelt speech before the tribunal, pursuant to how

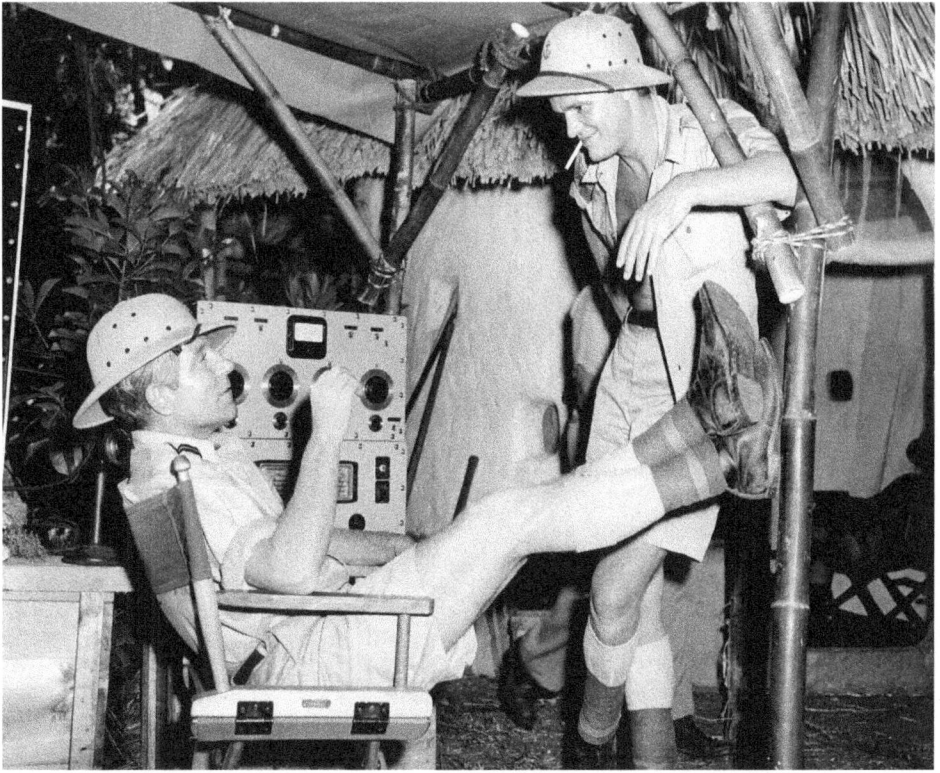

With Peter van Eyck.

fantastic a person Clement is, a speech about how, even though Clement was using another man's name, the courage which Clement demonstrated at the Battle of Koufra was genuine, and that, therefore, Clement's decoration was very well-deserved, no matter what name he received it under. "We all would have died, if not for this man," Varenne stirringly rhapsodizes about Clement. "He has no fear of life or death, and he has looked after all of us like a father. If this man was a scoundrel, then he's been reborn in discipline. He masqueraded as another, it is true. But, in this masquerade, he has served his country, well. No matter what sentence you pass, this man is, in my opinion, more than worthy of sharing the name of Maurice Lafarge." Varenne adds that Clement is actually honoring the real Lafarge by receiving honors under the other man's name, and he is glad that the two men's identities are inextricably linked forever, because both men are heroes.

While Colonel de Boivin respects Lafarge's heroism and leadership just as much as the rest of the men do, it is still upon him to pronounce sentence, which he does with some reluctance. Clement is taken outside to the parade grounds, where he is stripped of his Lieutenant's stripes and court-martialed to the rank of Private, Second Class. After the ceremony, Boivin tells Clement that he may remain in the Free French Army under another name—any name of his choosing—but Clement basically tells him that, in this cold and random world, names are utterly meaningless. De Boivin, as part of pronouncing sentence on Clement, next sentences Clement to serve in the most dangerous part of the front lines, but he tells Clement that he won't have to go it alone: "Four men with whom you have served [here in Africa] have requested to be sent to the front with you. I congratulate you on having such dedicated friends." People will actually die for their good friend, Gabin; in this movie, as in many of Jean Gabin's French movies, the friendship and brotherhood of men is the strongest and most regenerative force in the world.

The Impostor ends with one last pitched-battle, a battle which, according to a title that's superimposed over the action, is taking place, "Before the Last Oasis of the Fezzan, in March of 1942." Clement is sent to the front lines with Varenne, Cochery, and Bouteau. He crawls through the brush alone, sneaks through the trees, and 'takes out' an entire foxhole of Germans with a grenade, just as they are riddling him with bullets. He falls forward, dying on-screen. (Cut to nine years after *Impostor* was released: It is now 1953, and Jean Gabin is asked, by the great French suspense-film director, Henri-Georges Cluzot, to play one of the leading roles in the internationally renowned suspense classic, *The Wages of Fear*. Gabin refuses the role, telling the film's producer that he cannot accept it because the characters he plays must never die on-screen. There is obviously another reason Gabin doesn't want to appear in this film, however, because his characters do die on screen, not only in *The Impostor*, but also in *La Bandera, Pepe Le Moko, La Bete humaine, Le Jour se leve, Le Quai des brumes,* and dozens of other films in which the actor will appear throughout his lengthy career.)

The Impostor's final scene takes place a bit later: Monge, the farmer from Normandy, walks alone in a graveyard, and he comes upon an unmarked grave. This, of course, is the grave which belongs to Clement. "Sleep well, my friend," good-hearted Monge tells Clement, as the film fades to black.

While *The Impostor's* patriotic dialogue and speech-making are a bit over-wrought (Gabin's French movies never had this much dialogue, and it's a big reason why Gabin preferred making movies in France, where he felt that filmmakers really knew how to present him) it is, nevertheless, a very entertaining Gabin adventure, in which Julien Duvivier proved that he could fashion just as great of a war movie in the U.S. as he did back home in France, which is where he and Gabin made *La Bandera* together, in 1935. After *The Impostor*, Gabin and Duvivier wouldn't team up again for another fourteen years, until 1957, which is when the two of them would reunite for a bizarre and wonderful film noir together, *Voici le temps des assassins (Time of the Assassins)*.

In the five year period during which I wrote this book, the American motion picture *The Impostor* was unavailable for me to see in America. Universal Pictures, in Los Angeles, had an archival print, which they were unable to show me, due to what they deemed to be its unprojectable condition; as a result, I had to go to France, in 2004, to view a thirty-five millimeter print, supplied by the French Ministry of Culture, at the screening facilities of the Cinematheque Francaise. (Yes, it's true: I had to go all the way to France, to watch an American movie!) In 2007, the film was finally restored digitally, and released on DVD in

France (the original English-language print, with removable French subtitles) but, as of this printing, it is still not available on home video in America—the very country in which it was made. But since *Moontide,* Jean Gabin's only other American film, was finally released on DVD in 2008, after decades of being considered 'M.I.A.,' hope springs eternal.

What a Critic Said at the Time: "Jean Gabin benefits by a strong, dramatically-impelled story of the Free French in Africa. The pic is the first in which the Free French have, in any measure, been depicted. A well-balanced vehicle for Jean Gabin's personal talents... *The Impostor* offers Jean Gabin a forceful opportunity for a top characterization. He underplays and makes the part believable and the spectator is, at all times, sympathetic." (*Hollywood Reporter*, 2-4-44 issue. Critic: A. May.)

⚜

THE FILMS
CYCLE FOUR

Gabin Returns to France and Makes Films.
The Public is not yet ready to embrace him, as they did before the War.

FILM Nos. 34 TO 46, 1946 — 1953.

IN 1942, JEAN GABIN FILMED THE ONLY TWO AMERICAN PICTURES HE WOULD ever make, *Moontide* and *Imfpostor,* and between 1943 and 1945, he returned to France, where he served in General Charles de Gaulle's Free French Armed Forces.

Between 1946 and 1953, Gabin tried to make a comeback in France, appearing in twelve films: Some of these pictures were just as fantastic as ones he made in France before the War, while others were merely 'pretty good' (and a very few are even 'not that good'). But whether the pictures Gabin made during this cycle of his career were brilliant or not so brilliant, French audiences just didn't up to see them, feeling that Gabin had deserted them when he'd moved to Hollywood. Plus, while Gabin was still extremely handsome during this post-War period, his hair had, in the four years in which he's been away from the camera, gone suddenly white, and he'd also put on a bit of weight, which made him look avuncular.

In a few of these 1946-to-1953 films, Gabin continued to play his tragic, working-class drifters, who were fated for bad endings, but in most of the films (not only during this new cycle, but also for the rest of his career) he would now be playing a new kind of character externally, albeit one who exhibited the same quiet, somber persona which had been a hallmark of his mid-to-late 1930s' movie characters: He would now begin playing *bourgeois* businessmen, smooth criminals, and cops. (In other words: The clothes were fancier, but the quiet, world-weary persona was the same.)

A number of the films which Gabin would make during this period were co-productions between France and Italy and, in fact, throughout his later life, Gabin would often refer to this period, in which the Italians loved him more than the French did, as "my Italian campaign."

FILM 34

MARTIN ROUMAGNAC

France, 1946

Directed by Georges Lacombe. Produced by Marc le Pellitier and P.E. Decharme. Screenplay by Pierre Very and Georges Lacombe. Based Upon the Novel by Pierre Rene Wolf. Director of Photography (black and white), Roger Hubert. Editor, Germaine Artus. Music by Giovanni Fusco and Marcel Mirouze, Featuring the Tzigane [Gypsy] Orchestra. Production Designer, Georges Wakhevitch. (GENRE: ROMANTIC DRAMA) An Alcina Production. Running Time, 1 hour 55 minutes (in Europe). Released in France on December 18, 1946, by Gaumont/CPLF. Released in the United States (NYC-only) on September 3, 1948 (at 1 hour 20 minutes) with English Subtitles by Lopert Pictures, as "THE ROOM UPSTAIRS."

"Your music is dripping into my soup."
— *Gabin doesn't like a violin player hovering over him at a fancy restaurant,*
in "Martin Roumagnac"

While it's weird enough that most of Jean Gabin's great genre pictures aren't known in the United States, it is completely inexcusable that *Martin Roumagnac* isn't known in the U.S., not just because it's a great, gripping, and intense melodrama, but mostly because in this picture, Gabin would co-star for the one-and-only-time in his entire career alongside the actress who has always been considered to be one of the hugest international movie stars in the world (including the U.S.) his real-life lover, Marlene Dietrich. (The pair would be together off-and-on, in Europe and in the United States, between 1941 and 1946, and Gabin would remain, according to Dietrich in her autobiography, "The great love of my life.") While all of Dietrich's films continue to enjoy extreme popularity in the United States, *Martin Roumagnac* has never really been a known commodity in North America. Briefly, back in 1948, two years after the film made its bow in France, it was barely released in the U.S., at only one New York City art-house theater, by the now-defunct-for-decades B-picture distributor Lopert Pictures, a company which cut the film by thirty-five minutes and retitled it as *The Room Upstairs*. Marlene Dietrich's character in *Martin Roumagnac* is a prostitute, a profession which the censorious American Hays Code could simply not abide in 1948, therefore in Lopert's truncated American-release version, according to sources from the time the film was released, all references to the fact that Dietrich's character *hooked* for a living were, apparently, excised. (This must have rendered the American release print senseless, because the entire film is about prostitution.) *Martin Roumagnac*, in its complete version, is just as great as any of Dietrich's other pictures which cinephiles around the world have always enjoyed and treasured, and if you've ever loved any other great Dietrich movies, such as *Der Blaue Engel* (*The Blue Angel*), *Morocco, Desire,* or *Shanghai Express,* you'll love *Martin Roumagnac,* as well.

Martin Roumagnac constitutes an important part of the Jean Gabin canon for another reason (besides 'the Dietrich factor'), which is that it possessed, at the time it was made, the largest budget of any of Jean Gabin's starring-role movies. Probably owing to the fact that international mega-star Marlene Dietrich was involved with *Roumagnac,* Gabin was second-billed in the film's opening credits, even though the film has been named for the character *he* plays.

After taking a four year break from making movies to serve in the French military (Gabin's last movie, Julien Duvivier's *The Impostor*, was filmed in late 1942 and released in 1944), here, in *Martin Roumagnac,* we would find him yet again playing the proletarian drifter, the character which he customarily played before the War, although he now looks physically different than when we last saw him in *The Impostor,* because the War, not to mention all of the *great food* which he ate after the war was over, had seriously aged him: In *Martin Roumagnac,* Jean Gabin doesn't look four years older than he looked in *The Impostor*—he looks ten or twenty years older. And even though he's definitely still handsome, this is the first picture in which the actor's formerly-blonde hair is now snowy white, and where he's packing on a little bit of paunch.

I'm going to be spending a little more time talking about *Martin Roumagnac* than I am about the other movies in this book, not only because *Roumagnac* is more densely 'plot-heavy' than are Gabin's other pictures (read: more stuff happens in it), but also because it's historically important, being that it is cinema history's sole on-screen team-up of Marlene Dietrich and Jean Gabin.

The uncut print of *Martin Roumagnac* was finally, and for the very first time, released on home video in France, in 2004, without English subtitles or dubbing, and this DVD represented the first time the picture had been seen, even in France, the country of its production, for more than fifty years, because Jean Gabin himself demanded, very famously, that the movie be taken off the market. There has always beeen a great deal of speculation among Gabin fans about why Gabin didn't want the movie around, and many believe that it was probably because Dietrich and Gabin were, by each of their own, individual admissions, the one great love of one another's lives, and the film obviously reminded Gabin too much of Marlene.

The film, which was lushly photographed in black and white by the cinematographer Roger Hubert, takes place in the bucolic French provinces, and it opens at the bird-and-feed store owned by Ferrand, who's played by a terrific French stage actor, the stocky and always-disheveled-looking Daniel Y'd, a guy who, like his countryman and fellow Gabin co-star Michel Simon, bears a rather striking resemblance to Charles Laughton.

As the film begins, a little boy enters the shop asking for Mr. Ferrand, and Ferrand tells the kid that he's not the Ferrand for whom the store is named, nor is he even 'Ferrand Junior' ('the other Ferrand's son'), who took over the shop when the original Ferrand passed away. Jean Y'd's Ferrand is a completely different Ferrand, and weirdly, as the character will point out in the film several times, he's no relation to the original owners, who were named Ferrand, as well—it's just a coincidence. After the kid leaves, a handsome and well-dressed young man enters the store, and he's played by Daniel Gelin, one of France's first of the new, post-War matinee idols, a guy who would also become Jean Gabin's very good friend in real life. Gelin's character has no name: He's simply called *Le Surveillant*, which means 'surveyor,' but it also means, in slang, 'secret lover' or 'secret admirer.' (Gelin, who was reportedly a troubled man in real life, bears more than a passing resemblance to that very good American film actor, Farley Granger.) Ferrand tells the Surveyor that he's from Australia, and he even indicates Australia, by tapping the ground ('down-under,' get it?) with his foot. At this point, the Surveyor begins trying to bond with him, by telling him that he's not local to these parts, either. Then, a third guy, a dandy with a mustache, enters the store (he looks a lot like the American matinee idol Melvyn Douglas), and this third-guy and the Surveyor have something in common: They've both come into the shop searching for Blanche Ferrand, a woman who continues to live, and work as a prostitute, in the store's 'Room Upstairs,' which is the title, of course, of the film's truncated American version.

The dandy is disappointed that Blanche isn't in—anyway, at least Ferrand is telling the guy that she's not in. Apparently, Blanche and the dandy had scheduled an appointment for today, and upon hearing that she's not on the premises; he looks like somebody's just shot his dog: "What do you mean, she's not here? She knew I was coming! How could she have gone out?" Ferrand now elucidates a bit further, telling the disappointed-looking john that Blanche is "out, shopping," and the guy angrily snarks-back, "Ahhhh! Women always want to shop!"

As I've already mentioned, Daniel Gelin's young Surveyor is still there, in the shop. He has never met Blanche in person, but knows her by reputation, which is why he's shown up today (like everybody else in the movie, he too wants to be with her), and since Blanche isn't around, he's now deciding that, so that the day shouldn't be a total loss, he'll just buy a bird. (What a novel idea for a pet store: Come to buy a bird, and stay for sex with Marlene Dietrich!) Ferrand tells the Surveyor that he's welcome to buy as many birds as he wants to, because he can't stand having them around: "They're dirty and noisy. They're just a whim for my niece. We used to sell only [garden] seeds here, but no—my niece thought we should also be selling birds!" (Of course, it's always good to have caged birds in a film because, as *On the Waterfront*, *Birdman of Alcatraz*, and *The Shawshank Redemption* have all taught us, caged movie-birds always represent 'freedom,' or else freedom's redheaded stepchild, 'lack of freedom'.) While Ferrand has, in this scene, just claimed to be Blanche's Uncle, we'll find out, much later in the picture, that the true nature of their relationship isn't exactly what he's claiming it to be.

As it turns out, Blanche has really been here in the shop the whole time: She wasn't out shopping at all, in fact she was really just upstairs shagging a customer senseless, and not just any guy, but an incredibly-frightened-looking guy who now emerges from the bedroom with her and proceeds to haul ass out of the store as fast as he can, not wanting to be seen in the company of *une prostituee*. (Illicit stuff is always fun—until we get caught!)

When Blanche sets eyes upon the young and handsome Surveyor, who's still present, she's intrigued. Just like the Stella-Marie-character who toyed with the young Jean Gabin in 1931's *Pour un soir..!*, Blanche now asks the Surveyor, suggestively, what he would like, and too shy, initially, to talk to her, he just points to a pair of white songbirds—birds which coo away, as though they're meant for each other. (The Surveyor's just met Blanche for the first time, but we can see in his eyes that he already believes that she should be 'meant' for him—and not just for an hour, either!) "Songbirds are a species which can only live by twos," Blanche lectures to her newest young admirer, alluding to her own need to always have men around, but the Surveyor only wants one of the songbirds, in spite of the fact, as she's now telling him, that the two birds would die, would they ever to be separated. As she rings up his purchase, convincing him to take both of the birds (and he's not that hard to convince, since he's been *thinking with his schmeckle* ever since he got there), she tells him again that it distresses her, when she has to "separate the lovebirds." Well, needless to say, he's so instantly smitten by her (and nervous around her) that he *almost* leaves without paying for the birds, and then, after he finally *does* pay for them, he leaves the store empty-handed. (It's obvious to Blanche that this guy is going to be very easy for her to toy with.)

Later that night, Ferrand and his 'niece' Blanche are upstairs, swigging down some post-prandial coffee, while Blanche is busily hemming a dress. Ferrand asks her if she's still dating the wealthy Consul, a guy whom she's been seeing off-and-on because, in addition to whoring herself out, Blanche also happens to be the sometimes-mistress of a moneyed (not to mention, married) French Consul, a guy by the name of Laubry. "When I call him," she explains disappointedly to her 'Uncle,' "his wife always answers the phone." Undoubtedly, Blanche is just hanging with Laubry for his money because, later in the film, when we finally get to meet him, we'll see that, in both the looks and personality departments, *this guy's no bargain*. Blanche wants to leave the little feed store/whorehouse and relocate somewhere else—somewhere (anywhere) where she'll be able to make a fresh start: "Everything here is so small," she opines of her little town, "and everyone is so narrow-minded." She craves a big life (and why shouldn't she? She's Marlene Dietrich, and she's way too bigger-than-life to be here in a small town, *selling out her coochie* for a few dusty *sous*). Ferrand tells Blanche to be happy, because the shop is their 'front.' ("It's our façade—our appearance of respectability.") Blanche has been selling herself out of the store's upstairs room for two years now.

Director Georges Lacombe next gives us an interesting optical wipe, in which Blanche pushes open a closet door, and with this push, we also wipe to the inside of a smoky boxing arena. It is here that we will first meet Martin Roumagnac (Jean Gabin), a scrappy working-class fortysomething, whose friend and co-worker Paulo (Marcel Peres) sits on his right side, watching the grueling match with him. Martin's there today in support of his favorite local boxer, Dupuy (a 'lightweight'), while Paulo favors Dupuy's opponent. "Your boy is done! He's cooked," Martin razzes his pal. "He's good for nothing!"

Blanche enters the boxing ring: No doubt, she frequents the club, selling something a little more enticing than peanuts and popcorn, and the sight of such a regal-looking woman in such a low-rent dive instantly causes all of the working-class audience members to stand up and take notice (literally), especially one dark-haired high school-looking boy who elbows his friend: "Hey, you! Check out what just came in!"

There's an empty seat available on Martin's left, and Blanche asks him if it's taken. Not paying attention to her, because he's more interested in the fight, he mutters (without paying any attention to her) that the seat is free, but when he finally does deign to look over at her, he's instantly smitten, just like every other guy in the movie, and she looks relentlessly amused by the insane degree to which all of the guys in the place seem to be loving this stupid/brutal boxing match. Then, suddenly, she looks distressed because, whether this is true or not, she tells Martin that she's just lost her lucky four-leaf clover, which she's brought along with her today, "… for good luck." Martin Gabin-Shrugs, telling her not to worry about having lost it since, as he puts it, "A clover isn't silver. And even if it were, money cannot make happiness." She's intrigued by this simple working-man, a guy who looks quite happy with his little non-moneyed life, especially when she's a person who's biggest goal in life is to go somewhere else, 'to start over, fresh' in a place where she can get *lots* of money (and, probably, not as a prostitute). "What *is* happiness?" Blanche asks Martin who, the truth be told, is more interested in watching the fight, and he replies that he has no clue. He next turns his full-attention from the fight to her, and starts staring at her unbrokenly, as if he's an animal, and it's really funny. When Gabin stared at Michele Morgan with the same intensity in *Le Recif de corail*, it freaked her out, and she told Gabin's character that she didn't like being looked-at in that way, although very clearly, she loved every single second of it, just like Marlene Dietrich is really loving Gabin's staring at her, like she's a big plate of *bifteck et frites*, right now.

Blanche finally opines that she thinks boxing is disgusting, which makes it even more clear to us that she's shown up at the arena simply to look for men. (However, even while she's saying that boxing horrifies her, she does look more than a little turned-on by it!) Martin continues to check her out brutishly, but she doesn't move, and simply stares right back at him. At this point, a guy who used to be sitting on Martin's left-hand side, in the seat which Blanche has taken over, now returns, and asks her if he can have his seat back. "Sure," she replies, amazed that more than one man in this room is more interested in watching boxing, than in looking at her. It's not that all the guys in the room aren't hot for her because, clearly, they are. It's just that sports-spectatorship, unlike women, can't hurt you! (Unless you get hit in the nose by a fly-ball.)

Blanche leaves, heading out through the exit door and, after a few moments, we see where Martin's true loyalties lie: He raises up out of his seat and makes for the lobby to find her, but she's already gone, and so he now decides to go home as well, and just as he's leaving the building, he's approached by another woman, a hot blonde (she's played by Colette Georges) who's been waiting for him, very specifically: "Martin, I've been looking for you for days. I haven't seen you anywhere—even where you work." (Yikes! *Stalker-alert!*) He tells her that his absence from all of the places where she's been looking for him is easy to explain, because he hasn't been at his work-site for over a month: Martin's a construction foreman, but he's been taking a lot of time-off lately, mostly to walk through the woods, commiserating with nature, since Martin, like all of Jean Gabin's working-man characters, is a true man-of-the-earth.

Right after Martin has left the arena, he comes upon Rimbaut (Lucien Nat), a hospital administrator who's hired Martin to supervise the construction of his brand new clinic building. The guy tells Martin that he needs to see him tomorrow, and could Martin possibly meet him at the town's big central café at eleven a.m.? Rimbaut looks down at the ground and sees the four-leaf-clover which Blanche mentioned that she had dropped. (Hmm... So she really did have one, after all.)

Cut to the construction site: Martin's boss, contractor Gargame (Henri Poupon, who played Gabin's sick wife's doctor, in *Remorques*), has a father-son relationship with Martin, and has been contributing to Martin's relative success in the building field for many years. (Martin started out working for Gargame years ago, as a laborer, and now, not only as he risen to the position of Chief Foreman, but Gargame has additionally been grooming him to someday take over *the whole schmeer*.) It's a testament to Jean Gabin's likeability, that Gargame really adores Martin, even though Martin slacks-off sometimes, whenever he doesn't feel too much like working. (Martin's not a lazybones, though: Like all of Jean Gabin's other, working-man characters, 'work always comes first' with him; it's just that Gabin's Martin Roumagnac-character, like all of Gabin's movie characters, is a rugged individualist, and always does exactly what he wants.) Martin doesn't take Gargame's respect for him lightly though, and he takes this opportunity to let Gargame know that he's grateful for all of the responsibilities which his boss has always given him: "If I'm a good worker today, Mr. Gargame, it's all because of your support. I definitely don't take you for granted."

After work, Martin returns home to his little house, where his protectively-tough spinster sister Jeanne, who's played by Margo Lion, spends her entire life taking care of him. (Lion, Marlene Dietrich's real-life friend, met Jean Gabin when the two appeared in G.W. Pabst's great 1933 ensemble comedy, *Du haut en bas* [Gabin played the soccer player Charles Boulla, and Lion, as we remember, played the *ritzy-titsy housewife* Mrs. Binder], and it is also Lion who, according to some accounts, introduced Dietrich to Gabin in real-life.) Martin asks Jeanne where his shoes are and, instantaneously, she presents *los zapatos* to him, and right on cue. Ever a dutiful older sister, Jeanne has spent the last few hours buffing Martin's shoes to a mirror-finish, and she's not just fixing his shoes, either: Tonight, in fact, she's cooked him some very tasty french fries as well. Jeanne tells her brother that, while she realizes he always needs his freedom, like all of Gabin's 1930s and 1940s movie characters do, that she would still like to know what time he's going to be coming home each evening, if only so that she'll better know when she should have his meals prepared: "I can't cook just like that," she tells him, adding that he is her "… purgatory here on earth," but it's a purgatory which we can tell she really enjoys: Older sister Jeanne adores her brother, just like any mother who really loves her son, and is determined to spend the rest of her life taking care of him. While this might not be the best of all possible situations for a woman to be in, she definitely respects that her own role in life, is to be a helpful big-sister. Instead of answering Jeanne's constant barrage of wife-like, "where-have-you-been"-type questioning, Martin just stomps down into the basement, and she immediately surrenders to his Gabinian Quietude, asking him, "Hey, Martin: As long as you're going down there, would you mind bringing up some mustard?"

The next morning, Martin meets Rimbaut, the new hospital's principal administrator, at the local café, just as they had earlier discussed. "I'm not in agreement with your architect," Rimbaut tells Martin, and we can tell that Martin's mind is everywhere else in the whole world except on his work and, as the two continue talking, Martin now sees Blanche walking by with her bicycle, and he waves her over to the table, inviting her to join them for a glass of wine—an offer which she accepts very graciously. (Acting the total gentleman, Martin even walks her bicycle over to the table!) Not only does Blanche know Martin, but we can tell that she's also been acquainted with Rimbaut and that, rather obviously, Rimbaut is one of her clients. (In fact, Rimbaut was the embarrassed john whom we saw at the beginning of the picture—the guy who was running out of Blanche's room upstairs.) Blanche explains to Rimbaut that she's only just met Martin, at the boxing arena.

At that moment, another woman happens along, and this one isn't 1/100th as hot as Marlene Dietrich, is: It's Rimbaut's shrewish Margaret Dumontesque wife, Mrs. Rimbaut (Colette Regis), who has come to bring her husband home. Martin invites Madame Rimbaut to join them and instead, she starts bragging, a little too loudly (to make all of the café's alcohol-consuming patrons feel horible about themselves), that she "never drinks." (What a boring, fat load this one is! It's no wonder that henpecked Rimbaut has to go elsewhere to get his jollies!) She then tells her husband (mercifully, whispering this into his ear), "If you're enjoying your *happy widows* [and here, of course, she's referencing Blanche, because the phrase 'happy widow' is French slang, meaning 'whore'], at least don't show it too much!"

After the Battling Rimbauts leave, the waiter serves Martin and Blanche, and begins joking around with them. Blanche tells Martin that she's had to ride her bike from one side of the village to the other, and she apologizes to him, because her hair is a mess. Obviously, she wants to be perfect around 'real man' Martin who, very clearly, she's responding to in a much more real way than the way in which she responds to the steady-stream of other men who make up her steady clientele. He asks her what she does for a living (uh-oh!), and she's not exactly lying when she tells him that she "take[s] care of little tweeter birds." He tells that he's about to begin supervising the construction of a hospital for Rimbaut, the guy who's just made himself scarce, but that construction on the place hasn't started yet: He then changes the subject (quickly), because it's much more interesting for him to ask her '20-questions' about herself: He asks her if she's a foreigner, and she responds that she was born in Australia. He wonders aloud about how it is that the two of them have never come to meet before now, since they both live in the same town, and it's now her turn to change the subject, when next she asks him if he likes birds. ("Sure," he grins. "On trees." And what Martin reveals about himself next, is Simple Gabinian-Truth: "I'm not a complicated man.") Blanche admits to him that she doesn't much like most people, because she finds them to be sad, and Martin replies that in his estimation, this is only because she probably "doesn't know what to do with them." (Author's Note: Oh yes, she does!) She tells him that she can't believe it took a four-leaf-clover for them to meet, and he lets her know that he likes "natural things" (like four-leaf clovers) and that, to him, "life is beautiful." Comfortable around Blanche, he even (and this is completely uncharacteristic for Jean Gabin's movie characters) opens up to her, if only *a smidgen:* "I can do things with my hands, so I'm happy. I'm a person who likes sensations."

Blanche now tells Martin what we already heard her telling Ferrand earlier, which is that she doesn't want to stay in this town anymore, and Martin next walks her, and her bicycle, through the crowded streets. When she tells him that she's always wished that she could live in a fancy, Spanish-style villa, he immediately offers to build her one, and he's not kidding about that, either. (Oh, shit! He's being too nice to her! Based upon this offer which he's just made to her, we now know that any future relationship they might have is totally doomed.) She tells him that she once rented a villa in Australia, a long time ago (very briefly), but we don't know whether she's telling him the truth or not.

The next day, Martin's on the construction site of Rimbaut's new hospital building, and he's in the middle of a big pow-wow with Rimbaut. Blanche surprises Martin with a picnic lunch, and he's really happy about the fact that she's brought the grub, but tells her that he doesn't want to eat at the work-site with all of the other guys who, he knows, will be watching the two of them with jealousy (that green-eyed monster!) in their eyes. He tells Blanche that instead, and with her permission, he'd like to take her to a special place, "... a place with water and trees." She tells him that, while water and trees are what she used to like about Australia, she'd like to stay local today, since they still don't know each other that well: "Let's wait a day or two. Your landscape will not fly away." But Jean Gabin, who's always a force-of-nature, won't listen: "It's only fifteen minutes away. Let's go right now." (And who can refuse an offer made by Jean Gabin?) Even though Blanche 'puts out' right away for guys who pay for her up front, Martin doesn't know she's a prostitute, she really likes him (maybe), and she's determined to make him *really* like her as well, even though, of course, she's also going to start toying with him, since it's in her nature to do so.

Blanche and Martin arrive at the little meadow which he wanted to show her, and we can tell, by her very real smile that she's (beyond) happy that she's changed her mind about *not* coming along with him, because she's instantly enchanted by the place. (Heavenly music, *a la Gone with the Wind*, wells up on the soundtrack, and the film's lush black and white cinematography looks extra-enchanting in this exotically-foresty-scene). He tells her, "It's so beautiful here, you just have to kneel down!" (Leave it to the French, to throw in a not-so-veiled reference to *fellatio!*) "I can't resist you," she tells him, finally. He tells her that he'd like to take her to another place, this coming Sunday. Even though Martin is strictly an overalls-and-workboots-guy, he always wears a suit (ill-fitting, but it's probably his only one), whenever he takes Blanche out, even when they're just going out to sit in a field. (When Jean Gabin deigns to—horror-of-horrors—put on a suit, that must mean that he really likes you!)

Martin shows Blanche the empty spot where he'd like to build her a villa and, while there's no villa there as yet, there *is* a little perfectly-placed (for dalliances) pigeon shed. She asks him if they can go inside and if the place belongs to anybody, and Martin just Gabin-Shrugs: "It doesn't matter. I don't have a sense of ownership."

She talks about how she sells caged birds, and he tells her that, in his opinion, "Homes are cages." (Never before has free-wheelin' Jean Gabin uttered his movie-persona's mission statement, so very succinctly.) He tells her that he builds only functional buildings, "… like schools and hospitals, and no arty stuff (sorry, Frank Gehry), and that he never has any time for himself. ("Even if I wanted to build myself a house, I wouldn't have the time.") But it's clear that he wants to break his rule, and build her something with flash.

Then, thunder and lightning start putting on a private little show for them overhead, and he suggests they retreat into the shed to stay dry. (God has given Martin Roumagnac the perfect make-out line!) As they make for the shed, trying to stay dry, she tells him she's "not used to running," and we totally believe it because, even though Blanche is a hooker, she's definitely a classy one, inasmuch as any maneating hooker can be considered to be classy.

Martin and Blanche are now safely ensconced in the shed, a perfect place for their first steamy liplock—if one can ignore the cacophony of the pigeons who reside there. She looks deeply into his eyes and tells him that she hopes the storm won't last long, but when she says it, we can tell that she really hopes it will! The two of them finally kiss for the very first time (even though they've already known each other for probably several weeks now), and as their lips seal together in tender suction, director Lacombe pans to the shed's old, wooden front door, which slams shut three times from the wind —bang, bang, bang! (How's that for sexual metaphor?) When Lacombe dissolves back to the couple (we can only assume a few minutes later, and post-coitally), Blanche references both the rain and Martin's sexual prowess: "It stormed… but it never rained!"

Now, it's probably a few months later, and director Lacombe takes us back to the construction site of the soon-to-be hospital: Martin's busy supervising his dedicated crew and Blanche pays him another surprise visit, and this time, in a *multo*-fetching dress, asking him, sexily, if she's "disturbing" him. (Well, whether or not she's disturbing him, she's certainly disturbing the film's male audience members—and in a good way!) This scene is important dramatically, because it's the first scene in which Martin and Blanche change from using the polite French tense of the word 'you'—'*vous*'—with each other, in favor of the more familiar,

With real-life lover Marlene Dietrich.

'*tu*.' Martin's big sister Jeanne is at the job site, and she and Gargame are busily cooking up a huge pot of *crew-stew* together and, at the same time, they're whispering comments to each other, pursuant to how everyone in town knows that Blanche is a prostitute—everyone, that is, except for Martin. ("He doesn't know what he's getting himself into," Jeanne frowns, at Gargame.) Martin and Blanche enjoy a picnic on the grass, in full-view of the construction crew, and the other guys all look jealous that Martin has such a hot lunch date, while they just have thermoses.

This is the moment in which Blanche will now begin her manipulation of Martin, which we saw coming. Blanche genuinely loves Martin but, as I've already mentioned, larceny is part of her character, and she pouts to him that she hasn't seen too much of him for the last several days, to which he replies that it's only because, in his free time, he's been away, building her a 'dream villa.' She replies, "If you continue not being around, I shall be jealous of the villa." (That's right, Martin's building Blanche her dream house, and all she can say, is that the time he's spending working on it, is taking away from the time which he should be spending with her!) Since she hasn't seen the villa yet, because he doesn't want to show it to her until it's all ready, he's not taking her words to heart, because he knows that when she sees the finished product, she'll be very happy indeed. Martin is building the villa right next to that crusty old pigeon shack in which he and Blanche shared their first tryst, and his idea is that, even after the villa is built, the two of them can continue to make love in the pigeon shed, and this is a funny-subtle joke on the part of the filmmakers: Here's a working-class guy, and when he thinks about sex, he still regards it as being a shameful (yet necessary) activity, which can only be performed in a strictly functional environment. (If a Motel 6 or a Marriott Courtyard Inn isn't available, then a little wooden pigeon shed will surely suffice.)

Finally, the day comes when the villa is completely finished and, when Martin shows it to Blanche for the first time, she's shocked by how opulent, and how beautiful, it is. (Before, Martin said that he only built functional properties, but this place is as ornate as the Vatican itself.) "There are three *rooms upstairs*," he brags to her, when they arrive at the new villa, and he can't figure out why she winces right after he says, "room upstairs." (He still doesn't know that she plies her sexy trade, in a 'room upstairs;' to her, 'room upstairs' is uncomfortable code for the naked activities in which she engages to support herself and her 'Uncle.') Blanche is touched by the fact that Martin has made this beautiful house all for her, and the two of them next make hot sweet love, as director Lacombe fades out.

Meanwhile, Gargame is becoming infuriated with Martin, who's always, historically, missed *some* work, but who has now, of late, been missing more work than ever, because he's been otherwise occupied, in building this vanity property for Blanche. But Martin can't live on love alone: He still needs *home cookin',* and so that night, he plods home to Big-Sister Jeanne. He won't be staying long, however, because he's only returned home for a brief visit—to chow down, and to pick up his suitcase. ("And not the leather one," he orders his sister, "the crocodile one!") That's right: Martin's never cared about fineries before, but now that he's with a 'fancy' lady for the very first time in his life, he wants to keep up with the Joneses! He tells Jeanne that he's going off to Paris, "to buy some building materials," because he wants to fix the pigeon shack up, as a permanent place for himself to live. (In Martin's skewed/idealized world, he'll be living in the little pigeon shack on his beloved Blanche's property, so that he can be at her beck-and-call 24/7, and the fact that he wants to live in the pigeon shack is important to the film's narrative, because the word 'pigeon' [which is the same in French, as it is in English], is also a slang term in French, which means, 'a guy who's getting used by a woman.') Jeanne now starts railing on her brother for thinking with the wrong part of his anatomy but, as we all know, Jean Gabin doesn't like to be on the receiving end of bitchy treatment from any woman—lovers and family members alike—and he now tells her that she has no right to talk to him in such a patronizing tone. Jeanne finally confronts Martin about how he's become blind to the fact that Blanche is just using him, and she starts calling him 'Monsieur,' in a pejorative way which is slang among the French working-class, and which means 'rich man:' "*Monsieur* buys land! *Monsieur* builds a villa! *Monsieur* goes to Paris! Do you think you're a billionaire? Don't you see all of your hard-earned savings blowing away?" Martin gets infuriated, and Gabin-Outbursts that he can spend his money however he wants to; obviously, having an affair with this classy-looking woman—even though unbeknownst to Martin, Blanche (like him) is strictly working-class—represents, to Martin, a little vacation from his non-eventful real-life. (Blanche Ferrand is this movie's living embodiment of what happens when every man's fantasy becomes chillingly real.)

Every French movie always has to have its share of bar and café scenes' and *Martin Roumagnac* is no different: Next, we're in the town's local bistro, on a lazy Sunday afternoon. Everybody in town seemingly lunches at the same place (in a small town, everybody knows each other). The young dark-haired Surveyor is even there, and he's sitting at a small, round table by himself, reading, when Blanche shows up with both Martin and her 'Uncle,' Ferrand in tow. Hospital-mogul Rimbaut is there as well, with his shrewish wife, and when Mrs. Rimbaut sees Blanche, she tells her husband that in her opinion, "…that woman is completely ridiculous." (In all actuality, uptight Mrs. Rimbaut is way more ridiculous than Blanche has ever been.) Blanche sits down for lunch with her 'Uncle' and Martin and, as soon as Blanche and Ferrand get settled, 'man-of-the-people' Martin now excuses himself from their presence, and starts good-naturedly banking around the room like an errant pinball, greeting everybody. Everybody in town likes good-old Martin (he's 'everybody's pal,' just like most of Jean Gabin's Movie Characters are), even though they're all worried about him, because they all know that Blanche is a prostitute, while he still does not. During Martin's momentary absence from her table, Blanche recognizes the Surveyor, and smiles at him warmly.

One table in the bistro is full of hearty working men who are in the midst of a scintillating conversation about masonry, and they're all looking at Blanche, as they talk: "Look! The happy widow is into masonry." (Masonry = Martin.) They're all laughing at Martin, who doesn't know that he's being played, even though again, they all genuinely like him.

'Uncle' Ferrand really likes Martin, but wishes that his 'niece' would spend more of her time with her moneyed consul, Laubry, instead. He asks her, while Martin continues glad-handing-away at the other tables, if she's going to be seeing Laubry anytime soon, and Blanche replies that she doesn't really need to, because Martin's no slouch in the 'giving-her-expensive-stuff-department,' especially since he's been building her *that sweet villa*.

As he continues his table-to-table jaunt, Martin is now asking Mr. Rimbaut how the hospital construction has been going lately, since Mr. Gargame has had to hire a temporary supervisor in Martin's absence (and Martin's not even sore about it, since he's been pre-occupied with Blanche), and meanwhile Blanche continues to check out the still-reading Surveyor. Martin then returns to Blanche and Ferrand's table and sits down with them, apologizing for his absence, and meanwhile, over at Rimbaut's table, we see that even Rimbaut himself is now commenting to his wife about how, in his opinion, he knows Martin is being used: "I guess Martin doesn't mind wearing horns," he tells his wife. (It's a French expression, meaning, 'to be used by somebody.') She retorts, "Yeah, like all the other rubes who get close to her." (Of course, when she says this, she's really taking a dig at her own husband, but he's too dim to figure out what she's actually saying.)

A few days later, acting the part of the big-shot, Martin takes Blanche to a fancy hotel in

Paris and, hilariously, instead of underscoring the scene with the usual lovey-dovey music, director Lacombe has thrown-in some frightening horror movie music. The Eiffel Tower is right outside the hotel window, and Martin points out Paris's swanky Montparnasse-section to Blanche, trying to appear sophisticated to her, but she tells him that she already knows the area. (She's obviously turned more than a few tricks in Gay Paree.) "Here in Paris, everybody goes fast," Blanche tells Martin, but, as he reminds her (Jean Gabin characters are always slow and sure), "Patience is more important than going quickly." After their small-talk, Martin and Blanche are about to go out to dinner, but instead, she whips off her skirt, and he gets so hot for her, that they make love instead.

After 'their sex,' Martin and Blanche get all gussied-up in fancy eveningwear, and head out to dinner. (A very strange continuity mistake in the film, is: Right after they fuck, Blanche suddenly has a completely new and extremely fancy hairstyle. Did Martin *style her hair* after they had sex? Where in hell did that fancy new 'do' come from, anyway?!)

The two enter a mega-fancy Moroccan restaurant called Boubtichili, where a *Tzigan* (that's French, for 'gypsy') orchestra is playing, very energetically, against the back wall's huge backdrop of an ancient Grecian city. The tables' centerpieces are cellos, and we can tell that homespun Martin isn't used to being in such a fancy place. (In a hilarious sight gag, we see that Martin doesn't even know which of the two forks to use, and he decides, finally, to start alternating, keeping one in each hand!) Coming to his aide, a waiter (a fellow working-class guy who can immediately recognize a 'brother') brings Martin a third fork on a plate (great, that only makes it worse!), and we can tell that Martin would rather be somewhere else (anywhere else) but here. Referring to all of the spit-and-polished diners who are filling the place up to the rafters, Martin tells Blanche, "All these people—they must be a bore, during the day!" (They're probably not "a bore," though, 'cause *Blanche probably fucks 'em*, during the day!) The Gypsy musicians, who travel from table to table, next ask Martin if he's got a song request, and he asks to hear an old peasant song. Not knowing it, the musicians instead favor Martin and Blanche with a classical piece, and Martin gets irked, when they start shoving the violin right up into his face. He even asks the Head Violinist, "Do you really want your music to drip into my coffee? Isn't it sugary enough?" Blanche looks on amusedly, and suddenly, Martin looks *way* self-conscious, telling her that he's sorry he's ruining her night, and that he's very aware he's an uncouth brute. This scene calls to mind that almost-identical scene in 1931's *Gloria*, in which a similarly uncomfortable Gabin dined in that too *chi-chi* upper-class restaurant, completely unaware of the protocol of the rich and lazy.

After sex and food, Blanche now wants to dance, but Martin doesn't. (He tells her he doesn't know any of "those fancy, Parisian dances.") At that moment, a well-heeled guy (Jean Gosselin) appears at the table, asks Martin's permission to dance with Blanche, and Martin gladly allows it, mostly because he just wants to go outside, get some air, and have a smoke, even though the waitress only has fancy Oriental cigarettes to sell him, which he buys reluctantly, because there aren't any 'real' cigarettes in the place. The guy whom Blanche is dancing with, of course, is one of her ex-johns, and when Martin's outside, the guy tells her that he recognized her as soon as she came in, and right away. She tells this ex-john, trying to blow him off, that she's become married recently, and that her brand-new husband died shortly after the ceremony, so that currently she's a widow and is not yet ready to engage in new affairs—and she's not lying to the guy, completely: While Blanche isn't married now, she was, as we're now learning, married a few years back, to a guy who died and left her penniless. (So, she really is a legitimate widow, and her deceased husband was probably the original Ferrand, the guy for whom the pet store has been named, which means that 'Uncle' Ferrand, the store's current owner, is not really her Uncle, but actually her dead husband's brother—which also means that Jean Y'd's 'Uncle Ferrand' character is actually Blanche's brother-in-law!)

Exactly like Gabin's character did in *Gloria*, Martin now stands outside the restaurant chatting with the doorman, and looks incredibly relieved to be free, and he's even smiling and telling the guy, "Now I can breathe!" The doorman recognizes Martin as being a fellow 'Johnny Punchclock,' and the two immediately start bonding like brothers long-separated. Martin tells the guy that he's a builder, and the doorman replies that he himself used to be a watchmaker, that is, before he fell into the extremely un-prestigious door-opening-field. (The guy brags, extending his hands wide, "I made chronometers this big!") Martin tells the guy that he loves working with his hands as well, and the doorman tells him that his own dream would be to have a house in which he can 'work wood.' (Martin is definitely much more comfortable outside the restaurant with this guy, than he was inside, with all of the stuffy swells.)

Eventually, Martin makes his way back into the restaurant, and because he wants Blanche to be happy, and because he also wants to make it up to her for his boredom with the evening, he buys her the restaurant's wall sconces, which she had been admiring all evening, telling her that he'll put them up on the walls in her new villa.

Director Lacombe next cuts to the villa, and the first thing we see there, are those very same sconces, which now line the walls. The villa is completely finished, and it's as exquisite on the inside, as it is on the outside. At great personal expense, Martin's even hired Blanche her own personal Chambermaid (Jane Marguenat), a woman who, when we first see her, happens to be bringing Blanche a letter from the rich Consul, Laubry, with whom she sometimes keeps company. In the letter, Laubry is informing Blanche that his wife has just died, which is exactly what he's been praying for, and that now, he and Blanche are free to be together forever, should she have any interest in doing that. Martin asks Blanche who the letter is from, and she lies to him, telling him that it's from an old, platonic friend. (But Martin is Jean Gabin, and Jean Gabin's movie characters can sometimes see through the tunnelvision of their own horniness, and 'make good calls.') He asks her, cautiously (since she's got the upper hand, and he doesn't want to lose her), if she's absolutely sure that this letter wasn't written by some other boyfriend of hers. She asks Martin if her Consul friend can come and stay with them for a few days, at the villa, and Martin, who's satisfied that she's not involved with the guy sexually, gives her the go-ahead. Just when we thought Martin was coming to his senses, and thinking with his big head, he's just made another big-whopper-of-a-mistake.

Then, Martin does something which makes him the biggest rube/dupe of all time: While Martin built the villa for Blanche to live in, he's the owner of the place. And now comes the moment in our story in which he hands her the deed, signing the place over to her, lock-stock-and-sconces—now, and for all time. "But I didn't pay for it," she pouts, mock-shocked, and with absolutely zero conviction. Viewers of this movie might be tempted to guess that maybe, one reason Jean Gabin didn't want this film shown, might be because in the film, his character gets used a lot and doesn't act so smart—but this probably isn't the case because in the 1950s, the actor will star in a few other movies in which the woman-characters will also be using him just like Blanche is using his character in this film, but Gabin wouldn't have a problem with those other films, all of which would continue to remain in circulation.

One afternoon, while Martin is away (and probably, spending some more money on Blanche), Blanche is in the villa's garden, perched on a ladder, and decorating the front of the house with strands of ivy. Daniel Gelin's shy, young Surveyor comes to see her and apologizes for bothering her at her home, and this is the moment in which she asks him to please stop writing her letters; it's also the moment, in which we're first learning that *this infatuated young dude* has been writing her tortured letters, in which he's been professing his undying love to her. She wants to let him down easily because he's young, although she doesn't have to be as gentle with Martin, because Martin's older, and more foolish and guileless—therefore, he's also a whale-of-a-lot more fun to take advantage of. She tells the Surveyor, matter-of-factly, "You love me… but I don't love you" and, when she's making this pronouncement (and he's struck-dumb by the finality of it), he looks just like a puppy who's just gotten kicked in the head. But she next makes him feel just a tiny bit better, by adding a tender post-script to her harsh words: "Anyway, the most important thing in life, is to love… not to be loved. You're lucky that you can feel those feelings, because there are so few people who actually can." (Here, of course, Blanche is talking about herself.)

While this pathetic little scene is playing itself out, Martin's in a local tavern, to which his boss, Gargame, who's playing pool, has summoned him with great urgency. Gargame is worried about his surrogate 'son' Martin, and it's now time for a little paternal scolding: He tells Martin that Rimbaut took away the Gargame Company's hospital-building contract, just because Martin was unable to commit to the project, and also because Martin's replacement supervisor just wasn't working out. What Gargame is really telling Martin here, is that Martin's absence from work has hurt not just Martin, but also the financial state of the entire construction company. He tells Martin that he *does* have a couple of projects which he'd like him to work on, projects which need to be completed by the end of the month, but not if Martin's going to be disappearing again. (When eternal drifter Gabin takes a notion to drift, he's never trying to hurt other people—that's just his way.) Next, Gargame calls Martin on how stupid the younger man has been acting lately by choosing to continue his affair with a woman who obviously has zero regard for him (or, for anybody else, for that matter): "What you're doing with that woman is stupid, Martin. You're not behaving properly." One of Martin's jobs, as Gargame's main foreman, has always been to hire all of the company's laborers and, on that note, Gargame tells him, "Your absence is keeping whole crews unemployed, too. And by the way, not only does the whole town know what you're doing with that [manipulative] woman, but the *Bank Nationale de Paris* is building its new headquarters, and they've decided to go with another construction company instead of us, because even the guys at the bank know that you're too busy, screwing around!" Martin, in typical Jean Gabin fashion, doesn't get riled-up because, in spite of everybody's bitching at him, he's still head-over-heels in love with Blanche. Martin wants this whole conversation to end, so he now Gabin-Outbursts at his boss—and we can tell that it's probably the first time he's ever talked-back to this father-like guy—"So? I missed my shot in life. Okay, that's fine! I don't care! Just let it go!" Gargame didn't expect that kind of a response from a person whom he has always treated like a son.

On the way out of the pool hall, Martin telephones Blanche at the villa from the bar's payphone, because he's got something on his mind: "Blanche, you know, ever since your friend the Consul arrived a week ago, I haven't seen you at all." She says—not really wanting to see Martin, while she's 'otherwise occupied'—"Fine. Come over to the villa tonight, at eight-o'-clock," and hangs up. Ferrand has been in the room with Blanche during Martin's call, and tells her 'Uncle' that she's invited Martin over, tonight, "… just to calm him. Otherwise, he'll make a fuss." (She's obviously heard of those famous Gabin-Outbursts!) While Ferrand likes Martin, he really thinks that Blanche should be devoting her time, not to mention the rest of her life, to her rich visitor: "You've been spending a lot of time with the Consul this week. Are you going to marry him?" She replies that she's not sure, because the guy just talks about politics all the time and that, when he does, it just bores her to tears. She admits to Ferrand that she's using Consul Laubry just for his money, just as she's using Martin, too, for the 'free villa,' even though she's not specifically mentioning that subject.

Cut to that night, and to the villa's living room: Amusingly, when we first meet Laubry in-person (he's played by Marcel Herrand), he's pontificating about politics, *ad nauseam*, just like Blanche said he did, and Martin's there too, sipping coffee with Laubry, Blanche, and Ferrand. Martin and the Consul, two men from wildly different backgrounds, seem to really like each other. There's no name-calling and jealousy, like we thought we'd be seeing in a 'love triangle' scene like this, simply because Martin doesn't know he's part of a love triangle—he still hasn't figured out that Blanche is screwing Laubry, since he believed her when she told him that it was platonic between them. Martin even tells Laubry that he was saddened to hear about the death of the guy's wife, to which Laubry, nonchalantly (shouldn't he look more emotional when somebody's referencing his dearly-departed?) replies, "Well, we knew she was going to die." With even less conviction, Laubry next starts feigning loss, and he doesn't do that too convincingly, either. ("There's such a void in my life, since my wife died," the guy stage-acts; the Consul is just as cold as Blanche, and they probably thaw each other's coldness out, during their sex.) When Laubry heads upstairs ("all by my lonesome," he purrs, winking at Blanche) to "get a little shut-eye," Martin assesses the guy's character in a favorable way, for Blanche and Ferrand: "He's an interesting guy, that Consul. He's educated!" As Laubry continues his Matterhornian climb up the stairs, Blanche even throws a little Shakespeare at him: "May good dreams be a part of your sleep!'" (This is secret code, no doubt, for "Meet me in my bedroom in ten minutes.")

Blanche enters her own *boudoir*, and positions herself at the door theatrically, her face racked with confusion; obviously, she's trying to figure out which of the two men she's going to be sleeping with this evening, and we know already that it's going to be one of them, since she's already changed into a very-sexy nightgown.

When Laubry goes to sleep, Blanche surprises Martin (and us) by visiting Martin where he's staying, out in the pigeon house. (Well, maybe it's not really such a big surprise; after all, Blanche is using both of the two guys—one for money and prestige, and the other for a house—and of the two guys, Martin is the only one who actually looks virile.) And of course, Martin's excited that she's shown up (you'd be happy, too, if Marlene Dietrich showed up at your house in a slinky nightie), braying, "I thought you'd never come. I'm lost without you!" The pigeon house has a fireplace inside, and she tells him that the next time she comes over, she'd like it if he'd have the embers all glowing and ready.

It's now the next morning, and Blanche and Martin are freshly-fucked. The sun is filtering through the trees, and Martin tells her that he hopes Laubry will be going home today, and he also starts (wimpily) professing more of his love, to her: "Ahh, Blanche! *Je t'aime, je t'aime, je t'aime!*" If you haven't already figured out that Martin's setting himself up for the big-fall-of-a-lifetime, you've never seen a movie before.

Martin gets in his fancy new car which he's just bought (yes, he's spent the remainder of his life's savings buying a fancy ride, so that he can cart Blanche around with his head held high!), and he next heads over to the local Mobil Oil station. The attendant, Annette (Odette Barencey), who knows Martin, asks him if he's on her way over to the villa to visit Blanche, and he tells her that he is. But when Martin arrives at the place to surprise his lady-love, she's not there. Blanche's Maid tells Martin that her mistress has gone off to the small, nearby town of Moulin-Chaumette for the day, and so Moulin-Chaumette becomes Martin's next stop.

What's Blanche doing in Moulin-Chaumette? Well, she's there lunching with Laubry, at one of the little berg's quaint luncheries. "Such exquisite cakes," Laubry smiles, staring right into Blanche's cleavage as he utters the word 'cakes!' He's trying to impress her with his knowledge of flowers, but she isn't paying any attention to him at all; instead, she looks far away, still thinking, no doubt, about her previous night's lovemaking with Martin. "I like the language of flowers," Laubry continues dreamily, "because daisies mean love." She asks him, snarkily, if he believes that 'the language of flowers' is a necessary pre-requisite to becoming a Consul, and not understanding that she's just put him down, he next asks her to marry him! ("So: How about the two of us uniting our states of being widows?") Once Laubry starts talking, he too, just like the also normally quiet Martin, can't stop the floodgates of his mouth from pouring forth his eternal love for Blanche, this hypnotic woman with the heart-of-stone, and he now admits to Blanche that he's waited for two years for his wife to kick off, so that he could be with her. (Near the beginning of the film, when Blanche and Martin were at the boxing arena, he told her that he'd been waiting for a woman like her for years, and it often seems like everyone in this movie, just like in life, waits and waits for that one great emotionally and/or physically unavailable person to become available—and, of course, they never do.) Laubry tries to give Blanche some reasons that he believes the two of them are so similar: "Ambition is a mortal sin, and we're both guilty of that sin, so it's natural that we should wind up together—don't you think? Anyway, now I'm free, and don't forget—I'm rich!" (What a fool! Why do all these guys want to give Blanche all of their money? Forget the expression, 'Keep it in your pants;' these guys should really start thinking about 'keeping it in their wallets!') She tells him, agreeing with what he's just told her about ambition, "Ambition is worth all of the seven mortal sins altogether," and he then lets her in on the fact that he knows what she does in 'the room upstairs,' but that he still loves her anyway, and that he'd never judge her for it: "Come on now, Blanche, you're smart. You're not really just the owner of a bird shop, are you? And you're really not from Australia, either. I fully realize that I'm talking to a woman who has seen and done a lot of things."

At that moment, Martin surprises both Blanche and Laubry by walking into the restaurant, pretending that he's just shown up there accidentally. Laubry was happy to meet Martin at the Villa, but the fact that Martin's just shown up here, at a restaurant in another town, is a bit too 'on the calculated side' for his tastes, so he's now much less friendly to Martin than he was before. Martin sits down with the two of them (Blanche and Laubry look very uncomfortable) and orders himself a cup of herbal tea. "It's really nice out today," Blanche opines, nervously fumfering for something to say, something that will break-up the tension that's just set over the table like one of London's thickest fogs. Martin now tells them, which is true, that he once remodeled this particular restaurant, which is why he knows it so well, and, after making this pronouncement, he pours himself a glass of water, and Laubry next asks him, obviously expecting a fight, "Are water drinkers *mean?*" Blanche notices that the normally-calm and stoic Martin seems atypically-edgy and even angry and, at this point, Martin's friend Paulo, the buddy with whom he was sitting at the boxing arena near the beginning of the film, rushes into the restaurant, out-of-breath, and breaks up the seated trio's tension by adding some all-new tension into the admixture: "I'm sorry to bother you here, Martin," he pants, "but there's been a problem on that bridge project we're working on. [Here, Paulo is referring to a new project which Gargame told Martin he wanted him to supervise, back when the two of them were having their man-to-man chat, in the bar.] The scaffolding fell and several men were hurt—one, in particular, very badly." Martin asks Paulo how he knew that he (Martin) was at the restaurant, and Paulo remarks, indicating Blanche, "Madame's maid told me you would be here." (Meaning, of course, that Paulo went over to the villa to find Martin before he showed up here, at the restaurant and, of course, Laubry doesn't like hearing that, either!) Martin leaves with Paulo, much to Laubry's great relief. (Even in those movies in which Jean Gabin is thinking with his 'little head,' he's never less than one hundred-percent practical and, when push comes to shove, he still has more allegiance to the brotherhood of his fellow men than he does to women, no matter how prepossessing, and how 'Dietrichy,' the women are.) Laubry now, for the first time, actually feels threatened by Martin, not because Martin was acting threatening, but just because of Martin's presence. "So he really knows how to find you, doesn't he, Blanche? He's really in love with you, isn't he?"

Laubry then repeats his marriage-offer to Blanche, and this time more directly than he did last time, and her answer is eloquent: "You asked a question to the intelligent part of me, and intelligence requires time to answer. When people talk to the heart, it answers fast. But when you talk to the intelligence, it requires more time." So: What Blanche is really telling Laubry here, is that he doesn't appeal to her heart, but only to her intelligence, and when she's talking about intelligence, she's really referring to her own intelligence, where it comes to finding guys who can make her fiduciary problems go away. Laubry is just as much a marionette to Blanche as are all of the rest of the guys in the picture (Martin; the *Surveillant;* Rimbaut), and she hasn't ruled-out his offer, 100%—she's just telling him that she needs more time to think about it.

Martin arrives at the construction site of the bridge with Paulo at his side and, at this point, another foreman (played by Julien Maffre), a new guy whom Gargame has hired to replace Martin in Martin's absence, tells Martin that the badly-injured man's vertebral column has been crushed. Paulo, and Martin's sister, Jeanne (who's there as well) are mad, because they both know that if Martin had been there to supervise, that there wouldn't have been any accident at all. The injured guy, we're now learning, has three children, but never thought he would get hurt, so he never paid into his hospitalization plan.

The next night, Martin visits Blanche in her villa's bedroom. He tells her he waited for her all night in the pigeon house (!), and that he's mad because she didn't show up: "I was ridiculous in waiting for you all night. So tell me: Why didn't you come?! Did he [Laubry] spend the night with you?" She brushes the question off, and tells Martin to go back to his pigeon house (and she next actually refers to the pigeon house, as being Martin's 'stable,' which is even more demeaning than when she's just called it a 'pigeon shack'). He's tried, with a Gabin-Outburst, to let her know that 'he's the boss'… but now, with her cutting remark about the stable, she's just made him see for the first time that, in their relationship (such as it is), she's the one who wears the pants.

A bit later, Ferrand, Blanche, and Laubry breakfast together on the villa's veranda. Turns out, Blanche wasn't really with Laubry the night before—she just didn't tell Martin that she wasn't with Laubry, because she wanted to piss Martin off. Blanche asks Laubry if he slept well, and he replies that he would have, but that he was awakened early in the morning, by the sound of a slamming door. (*Of course,* the door slammed during Martin and Blanche's fight: "Oh, that was just the wind blowing the door shut," she lies. "We have a bit of a draft in this house.") He tells her he heard someone screaming, and she tries to quell his anxiety, by telling him that it was she who was screaming, but he knows that's a total crock: "That's funny," he tells her, trying to bust her, "because it sounded just like your friend, Martin Roumagnac. Anyway, I know Roumagnac is on familiar terms with you. I'm not stupid, you know. I see him calling you '*tu!*') Of course, this guy hasn't yet learned one of the Most Important Lessons in Movies, which is that you never, ever mess with Marlene Dietrich—and so Blanche, immediately, starts whaling on him: "Don't you ever talk to *me* that way, Mister! You and I aren't married... yet!" (That's a pretty funny statement for her to be making, because it implies that when one is married, one has the *de facto* right—and even the responsibility—to freak-out on one's marriage partner.) She continues, "Anyway, our upcoming marriage, *if* I decide to let it happen, will only be a business arrangement on both sides. You *know* there's no love between us." (He gives her money, while she gives him *booty*, and functions as his stylish arm-candy.) After a beat, and wanting to get the last word in, Laubry tells her that he agrees, although we know that he really *does* love her, with her assessment of their situation: "I like Roumagnac too, Blanche. But what bothers me about him, is that he's common. Look, when we get married, I don't care if you're with other men. [Author's Note: What a wimp!] But you shouldn't choose them from the lower-class, like you have with [Roumagnac]. He doesn't have good manners or speak in 'high French.' [Like many Jean Gabin characters and also, apparently, like Jean Gabin in real life, Martin Roumagnac speaks in a lot of slang.] He smells like masonry and thick red wine. You can't tell me that it never bothers you."

As Laubry continues disparaging Martin, Blanche gets really angry, and begins defending her working-class lover. (After all, in spite of appearances, she's working-class, too.) Even though Blanche is using Martin just like she's using Laubry, and just like she uses *all guys*, she does have some genuine feelings for him because after all, Martin is Jean Gabin and, as Jean Gabin, he's obviously the most real and unaffected person she's ever met: "Martin's smell bothers me less than the smell of that cadaver—your wife! For two years, while you were waiting for her to die, you were already burying her, with your thoughts!" Then, the ball's in Laubry's court, and it's his turn to return her bitchy volley: "Today, you're [making love to] the mason. Tomorrow it might be the people working in the house—the gardener, or even the butler!" Then, Blanche gets back on her 'dead wife-trip:' "You brought me a cadaver for an engagement gift. You're an idiot! Roumagnac is worth a hundred times more than you are!" What we're seeing here, for the first time in the film, is that, in spite of all of her problems (and even she probably didn't even realize this until this very second), Blanche really *is* head-over-heels in love with Martin, and she's probably in love for the very first time in her whole life, and it's crept up on her completely unexpectedly. (In that old Gabin picture from 1931, *Pour un soir..!*, Stella-Marie, the prostitute who was manipulating a much younger Jean Gabin, told her sister Monique that in this life, there is no 'love,' only 'lust,' and Blanche probably believed the very same thing—that is, until now!)

Then, we get a little bad news, but thankfully it's news which is mostly unrelated to the plight of our central characters: We're learning now that the construction worker who took a dive off of that scaffold at the bridge site has just passed away in the hospital. Martin, feeling badly because he wasn't there to protect the guy from danger when the accident happens, goes into a restaurant which is owned by his friend Bonnemain (Charles Lemontier), and now hits Bonnemain up for a loan, for some money to give to the fallen man's family. When Martin leaves, Bonnemain sits down with his wait-staff (the eatery hasn't opened for dinner yet), plays cards, and tells them that in his opinion, Martin should have asked Ferrand for the money, instead of asking him for it. (Bonnemain's an important and not-so-minor character in the film, because he knows something which we don't know, namely that disheveled old Ferrand, the bird store owner who lets Blanche turn tricks because he's always pleading poverty, actually has big bucks! The bird store, as it turns out, is really just a front, not just for Blanche's whoring, but for some of Ferrand's large-scale criminal operations, which have netted the guy some pretty heavy green over the years—money which even Blanche doesn't know he has. The old creep actually makes her turn tricks because he keeps telling her how poor they are, and yet they're not!) The waiters, just like everybody else in town are, of course, all talking about how Martin is being conned, and some of these waiters have been (by their very own admission in this scene) Blanche's customers, as well. Martin overhears all of this as he's walking out and, even though he's finally figuring out that what they're saying about him his true—that he's been played for a sucker—he's still getting mad at them, anyway. He now grabs Bonnemain, like he's going to punch him out. "What the hell are you saying? You're just jealous, because you can't have Blanche, and I can! You're mad, because she's mine!" (Can Martin really be this dumb? Will he come to his senses? We hope so!)

Next, Rimbaut, the big-time hospital-owner, comes to the villa to visit Blanche. He, like lots of other guys in the picture, doesn't see Blanche anymore either, now that she's with Martin, and he too, just like Laubry a few scenes ago, is now pathetically putting it all on the line for her: "Even though I'm married, I can't live without you! I just want to know if I'm still in the game!" She tells him, totally freezing him out, that he was never actually 'in the game' to begin with. For a big businessman, this Rimbaut guy's a pretty big whiner: "Look, I know you're very attached to Roumagnac, Blanche, and that he doesn't have any money. Well, I have money, and I have weighty political connections. Maybe I can help your friend Roumagnac out a little bit. But to do that, I need you." (This 'wealth and political connections'-thing, is the same load of bunk which the Consul was just feeding Blanche, a few scenes ago.) She tells Rimbaut to go home to his wife and, to make sure he doesn't come back, she even throws in a dollop of smooth, creamy venom: "You're dead to me!" He starts screaming at her, something along the lines of, "... the dead come back! You'll see me again!" Ferrand then enters the room to make sure she's okay, but he's way too helpless-looking, out of shape and disheveled to actually do anything, in case any violence is going on. He's smoking a huge pipe, and his big messy hair hangs over his forehead, in a rat's nest.

Martin, not having seen Blanche for days, wanders into the bird-and-feed shop looking for her, and Ferrand lies, telling him that she's not there, but she really is. Sure enough, Blanche then wafts downstairs, and Martin, who's now finally figured out the truth about Blanche (and he's figured it out much later than all of the other characters in the movie, and looks really embarrassed about his naiveté), asks her whom she's been with, upstairs: "Are you going to tell me that you're all alone up there? I'm not crazy! I understand what's going on in the room upstairs! It starts in the store, and it ends on the bed! SLUT!" Martin storms out, and Blanche confesses to Ferrand that she's now more "fed up" than ever before, and that she's going to be leaving town permanently, and right away. Rattled by just having been chewed-out by Martin, she now throws open all of the cages and lets all of the birds fly free, a symbol of the freedom which she herself wishes to have, and Ferrand is incredulous: "What are you doing? Those birds don't make a lot of money, but they make us some!" (He doesn't need money, but he doesn't want her to know that. [Everybody in this movie is screwing everybody else over—friend and relatives, alike!]) Some heavenly music starts dripping from the soundtrack, as Blanche announces to Ferrand, "Maybe, when I leave here [for my uncertain future], I'll die—but maybe, there's just as good [of] a chance that I'll be free!"

Next, we cut to the somber funeral for the fallen construction worker. Martin's sister Jeanne walks alongside the worker's small children and widow, and the widow's face is, of course, completely obfuscated by the appropriate black veil. Gargame and Martin are both present as well, and Gargame seems genuinely-touched that Martin's been going around asking for money, to help out the guy's family. (Martin would probably have given some of his own money, but he doesn't have any anymore—he's already spent everything he had on Blanche's villa, and on his new car.) Gargame informs Martin that Blanche sold her bird store the previous day, and that she's probably going to be leaving town, and Martin takes this horrible news in quietly, but Gargame would love to be able to see the stoic guy react: "You know Martin, just for once, I'd like to see you have a reaction. Behave like a man!" (The Gabin-Quietude, which serves Our Hero very nicely in many movies just doesn't fly with Martin's boss, a guy who's used to people actually conversing with him, and exchanging ideas on a back-and-forth basis.) Some churchy-sounding music next floods the soundtrack, as Martin makes a dash for his car to head for the bird shop, hoping that maybe he'll be able to head Blanche off at the pass, and apologize for what he said to her the last time they spoke (when he called her a 'whore'), before she leaves town forever.

Martin gets to the bird shop, but he's too late: She's gone. And while it's true that Blanche really *did* love Martin, she apparently loves freedom all the more. A new owner (Paul Faivre) has already taken possession of the store, and he's a kindly old geezer who bought the place two weeks ago (but Blanche and Ferrand 'kept mum' about the sale). The new owner tells Martin that he won't be selling birds in the shop anymore, since they're too noisy and messy, and that he'll probably just start selling animal feed, or else that maybe, he'll just sell some animals that aren't as noisy as birds.

Martin thinks that Blanche may have returned to the villa to 'say goodbye to it' before her departure to wherever it is that she's going, so that's where his next stop will be, although first, he's going to have to stop over at the Mobil Oil station, where he'll once again chat-up

Annette, the gas attendant lady, as he fills-up for the big ride.

Martin finally arrives at the villa and, as it turns out, he was dead-right: Blanche *is* there, and she's tearing up the deed—the proof of her ownership of the property. Why would she do that? Maybe she's not totally mercenary, after all! Maybe she really does just want to be free, and maybe she really *is* a good person (and maybe she really does love Martin)!

"Am I bothering you?" Martin asks her in an accusatory tone, as he bursts through the front door, not even stopping to learn the truth (which he'd definitely be happy with). "This villa cost a lot of money, and I know you're trying to take the money out!" Martin slaps her, guessing incorrectly that Laubry is there with her: "So, you're into politics, huh? You've always been a liar!" She snipes at him that his hands are dirty (no subtext; they're actually just really black and crusty!), and that he smells of Pernod, the French worker's beverage of choice (it goes well with accordion music!), and then he does the only thing a man can ever really do, when he's finally had enough:

Martin strangles Blanche, until she starts begging for mercy!

Then, he starts running around the room tearing the whole place apart, just like Orson Welles in *Citizen Kane*, while continuing to damn her with her every prostitute-related epithet he can think of. When Blanche catches her breath, she tells Martin truthfully, that she's not seeing Laubry anymore, that she's given him up for good, and that she's just going off to be alone, and without any man at all. Still enraged however, because this true explanation of hers isn't good enough for him, he bats the sconces off the wall with his fists, the room catches fire, and the fire quickly spreads through the entire villa. Martin runs outside, unable to save Blanche who, just like her house, is now also engulfed in flames.

Blanche burns to death.

Martin arrives back at his sister Jeanne's place, and she's very clearly worried, because she hasn't seen him for a long time: "Where are you coming from? I've been waiting for you!" Still tripping-out over what's just happened, Martin has no explanation for her, and Jeanne scolds him (he's ever her 'baby brother'). She notices, then, that he seems to have cut his hand, and she asks him how it happened: "Did you hit someone? Do you still have problems with that woman? Well, never talk about her to me again! It's going to be over between you and her, do you understand?" (It's more *over* than Jeanne can even begin to understand!) Martin then admits to Jeanne that he's just killed Blanche, and it's weird that he's using that specific word, because he didn't really kill her—it was more like, 'he was just unable to save her.' In fact, he feels so horrible about Blanche's death that, at least, at this particular moment (he'll vacillate a little bit as the film continues), he doesn't want to go on living:

> JEANNE: You killed her? That isn't true!
> MARTIN: Yes. It is true.
> JEANNE: But they'll take you away! Was it at her shop?
> MARTIN: No. At the villa.
> JEANNE: Did anybody see you?

MARTIN: No.

JEANNE (freaking out): Well… don't just sit there!

Jeanne, immediately and instinctively, goes into protective 'Mama-Bear Mode,' helping her brother to create a good alibi for himself: "Well, okay: A lot of people were around her. Nobody will ever know it was you." But just in case anybody should figure out that it was Martin who set the fire, whether he did it on purpose or not, Jeanne, very smartly, proceeds to set the wall clock back to 1:00 p.m., which is the time that Blanche burned up. She next tells Martin, "Okay, here's your story: If anybody asks you, you've been here all day, and we've been eating lunch."

Right after Jeanne's re-set the clock, the happy-go-lucky Mailman knocks and brings Martin and Jeanne their daily junk mail. He looks up at the clock, and notices that it is (he thinks) 1:00 p.m. Martin's been putting on a façade of calmness the whole time that the Mailman's been there, and the second the guy leaves, after Jeanne and Martin have given him a glass of wine which he's accepted readily (here's a guy who's definitely in love with 'the good grape'), Martin's as close to being a nervous wreck as Jean Gabin can ever truly be, which is to say that he's just sitting there calmly, staring down at the floor, and displaying no facial expressions at all. Jeanne comforts him, by rationalizing further: "Anyway, that Blanche—she was seeing a lot of people. So her killer could have been any one of dozens of jealous guys."

But Martin doesn't want to hear any more about it, and he stifles Jeanne by telling her that he loved Blanche: "Anyway, how could *you* understand?" (What a mean dig for Martin to make at his sister. He's basically telling Jeanne—this good woman who has dedicated her whole life to taking care of him—that she's an old spinster who'll never know anything of love!) He then adds, trying to remain level-headed, "Anyway, if they do put me on trial, I will defend myself, and they won't get me." We can tell though, from his world-weary expression, that he's totally resigned to whatever fate may bring, and that he really doesn't care whether the authorities are going to be guillotining him, or not. (In fact, he'd probably prefer that they do.)

Cut to the next scene: Martin's been caught and jailed, and his court-appointed lawyer, who's played by Jean Darcante, paces Martin's cell. Now that Martin's experiencing jail for the first time in his life, he doesn't want to be there anymore and, in fact, while in only the previous scene he was saying that he wanted to be guillotined, now, suddenly, he's done an about-face, and has become obsessed with his own personal freedom, and with how quickly he can attain it. Martin tells his 'mouthpiece,' that he's going to be pleading innocent, since he didn't kill Blanche on purpose. (In his own view, which is more or less true, he didn't burn her up—the house did!) The Lawyer tells Martin that if he does plead guilty to the murder, that he'll probably receive only the minimum sentence, because the Lawyer thinks that he can prove, based upon the way that Blanche used a lot of men (including Martin), that she was a real con-artist. ("Just tell the Judge that she didn't make things easy for you!")

Next, we see Gargame and other passers-by filling up the town square, and many of them are picking up the latest edition of the newspaper. (Headline: "MARTIN ROUMAGNAC: ACCUSED OF MURDER!") Martin's everybody-in-town's friend, and all of the people who pick up newspapers are shocked and astounded. Meanwhile, in a local corner bar, a radio announcer whom we can hear over the din of clanking glasses solemnly proclaims, "Martin Roumagnac believes in Fate," and he's not saying it in a favorable way, either. The radio next reports that a letter which has been written on Martin's behalf was sent to the prosecuting attorney by, of all people, Laubry! As it's turning out, the Consul is a much-nicer person than we thought he was. Currently, he's away on business in the Netherlands, which is where he's mailed this letter from, and, while it's not stated in the film specifically, we can tell that he probably thought that he, himself, would be a murder suspect, and so he skipped town. Well, he needn't have bothered, because now, as the radio announcer is alerting us, the Judge on the case (the trial hasn't yet begun) has already excused Laubry from the witness stand, because the forensics lab, in checking out the villa, couldn't find any evidence to suggest that Laubry was present on the day in which Blanche was transmogrified into a krispy kritter and, at this point in the action, the non-fickle finger(prints) of fate are all pointing toward Martin. One 'ornery old cuss in the bar, a pool-playing old codger who obviously likes Martin, tells Paulo, who happens to be playing a round with him, "Maybe Martin's not guilty. I mean, if there was a fire, wouldn't the fire have burned his fingerprints?" Paulo believes Martin to be innocent, as well: "The press is trying to make Martin guilty, but that's just plain meanness." Nobody in town, with the exception of that crappy old newspaper editor who wrote, "Do you really think you'll win, Martin" thinks that good old Martin would be guilty of as heinous a crime as outright premeditated murder. Maybe he's guilty of thinking with the wrong head, but ultimately, to paraphrase Woody Allen from *Love and Death*, "isn't all mankind guilty of that very crime?"

The final act of the film should be subtitled "The Trial of Martin Roumagnac," because that's exactly what it is: Annette the Mobil Oil pump-*jockatrix* is there, and so is the love-tormented young Surveyor (Daniel Gelin), who sits alone in the back row of the courtroom's audience area. 'Guest-of-Honor' Martin gets a privileged seat above everybody else on a raised platform, and not only does he *not* look freaked out and scared by the fact that he's on trial for murder, but he actually looks sleepy, as though he just wishes that this whole fandango would be over already, so he can get some peace. (It's just like in those other movies, in which Gabin's characters always stay a bit too calm, during their own police interrogations.)

Gas-lady Annette looks up at Martin, and apologizes to him for the fact that she's been called to the stand today to testify on behalf of the prosecution, since she genuinely likes him: "I have nothing against you personally, Mr. Roumagnac, but it's true: You were at my gas station." Martin's Attorney asks the woman if she can prove that Martin was at her filling station on the day of Blanche's death, and she replies that she can't prove the exact date, so the Judge summarily dismisses her. (Chalk up one point for The Gabin Defense! Not that the lackadaisical/bordering on soporific Martin even cares.)

Day One of the trial has now run its course, and Martin's now back in his jail cell and staring out the barred-window, looking just like Francois in *Le Jour se leve*, the murderous young Gabin character who sat alone in his darkened attic, waiting for the cops to come and drag his ass off to jail. (Through a weird twist of moviefate, scheming Blanche is the one who's now free, while *Martin* is the one who's become the 'caged bird.') The evening's newest and most up-to-the-minute newspaper headline proclaims that nobody knows where one of the key witnesses—Blanche's 'Uncle' Ferrand—is, and that it's too bad, because his testimony would have been considered very important for both sides.

The Trial, Day #2: The Mailman, just as Martin's sister thought he would be, is on the stand now, and he's telling the court that he was at Martin and Jeanne's house with them at 1:00 p.m., which is the time that Blanche's villa is supposed to have burned down (according to his testimony, anyway) thus placing Martin, very squarely, *not* at the scene-of-the-crime. The Prosecuting Attorney (he's played by Paul Amiot, who also played the lawyer, Merlu, in the 1932 Gabin flick, *Coeur de lilas,* and Gabin's partner in the missing 1933 Coast Guard adventure, *L'Etoile de Valencia*) interrogates this postman, a guy who, as we already saw, definitely loves *vino:* "So, my client and his sister invited you for a glass of wine, didn't they? And you can't turn down a glass of wine, can you? And since you were drinking, isn't it possible that you don't really even know what time you were actually in the Roumagnacs' home?" (The Prosecutor has figured out already that it's possible Martin and Jeanne were trying to get the guy drunk, so that he wouldn't remember time properly.) "They *did* offer some wine to me," the Mailman replies, "and I took it. I've never missed my schedule a day in my life, and I didn't miss it that day, either." The Mailman then smiles a big gap-toothed smile, and looks like he's having nothing but fun, being part of such a big trial: Definitely, these proceedings are a big event for a guy like him who spends his whole life *schlepping* around a smelly wet leather bag full of Hammacher-Schlemmer catalogs!

Many optical wipes are used during the trial, which is director Georges Lacombe's way of showing us that time is passing. The Judge (he's played by Marcel Andre), having already heard days and days worth of testimony, next tells all-assembled that he has been convinced completely of Martin Roumagnac's guilt, however Martin's lawyer won't stand for it: "Why are you trying to make my client guilty, when he is not? He was having his lunch at home when the crime is supposed to have been committed—and anyway, so what if my client likes women? Men are like moths to their light! If I may borrow the words of Mr. Roumagnac's sister [Jeanne said the same thing when she was on the stand in her brother's defense, a few scenes ago], 'There has never been a murderer in the Roumagnac family.'"

Martin's lawyer is so persuasive, and everybody in town continues to love Martin so much (even in spite of the fact that they think he should have known better than to get involved with a saddle-tramp like Blanche), that all of the audience members in the courtroom now applaud when he proclaims his client's innocence. Everybody in the room is supporting

Martin, which is a nice twist because earlier in the picture, some of those same exact people were making fun of him.

The Judge asks Martin if he has anything to say in his own defense, but Martin just shakes his head. "No," he whispers softly and resignedly, as everybody cranes their necks in to hear him, "I told you I'm innocent. That's all." Then, unexpectedly, Blanche's 'uncle-slash-brother-in-law' Ferrand arrives, looking, if this is even possible, even more disheveled (and hobbled-over and ratty) than usual. The Judge wants to hear Ferrand's testimony, since he has a feeling that it might corroborate the fact that Martin is guilty, which is what we know the Judge already thinks anyway, but Martin's lawyer won't hear of it: "Look, it's too late in the trial for this man, Mr. Ferrand, to speak. We've already weighed all of the evidence. The defendant—my client, Mr. Roumagnac—is supposed to be the last person to talk, and he already has. So this trial is over. Martin Roumagnac is simply not guilty." The Judge won't give Martin's lawyer that satisfaction, though, and he lets loose with a mighty cry of "Overruled!" He then places Ferrand on the stand anyway, asking him why he didn't show up before, when he was originally summoned, to which the majorly depressed-looking Ferrand replies, "Because, for the few months since Blanche's death, I have been by myself, dreaming only of my own death." (He was so overcome by Blanche's death that, apparently, he had himself committed into a mental hospital. As we already know, Ferrand's a raw-nerve, a guy with the most fragile constitution of any human being who's ever lived.) He continues, "On the day of the murder, Martin came into my store and met the new owner. I never got the impression that Martin could murder anybody." (The New Owner must have called Ferrand and alerted him that Martin had stopped by. Is Uncle Ferrand defending his niece/sister-in-law's killer, because he knows that Blanche truly loved Martin? Most probably, yes.) Martin, who's starting to go a little stir-crazy now, starts yelling out, during his own trial, that everybody should just "hurry up" and "finish this craziness," so that he can go back to his cell and rest. He also admits to the court, of his own volition and without being asked (thereby breaking his own self-imposed 'Jean Gabin Silence-Rule'), that he really loved Blanche, and that his life didn't start until he met her. (Apparently, at least in the world of this film, in France, one can speak out at one's own trial anytime one wishes to, without being considered out-of-order; French trials are [at least as they're being portrayed in *Martin Roumagnac*] a lot like those British Parliament meetings they're always showing on C-SPAN, in which each person gets to talk and interrupt and harrumph everybody else as much as he wants, without any fear of repercussion.) At this point, Martin even waves his own lawyer away, when the guy is only trying to help him. (Martin is so sick and tired of this case, he doesn't even feel like being defended anymore.)

"The past of your niece is murky," Martin's lawyer tells Ferrand. "She earned money from, shall we say, 'nightlife.' Why is it that she was in Paris, sometimes? Can you tell us?" Ferrand replies that, as far as he knows, "She used to go to Paris sometimes, to learn how to paint, because women have to be 'agreeable' when they are married." (Ferrand really believes what he's just said too, because 'painting' is probably *exactly* what Blanche told Ferrand she was doing, in the City of Lights.) Ferrand tells the court that he believes both Blanche and Martin to be innocent of whatever everybody is saying about them. (Ferrand still likes Martin, even if Martin *was* accidentally responsible for Blanche's death, which is what Ferrand believes to be true.)

Martin's lawyer tells the court that Laubry offered Blanche a fortune to marry him, and he then shows the Judge a letter which Laubry wrote to Blanche which seems to have proven it. He adds also that Blanche wasn't interested in Laubry's money, because she loved Martin more than she loved Laubry, and that Martin loved her right back, which is why Martin would have never intentionally killed Blanche. (As the Lawyer is now telling the Judge, "When would you actually kill somebody that you really love?") The Judge accuses Martin, "You were jealous of this other guy, and you wanted to prevent her from seeing him, didn't you?" "It's true," Martin's lawyer tells him, addressing his client directly. "Blanche didn't want to see Mr. Laubry. She only wanted to see you."

Martin starts looking really embarrassed about the few Gabin-Outbursts which he's let slip during the trial, because he's just learned now and for the first time, during Ferrand's testimony, that Blanche really *did* love him as much as he loved her, and that she didn't love Laubry at all, *and* he's also learning now that she stopped hanging out with Laubry very specifically because Laubry said shitty things about Martin, and that Blanche just didn't like it.

After some deliberation (in film terms, that means after a slow dissolve), the Jury has its say-so, and declares Martin to be innocent of all charges. Blanche's death is ruled to have been an accident, and Martin is free. Everyone in the courtroom cheers and, as the audience filters out, only Martin remains. His lawyer escorts him out and he looks miserable, even though it's just been determined that he's not guilty, because he misses Blanche so much. Even though Martin's not in trouble anymore as far as the legal system goes, he knows in his own mind that he, and he alone, is the one who was responsible for her death, even if it wasn't intentional; and even though the law won't be punishing him, we can already guess that his own guilty conscience will. After Martin and his attorney have left the courtroom, only one attendee is left: It's Daniel Gelin's lonely, obsessed, young Surveyor. He's just sitting there. And sitting. And thinking...

Back at Martin and Jeanne's house that night, everyone in town has come together, to throw Martin a big celebration party, and even Mr. Gargame himself is there. All of the partygoers look ludicrously happy—all, that is, except for Martin, who's more miserable-looking, and more Gabin-Expressionless, than he's been in the entire movie. In the kitchen, Jeanne's cooking-up-a-storm with a girlfriend, a woman who's telling her, "I know you've been through hell. Well, thank God all of the bad is over!" And guess who else is making the scene at our big shindig: It's the happy-go-lucky Mailman who, loaded out of his mind tonight, as per usual, is telling everybody he knows that Martin is free, very specifically because of his (the Mailman's) own personal testimony.

Gargame starts handing guests copies of the evening's newly-released newspaper, the headline of which proclaims, "MARTIN ROUMAGNAC IS FREE," and Jeanne places a comforting arm around her brother's shoulder. ("It's all over, honey.") Paulo even makes a funny toast to Martin: "To the good health—of your attorney!" (Even in old movies, they still have 'lawyer jokes!') Instead of laughing, Martin now has a huge Gabin-Outburst (he has a lot of them in this picture, as opposed to just the usual one or two): "Shut-up, all of you! Leave me alone! None of you knows anything, and you all just talk about what you don't know!" He stampedes into his bedroom, slamming the door behind him, and now he's all alone in the dark, just like he was in jail. (What Martin's just screamed out at his friends, is almost exactly what Gabin's character yelled-out to the crowd at the end of *Le Jour se leve*, when his character told the congregating lookieloos, who were crowded beneath his window, to go home and to leave him alone.) While the partiers revel below, Martin just stands there in his bedroom, expressionlessly.

Downstairs, somebody unexpected is showing up at the party: We now see the lone figure of the Surveyor lurking outside Jeanne and Martin's house in the shadows—and he's got a gun! Quiet and unassuming throughout the film, this young and tortured admirer of Blanche's has come to kill Martin Roumagnac because, in his mind, Martin is the one who's taken Blanche away from this world. (The Surveyor-character is a 'Gallic Norman Bates,' but with only about half of Bates' creepiness.) Martin knows that the young guy is right outside his window, pointing a gun at him and, rather than back away from the window to save himself, he quietly backs right into the window, wanting to die, needing to be free of the misery that a life without Blanche Ferrand will be sure to bring him. Then— CRACK! CRACK! The Surveyor pumps two shots into Martin's back, and Blanche's four-leaf clover, which, as we're now finding out, Martin has been holding for the whole evening (and maybe, he was even holding it during his trial) drops out of his hand. (Sounds silly, but the moment is very poetic.) The last thing which our tortured Martin Roumagnac does, before he falls down dead onto the floor, is to walk around the room, turning off the one small lightbulb which has remained on during the scene. He then falls to the ground, dead (and this whole scene, from beginning to end, is very surreal, and very David Lynch-like).

As Martin lies dead on the floor, the voice of a female partier from below is now yelling up to him: "Life is beautiful, Martin! [It's the same exact sentiment which Martin had expressed near the beginning of the film, when he first met Blanche at the boxing ring.] Come down! Everyone is saying goodbye to you!" Little does everybody present know, that Martin is dead, and that they're all really saying goodbye to him, and forever, whether they know it or not. Next to Martin's body, on the cold wooden floor, there's a copy of that newspaper with the "Martin Roumagnac is Free" headline spread across its top, and now, of course, Martin Roumagnac truly *is* free.

Martin Roumagnac is a very good and consistently engaging movie, one which manages to carefully avoid melodrama at every step, and it succeeds wildly, even in spite of the uniformly lukewarm reviews which the film received on both sides of the Atlantic when it was first released. Not only is the picture great dramatically, but it's also helped immeasurably by the beautiful, pastoral look which the film's cinematographer Roger Hubert, has given to the villa scenes.

When *Roumagnac* was released on DVD in France, in 2004, it was the first time in which the film had been seen anywhere in the world, even in its native France, in almost fifty years, and probably, it's not just because Jean Gabin didn't want it shown: Even when the picture was first released theatrically in France, back in 1946, the film's distributor, Alacine, didn't put too much time, effort, or money into advertising because, as I have already mentioned in the biography section of this book, French audiences were still punishing Gabin for deserting them during WWII. In any case, *Martin Roumagnac* is a very worthwhile Jean Gabin movie and, in fact, according to author Ean Wood in his 2002 book *Dietrich: A Biography*, the film almost had a sequel, which was to be called *Premiere mondiale* (*World Premiere*), however, this film was never made, because Gabin and Marlene Dietrich broke off their real life, five-year love-affair shortly after *Martin Roumagnac* was released, and the two of them never saw each other in person again, after the evening of the film's star-studded Paris premiere, which took place at the beginning of 1946. (Since Martin and Blanche both die in *Martin Roumagnac*, *Premiere mondiale* would, more accurately, had to have been a *prequel*.) In 1949, also according to Ean Wood, a British journalist apparently asked Jean Gabin if he would ever make another picture with Marlene Dietrich (who, at this point, Gabin hadn't even seen in-person, for two years), and Gabin's reply was reportedly as curt as it was simple: "*The old lady is too unstable.*" (These probably weren't his true feelings because, as I've mentioned, Gabin and Dietrich would love each other for the rest of their lives, even though they never saw each other again after the premiere of the film.)

Be that as it may, *Martin Roumagnac* is a great film, and one which definitely deserves a million times more recognition than it has ever received. Marlene Dietrich's Blanche character is just as great a 'Blanche' as that other, 'more known' Blanche of the stage and screen, Blanche DuBois, from Tennessee Williams' Pulitzer-winning play, *A Streetcar Named Desire*. Just like Dietrich's 'Blanche' in *Martin Roumagnac*, so too Williams' Blanche DuBois-character is a working-class prostitute who pretends to be high-class, because she has so much disdain for her common life. Similarly, Jean Gabin's inarticulate, rough-hewn Martin is just as great of a 'working-class guy, who pines after a woman who's pretending *not* to be prostitute,' as is Stanley Kowalski in *Streetcar*, and if you haven't yet figured out where I'm going with this: The French film *Martin Roumagnac* premiered in Paris on December 18, 1946, and the stage play of *A Streetcar Named Desire*, which sets it scene in New Orleans' *French* quarter, opened at New York City's Ethel Barrymore Theater almost exactly one year later, on December 3, 1947! Is it possible that Tennessee Williams visited Paris, saw the film of *Martin Roumagnac*, and then became suddenly inspired to 'write' his 'original' play, *A Streetcar Named Desire*? Since *Martin Roumagnac* is the one film of Marlene Dietrich's sound movie career which was never properly released in the United States, except for its barely-advertised one-week run in one New York cinema in its heavily-truncated version, is it possible that the backers of the Williams play somehow squelched *Roumagnac's* American release because they didn't want American audiences to discover the similarities between the two works? I would never want to accuse Tennessee Williams of plagiarism but, suffice it to say, watch George Lacombe's 1946 film, *Martin Roumagnac,* and then watch director Elia Kazan's 1954 film version of Williams' *A Streetcar Named Desire,* and decide for yourself!

What a Critic Said at the Time (Reviewing the shortened American-release version): "A curiously uninspired treatment of a crude and conventional theme. Gabin seldom takes off his hat, which is an old Gabin way of showing contempt for urbanites." (New York *Times,* 9-4-48 issue. Critic: Bosley Crowther.)

With Colette Mars.

FILM 35

Miroir

France, 1947

(Literal English Translation: "MIRROR") Directed and Edited by Raymond Lamy. Produced by Marcel Bryau. Written by Paul Olivier and Carlo Rim. Music by Maurice Yvain. Director of Photography (black and white), Roger Hubert. Production Designer, George Wakhevitch. (GENRES: DRAMA/CRIME) An Alacine Production. Running Time, 1 hour 35 minutes. Released in France by Gaumont-Eagle Lion, on May 2, 1947. Never Released Theatrically in the United States.

"I'm a little overworked lately."
— Gabin to his Mistress, right after he's shot his best friend, in "Miroir"

Miroir was a transitional film for Jean Gabin. It marked, for the most part, the end of his 'working class, tragic drifter movie-period,' and the beginning of his '*bourgeois*, rich guy period' (1947, to the end of his life/career in 1976), in which he'll play an older business patriarch/captain of industry, a guy who's successful, and who has also come-up from working-class roots. And we actually get to see his transition on screen (it's partially why the movie is called *Miroir* [or, in English, *Mirror*]) because, while his character is now a wealthy businessman, the picture's director, Raymond Lamy, a film editor who would direct only a few films, is going to flash back, and we'll be able to see Gabin's same character as a younger man, when he *used to be* a working-class drifter. (So: We're lucky because, in a sense, we're getting both the 'old' and the 'new' Movie-Gabins, in this one film.)

The film opens in present day Paris, at a meeting of big business muckimucks.

At the head of the table—it's big-time captain-of-industry/owner-of-many-companies Pierre Lussac (Jean Gabin). Pierre's a gangster, too, but one with scruples. A gentleman-criminal (for the remaining twenty-nine years of his career, Gabin is going to be playing *lots* of them), his businesses aren't always 'completely above-board' but at least he, himself, is always honest: Jean Gabin's businessmen characters will never rip anybody off, nor will they ever double-cross anybody and, in those pictures in which he's a bad guy, he's always an 'honest' bad guy.

Pierre's also a family man: His son, Charles (Daniel Gelin, who played the young Surveyor,

Gabin's rival for Marlene Dietrich's affections in the previous year's *Martin Roumagnac* [a film which was produced by the same company which also produced *Miroir*, Alacine]) is a young and honest trial lawyer, the one Lussac family-member who didn't go into crime. (*I know, I know:* 'Honest' and 'lawyer' are an oxymoron—but just go with it!) When we first meet Charles, he's just finished prosecuting a crooked cop.

Attorneys in France, at the time the movie was made, weren't that well paid, and since father Pierre is the successful one in the family, he buys his son a fancy new apartment, as a present. "It's amazing," Charles enthuses, gawking at the luxurious pad with delight, especially because one of the bedrooms has been converted to a very cool-looking office. Pierre's married to a young woman who's his son Charles' age (the recurring joke in the film, is that Charles' step-mom is his own age), and Charles himself is about to get married too, and to a woman called Juliette Monfort (Colette Richard), but Pierre frowns on the marriage because this, after all, is class-conscious France, and Juliette comes from a family of *bakers*. (We'll see the same problem rearing it's ugly head again seventeen years later, in another Gabin picture, a 1964 comedy called *L'Age ingrat*, in which Gabin's wealthy shipping magnate-character will frown on his daughter's marrying the son of a middle-class grocery story owner.) It's a weird plot-point because before Pierre Lusac became rich, he too was working-class. In many of Gabin's other films which he would make after *Miroir*, but not in all of them, Jean Gabin's 'wealthy, *bourgeois* business characters' will usually embrace their working-class roots, but in this picture, he's trying to block them out completely. Pierre's 'got his hands in everything,' since he's not only a shipping magnate, but is also the owner of a popular newspaper, as well as of many of France's fastest race horses.

Tonight, Pierre's going to be meeting up with some potential new business partners, at the fancy boxing ring which he owns, the trendily-named 'Le Ring,' which takes up a large back room of its own at the Folies-Bergere, in Paris's hooker-filled Pigalle section. While Pierre is busy solidifying his evening plans, a woman enters his office, and she's only a woman very nominally because, in fact, she's a *Nun* (she's played by a one-named actress called Sylvie), who's come to Pierre to ask him for money, for the construction of a new church. (In lots of French films and, of course, in *Godfather III*, the Church is always depicted as being a bunch of greedy property-hounds.) Nunzilla hands Pierre the blueprints which her architect has made and, after considering them very briefly, he tells her that they're far too opulent: "If you're going to go that route, you guys should just build a casino," he tells her—and he's not even joking about that!

That night at Le Ring, Pierre has set up a show of what we today—or at least, what "we, back in 1983"—called 'Female Foxy Boxing,' to woo potential business partners to sink their cash into his various ventures. An old-time military guy and sometimes-business partner of Pierre's, The General (Jacques Mattler), has shown up, as has an unexpected and unwelcome guest, Manfredini (Rene Hell; yes, that's his real name!), a shifty old gangster from Nice. Apparently, Pierre and Manfredini were partners in some business dealings years before in which Manfredini screwed Pierre over so, as a result, Pierre's not too happy to see him again;

in this scene, Pierre even asks Manfredini if he's shown up tonight, after all these years, to screw him over again! Manfredini tells Pierre that they should let bygones be bygones and re-start their partnership, even though the two of them have had problems (to say the least) in the past, but Pierre doesn't really want to talk to the guy any more, and so he excuses himself.

The next stop for Pierre is a walk through his casino, where he meets-and-greets all of the big high-rollers, and also runs a spot-check on his employees. A wealthy-looking Baron (Felicien Tramel) is playing cards and, of course, Jean Gabin movies are always crawling with Baron-characters—*Chacun sa chance* (1930), *Les Bas-fonds* (1936); *Le Baron d'ecluse* (1959); *Le Jardiner d'Argenteuil* (1966)—both real Barons, as well as fake ones. This Baron, in particular, seems to be very lucky, and the croupier, whose name is St. Eloi (Henri Cremieux), is kissing his ass, telling him that he'll probably be breaking the bank tonight, which doesn't sound too wonderful to Pierre, who's just overheard him saying it. Pierre pulls the handle on a slot machine and, just like with American television's lovable 'Fonzie' character, the coins avalanche-out! Pierre tells St. Eloi that tonight, he intends to sort out all of the casino's problems: Mainly, the place has become quite the money-drain lately, since customers are winning more money than they're supposed to be, and, at the same time, Pierre's also recently gotten wind of the fact that some of his employees might even be doing a little skimming.

At the end of the evening, the Baron enters Pierre's office and hands over his winnings, and this is where we find out that he's not a real Baron, nor is he even a real card-sharp: He's just a shill who works for Pierre, and Pierre keeps him on, even though the guy used to be a crook, because he genuinely likes the guy. This *faux* Baron has come to tell Pierre that he doesn't want to work in the casino anymore, because he wants to change his life, so Pierre, who's eternally the Good Boss, calmly tells him, "Okay. I'll let you work in my stables if you want to, and you can help me take care of my racehorses. If you do a good job, I'll give you fifteen percent of what I make on the ponies, when they win." The Baron really loves Pierre and in fact, so do all of the casino's other workers, all of whom would go through hell and high water for their tough but tender boss. As soon as the Baron leaves, other employees start entering Pierre's office one-by-one, because each one wants to have his or her own problems addressed by the boss too, and it's just like the scene at the beginning of the first *Godfather* in which, one at a time, friends and would-be friends all found their way into Don Vito Corleone's study, where they illuminated the great patriarch on all of the problems in their own lives, which they wanted him to fix. One reason that all of Pierre's employees love him so much is that, at the end of each evening, he always makes time to hear everybody's concerns, which is very modern of him to do. (Jean Gabin invented 'corporate management-training.')

The strikingly beautiful Lulu (Martine Carol), a would-be actress, next enters Pierre's office crying, because she's just lost big, at the gaming tables. She doesn't work at the casino, but Pierre has apparently loaned her some money to play with since, as a good businessman, he knows it's good for the casino to have a mega-hot girl around—Lulu's even known around the place as 'The Princess,' but not in any kind of a pejorative manner, because everybody there truly likes her. She's flat-broke and needs a loan, and Pierre tells her that he'll be happy to provide her with a little more *scratch* on one condition, which is that if she ever gets a big part in a movie or in a play, that she's going to have to pay him back out of her earnings. Of course, she accepts readily.

Next, the casino's sad-sack Bartender (Robert Le Ray) enters Pierre's office and tells Pierre that his family is mad at him, because he's been working at Carlo's female foxy-boxing show, and his family feels that the show is sleazy. Pierre likes the Bartender, and knows that the guy is a really good worker, and that he's just cracking up, because he also happens to be *a real nebbish* who has no life nor any social skills, so Pierre makes him an offer, too: He points Lulu out to him (she's playing in the casino, again), and asks him if he'd be interested in taking a vacation with "a pretty young girl." Pierre has just successfully *pimped Lulu-out* to the Bartender, and the new couple now walks away, arm-in-arm. The Bartender, who was sullen only moments ago, now looks like it's the best day of his whole life, although Lulu looks beyond grossed-out: She's just going out with the guy to placate her boss, because he's always so good to her.

Next up in Pierre's office, it's Pierre's assistant (Marcel Dieudonne), who informs Pierre that one of Pierre's best men has just been shot to death. The assistant doesn't address his boss as 'Pierre' but, instead, by an ancient nickname of Pierre's, *'Miroir'* ('The Mirror'), the meaning of which we'll be learning about later in the picture. Finally, Pierre's mistress-on-the-side, sultry brunette, Cleo (Colette Mars), who sings in the casino's nightclub, enters his office, and tells Pierre that she still loves him, and that she always will.

And just when it seems like life can't get any more complicated than it already is, and just as Pierre is making egress from his casino to go home for the night—BANG!—somebody off-screen has just taken a shot at him. Was it one of Manfredini's men? Was the whole meeting with Manfredini, in which Manfredini put on his whole, "Let's let bygones be bygones and work together"-*shtick*, just a trap to lull Pierre into a false sense of stability? Pierre is played by Jean Gabin though, and Jean Gabin never looks frightened—even when people are trying to kill him! He just alerts his security guys that they're going to have to be extra watchful from now on, and he then leaves, walking out into the night streets, all by himself.

Pierre doesn't only own a small Foxy Boxing ring at the Folies, either; he also owns a real Paris boxing ring on the other side of town, and next, on his way home, he stops-off there first, taking some time out to watch a young pugilist, 'Battling Joe' (Jacques Sernas), who happens to be married to Lulu ('The Princess'), as he's doing his training. Joe is bummed-out because, as an amateur boxer, he doesn't make enough money to support his wife properly, and he knows full-well that she sometimes has to prostitute herself, just so the two of them can eat. Joe asks Pierre where Lulu is, and Pierre lies to the guy (not wanting to say, "Oh, I just set your wife up with a *nerd*"), but only to spare the young guy's feelings: He tells Joe that Lulu told him that she was going to the country, to visit relatives. Joe's not stupid or punch-drunk though, and he totally knows the score, confidently changing the subject by telling Pierre that, now that he knows he's going to be winning the following evening's big prize fight, with the big money he's going to be making, he'll be able to "… take [Lulu] out of this horrible life[style]." Pierre, like just about all Jean Gabin characters, has a good heart, and we can tell just by looking at his face that he feels badly about what he's just done to Lulu and Joe; in fact, the reason that he's come to see Joe, even though he doesn't say it (with Gabin, the most important things are always unspoken), is *exactly* because he feels so badly about it.

Manfredini, with some of his 'boys' in tow, has followed Pierre over to the arena and, not willing to take no for an answer, reminds Pierre that it will be in Pierre's best interest to go into business with him, and Pierre again restates the fact that he is sublimely uninterested. In every film in which Gabin plays a wealthy boss, and *Miroir* will be the first of many films like this to come, he almost always works alone, and his is always the final say, which is exactly what he's letting Manfredini know in this sequence. Pierre's then saved by the bell because, at this very moment, his son Charles comes to see him, to plead with his father to allow the marriage between himself and baker's daughter, Juliette. Pierre's now caving a bit, finally giving his o.k. to the union, and most probably, because he knows that he hasn't been too honest with Charles about things either, like (for example) about the fact that he's not even Charles' real father! Pierre tells Charles, gently, "You and Juliette come from different classes. But if you want to marry her, you can." At this point, one of Manfredini's smart-ass henchmen who's remained in the room during the whole father/son meeting, checks-out both Pierre and Charles, and passive-aggressively smirks at Pierre, "Hey! How come your son don't look like you?!" In his office a few days later, Pierre receives a telegram from Nice. It's from one of Manfredini's underbosses, and he's informing Pierre that Manfredini has just been rubbed-out. Manfredini's gang thinks Pierre is the guy who was responsible, even though he wasn't, and the telegram warns, "*We're coming for you, Lussac!*" But Pierre doesn't look scared, remaining Gabin-Calm even when, in the next scene, some of Manfredini's hoods are going to start shooting-up many of the places which Pierre owns, including a fancy restaurant.

The next morning, we see Pierre's old friend Ruffaut (Paul Oettly), Charles' real father, for the very first time, when Ruffaut's being released from jail. (Years before Pierre found out that Ruffaut was in jail in Paris, he thought Ruffaut was hiding out in Venezuela.) Pierre hopes that Ruffaut won't make any attempts to see Charles.

That night, *chez* Pierre, Pierre's much-younger wife, Anna (Gisele Preville) has invited Juliet Monforte's baker parents, Antoine and Cleo Monforte (Robert Moor and Gisele Preville) for dinner, as well as Bechard the Priest (Paul Faivre), plus a Bishop and a bunch of other fancy swells. (In another of the movie's knocks at organized religion, we're seeing here that members of the clergy really get off on hanging around with dyed-in-the-wool gangsters!) Anna is deciding out loud that champagne will be served all the way through the meal instead of before, as is custom in their household. Indeed, Pierre Lussac is so fabulously wealthy, he's even got his own brand of champagne, called *Veuve Pigeon* and, as we already know from *Martin Roumagnac*, the movie which Gabin made right before this one, the word 'pigeon' in French is slang, meaning 'rube,' 'goof,' or 'dupe.' As smart as Gabin's Pierre Lussac is in this movie, obviously, Manfredini's men think he's a guy who can be pushed around.

Juliette's dad Antoine tells Pierre that he wants his daughter's wedding to be simple, and Pierre seconds the idea, telling his wife that he thinks Charles and Juliette should have their wedding right here, at his house. Pierre has a slot machine in his living room and, during cocktail hour, everybody takes turns playing it—even (of course!) the Priest.

Director Raymond Lamy match-cuts this shot with another shot—this one, of a second slot machine at Pierre's casino. It's now the next day, and Pierre pulls the arm of his slot machine, winning again. At that moment, a cop, Inspector Ballestra (Charles Lemontier, who played the Restaurateur in *Martin Roumagnac*) comes in to check on a lead which he's received, no doubt, from one of Manfredi's men, which is that some of Pierre's games might be fixed, but Pierre shows him his records, which state that he and his casino are always (unfortunately) losing, and that the customers are always winning. He assures Ballestra that everything at his casino is always above-board, and simultaneously, at home, Anna is printing out the wedding invitations, as some Chopin music wafts in the background.

Meanwhile, at the casino's nightclub, Pierre's sometimes-mistress Cleo is warbling-out a torchy tune, which is about, according to its lyrics, a guy who's "secretive," and who "hides things." Clearly, she's singing about Pierre, and he watches her performance expressionlessly, not even wincing at the lyrics, which are very obviously directed right at him. (Sample: "I know you're a liar—but I love you, anywaaaay...") After the show, Pierre makes his way into Cleo's dressing room, where he offers her his very concise review of the song (he tells her, "Baby, you've got problems!"), but *he's* clearly the one with problems: Even though now, at his present stage in life, he's a capitalist money-machine, he wishes he could go back to the good and simple old-days before he made his money, the days when he was just a normal, working-class guy, and life was much easier. Cleo tells Pierre that she thinks Pierre should leave Anna for her ("Get rid of your wife. I've always been yours, anyway"), and Cleo's feelings for Pierre aren't exactly one-sided either because Pierre, too, is starting to think that he might want Cleo in his life, on a full-time basis. (He doesn't *really* think she's nutty, like he has just intimated.)

Manfredini's men come to see Pierre, and now that Manfredini's pushing up daisies, the Manfredini Organization's new boss, Manfredini's former underboss Folco (Antonin Berval), is in charge. Folco, who is an ex-boxer himself, tells Pierre, "Look here, Lussac: I think you're the one who killed Mr. Manfredini. But if you go into business with me, I'll forget about it, okay?" That night, Battling Joe fights Kid Leon (Maurice Regamey), who happens to be managed by Folco, himself. Joe seems to be winning, and his wife Lulu, who's back from her tryst with St. Eloi, the nerdy sad-sack croupier, is in attendance, looking pleased with how her husband is performing in the fight.

The very next morning, it's time for Charles and Julia's wedding at the Lussac residence: All of the assembled guests are dressed in black tie, and Pierre wears white gloves, which look really uncomfortable on him; Pierre Lussac is rich but, like all Jean Gabin movie characters, he's also (aside from the fact that, in this picture, his character doesn't want his son marrying 'poor people') unpretentious. The Reverend performs the service, and he declares, without any trace of irony, "I like when virtuous people get married!" 'The Rev.' then thanks Pierre—it's kind of bad taste to do this in front of the guests but, then again, in the world of this movie, the Church = Bad Taste—for helping the dioses out with a very recent donation which, as we're finding out now, he's recently made. Pierre's assistant then interrupts the proceedings, to whisper into his boss's ear and inform him about Lussac Industries' newest problem: "I don't mean to interrupt you, sir. But I must inform you that the new ship you've just purchased—well, it's just exploded at sea, and we believe that Folco's men are responsible." Finding out about this during his daughter's wedding is bad enough, but to make matters worse, four of Folco's men (they're played by Fernand Flamet, Manuel Gary, an actor called 'Josselin,' and Julien Maffre [the worker who fell off the scaffold in *Martin Roumagnac*]) now show up at the ceremony, and start intimidating everybody with their scary-silence; Pierre sees the hoods, who are standing together in the back of the room, and shoots them all an incredible, 'I'm-not-afraid-of-you-guys'-scowl, for even having dared to show up. After the service, the thugs stick around for the party, and one of them even whispers, skeevily, to Pierre, "Your casino is failing, you know. You're headed for a big fall, my friend!"

Even though Folco's men have just told Pierre that everything in his organization is, or will be, going to pot, Pierre remains completely unafraid of them, knowing that everything the Folco-guys are telling him is untrue, and that they're just trying to freak him out. Pierre, then, overhears Juliette's Mother, telling another guest about how her daughter is marrying the daughter of an 'adventurer,' which is her polite way of saying that she thinks Pierre is a gangster, to which Pierre smoothly replies, "You are in no position to talk. You're a family of bakers!"

That night, Pierre knocks at his wife Anna's door, and she's in bed looking depressed, because she believes what Folco's men have said about Pierre's running out of money, and the thought of living without money has given her insomnia! He tries to convince her otherwise but, this time, when he goes over to the slot-machine in his house, and yanks on the arm, it doesn't pay off, and probably, for the very first time. For the first time in his entire adult life, Pierre has just lost and, hopefully, this loss is not predicative of things to come.

Back in Marseilles, Folco and his men are sitting around and telling the true and legendary story of the man whom they're up against, Pierre 'The Mirror' Lussac: Director Raymond Lamy now flashes back to twenty years before the story which we're now watching started, to 1915, and we now get to see what Pierre was doing in life, when he was younger (before he became a tycoon):

Young Pierre, who's also played by Jean Gabin (with dyed jet-black hair since, in real life, his hair was now silvery-white), was a poor French working-class anarchist who hated the establishment: In 1915, young French anarchists fought (with weapons) not only against the wealthy, moneyed *bourgeoisie*, but also against the trade unions, which they saw as being completely corrupt, and not helping the workers whom they claimed to be representing at all. (Just like today!) French Anarchists, at the time, referred to the union bosses as being 'the dictatorship of the proletariat,' because the men in charge of the unions were, to the anarchists' way of thinking, more interested in lining their own pockets than they were in helping the working people whom they were supposed to be serving. When we first see 'young Pierre,' he and his two Anarchist-pals, Ruffaut and Le Roy (Robert Arnoux) are lobbing Molotov cocktails through the window of a wealthy union boss's house, and the police are engaged in a shoot-out with Pierre, Ruffaut, and Le Roy. When director Raymond Lamy cuts back to 'the present day,' which he's going to be doing next, we'll now learn that the reason Ruffaut, Charles' real dad, has been in jail for twenty years, is because he wouldn't give up his two friends, Pierre and Le Roy, when they nabbed Ruffaut for some of the more violent crimes in which the three friends engaged, when they were young Anarchists.

End of Flashback.

In the present day, again, Pierre knows that Ruffaut has just been released from prison, and he means to nip any potential problems associated with his release in the bud, by telling Charles carefully, "What would you say if I told you that you're not my real son?" Stoic, just like his Gabinian step-dad, Charles mutters calmly that he doesn't know: "I guess I would have nothing to say."

Ruffaut is now not only out of prison, but he's also in-hiding, and somewhere in Paris. Pierre knows exactly where to find him because it's an alley where he, Ruffaut, and Le Roy used to hang-out twenty years ago, whenever they were trying to ditch the police. When the two old friends are reunited after twenty years, the first thing Ruffaut asks about, of course, is Charles: "Do you have any news of Charles? Is he getting married?" Pierre changes the subject by asking Ruffaut, somewhat snidely, if he still considers himself to be an Anarchist. In *Miroir*, just like in a number of his other films (like *La Bandera* and *Quai des brumes*), Jean Gabin hates things and people that remind him of his characters' shady pasts.

Ruffaut wants to meet Charles, to tell him that he's his real dad, and to brag to his son that he's still an Anarchist: While times have changed, and while Pierre and Le Roy have switched over to the other (to the establishment) side—in fact, Le Roy, the third friend, has even become a *cop!*—Ruffaut has not changed. Since Pierre doesn't want Ruffaut to interfere with his, and with Charles,' present life, he now shoots his old friend Ruffaut to death.

Then, silently, Pierre heads over to Cleo's apartment, and tells her cryptically that he feels "very overworked lately" (!), and she gives him a choice of cognac or Calvados, the French apple-brandy which Gabin apparently loved in real life (in fact, there's even a drink, which is listed in many of today's bartending books, that's made out of Calvados, and which is actually called a 'Jean Gabin' [I've supplied the recipe at the end of Volume 2, just in case you get thirsty]), and tells him she's just received a telephone call, stating that some people want to take revenge on Pierre for Manfredini's death. But of course, Pierre is not afraid.

The next day, Pierre attends Ruffaut's funeral, and nobody knows that he, himself, is the one who shot his old friend. Folco's men arrive for the film's climactic big shoot-out-with-Pierre, at the cemetery. It's the film's genuinely exciting big-finish, and we get to see gangsters shooting at each other from behind graves, while headstones explode into dust. Pierre seems to be the last survivor—but then he, too, gets shot to death. Le Roy, the cop (Pierre's old friend) examines the body of his lifelong friend and, as the film ends, he tells another cop that the reason Pierre Lussac was called 'Miroir,' is because back when the two of them were Anarchists together, Pierre saved Ruffaut's life: Apparently, and we're going to be seeing this now in Raymond Lamy's newly-offered flashback, Pierre noticed in a mirror's reflection that a cop was about to shoot Ruffaut, so he valiantly pushed Ruffaut out of the way to stop it from happening. (So weirdly, in 1915, Pierre saved his friend Ruffaut's life and 'today,' in present-day 1935, he's just ended it!)

Director Raymond Lamy's *Miroir* is a chilling movie about how, to paraphrase the poster for director P.T. Anderson's dazzling 1999 San Fernando Valley-epic *Magnolia*, "You might be done with the past… but the past isn't done with you:" *Miroir* seamlessly knits together Jean Gabin's young, working-class drifter-character, with the character he's going to start playing in a lot of the films which he'll be making throughout the 1950s and 1960s, the 'older, *bourgeois* industry captain-guy.' This is the film in which we actually get to see (visually) the transformation of Jean Gabin's Movie Persona, from the young, working-class, tragic drifter guy, whom he plays in the flashbacks, to the wealthy, *bourgeois*, captain-of-industry-guy, and it's also one of only two feature films which Raymond Lamy, one of France's most accomplished film editors, would ever direct, although he *was* Georges Lacombe's assistant director on *Martin Roumagnac,* and Jean Gabin personally invited Lamy to direct *Miroir*. It's hard to describe Lamy's directorial style which, for want of better terminology, I'll just describe (based upon my one viewing of *Miroir*) as being no more than good, serviceable, and appropriately invisible, which is to say that Lamy doesn't use any fancy or flashy visual tricks, like a lot of today's directors use (those irritating tricks, which only serve to pull us out of the story). *Miroir* has no credited film editor, which leads me to believe that Lamy, because his 'real career' was that of a film editor, probably cut *Miroir* himself.

Miroir was considered unavailable, even in France, for almost sixty years. In 2004, knowing that there was no other way to see it, I traveled to Brussels, where I was able to view a very good 35-millimeter print of the film at the Royal Cinematheque of Belgium. Too bad I'm not a psychic though, because two years after my Belgium trip, the film was finally restored, and released on DVD in France (French only; no English subtitles) in November of 2006. (Sigh!)

What a Critic Says Today: "If Raymond Lamy, who produced *Miroir* in 1947, does not have the visual ability of Duvivier, the film, at least, holds our interest… Jean Gabin is excellent, in this relatively ignored film." (From *dvdcritiques.com*, 11-15-2006 issue. Critic: Julien Sabatier.)

Top: With Isa Miranda. Above: With Vera Talchi.

FILM 36

Au-dela des Grilles

Italy/France, 1947

(Literal English Translation: "BEYOND THE GATES") Directed by Rene Clement. Produced by Giorgio Agliani and Alfredo Guarini. Screenplay by Jean Aurenche, Pierre Bost, Alfredo Guarini, and Jean Jeannin. Based Upon a Story by Alfredo Guarini and Cesare Zavattini. Director of Photography (black and white), Louis Page. Editor, Mario Serandrei. Production Designers, Piero Filippone and Luigi Gervasi. Music by Renzo Rossellini and Roman Vlad. (GENRE: DRAMA) A Production of Francoriz Production (France)/Alfredo Guraini Producione and Italia Produzione (Italy). Running Time, 1 hour 35 minutes. Released in France by Francinex, on November 16, 1949. Released in the United States with English Subtitles as "THE WALLS OF MALAPAGA" on March 20, 1950, by Films International of America, Inc.

"Police! He's right here! Come and get him!"
—*A teen-aged girl is mad that her mom is dating Gabin instead of her,
so she tries turning him in to the police, in "Au-dela des grilles"*

Martin Roumagnac and *Miroir*, Jean Gabin's first two post-World War II movies, made on his home-turf (*'La France'*), both vanished quickly from the box office in their native country. (*Miroir* never saw the light of day in the U.S. at all, and *Roumagnac* did, but only in a severely-truncated version, in spite of the fact that both movies are very good.) Gabin hadn't yet figured out that the main reason French audiences weren't coming to see his films, was because he had (they thought) deserted him when he went to the United States in 1941 and 1942; in his mind, the reason they weren't turning up to see him in *Martin Roumagnac* and *Miroir* is because, in those movies, he played a rich guy, and maybe they really wanted to see him only as the kind of tragic drifter-character whom he had played before the War. So, for his next movie ("... *fifteen million Frenchmen can't be wrong*," as a singing chorus trilled in Mel Brooks' classic 1974 comedy, *Blazing Saddles*), Gabin decided to give his audience what he felt it wanted: In the young director Rene Clement's *Au-dela des grilles*, Gabin would throw a little blonde hair dye into his suddenly-silver mane, *drifting-tragically* for one last time: *Au-dela des grilles* is a great (and haunting, and emotional) piece of cinema, a slice of Poetic Realism which was released a decade after Poetic Realism, as a film movement, had already died-out, but which is just as strong (and dark and powerful) as Gabin's other Poetic-Realist pictures, and not just *Le Jour se leve* and *Quai des brumes*, but also *La Bandera, La Bete humaine,* and *Remorques.* In fact, *Au-dela des grilles*, which has today been completely forgotten in the United States was, *once upon a time* (and for one brief and *extremely fleeting* moment) actually treasured in the U.S., because the film, which was released in America as *The Walls of Malapaga*, took home the Best Foreign-Language Film Oscar at 1949's U.S. Academy Awards! In the U.S., we fondly remember Oscar's Best Foreign Film winners which came both before and after *Au-dela des grilles*—namely, De Sica's *Bicycle Thieves* and Kurosawa's *Rashomon*—but *Au-dela*, which is equally as great as those other pictures, today merits nary even a footnote, in North America.

Post-World War II, French producers, with the exception of the Alacine company, which made both *Martin Roumagnac* and *Miroir,* weren't interested in making Jean Gabin movies at all (or movies with *any* 40+ year-old actor, for that matter); just like in today's movie industry, they were more interested in producing movies which showcased 'newer' and 'younger' stars. So Rene Clement attained half of the financing for *Au-dela des grilles* not from France, but from Italy, where 'Poetic Realism's post-World-War II cousin, Neo Realism' was now in full-flower, and *Au-dela* is definitely a work of Italian Neo-Realism which, like French Poetic Realism, is a dark genre of film predicated on the experiences of the working man. *Au-dela's* cadre of talented screenwriters was headed-up by Cesare Zavattini, whose heart-tugging writing had audiences around the world 'getting out their handkerchiefs,' from the sheer emotion of the two great Neo-Realist films which he had previously co-written, both of which had already won Best Foreign Film Oscars at the American Academy Awards—1946's *Ladri de biciclette* (*Bicycle Thieves*), and 1947's *Scuiscia* (*Shoeshine*)—both of which happened to have been directed by Vittorio De Sica.

Au-dela des grilles updates Gabin's pre-war, 'tragic-drifter-in-hiding-from-a-crime-he-committed-in-a-faraway-place-before-the-movie-started'-trope, and this time out, his safe haven (the protective 'Casbah' of this film) is a French Merchant Marine ship, in whose protective bowels (the police are not allowed on the ship) he intends to stay, and for as long as possible.

Gabin's Pierre has eluded Paris authorities, having murdered his twenty-two-year-old girlfriend, because she told him that he was "too old for her." To avoid the police, he's just sailed away with the French Merchant Marines, hiding in the hull of the ship, a place which, just like the Casbah, international police are not permitted entrance.

While Pierre would be content to stay down in the ship forever, a nasty toothache compels him to leave, risking life-and-limb to run through the war-torn streets of Genoa, in search of a good dentist. On land for only several minutes, Pierre is mugged, just like Gabin's character had been mugged at the beginning of *La Bandera*, and with no money to pay a dentist, he finds a quack, a guy who, since he can't be paid, offers Pierre to yank his tooth free-of-charge, and without anesthetic. (In true tough-guy style, Gabin doesn't even wince during this very painful experience.)

But it won't be long—also, *La Bandera*-style—before Pierre gets overwhelmed with guilt about the murder which he has committed, and knowing, as in other Gabin films, that the fate of a silver-screen killer, will always be to get caught (since "Crime Does Not Pay!"), he resignedly decides to turn himself in, to the local authorities.

But fate now throws Gabin a nice (for a change) curve or, more accurately (and more scintillatingly), *curves:* Entering the local police station, Pierre encounters the shapely Marta, who's played by the '*eh comment!*' ('and how!') brunette of the picture, Isa Miranda, the sultry lady-restaurateur who runs the *trattoria* next door to the police station, a woman who delivers daily pesto to Genoa's Carbo-Loading 5-0. Marta and Pierre are instantly intrigued by each other, and it's not long before he's in her restaurant, charming his way into a free meal. (Jean Gabin is free-wheelin… and free-*mealin'!*) Then (a big high-five for Gabin!), he charms his way into her home as well, where she gives him an extra helping of good, sweet loving, even though he's already confessed his crime to her.

Marta's precocious fourteen-year-old daughter, Ceccina (Vera Talchi) is similarly smitten by Pierre, and Pierre helps the comely mother-and-daughter team, by duking it out with Marta's psychotic and psychotically-unemployed ex-husband, Manfredini (Andrea Checchi), a guy who's made a full career out of attempting to kidnap his daughter Ceccina, and as often as he can. Mother and sexually-burgeoning daughter are both jealous of each other's attentions to and from Pierre, yet they both adore him, so they both agree that they will never divulge his secrets.

But soon, in the words of George Harrison, "it's all too much" for Ceccina: She knows she doesn't have a *Chinaman's chance* with the handsome, older man who's diddling mamma-bear, so this jealous 'Bad Seed' decides to narc on him, writing "Pierre is here!" on the sidewalks with chalk, and drawing arrows which lead toward her mom's apartment building. At the end of the film, Pierre, knowing that his Fate can only be to get caught, walks purposefully through Genoa's city walls—the 'Walls of Malapaga' of the film's American release title (they're just like the gates which separate the Casbah from the port, in *Pepe Le Moko*)—where the cops are already in waiting, to escort him to his presumably less-than-satisfactory fate.

Au-dela des grilles is as cool as any of Jean Gabin's other coolest movies (by which I mean: most of them), and it definitely deserves its own spot in the pantheon of great movies, which is where this film actually *used to be,* before film history somehow wiped it out of the collective memory (at least, in America). The film's young director, Rene Clement, who would direct Jean Gabin in only this one movie, was thirty-four when he made *Au-dela*, and he is mostly known in the United States today for one movie, his lush, color 1960 thriller *Plein soleil* (*Purple Noon*) starring Alain Delon, a film which introduced movie audiences, for the very first time, to novelist Patricia Highsmith's popular 'Talented Mr. Ripley' character.

By the way: When the film played in a single New York art-house cinema, in March of 1950, it was preceded by two short subjects—a cartoon called "Geometry Lesson," and a fashion documentary about Christian Dior!

A Great Post-Script/Update to this Chapter (a/k/a, "Yes, Virginia, There IS a God!"): On February 25, 2007, at the 79th Annual Academy Awards presentation, a film clip montage of 'Best Foreign-Language Films,' which was assembled by the Italian director Guiseppe Tornatore (*Cinema Paradiso*) was presented, and guess what: They showed Gabin in not one, but *two* clips from *Au-dela des grilles!* In 2007, for two brief, shining moments, *Au-dela des grilles* returned to America.

What a Critic Said at the Time: "A pulsating drama of frustration... an exciting fusion of Italian and Gallic talents. Excellent directing, a fine script, and imaginative photography. Gabin plays the fugitive with his usual understatement. It is an excellent performance." (*Variety*, 10-26-49 issue. Critic: "Kahn. [Nat Kahn.]" Reviewed at Cannes Film Festival.)
What Another Critic Said at the Time: "Not since our old friend, Jean Gabin, appeared in the French film *Quai des brumes* have we seen him in a picture of such strength and eloquence as *The Walls of Malapaga*. The feeling for human beings caught in the undertow of life is of a most tender and tolerant nature, delivered under the excellent direction of Rene Clement, makes for a full and forceful film. Mr. Gabin has the star role, and he plays it excellently." (New York *Times*, 3-21-50 issue. Critic: Bosley Crowther.)

BONUS CHAPTER
(A stage play starring Jean Gabin)

LA SOIF ("THE THIRST")

*A synopsis of an original stage play, in three acts (1949), written
(especially for Jean Gabin) and directed by Henri Bernstein.*

This is the only stage play in which Jean Gabin would ever appear during the entirety of his 1930 to 1976 film career. Gabin's good friend, the author Henri Bernstein, wrote this piece specifically for Gabin (and for Gabin's friends, Madeleine Robinson and Claude Dauphin—which explains why their characters in the play have the same first names that the actors had, in real life). *La Soif* was presented, beginning on February 8th, 1949, at the Opera Theatre, at 100 rue Richelieu, Paris. This synopsis of the theatrical production is offered here, to give the reader a feeling of 'what it would have been like to have seen Jean Gabin on stage.'

(With *La Soif*, Jean Gabin attained the wish which he had since he was young: Now, finally, he was able to perform on stage, in a 'serious, dramatic play.')

SETTING
The play takes place in Ville d'Avray France, in a country home.

CHARACTERS
Jean Gabin plays the role of 'Jean Galone;' Madeleine Robinson plays 'Madeleine Rony;'
Claude Dauphin plays 'Claude Darois;' Aline Bertrand plays 'Suzanne Langlois;'
and Guy Saint-Clair plays 'Jacques.'

ACT ONE
SCENE ONE
Best friends Claude and Jean haven't seen each other for a long time, because Jean has been traveling in the Pacific for quite awhile. Dr. Claude talks about his passion for science and research (and dancing; it's what he does at night, to 'blow off steam'), and the two men make jokes about women and love. Jean tells Claude, "I remember always having seen women fall

On stage with Madeleine Robinson.

at your feet... yet you never sleep with them!"

SCENE TWO

Jacques Legrand, a young student-painter, comes to tell his teacher, Jean, that he is leaving Ville d'Avray. The reason he gives, is that the artistic life isn't as glamorous for him, as it is for Jean.

SCENE THREE

It is revealed here that Jean lost his wife, Noella, before the beginning of the play. He's closed off most of the rooms in the house, living only in his living room, and since Noella died, he has been unable to paint. Jean is depressed, and Claude wants to help his friend, so Claude brings the fact to Jean's attention, that a journalist has just written an article in the newspaper about Jean's loneliness. (Jean sees the newspaper during this scene, and shouts out: "This is an intrusion!")

SCENE FOUR

Madeleine, a beautiful young woman, passes by Jean's garden. She sees him singing softly to himself, and stops to introduce herself. She asks Jean to paint a portrait of her, but he flatly refuses to do so.

SCENE FIVE

Jean has changed his mind about painting Madeleine, with whom he's become, very obviously, smitten. He agrees to give her one hour of his time, although he insists that Claude has to dance for them, first. ("No dancing... no drawing!")

SCENE SIX

Madeleine tells Jean that she's heard him singing, and she asks him if he'll sing a song to her, while he paints. Begrudgingly, he starts singing as she poses. (Lyrics: "Thanks to the propeller, the boat glides upon the flat current, which looks like a mirror/The larks loop over our heads, from dawn until the night.")

BLACKOUT

(A Unique Scene, which Takes Place Between the First and Second Acts)

We see now that Jean's completed his portrait painting of Madeleine, and that it's beautiful. He talks about his travels in the Pacific, and calls them a mistake because, as he's admitting to her now, he loves Paris. He tells her that his wife, Noella, made him promise that he would keep painting 'no matter what,' but that the act of putting the brush to canvas seems dull to him now. Although he has just completed the painting, he tells her to stay, because he's really enjoying her company. Madeleine opens up to him now, telling him that she will be divorcing. They bond over their mutual feelings of loss, and he's a little bit hurt when she's admits, now, that the reason she needs a portrait of herself, is because she wants to give it to her lover, a man named Sebastian Delrieux, who happens to be dying. Jean tells Madeleine that he sees women as being beautiful flowers and that, in his opinion, "*all men are aloof.*" He asks Madeleine to stay for dinner, but she tells him she has to go; however, she gives him her address.

ACT TWO

SCENE ONE

A blackboard at the side of the stage tells us that it is now 'March,' and that it is also two years and two months later: We're now in a beautiful Paris salon. As it turns out, Madeleine knows Dr. Claude, as well. (They probably met when she was hanging around with Jean, when Jean was painting her.) She has worked for him, typing up some of his medical notes, and he tells her that she's a good writer, and that she should think about writing her own book. Madeleine, as it turns out, has been romantically involved with Jean, and living with him for two years, while she is also seeing Claude on the side, at the same time. Claude tells Madeleine that, as soon as Jean finishes painting his new work, a fresco, that he and Madeleine will tell him about their affair.

SCENE TWO

Madeleine's best friend, Suzanne Langlois, comes to visit her. The two women haven't seen each other for nine years. Suzanne is a nurse who has spent the last several years working in Indochina. Claude offers her a job.

SCENE THREE

Madeleine tells Suzanne, that she feels that she's no longer in love with the always-brooding

Jean, and that she feels Jean will never truly get over his wife, Noella's, death. She tells Suzanne that she's tried to tell this to Jean on many occasions, but that he never pays attention, when she talks to him. She also tells Suzanne that she's fallen in love with Claude, in spite of the fact that this "dancing doctor" is *a pretty big player.*

SCENE FOUR:

Jacques, the young student-painter who used to be mentored by Jean, comes to visit the older man. He tells Jean that he is in love with his girlfriend, Ingrid but that he also loves another woman. Jean tells Jacques that he is deceiving both women.

SCENE FIVE:

Jean arrives home and finds out that Madeleine's there, *and* that she's been messing around with Claude. (He's been sitting outside of Claude's house in his car, spying on them!) Madeleine tells Jean that she and Claude are going to be getting married. She wants to fight with Jean, but Jean just throws the two of them out, and silently goes about cleaning his rooms. [Author's Note: Talk about Jean Gabin 'not getting riled-up!'] But this bothers Jean more than he's letting on, and he collapses. Madeleine runs back into the house and whispers "I love you" to him.

SCENE SIX

Jean is now in the hospital, and has been diagnosed with internal bleeding. Madeleine's friend Suzanne is taking care of him.

ACT THREE
SCENE ONE

The blackboard on the side of the stage tells us that it is now April, and that it is also thirty-four days later. Jean is in the hospital—weak, pale, and barely able to speak. Suzanne tells him, "Madeleine will mourn you. But she will still marry Claude, anyway."

SCENE TWO

Claude is getting mad at Madeleine because, apparently, she's been spending a lot of time visiting Jean in the hospital, and he's feeling threatened by her.

SCENE THREE

Claude visits Jean in the hospital. Claude tells Jean that Madeleine prefers him (Jean), and that he (Claude) doesn't want to marry her, anymore. The two men both agree that their friendship is ruined, because Madeleine has played both men against each other. Jean, who's a man of much common sense, tells Claude that he should stay with Madeleine, and that he doesn't want her to be alone in the world, because she's passionate (and *crazy*)!

SCENE FOUR

Jean is back home after his hospital stay, and Madeleine is now sitting with him, holding his hand in the room. He is making a new painting of her. The old portrait of Noella, which used to hang in the living room, has been replaced by that first portrait of Madeleine, which he had made two years earlier. Madeleine tells Jean that she's really enjoying "these divine days" which she's been spending with him, and he tells her that he's sorry that she sometimes has to see his depression. He tells her she is "a most beautiful rose, who has fallen from the sky."

SCENE FIVE

While Jean is at home, he still needs a doctor to attend to him occasionally, and Claude recommends a new physician to him. (The two men have remained friends, in spite of everything.) Jean and Claude speak together about the joys of life and health. When Jean leaves the room, Madeleine and Claude talk. She tells him he looks unhappy, and he tells her that he'll always love her and that, hopefully, one day, his feelings for her will "become faint." He adds, "The unknown always overwhelms us: Such is my destiny." Claude does a last dance for her, before he leaves.

SCENE SIX

Madeleine and Jean declare their love to each other, in a very tender way. Suzanne comes in to give Jean an injection. He takes a drink and compares '*la soif* (the thirst) for alcohol to "the thirst for finding the right colors and shades, in my paintings." He tells Suzanne, "As long as I have the thirst, I will always be able to paint." He goes upstairs to his bedroom alone, without having received his injection.

(Author's Note: *Thank you to Delphine Chabre, for translating the play into English.*)

THE END

An unnamed New York *Times* critic was on-hand, in Paris, for the opening night of *"LA SOIF,"* on February 8, 1949, and this is what he wrote about it:

"Henri Bernstein, playwright-producer... tonight presented his first [new] play since 1939. The audience applauded the excellent acting of the cast, headed by Jean Gabin, film star.

"'*La Soif* ('Thirst') appeared to be little more than a stylized repetition of 'the eternal triangle.' Although the play [feels like it was written] twenty or thirty years ago, the direction and acting are extremely up-to-date. The acting, by all parties concerned, left nothing to be desired, especially the scene in which Gabin suffers a heart attack.

"While the plot was extremely obvious, everyone appeared to be satisfied that Bernstein had given Gabin the opportunity to make love to Mademoiselle [Madeleine] Robinson." (New York *Times*, 2-9-1949 issue.)

Top: In conference. Above: With Antonietta Patrosi.

FILM 37

POUR L'AMOUR DU CIEL

Italy/France, 1951

(Approximate English Translation: "FOR THE LOVE OF HEAVEN") Directed by Luigi Zampa. Produced by Golfiero Colonna and Carlo Civallero. Screenplay by Vitaliano Brancati, Suso Cecchi d'Amico, Diego Fabbri, Giorgio Moser, and Henri Jeanson. Based Upon a Story by Cesare Zavattini. Director of Photography (black and white), Carlo Montuori. Editor, Eraldo da Roma. Music by Nino Rota. Production Designer, Gastone Medin. (GENRE: COMEDY) A Production of Cines Films (Italy) and Pathe Cinema (France). Running Time, 1 hour 21 minutes. Released in France on February 14, 1951, by Pathe-Carette. Released in the United States with English Subtitles, as "HIS LAST TWELVE HOURS," on November 12, 1953, by Italian Film Export.

"We have a tradition in this family: Whoever's celebrating a birthday
gets to cut the beast!"
*— Gabin's cuckolded wife tells her dinner guests about a family turkey-carving
tradition, in "Pour l'amour du ciel"*

Right after *Au-dela des grilles*, the Italian-French co-production which Gabin made in 1949, Gabin joined up with the Italians for another team-up which also, like *Grilles*, was co-authored by the legendary screenwriter of Neo-Realistic cinema, Cesare Zavattini— *Pour l'amour du ciel* (literally: *"For the Love of Heaven"*). Unlike *Au-dela*, however, this one's definitely a comedy (it's Gabin's first comedy, since Duvivier's lottery ticket-extravaganza *La Belle equipe*, back in '35), although Gabin plays it straight, which makes the film, and Gabin himself, come across as being 'even more funny.' *Pour l'amour du ciel* is not just a comedy, but a Capraesque comedy, which shares that the time-honored (and in some other movies, but not this one, *timeworn*) trope, in which 'a wealthy, out-of-touch guy learns humility by getting to know real, working-class people.'

As *Pour l'amour* opens, millionaire leather-and-skins company magnate Carlo Bacchi (Gabin), President of the eponymously-named 'Bacchineau Corporation,' is meeting with American business-types, in his lush/plush Rome office. It's Carlo's birthday today, and schoolgirls of elementary age are in Carlo's outer offices, holding flowers, and sitting alongside various of the town's leading officials. All of them are waiting patiently for Carlo to come out, so they can start singing "Happy Birthday" to him, on behalf of the entire town. (Carlo Bacchi is even more important in Rome, as we're going to be finding out, than are most of Rome's politicians!) Rome's nerdy Mayor even proclaims, angrily, that if Carlo doesn't come out of his office in about five seconds, he's going to be leaving. This relentlessly-milquetoast civic leader is pissed beyond belief that he has to defer, by dint of Carlo's personal monetary worth, to the whims of a leather salesman, when he, himself, happens to be the boss of an entire city!

The Americans meeting with Carlo, who include the American 'Big-Boss' Mr. Trevor (Frank Colson), are signing a contract with him, the result of which will be that Bacchi's furs and leathers will be sold in the U.S. All of the visitors are kissing Carlo's ass, which he's savvy enough to spot, and which he 'calls them all on,' as soon as they start doing it. And just as he's about to 'scratch-out his *Jean* Hancock,' Carlo, completely impromptu (to screw with his guests), suddenly decides that he'll sign-off on *some* of the agreement, but not all of it. Mr. Trevor tries to stand up to Carlo (bad idea to stand up to Jean Gabin), incensed that Carlo doesn't approve of the entirety of the agreement, and Carlo calmly gives his reason for being selective about where he places his signature: "Europe is already under your American vice-grip. I will not stand by and watch you taking advantage of us Europeans anymore. I will not sign those parts of your document which will forever condemn me to being just a cog in the American machine!" (The film's very sparse release in the United States, at one art-house theater in NYC three years after its French theatrical release, might have had something to do with the anti-American nature of Gabin's speech, in this scene.)

The Americans shuffle out of the conference room angrily and, at that moment, Carlo's wife Margot (Mariella Lotti) is calling from home. She's planned a very fancy birthday dinner for her husband, with a lot of their fancy friends in attendance, and he tells her, emotionlessly, that he'll be late, and it's no matter to him at all that the dinner's getting cold. It's not only Carlo's birthday, but it also happens to be the birthday of Carlo's own Patron Saint, and he just doesn't care. And when he finally does deign to emerge from the bowels of his inner-office, and the kids start singing-out their good wishes to him, Carlo, Ebeneezer Scrooge-like, just doesn't care, and little feelings are getting hurt, right in front of our very eyes. When Carlo heads out into the hallway, to avoid more first-grade theatrics, he walks right into a viper pit: It's the employees from his factory, and they're all shouting about how they want "more break time," not to mention a sizable raise. One worker (he's played by Piero Pastore) even points a finger at Carlo, and not so timidly, either: "Mr. Bacchi, I've been working for you for more than ten years, and I need more money! My Union says I'm entitled!" "I don't care what your Union wants," Carlo sneers at poor little Johnny Punchclock—or, as they might say it in good-ol' Viva-Italia, '*Giuseppe Punchclock-o.*' (In most of the films in which he plays rich businessmen, Gabin's characters side with the people who work for them, since his characters were usually working-class before they became rich, but not in this one, and not in 1947's *Miroir*, either.) Just like in Dickens' *Christmas Carol*, we know that time is drawing near for the unfeeling Carlo Bacchi to somehow 'learn humility.' Carlo tells his assembled workers that he *will* give them raises, but he doesn't say it in the most diplomatic way: "You guys can all shut up, because I signed a contract yesterday with your union, guaranteeing you all work for two more years. And listen: I don't want any more trouble. I promise I will get into a fight with you, if a fight is what you want—but I won't do it tonight." As Carlo leaves his building, he notices that somebody has scrawled an insult about him on the wall, however we can't make out what the words say.

When Carlo arrives home to his mansion, he's first greeted by his dedicated Butler (Bruno Corelli): "Some flowers for your birthday, Mr. Bacchi?" the Butler brown-noses, pointing out a recently-delivered bouquet on the entryway credenza, to which Carlo very succinctly replies, "Who cares?" It's a tribute to how great an actor Jean Gabin is that, even though he's being a complete asshole in this movie, we still manage to like him anyway, because he's taking such great pleasure in playing an jerk, that we're totally *with* him, even though, at the same time, we also want him to get what's coming to him and, even more than that, we want him to learn how to be nice. (Carlo Bacchi is the ultimate 'man you love to hate.')

Entering his living room, Carlo first comes upon his seven-year-old daughter Anna (Antonietta Patrosi), his wife Margot, and a group of Margot and Carlo's well-heeled friends—including Monsignor Biamonti (Aldo Bettoni)—all of whom have been waiting patiently for his arrival. (As we already saw in *Miroir*, 'Churchies' really get off on hanging around with Big Business-types: French and Italian filmmakers really love getting in their digs at Catholicism—both of their countries' 'religion-of-choice.') The Monsignor crows at Carlo, "I just stayed at that new hotel [which] you recently built. It's really fantastic." Carlo asks the Monsignor how the Pope, an old acquaintance of his, is doing, and Biamonti replies that the extremely-ill Pontiff's health isn't getting any better. Other guests around the Bacchi table include an effete, mustached Duke friend-of-the-family (he's played by Carlo Sposito) who also doubles as Carlo's attorney, and Margot's friend, Lidia Guidi (Elli Parvo), with whom Carlo happens to be having an affair—and right behind her back! Weirdly, Carlo's wife, Margot, is wearing a black dress, while mistress Lidia is adorned in the white one. (In the ahead-of-its-time world of this film, wives are evil—but mistresses are good!)

An elderly Housekeeper/cook now hefts an enormous turkey over to the table, and Margot Bacchi informs her guests, "We have a tradition in this family: Whoever has a birthday gets to cut the beast!" A second old housekeeper next enters the dining room, to alert Carlo about the fact that there's a phone call for him, from the American Mr. Trevor, and Carlo promptly chews her out for bothering him and his guests, while they're *'in medias pollo'* ('in the middle of chicken'), which is pretty impolitic of him, considering that this particular maid also happens to be his own elderly, maiden Aunt (she's played by Bella Starace Sainati), whom he's got working for him in perpetually-indentured servitude. He screams at her that she should never answer the phone, but she tells him that Mr. Trevor says he forgot an important signature on the contract, and that he's going to be needing it before he gets on the plane, back to America. Carlo excuses himself and leaves the room, grumbling to his guests that he'll be back in a little while.

Carlo drives (by himself, with no driver) to the airport, where he meets Mr. Trevor on the tarmac, just as Trevor's plane is about to take off. He signs the contract, leaves, walks out into the street, and then CRUNCH! He is instantly run-over by a truck! Carlo Bacchi is dead!

The Truck Driver (Dino Raffaelli) who's just smashed the C-Man into *pavement pizza (rustica)* immediately goes into shock: "I don't understand it! He just went under my wheels!" And then, Carlo ascends to Heaven, just like in the American feature film comedy, *Heaven Can Wait*. (This is Gabin's only picture, out of the ninety-five he made, which has 'fantasy elements' in it.) Right before our eyes, we next see Carlo walking through the clouds alone (of course!), and he's still wearing the same dark suit which he was wearing on Earth. (Apparently, according to this film, when you die, you get to take your wardrobe with you.) A beautiful faceless Angel (she's voiced by Paula Dehelly) appears and, without even greeting her, or flirting with her, he immediately (it's second-nature to him) begins negotiating: "I'm not supposed to be dead at my age! This is a mistake!" (But of course, she's heard this kind of *mishegoss* before.) She orders him to 'show her his soul,' and he tells her he has no idea how to do that, so she informs him that it's 'written on his sleeve'—and sure enough, when Carlo checks out his arm, he notices that he's got a long vertical white stripe painted down the length of his jacket-arm, which is meant, of course, to signify his 'corrupt soul:' "You've done bad things to people, Carlo," the Angel tells him. "It's written on your arm. So I have no choice, but to send you to Hell." And of course, since Carlo is played by Jean Gabin, he naturally keeps his cool, and doesn't get flustered one iota: "I can't go to Hell! I'm a good man! God doesn't know everything! [Carlo Bacchi is such a ballsy cat, he can even take issue with 'The Big Guy!'] Anyway, "Why is 'Hell' the only word in your mouth?" He then starts threatening her gently, as though he's talking to an underling who isn't doing her job properly: "You'd better be careful about what you're going to do with me, because I'm a practicing Catholic! Right before I came up here, I was even having dinner with the Monsignor, and he'll give me a good reference! Plus, during the Pope's recent illness, I was hoping for the best for him. You can't condemn me on looks, alone. I've always celebrated all of the holidays!"

Just like in *A Christmas Carol*, the Angel next tells Carlo that it's time to examine his life since, to quote Socrates, "the life unexamined, isn't worth living," and she indicates a blank wall, where The Greatest Hits of Carlo Bacchi's Life will now magically appear as 'streaming video:' In 'Clip #1,' Carlo sees a disgruntled employee whose face we cannot make out, tagging an insult about Carlo on the wall outside of the Bacchi Industries building (it's the graffito which we half-saw earlier in the picture), although, even now, we're still unable to make out the words. 'Clip #2,' which follows, is a moment from the dinner party which Carlo has just left, and we see that, when he was there, he was holding hands with his mistress, Lidia, under the table, while his wife Margot was sitting right nearby, and not noticing. Carlo tells the Angel that he's done good things in his life too, and that he was always, *especially,* a good son, and she replies, "Well, you may have been a good son, but you're not a very good nephew: Here's your poor Aunt, who works for you like a slave!" Another clip finds Carlo slapping the face of a dark-haired man (probably, it's somebody who works for him), and after watching the clip, Carlo defends himself to the Angel, actually telling her that he's not responsible for his organs! ("I have a bad temper—but a good heart!") Then, it's an Eisensteinian-montage of Carlo, *in flagrante delicto* with all of the women whom he's fucked throughout his life, and we learn that their names are Rose, Villaine, Jeannete, and Anne-Marie. (One of the women was even a circus performer!) Then, it's a second montage, and this one features still photos of an entire nursery's-worth of illegitimate babies who were fathered by Carlo, with the aforementioned chickadees. The Angel scolds Carlo: "These are the fruits of your illegitimate loves! You didn't believe any of these women when they told you they were pregnant." Carlo now rationalizes, telling her that he didn't believe any of the women when they (all!) told him they were pregnant, but that now, it doesn't matter: "Anyway, all of that stuff happened when I was younger, so it's not my problem." Carlo (and we) now also gets a quick shot of himself from the distant past, and we can tell it's supposed to be the distant past, because his hair has been dyed-black, and he's biting a woman, playfully. (He even smiles when he's with this one particular woman, and smiling is something that, we can tell, he doesn't do too much of, anymore.) "I was nice when I was poor," he Gabin-Shrugs at the Angel. Finally, she reminds him that he lost whatever was left of his innocence, which he never actually had, when he married Margot—which he did, only because her father was rich. (*So:* This is how Carlo made his money: He married into it!) "Carlo, you've always had ulterior motives for everything you did in your life. You were impertinent, you were fond of debauchery, and you were a liar." But of course, Carlo just hears what he wants to hear: "Well, I didn't commit any crimes!" (Carlo Bacchi, like many of the on-screen characters who are played by Woody Allen, always 'creates his own moral universe.') "At my burial, they will praise me," Carlo tells her. "I love pretty girls and money. If I were rich by birth, instead of through marriage, I would probably be more refined—I would be more interested in books and music, and so forth. But I'm not, and that's life." She then reminds him of his very worst crime of all: "Your worst sin was committed over *Santini*." He tells her, truthfully, that he doesn't know anybody named Santini.

She's talking about Amedeo Santini, a man whom Bacchi has apparently hurt, without ever having met him in-person: "Mr. Santini often screams your name out in despair," the Angel informs Carlo. It's now starting to get dark, signifying that Carlo is very clearly starting his descent down to Hell, so he now starts trying to negotiate with her again: "Look, just give me twenty-four hours more on earth, and I'll fix whatever it is that I did wrong." Just like Carlo is used to making deals, so the Angel is now making a Monty Hall-esque deal with him: She tells him that she'll give him twelve hours to return to earth (*His Last Twelve Hours* was the film's 1953 American release title), to make amends to as many people as he can, and Carlo jumps at the chance for a few more hours of life (businessman love challenges!): "I promise you that twelve hours from now—I will have become a Saint!"

The Angel returns Carlo to Earth, and he wakes up, miraculously, from beneath the truck which hit him. The crowd can't believe that this guy, who actually 'seemed dead' just a couple of minutes ago, is now up and walking around! Carlo dusts himself off, tells the driver "no hard feelings," and returns home to his mansion and to the dinner table, as though he's just getting back from meeting the Americans at the airport, which, for all practical purposes, he is. He politely tells his guests, including the Monsignor, that he's sorry, but that they're all going to have to leave, and right now. (After an out-of-body experience, coffee and profiteroles are a little on the anti-climactic side!) The guests all mention to each other that Carlo looks shaken, and Margot even tells him that he looks "as pale as death," but he assures everybody that nothing's wrong. He then goes over to the phone, and calls his secretary at her home (not bothering to ask her if he's interrupting her dinner), and orders her to call down to his factory, to see if his company, which employs thousands of people, has anybody named 'Santini,' and adds that he must find this man—and *tonight*. Margot reminds Carlo that it's late, and that he shouldn't be worrying about work at this hour, and she also chides him, more gently than he deserves, because he hasn't yet eaten his dinner. The Monsignor, who's still on the premises, and who is continuing to enjoy the complimentary *medallions du veau*, resumes smooching Carlo's ass: "Carlo, your heart is so good!" Carlo, very quickly, and to get the ball rolling on 'adding a little good credit to his Karmic bank account,' immediately whips out his checkbook and writes a check, which he makes out to the Church in the amount of five million francs! The Monsignor can't believe it, but Carlo, who is now trying to turn-the-other-cheek (or in the case of Gabin who, by 1950, was already getting a tad paunchy, turning the other 'jowl'), tells the Monsignor that the amount of the check "is not excessive." Carlo now, once again, apologizes to his dinner guests, who are so intrigued by his weird behavior that they still haven't gone home, and he tells them that he has to go back to his office to pick something up which he has forgotten. And just as he starts heading out the door, he asks his little daughter Anna if she has a copy of the Gospels, since he knows he'd better start familiarizing himself with The Good Book, and fast! She tells him she doesn't have her Bible anymore, because she "gave it to some poor people, who looked like they really needed it." (In the world of this film, religion is an ineffective salve for poor people; religion's all they have, since this life sucks, and maybe—just maybe—'the next life' will be better.) Since Carlo now has it in mind that poor people are the only ones who tote Bibles around, he asks his apartment building's Doorman if the guy has a copy handy and, sure enough, the guy does—in fact, he even carries one right in the front pocket of his jacket! Carlo buys the book from the gentleman for *Les Big Bucks*, after managing to flip the guy's wig, by informing him, "Guess what, friend? I died at 9:04 p.m.—but now I'm back!" When Gabin walks off-screen, the guy, of course, crosses himself.

Carlo returns to his office, quickly bypassing the hastily-scrawled *graffito* which we can now read, for the first time—"Carlo Bacchi is a Thief and a Killer!" (Who wrote it? Was it The Mysterious Mr. Santini?) Carlo has called his board of executives back to work for an emergency night-meeting, and he tells all assembled, "This organization always donates to people who've already got a lot, right? Well, I've got a new idea: Let's start giving some money to people who only have a little, and let's quit talking all of our usual big-business nonsense!" The board members can't believe that their greedy, Type-A boss is talking like a kid who's taking-up donations for UNICEF: "Look: You all know that I own two-thirds of this company. So now, I've decided that all of our factory workers will profit: We're going to increase all of their paychecks, and they will, ultimately, all receive fifty to seventy-five percent of everything which this company makes!" (Where else but in an Italian movie will we ever see a company's big, capitalist boss 'seeing the light' and suddenly turning into SuperMarxist?)

Carlo's secretary's at home and she now telephones the office, to inform her boss that there is no Amedeo Santini employed by Bacchi Industries, although she *has* managed to find a local listing for an Amedeo Santini in the phone book, and she gives him the guy's home address.

Amedeo Santini is played by Julien Carette, who is second-billed in the film's promotional materials after Gabin, and we already know Carette, because he had already appeared with Gabin thrice before—as 'Cartier,' the drag-loving/"Marguerite"-singing actor in *La Grande illusion*, as Gabin's train engineer pal Pecqueux in *La Bete humaine,* and as Havelock, the ship's cook, in *Le Recif de corail.* Santini lives in an impoverished Roman slum, and when Carlo bursts into Santini's apartment, he immediately smells a gas leak, and sees a young man and woman making out. Carlo asks the young man if he's Santini, and the kiss-ee, Maria (Antonella Lualdi) pops up from underneath her young suitor and replies that Amedeo Santini is her Uncle, and that he's not home at the present time: "We're waiting for him to come back; we don't know where he is!"

A police officer then enters and briefs Maria on what's happening: "Miss, I'm afraid that your uncle, Signor Santini, is in the hospital. He's just tried to drown himself! Carlo, Maria, and her sexed-up boy-toy, Nanni (Tommasso Palotta, an actor who is also sometimes billed in other movies, as 'Maso Loti'), all head over to the hospital, to see him.

When Santini sees Carlo, he immediately freaks out, and Carlo can't figure out what the guy's so ticked-off about, since the two of them have never even met each other before. Carlo asks Santini what it is that he's done to hurt him and Santini, rather abrasively, snaps back, "You don't need to know people personally, to force them into suicide!" Santini next illuminates Carlo on why he tried to kill himself, and why he holds Carlo responsible, and we now get to see, in flashback, the events leading up to his suicide attempt, with Santini setting the scene for Carlo, and for us, in voice-over:

"Yesterday, I had a shoe that I needed to repair. I sent Marie, my niece, to the shoe repair store, but she came back empty-handed. The cobbler wanted three hundred *lire* to repair the shoe, up from one hundred-twenty, which is the price he always charged me before. I told him I wouldn't give him that much, so he wouldn't fix my shoe."

Next, in the flashback, we see Santini going into the store, himself, and telling the Shoemaker, who is played by the actor Dante Maggio (an actor who was known for speaking, in his films, in a very-pronounced 'Provencale' accent, an accent which you'll hear if you ever spend any time along the border of France and Italy), that he's calling the police, because in his humble opinion, the Shoemaker is a thief. The Shoemaker tells Santini it's not his fault, and that he's had to raise prices, because the leather he needs to fix shoes comes from Bacchi Industries, which has the monopoly on all of Italy's leather, and that Mr. Bacchi has apparently doubled the price of shoe leather to three times what it used to be, and therefore, he (the Shoemaker) just can't afford to buy any new leather, at all. The Shoemaker, even having just explained himself fully, is still so mad at Santini for yelling at him, that he decides to keep Santini's shoe.

Cut back to the hospital, present-day, where laid-up Santini informs Bacchi, *re:* The Shoemaker, "That jerk kept my shoe, because of you!" He then tells Bacchi (cut to Flashback #2) that, right after getting reamed-out by the shoe-dude, that he went to the Bacchi Company's offices himself, to try and have-speaks with Bacchi personally, but that he couldn't get in, so instead, he just plastered graffiti all over the wall. (In this film, amusingly, the graffiti-message keeps changing every time we see the wall, a device which is straight out of the earliest issues of *Mad Magazine*, in which the graffiti words always used to change, from panel-to-panel.) When we see the graffiti this time, it reads, '*Bacchi e un porco!*' (Bacchi is a pig!) While Santini's scrawling his festive 'Message to Love' on the wall, we see that he's only wearing one shoe, and that his other foot is bare-ass naked!

Director Zampa next cuts to the mansion of a wealthy government official, for whom Santini works (he's the official's valet/butler). He runs into the room, all fancied-out in his butler uniform, and wearing only one shoe. "The Cops didn't arrest me for the graffiti," Santini continues in his present-day voice-over, "because they know me as a valet to this very rich and powerful guy. Anyway, my esteemed boss saw that that I was late, and he didn't believe me when I told him that it was your fault, Mr. Bacchi—and so he fired me!" In this movie, just like in other Italian Neo-Realist films which were made at around the same time, in the late '40s, and in the early '50s, 'loss' is represented by an object—the shoe—just like it was also represented by a bicycle in De Sica's *Bicycle Thieves*, and by the old man's beloved missing dog in his *Umberto D.*, both of which were also, like this film, co-written by Cesare Zavattini. Frustrated that he's been fired, Santini heads back to the corporate offices of Bacchi Industries, and scribbles a new message onto the wall, "Carlo Bacchi is an Assassin," and then, immediately thereafter, he attempts suicide, by leaping into the river. Back in the hospital meanwhile, in 'the present day,' Santini completes his story, by telling Carlo, "I've been completely humiliated—and all because of you!"

Carlo knows that he's going to have to make amends to this guy, if he wants his afterlife to consist of fluffy clouds, as opposed to ass-burning fire. And, he's really going to have to hurry up about it too, because the clock is ticking faster than a 39-year-old-woman-without-a-husband. Carlo (this isn't his nature, you understand, but the man has no choice) now starts sucking-up to Santini: "I'm happy that I was finally able to meet you, Mr. Santini. I'll give you everything you want!" Carlo orders the nurse, first, to place Santini into a private room, and then secondly, to bill him (Carlo) for it—and then he gets an even better idea: He decides to bring Santini home with him to his own mansion, to recuperate in style. Santini's niece Maria, and her boyfriend Nanni, come along to Carlo's house as well, to make sure that everything is *kashrut-pareve (kosher-for-passover)*.

Carlo introduces Santini to his wife Margot, and instructs his Aunt/Servant to let Mr. Santini pick anything he wants from his own personal wardrobe. He tells Santini that he wants to make him happy, and also orders his Aunt to give Santini some warm milk and an expensive lamp (which, as he now tells the man, he can keep forever). He also treats young Maria to one of his wife Margot's fur coats, without even consulting Margot on it first, and a great twist in the film (a twist which we'll now see, for the first time), is that Santini is such a complete asshole (even more so than we even thought), that now he's *really* going to start taking advantage of Carlo's largesse (not that he hasn't been taking advantage of it already): *Pour l'amour du ciel* is the only Jean Gabin movie out of ninety-five in which a working man-character is portrayed as being a total jerk, instead of being saintly and even godlike. Santini tells Bacchi that he doesn't want the Butler to serve him his warm milk, and that he'd much prefer that Bacchi's pampered wife Margot should subjugate herself by serving it to him, personally. Carlo readily agrees, even though Margot gets all huffy about it, and he asks Santini a rhetorical question, although we can tell that he'd really much rather be kicking this advantage-taker a new ass. Carlo now asks Santini, "Isn't life beautiful?"

Santini isn't stupid though, which we already knew. (I mean, if you were a *true moron*, there's no way you would be able to expertly insinuate yourself into a plush situation like this), and he asks Carlo about why he's so interested in his happiness. Carlo doesn't know how to answer, so Santini next ups his larcenous ante: "You know, Mr. Bacchi, if you *really* want me to be happy, you should really buy me a house of my own!" Carlo, knowing he's only got a few hours left on Earth anyway (there's no point to being 'the richest man in the cemetery'), is caving to this guy's every demand, even the extra crazy demands which relate to free housing: "Okay, sure! Let's look through the real-estate ads, and I'll buy you a house right now!" Carlo's effeminate Duke-pal, who might even be renting a room from the Bacchis (he's always present in their house), advises him against it: Never before has he seen Carlo acting so fiscally irresponsible.

Carlo immediately starts house-hunting with Santini, Maria, and Nanni, and Santini is now bragging to all of Carlo's horrified neighbors that, "Mr. Bacchi is buying me a house!" (One neighbor even leans into another and opines, "For Bacchi to give a house is like me giving away a pack of cigarettes.") Santini tells Bacchi exactly what kind of a domicile he's got in mind for himself, too: "I want *that* house… the one over there—with the tower!" He indicates one of the largest mansions you'll ever see, one which truly *does* have a tower, and exclaims, "I want that house! It's Modern-Gothic!" The only pressing problem which we're going to be having though, as far as Carlo's buying Santini the house is concerned, is that the house's present owners have no interest in moving out, or in selling it.

The foursome arrives at the gigantic estate which Santini favors, to discover that it happens to be the home of Gigliosi (Nerio Bernardi), Italy's most famous baritone. The heavy-set singer has lost his voice, and wants to greet them personally, but is unable to do so, so he bangs on some piano keys, to alert his Wife (Marga Cella) that she's going to have be doing the talking for him: "My husband has lost his golden voice," she apologizes to Carlo, Nanni, and Maria, but Carlo stops the small-talk with a wave of his imposing Gabin hand, and gets right down to business: "I would like to buy your house right now!" As Carlo and the Gigliosis start discussing this sudden transaction, a famous Senator who knows Carlo (he's played by an actor called Autista Camion, which I'm not sure, but I think translates into English as, 'Autistic Truck') then emerges from one of the house's many upstairs rooms; as it turns out, the mansion doubles as a high-end brothel, which Gigliosi, in between making with the 'O Solo Mio-business,' runs! Carlo's mouth drops, and Gigliosi tells him that he should keep what he's seeing 'on the D.L.' (In other words: 'What happens at the baritone's house, stays at the baritone's house!'): "Here, we don't talk about politics, Mr. Bacchi. Do you catch my drift?" Maria's a bit naïve, and believes that the Senator actually lives upstairs, until Nanni sets her straight about the birds and the bees.

Carlo quickly buys the house (total escrow time = one minute), he and Gigliosi shake hands (but they don't spit on them first, like *cowpokes* do in every great western), and then, well—'it's a done-deal, amigo.' (Of course, most of the upstairs doors remain locked because, no doubt, there's still plenty of jiggery-pokery going on, behind them.) While Carlo is asking Gigliosi to turn the keys over to him, he sees, out of the corner of his eye, one of the house's (or one the world's, for that matter) least tasteful decorations: It's a nude female statue, replete with a mannish gargoyle-head and massive batwings! (*Fuuuck*, Santini was right, when he asked for 'gothic!') Madeleine, who's one of the prostitutes, emerges from behind the same door from which the Senator has just emerged; she doesn't know that the houses's new visitors already know the truth about what she does for a living, so she tries to keep up appearances (and her appearance is nice!), by introducing herself to them as a 'Viscountess!'

Santini thanks Carlo: "I'm glad you bought me a house. But I'm still not entirely happy, because I don't want my daughter marrying this worthless bum. I want her to marry somebody noble—like your Duke friend." Carlo, Nanni, Maria, and Santini now repair to Carlo's house to tell everybody the news and, of course, everybody present (Margot, the Duke, and the Butler) is horrified—especially, the foppish Duke who, very plainly, is not into girls.

As if things couldn't get any worse (although 'the law of movies' dictates that they always will), Carlo's mistress, Lidia, has picked this moment to confess her affair with Carlo, to Margot: "I know, from my Senator friend [it's not mentioned in the film but, no doubt, she's referring to the guy who was upstairs with Madeleine, the prostitute], that your husband has just gifted a seventy-five million *lire* house to some unknown guy, and it's especially horrible, because your husband was just about to buy me a villa with that money! [Shades of *Martin Roumagnac!*] Anyway, I'm telling you all of this, just because I don't want us to have any secrets." Carlo is forced to admit the truth about his infidelity (or, the truth about *this* infidelity, anyway) in front of both women, and he does it with the usual Gabin-Flair, not allowing himself to get riled up, at all: "Yes, she is my mistress," Carlo admits to Margot of Lidia, right in front of both women. Margot glowers at her errant husband, and instead of apologizing to her, he instead tries to placate Lidia, his mistress: "My buying a house for Mr. Santini doesn't have anything to do with the property which I'm *still* going to be buying for you!" Lidia, not caring about whether or not she's already destroyed the last vestigial traces of Margot's feelings, coldly replies, "You always told me that your wife was only the mother of your children!" Margot, who's beyond-angered at having to watch this horrorshow, screams out at her husband, "May God forgive you," and Lidia chimes in that God has absolutely nothing to do with any of the things that happen to be going on in this room, at this moment. Both women are angry at Carlo—and/plus, at the same time, The Thin White Duke is informing Maria that he's already engaged to somebody else (which seems next-to-impossible, but we'll let it slide).

"See you at God's side," Lidia bleats angrily at Carlo, storming out of the room, and not knowing that Carlo's going to be at God's Side—or at Satan's!—faster than she even knows. As Lidia leaves the room, she sneers in Margot's ear, "Your husband talks like someone who's dying."

Carlo heads up to his study, not wanting to spend the last two hours and four minutes of his life in an argument which he knows he'll never win. It's now 7:00 p.m. He sits down at his desk and makes notes for his family, pursuant to who they should telephone to settle his businesses when he's gone and, at that moment, his cute little daughter Anna comes in to see him. Even though Carlo and Anna love each other, he's obviously very remote with her, and director Zampa shows us that their relationship, while it's remote is, at the very least, effortlessly cordial: "I couldn't sleep," she tells her dad, "so I just came in to give you a kiss. Can I sit with you?" Then she notices his atypically-pale visage: "You look weird, daddy!" (He replies, "No… I'm the same," but she begs to differ.) She tells him, very intuitively, that he looks "far away," and she also asks him if the rather diffident behavior which he's been exhibiting tonight is her fault: "Have I done anything to make you mad? Do I sometimes pain you, Daddy?" "Of course not," he replies, then asking her, "Have I been nice with you, honey?" Honestly, as only a child can be, she replies, "Yes, daddy, you're always nice to me. But you don't keep your promises. When you saw me in the living room, that day when it was raining, we had hot chocolate together, and you told me that every week we would have hot chocolate together—but we never have. You used to play with me every weekend, too, but we haven't done that for a long time, either!" So Carlo, who has less than two remaining hours left on earth, now decides to take Anna for a walk through Rome and to a café where, very sweetly, he orders-up hot chocolate-for-two and tells her, conspiratorially, "I'm going to tell you a secret, Anna, and what I'm going to tell you is something that people won't believe: I just came back from Heaven, and I have to go back again, very soon. So when I don't come back, I don't want you to be angry with me, okay? I want you to promise me that you'll always be a good person. I have done bad things to people in my life, Anna—especially, to a man named Santini, who only had one shoe." Anna is not crying (she doesn't obviously know her dad well enough to be distraught, or else she's just too young to truly understand the concept of death), but like a good, stoic-little 'Junior Gabin,' she's very pragmatic about the whole thing, and she just wants to know more about the man with one shoe: "Did he have a wooden leg? Did you buy him a [replacement] shoe?" After a beat, Carlo smiles and replies, "No. I bought him a house."

Carlo takes Anna's hand, and brings her to see Santini's new mansion: Santini's there with the Duke, and Santini's livid, because Maria and the Duke aren't interested in each other at all, but our formerly-poor friend doesn't look too worried though, and he tells Carlo, confidently, "She's my niece. So I can *make* her marry him!" Santini, who's drunk with his newfound power, suddenly thinks he can have whatever he wants in life without any restrictions—and clearly, what the filmmakers are trying to tell us here, is that the *nouveaux rich* always love throwing their weight around, and in as vulgar a manner as they can! (Carlo, himself, is the poster-child for that sort of behavior.) Santini tells Maria that if she doesn't marry the Duke, he'll "give the house back to Mr. Bacchi," although we know he doesn't mean it. (He's crazy, but he's not that crazy!) Maria runs away and locks herself in one of the house's many bedrooms. Carlo comes in to talk to her, and she tells him, "You've been very nice to us, Mr. Bacchi. But I want to get married to Nanni—not to the Duke." Carlo checks his watch: It's now 7:45 p.m., which means that he's now only got '1:04' left on the clock before it's time for 'Death: The Sequel.' Little Anna has a talk with Maria too, and after the conversation (the little girl is persuasive and wise-beyond-her-years, but she's also real and [charmingly] non-precocious), Maria agrees reluctantly to marry the Duke, who still doesn't want to marry her, either. Maria genuinely loves Nanni, though (even more than she loves life itself), and she doesn't want to hurt him, so she asks Carlo if he can go and see Nanni on her behalf, to break their relationship off. Carlo does so willingly, telling Nanni (lyingly, and with complete Gabin-Stoicism), "Maria doesn't want to be with you, anymore." Nanni can tell that this isn't true, so he now goes to Maria, himself: "Tell me honestly that you don't love me anymore." Maria pushes Nanni out of the house, and little Anna cries because she knows, instinctively, that Marie and Nanni genuinely love each other, and that all of this bullshit is preventing true love from taking its course.

Carlo now has approximately ten minutes left before he must return to Heaven and he knows that the most important thing he's going to have to do, before he shuffles off this mortal coil for good, will be to make Nanni and Maria happy. He vocalizes to Santini that, even though he's just bought him the house, that it's his own name on the lease and not Santini's (and that 'The Gabin Giveth and the Gabin Taketh Away!'), Santini 'looks his Indian-giving gift horse in the mouth,' now sneering at Carlo, "You're a thief with a slappable face"—but Carlo doesn't care. He tosses Santini onto the street (literally), realizing, like the drifter characters which Gabin had only recently stopped playing, that he's fated for ill regardless of what he does, and he tells Santini, grinning widely at the man, "I know I'm damned—but it's okay!" Carlo immediately signs the house over to Nanni and Maria, and tells them to get married. Amedeo Santini, who has now become homeless just as fast as he had previously become a home-*owner*, starts shouting into the heavens that he's going to attempt suicide again. (There's only one thing in the world Santini truly loves, and it's sympathy.)

Carlo bids goodbye to his stoic (we told you she was 'a Little Gabin') young daughter Anna, and hands her over to Maria with these instructions: "Please: Take my daughter back to her mother for me." Anna is now crying, because what's about to happen to her father, is finally sinking in. "Be a good girl," he tells her. Then, he goes outside, and the same truck which ran him over before, now smashes into him for a second time, ending Carlo Bacchi's time in this realm forever. (Forgive the bad pun but: "He walked right into that one!")

Now in Heaven again, Carlo prostrates himself before the gossamer lady-Angel: "I know, I know. I didn't do a good enough job, fixing everything. Okay, so, fine: You can send me to Hell. I tried to make that guy Santini happy, but in the end, I just didn't care about doing it." (It was more worthwhile for Carlo to make Santini's niece and her boyfriend happy, because they are good people.) But then, Carlo gets some good news: The white stripe on the arm of his jacket has cleared up—and so, too, apparently, has his Bad Karma! The Angel tells him, "Maria and Nanni are now together, and they're happy, and they owe their happiness to you. You have made people happy. So now, you can stay here in Heaven!"

Jean Gabin walks off into the clouds, alone. (*Sure*, he walks off alone in lots of his movies, but this is the only movie in which, when he walks off alone, it's not sad, because he's walking-off into his Greater Gabin Glory!)

Pour l'amour du ciel is Italian Neo-Realism mixed with a pinch of Frank Capra, and a *soupçon* of *Heaven Can Wait*, and it's yet another wonderful Jean Gabin movie which definitely deserves some recognition in the United States, where it hasn't been seen since its initial 1953 release, at the usual 'one art-house theatre, in NYC.' The film also had an Italian title, *E piu facile che un camello*, which is a Biblical reference. ("It is easier for a camel to get through the gates of Heaven, than it is for a miscreant [to do so].") In the movie, Jean Gabin has twelve hours on earth to make everything in his life right, and the film's American release title, *His Last Twelve Hours*, is a direct reference to Christ's ordeal, which also is meant to have lasted twelve hours. *Pour l'amour du ciel* is an extraordinarily fun movie.

What a Critic Said at the Time: "The bulk of the acting burden falls to the talents of Jean Gabin and Julien Carrette, and they work well with the material. Luigi Zampa's direction shows imagination and so does Nino Rota's music." (*Variety*, 11-18-53 issue. Critic: "Mosk. [George Moskowitz.]" Reviewed in Paris.)

What a (Wrong-Headed!) Critic Said at the Time: "Limp and humorless, the film is brightened by an occasional witticism. Tedious." (New York *Times*, March 1953. Critic: Bosley Crowther.)

Gabin and Nicole Courcel.

FILM 38

LA MARIE DU PORT

France, 1950

(Literal English Translation: "MARIE OF THE PORT") Directed by Marcel Carne. Produced by Sacha Gordine. Screenplay by Marcel Carne, Louis Chavance, and Georges Ribemont-Dessaignes. Based Upon the Novel by Georges Simenon. Director of Photography (black and white), Henri Alekan. Music by Joseph Kosma. Editor, Leonide Azar. Production Designer, Alexandre Trauner. (GENRE: DRAMA) A Production of Films Sacha Gordine. Running Time, 1 hour 28 minutes (1 hour 40 minutes, in Germany). Released in France on February 25, 1950, by Les Films Corona. Released in the U.S. on July 23, 1951, with English Subtitles, by the Bellon-Foulke Company.

> "Our marriage is a ménage-a-trois: Boredom, you, and me."
> — *Jean Gabin's shrewish wife, in "La Marie du port"*

The whole point of this book, is that most Jean Gabin movies are great and so far, it's been true. The first thirty-seven Jean Gabin movies (all of the movies which he made in the 1930s and 1940s [the ones which I've talked about, so far]) were uniformly wonderful, the kind of great, life-changing movies that you can't wait to tell your friends to catch.

Unsentimental *La Marie du port* is Jean Gabin's 38th feature film, and the first one which I would characterize as being only 'pretty good' instead of 'great'—but it's not Gabin's fault, because he's just as captivating as ever, so possibly, the script read better than the finished film. (Everybody makes mistakes...)

La Marie du port is the third motion picture collaboration between Gabin and director Marcel Carne, who guided him through the brilliant *Quai des brumes* (1939) and *Le Jour se leve* (also '39), but whereas those films are gripping, intense, and absorbing, this one is a bit *slllllow*, and sometimes uninvolving, and it's obviously because this time out, Carne wouldn't be partnered-up with his screenwriter-of-choice, Jacques Prevert, who wrote both *Quai de brumes* and *Le Jour se leve*.

As the film opens, smooth, big-city resort-owner Henri Chatelard (Gabin) and his fiancée, Odille LeFlem (Blanchette Brunoy) are on the way to her father's funeral, heading from the big city of Cherbourg, in northern France, down to the port city of Provence in the south, and suddenly—POP!—they get a flat tire and, as Henri changes it, he berates Odille about her non-traditional (read: too colorful) choice of funeral attire—"You could have worn black!"—to which she not-so-guardedly replies, "I don't give a damn! When my father was alive, he never came to visit me. He should count himself lucky that I'm showing up for his funeral at all, no matter what I'm wearing." She lightens up a bit though, and tells Henri that she's glad he's come with her (it's the only time she'll be paying him a compliment in the whole movie), but he doesn't like conditional praise, and so he makes sure that he's able to get the last word in, edgewise: "Yeah, I just came, because I didn't have anything to do. I like to meet people, but I don't like funerals, so I'll probably just drop you off and go and sit in a bar."

Henri spends the whole funeral waiting it out, just like he said he would, at one of Provence's local boat bars, Josselin's Place, which is directly across the street from the cemetery, and Gabin, in this sequence, looks every inch the Big Movie Icon, as he leans casually against the bar alone, sipping his coffee. He starts chatting-up the aged proprietress, Madame Josselin (Jane Marken), and as we already know, Gabin's movie characters, whether they're rich or poor, almost-always prefer hanging around with people who are as unpretentious as he is.

As the funeral procession spills out of the cathedral and down the street, the town's handsome young barber, Marcel Viaud (Claude Romain, who looks very dapper in his white coat) stands outside of his shop, gawking at Odille's younger sister, eighteen-year-old Marie (Nicole Courcel), and this guy's got unrequited love written all over his mug. As the coffin and the mourners file past Josselin's, Henri sees it pass and, respectfully and comically, he takes his hat off for all of about two seconds, before re-attaching it very quickly. (As we learned in 1939's *Le Recif de corail*, Jean Gabin doesn't take his hat off for anybody!)

Post-burial that evening, the extended LeFlem family is having dinner at a relative's home, still *sans* Henri, who remains *au bar*. One of the concerned relations start wondering aloud, about "… what the kids are going to do," and what she's referring to here, is that Marie and Odile have three very young brothers and sisters, small children whom Marie has been helping to raise. Since old people always say exactly what they think, one ancient Aunt (Marie-Louise Godard) even opines to Marie, directly within Odille's earshot, that she hopes Marie doesn't "… wind up like her big sister." Most of the family members agree that Odille is wasting her time with Henri, a guy who, according to the world of this movie, is legendary in France for being a carefree womanizing dandy—in fact he's practically famous for it. All of the assembled relatives *pow-wow*, and they're now deciding that the children should probably be taken away to the country, to be raised by some older relations.

Down at the boat bar, a sailor (Jackie Blanchot) who happens to be a LeFlem family friend, tells Henri that he's trying to sell the fishing boat which Marie and Odille's dad owned, to make some money for the family and, at that moment, Marie comes in, and she and Henri lock eyes. In this scene, Henri is meeting his fiancée Odille's little sister for the first time, and he's instantly smitten with her, even though he's 46 and she's 18! She's come into the bar to try and procure a job, and when she sees Henri staring at her intently (he looks like a twelve-year-old in 1976 who's just caught his first glimpse of a Farrah Fawcett-Majors poster), she shyly inquires of him, "Do I know you?" "You should," he smiles at her. "I'm *almost* your brother-in-law." (The key word here, is, of course '*almost*...')

The next day, it's the public auction for the LeFlem family's fishing vessel. A large crowd which mostly consists of sailors shows up, and *le bateau* is up on the block first. Its starting price—*three million francaroonies*. Nobody wants to buy it (it's not the newest boat in the world), so the price immediately drops to two-point-five. Odille's watching the auction alongside Marie, and Marie tells her big sister, excitedly, that she just met Henri: "Your fiancé is so nice! And his hair is all white!" Odille cautions her that Henri is "*nice with all women*," and she looks more-than-a-smidgen threatened by the fact that her sister is taking notice of her 'almost-husband.' Odille says of Henri, characterizing the nature of their strange relationship for the first and only time in the film, "I'm not unhappy with him, and I guess it's fine that we're going to be married, but to tell you the truth, he's not my dream-man, either. My dream has always been to go to Paris, but I stopped in Cherbourg and met *him*. Anyway, if you want to, you can come back to Cherbourg with Henri and me." In this film, as in many other pictures which Gabin will start making in the 1950s, people just settle for their lifemates, often marrying people they don't even like, usually because the people they're about to marry have some money socked away; dramatically, it's not too interesting to meet characters who just don't care who they marry but, then again on the other hand, in real-life, we never wind up with the people we really want, anyway; so while the fact that the characters are apathetic isn't too interesting in a dramatic sense, the fact that they don't care is (I guess) true to life, although it also hurts the film: We're rooting for the characters to 'want' something, or somebody, and none of them (especially Odille) really seems to care too much. And while Henri isn't the person Odille really feels she should be with, he certainly *is* very successful, since he owns a huge hotel/resort/restaurant/movie theater-complex, in Cherbourg.

When we see Henri next, he's down at the Provence docks, having just placed the winning bid on the LeFlem fishing boat, and when he sees Odille and Marie there, he brags to them that he can now, finally, add 'fishing' into his varied group of enterprises, since the ocean is the one 'field' which he hasn't yet conquered; but Odille doesn't look all that impressed.

Over the next few days, Marie becomes acquainted with Marcel the barber, and it's clear that he likes her more than she likes him. It's also eminently clear that she's going to start using his attentions toward her to build herself up emotionally, while she's pining away in secret for Henri. When night falls, and Marcel sees Marie down at the docks, he immediately confesses his love to her, telling her that even though he doesn't really know her, and realizes that he has no right to say anything, he's heard she's going to be taking the job in the boat bar, and he tells her that he's worried about her safety there, since she's going to be serving drinks to a bunch of creepy/horny old seafarers. She tells him that she's taken the job, mostly just to "be around people," since her little brothers and sisters have already gone away to the country to live with cousins, and that being around people, *even if they're creepy and horny*, will keep her from feeling lonely. Marcel's brought Marie a little bottle of lavender perfume. (We already know he's not going to be 'getting her,' because he's being too nice.)

In Cherbourg now, Gabin's Henri, looking smooth in a black, button-down shirt and white topcoat, *a la* Pepe Le Moko, is listening to a football game on the radio, in his resort's well-appointed office. He's still engaged to Odille, and he seems happy about it, although it's very clear to us that her 'cold feet' will soon be growing even colder. A group of sailors-on-leave next enters the hotel, accompanied by a gaggle of women, who are either their girlfriends or hookers (or both!), and Henri rents them some rooms, throwing in a few complimentary bottles of wine.

Odille is quick to express her boredom with Henri, telling him, in this otherwise unexceptional film's best line of dialogue, "Our relationship is a *menage-a-trois: Boredom, you, and me.*" We can't really feel sorry for Henri, though, because he's not dumping her, like he should be doing. (He doesn't like her, she doesn't like him, and yet the two of them persist on getting married. We're sitting there watching this movie, and we're yelling out at the screen, "Do something, Gabin! Dump her!" But he won't dump her, and we like his Henri character less, because of it.) Since Odille is never nice to Henri in the story, and she's clearly just using him to attain a comfortable lifestyle for herself, it's not exactly clear why he's staying with her, although I'll bet she's a little minx between the sheets! (Come to think of it, maybe this is the perfect arrangement for a Jean Gabin movie character: In his first group of movies from the early '30s, Jean Gabin's characters always got hurt whenever they opened up to, and fell in love with, women; so maybe, a loveless marriage is the perfect thing for a Jean Gabin movie-character, because you can't get hurt by somebody whom you've never loved in the first place.) Funny thing about Odille, though: Even though she's very obviously bored with Henri, she still looks jealous, whenever she catches other women checking him out.

After Henri interviews a middle-aged boat captain, Dorchain (Rene Blancard), whom he's about to hire to take care of his newly-acquired fishing boat, he next pads downstairs to his hotel's front desk, where a wealthy-looking family from Paris is struggling with the Desk Clerk (Jean Clarieux) to obtain a room. The Clerk looks like he's at the end of his rope, and the family's Dad (his character is simply called 'the Malcontented Client,' and he's played by Robert Vattier) begins trying to throw his weight around, even screaming at Henri (which is *never* the best way to get Jean Gabin's attention), "See here! I want a room for my family, but your Clerk has just given it to a soccer team and their girlfriends!" Henri doesn't like whiners and so, very calmly, he puts this big snob in his place: "We gave the room to a football team, because we prefer them over you." The family's eighteen-year-old daughter (Louise Fouquet), who's very cute, is instantly (of course) smitten by Henri, and she pouts to him that "it sure would be nice" if he would let her family stay there. After checking out the lay of this young lady's pert 'land,' Henri decides that maybe, just maybe, he's been a bit too rough on the family and so, while he truly has no more rooms left to give, he placates the family by giving them free tickets to his resort's movie theater, which happens to be showing a 1945 French film version of Dostoevsky's *The Idiot* (which was directed by Georges Lampin, who will direct Jean Gabin in 1956, in a contemporarily-set film version of Dostoevsky's *Crime and Punishment* [*Crime et chatiment*]). Odille knows that Henri could have charged the cute girl's father a lot more for the room than what he was able to make from the soccer team, and she asks him bitchily why he "likes throwing money away." (Even if Odille doesn't 'get it,' we Super Gabin Fans sure do: Henri would rather populate his hotel with people who are nice and real, than with rich demanding snobs, who would probably be demanding new tablecloths, fresh *serviettes,* and the correct spoon and glass every five seconds; Henri Chatelard is rich, but he's not pretentious.)

In the next sequence, Henri and the family's eighteen-year-old daughter are taking in a movie in his theater (Jean Gabin moves fast!), and the two of them happily share a sandwich, while a newsreel unfolds on the screen in front of them. He's not hitting on her, and he won't, but we can tell that, for the time being anyway, she's a more-than-acceptable substitute for Odille's sister Marie, who's also eighteen, and who isn't in Cherbourg at the moment. (Henri's clearly getting a big charge out of sitting next to such fresh, young flesh!) The newsreel's Narrator is discussing a sea battle between the Americans and the Germans (*La Marie du port* sets its scene during WWII), and he's intoning, "… it's proof that when you have strength, you don't have to use it." The Narrator is talking about the American Navy, but he could just as well be talking about Jean Gabin.

Henri heads down into his newly-acquired fishing boat, and tells his new *aide-de-camp,* Dorchain, that he's going to need to order a better motor: "We've got to get this rust-bucket going. We've got to start catching some fish, so I can make my money back." Henri next rolls up his sleeves, and starts working on fixing the old engine himself, because even though he's made some money in life, he's still a Gabinian Man-of-the-People, who's never above getting his hands dirty.

Now horned-up from hanging around with a dusky eighteen-year-old, Henri takes a top-secret day-trip down to Provence to see the eighteen-year-old he really likes, Marie, his wife's hot little sister whom he's been thinking about ever since the day he met her. When he enters the boat bar where she works, an elderly guy is hitting on her (he's super old, so he's going about it in a sweet way, as opposed to a sleazy way), and she's telling the old geezer to get lost—so what we're seeing now, is that she's a lot tougher, and less demure, than we initially believed her to be. (Well, she *is* 'tough Odille's' sister, so the apple, apparently, doesn't fall far from the tree.) Henri tells Marie gently, that she should be nicer to the clientele, and she's so excited to see him, that she throws her arms around him. The bar's Owner (Camille Guerini) orders her, rather brusquely, to go off and clean some mugs, and Henri *chews the guy a new a-hole,* as Marie beams proudly at her knight in shining armor.

Director Carne next gives us all of the 'port at-night sequences' we can handle, and all of them are *tres-atmospherique:* It's down by the port that Marie is again, now, meeting with Marcel, her favorite 'obsessive barberboy.' Since Henri doesn't live here in Provence, where Marie lives, Marcel, since the last time we saw him a few scenes ago, has kind-of managed to wear her down a little (must have been that lavender perfume), and now we're noticing that she likes him more than she used to, and that it's very possible she may even have a little love for him, too (although, basically, he's just a placeholder until somebody a little more cosmopolitan—like Henri, for example—comes along): "I'm tired of being a servant in a bar," Marie complains to Marcel, adding that she'd like to go away forever, on a boat. Marcel is naïve, but he's not completely stupid, and he knows that she doesn't want to go on a boat with him, but with Henri, so he tries to nip her seafaring dreams in the bud, by proposing to her right there, but she sidesteps the question, telling him that her father thinks she's too young to get married. (Since her father has just died, using this as an excuse is kind of stretching it.)

In Cherbourg, Odille spends the day (just like a lot of pampered Beverly Hills *hausfraus*) lounging around in bed, trying to figure where Henri's gone off to, although she's pretty sure that he's gone to Provence, to hang out with Marie. Down in Provence, simultaneously, Marie's *near* a bed, but not in one: She's making-up a bed in the sailor bar's little 'hourly-room' hotel-area, when Henri comes in, and starts flirting with her. ("Hi, Marie! Are you getting that bed ready for me?!") She asks Henri, acting *faux*-demure, why he's being so forward with her, even though it's very clear to us, of course, that what he's saying to her, is turning her on, massively: "I'm just a child! Why are you around me? Do you want to help me make the bed… or are we just going to undo it?!" Even though Henri's already started the Flirtation Waltz, he feels a little uncomfortable about what he's started and, since she's obviously just made some of his mojo go away, by reminding him that she's 'just a little girl,' he now changes the subject, although not very well, by asking her, "So, uhh… what do you do with your boyfriend—that barber?" She innocently replies, "The usual. We just kiss each other and say that we love each other." Of course, she's never slept with Marcel, but she wants to make Henri jealous, by having him think that she has. Henri next asks Marie about "what else" she and Marcel do, to which she smilingly replies, "You're damned curious!" It is to Jean Gabin's credit that, when he asks her these sexy questions, he doesn't sound (too) creepy.

In his barbershop, meanwhile, Marcel is shaving a mustached Sailor (Joel Hammond) who, like anyone else in any small town, anywhere in the world, has been hearing all of the gossip about Marie's supposed affair with Henri, and it's unfounded gossip because, outside of the flirtation, nothing sexual has really happened between them yet. The Sailor tells Marcel that he's always known Marie to be a "slut." Marcel is shaving this ingrate, listening to him denigrate the girl of his dreams, and he's too wimpy to slash the guy's fuckin' throat—which is what he'd be doing, if he had any courage! Instead, he throws down his razor like a big wimp, and runs into Marie's sailor bar, acting completely hysterical: "Marie, listen to me! I know your sister's husband is after you. But don't you see? I love you more than he ever will!" Alternately leading Marcel on and ignoring him, Marie now has to do the latter, sighing (just like jaded Stella-Marie in 1931's *Pour un soir..!), "*Yeah, yeah. Everyone uses the word 'love.' But what does it mean?" This little mini-speech deflates Marcel like a flat tire and, as any student of 'Contemporary Dating 101' knows, Marie respects Henri more than she does Marcel, because

Henri never tells her he loves her. (Marcel, in other words, is much too needy.) She tells Marcel, "Ultimately, we can never be together. I am going to leave for Cherbourg with Henri, and maybe I'll stay there with him after he decides that he doesn't want my sister anymore." Marcel tells her that if she goes off with Henri, that he'll do something desperate to himself. (What's he gonna do? Swallow the blue liquid that cleans the combs?!) Henri walks by the harbor and sees Marcel and Marie together, and now it's his turn to get a bit jealous: "Do you often go and see your boyfriend on the harbor?" he asks her.

That night, Marie's alone in the bar, closing down the register, and Henri sits down beside her, needing to talk. She reminds him that he's told her in the past that he'd like to take her to Cherbourg with Odille and himself, and the answer which he now gives her ("That was just a joke!") makes her feel horrible. Henri likes Marie, but he's also 'level-headed Jean Gabin,' and he realizes that, ultimately, it's going to be a whole lot better for Marie to wind up with a guy her own age: "I can't take you to Cherbourg. I think that, if you really admit it to yourself, you have the same feelings for that barber that he has, for you. Of course you do! [The Illustrious and Exalted Jean Gabin Knows All!] Anyway, when you marry him, I promise I'll be the best man." Since Marie's young, and actually still has 'feelings' (!), she starts crying, and he makes her feel worse, by choosing this moment to parrot back to her exactly what she said in the past, to both him *and* Marcel: "What *is* love, anyway? What's the big deal?" He's now telling her exactly what she's always saying, but when he throws her own words back in her face, she can't bear it—so he just takes a pregnant pause, and tells it like it is: "You want me to ask you to marry you. But I don't want to!" We know that Henri has the same *real* feelings for Marie which she has for him, and that he's ignoring them, not because of her age, but because he's engaged to her big sister.

Marcel is 'feeling the pain' too, and in one of his many extremely pathetic moments in this movie —and this one is definitely the most pathetic of all—he actually throws himself drunkenly onto the street, and starts crying like a baby, and an old mustached drunk wanders by, shaking his head. (If this were *Bye, Bye Birdie*, Paul Lynde would shrug, and begin singing, "What's the Matter with Kids Today?") While too many coincidences in a movie sour the audience on what's happening, the coincidence which transpires in the next sequence, is a stone-doozy: Henri's driving his car at night, in Cherbourg. He's pre-occupied, obviously, by thoughts of Marie and, accidentally, he plows his car over the street-prone Marcel! Marcel, as we're going to find out shortly, has made the trip up north to Cherbourg, to convince Henri to stop messing with Marie, so that he can have her all to himself.

Henri runs into his resort-bar, where Odille happens to be present and, suddenly, he freaks-out on her (it's atypical for Gabin to do this in a movie, but here, not only is he doing it, but he's doing a crackerjack job): "I've got that boy Marcel, the one that likes your sister, in my car. I ran him over, accidentally. And we can't take him to the hospital, because they'll think I did it on purpose!" Odille tells Henri that she knows a good private doctor to whom they can bring him.

Henri drives Marcel to the Doctor (Emile Drain), who informs Marcel that he's suffered only "… a minor contusion of the tendon," and that he should be okay again, and very soon. Marcel, who's now bonding with his older 'rival' Henri, tells him, "Just don't tell my father [that I was drinking and lying in a road]!"

Back in Provence, at the same time, Marcel's family and friends don't know where he is—they have no idea that he's with Henri and Odille at their resort, and that the couple is hosting him, while his leg is healing. When Henri goes upstairs to his private quarters, his flirting-buzz is broken, when he walks in (to his extreme horror) on Marcel, who's in bed with Odille! She claims that she's just 'taking care of him,' and I guess we can buy that explanation, because she's fully dressed, he's under the covers, and she's far enough away from him, where it looks physically impossible that they were having sex.

"I don't want Marie to know that I'm here with you and Henri," Marcel tells Odille, after Henri storms out of the room, pissed. "She'll think I was sleeping with you, and then she won't go to America with me!" Marcel's big dream, we're learning now, is to go to America, to be "… a hairdresser for rich ladies. Did you know that in America, they don't dress women's hair? They just undo it!"

Henri starts playing *billotte* with some of his guests, and he then sulks into his movie theater, which is again showing the French film version of *The Idiot,* and this is some pretty self-reflexive humor on Julien Duviver's part, since the only idiot we're seeing in *our* movie (in *La Marie du port*) is Henri himself, because Henri never makes any attempts to extricate himself from any of these bad relationships which he's either in, or which he's trying to get himself into. "How can *The Idiot* be a romantic movie," he rhetorically asks some patrons, who ignore him as they file out at the film's end. He then goes into his restaurant, and a mystery fortysomething brunette, Francoise (Odette Laure) is sitting there, smiling at him. He takes a seat next to her, and she tells him she's from a nearby village, and that she has a little daughter who's eighteen (almost the same age as Marie is). Henri tells her, "I almost did something stupid with somebody who's about as young as your daughter, but I'm getting older, and I don't have any more time to be complicated." Here, he's brushing the brunette off, at the same time as he's telling her that he can't get involved with Marie as well and, in effect, he's 'killing two brunettes with one stone.' Francoise tells Henri that being alone has always been fine with her, and that she never has nightmares when she sleeps alone.

Back in Henri's office, Dorchain, the guy who's been taking care of Henri's new fishing boat for him, has come to tell him about some new problems with the vessel, but Henri, who's exhausted from a day of heavy soap-opera, tells him nicely that he doesn't want to hear about it right now. The two men drink together, and Dorchain tells Henri that everybody in town is wondering about Marcel's present whereabouts. (Dorchain, of course, already knows where Marcel is, because Henri's told him everything, but he's a loyal employee and friend, and so he's keeping his boss's secret.) Henri changes the subject, and starts talking about reselling the boat, since he's tired of sinking money into its upkeep, when it doesn't actually 'work.'

Dorchain, because 'fair-weather sailors, make fair-weather friends,' then meets Marie on the port (so much for keeping the boss's secrets), and engages her in a secret conversation:

"So: I'm not supposed to tell you this, but I know where your boyfriend, Marcel is." Why would Dorchain do this? Well, while he's a genuine friend to his boss, Henri, he also cares genuinely about Marie's welfare (in a non-sexual and—some might even say—paternal way), and he'd like to see a her (a/k/a/, 'a young person') winding up with her true love (as opposed to, for example, ensconcing herself in an affair, only for money-grubbing reasons, which is what everybody else in this movie seems to be doing). She tells Dorchain that she doesn't want to know where Marcel is, but it's clear from her dewy eyes that she does wants to know, and *stat!* So, he next tells her where she can find Marcel.

That night, Odille tells Henri that she's leaving him, and that she's going to Paris. (That's where the real rich guys go to meet young women.) She tells him she hopes they can part as friends, and that she's decided to call off their upcoming marriage, and now Henri's been duped twice: He told Marie he couldn't be with her, because he was going to marry her big sister, but now, the big sister is leaving him, and Marie is going back to be with Marcel! This, of course, leads Henri into our film's sole Gabin-Outburst: "You're accusing me of running after your little sister? How dare you! She's nothing but a kid!"

After Odille walks out, suitcase in hand, Marie, who's now wearing a beautiful peasant blouse, enters Henri's bedroom to say hi to him. (She usually wears her hair up in the picture, but she's now letting it down for the first time, and it's very lush and beautiful.) She white-lies to Henri, telling him that she was just in the neighborhood, and asks him if she's frightened him. "I'm afraid of nobody," he tells her. (This is *Simple Gabinian Truth*.) "But it's nice to see you, Marie. I thought I'd never see you again."

Now dispensing with the small talk, she just flat-out asks him why he doesn't want to be with her, or at least why he's pretending not to want to be with her: "Is it because I don't please you?" He tells her that she has pleased him! (So, as it's turning out, they did make love!) He now tries to act creepy, and to freak her out intentionally, because he knows that it's the only way he's ever going to be able to get her to quit him: "So, is it warm under your blouse? If you're not afraid of me, come sit here!" Marie hasn't come for a sit-down, though; she's only shown up to tell him that she's decided to go off and be with Marcel, and this admission causes Henri to open up with some of his own feelings for the only time in the film. ("It's stupid, Marie, but I always think about you.") But then, realizing that he must sound like a whiny girl, he pulls his emotions 'all-the-way-back-in:' "Look, I know Marcel wants to see you. He's an idiot—he adores you! Let's go and get him. I'll take you to where he is!"

Henri and Marie go upstairs to Odille's room, to get Marcel (she's still 'nursing him'), and (this isn't such a big surprise) this time out, Marcel is now *screwing* Odille! Henri and Marie are so staggeringly uncomfortable when they discover this unfortunate tableau which they see stretched out before them, that Henri laughs uncomfortably, and utters a nonchalantly-existentialist non-sequitur ("Oh, life!"). Marie is so unhinged, that she runs out of the room.

Marie knew she loved Marcel, but she didn't know how much she really loved him, until she saw what she's just seen. Now outside with Henri, pretending to be strong, she changes what she told Henri just a few minutes ago: "I lied to you, Henri. I didn't come here for Marcel. I came here for you." (Jean Gabin always gets his woman!)

Henri takes Marie into his movie theater, they sit down together side-by-side, and he now starts lecturing her, very gently: "Of course, I always knew that you loved me as much as I love you. So maybe love *does* exist. Of course it does! And the most important thing about love, is that people should talk about it, and believe in it." (Did Jean Gabin really say this? *Yes!* Usually, his movie characters aren't so verbal about love, but this Big Revelation which he's now making isn't really such a big stretch, because Jean Gabin, in his movies, is always the voice of reason, and the fact that he wants people to *open up about love*, and to be honest about it, is more than a reasonable statement for his character to be making, at this point in the movie.) Henri and Marie watch a film of a man in the South Pacific who's climbing down a palm tree and, as they watch some newsreel footage, he whispers to her, "It's unfortunate that life is so short, and that we give ourselves so many problems. Anyway, your sister Odille is leaving for Paris, and your boyfriend's leaving, as well: He wants to be a hairdresser for women on the *Queen Mary!*" (This is kind of a dig at Marcel, like, maybe, Henri's suggesting that Marcel is a little queeny, himself!) Henri adds that possibly, instead of selling his new (and horrible) boat, he'll instead sail it to the South Pacific all by himself. When she asks him why he wants to go it alone, he replies, "It's a small boat. There are a lot of girls in the South Pacific—and they, too have nice blouses." Yes, right after Henri has confessed his love to Marie, he's now telling her that he's leaving her, to go off with the fecund women of the South Pacific. (It's hard to love a movie in which the characters mess with each other and manipulate each other and don't know what they really want.) She can't take Henri's wishy-washiness, though, and so she now becomes pro-active: "Okay, Henri. This time, I'm leaving for good. I won't come back and bother you, anymore. I'm sorry I've wasted your time."

He drives her to the bus and, the whole way, she's giving him the silent treatment. He asks her if she's going to leave without saying anything, and she tells him, "You don't want me for anything. You just want to make me laugh—or something like that. Well, the day I commit suicide—you can laugh all you want." She gets out of the car, and he watches her board the out-of-town bus.

After Marie gets on the bus, a down-in-the-mouth Henri retreats into his resort's bar, feeling lonely, but also knowing that he's done the right thing by letting her go, because she's too young. Then, suddenly, there's a phone call for him: It's Odille, who's now informing him that she and Marcel will be leaving for Paris together, and Henri, who's not at all surprised, wishes the two of them well. At this point, Dorchain enters the bar, and starts talking to Henri about Marie. "I'm worried about the little one. She talked to me about drowning herself, once. And she seemed very serious about it!"

Drowning? Suddenly, Henri flips out! He knows he's got to get Marie back, so he jumps into his car, and races to get her off the bus, before it's too late, just like Dustin Hoffman going after Katharine Ross, at the end of *The Graduate!* He chases after the bus in his car, yelling, "Get off! I forgot to tell you something." Marie gets the bus driver to stop, and she now climbs back into Henri's car with him, and she's got a giant smile plastered across her face. Henri and Marie both look happy now, and he tells her, "I was afraid you might do something stupid. Kids do silly stuff! Anyway, I guess I like to do stupid stuff too, and if I didn't act stupid with you, I would do it with someone else—and I'd rather do it with you." In other words, I guess what he's really telling her, in his roundabout way, is: "*I love you, Marie!*"

Henri's fishing boat leaves port, helmed by Dorchain, to whom Henri has just sold it, and Henri remains onshore with Marie: The two are now, finally, '2gether4ever,' and he asks her if she still thinks about drowning, to which she replies that she was never really serious about that. He asks her if she'll marry him, and her luminous smile is all he needs for an answer. "If people come to the ceremony and think it's weird, because of our age difference," he tells her, "I'll just tell them that I'm actually your father, and that we're just at the Church, celebrating your Communion!"

La Marie du port is the first of nine Gabin films which would be based upon books by France's most prolific (Belgian-born) novelist of all time, the gleefully anti-Semitic novelist, and sometimes screenwriter (although, not of this film) Georges Simenon, who wrote four hundred and twenty-five books during his fifty-year career. (The author's intense anti-Semitism has everything to do with why he never caught on in the United States, in the same way in which he did in Europe.) Simenon is known, mostly, for his crime novels (he's 'the French Agatha Christie'), but he'd also write a lot of love stories and love-triangle books, and both his love stories and his crime books would often be turned into Jean Gabin movies, in the 1950s, '60s, and '70s.

While Gabin delivers one of his usual solid performances in this film, the movie itself is hard to like, because none of the characters knows what he or she really wants. Even though in real-life, we very often don't know what we want (most of the time, anyway), when we're buying movie tickets with our hard-earned coin, the filmmakers had *better* tell us what the characters want. Ambiguity is wonderful in movies, because it makes the audience active in putting the pieces of the story together but, on the other hand, wishy-washy characters who don't give a shit about anything aren't great, and it's why I can't really recommend *La Marie du port*. While the whole point of this book is that 'most Jean Gabin movies are great,' in the 1950s, *The World's Coolest Movie Star* appeared in a small group of eight-or-so 'not-so-great' love-triangle movies which have the exact same story-line as this one—movies that aren't all that interesting, because his characters never seem to want anything. (The others, besides this one, are *Victor; La Verite sur Bebe Donge; La Minute de verite; Fille dangereuse; La Vierge du Rhin; Le Sang a la tete;* and *Crime et chatiment.*) To elaborate a bit further: *La Marie du port* and these other seven films aren't that wonderful, for the same reason that all of Gabin's other eighty-something movies are fantastic: One of the things we like most about Jean Gabin (one of the character traits which made his movie persona so beloved) is that, when problems are going on all around him, he doesn't react—he just shrugs, and blows it off: Jean

Gabin's on-screen job, is to be 'the calm in the middle of the storm.' It's what we expect out of him, and usually, we get mad when he's *not* behaving this way. But in these eight movies, the female leads (his wives, girlfriends, or mistresses) are all using him. They don't really like him, he doesn't really like them, and we want him to fight back and *call them on their shit—* but he doesn't! He just remains stoic. Now probably, as I mentioned at the beginning of the book, the relative inaction of Gabin's characters from his post-1946 *bourgeois*-guy-films, is meant to be the filmmakers' subtly-ironic commentary on how lazy and stupid the rich are. ("The job of us *bourgeois,* is to be able to take a lot of shit in style," Gabin's character will say in another movie like this one, a 1958 effort called *Le Sang a la tete* [*Blood to the Head*]), but the only problem is, that it doesn't really work. These eight pictures lose our interest, because we want Gabin to take action. We *want* to root for him to get rid of these ladies who are sapping his strength like Kryptonite, but he won't do it! The movie he'll make right after this one, *Victor*, will be guilty of exactly the same crime.

What a Critic Said at the Time: "A well-made film that deals in adult emotions and should do well in arthouse situations. Gabin, aging but still dynamic, is excellent as the tight-lipped, self-sufficient restaurateur who finds his values late in life." (*Variety*, 4-26-50. Critic: "Hawk. [Robert F. Hawkins.]" Reviewed in Paris.)

What Another Critic Said at the Time: "A fable that has the nature of an after-dinner joke, it is complex and mature, yet queer and sometimes baffling. The man is played with superb sophistication and dry humor, by Jean Gabin." (New York *Times*, 7-26-51 issue. Critic: Bosley Crowther.)

FILM 39

Victor

France, 1951

Directed by Claude Heymann. Produced by Gilbert Cohen-Seat. Screenplay by Jean Ferry and Claude Heymann. Based Upon a Play by Henri Bernstein. Director of Photography (black and white), Lucien Joulin. Music by Marc Lanjean. Editor, Suzanne de Troeye. Production Designer, Emile Delfaur. (GENRE: DRAMA) A Production of M.A.I.S. Running Time, 1 hour 30 minutes. Released in France on June 13, 1951, by SRO. Never Released Theatrically in the United States.

A Concerned Ex-Lover (who is leaving Gabin): "What will become of you?"
Gabin (Shrugging; he neither knows, nor cares): "We'll see..."
— from "Victor"

E merging directly upon the heels of *La Marie du port*, *Victor* is the second Jean Gabin film in a row that's 'not so great' (instead of the usual 'fantastic, amazing, brilliant, wonderful, stupendous'), and not just because, like in *Marie*, the characters are wishy-washy and manipulative and don't really know what they want from each other, but also because *Victor's* director, Claude Heymann, who with this film, will be working with Gabin for the one and only time in both of their careers, has taken an ancient stage play which was written by Gabin's friend Henri Bernstein, for whom the actor had already starred in 1938's *Le Messager* (on film), and in 1949's *"La Soif"* (on stage) and transformed it into a movie, without any attempt to open it up: The way in which director Heymann has chosen to place his performers physically within the frame, looks, in most sequences, like stage-blocking, as opposed to movie-blocking. That is to say, in the film version of *Victor*, Heymann is going to film most scenes, showing two characters talking in the foreground, while a third remains in the background; then, they will all switch places, and one character will move to the front, and another will retreat into the shadows. (Anyway, no matter how you slice it, this visual strategy of the filmmaker's totally screams 'stage-play.')

Victor is the second picture, after 1947's *Miroir*, in which Jean Gabin will portray a gentleman-gangster (in this picture, a very small-time gentleman gangster), a guy who's always polite and honest, even while he's going about his dishonest criminal behavior.

Top: With Francoise Christophe. Above: With Jacques Castelot.

When we first see Victor Messerand (Gabin), he's headed back to the hooscow, for his umpteenth small crime. The Guard walks him back to his cell, and Victor Gabin-Shrugs resignedly, muttering something about how he guesses he's going to "have to get used to it again." Heymann compresses time and now, suddenly, it's one year later—in fact, it's Christmas-time. Victor is released from prison, and the jailhouse Priest tells him to try and stay away: "Try not to make the same mistakes yet again, Victor. Lord knows, there are a lot of temptations in the outside world."

Immediately of course, just as Victor is outside of the prison walls, 'Temptation #1' starts shaking her gorgeous ass at him: Beautiful Francoise (she's played by Francoise Christophe), who's dolled-up in a fancy fur coat, picks him up outside the prison gates. She looks like *the hot version* of Cruella DeVil from *101 Dalmatians* and, because of this costumic iconography, we can already tell that she's probably a pretty heavy-duty gold-digger.

Francoise is the not-too-faithful wife of Victor's wealthy (crime) boss, Marc (Jacques Castelot), a balding little homunculus, and she and Victor have been having an affair for years, and probably on the sly. Marc, who's always out of town on business, is too dumb to have figured out that his wife is engaging in illicit lovefests with Victor, and if he did, it would cause more problems than you'd ever want to know about, because Marc, as Victor's boss, represents the sole source of Victor's livelihood. While it's acceptable in France, and in French movies, for a man to have mistresses, it's never acceptable in any culture to sleep with your boss's wife. (*Wait!* Let me rephrase that: It's not acceptable to *get caught* sleeping with your boss's wife!) We can tell that Francoise just uses the balding and physically amorphous little Marc for his riches, and that she needs big, studly, earthy Victor for his more primal, 'Gabinnic qualities,' although we're still not sure if she actually loves either man—which is a major weakness in the film's narrative. (She 'vacillates' like it's nobody's business!)

Francoise takes Victor out for a drink, to lubricate him for a little post-prison love-makin.' A crime-crony of Victor's, Gratien (Camille Guerini, *La Marie du port's* bar proprietor) happens to be at the same tavern, doing a little kissy-face on his own girl, but Victor, who's focusing on Francoise, isn't paying any attention to him. Francoise starts kissing Victor, and he feels embarrassed because he's left prison without showering; like every one of the other smooth-criminals Jean Gabin will play in his post-World War II pictures, it's important for Victor to always be impeccably clean and well-dressed. (Gone, are the pre-War days, when Gabin's working-class drifter-characters used to feel uncomfortable, wearing ritzy clothing; in a good many of the movies Jean Gabin will make post-1950, *ritzy glad-rags* are exactly what Jean Gabin is going to be wearing although, as I mentioned in this book's introduction, he'll still continue, on occasion, to additionally make those movies in which he plays his time-honored 'working-class guy-character,' the guy who always feels the most comfortable in overalls and work boots.)

Victor wants to go over and say hi to Gratien, but Francoise advises him against it. ("Gratien's the reason you went to jail in the first place!") Because we've already seen thirty-eight previous Jean Gabin movies, we know already that, when his characters are being interrogated by the police, 'our Gabin' will never give up his friends, and we now learn that Victor, who is as loyal to his friends as are all of Jean Gabin Movie Characters, took the fall for Gratien, and by choice: "Nobody told me to take the blame. I did it because I wanted to." (Remember the Mantra: In Jean Gabin pictures, no matter which decade in which they are made, the Friendship of Other Men is always preferable to The Love of Fickle Women.) Victor and Gratien have been friends, ever since they fought alongside each other, back in WWII, and so especially, in this case, the allegiance which these two old war horses feel toward each other is definitely stronger than any allegiance which Victor might feel toward any broad—even a totally smokin' broad, like Francoise.

After their drink, Francoise invites Victor up to Marc's mansion, since Marc's away, but Victor, who's one of those consummate Gabin Movie-Loners, would rather be on his own for a while, before he returns to his life of (small) crime, if indeed 'more crime' is going to be what he'll now choose to pursue. He tells Francoise that he wants to start over, fresh. ("I'm going to make myself into a better man, and then you'll love me more!") But of course, the reason she's so hot for him, is that he's not 'better.'

Since Victor, who is perennially 'Gabin-Transient,' has no home to call his own (even though Gabin is older, his movie characters still have a few 'existential drifts' left in them), he next lopes over to his cousins' house, and the only person at home happens to be his Aunt Martine, played by Lyane Morice, who hugs him and invites him to the restaurant she owns, for a 'welcome home-meal.' He politely declines though, actually telling her, and in these exact words, "Thanks. But I'm just going to drift around for awhile." (!)

Next stop for Victor: It's the home of another crime-buddy, mustached Genoust (Jacques Morel), another cog in Marc's crime gang. "So when are we going back to work?" Genoust excitedly inquires of Victor. But Victor just Gabin-Shrugs, telling Genoust that he probably won't be getting back to work that soon. ("I want to lay low for a little while.") "Cool," Genoust replies, "but I know Marc's going to have a lot of stuff for us to do, after the first of the year." In the meantime, Dijon invites Marc to enjoy Christmas day festivities up at Marc's country cabin, a cozy little enclave which all of Marc's foot-soldiers are entitled to use, whenever Marc's away on (his international drug) business(es)—which he is, a great deal of the time.

While Victor and Genoust are up at the cabin, Genoust starts renewing his pleas for Victor to go back to work with him, and with the rest of Marc's gang, and immediately, if not sooner: "If you have reservations about continuing to work for Marc, maybe I can ask Marc to give us a bigger cut on the next job." At this point, a gorgeous young brunette enters. She's Marianne (Brigitte Auber), and she's been sent over by Marc, to act as the organization's new sexy secretary: Marc, who has no idea that Victor is making it with Marc's own wife, Francoise, has probably sent Marianne over to the cabin, as enticement for Victor to stay on with the organization. Marianne tells Genoust and Victor that she's going to start working for them after the holidays have run their course, and that she's only come by today for a 'meet-and-greet.' Victor, although he's twenty-some years older than Marianne at least, thinks that she's pretty darn cute, and *vice-versa*. (Just like in *La Marie du port*, and in a bunch of other Gabin Movies which he'll be making over the next twenty-some years, all luscious twenty-year-old girls will always have a '*thang*' for older Gabin, who's manliness is as ageless as the Seven Seas.)

The next night is Christmas Eve, and Victor and Francoise share dinner together, over at Marc's mansion (in Marc's absence, of course), followed by a bout of hot, off-screen *Christmas Sex*. Post-coitally, she confides to Victor that she's no longer interested in Marc: "I only want you, Victor. Please say you'll marry me!" (Let's note, here, that she's not actually confessing her love to Victor; she's just telling him that she's hot for him.) Victor tells Francoise, Gabin-Dispassionately, that ultimately, the two of them are probably fated *not* to be together, since they come from different worlds, and that, even though he's been trying to better himself, and even though he suspects that he'll always 'do all right,' he knows he'll never really make *bukku* bucks, and that Francoise will never be able to live without the luxuries which Marc has always been able to give her.

Now: *Surprise!* Marc's decided to return home early, to be with his wife for Christmas, and hearing Marc bounding up the stairs, Victor now skedaddles out the back door. Husband and (nervously out-of-breath) wife light the Christmas tree together and, just then, she jumps when the phone rings. Jokingly, and unaware that she's been seeing Victor, Marc now ribs her: "Answer the phone! It might be the man of your dreams!"

Francoise doesn't know that Marc was just kidding around and, perhaps a bit paranoically, she thinks that he must somehow know all about her affair with Victor—which, very plainly, he doesn't—so she cops to it. Marc is more than shocked, because now, she's telling him that she loves Victor, and that she's going to be running away with him, and very soon.

As Marc and Francoise now start engaging in the kind of stiff tiff which is always an unpleasant by-product of such admissions of infidelity, director Heymann now cuts away to Victor, who's out on the street in front of Marc and Francoise's apartment. As he looks up into their window, he sees that Marc's fist is raised, as if he's going to start beating the stuffing out of his wife so, completely unafraid of his boss, Victor bolts up the stairs, instantly ready to duke it out with him. Even though Marc's a tiny little wimp, the two men have been friends in the past—in fact, they've been 'tight' right up until this very moment—and Victor doesn't really want to do the guy any damage. The building's Landlady (Jane Morlet), who is very clearly on Victor's side (like everybody else in every Gabin movie, she instinctively sides with Jean Gabin), tells him not to fight with Marc: "Stop it, Victor! You're not like those people. You're normal!"

When Victor and Marc are face-to-face, Victor tells Marc, very truthfully, that he's never meant to cause any problems with him: "You're my boss, Marc. And even though you're probably not going to believe me, I still consider you to be my friend. Francoise came to visit me in jail, and I fell in love with her. It wasn't her fault—I'm the one who initiated the affair." Tiny Marc is intimidated by big, brawny Victor, even though Victor works for *him*, and he sheepishly asks Victor, "So, do you think you're going to marry my wife?!"

It's *not for nothing* that Marc's a big-time crime boss though and, at this point, the little guy summons up just enough steeliness to try and threaten Victor: "I'll have you know that you're at my house, and that you're still on parole. So, I'm going to ask you to leave my wife and me alone, or I'll call the police right now and tell them that you're here!" Without even thinking about it, Victor now launches himself into *Jean Gabin Primal Mode*, and throws Marc against up the wall, getting right up in the other fella's face, in a Gabin-Outburst: "I could kill you, but I won't. Ultimately, Francoise is going to have to choose between us." Victor lets go of Marc, and then retreats to the back of the room, to give Francoise and Marc a few seconds to decide what they're going to do about their marriage. (With Gabin standing in the background, and Marc and Francoise remaining in the foreground, we're definitely looking at the blocking of a stage-play.)

Francoise then tells Marc (and this is the direct gainsay of what she said to Victor, just before Marc arrived), "I want to be with you, Marc, and you only! We're made for each other!" (She's playing the two men against each other and probably, if she were to look deep within herself, we'd see that in the end, she's in it for herself, and that she isn't really interested in either one of them, and that 'playing men against each other' is just a game which keeps her from boredom.) Marc crosses his arms: "Well, if that's true, go and tell him that." Marc's not dumb, though: He *knows* that she wants to be with Victor, and even though he can accept it, he'd definitely hate losing her, because—well, look at her! (*She's hot!*)

In front of both men, Francoise next changes her tune yet again, now claiming to Marc that she likes Victor better than she likes him—and, mind you, this is only seconds after she had just said the exact opposite: "You're right, Marc: I *do* love Victor more. Just let me leave you now, and without a fight." Marc tells her that it's fine by him if she leaves, but on one condition, and one condition only: "Everything you own is something I've given you. So before you leave, you have to give me everything—including your dress!" As she strips down to her bra and panties (because, in The Gangster World, public humiliation is The Name of the Game), Marc continues driving his stupid point home: "Victor will never be able to give you what I gave you!" She tells Marc that she's always considered herself to be no more than a possession to him, and one that is no different than any of the other fancy trinkets which fill his apartment; she reminds him, too, that she can't be bought, which is an intensely goofy statement for her to be making, because we already see that *she has a Ph.D in 'being bought!'*

Victor now takes Francoise away, with a mighty cry of *"Allons-y"* ("let's go!"), and Marc doesn't even try to stop them. As Francoise, who is now free from Marc, walks down the street with Victor, Victor tells her that, even though she's coming away with him right now, he knows *where it's at:* "I *know* you love Marc. I also know that he bought you, just like he's always bought everything else in his life, and that you two have always just been trophies for each other." Next, director Heymann and his co-scenarist Jean Ferry (the two men adapted Henri Bernstein's play, for the screen) give us the movie's one very cool plot twist: After rescuing Francoise from Marc, Victor next dumps Francoise's sorry ass, right then and there (right on the street!), as payback for that fact that she's embarrassed him, by playing him against Marc. Jean Gabin will not stoop to any woman's manipulations—and clearly, this woman must be punished! Now, Francoise has neither Victor nor Marc, she's just been publicly humiliated twice in the space of about five minutes, and Victor's happy that he's gotten the upper-hand on her, and he looks really excited, too: Now, no doubt, he will be free to pursue the beautiful young Marianne. As Victor walks away alone, the Landlady of Marc's building leans out the window, shaking out some laundry, and singing a song to herself, the lyrics of which are commenting, in the style of a Greek Chorus, on the *love-triangle-action* which we've just been seeing. (SAMPLE LYRIC: "With lots of jewels, I can buy the one I want…") While the lady continues to trill, director Heymann pans over to Francoise, who's standing out on the empty street, now on her own, crying herself a river.

Now that Victor's out of Marc's and Francoise's various grips (and, *he thinks*, out of the crime world), he's free to 'go legit;' in fact, unbenknownst to everybody he knows, he's already been brewing-up a little business venture of his own, and it's 100%-legal: Victor, as we'll now learn, isn't *just* a criminal, but he's also a very skilled engineer and, for the last several years, he's been quietly renting out a machine shop in which, in between jail terms, he's invented the world's most powerful electrical generator, which he's christened 'The Accumulator.' Victor has his new and *hot* secretary, Marianne, come over to the shop, to dictate a letter to the International Motors Company, which has been chomping at the bit to buy the patent from him: "Dear Sirs: I would like to accept your offer of two million francs, for the machine which I have invented—the Accumulator. This letter confirms my acceptance of your deal."

This is the first time Marianne is hearing about Victor's millions and, like all women when they hear about guys with money (even 'good women'), she now looks like she's going to have a *petit mort* ('little death'[a/k/a: orgasm]), right there on the spot: "Ooooooh! Two million is quite a lot!" Even though he doesn't know her that well, Victor uses this moment, during which Marianne's defenses are down—a moment in which, no doubt, she's imagining herself floating on a magic carpet made out of a giant thousand-franc note—to propose to her. (Whether Victor is serious about his proposal or not, he knows that suggesting such a union, is a great way to get any woman's skirt flying above her head.) He invites her out for drinks and dancing, which she accepts, gladly.

Victor's Bank Director friend (he's played by Jean-Paul Moulinot) next enters the machine shop, and the guy is positively frothing-over with good news: He's the sharp-eyed moneyman who's brokered that big deal between Victor and International Motors, and he's come to tell Victor that he's been able to up International Motor's initial offer from two million francs, to just over forty million. Now Victor, who was formerly just a working stiff, is even more mad-rich than his (former) mega-rich boss Marc is! Marianne plops herself down onto Victor's lap, the prospect of forty million *shekels* making her look like she's ready to experience another 'Big O:' "Tell me again about how much they're going to be paying you, Victor. Oh my God, you are soooo rich!" (In this film, all of the female characters—even Marianne, the nice one whom we actually like—are all hardcore money-grubbers!) Instead of looking excited about being as newly mega-rich as a Rothschild, Victor, very realistically, starts worrying now about the complications which will come in his life from having so much money; he's now thinking out loud about the probability that everybody he has ever met in his life will soon be coming out of the woodwork, to try and 'borrow' some of his cash, and this whole sequence is horribly shot and edited, with the actors placed in the wrong parts of the frame, by director Heymann: Each actor, in his close-up, is looking off into the wrong direction so that, instead of seeming that the actors are looking at each other, which is what they're supposed to be doing, it instead appears that each one is looking at an unseen 'mystery object,' off-screen; it's no wonder that Quality-Conscious Jean Gabin and director Claude Heymann would only work together on this one film.

Victor goes back to Marc's mansion, and even though he's not really the vindictive sort, he gloats to his ex-boss about how he no longer needs to work for him. ("I've just become even richer than you are!") Now that Victor is filthy-rich, Marc, of course, tells him that, since he's helped Victor out of innumerable jams in the past, that he is entitled to at least a small piece of Victor's newfound fortune, and Marc has some different news, too—news, which isn't that great: He tells Victor about a shocking headline which has just appeared in today's newspaper: Apparently, the police think they may have finally pieced together information leading to an unsolved, ancient money-laundering crime which involved five-million francs, and they believe the culprit to have been Marc. Marc tells Victor that Victor "owes him one," and that he expects Victor to take the fall for him, while he flees. ("You owe me that much, Victor, for all the times when I carried you, when *you* were in trouble.") Victor waves his ex-boss off, though: "No way. Not interested. I'm rich, now. I'm not involved with crime anymore, and I'm not going to jail for something we did years ago." Marc won't take no for an answer, though: "The reason you were released from jail just now, was all my doing, Victor, in case you haven't figured that out. I wrote a letter to the parole board, telling them that you're a good man. Plus, if you remember, when it comes to that old job which I'm now being accused of pulling, I let you keep half of the take—five million francs. So it's payback time, and you can't deny me. You've got to help me out with this."

Victor puts his foot down, though, telling Marc that there's no way he's going to be going back to jail for him, or, for that matter, for anybody. So Marc now switches over to a 'kinder, gentler' tone, and asks him for a more doable favor: "Look, Victor: If you won't go to jail for me, then will you at least do one thing? Do you still love Francoise?" (Victor 'Gabin-Shrugs;' he has no idea if he loves Francoise, whose ass he dumped out on the street, and neither do we—and we wish we did!) Marc continues, "Well, *I* love her—she's silly, but she's dear. Now, do just one thing for me: Will you be her friend? I need to know." Wailing police sirens can now be heard, drawing closer to the apartment, and Marc knows now, that the jig is up. Victor suggests to Marc that he should *amscray* out the back, find Francoise (wherever she happens to be right now, because neither of the two men know, since they've both dumped her), and take her with him to another country, to hide out. But Marc tells Victor that this is a bad idea because, in case he (Marc) should get arrested, Francoise will be arrested as well, as an accessory. Victor next tells Marc that if he gives himself up, he'll probably only be required to serve half of a four year sentence, and now, in retrospect, Marc likes Victor's first idea better, so he agrees to try and flee from France, and all by himself. Edging quickly toward the back door, Marc reminds Victor to always be a friend to Francoise for him, and he then *books-out* through the back door, before the cops can catch him. Turns out, he ran for nothing (at least, at this moment). While it's true that cop cars *were* speeding up the street, they weren't going toward Marc's house: They were actually responding to a call which was coming in from somewhere else. Marc makes for the airport, rents a small plane, gets in, takes off and (we saw this coming), intentionally crashes it off-screen, killing himself instantly!

We now get to meet the distinguished President of International Motors (he's played by Pierre Mondy), the guy who bought Victor's generator for forty million francs. The president has brought a check for the forty million with him, and he pays Victor in full, offering, as he hands it to him, to teach Victor how to invest: "Since you're clearly a guy who likes beautiful women, Victor, you're going to need to put your money into investments, so that the ladies won't be spending it."

Cut to 'many years later:'

Francoise and Victor run into each other on the street, accidentally, and Francoise looks about twenty years older than she did the last time we saw her, but Victor looks exactly the same. (Whoopsie-daisy!) She obviously hasn't seen Victor for years, and clearly, we can tell from the way she's now molesting him with her eyes, that she's still interested in him, but won't admit it, because she has no idea that he ever sold his generator idea many years ago, and that he's been a multi-millionaire for years: She thinks he's still poor as the day he dumped her those many years ago and, narratively, this doesn't make a lick of sense, because then, just like now, financial newspapers the world over have always informed *everybody with reading skills* about all of the big business deals-of-the-day, and about who all of the newly-made moguls are (so it's hard for somebody who's watching this movie, today, to fathom that Francoise wouldn't have known that Victor sold his machine for forty million francs many years before, especially because forty million francs in 1951, is probably closer to 400 million, today. You'd think that, over the years, even if Francoise didn't read the *Financial Times*, she'd still have some inkling that her ex-lover is one of the wealthiest men in France)!

"How's it going with your little machine?" she asks him, condescendingly. He can't believe that she doesn't know that he sold it and became rich off of it years ago, so he pretends with her, as the two of them are engaging in this conversation, that he's still poor and struggling. She apologizes for playing him against Marc when they were younger: "I betrayed your tenderness more than once, because I was miserable. I only loved one man, and you have to know, Victor, that [and here comes a really bizarre surprise admission, which we're *not* expecting:] Marc is the one [whom] I have always loved. Not you!" Clearly, from the moony way in which she's looking at Victor, we can tell that Victor is really the only man for whom she's ever carried a torch, but that she doesn't want to say it outright, because she knows as well as we do that stoic Jean Gabin isn't the world's best reactor. (Francoise is so cold-hearted, she's still playing Victor against Marc, even though Marc's been in the ground, for years.)

Victor has clearly retained a few, stray feelings for Francoise over the years, but he now has even less tolerance for her flighty, mind-changing weirdness than ever, so he very soberly nips the rest of their conversation in the bud, telling her that this is the last time the two of them will ever be seeing each other. She agrees, trying to hide her tears, because she doesn't want Victor to see that she still cares, and tells him that she's going away again, and that she still has much of the money which Marc left her in his will, years ago (so that she has been, and will continue to be, okay); she *does* ask Victor however, if, before she leaves, he can hold her hand just one more time, for old time's sake: "If you hold my hand for just a few moments, it will mean that you forgive me for all the trouble I put you through in the past." She asks Victor, still believing him to be poor, about what's going to become of him and, with a mischievous Gabin-Shrug, he poker-facedly responds, "We'll see…"

Of course, because Victor is Jean Gabin, and because *Francoise is a woman*, she now does another one of her sudden about-faces and, unable to hold her true feelings in, she confesses to Victor that what she's just said about loving Marc instead of him isn't true, and this confession is delivered in complete stream-of-consciousness: "Oh, Victor! You make me want to laugh! I didn't want to hurt you, but you still look like you don't even care! I'm still a woman! While Marc will always be my one-and-only, I'd still have enough love for you—if only, you'd want it…"

Victor tells Francoise that he is already married, and "…to a nice woman named Marianne." Francoise asks Victor if Marianne loves him back, and he shrugs, saying that he doesn't really know. Obviously lonely, even with all of her MarcMoney, she next asks Victor, point-blank, "What if I asked you to divorce this Marianne and marry me?" Victor's reply is no more than the least-perceptible of all Gabin-Shrugs and next, feeling suddenly embarrassed for having just put what at least for the past few moments have passed for her true feelings on the line for once in her entire life, Francoise now tries to save face, pretending that she just doesn't care: "Well, forget I said anything. Just go home to your Marianne!"

When Victor goes home to Marianne, he finds, unexpectedly (to him *and* to us), that she's just left *him!* According to a note which she's left, she's gone to the airport, because she wants to "…start a new life somewhere else." (Probably, she's gone off with another guy and, even more probably, he's younger than Victor, although the film never tells us where she's going, or whom she's going with.) Victor high-tails it over to to *el aeropuerto* to try and stop Marianne from blowing town, *a la* the famous Bogart/Bergman 'landing-strip ending,' from *Casablanca,* in the hopes that they can be together, but the film then abruptly ends, even before he can confront her. Jean Gabin walks away alone, just like he always did in most of his movies from the mid-to-late '30s, although the difference between this movie and those older movies is that, this time out, we're not worried about what will become of him, because fate is being uncharacteristically kind to him: *He's bloody rich!*

Victor is a very standard Jean Gabin Love Triangle Flick, of which the 1950s, as I've already mentioned, provided eight prime examples. Just as in *La Marie du port*, we can't really get too invested with the story or in the characters, because we're not sure if they really even like each other or not, and if the characters don't care, well then—why on earth should we? At the end of Claude Heymann's film, Francoise and Victor remain alone, because they were both too jaded, and/or, maybe even too shy to ever admit their true feelings to one another. Now in real life, we do this to ourselves all the time (sabotaging our own future happinesses, by never telling the people we love how much we really love them), but in a movie, we as an audience need to see some resolution; we have to understand fully how the characters feel about each other in every movie, no matter what your pretentious friends will tell you, whether it's a big Hollywood blockbuster, or a tiny little art movie. With *Victor*, we don't know anything, except that soon the movie will be over and we can go eat!

What a Critic Said at the Time: "This film, based on [a] recently successful play, inherits too much of the stagy talk and action to make [it] acceptable art-house fare. Full of long, actionless passages and static direction. Gabin, as Victor, seems sheepish." (*Variety*, 7-11-51 issue. Critic: "Mosk. [George Moskowitz.]" Reviewed in Paris.)

Top: Back in the trainyard, for the first time since "La Bete humaine." Above: With Simone Valere.

FILM 40

LA NUIT EST MON ROYAUME

France, 1951

(Literal English Translation: "THE NIGHT IS MY KINGDOM") Directed by Georges Lacombe. Produced by Pierre Gerin and Robert Prevot. Screenplay by Charles Spaak. Based Upon a Story by Marcel Rivet. Director of Photography (black and white), Philippe Agostini. Music by Yves Baudrier. Editor, Henri Taverna. Production Designers, Rino Mondellini and Rene Moulaert. (GENRE: DRAMA). An L.P.C. Production. Running Time, 1 hour 50 minutes. Released in France on November 7, 1951, by DisCina. Released in the United States by Arthur Davis Associates with English Subtitles, on September 29, 1953.

"Everyone who can see has lied to me!"
— *Gabin, after going blind, in "La Nuit est mon royaume"*

Forty years before Al Pacino would assay the role of 'a charming-blind-guy-getting-involved-in-fun-hijinks,' in Martin Brest's *Scent of A Woman*, Gabin trudged that field, carefully, and with a cane, in the tremendously entertaining *La Nuit est mon royaume* (*The Night is My Kingdom*). After the fairly uninteresting double-header of *La Marie du port* and *Victor*, Gabin knew he needed to pick a winner, so he hired his old friend Charles Spaak, who put him through some of his best paces in the '30s (*La Bandera*, *Les Bas-fonds*, *La Belle equipe*, *La Grande illusion*, *Le Recif de corail*, and *Remorques*), to adapt Marcel Rivet's short story, and the resulting picture is a powerhouse, which definitely represents Gabin's return to great material. And although it garnered some pretty great reviews, and even a well-deserved Best Actor trophy for Gabin at 1951's Venice Film Festival (and on the heels of this award, a token U.S. art-house release), at this point, Gabin was still be three years away from regaining his pre-war popularity, in his native France.

In *Royaume*, Jean Gabin is, just as he did thirteen years earlier in Renoir's *La Bete humaine*, playing the role of a train engineer and, as the film begins, Gabin's Raymond Pinsard daringly rescues the out-of-control train which is under his stewardship, as it brakelessly careens toward its doom (the opening of the film could basically be considered, "*Runaway Train '51*"), and he is able to heroically save it, although he has similarly been *unable* to preserve the life of his co-engineer friend, Loustaud (Paul Azais), when both of them are suddenly thrown from the locomotive.

Raymond receives the *Chevalier du Legion* medal for his heroic train-saving, but can't properly enjoy it, and not just because his friend has died, but also because the accident has left him blind, and he must now be led around by his elderly mother (Cecile Didier). Witnessing this 'forced-emasculation-through-blindness' of Alpha-Male Gabin will be a new rub for his audiences, but he bears it all with Jean Gabin's 'whatever happens, happens'-brand of stoicism. Raymond tells the crowd of French dignitaries who have gathered to present him with his medal, "There are 25,000 blind people in France. Don't pity me," and he adds, quite poetically, that it may even be a blessing that he's now blind: "Some people blind canaries to make them sing," he sighs.

It's not that his newfound blindness doesn't bother Raymond, completely: In the one outburst of emotion which Gabin will be allowed in each film—and this time, it will come at his mother's dinner table, when he's dining with close relatives—he'll cry out, "Can't you see I'm unhappy! I'm sick to death of goodness! Everyone who can see has lied to me!" After he's finished 'letting-it-all-hang-out' in this manner he'll immediately retreat, just like in every Gabin film, back to into his shell-of-stoicism, never referencing this outpouring again.

Raymond's doting old Mom, in due course, enrolls him in a school for the blind, where he instantly falls in love (love is blind, get it?) with the equally non-sighted (and, did we mention, hot?) Braille teacher, Louise Louveau (Simone Valerie). Our 'handicapable' hero Raymond manages to keep his good humor intact, squeezing comically into a tight little kid-sized school desk, and playfully giving wrong and even *double-entendre*-laden answers to the other students in the class (his classmates are mostly children), who seem to be having no end of problems answering the questions in their Braille books.

Louise insists that Raymond should hunker down—and not only on top of her, but also to learn his Braille lessons, but he just Gabin-Shrugs, telling her that it's not important for him to learn Braille, because soon, based upon what his mother has told him, he'll have the operation which will enable him to see again.

The Louise-Raymond romance blooms, and Louise confides to her colleagues, "He is the most moving case I've ever seen," much to the chagrin, of course, of Louise's jealous, fully-seeing boyfriend, Lionel (Gerard Oury, an actor who will eventually become a director of some very popular French comedies—most notably, of 1966's World War II epic *La Grande vadrouilles*, a movie which remains, to this very day, France's very biggest indigenous boxoffice hit of all time), who runs the school. Lionel tells Louise that he didn't see her affair with Raymond coming, and she replies, "How blind you've been," before traipsing away, rather dramatically, with her little seeing-eye dog, Polka, at her side.

Lionel becomes so threatened by Raymond's attentions toward his girlfriend, that he jealously and maliciously tells Raymond a truth to which only he and the nun with whom he co-runs the school are privy, which is that Raymond will never regain his sight. As resigned to cruel fate as Jean Gabin is in all of his movies, Raymond sneaks out of the school, using his now-supersonic deaf man-hearing skills to follow piercing train sounds through the night, and he is now ready, with great solemnity, to throw himself in front of the first train that passes, thus ending it all—but right before he does this, he's heroically rescued by his concerned brother-in-law, Jean (Jacques Dynam), who arrives at the tracks, just in the nick of time. (You've heard of *deus ex machina?* Well, this is brother-in-law-ex-machina!)

Eventually, Raymond learns to accept his blindness and, before long, he's even back at the school learning Braille, while Louise's hand sensuously guides his own hand over the little dots. (He's also learned how to build fabulous radios for everybody in town.) "Misfortune makes men like sheep," Louise tells Raymond admiringly, "but you've remained a man!" Yes, even though he's blind, Jean Gabin is, for a welcome change, actually allowed to experience a completely positive happy ending, although the tragic rub, is that he won't be able to *see* his happy ending.

La Nuit est mon royaume features not only one of the coolest-sounding titles of any movie ever made anywhere in the world, but more importantly, it's a terrific Jean Gabin movie, and one which benefits not only from great performances, writing, and directing, but also from a hypnotically-beautiful musical score which was composed by Yves Baudrier. While the film was released at two art-house cinemas in the U.S. in the 1950s, it is unknown in America today, and I was able to view the only surviving English-subtitled print at UCLA's Film Archives in Los Angeles. Hopefully, one day there will be more prints of *La Nuit est mon royaume* for the rest of the world, outside of France, to enjoy.

What a Critic Said at the Time: "This is an offbeat film, done with reserve and intelligence. The Jean Gabin name may get it some trade in America. Jean Gabin is excellent as the maimed engineer whose dynamic spirit, and zest for life, finally, help him [to] overcome his handicap." (*Variety*, 9-26-51 issue. Critic: "Mosk. [George Moskowitz.]" Reviewed at Venice Film Festival.)

What Another Critic Said at the Time: "The problem of showing the sensations of a man who cannot see is conveyed with fine precision by the sturdy and solemn Mr. Gabin. An odd and difficult assignment is undertaken by Jean Gabin in *The Night is My Kingdom*. He works at it hard, and with sincerity." (New York *Times*, 10-3-53 issue. Critic: Bosley Crowther.)

With Carla Del Poggio.

FILM 41

FILLE DANGEREUSE

France/Italy, 1952

(Literal English Translation: "DANGEROUS WOMAN") Directed by Guido Brigone. Produced by Carlo Musso, Gualberto Bagnoli, Carlo Bugnani, and Armando Morandi. Screenplay by Guido Brignone and Alessandro De Stefani. Based Upon a Play by Sabatino Lopez. Director of Photography (black and white), Mario Montuori. Editor, Jolanda Benvenutti. Music by Milan Bixio. Production Designer, Ottavio Scotti. (GENRE: MELODRAMA) A Production of Societe Generale de Cinematographe (France) and Titanus (Italy). Running Time, 1 hour 35 minutes. Released in France on January 16, 1952, by Societe Generale de Cinematographie. Never Released Theatrically in the United States.

> "I'd like to go somewhere else, just so you could write letters to me
> and I could read them."
> — *A manipulative grifter-girl messes with Gabin's mind, shortly before
> she screws him over, in "Fille dangereuse"*

After the not-so-intriguing *La Marie du port* and *Victor*, here comes a third 'not-so-intriguing' movie in which a girl is messing with Jean Gabin and he doesn't fight back—and we really want him to! It's director Guido Brignone's French/Italian production of *Fille dangereuse* (or, in English, *Dangerous Woman*).

We're in Rome: As the film opens, a patient is wheeled into medical school operating theater, where we'll first meet Dr. Antonio Sanna (a/k/a, Jean Gabin) in the first of three movies from the 1950s in which he'd be playing doctors (the other two, were 1952's *La Minute de verite* and 1956's *La Cas du docteur Laurent*). He's teaching his very-attentive class about the little anaesthetized kid who's splayed out on the table in front of him, and telling his students that, in his opinion, "… the most important thing we can all do, and not just in medicine but in life as well, is to always be looking for symptoms," even when the patient— or, by extension (as we're going to be seeing in this picture) when the love relationship— appears to be healthy, so we already know that we're watching a movie which is going to be dealing with the symptoms of somebody's failing relationship. He tells his students that, very often, a 'crazy' person and a 'normal' person might have the same disease, but that the normal person will heal naturally, while the crazy person won't heal at all, or else, he'll just get worse. (Hmm... haven't read that one in the *AMA Journal* before; guess that's why they call it, '*Gabin-o-pathic Medicine!*')

Post-operatively, Antonio's now in the office of the hospital's Chief Administrator (he's played by the great Italian character actor, Paolo Stoppa), who's happy to inform Antonio that he's hand-picked him to be the Chief Administrator of another hospital—in fact, it's a brand-spankin' new hospital, in Bologna. While Antonio knows that being chosen like this is a great honor, he doesn't want to leave his present position, because he feels allegiance toward both his students and his present patients, many of whom, as he's now reminding the Administrator, happen to be war veterans. To put it mildly, Antonio just doesn't want to go, but the Administrator simply won't hear of it: "You have to detach from this job," he tells Antonio.

After a little quiet soul-searching (it's Jean Gabin's specialty), Antonio changes his mind, and decides to accept the position, and that night when he goes home, he lays it on the line with his wife, Maria (Carla Del Poggio). Antonio and Maria Sanna really love each other, and while she's not so keen on leaving her present set-up in Rome, she's obviously one of those good, selfless wives who'd go to the moon and back, for her husband. (Thankfully, Bologna's only about half-as-far as *la luna*.) The couple is going to be leaving Rome immediately (the next morning, in fact), but tonight, to celebrate, Antonio tells Maria that they're going to be taking in the Circus at the Teatro del Pavone, to celebrate his new gig. (In this movie, there's no need for suitcase packing! I guess their clothes are already 'just there!')

Needless to say, Antonio and Maria Sanna will never get to Bologna because Cruel Fate intervenes, just like 'she' does in most Jean Gabin pictures: The circus's strongman, Serge (another great Italian movie performer, Serge Reggiani, who'd continue to appear in European movies all the way up until his death in 2004), shares his dressing room with Daisy, who's played by the smokin'-hot Jane Russell-clone, Silvana Pampanini. Serge and Daisy are billed as a brother-sister act, *a la* Gabin and Josephine Baker in *Zou Zou*, although they look nothing alike, because they're actually boyfriend and girlfriend! As part of their act, they use the fictitious stage-name of 'Parnell' which, if it were their real surname, would make them both *Irish!*

Suddenly, during the evening's performance—KLUNK!—Serge takes a big fall, off of the trapeze. (Remember *Varietes*, Gabin's 1935 trapeze picture? The French really love setting their movies in circuses because thematically, the trapeze represents 'that oh-so-thin line we're all walking on.') Antonio rushes the stage, and orders the bystanders to call for an ambulance; and just when we're beginning to think that good old Jean Gabin would never be interested in such ephemera, he asks Serge, just as Serge begins passing out, what kind of medical insurance he carries. (Told you Gabin was always level-headed!)

And when Serge goes into a coma—*he stays in a coma!* Morning comes, and the trapezist has already been taken to Antonio's hospital in Rome, and when next we see him, he's being operated-on by Antonio, and Antonio's even got this one special nurse standing next to him, a woman whose sole job, or so it would appear, is to mop away all of the precious drops of Gabinsweat. According to the O.R.'s wall clock, an hour has passed and, after the operation, which was a success, Serge is still out-cold, but Antonio tells *mega-hot* Daisy that her brother will be back on his feet, and in no time, flat. Daisy is so overwhelmed with happiness, that she actually kisses Antonio sensuously, down the entire length of his arm.

Daisy tells Antonio that she prayed during the operation, although she looks, just like Gabin's own character in 1938's *Le Recif de corail,* like she's probably never seen a Bible before in her whole life: "You did *more* than just save him, Dr. Sanna," she coos. "I have a debt to you. You can ask of me whatever you want!" Of course, she'd love the uber-masculine Antonio to make love to her but, as we already know, Jean Gabin doesn't get involved with 'OGL' ('other guys' ladies') or, at least, he resists it for as long as he can! Antonio's very professional (he never mixes comas with pleasure) and he advises her (but not exactly in the verbiage which I'm about to use) to 'not let the door hit her ass on the way out.'

Daisy retreats to Serge's bedside, where he remains comatose, and he's now wearing a neckbrace, due to the damage which he had sustained in the fall. Serge has been placed in a non-private, double room, which has been bifurcated down the middle by a very prominent curtain and, while we can't see the other patient with whom he's sharing the room, we can definitely hear the guy, and this Patient X's voice is superimposed over close-ups of Serge's inert, comatose face; in effect, then, this unseen other patient's wild and, no doubt, pharmaceutically-induced musings become 'Serge's words.' (It's a very cool stylistic device, which director Brignone is using in this scene, and to great effect.) "What right do they have to force me to live?" the Unseen Patient cries out to his equally-Unseen Visitor. "The nurse told me I'm a maniac. If they force me to live, I'll kill them!" The guy is clearly crazy-like-a-fox, and he now continues spouting out a lot of frenetic, booga-booga/blarney, including, "I can't see! *Only the dead can see!*" On the other side of the curtain, Daisy now starts whispering to Serge, hoping that he can hear her sultry voice from within the depths of his coma, and she now informs him that he's just been operated-on by "...the greatest Doctor in the world: Doctor Antonio Sanna!"

The next day, Serge has emerged from the chrysalis of his coma, and Antonio is telling him that he's going to have to remain in the hospital for a period of several weeks, to recuperate. In the meantime, Daisy's become friendly with Dr. And Mrs. Sanna: She's starting to hang around with the two of them a lot, and is quickly becoming, in effect, their hot third-wheel. Maria Sanna, never thinking that her 'good' husband would ever dare to cheat on her (well, he hasn't, yet... at least, not with Daisy) even drops her husband and Daisy off at the hospital together, and by doing so, of course, she's just become unwillingly complicit in the future Daisy/Antonio affair which we can guess is going to be happening, just around the corner.

Daisy enters Serge's hospital room herself, and surprise—Serge is not only back from the Land of the Dead but, jarringly, he's sitting bolt-upright, and he looks spooky (just like Linda Blair in the throes of demonic possession), and he instantly begins accusing her of having an affair with the Doctor. ("You're betraying me with your eyes!") Apparently, that trapeze 'accident' which turned Serge into an old-broke pony (he's no longer in his coma, but will remain, at least for awhile, physically paralyzed) was caused by Daisy, who didn't push the bar high enough on purpose, because she knew that Serge happened to have been carrying a very heavy insurance policy and, as we're now finding out, the two of them worked it all out together before the accident, that she would miscalculate the position of the bar, sacrificing his health on purpose, so that they would both become rich. We're now wondering: Will Daisy double-cross Serge, and try to keep all of the money for herself? (We shall see!)

After visiting with Serge, Daisy next sashays into Antonio's office and tries to coax him out of his Gabinian-Shell, inquiring, "Are you always so silent with everyone?" (Of course he is, lady! He's Jean Gabin! Didn't you get the memo?!) She's mad, because he's not going nuts for her, like every other guy with whom she's ever flirted has always done, and so she calls him on it. ("You never even look at me!") Since this rather frantic line of questioning isn't really getting her anywhere, and because Antonio's not coming around in the way in which most healthy guys between 18 and 80 always do when they're around her, she next, *per* Christopher Guest in *Spinal Tap*, turns her whole Hotsty-Totsy act 'up to eleven,' immediately getting down to brass tax: "So, listen, Doctor, I need a statement from you for my brother's insurance company, saying that he will never be able to go back to the trapeze again. Can you do that for me?"

Antonio's mouth drops: "Not only can I not sign a paper saying that your brother will never work again, but I can't even do the opposite!" Daisy now really starts making with the poutiness, and she says, using her best *femme-fatale* wiles, that she'll happily give Antonio a cut of any money which she might be able to retrieve out of the situation. Of course, Antonio looks horrified: He can't believe this girl wants to cash in on her own brother's accident, and Antonio's so honest, it's not even occurring to him that she's the one who actually made it happen, and she now tries to calm the savage, Gabinian beast—"Oh, don't be angry with me!"—but it's too late, because a volcanic Gabin-Outburst is just on the horizon (sailor, take warning!): "Young lady, you are corrupt! This is the first time anyone has ever asked me to do this before!" What he's saying is believable, because *Fille dangereuse* was made in 1952, which is decades before the entire world became scam-and-frivolous lawsuit-happy. He bids her goodbye.

At this point, a Nurse (Diane Baker) enters the hospital room, and tells Serge that soon, while he will probably be able to walk again, he will still need to be in a harness, and for several months. When the Nurse leaves, Daisy continues her subterfuge-talk with Serge: "Dr. Sanna is not an easy man to crack, what with his *morals* and his *conscience!* But you'd better believe that I'll get through to him." The Administrator then comes in, and tells Daisy that the harness which Serge will need is going to cost one hundred-thousand francs, and Daisy knows that she's definitely not going to be able to afford that chunk o' change on carnival pay.

Within moments, Daisy is back in Antonio's office and, even though he's thrown her out twice before, we can tell he's starting to change his mind about her: This time, he's delighted that she's come to see him, and she tells him that she feels terrible, because she can't pay her 'brother's' hospital bills, but that she will soon be able to, as soon as she goes back to work at the circus and starts earning some money, again. Of course, Antonio (Jean Gabin is only flesh-and-blood!) is falling in love with Daisy, against his better judgment, and he tears up her outstanding bill, right in front of her. For a smart-cookie, Jean Gabin's Movie Characters sometimes tend to get led around by their *coq-au-vins* and, as I've already said, we always like him better in those movies in which his characters don't allow themselves to get used so easily.

Daisy pretends to be horrified when Antonio insists that she doesn't have to pay, and that in effect, the whole operation and hospital stay have now been, officially, 'comped.' She now starts making with the phony-baloney crocodile tears. ("You think I can accept this charity?") Then, Daisy and Antonio kiss, passionately: She's crazy, he's crazy-horny, and together—they're doomed!

It's not long, before Daisy's in Antonio's car, and not much longer than that, before they're making love in a *frou-frou* hotel. He asks her, very carefully, about something he's been thinking about: "I don't want you to get mad at me for wondering what I'm wondering, but: Could you have possibly *not* have pushed the trapeze bar far enough, on purpose?" She answers, not-so-cryptically, that she'd never hurt her 'brother,' on purpose or otherwise.

Daisy likes to make love a lot—in fact, many times in a row. (After a few sultry hours with this incredible woman, Gabin definitely needs a great big bottle of Evian!) Antonio then asks her if her predilection for always wanting way-too-much sex might possibly have something to do with the fact that she fears death, and always needs to be doing something fun (or, in today's parlance, something 'extreme')—something like 'having sex' or 'swinging on a trapeze,' as a way of proving to herself that she's really alive, and that she can really 'feel.' Daisy admits to none-of-the-above, although she does concede that her business, is 'to act.' (Is she acting now, with Dr. Sanna? Of course she is! Quick, Gabin! Wake up and smell the larceny!)

Post-coitally, Antonio now stretches out, yawns, and smiles, and exclaims to his half-naked audience of one that he feels like a kid today. She tells Antonio that he's a very romantic person, and bets that he'd write very sweet love letters to her, if she asked him to. ("I'd like to go somewhere else," she tells him, poetically, "just so you could write letters to me, and I could read them.") She tells him she's jealous of how calm he always is, since her own mind is always in utter chaos, and then, after he's already torn-up her bill (*and torn her up),* she now gives him some bad news: She tells him, turning her emotions around on a dime (like the wishy-washy Francoise-character, in Claude Heymann's *Victor*) that their affair cannot continue beyond today, and that she's going to be going away without Antonio, and also without her 'brother,' Serge, to another country—somewhere where she'll be able to start her life over in peace, free of all men, just like Blanche in *Martin Roumagnac* and Marie in *La Marie du port.*

Now, it's time for director Brignone to show us a little bit of Dr. Antonio Sanna's home life: Antonio's fourteen-year-old son Mario (Enrico Olvieri), and Mario's pal Gianni, both junior high school-aged, are riding the bus home from school, which now happens to be passing the local love motel, where Marco's dad is *porking* Daisy. Gianni nudges Mario: "Hey! Isn't that your dad's car, in front of that hotel?" Mario is pretty calm about it—after all, he's supposed to be 'Jean Gabin's son:' "Oh, yeah. He's probably seeing a patient." But of course Mario knows what his dad is doing in there: He's a teen-age boy, so his 'real brain'— the one below the stomach and above the kneecaps—is preternaturally wise about life.

At the same time, having been released from the hospital, Serge is now at home, at the apartment which he and Daisy have rented, in Rome. He sits alone in a chair, flicking the light-switch on and off, exactly like Glenn Close will do three decades later in *Fatal Attraction,* and wondering about where Daisy may have gone. Like little Mario, though, Serge pretty much already *knows* what she's up to.

That night, post-tryst, Antonio arrives home and Maria and Marco are waiting for him at the dinner table. Mario tries to get his dad to admit to some illicit behavior, but since he loves his dad, he does it super-carefully: "So, uh... One of my friends from school was sick today [it's true, and here, Marco's talking about another kid in his class, but *not* his buddy, Gianni], and the [specialist] he needed [read: *Dad*] wasn't around. We couldn't find you. Everyone was scared, and the hospital couldn't find you, either. Were you taking care of another sick person, somewhere else?" (This is actually, more or less, the truth: Daisy is a very sick person!) Maria is a bit more naïve than is her son, when it comes to *les affaires des coeurs*, and she doesn't think her husband would ever run around on her, so she's oblivious to her son's rather indirect accusations.

The next day, Mario buys the morning newspaper, and a full-paged advertisement on the back, proclaims that the Circus has extended its stay in Rome, and that its featured performer is "Daisy Parnell—The Dangerous Woman!" At the same time, dutiful Maria Sanna has ventured over to her husband's hospital, where she talks to one of his associates, Dr. Bacca (Robert Arnoux), and asks him if he's noticed her husband acting "weirdly," lately. Bacca responds that he hasn't, and he's such an egg-heady-looking-guy, we know that he's probably telling the truth. Bacca, who's lost in his own world of test tubes, beakers, and microbes, now dopily gives Maria a special prescription: "Go home and smile! Smiles have big healing power!" As little Alvy Singer (Woody, Jr.) would one day be seen to comment in *Annie Hall,* to a similarly-delusional-looking grownup (the character 'Joey Nichols,' who puts nickels on his forehead), "What an asshole!"

But Dr. Bacca isn't as oblivious as he's just pretended to be: He certainly knows all about his friend's affair with the hotsy-totsy acrobatrix, which has now been going on for quite some time. He goes into Antonio's office (Antonio's been in the building for the whole time) and alerts him, "Your wife was just here. I know there's nothing between you and that woman [Bacca winks, as he says this], but your wife suspects that something's up." Antonio just Gabin-Shrugs: "Who cares? I mean, look at Walter Grimaldi [another Doctor-friend of Sanna and Bacca's]: For Chrissakes, Grimaldi's sleeping with his maid!" Bacca says he's just telling Antonio this to unburden his own conscience, and Antonio replies, curtly, "You deal with your conscience, and I'll deal with mine!" In France, it's common (yesterday, today, and tomorrow) for married men to have mistresses, and for wives to just deal with it. (I'm not saying it's right; I'm just saying it! The French, unlike us puritanical Americans, are actually able to separate 'sex' from 'love.') The fact that he's ensconsed in a hot, sweaty, sexual affair doesn't bother Antonio, and because he's okay with it—well, we're okay with it, too.

Back at home, Serge's head remains in a neckbrace, which he's now covered with a smart black turtleneck (and with his head popping-up out of the tube neck, he bears more than a passing resemblance to Eric von Stroheim's Colonel von Rauffenstein, in *La Grande illusion*). Daisy's sitting with him, and he tells her that he doesn't want to be locked up at home anymore, and that he's starting to get antsy, so she mollifies him by telling him that they should be receiving their money from the insurance settlement any day now because in the heat of passion, Antonio, against his better judgment, signed off on it. Serge warns Daisy that, when they *do* get the bread, she'd do well to remember that half of it belongs to him, and that she'd better not be tossing it around on herself, and on her new boyfriend, *Dr. S.* Just thinking about Daisy screwing Antonio has whipped Serge into such a froth, that he slaps her face— and hard! He's full of jealousy over his girlfriend's relationship with Dr. Antonio, even though at the same time, he's needed her to make love with him, so that they can collect that big insurance windfall. Serge, even though he wants the money just as badly as she does, now crazily accuses her of being (in these exact words) a "mercenary bitch."

Soon, Serge is able to walk again, and his first stop is the Sannas' house, where he confronts Maria Sanna: "I need to see your husband, ma'am. He's not at the hospital." (Is Serge going to tell Maria that her husband is really out, making it with Daisy?) Luckily, Antonio has picked this exact moment, to come home from work: "Your patient is here," Maria tells her husband, still not knowing that he's screwing this swarthy hombre's sister. Like all good wives do, she clears the room, so that the two guys can 'make with the man talk.'

Antonio tells Serge to be brief in whatever he's come to tell him about, and Serge pretends, for a moment, to be a nice guy: "You saved me, Dr. Sanna. I want to do a service for you, so that we'll be equal." Satisfied that Maria's not within earshot, Serge next let's his true, bullying colors shine-through: "I know you're screwing Daisy. And if you want to know why she didn't make it to your little assignation today, it's because I hit her! That's the only way to get through to her. And by the way: She's not my sister. She's my girlfriend—just like she's yours!"

Serge next reveals that Daisy is neither Italian nor Irish: "I met her in a disgusting area of Hungary [!], when the Circus was performing there, and I fell for her. It took me two years to figure out what she's all about. I didn't know she would dump me for you." Antonio counters, "You came here to tell me that she's a whore?" Serge now threatens Antonio ("You should be careful, Doctor!"), and then storms out, after 'putting his nice guy-face' back on for a second, while he's bidding goodbye to Maria.

Antonio now sits alone in the dark, in his study, in total stonefaced 'Jean Gabinian Silence.' When Maria comes in, she calmly makes her husband aware that she knows all about his affair (if she didn't, she would be stupid, and she's not), and she asks him, calmly, if he thinks that their marriage can continue.

"How you've changed," Maria accuses Antonio—meaning, probably, that this is the first time he's ever cheated on her. Even though, as we're finding out in this scene, and based upon what she's now telling him, they've been growing apart for quite some time, Antonio genuinely loves his wife, and wants her to give him another chance: "Look, my having an affair with the trapeze-girl was a bad mistake. So, what if I told you that it's all over between her and me?" Maria looks at her husband with the appropriate amount of skepticism.

Now, we're back in Antonio's medical class, and we get to see the small boy who Antonio was consoling in front of the class, at the beginning of the film. The kid has recurring hepatitis which, apparently, has no signs of improving: "Sometimes your nervous system complicates things," he tells the boy, and here, Antonio is referring (not-so-obliquely) to his own extra-marital problems. Hot Daisy happens to be sitting in on the class (she's way up in the back row), and all of the young male medical students now start eyeing her, nudging each other, and giving each other a bunch of 'she's the hostess with the mostess' looks. "That's the professor's mistress!" one Student grins widely, happy to be privy to somebody else's private life.

After class, Antonio corners Daisy in the hallway. (To him, it's not cool for 'the mistress' to show up at 'the lover's' place of work): "You want to shame me, in front of my students?" he scolds her. "You used me to get rid of your gigolo—isn't that enough? You disgust me! You have resources now, so just go away! Leave me alone!" Antonio means to make everything right again between himself and his wife, and having Daisy around is throwing a wrench into his plans for matrimonial happiness. Not easily deterred, she tells him that she's leaving the hospital now and that if he wants to see her, for any reason, that she'll "... be at the inn... where we first made love!"

And then (this movie will never be retitled *The Joys of Self-Control)*, in the next scene, Daisy and Antonio are again in bed together, at that very inn. Antonio hates everything that Daisy's done to mess up his life, but he's still Gabin and, even though the 'big head' is level-headed, 'the other head' is always ready for action! (Guess this really does make Jean Gabin an 'everyman,' because everybody, even the smartest people, sometimes thinks with the wrong part of his anatomy. Jean Gabin characters are never weak—they're just human. [Intellectually, Antonio really does hate Daisy, but... damn, she's fine!]) She tells him, "I knew you'd come back for me. I'm poison, I know. But for you, I'm a healing poison."

Dr. Bacca, Antonio's associate at the Clinic, now arrives at the Sanna house to visit Maria, who's packing her suitcase, preparatory to leaving her husband: "I told Antonio that I was leaving," she discloses to her husband's friend, "and he said, 'just leave.' Antonio hasn't slept at home in more than a month. I've been making his bed every morning, so that Mario won't know that his father hasn't been here." Bacca, instead of pleading with Maria to stay with Antonio (he's a friend of both Antonio's and Maria's, just like how in *Le Tunnel*, Freddie Robbins was a friend to both Gabin's 'Mac'-character, and also to Mac's wife, Ruth), now helps her with her exit-plan: "I'll go to the train station for you, and buy tickets out of Rome for you and for Mario—if that's what you want." (In case you're wondering: Bacca's *not* having an affair with Maria.) At that moment, Mario runs into the room and tells his mom that he's called the hospital looking for his father, and that the switchboard-operator told him his dad wasn't there. Of course, where he *is*, is in the motel room with Daisy where, when we next see the two of them, she's telling him, "If you were mine, I wouldn't let you leave." But he's got to leave, because he's got a surgery to perform—and he's late for it!

In the Very Earnest Surgery Scene which follows, Antonio's operating on Mario's friend Gianni, the one with whom Mario was sitting on the school bus, because the boy, subsequently to the last time we saw him, has been involved in a horrible accident, and Antonio, the doctor who's supposed to be performing the young man's surgery, has been so busy *plucking Daisy* (so to speak), that he's shown up late for it. And because *Fille dangereuse* is a melodrama, Gianni naturally flatlines right there on the operating table. Antonio has arrived at the hospital too late.

Embarrassed for himself, Antonio now, and as he did before, retreats into the inner-sanctum of his private office, where he sits, 'Gabin-Alone'—just like in '39's *Le Jour se leve*—puffing on a refreshing French cigarette. Other doctors come to see Antonio to console him, and to tell him it's not his fault that the patient died, and stoically, Antonio now tells them that he intends to quit the medical profession, because it just doesn't interest him anymore. The other doctors tell him that they'd miss the hell out of him if he quit, even if he does sometimes mess up the occasional life-or-death surgery.

In the next sequence, Serge makes an appearance at Antonio's home one more time, and Antonio's alone there, since Maria and Mario have now left him. "I thought we said everything we had to say to each other," Sanna tells Serge, not wanting to encourage conversation, and Serge, instead of being angry toward Antonio, is now acting (the key word being, 'acting') brotherly toward him, because they've both shared the same amazing experience (Daisy): "I can't get mad at you, Doc. I know that once you've gotten Daisy under your skin, she's hard to forget." Antonio wants Serge to get to the point, and so he asks Serge what he's come here, for. (I mean, we know that this nasty-ass con-artist guy hasn't just dropped by for a cup of General Foods Café Suisse Mocha!)

"I need money, Doc. I don't have the right to ask you—but I have to." Antonio's already figured out that he's going to have to pay this guy off to get him out of his life for good, and so, resignedly, he asks Serge how much he needs, and Serge's answer is a very brusquely-offered muttering of, "Whatever you can spare." Antonio, wordlessly, writes Serge a check and then, right after Serge has received the funds for which he's just lobbied, Serge tears the check up, screaming out that he doesn't need Antonio's charity. (Wow, what a *schizo freak!* Daisy did exactly the same thing, earlier in the movie: Remember when she asked Antonio for money, and then she got pissed-off when he gave it to her?) This is the scene in the movie where we're having the least amount of sympathy for Jean Gabin's character: Why is Antonio caving-in to this guy's crazy demands? (Why is he not knocking this greasy freak out on his ass?) Even though we, the movie's audience, depend on Jean Gabin to be stoic and resigned to his fate, we'd still love to see him clock this guy like it's eight-thirty! (Serge Reggiani was always great at playing menacing characters, although a contemporary critic, Andy Klein, who writes for Los Angeles *City Beat,* has proclaimed that Reggiani's "striking resemblance to [the British comedian] Rowan Atkinson retroactively hurts his performance[s].")

Next, we see Maria and Mario leaving town, *via* train. "You think dad's going to pick us up on the other end," Mario asks his mom, hopefully not realizing that they are going *away* from Antonio, and not toward him. Mario tells his mom also that he wants to go to the hospital and visit Gianni, unaware that his best friend has just succumbed, under his father's own knife. (Uh-oh! This is a lifetime of therapy waiting to happen!)

Hours after Serge has come to visit Antonio at home, it's now Daisy's turn to visit him, but she couldn't have picked a worse time, because Maria has decided to give her husband one more chance, and she and Mario have taken the train back to Rome—and back to their house. (Talk about bad timing!) When Maria and Mario get home, they see Daisy sitting in the front parlor with Antonio, and Marie orders the hot homewrecker to get the hell out of her house.

Confronted by both his wife and his mistress (not to mention his confused-looking son) at the same time, he tells Daisy to go and wait for him in his car, telling her that he'll be with her in a minute, and this doesn't sound very promising for Maria: It sounds instead like Antonio and Daisy are going off to enjoy another love making session! With son and mistress safely out of the room, Maria and Antonio now engage in a confrontation about Daisy. "I don't really even know her name, or even if she really loves me," he tells his wife calmly, "but I'm leaving with her, anyway." Maria is more than indignant: "You're going to leave me for *her?* After I just came back to give you another chance? I'm your wife! Can't you see that one day this tramp will dump you anyway, and for another guy who's got some money?" Then, Maria makes with a line which you will never hear a woman utter in any American movie: "With my help and love—I know you'll come back!" (That's right, in French films—and we'll be seeing this in a few more films which Gabin will be making in the 1950s in which his characters will take mistresses—when the 'husband-characters' are cheating on their wives, the wives *always* feel responsible, as if the reason their husbands are cheating on them is all their fault, because they're not being 'supportive-enough wives!') Maria asks Antonio, pathetically, what she can do to make the marriage better, instead of asking him what *he* can do to make it better!

Daisy sits out in Antonio's car, waiting for him—and is she in for a big surprise! Instead of her illicit married lover, Antonio, climbing into the car with her, Maria gets in, and in the incredible scene that takes place next, Maria cranks the engine up to about a hundred miles per hour and starts flooring-it, like a bat out of hell. (It's a very wild variation on every great suspense movie's time-tested, 'If I can't have him, nobody can' moment.) Maria, rather impetuously, drives both herself and Daisy off of a nearby cliff, figuring that if she and the Other Woman are both dead, that neither of them will get Antonio. (She's cutting off her nose/life to spite her face/husband.) Since Maria was very level-headed and mild in the rest of the film, her behavior, at this moment, is coming as quite a shock to us, but since we know also that she's a strong woman, it's not stretching things to think that she *could* perpetrate such a bizarre act.

Daisy, 'the trollop,' dies in the crash, and of course Maria, 'the good wife,' lives. (Morality Rules!) Maria has been injured pretty badly, though, and when we next see Antonio, he's (confidently) performing the operation which will save her life—and of course, it's a smashing success. Maria emerges, out from under the ether, completely healed and back to normal, and the fact that Antonio's been able to save his wife makes him decide to *not* quit being a doctor, and now, it seems that he loves his wife (not that he ever didn't) more than ever. (It's bad that Maria took that decision to drive herself and the other woman over the cliff, but at least, it got her husband's attention: Jean Gabin is so stoic that sometimes, the only way to get his attention, is to drive off of a major precipice!) Mario forgives his father too, and once again, the Sannas become A Happy Family, and everybody lives—well, I won't exactly say happily ever after, but I will say, 'Happily Ever After's Red-Headed Step-Cousin, 'French-Happily Ever After,' the definition of which might be: "Mostly happy, except that, after the film is over, the characters will probably just continue to repress all the stuff in their lives that isn't so happy, and will also keep screwing other people to whom they're *not* married."

This picture was released in Italy under the title, *Bufere.* The word '*Bufere*' has no meaning in French, but it's a French-Italian co-production, and there *is* a word in Italian, '*bufera*' (with an 'a') which means stormy; so maybe, this secondary title was meant to suggest the Daisy character's stormy temperament.

What a Critic Said at the Time: "This French/Italian co-production lacks credibility. It would lack authenticity, even if Gabin played a head-honcho boss of the Hospital Beaujon [Author's Note: Large and famous hospital, in Paris.] Gabin's performance is as conscientious as it deserves to be." (*Radio Cinema Television* Magazine, Paris, 6-14-53 issue. Critic: Marcel Huret.)

What Another Critic Said at the Time: "This is a drama that brings a lot of unintentional laughter—it's an involuntary comedy. Everybody speaks French with a Roman accent in this little Italian town—everybody except one, Gabin. His accent is a mix of accents from Rome and from Belleville." (*Noir et Blanc* Magazine, 6-24-53 issue. Critic: H. Lanwick.)

With Danielle Darrieux.

FILM 42

La Verite sur Bebe Donge

France, 1952

(Literal English Translation: "THE TRUTH ABOUT BEBE DONGE") Directed by Henri Decoin. Produced by Francois Carron. Screenplay by Maurice Auberge. Based Upon the Novel by Georges Simonton. Director of Photography (black and white), Leone-Henri Burl. Editor, Annick Millet. Music by Jean-Jacques Gruenwald. Production Designer, Jean Douarino. (GENRE: MELODRAMA) A Production of OGDC and Union Generale Cinematographique (UGC). Running Time: 2 hours 4 minutes. Released in France on February 15, 1952, by Alliance Generale de Distribution Cinematographique. Released in Great Britain with English Subtitles, as "THE TRUTH OF OUR MARRIAGE." Never Released Theatrically in the United States.

"If you can't get them immediately… you still get them!"
— Gabin's character, talking about the few women on earth who would dare to play hard-to-get with him, in "La Verite sur Bebe Donge"

What would you do if everybody you ever met in your entire life—trusted friends and family alike—was trying to screw you over, and each one had been doing it for years, only you were so good and so kind, you didn't know it? Nope, it's not *a typical day in Los Angeles;* it's actually the idea behind the overlong and 'just kind-of-good' Gabin soaper, *La Verite sur Bebe Donge (The Truth About Bebe Donge),* the fourth movie in just two years in which a woman takes advantage of 'wealthy/*bourgeois*' Gabin, and he knows she's doing it, but doesn't fight back (*La Marie du port, Victor,* and *Fille dangereuse* were the previous ones), and so we lose interest in his character because of it. Another strike against this film, is that it's got so many flashbacks-within-flashbacks that, at certain points in the narrative, it becomes impossible to tell whether the moment we're looking at is taking place 'today,' or 'years ago.' (But more on that, soon…)

Donge, the second of the nine films Gabin would make which were based upon novels by Georges Simenon (the first was *La Marie du port*) opens with some great piano music performed by the film's composer, Jean-Jacques Gruenwald, music which is accompanied by an existentially pessimistic on-screen quote from Vladimir Jankelevitch (1903-1985), one of

France's most popular philosophers and musicians: "In truth, I tell you that we have passed through birth, to start all over again. It's supposed to be your turn, but it's just one turn for nothing." In other words: We're all going to be living the same shitty life over and over again, and for no reason.

Francois Donge (Gabin), the wealthy owner of the Donge Tannery (his company supplies France with leather and furs, which is exactly what Gabin's Carlo Bacchi character also did, in *Pour l'amour du ciel*) is a patient in a large, Parisian hospital (in this movie, *he's* the patient), the *Clinique Jalabert*. For the last several weeks, Francois has been in and out of a mighty coma, which was induced, he thought (at least, for awhile) by a plateful of bad oysters, and he doesn't know that his scheming young brunette wife Elisabeth who's nickname is 'Bebe' (it's similar to calling somebody 'Baby Doll,' in English), who's played by the great star Danielle Darrieux (when this film was made, she was the ex-wife of the film's director, Henri Decoin), has poisoned him with mercury, as a way of discreetly offing him, and getting at his fortune. This movie was made right after *Fille dangereuse* and, because of the hospital setting, and because it's got a female character who's using Gabin's character for his riches, it's basically "*Fille Dangereuse, Part Two.*"

As the film begins, Francois emerges from his coma, and his gold-digging wife Bebe pretends to be excited about it. (To Dr. Jalabert: "Doctor, look! He's coming back!" Then, to her husband, with a fake smile: "Gee, honey, you really frightened us!") But just as soon as Francois' eyes are open, he's out-like-a-light again, and even though he's dead-to-the-world, director Decoin now starts giving us Francois' thoughts in voice-over, which is very similar to what director Billy Wilder did at the beginning of *Sunset Blvd.*, which was made two years before this film (and quite possibly, Wilder's film was an inspiration for this film's voice-over device: As *Sunset Blvd.* opens, as you remember, William Holden's character is dead in Norma Desmond's swimming pool, and it is his 'dead man's voice-over narration' which carries us through the film). Francois' voice-over (this guy is more intuitive when he's unconscious, than most of us are, conscious) tells us that he thinks his wife, not to mention everybody else he knows as well, is just using him for his money: "They all think I'm far away. Well, they don't know how true that is. I'm far away from all of them!" (This is nothing new, though: Tragic Drifter-Gabin is almost always 'far away from everybody,' and this time, his character has drifted not to 'Spain' or to 'Le Havre,' as he did back in his 1930s' pictures, but to *Comaland,* and believe you, me—it's the same difference!) Bebe tells the hospital staff that she doesn't want too many visitors coming into the room: Very obviously, she wants to be there all by herself, no doubt as a way of making all of her poisoning and mercy-killing activities easier to perpetrate.

Later that day, when Francois emerges for a second time from his off-again/on-again coma, he immediately asks his physician Dr. Jalabert (Jacques Castelot), who's standing over him, "What did they put in my stomach?" Jalabert, who is also, incidentally, Francois' long-time friend, tells him that the pain in his stomach is due to a bleeding ulcer which hasn't yet healed. Before Francois slips away again—which is what he's going to be doing about four seconds from now—he tells Jalabert that, in his delicate condition, all he wants is "a little dignity," and doesn't want any of his friends to see him in this horrible state.

Francois' whole family has been fully-aware for years that Bebe is 'koo-koo-nutty,' but they've never been able to persuade mule-stubborn Francois to divorce her. This is one of those movies like *La Marie du port*, *Victor*, and *Fille dangereuse*, in which Gabin's character, while he's meant to be a very smart guy, is closing his eyes to the fact that a woman is using him and taking advantage of him, because he's hot for her. (AND/OR: He knows he's being taken advantage of, but just doesn't care, since we're all cruelly-fated in this life, and the few scattered hours of tainted love which we get in this too-fast-moving interim between life and death—even when that love is coming to us in the form of a compulsively-avaricious harridan—is all we can ever hope for.)

While Francois must remain in the hospital, Bebe gets to go home each night, and one of the things she does at home, during the flick's opening moments, is to write her sister a letter, the subject of which is chocolate: Bebe is a major chocoholic, and what we're looking at here, even though we don't know this yet, is actually a scene from the end of the movie, which director Decoin has chosen to tease us with at the beginning of the flick—which means, of course, that whatever Bebe's chocolate-compulsion is about, will somehow be important (at least, we'd better hope it will be) to the rest of the film. At the same moment during which she's writing the letter, Georges (Daniel Lecourtois), Francois' younger (by just a few years) brother, arrives at Bebe and Francois' tony manse, to check up on his brother's wife (either Georges and Bebe are having an affair, or else Georges just suspects that Bebe's screwing her brother over, and wants to see what she's up to), and when she hears him coming, she leaves the house quickly, sneaking through the servant's entrance, and driving off to the hospital for another of her visits with her sometimes-out-of-it husband. (Bebe visits Francois in his hospital room several times a day, and whenever Francois is under, director Decoin gives us a recurring shot, in which Bebe is standing against the white, brick hospital room wall, her hair bobbed scarily upwards, like the *Bride of Frankenstein:* What you notice immediately about this movie is that, in those scenes in which Bebe feels herself going crazy, her hair is always up, but that her coif is down during those rare moments in her life in which she's not engaging in any behavior which is particularly avaricious.)

Now, we flash backwards to the days before the stinging taint of mercury screwed-up Francois' system: Indeed, Decoin is now showing us those months directly before Francois met Bebe, when Francois was just a successful 48-year-old bachelor-about town, juggling loads of simultaneous girlfriends, many of whom were either widows, or else 'desperate housewives' who spent their daylight hours cheating on their unsuspecting husbands. In his voice-over, Francois even tells us that it's fun to have sex with a lot of women and, preferably, as many as you can get! ("Some people," he tells 'us,' "stay virtuous. But in high society—we don't.") Even though, post-WWII, Jean Gabin would now be playing rich, *bourgeois* guys in bespoke suits, his heart-of-hearts remains with the working-class, and therefore this line of voice-over narration is more-or-less a dig at the character which he's playing in his own movie. (In other words, the whole movie is a piss-take at the pretentions of the rich, and like all of Gabin's movies, it's made for the actor's favored 'regular, working-class audiences.') After sex, Francois always tells his girl-of-the-moment, whomever she may be, that he "has an appointment to go and see his brother, George" (it's his convenient 'out-clause'), but the women to whom Francois makes love in this movie have all been conceived by screenwriter Maurice Auberge as being smart cookies who know that he's really just leaving them to go off and have affairs with other women.

As our flashback continues, night has fallen, and Francois climbs into a taxi with Nadine (Gaby Bruyere), a mega-hot society babe who's been sitting in a cab waiting for him (while he's been finishing his assignation with the other chick)! Nadine and Francois are just occasional lovers, but she also happens to be one of his most important fur-suppliers (*and in more ways than one*)! Francois asks her how the *lecume* (merchandise) is.

Nadine knows that Francois is actually on his way to meet yet another mistress—his third woman of the day (his second woman, after her), and she's not afraid to call him on it: "Is it for your brother's happiness that you have an appointment every night at nine p.m., or is it for something else?" In this film, just like in all of the other movies in which Gabin's character takes mistresses, the mistresses, ultimately, can never get too mad at him because in Europe, as I've already mentioned in other chapters, it's understood that a man needs many women. (Remember the toast that sea-captain Russell Crowe made with his crew in Peter Weir's glossy 2003 nautical epic, *Master and Commander*: "To my wife and my mistress; *may they never meet!*") In Francois' voice-over, he tells us he can get any woman he wants; in fact, Gabin's character in this movie is *so* cool, he can brag to us about landing women, even while he's in the hoary depths of a coma. Francois even has a motto, which is related to the few women on earth who would ever dare to play hard-to-get with him: "If you can't get them immediately… you still get them!"

Nadine drops Francois off at the train station and, when he arrives at his destination, he's actually got yet another mistress (this is his fourth woman in one day, if you're counting) who's waiting for him and, after he's finished 'doing his business' with this particular lady, whose name is Madame d'Ortemont (Gabrielle Dorzat), she asks him when she will be able to see him again, and again, he performs his usual *shtick*, related to how he has to go and see his brother—which of course, as always, works like a charm. She keeps trying to smooch him and rub-up on him, but he pushes her away. ("I told you! My brother needs me!") She tells him he would make a "detestable huband," but what we're actually seeing, is that his badass disregard for her feelings, is exactly what makes him so desirable to her. And back on the train that night, as he's heading back home to Paris, Francois next runs into an old Judge-friend (Marcel Andre), who greets him thusly: "Well, I'll be! It's Francois Donge, the future President of France!" (As JFK and Bill Clinton have already proven in America, lots of great horndogs can get to be President!)

Now, director Decoin flashes-forward to the time when Francois will be meeting his future wife, Bebe, for the first time: Francois' older brother, Georges, is about to get married to a wealthy society woman, Jeanne (Claude Genia), who happens to be heiress to a whopping family fortune of her own: Jeanne's father, who's now pushing up *les daisies*, had apparently owned all kinds of fancy shops and stocks, and the biggest success of his lifetime, is that he happened to have created a toothpaste which removed the nicotine from smokers' teeth. (In France, that would sell a zillion packs!) Francois and Georges, as we're now figuring out, are like the direct antecedents of the inveterate, women-conning lotharios who were assayed by Steve Martin and Michael Caine in 1989's *Dirty Rotten Scoundrels,* or in that film's predecessor, 1967's *Bedtime Stories,* which paired Marlon Brando with David Niven. Georges tells Francois that he wants to introduce him to Jeanne's younger sister, Bebe (this is the scene in which he, and we, will first make her acquaintance), a woman who, as he's now telling his little brother (although not in these exact words), happens to be *quite the little hotty.* Georges gives Francois a preview-of-coming-attractions, pursuant to why he believes it would behoove the two of them to marry the two sisters: "Jeanne and her sister are going to inherit their dad's whole fortune. Why shouldn't the two of us be in on it?" But Georges wants Bebe to meet Francois subtly, so that she won't suspect any funny business: "I'll have her meet you through this old lady-matchmaker I know. That way, it won't seem like what we're doing is too obvious."

The Matchmaker, who actress Yvonne Claudie plays as being 'an old lady who's seen it all,' is endlessly amused by the fact that these two brothers, each one individually wealthier than most small countries, are hankering for these two sisters who are also wealthy, but who are less wealthy than they are. The rich, who are never satisfied with their lots in life, this movie seems to say, always want more, more, more, and the Matchmaker*euse* even calls them on it: "You guys always have a lot of women. What on earth do either one of you want to get married for?" Still, she agrees, against her better judgment, to introduce Bebe to Francois. (If she introduces them, she gets a cut, so she's just as greedy as they are) She tells Francois that she will introduce him to Bebe, but that she won't do it immediately because, as she's now telling him, "you're an inveterate cheat, and you're not ready to meet a nice woman yet." (The joke, of course—the punchline of which we already know—is that Bebe is going to turn out to be the most *un-nice* woman Francois has ever met in his entire life.) This Matchmaker has a pretty cold idea about modern-day, 'man-and-lady relations:' "Marrying for love is in the past. We're in France—not the Mediterranean! It's never good to harbor romantic dreams." Funny, that this movie, which was made in France, 'the Capital of Romance,' is so down on love; this movie is kind of thumbing its nose at the fact that the rest of the world believes the French to be so *tres romantique,* and since American motion picture distributors liked to import romantic French films to the U.S., it's no wonder that such *unloving* French entertainment as this film—or like *Fille dangereuse,* right before it—never saw the light of day in the United States.

Francois is a very pragmatic guy, and doesn't want to work on Bebe if he's not going to be getting anything out of it: "Are you sure we'll be able to get all of the girls' money?" Francois asks George, to which his brother replies enthusiastically, "Of course we will! Their parents have left it for them—and they will leave it for us."

As it turns out, Francois won't have to wait too long for the Matchmaker to introduce him to Bebe, because Bebe's been right there in the house with them for the whole time. Remember how, at the beginning of the film, we saw Bebe up in her study, writing a letter about chocolate? Well, when Bebe wafts down the staircase in this sequence, in these final moments before she's about to meet Francois for the first time, she's munching-out on a chocolate, and childishly hiding the wrapper in the planter at the foot of the stairwell.

Francois is taken by Bebe immediately (as he'll eventually, also, be 'taken' by her, in another way—in the grifting-sense), and he tells her that she looks, in real life, exactly the same way that she looks in her portrait, which happens to be looming over them on the wall directly above where she now happens to be standing.

Dissolve to later that night: Georges, Francois, Bebe, and Jeanne are playing cards, and making some small-talk about the French military. Francois mentions how, even in the army, dishonesty in business, mostly *via* the bootlegging of cigarettes and booze, is practiced widely: "Some in the army earn their money honestly—but many do not." Maybe, this is Francois's roundabout way of telling Bebe that, even though he's just met her, he knows she's not completely honest, and that she should definitely be watching her step around him, since he's perfectly capable of being dishonest, as well.

The date progresses to its inevitable 'Francois and Bebe, Alone-on-the-Veranda-moment' and, just like they used to say in those pumped-up Simpson-Bruckenheimer action flicks from the 80's—The Heat is On!

When Francois leaves, at the end of the evening, the Matchmaker corners him in the hallway. ("So? Did you like her?") He pretends he wasn't interested in Bebe and sighs, with a Gabin-Shrug, "Aaahh, I don't know. She's just a kid!" (But he's not saying that he *doesn't* like her, and the Matchmaker is smart enough to have picked up on that.) Then, separately, the Matchmaker asks Bebe what she thought about Francois, and her reply is a very astute, "He's strong—but I think he's a liar." (Whoa! Talk about the pot calling the kettle black!) The Matchmaker tells her that, whether or not she and Francois like each other that, at the very least, her sister Jeanne will be happy with Francois' brother, Georges. Bebe next replies, very coolly, "Anyway, love does not exist." This is the same exact sentiment which was uttered by the Matchmaker-lady, a few scenes ago, and it's also what some of the other world-weary *femmes-fatale,* in a few earlier Gabin movies—the Stella-Marie character in 1931's *Pour un soir..!,* Jeanne in that same year's *Paris-Beguin,* and Odette in *La Marie du port*—have been spouting-out. "I'm so happy!" the Matchmaker calls out. "Everyone's in love!" This is a great line, because all of the characters have already told us that, in each of their individual belief systems, there's no such thing as love, and so when's she's shouting out that "everyone's in love," what she really means, is: "Let the games begin!" Then, because this is a French movie, and the 'serious' screenwriter has to pump-up the dialogue with some ambiguous horseshit which has nothing to do with anything, the scene fades out, just as the Matchmaker asks Bebe some random question about the quality of a certain kind of lentils!

Now, we're going to be flashing-forward again: Francois and Bebe must have been dating for quite some time now, because we're now at the point in our narrative in which Francois and Bebe are first discussing the possibility of marrying each other. They talk about the abstract concept of 'love,' and Francois is even colder about the subject than she is: He Gabin-Shrugs, telling her (and this is some overly-florid screenwriting, but, whatever: It's okay), "You know, love is like anything else: You just make it up. The only word that is important is not 'love,' but '*live*.' All of the other words are too big—they block my view. The bigger the words are, the less you can see what's behind them."

Director Decoin next gets us to the church on time (thank you, David Bowie) and we're now guests at a big fancypants double-wedding ceremony, in which Georges is marrying Jeanne, and in which Francois, too, is tying-the-knot (with Bebe). Francois looks bored during the wedding and, very comically, he's staring down at the floor, instead of staring at his fetching gold-digger-to be. During the ceremony, while the Priest prattles on, Francois even whispers in Bebe's ear the same thing he told her before, although it seems a tad inappropriate during a wedding ceremony—namely, that, "Love is something you make up." What he's really telling her, is: "Okay, now that we're getting married, remember: You'd better not screw me over, cutey! You'd best watch your ass," and we, the movie's audience, are happy that he's saying it, because here, for the only time in the movie, he's not being a total pushover: He's telling her not to fuck with him, and we're liking him a whole lot better than we did before, because of it. She knows, all too well, what he means, and with a smile, she replies, "Is this the best time to talk about it?" Bebe and Francois are aware that they're both just marrying each other so that they can screw each other over financially, and get their hands on each other's money.

Now, the barrage of flashbacks-embedded-within-flashbacks ceases (for awhile, anyway), and we're back in the hospital in the present day which, as we're now starting to figure out, is about one year after their wedding (she started working fast, as far as the poisoning went): Francois snaps out of his coma for the ten-thousandth time in the movie, and not only is Bebe there, but Georges is standing there, right next to her. Francois has been conscious for only about three seconds, when Bebe makes a sudden announcement, a statement which is no doubt calculated to send him spinning back into la-la land again: "I want a divorce!" While Francois has 'been under,' Bebe's been embezzling from his company, a little bit at a time, so that the money-withdrawals are hardly noticeable, and now that Francois has been drained of everything but mercury, she no longer has any use for him. Francois, although he doesn't know it, due to his physical state, is unable to pay the hospital the two hundred thousand-franc hospital bill which he owes, and Georges is taking care of his affairs, for him. (Uh-oh!) Georges writes a check, and he and Dr. Jalabert take a walk down the hallway, together. They begin discussing the fact that somebody should probably be bringing Francois some healing waters from Vichy. (It's more clear to us than ever now, that Georges is probably in on Bebe's scheme to defraud Francois.)

Francois is in-and-out of Comaland for awhile, and the next time he wakes up, he starts puking his guts out (mercifully, off-screen), but as sick as he is, he's still Gabin, and he still has it in him to flirt with the cute nurse (played by Juliette Faber), who's now come in to check-up on him: "What's your name," he asks her with a surfeit of charm, and tickled, the young woman tells him (Francois has got a rather nasty case of bed-head) that he looks like "a furry little animal." As she combs his hair, he lets on to her that he knows about everything that his scheming family members are doing to him: "I think my wife tried to poison me… but anyway, don't worry about it, because it's not your business." (What he's really saying here of course, 'in code,' is: "Helllp! Get me the hell outta herrrrre!") Then, he starts hallucinating and asks for his coat, even though he knows full-well that, in his present physical condition, he's not going anywhere. He insists that the Nurse should take five thousand francs out of his pocket to buy herself something nice, which she does, although she's embarrassed about it, and she next goes into Dr. Jalabert's office, and tells him about the free money with which Francois has just gifted her. Jalabert just shrugs: "Well, if he said you can have it, then you should have it."

Meanwhile, Bebe's not worrying too much about Francois' physical condition: She's spending her day, not visiting her husband, but buying herself an expensive dress for a big party which she's going to be throwing at her home that night, a one-year anniversary party for herself and Francois, even though Francois, who is laid-up in the hospital, won't even be able to attend.

Dr. Jalabert visits his friend Francois (he's one of the few people left in Francois' life who's still honest with him—or so we hope!): "I don't mean to upset you, Francois. But I think your wife has been seen in the streets, lately." (In other words, she might be a prostitute.) Francois, who is as resigned to bad news as are all of Jean Gabin characters, just shrugs, replying, "Yeah, well, it's not important that she's in the streets. It's important that I'm alive!" (Yeah, you go, J.G.! Gabin-the-Man is lookin' out for number one!) The Doctor tells Francois that the mercury, which remains in his body, is starting to affect his kidneys, and it's not long before Francois is hallucinating again: During this particular hallucination, he thinks Bebe is in the room with him, but it's really just that nice, hair-combing Nurse whom he had earlier allowed to fondle his wallet.

Flashback time again: Francois and Bebe are on a train, headed out of Paris. They're off on their honeymoon trip, and before they can get to their final destination, Naples, they're going to be making a couple of other stops: First, they're going to enjoy a night out on the Cote d'Azur, where Francois needs to go on his company's behalf, since he's got to personally inspect all of his company's 'leather-cows,' by himself. Also, at this point in his life, Francois is going to be starting up a new venture (especially, now that he's presumably got his new wife's capital, in addition to his own): Apparently, at least in the world of this film, there's something in cow's milk which can be used in the creation of plastics, and he wants to be right there on the ground floor of this burgeoning, new field. The second night, he and Bebe will go to Nice, where Francois has an appointment with his own, personal shoemaker, and then, finally, on the third night, they will be in *Napoli*.

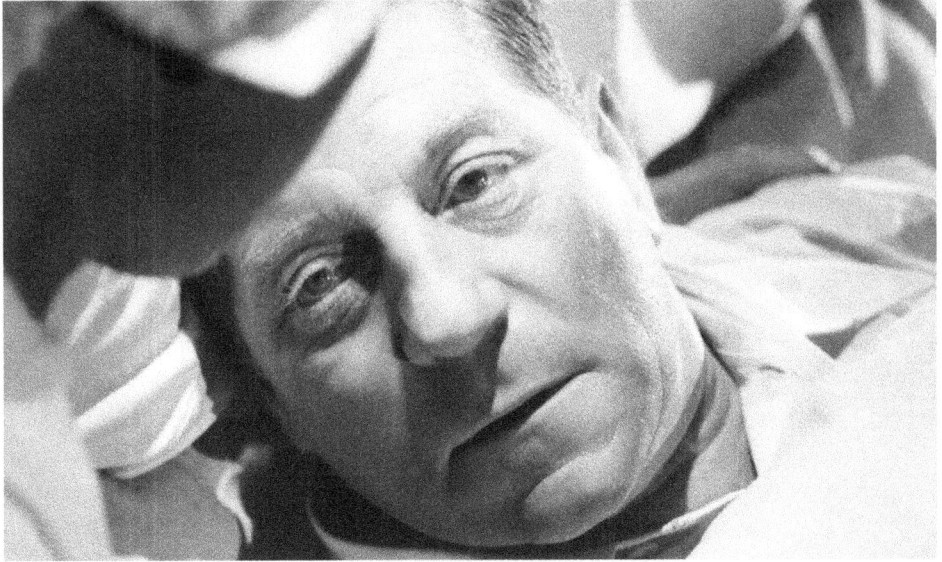

The stinging taint of mercury.

When Bebe and Francois arrive at their Cote d'Azur hotel it's raining and rather heavily, too. They take the elevator up to the room, listening to the patter of the rain, and both of them look happy (and by the way, this is the only moment in the entire film in which both of them look that way at the same time). In the hotel room, Francois orders some drinks, and the Bellboy gives them a funny look: Nobody has to say anything, but we know, just from how the Bellboy is staring at Francois, that he's seen Francois at the hotel before many times and, no doubt, in the company of other women.

After their sex, Bebe asks Francois if she's been a disappointment to him in the lovemaking department. She tells him she feels like they can't hide anything from each other, even though it's very clear that they hide absolutely everything from each other, and she also tells him, not really believing what she's saying herself but wanting to set him up with a little false security, "If you ever have someone else in your life (read: more mistresses), it's fine by me—just let me know!" She then asks him if he thinks she's stupid, to which he smirkingly replies, "No, Bebe. You're not stupid. You're like all women: You're just trying to get your life secured. You don't want to be forty, with wrinkles, and still not married." (!) She tells him, next, that she feels she'll probably be disappointing him in some of the other wifely areas: "I'm bad at cooking and housecleaning, you know. And I'm not interested in having any children." She then gets to utter a great Georges Simenon-penned soliloquy, which seems like it could have emerged right out of a David Lynch movie: "I'm not a mother hen. I'm not here to pop an egg out. Children are like fruit. I just want to love *you*." Bebe tells Francois that "being married is definitely better than being alone" (which doesn't, by any means, sound like any kind of a great recommendation for marriage). Needless to say, Francois won't have to wait that long before he starts shagging a new mistress because, in the next scene, which takes place a few days after his and Bebe's honeymoon, he's now cavorting with his hot fortysomething, blonde Secretary (Meg Lemonnier, who acted opposite Gabin in the final stage play in which he performed before his film career took off, 1930's "*Arsene Lupin, le Banquier.*")

The honeymoon now over, Bebe is setting-up shop, and moving into Francois' mansion. In the film's lightest moment, and this is definitely one of the funniest moments in any Gabin movie, there's a hilarious-looking portrait on the living room wall of Francois' lookalike grandfather (it's really a painting of Jean Gabin with giant, white muttonchops, and it looks like a prop from one of those Three Stooges shorts in which Shemp Howard used to play his own grandfather), and in the painting, the grandpa is comedically rolling his eyes. (Even dead, this 'Gabin Ancestor' [*Gabincestor!*] is commenting on the ridiculousness of the film's central characters.) The painting bugs Bebe, because it's practically calling her to the mat on the subject of her lifetime of dishonesty and duplicity. ("The man in the picture is staring at me. It frightens me.") Francois replies, more attached to the picture of his dead grandfather than he is to his live, flesh-and-blood, virago-of-a-wife, "Well, then don't look at it." She then asks Francois if his secretary is a "natural blonde" which, of course, is her not-so-subtle way of busting him on his cavorting. He tells Bebe that it's over between himself and his secretary, although we know that, when it comes to Gabin—it's never over!

Next, it's a trip to Francois' factory, *Le Tannerie Donge* which is, shortly thereafter, followed by a husband-and-wife drive-by of a potential real estate purchase. There's a fancy mansion for sale in the wealthy Parisian suburb of Neuilly (the 'Beverly Hills of Paris'), and Francois tells Bebe that maybe he'll buy it for the four of them (for himself, Bebe, Georges, and Jeanne). As he also tells her, "We can live in it together, and then—who knows? Maybe a creature [*baby!*] will come." (Even though Bebe said she didn't want children, Francois is still trying to lubricate her into wanting them, by supplying her with 'every woman's ultimate KY-jelly'—a house.) It's clear, too, that she might be changing her mind about her rock-solid no children-rule, because she's already changed her mind about not cooking for Francois, and one thing leads to another, right? As Francois boards the train for another out-of-town business (wait, scratch that: make that, 'monkey business') trip, she runs after him with a lunchbag, screaming, "Wait! I made you food!"

Flashback over.

Now, we're back in the hospital, and it's present day.

Francois is now hallucinating more wildly than ever, and screaming out some really crazy things ("It has two heads, an apartment, taxes, a short life..." [Is his sub-conscious, which often does the talking for him, referencing himself and his 'big head and little head,' or is he just talking about his two-faced wife?]). Dr. Jalabert asks Francois how his recurring headaches are, and Francois replies, able to speak cohesively for a few minutes in the midst of his *freak out*, that he hasn't had one for a day or two. Jalabert comforts him slightly, by telling him that in one or two more days he can go home, and so that we, the audience, will understand that Jalabert is a 'for-real Doctor' (that he's not, in other words, *per* the American commercial, just 'playing one, on t.v.'), he even lets fly with a salvo of complicated med-school lingo ("Drink lots of liquids!"). When Drouin (Marcel Andre), Francois' lawyer and friend, visits that day (we sure hope that he and Francois are going to be writing Bebe out of the will), he tells Francois that, even though Bebe is ruining Francois financially, he and Francois should, at least, be able to get back much of the money which Bebe stole and, at the most, get her sent away to jail for a long, long time: "Truth fighting Law is like a pot of clay fighting against steel. I hope you have many years ahead of you Francois, but if you were dead, it would be totally clear that she killed you." Even though she's totally screwed him over, Francois still doesn't want Bebe to be arrested; he still has some feelings for her (*cock feelings;* and as every man knows, these feelings often override our 'actual' brains)! Francois reveals to Jalabert that he genuinely loves Bebe (No, Gabin! Stop!): "If only she could believe me that I love her." He then adds, wistfully, "If only she could cry…"

Also in the present day, while Francois is lying inert in his hospital bed, Bebe is continuing to prepare for her big party. In this scene, we're finding out that over the ten years in which Bebe and Francois have been married, they've actually had 'a little creature' (a son) after all, little Jean-Marc (Jean-Marc Tennberg), and apparently, 'little J-M' doesn't know his dad Francois too well, because Francois is always away on business. (Read: having affairs). "Got to make the evening a success," Bebe chants weirdly to herself, as she runs around, checking on how the caterers are coming along with *les viandes.* And meanwhile, back at the Clinique Jalabert, Dr. Jalabert is rapping (in the old, old-school sense) to another M.D., Dr. Gasparre of Toulouse (Maurice Bennard), a kidney specialist, about the things that they might be able to do to help Francois. And then (it's plot-twist time again, boys and girls) we see Francois' lawyer, Drouin, riding in a horse-and-carriage with Bebe: Yes, as we've already surmised, Drouin has been involved with Bebe in the whole Screwing-Over of Francois Department, and the two of them are also, of course, having an affair. In this scene, Bebe even tells Drouin about how exactly it was that she poisoned her hubby: "I went to Francois' tannery while he was away with one of his mistresses, got the poison, and put it in my make-up box—four grams of it." Drouin asks her if she's worried about being condemned for her actions, even though he's the one who, as it's turning out, has been coaching her through them, and she replies, totally okay with whatever the outcome may be (she's being 'Frenchly-fatalistic,' here) that she is. (What a depressing movie! Everybody is screwing everybody else over, and nobody has any loyalty to anybody else!)

In the hospital, Francois is now delirious again, and he's prattling on (about women's dresses!), as Georges and Dr. Jalabert look on, concernedly. Then, it's a flashback to Bebe and Francois' wedding party, ten years ago: Francois looks Gabin-Cool in his tux, and Bebe looks good enough to eat! The Matchmaker-lady, who is present, asks everyone within earshot, "Don't you think her dress is daring?" Francois tells Bebe that he's going to have to be cutting their honeymoon-period short, because he's going to be leaving for Sweden the following morning on a business trip, so he turns in early, on their wedding night. Clearly, he knows that he's going to be needing all of the energy he can muster, for *Sexy Sweden.*

He can't sleep that night though, because he hears a noise which is coming from out in the hallway; Bebe's out there on a ladder, trying clumsily to remove the freaky painting of Francois' grandfather from the wall. When he goes into hallway and sees what she's doing, he tells her to leave the painting alone, and she actually threatens him, and it's the first time in Bebe and Francois' marriage in which she's doing that. (What a special moment!) She tells him that the day he's not around anymore, which he takes to mean that she might try to bump him off, she'll *definitely* be removing the painting from of the wall. Why doesn't Francois dump Bebe then and there, if he already knows she's going to try and kill him? (There's 'that old Gabinian-resignedness, for you!')

Francois, of course, did *not* go to Sweden, as he told Bebe he was doing: As we're going to be seeing in this scene, he was really just across town, enjoying a dirty weekend with his hot Secretary. A few days later, when he returns home, Bebe accepts him back happily, with a sultry cry of, "Let's pick up where we left off before you left," and before you can say, "*J'en ai marre*," the two of them are happily making love in semi-happily-married semi-bliss. Post-coitally, Francois tells Bebe that she just can't "grasp" him although, from our perspective, it looks like the two of them are grasping each other just fine! She notices a blonde hair on his jacket (the Secretary's) and confronts him about 'the cross-town traffic' ("I thought you said you weren't seeing her anymore!"), but Francois remains Gabin-Calm: "I sleep with a few people, and that's the truth about life. Do you want me to fire her?" Bebe calms down, and starts acting realistic about it: "No. She's a nice secretary. You might as well keep her. She's a hard worker." (!) He finishes off the conversation: "Good. Then I don't see what the problem is..."

Francois thinks that this is the end of the story—that his dalliances have been brought to the fore and examined and can now be (literally) put to bed, but for Bebe, it's not over. (For her, it's just beginning!) She asks him if he thinks that they should divorce, and if he agrees with her that, maybe, it was wrong for them to be married in the first place. She also asks him, in the same breath (and remember, this is right after they got married) if he wants to have a child.

Then, it's time for a Gabin-Outburst: Francois is tired of that fact that Bebe routinely vacillates back and forth about what she wants and doesn't want out of life, so he throws her down on the bed and starts shouting at her, and he even slaps her face: "You're crazy! You already told me you don't want a kid!" Then, they hug (!), the face-slaps having just tenderized her for more lovemaking! (Talk about how 'the best part of fighting is making up.' This unhealthy couple fights and makes up, every five seconds.)

The morning after this big *contretemps*, in the same flashback, we see that Francois has finally purchased that huge house which he had driven past earlier in the film (that big suburban mansion which he's been salivating over), and he tells Georges that Jeanne and Bebe can live there alone. ("That will leave us free to do what—or, more accurately, '*whom*'— we want!") Jeanne seems accepting of the two guys' behavior, telling her sister Bebe that they probably won't be able to change Francois and Georges, because "... they're just part of the male tradition!" The brothers install the women in the house, all by themselves.

Now, we get another glimpse of Francois and Bebe's wedding party. (The zillion flashbacks in this movie, which are embedded, like Russian nesting dolls, within other flashbacks, actually draw us out of the film, because every time a new flashback happens, it takes us a few moments for us to orient ourselves as to when exactly the flashback in question is taking place, or even whether or not the scene in question is even a flashback at all!) "Happiness suits you," the Matchmaker tells Francois. He's surrounded by business clients, and is in the middle of telling them about how well everything has been going with some ventures which he's been conducting in South America and in Asia. Dr. Jalabert is attending the party too, with his own wife, and Bebe is off in another corner, on her own wedding night, flirting with another doctor, who happens to be black. (One *tres*-racist society glamazon who's present at the party is really looking down her nose at the guy, actually whispering to another lady, "He doesn't *look* like a surgeon!") Some of the older Doctors in the room are voicing amazement that a black man has been accepted by the French medical profession. ("I didn't know we had any black surgeons in France!") Another guy, who can't believe it either, is heard to say, "Guess what: In America, they have lots of them! I even met a black psychoanalyst there!" The filmmakers don't seem racist though, because just like with many of the other movies which Gabin would make during this, his 'wealthy, *bourgeois*, captain-of-industry cycle,' the filmmakers are using the subject of racism to comment, albeit subtly, on how stupid, and how small-minded, the upper-classes can be.

During the party, an expensive dress which Bebe has ordered arrives, and always the attention whore, she slips into it, ready to model it for her guests. Jeanne loves Bebe's new frock, and talks about the way she thinks that it should fall along her shoulders. (Georges is really taking her in, ensconced in watching his brother's new wife, hungrily.) A guest comments to Bebe about how she's noticed that there are no telephones in the house: Yes, friends, Francois and Georges have installed their women in a house without phones, so that the women can't call and check up on them!

Back in the hospital, present day (at least, we'd better hope it is!), Jalabert and some other doctors are talking about Francois' quickly-failing kidneys (the docs have been running some tests on his kidney cells), and *Our Man* is awake and alert, hearing every single word that they're emitting on the subject of his delicate condition. The doctors are talking about removing one of Francois' kidneys, although they also realize that, by doing so, they'll only be giving Francois a slightly-better chance of surviving than he already has, which is basically nil to begin with. Francois announces to the doctors that he wants to live, adding that this belief of his should keep him alive for years.

Bebe visits Francois, once again. He tells her (and this, no doubt, makes her *really* happy) that he's going to have a kidney removed and that, if he survives the operation, he thinks the two of them should, with any remaining time which he may have left, only do things which make them happy, because he loves her so much. (Yes, Francois remains, even after ten bizarre years, head-over-heels in love with his wife, even after she's poisoned him and taken most of his money! [As Eddie Murphy's Velvet Jones character used to say on *Saturday Night Live*, back in the '80s, Francois has truly been "kicked in the butt by love!"]) After his admission, she cruelly replies, "But I don't love *you* anymore," and this is where he very suddenly changes his tone, letting her know that he's not completely out of it, and that she'd better 'watch her p's and q's' (i.e., cease-and-desist, in the 'trying to kill him'-department): "If I die, Bebe, the world will condemn our child, because of the way we made him." (Author's Note: Bebe became pregnant before she and Francois were married.) She's not put off by that sentiment though, and coldly exclaims, "He'll be able to live without us. We are nothing to him. Besides—you can't start your life twice." (Damn, this one's mean!) Even though, earlier in the film, Francois remarked that 'to live' is more important than 'to love,' he's now, just seconds after he's said it, kind of recanting, telling her that he knows, full well, that love *does* exist, and that when it happens, it's always a genuine miracle, even if one is feeling that love toward a person who doesn't love him (or her) back. He admits that he hates how she's never emotional ("If you could just cry, at least!"), even though, when push comes to shove, he's not necessarily the most emotionally-available guy in the world, either. She tells him that ultimately, there can be no hope for their marriage, and that he'll never be able to make everything right. Not only is Francois not mad at Bebe for having poisoning him but, in some way which we can't understand, because he never addresses the issue, he probably even thinks that he's deserved to be poisoned by her, because of his incessant philandering. (Jean Gabin's movie characters, no matter what decade the films are made in, always realize that, in the end, no-one can never really escape fate—so why fight it? Let's all just have some hot, sweaty fun on the way to, per Andy Warhol, 'The Exploding Plastic Inevitable.')

Now, it's time for the big and dramatic kidney operation scene for which we've all been waiting so patiently: Doctor Jalabert tells Francois that he'll now be anesthetizing him, and that if he has anything to say, he'd better say it now. Francois, resigned to 'whatever happens,' and not in the best of moods either, replies—and we wouldn't expect any less from tough-as-nails Gabin—"Just leave me alone!" Director Decoin now cross-cuts between the operation, and a new party, which happens to be going on at Francois and Bebe's house at the same time as the operation; Bebe, Georges, and Jeanne are such terrible people, they're not even at the hospital during Francois' big surgery—they're at a party celebrating, and they're not celebrating Francois and Bebe's anniversary, but the fact that Francois will soon, if all goes according to Bebe's plan, be dead, and that the three of them will be in group-possession of all of his *munnah-hunnah;* yes, Francois is getting double-crossed, and not just by his own wife and his wife's sister, and his own lawyer, but even (also) by his own brother! In *La Verite sur Bebe Donge*, everybody sucks, and nobody (to quote the bumper-sticker) *swallows.* As Francois starts going under, he calls out to the absent Bebe, hallucinating that she's in the room with him: "We can start again, my love! I'm going to liiiive!"

Next, Drouin, Francois' lawyer, arrives at Bebe's simultaneously-occuring party, and tells all-assembled that Francois has just died on the operating table. Wordlessly, Bebe pads up to her room, needing some time alone. She wanted her husband dead and, while she doesn't feel any guilt about her part in his demise, she's still a bit weirded-out that it's really, actually, happened. When she reappears next at her party, it's with suitcase in hand, and she tells her roomful of guests, with a faraway (medicated, if you ask me) look in her eyes, that she's leaving and, as it turns out, she's not going to be going far because, just as she's about to leave, Dr. Jalabert, the one guy in the movie who was Francois' true friend (the one person who wasn't fucking him over) arrives with a cop in tow—a cop who's ready to arrest her for the murder of her husband.

After the police take Bebe away, George finds a note on her dresser, the note which she was writing at the beginning of the film. (It reads, "To be opened after my arrest.") In the envelope, besides a letter of confession about the crime (which also mentions that her sister Jeanne can help herself to as much of Bebe's uneaten chocolate as she wants!), is the empty container of mercury powder—in fact, a few traces of the stuff even dust the bottom of the box. She leaves now, without kissing her son Jean-Marc goodbye, and as the cop car carrying Bebe drives away, director Henri Decoin irises-out very slowly, just like how directors used to do it in the silent movies, of which this movie is just as over-the-top melodramatic.

The story which is portrayed in *La Verite sur Bebe Donge*—'philandering lothario gets injured or bumped-off by one of the scores of women he's using and discarding like old Kleenex'—will play itself out in lots of European films, and three of the best known and much better examples, are Henri Georges-Cluzot's amazing Simone Signoret picture, *Diabolique* (1954), Francois Truffaut's 1972 *L'Homme qui aimait les femmes [The Man Who Loved Women]*, and Fellini's 1981 *La Citta delle donne [City of Women]*, all films in which a man's past comes back to haunt him, when all of his old flames get together, to make his life a living hell. Those films are all better than this one, but *Bebe Donge*, in spite of the fact that it's boring and confusing, has one great element which those other films don't have—*Jean Gabin*. And besides, it's impossible to 100%-hate a movie in which the dying man's last words are a shouted-out-in-anger cry of, "Just leave me alone!"

The 1950s will find Gabin starring in a few more movies in which he plays a rich guy, and ladies are fucking him over and he's not fighting back so we can't really like him. But mercifully, he'll also (and mostly) make a lot of fantastic movies during the 1950s, as well—films like *Le Plaisir*, one of the actor's best films, which I'm going to tell you about next.

What a Critic Said at the Time: "[In *La Verite sur Bebe Donge*], narrative is sacrificed to mood, atmosphere to character study. Gabin is excellent, as an extrovert whose final realization about life comes too late. The film's overlong playing time could be pruned." (*Variety*, 3-19-52. Critic: "Mosk. [George Moskowitz.]" Reviewed in Paris.)

Top: Communion. Above: A luncheon for working girls.

FILM 43

LE PLAISIR

France, 1952

(Literal Translation: "THE PLEASURE") Directed by Max Ophuls. Produced by Edouard Harispuru, M. Kieffer, and Max Ophuls. Screenplay by Jacques Nathanson and (uncredited) Max Ophuls. Based Upon the Stories of Guy de Maupassant. Original Music by Joe Hajos. Non-Original Music by Edmond Audran, Jacques Offenbach, and Robert Planquette. Directors of Photography (black and white), Philippe Agostini (story: "Le Modele") and Christian Matras (stories: "Le Masque" and "La Maison Tellier"). Editor, Leonide Azar. Production Designers, Jean D'Eaubonne, Robert Christides, and Jacques Guth. Costumes Designed by Georges Annenkov. (GENRES: COMEDY/DRAMA) Running Time: 1 hour 33 minutes. A Production of Stera Film/Compangie Commerciale Francaise Cinematographique (CCFC). Released in France by CCFC on February 29, 1952. Released in the United States with English Subtitles as "HOUSE OF PLEASURE," by Arthur Mayer-Edward Kingsley, Inc., on May 19, 1954.

"How about a little kiss, doll?"
— *Farmer Jean Gabin loves prostitutes, in "Le Plaisir"*

After his spate of practically back-to-back, not-so-great, early 1950's love-triangle movies in which women take advantage of Gabin's characters, and we lose interest in him because he doesn't fight back— *La Marie du Port; Victor; Fille dangereuse; Bebe Donge*—Gabin is now back-on-track, at least for awhile, and taking a reprieve from playing his philandering captains-of-industry-characters, returning to his working-class roots to play an atypically (for Gabin) happy life-loving farmer, in the third segment of the fantastic anthology picture *Le Plaisir*, the magical film which was adapted from the stories of Guy de Maupassant, and principally from Maupassant's 1881 book of short stories, *La Maison Tellier* (*The House of Tellier*). *Le Plaisir* is not only a wonderfully-ebullient movie, which is fairly abrim with real honest-to-goodness life, but it is also considered, throughout the world, to be one of France's very best movies of all time. The picture's English-subtitled/French-language American release print is narrated in English by Peter Ustinov, who serves as the voice of the storyteller Maupassant, and it is this version which is currently available in the U.S. (as an out-of-print

VHS tape, which is usually pretty easy to find on eBay).

While Maupassant (1850-1893) was mostly known for his horror stories (as far as tone is considered, he might be considered a cousin to Edgar Allen Poe), the final two of the three stories which comprise *Le Plaisir* are happy and upbeat, which is especially funny, because the film's third and longest story is a heartfelt ode to prostitution, the profession of which de Maupassant was, apparently, a very big fan: The author died of syphilis at the age of forty-three and, apparently, as he fell deeper and deeper into the disease (according to his biographers, anyway), he very often believed that *his furniture was trying to attack him!*

Le Plaisir represents the only film in which Gabin would ever work for the visionary French/German-born director, Max Ophuls, all of whose films are whirling, colorful (even when they're in black and white), *fin-de-siecle*/dress-up spectacles, which present daily life as being a fun, visual, swirling parade, and in this respect, Ophuls is very much a cousin to Federico Fellini: Some French critics, back in the '50s, which is when Ophuls made most of his movies, didn't enjoy Ophuls' continually-swirling camera, but he's been re-evaluated today in his home country of France, and the director's countrymen now consider him to be one of the finest directors of all time. (American film critics, however, have always considered Ophuls to be one of the world's greatest directors, and were the first to recognize his greatness, even before the French did, and a number of today's biggest American directors—with the emphasis on Spike Lee and the Coen Brothers—would probably have never broken out the dolly tracks and spun their cameras around their actors, had it not been for Max Ophuls having done it first.) It's too bad that Gabin will work with Ophuls only on this one picture, because Ophuls seems to have brought out the best in *Our Favorite Actor:* In his most recent, early '50s pictures, Gabin had been *extra* dour (especially, in *Marie du port, Victor, Fille dangereuse,* and *Bebe Donge*), but in *Le Plaisir,* J.G. is continually smiling and light-hearted.

The film takes place in the mid 19th-century, and the first and shortest of its tales is an adaptation of Maupassant's short story, "*Le Masque.*" The picture opens with a fancy Parisian dress ball, in which revelers spin and dance (and we get to see up lots of the dancing girls' skirts)! A jaunty-looking regular enters, a 'Mr. Ambroise' (Jean Galland), and Our Narrator tells us that Ambroise had always been recognized as being France's finest dancer of the *quadrille* (the precursor to American 'square dancing,' because it involved four couples, moving in formation), and that he would always show up as needed, to substitute for the show's main hoofer, whenever the guy would 'take ill.' We get to see Ambroise dancing and, if you think that '*Feet of Flames*' is a 21st century invention, *well, you've got it all wrong, my brother!* Ambroise dances fantastically, and makes the women and men in the place take notice; in fact, at one point, he gets so caught-up in the excitement of what he's doing, that he actually passes out cold! A Doctor who is played by Claude Dauphin (who appeared with Gabin on-stage, in 1949's "*La Soif*") is quickly summoned. He takes Ambroise into the club's back room to work on him and, as it's turning out, Ambroise's handsomely-smooth, *young-'n-mustached* face, is really just a mask. The Doctor removes it, to reveal that Ambroise is actually a very old man; in fact, there's no way that he could be a day under eighty!

The Doctor takes Ambroise home, and Ambroise's dutiful wife Denise (Gaby Morlay, from *le Messager*) tells the medic that her husband, when he was younger, was always a favorite of the ladies, and not just because of his otherworldly dancing acumen, but also because he was one of Paris's best haircutters, at the fancy Martel Hair Salon. She tells the Doctor that the day Ambroise found his first gray hair, he became depressed, and that as the decades began to pass, he felt embarrassed that was now too old to appeal to young women, and that this is the reason he began wearing his mask. (The moment is very sweet, because Denise is telling the doctor that, even though she's basically no more than his maid now, she still wouldn't trade him for the world.) The Ambroise story, which is the shortest in the film, is simple and beautifully rendered, and when the Doctor pulls off Ambroise's mask to reveal that he's really an old man, instead of the young man whom we initially believed him to be, we're witness to a moment which is powerful without words; when we see Ambroise's real face, we understand why he wore the mask, even before Denise told the Doctor why he was: We all fear getting old, and this is a great movie moment which will stay with everyone who sees it.

In the Second Story, "*Le Modele*" (these stories are so good, we almost forgot that we haven't yet seen Jean Gabin, who won't appear until halfway into the film's third, and longest, story), young Daniel Gelin (from *Miroir* and *Martin Roumagnac*) stars as a poor (yet 'rich with his own ego-mania') portrait painter named Jean, whose muse, the beautiful Josephine, is played by Simone Simon. (With *Le Plaisir*, Simon will now have appeared in a third picture with Gabin although, this time out, they won't be appearing in any scenes, together.) Jean and Josephine—'painter' and '*paintee*'—love each other more than any couple you've ever seen before in your life, and Ophuls now presents us with a brief montage, which consists of a number of ultra-quick shots, in which Jean is telling us, and in which Ophuls is showing us, in titillating close-ups, what his favorite of her body parts of hers, are (her shoulder; her eyes; her smile), and we get to see these anatomical features, in quick succession.

Then: *It's Kiss of Death Time for their relationship:*

Jean sells his paintings and becomes wealthy, and so naturally, he wants to trade-up girlwise, which is daffy on his part, because there's no such thing as trading up from the smoldering Simone-Simon (but, whatever)! Because Jean has spent so many years telling Josephine how fantastic she is, naturally, she doesn't want to leave, because she's grown so dependent on him. She tries, very carefully, to confront him, and to ask him why he doesn't love her anymore, but he's a rich artist, and so also naturally, he has now decided that he doesn't ever want to see her, ever again. Jean's best friend Joseph, who's played by the *super-suave* Jean Servais (an actor who's known by movie junkies throughout Europe *and* the U.S. for his starring role as the ultra-smooth gentleman-gangster Le Stephanois, in director Jules Dassin's landmark 1955 French *film noir* caper-flick, *Rififi*), is given the duty of 'dumping Josephine' for him. (In fact, Servais also provides 'Guy de Maupassant's voice-over narration' in *Le Plaisir's* original French release-print, in lieu of Peter Ustinov.) And because Ophuls and Maupassant and Fellini (and, come to think of it, *Shakespeare*) never want us to forget that 'all of life is just a play,' Joseph coldly plays the piano, while he's telling Josephine that Jean is dumping her, and he's underscoring his severe words with some equally-severe pounding on the 88 keys. Joseph tells Josephine, "He's dumping you, because his family wants him to marry a wealthy girl." (Piano: PA-DUM!) Josephine claws her way into Jean's study, and tells him that if he dumps her, she'll jump out the window and, not believing that she'll actually defenestrate herself, he very savagely points to the window and mutters, "Okay, there's the window. Go and do it!" She runs up the stairs and jumps, and Ophuls photographs this moment expertly, from Josephine's point-of-view, so that it feels like we've broken free from our moorings in the movie theatre, or in front of the t.v., and jumped out of the window with her. (This is a breathtaking and extremely dynamic movie moment, one which puts us into the action in a way which even 3-D could never hope to replicate!)

Miraculously, Josephine's not dead, but she *has* broken four-out-of-four limbs. Ophuls next dissolves to a shot of Jean and Josephine on the beach, and Jean is pushing Josephine in a wheelchair. In lesser hands than Ophuls,' a moment like this might ordinarily have come across as being corny, but the director makes it really tender and poignant. The film's Narrator (Ustinov or Servais [or, in the film's *German* release version, *Anton Walbrook*]) tells us, that the moment when Josephine jumped out the window, is the moment during which Jean really knew how much he loved her. Ustinov-as-Narrator: "Maybe it was her lunacy that drew him to her... I don't know...")

Next, it's time for Story #3, the longest story of the film, "*La Maison Tellier*" (or, in English, "Madame Tellier's House") which is set in what the Narrator tells us, is Paris's best-loved "Whorehouse #3." (That's really the place's name! It says so, right there on the shingle!)

> NARRATOR: This story is really a joyous celebration, and not so much of prostitution, which it is, but of love in all of its many forms. Every weekend, all the men of Paris go to Whorehouse #3. There is one entryway for the rich—mayors, doctors, lawyers, the tax collector, the banker's son—and another for the poor (for the working-class people and the sailors). And all of them are together, in their love of the bawdy women. The men go there to sip their Calvados, to tease the girls, and to talk to the Madame.

"I never approved of this place when I was running Paris," the Mayor (he's played by Rene Blancard) tells his friends, in the same exact beat in which he's running into the house with a huge, excited smile on his face. But he's happy for nothing, because tonight, the place isn't open. There's a big sign on the door which actually reads, "Closed, for a [religious] Confirmation," and the Mayor and his buddies, who are the community's leading lights, now decide, because they are unable to go inside, to sit by the Seine together, where they'll now ruminate about how one of their group stupidly became sick from eating mushrooms today, since 'shrooms aren't in season.

The fact that the sign on the door is announcing that the place is closed for a confirmation, happens to be true, too: Madame Tellier's thirteen-year-old niece, Constance, is about to be confirmed, in the Norman town of Clecy (it's where France's famous Calvados rum comes from), and the girl's father, who also happens to be the Madame's cousin, a simple farmer named Joseph Rivet (Jean Gabin), has invited her and all of her ladies to be his guests for the big event: There aren't too many family members in the Rivet clan, and Joseph wants to fill the church up, so the prostitutes get dressed-up in their fineries, buy themselves train tickets to Clecy, and head off to the communion. (Madame Tellier is played by the luminous Madeleine Renaud, who played the object of Jean Gabin's affections in three previous films—1932's *La Belle Mariniere*, 1933's *Le Tunnel*, and 1934's *Maria Chapdelaine*. *Le Plaisir* would mark Renaud's first time in front of the cameras in eight years.)

The next sequence, in which Madame Tellier and her Girls ('Rosa' is played by Danielle Darrieux; 'Louise,' by Mathilde Casadeus; 'Flora,' by Gina Leclerc; 'Fernande,' by Paulette Dubost; and 'Raphaele,' by Mila Parely) are traveling up north *via* train, is great: 'Fellow Travelers' (*not Communists,* just *people on the train*) really love the girls, and one man, a Hosiery Salesman who gets on at the 'Bolbec' stop (he's played by Pierre Brasseur, Gabin's rival-in-love for Michele Morgan, in *Quai des brumes*) even offers to give each girl a free pair of the stockings which he's selling, as long as each lady will try-on the footwear right in front of him, which they of course all do, and very gracefully! The hookers next all begin singing cheerfully, and this *trollop-trilling* is infectious to the other passengers. ('The Joy of Music' is the only infection which these ladies of easy virtue are spreading on this trip.) Everybody enjoys the happy presence of Mme. Tellier and her ladies—everybody, in fact, except for an angry-looking elderly couple who get off in Motteville (they're played by Charles Vissieres and Zelie Yzelle), and they're angry of course, because they've had to share the car with a bunch of girls who, as the aged wife is now pointing out very pointedly, are "sluts." (The Narrator tells us that, in his opinion, this prudish old lady has "… eyes like poached eggs.") (!)

The train arrives finally in bucolic Clecy and, when we first see Joseph Rivet (Gabin), he's walking through the country, pushing his cart (think: Tevye from *Fiddler on the Roof, sans yarmulke*), all ready to celebrate his daughter's big day. When the train arrives in Joseph's small village, he picks the girls up in his horse-drawn cart, and when he arrives home with them, at his family farm, he has a hell of a lot of fun helping each individual girl down from the cart, although his wife, Mrs. Rivet, who's played by Helena Manson, doesn't seem to be having as much fun as her husband is having! Very quickly, all of the good-naturedly wanton *prosties* fill the dreary village with much needed sunshine, and they quickly become beloved by all of the village's residents, none of whom realizes that they are prostitutes. (The citizens of Clecy are so sweetly naïve, they merely believe the women to be a bunch of really sophisticated big city women who just so happen to have great attitudes and sexy clothes.)

Next, it's an outdoor pre-Communion lunch at the Rivet home, and this is the scene in which we learn that the prostitutes have all pooled money, which they've earned on their knees and backs, to buy Constance a communion dress. Joseph genuinely likes all of the women (who wouldn't?), and because the other citizens of Clecy are finally starting to figure out what the women do to make money, he even defends what they do for a living during the pre-meal prayer, making sure that Tellier and her girls know that "… the good Lord knows everything;" what he's saying, in other words, is that God knows what these ladies do, and that He loves them, anyway. (And even if the Lord doesn't love them—*Joseph sure as hell does!*)

The night before Her Big Day, young Constance (Jocelyne Jany) is nervous and can't sleep, and Madame Tellier asks her where her mom is. (Clearly, Mrs. Rivet, who's mega-pissed that her husband has prostitutes in her house, is away, spending the night at a neighbor's house.) The next day at the Confirmation, Rivet walks the women into the Church, and when the men of the town see them, they all immediately begin *lusting away in the pews!* (One especially excited-guy even exclaims, "They bring the perfume of the city into our church!") When the ceremony finally starts, it's so beautiful that everyone in attendance (even the prostitutes, and all of the men) begin crying with happiness and, as far as the prostitutes are concerned, Ophuls is able to convey the notion to us that they're also crying because they feel suddenly guilty about how they earn their daily bread. Even Gabin's Joseph character is on the verge of tears, but don't worry: He's Gabin, so he won't be bawling away like a sissy. (Heaven forefend!)

After the Communion, Joseph throws a second big outdoor meal, a massive dinner, and he's set up a long table with all kinds of food and drink, right next to his barn. He is drunk and happy, and now waxes again about how great it is that all of the guests are there, and Madame Tellier tells him laughingly that he's so drunk, this is the fourth time in as many minutes in which he's made the same exact speech! He requests, during his toast, that Mme. Tellier and her women should stay longer, but they inform him that they're due back in Paris, and that they're going to be leaving on the next train, and also that they're going to need him to give them a ride back to the station, on his horse-drawn cart.

As the women are all getting ready to leave, Joseph tiptoes into his favorite prostitute, Madame Rosa's room, to say goodbye. We're not sure what's going on in there, beyond the closed door upon which Ophuls is focusing his camera, but we suddenly hear the sound of a woman screaming, and she now throws him out of the room, screaming at him that he should get out, but Joseph's such a good-natured guy, he's probably just copped a little feel (and can you really fault him for that?) His wife is downstairs when this happens, and naturally, she becomes livid, so he apologizes to her (it's heartfelt) and drives all of the ladies back to the station.

Le Plaisir is a fun (and spirited, and even uplifting) film, which sends you home with a smile when it's all over (or if you're already home when you're watching it, it sends you into the next room, with a smile)! It's relentlessly cheerful (except for *the girl-throwing-herself-out-the-window-scene*, but even that story ends happily), without ever once sinking into mawkishness, and Ophuls directs the picture with his famously-deft and light-fingered, touch, which you can also see in the other films which he made, from the '30s through the

'50s, especially *La Ronde* (1950), *The Earrings of Madame D'* (1953), and *Lola Montes* (1955). *Le Plaisir* would even be nominated for an American Academy Award in 1954 (for "Best Art Decoration/Set Decoration, Black and White: Jean d'Eaubonne, Robert Christides, and Jacques Guth"). In the original French release prints which were struck in 1952, the film's three stories were apparently presented in a different order, although now, all existing prints of the film throughout the world are uniform, and the stories are presented in the order in which I've just described them. In the original French print which premiered in Paris in 1952, the story, "*Le Modele*" came first, "*House of Tellier*" (the longest one) showed up in the middle, and the sad "*Le Masque*" came third, so that in effect, the two shorter stories were book-ending the longer one, and the sad story came last, but of course, America always demands 'a happy ending,' which is why the order was originally changed when the movie reached U.S. shores. And before I move on, here's a fun, biographical detail about Max Ophuls: He was born 'Oppenheimer,' but changed his name to avoid embarrassing his wealthy, German, store-owning family—a family which apparently looked down on 'lowly show business.'

What a Critic Said at the Time: "Technically stunning, with top-level marquee names both for here [France] and the U.S. Jean Gabin shows his his dynamic qualities, as a farmer who falls in love with [a prostitute. The film is] technically sunny." (*Variety*, 4-2-52 issue. Critic: "Mosk. [George Moskowitz.]" Reviewed in Paris.)

What Another Critic Said at the Time: "[The film gives us] three ironic comments on the natures of civilized men, and it mixes limpid candor with polite gentility. It's a delightful gem... a gay and tasteful little trinket of sweet sentiment and restrained ribaldry. Everybody does a perfectly balanced job. Jean Gabin is magnificently puffed and curious. *Le Plaisir* affords such pleasures as are few and unrestrained in this hard world." (New York *Times*, 5-27-54 issue. Critic: Bosley Crowther.)

With Michele Morgan, in their first film together in thirteen years.

FILM 44

LA MINUTE DE VERITE

France/Italy, 1952

(Literal English Translation: "THE MOMENT OF TRUTH") Directed by Jean Delannoy. Produced by Leon Carel, Henry Deutschmeister, and Alfred Stoger. Written by Jean Delannoy, Henri Jeanson, Roland Laudenbach, and Robert Thoeren. Music by Paul Misraki, Georges Van Parys, and Winifred Zillig. Directors of Photography (black and white), Gianni DiVananzo, Luise Holscher, and Robert Lefebvre. Editor, James Cuenet. Production Designer, Serge Pimenoff. (GENRE: MELODRAMA) Running Time, 1 hour 40 minutes. A Production of Cines Films (Italy), London Films (France), and Wiener Mundus-Film (Austria). Released in France on October 22, 1952, by Gaumont. Released in the U.S. with English Subtitles (in NYC, on April 26, 1954 and in Los Angeles, on May 7, 1954), by Arlan Films.

"Of course I was cheating on you with Madame Meurier. She was nice to me. And you are an iceberg!"
— *Gabin explains his cheating heart to his emotionally-distant wife Michele Morgan, in " La Minute de verite"*

After starring as a happy farmer in Ophuls' wonderful *Le Plaisir*, Gabin will now return to making another one of those 'pretty-good-but-I-wish-it-were-better'/paint-by-numbers *soupers* in which he plays 'a wealthy, *bourgeois* guy who's been getting screwed over by his woman (his wife or his fiancée) for so long, that he's become too lazy and comfortable to fight back.' *La Minute de verite* (*The Moment of Truth*) is a film which tends to be a tad better than its four predecessors-with-the-exact-same-storyline (*La Marie du port*, *Victor*, *Fille dangereuse*, and *Bebe Donge*), just by virtue of its 'stunt casting,' because it's a picture which reunites France's Most Popular Movie Couple of the Late 1930s, Jean Gabin and Michele Morgan, for the first time in over a decade (since *Remorques*), and while it's pretty good, it's still not great, because it's hard to root for 'idle-rich' characters who don't even know what they want, and who don't allow themselves to get too excited about anything. Even if the filmmakers are using the film as a platform to make fun of the rich, and to show how bored the rich are, we still need a little bit more.

In this picture, Jean Gabin and Michele Morgan, more than ten years after they were lovers in real life, play a *bourgeois* couple who've been married for ten years, and they're going to be spending most of the movie discussing and examining their marital troubles and infidelities, at great length. (The film will also present us with *many* unnecessary flashbacks which, just as with *La Verite sur Bebe Donge,* only serve to confuse us temporally because, quite often, we're not sure if the scenes are taking place in the present or in the past.) The film's subject matter makes it a close kin to much better and more well-known, and more vital, marriage-on-the-downswing-movies, like Mike Nichols' *Who's Afraid of Virginia Woolf* and Ingmar Bergman's *Scenes from a Marriage,* by fourteen and twenty-one years, respectively. *Minute* is the first of six Gabin pictures which will be directed by the actor's real-life good friend, Jean Delannoy, a guy who's adept in any genre you can throw at him (crime, romance, *etc.*), and this film wasn't the first one in which Delannoy and Gabin would find themselves working together: Twenty years earlier, in 1932, Delannoy was the film editor on Gabin's early comedy, *La Belle Mariniere.*

Minute opens with a shot of the Eiffel Tower, which places us (at least, we'd better hope!), in Paris. When we first meet Gabin's character, 'Dr. Pierre Richard' (not to be confused with the real-life 'Pierre Richard,' one of France's great movie stars, who's known in the U.S. mostly on the strengths of his popular 1973 comedy, *The Tall Blonde Man with One Black Shoe*), he is helping his eight-year-old daughter Simone (Marie-France) study for a test. He deftly makes her think that she's figuring out the answers all by herself, by providing her with very-subtle clues, so that each time she answers a question correctly, she excitedly tells him that he owes her ten francs! Pierre, although he's not the most demonstrative guy on earth is, nevertheless, a good dad, and he also happens to be the only parent of the two who's actively involved with Simone's hands-on raising, since his wife Madeleine (Morgan), a stage actress who's depressed about the shitty reviews she's been getting for the play in which she's currently appearing, wiles-away the daylight hours in bed, *or so we think* (at least, that's what we think right now), being pampered and served by her dutiful Maid (who's played by Jacqueline Canterelle).

On his way to work this particular morning, Pierre peeks into wife's Madeleine's room to say goodbye to her, tells her that the Maid will be taking Simone to school as she does each morning, and then jokes gently with her about the prone position in which she chooses to spend each day: "Are you sure you're not sleeping enough?!" (It's a benign version of that very famous scene which we'll be seeing eighteen years later in Mike Nichols' 1971 film *Carnal Knowledge,* in which Jack Nicholson will berate his depressed wife, who's played by Ann-Margret, because she sleeps all day, while he's off in the trenches, 'busting his ass.') And just as Pierre's leaving for work today, Madeleine tiredly reads him one of her not-so-stellar newspaper reviews, in which the critic has remarked that she comes across, in her performance, as being "cold, like an iceberg." 'Gabin-Eloquent'-Pierre, who never talks unless he absolutely has to, doesn't say anything at all: He just kisses her goodbye gently, and she tells him that she'll probably "get up in a little while" and that, when she does, she intends to spend the day, "trying-on clothes."

Dr. Pierre works out of a suit of fancy offices, from which he services a very upper-class clientele. He's only been at work for a few minutes on this particular day, when a bicycle messenger whom he knows enters, telling him that there's a young transient down at a flophouse on the 'other (read: *bad*) side of town,' who has tried to commit suicide, by asphyxiating himself. And when the expensively-dressed Pierre makes his way over to the skeevy flophouse, the place's down-on-their-luck residents are naturally skeptical of him. In *La Minute de verite*, unlike in Gabin's other 'rich, *bourgeois*-guy' pictures from the 1950s, there's no evidence at all that his character used to be working-class before he got rich. (In this movie, he was a rich guy, right out of the gate.) The flophouse's Landlady (Yvonne Yam) tells Pierre that he's not "the kind of doctor we asked for" (meaning: "He's not poor, like we are"), but he ignores her, and immediately begins ministering to the out-cold, handsome, and dark-haired 'almost-suicide.' As Pierre completes his examination of the thirtysomething guy, he looks over at the bureau of drawers next to the young man's bed and, suddenly, his eyes fix upon what appears to be a recently-snapped photograph of that very same young man, cuddling up with Madeleine. (That's right: Pierre's come to save a man, only to discover that the guy has been sleeping with his wife! Which means: Madeleine's not always in bed like she always says she is… or at least, when she is in bed—she's not alone!) The young guy, as it's going to be turning out, is the bohemian painter Daniel Prevost, and he's played by Daniel Gelin, who we've already seen in three previous Gabin pictures—*Martin Roumagnac, Miroir,* and *Le Plaisir. La Minute de verite* is a very important part of the Jean Gabin Movie Canon, because it represents the first of many films Gabin will make in the 1950s, in which his characters will be competing with much-younger men for the affections—or, more accurately, *afflictions*—of various, crazy women.

As Pierre examines Daniel, residents of the flophouse, responding to his gentle manner, are growing, in spite of their initial reticence, to like him, and many of them are now standing around, whispering to each other about how great a doctor he's turned out to be, in spite of the fact that he's rich and they're poor. Not realizing that Madeleine is Pierre's wife, the Landlady now begins bragging to him: "The lady in the picture with Daniel—Miss Madeleine, her name is—is very faithful to him. She's been coming to visit him every day. We think that he even attempted suicide because yesterday, when she visited him, she told him that she wouldn't be seeing him anymore." As if this isn't a hard-enough pill for Pierre to swallow, he also sees that Daniel, who's still 'out-of-it,' has a brooch affixed to his lapel—and it's not just any brooch, either, but one which Pierre recognizes, because he's the one who gave it to Madeleine ten years ago, when they were first married. (When none of the flophouse's residents are looking in his direction, Pierre quickly snatches the bauble back.) Pierre, who is apparently just as much of a 'detective' as he is a doctor, also notices his wife's very distinctive shade of lipstick on what appears to be a recently-smoked cigarette which has been stubbed-out in the ashtray next to the younger man's bed.

That night, Madeleine's performing in her current play, the one in which the critic wrote that she's "iceberg-like," and Pierre comes to see it, and her big soliloquy in the production includes the line, "I'm not the same woman I was before;" we can figure out already that the line will probably, if we're lucky, resonate with the ever-unfolding drama in the Pierre/Madeleine marriage. Tonight happens to be Pierre and Madeleine's tenth anniversary and, during intermission, when he comes backstage to greet her, she tells him that she'll meet him at home later, for a late-night anniversary dinner. Obviously, she has no idea that her husband has just learned about her affair with Daniel.

Later that night at home, Madeleine has prepared Pierre a candlelit anniversary dinner, and she's *so* conceited that, to get him into a 'sexy, anniversary mood,' she plays him a record album recording of her own voice which she's made for him (shades of when Gabin's wife-character did the exact same thing, in 1938's *Le Messager*). This is an overly-dramatic flourish from an overly-dramatic person, but it's psychologically-interesting, nonetheless, because it shows us that it's hard for Madeleine to communicate her feelings in real-life, when she's not on-stage. Madeleine has, *via* the record, managed to separate her voice out from herself, and director Delannoy is showing us here, that Madeleine is a person who is very much removed from her real-life self, a removal which, in her own mind at least, gives her the license to cheat on Pierre. (Today, we refer to this kind of mildly-sociopathic behavior as, 'compartmentalizing.') Besides the record album, Madeleine, at this point, also presents Pierre with a wrapped gift—a toy knight on a horse. And now, he's got a gift for her, too! Passive-aggressively, he hands her the photograph of herself with Daniel, which he had managed to snag from from Daniel's bedside, at the flophouse. (In the parlance of Desi Arnaz, "Lucy's got some 'splaining to do!")

Because Pierre is played by Jean Gabin, we're noticing that Pierre isn't getting riled up at all, now that he's confronting Madeleine on her infidelities and, in the same beat in which he's telling her he knows, *per* Lennon and McCartney, "What Goes On," he's also letting her know that he doesn't even know how to react to his new discovery, since the wound is so fresh, and he now starts lecturing her, in a salvo of no-nonsense 'Gabin Monotone:' "Some men leave when they find out that their wives have cheated. Some get drunk. Others don't give a damn." He doesn't tell her which one of those things *he's* thinking about doing but, because he's played by Jean Gabin, we can figure out that, more than likely, he'll be 'choosing Door #3!' What Pierre is the most pissed-off about, even more so than the fact that Madeleine's been cheating on him (since cheating, in France, and especially in old French movies, is actually considered to be 'part' of the marriage, and mistresses, as I've already mentioned in my discussions of previous Gabin movies, are as common among the French upper-classes as breathing), is that their daughter Simone has, just today, received high marks on a test at school—and Madeleine doesn't even seem to care.

Within a few seconds however, Pierre is back to confronting Madeleine about 'her cheating heart' again, and not sure how to answer his questions, she instead starts crying, but obviously, she's only crying crocodile tears (remember: She's an actor, so she can turn it on and off, at will), because clearly, this marriage has "Lost That Lovin' Feelin." Pierre then responds with a 'mini Gabin-Outburst:' "Only a few minutes ago, on your record, you told me that you love me, and yet just today, I discovered that you've been cheating on me. I'll never understand you! And on top of that, you're crying! Who are you crying about? Yourself? Do you have an excuse for your behavior?"

Pierre next asks Madeleine where she met Daniel, and she replies that they met at a nightclub *eight years ago*, in 1944, which was two years into Madeleine's marriage to Pierre. (So, she's actually been cheating on Pierre with Daniel for eight whole years, and tonight is the first time that Pierre [who's a smart guy, which means that Madeleine is good at subterfuge] has caught on to the deception.) And just when Pierre's really about to lose it with her, she takes the pre-emptive strike, alerting him that she knows that, just like she's been cheating on him for almost the entire length of their marriage, so too has *he* been cheating on *her* for the whole time, as well. We next flash back eight years ago, to 1944, and each time Jean Delannoy begins a flashback sequence, he's going to be zooming in on Madeleine's spinning, personalized record album, a device which the director has more than obviously borrowed from 1941's classic Cary Grant-Irene Dunne weepie, *Penny Serenade.*

In this flashback, Pierre and Madeleine who, at this point, have been married for two years, are attending a swank, fancy-dress ball, and both of them are dancing with other people. (The War is on, but many of Paris's most fancily-dressed swells are still kicking up their heels.) Pierre's tripping-the-light-fantastic with one of what will turn out to be his many mistresses, Madame Balinga, who's played by Doris Duranti, and as we're watching the two of them *boot-scooting* together, Madeleine's telling Pierre (and us) in the voice-over which she's delivering in the Present-Day, on their Tenth Anniversary Night, about this mystery lady: "Your Madame Balinga certainly had quite the reputation, Pierre: She had a certain weakness for doctors."

After this Dance Party scene, Delannoy now flashes-forward to a subsequent event which, apparently, also took place, back in '44: Pierre and Madame Balinga are canoodling in a darkened theater's front row (Pierre told Madeleine he was 'going out with male friends tonight. [Whoops!], and completely unbeknownst to the illicit couple, Madeleine is sitting in the row right behind them.) With a devious smile on her lips, Madeleine counts to three, and then burns the shocked Balinga's back with a cigarette, feigning contriteness directly afterwards: "I am sooo sorry, Madame Balinga! I didn't do it on purpose!"

Now, back in 'Present Day 1952' (during our 10th Anniversary Dinner-and-Marital-Accusations-Fest), Madeleine is now also accusing Pierre of sleeping with another woman, as well, Madame Meunier (who's played by Lea di Leo), the married nurse who works at his office. Instead of getting mad again though, Pierre just throws it back into her face, demanding more information about her own clandestine relationship (a/k/a, her eight-year *fuckathon* with Daniel).

Now, we get a flashback of the very first night that Madeleine and Daniel ever met, which was also in 1944: Jean Delannoy is taking us to Paris's trendy *Zero de conduit* ('Zero for Conduct') nightclub (the name of the club is a tribute to the incredibly famous French film of the same name, which was directed by wunderkind Jean Vigo in 1933, and it's a very funny name for a nightclub, because in nightclubs, nobody's conduct is ever too sparkling), where Daniel's performing on stage, and his act (or his performance art-piece, if you will), revolves around his painting-to-the-music on a huge canvas, for the club's besotted patrons, while a smooth jazz band lays down its reet beats behind him. Daniel's already drawn a robustly-fecund nude female torso and, noticing Madeleine for the first time, he quickly adds her head onto it! Not embarrassed to find this representation of herself on display in front of such a large crowd (actresses dig any kind of attention they can get), she blushes, and it's not too long, naturally, before she's over at Daniel's tiny artist's hovel. Ostensibly, she's adjourned to his pad just for coffee but, thanks to the German bombs which have just started raining down outside (we hear, but cannot see them), she's not going anywhere, at least for awhile. Daniel leans out the window, utters a calculatedly skirt-dropping prayer for world peace, and then right on cue, and just like he knew she would, she jumps his bones, and the two new friends dip out of frame, making *hot, sweet, French love* for the very first time.

It's time for an optical dissolve, which now takes us to a few months later in the same 1944 flashback: While Madeleine and Danny Boy have been illicitly shagging like minxes for only a few months at this point, Daniel is already accusing Madeleine of remaining with Pierre only for his money, and she's so smitten by Daniel that, when he's chewing her out like this, she doesn't even get mad at him; in fact, it kind of turns her on since, as we've already seen, Daniel, like every artist (or would-be artist) on earth, is an emotional volcano, while her husband Pierre is 'Gabinly Quiet' and reserved. Now comparing himself and Madeleine with Tristan and Isolde, Daniel recites a love poem to her: It's Guillaume Apollinaire's "*Le Pont Mirabeau.*"

Apollinaire was the French poet of Polish extraction who engaged in some real-life larceny of his own: In 1911, he actually stole the *Mona Lisa* from the Louvre and kept it for nine days, before being jailed! The poem is, on the surface, about two lovers who meet on Paris's famous Mirabeau bridge which overlooks the Seine and, in fact, the bridge and the poem about the bridge are inseparable in the French national consciousness, even to the extent that if you go to Paris today, you'll notice that the first verse and chorus of that poem have been carved into the end of the bridge's wall, and by whom—nobody knows.

Rock-and-roll buffs might be interested in learning that, in the 1980s, Jem Finer of the Irish rock band the Pogues even set this beloved poem to music. According to "*Le Pont Mirabeau*'s" (or, in English, "Mirabeau Point's") enchanted verses, true lovers are always a rock of stability for each other, no matter what chaos is ensuing all around them.

After Daniel has finished reciting the poem, he surprises Madeleine by presenting her with a sexy new painting he's drawn of her, in which she's wearing even fewer clothes than she was wearing in the last one... if that's even possible! The painting is an impressionistic piece, which means that, while it's ostensibly a painting of Madeleine, the face, which is really just a mess of squiggles, is very vague, and could actually be anybody.

Now, once again, 'in the present' (1952/Pierre and Madeleine's house/10th-Anniversary Night), Pierre is horrified to discover (and he's discovering this at the same time that we're discovering it), that this very same nudie painting is none other than the painting which today hangs over Madeleine and Pierre's fireplace, in their own living room. (What a *slap-in-the-kisser* for any husband, to find that a painting which has been on display in his own house for more than eight years has actually been made by his wife's illicit lover!) Pierre now starts mocking the painting, a piece of 'art' which, up to this moment, he used to really like.

Now, the film is going to start really getting confusing, *a la Bebe Donge,* by delivering so many flashbacks-piled-upon-even-more-flashbacks (piled-upon-flash-forwards) that, often, it will be well-nigh impossible to ascertain whether we're looking at a moment which is happening now or in the past.

In the next wartime flashback, we see Madeleine chit-chatting with her plain-Jane sister Monique (Simone Paris), a woman whose baby has been fathered by *a man to whom she ain't hitched.* Apparently, the baby is very sick, and in dire need of penicillin, and the problem is, it's wartime, and civilians can't get too many *meds.* Madeleine tells Monique that her own illicit man, Daniel, is not just a painter, but also a freedom-fighter in the French Resistance, and that Daniel might very well have access to penicillin, as well as to other *medicaments* which soldiers, and women with sick children, must have. Madeleine's excited to help Jane out, not just because Jane's her sister but obviously also because it will afford her an opportunity to see Daniel again. At first, when Madeleine and Daniel meet up, he tells her that he can't steal the penicillin for her, because it would be too risky, but after a fiery bout of off-screen lovemaking… he changes his mind.

As Madeleine now tells Pierre on their Present Day Anniversary Night, "That was the first time I didn't trust you: You're my husband, and you're a doctor, but you wouldn't help me get any penicillin, so I had to get it from Daniel. So, in a way, your not giving me the penicillin I asked you for, is what pushed me further into Daniel's arms." (What a conniver! She's actually blaming her own infidelities on her husband! Talk about 'grasping at straws!') "He had the guts to steal for me," Madeleine continues. "But you, Pierre… you don't have the guts to do anything!"

Next, we see Madeleine on stage, in yet another 1944 flashback (what would we do without 'em?), appearing in a production of *Romeo and Juliet.* Of course, she's preoccupied with her own personal Romeo, Daniel, whom she'll be seeing after the evening's show, the result being, of course, that she is unable to focus properly on the Bard's great lines; she even goes so far as to tell the play's director, by way of apology, that she's "in a fog," and damn if she hasn't even forgotten one of the play's coolest lines—"Love is stronger than death."

That same night in 1944, post the evening's *Romeo and Juliet* performance (and also, *post-Daniel-screw*), Madeleine arrives home. Pierre asks her why she's so late, and she outright lies, telling him that she was hanging out with some friends from the production, and Pierre doesn't even question her about it. (Remember: It's still a full eight years before he's going to be figuring out that she's been cheating on him with Daniel.) She next tells him that she's going to be leaving Paris for awhile, to play "Antigone" in Switzerland. (Funny, that Madeleine mentions she's going to be playing Antigone, because Madeleine's the living-embodiment of Sophocles' strong-willed, 'do-whatever-the-hell-she-wants' 5th-century gal, whose most famous line in the Greek scribe's play, happens to have been the very resonant—as far as Madeleine and Pierre's relationship is concerned—"we die, forever.") It's easy to figure out that she's really just leaving Paris to be with Daniel, and that there's not really any "Antigone" play being mounted, anywhere at all. (Somebody's getting mounted—but it's not Antigone!)

In the present day again, Pierre now tells Madeleine, "You only had one thought that night: To get away from me, and as quickly as possible. But may I tell you something? I'm not jealous of Daniel, because he can't give you the lush lifestyle that you're used to, and I can. And money is what's important to you—not love." (Love may very well, *per* Shakespeare, be 'stronger than death,' but one thing's for sure—it sure is a whole lot weaker than money!) And now that Pierre has learned the true extent of his wife's eight-years-worth of infidelities, everything is becoming crystal clear to him, and he's also recognizing, now and for the first time, just how much his own home has grown to reflect her taste in the other man: Not just one, but in fact all of the paintings in Pierre's home—all paintings which, at one time or another, have been introduced into the house by Madeleine—were painted by Daniel! (So, when *isn't* the wife the interior decorator?)

1944, Again: After Madeleine's Cairo-tryst with Daniel, she goes back to Paris, but doesn't return home immediately: She stays with friends, not telling Pierre that she's come back, because she wants to spy on him. Of course, she sees his car parked in front of a love-motel, and when he walks over to the car and sees her there, he tells her, with a totally straight face, that he's just been "with the tax guy." She asks him if the "tax guy" needs a lot of care, and completely Gabin-Stoic, Pierre replies, "Oh, yes. In fact, I'll have to come here often!" Comically, even though she's just caught him *in flagrante delicto* with another woman, Madeleine and Pierre decide to go out to dinner together, anyway. (In France, money is stronger than love—and *food* is stronger than love and money, put together.)

In another 1944 flashback, which we're going to be seeing next, Madeleine's now in Switzerland (she really gets around!) with her theater troupe, and when she and some of her friends enter a local church, they come upon a stained-glass window which features the face of Mary—and weirdly, the image of Mary has been based very clearly upon Madeleine's face, and it is from this accidental stained-glass window-sighting that she learns that Daniel, whom she has been unable to track down in Paris, of late, might be in Switzerland. When Madeleine's friends remark, *re:* the window, "Mary looks like you," she looks embarrassed, telling them that she "knew the artist a long time ago, but not too well." A helpful Priest (Lucien Doral), who's excited to have the subject of his window standing right in front of him (it's a whole hell of a lot better than seeing the face of the Holy Virgin in your grilled cheese sandwich), tells Madeline that if she's interested in visiting the creator of the glass window, that he lives close by; he then gives her Daniel's local address.

"Present Day 1952/10th Anniversary Night:" Pierre's now laughing off Madeleine's Swiss Tryst ("So! I guess you've never cheated on me under three thousand meters of altitude!"), and he's deciding, after all of these years of deceit, that the two of them should separate, and for good: "There is nothing left to our marriage, but the fact that we are comfortable with each other—and that is not enough of a reason [for us] to stay together." Finally, Jean Delannoy has given us some much-needed explanation of just why Madeleine and Pierre have stayed together for all of these years: They're just comfortable with each other. (We kind of knew it anyway, but it's a relief to hear a character actually copping to it!) "We can end our marriage now," he continues, finishing off his diatribe with a comment which is really below-the-belt: "Anyway… you were always a whore!" Irately, she lets Pierre know that he has no right to judge her because, when she and Pierre first met (in Nice, in 1942), she never hid anything from him about her past, and that he knew, even before they were married, that she had been with a variety of men. She now tells him, "I love Daniel, and so very often, I've thought about leaving you, too. You're always very calm—more calm than anybody I've ever met, and I'm bored to tears with that. Plus, whenever I've traveled outside of Paris to appear on the stage, you've never even once come to visit me." While this evening represents the first time the two of them have ever brought up the subject of divorce, it's very clearly been on both of their minds for most of their marriage because, in a brand new 1944 Flashback which we'll be seeing next, Daniel takes Madeleine to a meadow, where he surprises her by showing her a little shack he's rented for the two of them. (It's reminiscent of the scene in *Martin Roumagnac,* in which Gabin built that little countryside villa for Marlene Dietrich.) He tells her, "We will really celebrate here, after your divorce. In fact, if you want me to, I will call your husband and make an appointment with him—to tell him that you will be leaving him for me!"

One morning, in what must be 'Present Day 1952' (and maybe, a few months before '10th Anniversary-Night,' although it's hard to tell, because director Delannoy doesn't set the scene up properly, editing-wise), while Madeleine's lounging about in bed, Pierre tells her that he's "going away for the day," and he leaves her the phone number where he can be reached, and "only in an extreme emergency." At first, she's freaked, because she thinks, as we do, that he's gone off to spend the day with one of his endless-supply of mistresses, but when she cabs it over to the address which corresponds to the phone number he's given her, she's relieved to find out that he's not with a woman at all, but that he's ministering to a little boy who's in a coma! (This is the movie's one great scene, because it's the one moment in the whole picture, outside of that bit at the beginning in which Pierre was helping his daughter with her homework, in which one of the characters is actually doing something selfless, instead of selfish.) In this scene, we're learning that Pierre's always been a secret guardian angel to this fatherless boy, whom he apparently saved when the boy's mom left her husband (the boy's dad) to take up with another guy. (Could Pierre be the kid's real dad? Maybe, but the filmmakers never tell us, and I didn't even make the association until several months after

I originally wrote this chapter, and began re-writing it. It's hard to guess if Pierre's this kid's dad or not, because everybody's behavior in this movie is pretty cryptic, to begin with.) That same evening—the night following the day when she's made this discovery—Madeleine is temporarily happy with Pierre, and she stares at him, for the one-and-only time in the whole movie, with real love, and we can tell, just based upon watching this one scene, that the few moments they've had like this, have something to do, even more than money, with why they got married. (I mean, there has to have been some love there, at least initially, even in the worst marriages—right?) As Madeleine is now telling Pierre, in voice-over, "When I found out that you had been helping the boy, I had the impression that I was meeting you for the first time, and that I had become your wife all over again."

Next, again back in 1944, Madeleine's up in Daniel's artist's hovel, and she's crying. A bit coldly, her young lover tells her that her eyes "look like muddy water," and he asks her if she's talked to her husband about leaving him yet, and he then (this is no way to keep a girl!) starts berating her, even before he gets his answer: "Of course you didn't talk to him. You didn't have the guts, did you?" Next, in a flashback-within-a-flashback, we see that once, Daniel even pretended to phone Pierre, and to have a confrontation with him, just to freak Madeleine out, but that he was really just calling the recorded message which tells you what the correct time of day is!

And, wouldn't you know it: Tonight, during 'The Big 1952 Anniversary Night Reality-Check' (which is eight years after the flashback which we've just witnessed), and just as Madeleine has finally agreed to leave Pierre for Daniel, she's now opening-up a shocking letter which has arrived in the day's mail. And get this: It's a suicide note from Daniel (he wrote it the day before, moments before he killed himself), and in it, he's telling her that he's finally accepted that he'll never be able to have her all to himself and that for him, the only remaining option is death.

What makes Jean Delannoy's *La Minute de verite* different from American films about infidelity is that, in 'American Infidelity Pictures' (*Fatal Attraction*, *Kramer vs. Kramer*, etc.), there is usually more obvious hatred between the arguing/cheating married couples while, in *Minute*, even though Pierre and Madeleine talk about each other's infidelities and call each other 'liars' a lot, there is very little outright hostility between them, except for those couple of angry outbursts which they both exchange on either side. This troubled couple has actually gone past anger, into completely tuning each other out. *La Minute de verite* has no scenes in which the couple screams or breaks stuff, like the characters in *Who's Afraid of Virginia Woolf* do, and it's too bad, because that's exactly what we want to see!

The ending of *La Minute de verite* is just as ambiguous as is the rest of the picture: We're not sure whether Pierre and Madeleine are going to remain married or not, although it's possible they will stay '*un*-happily married' (unless Madeleine finds a new guy to fuck on the side), because Daniel's dead now, and she has nowhere else to go.

Fun-Fact #1: As *La Minute de verite* was a French/Italian co-production, which was financed with money from both countries, Jean Delannoy was asked by the producers to re-shoot all of the scenes which featured Daniel Gelin's 'Daniel Prevost'-character with an Italian actor, specifically for the film's Italian release: In the Italian-release version, Gabin and Morgan play opposite not Daniel Gelin as the painter Daniel Prevost, but a big Italian box-office star-of-the-time, Walter Chiari. In the Italian-language version, which I did not see (I saw the French one, with Gelin), Gabin and Morgan are speaking French, and have been dubbed into Italian, by other actors. Weirdly, when the French-language version of the film was released in Paris, one of the movie posters touted it as being 'a film co-starring Jean Gabin, Michele Morgan, and *Walter Chiari*, even though, when viewers ventured into the theater, they saw not Chiari, but Daniel Gelin. Oh, what a tangled web movie company publicity departments weave when they decide not to cough up enough bread to make their posters correctly! (Plus, Daniel Gelin must have felt awful, seeing somebody else's name up on the French poster, when it was he, who was in the movie.)

Fun-Fact #2: Guess who director Jean Delannoy's most famous American relative was? Well, here's more than a hint (in fact, here's the answer): In America, the original, French family name, 'Delannoy,' was shortened to 'Delano;' that's right, Jean Delannoy's most famous American relative, was President Franklin Delano Roosevelt!

Fun-Fact #3: 'Sublime-to-the-Ridiculous-Department:' When this dour/sour doomed marriage-tragedy opened in New York City in April of 1954, at one art-house cinema, it was preceded by a UPA cartoon short, "Howdy Doody and His Magic Hat." (Gabin + Doody! What a magical combination!)

What a Critic Said at the Time: "Neither emotionally convincing, nor is it otherwise very interesting. Unexciting [and] emotionally flat. The performances are indifferent." (New York *Times*, 4-24-54 issue. Critic: Bosley Crowther.)

What Another Critic Said at the Time: "Gabin is ingratiating as the Doctor who is faced with the dilemma of an unfaithful wife whom he adores, but director Jean Delannoy has not injected [any] warmth or passion into the proceedings, [which gives] the wife's love affair a decidedly unclear ring, detracting from the [film]." (*Variety*, 11-19-52 issue. Critic: "Mosk. [George Moskowitz.]" Reviewed in Paris.)

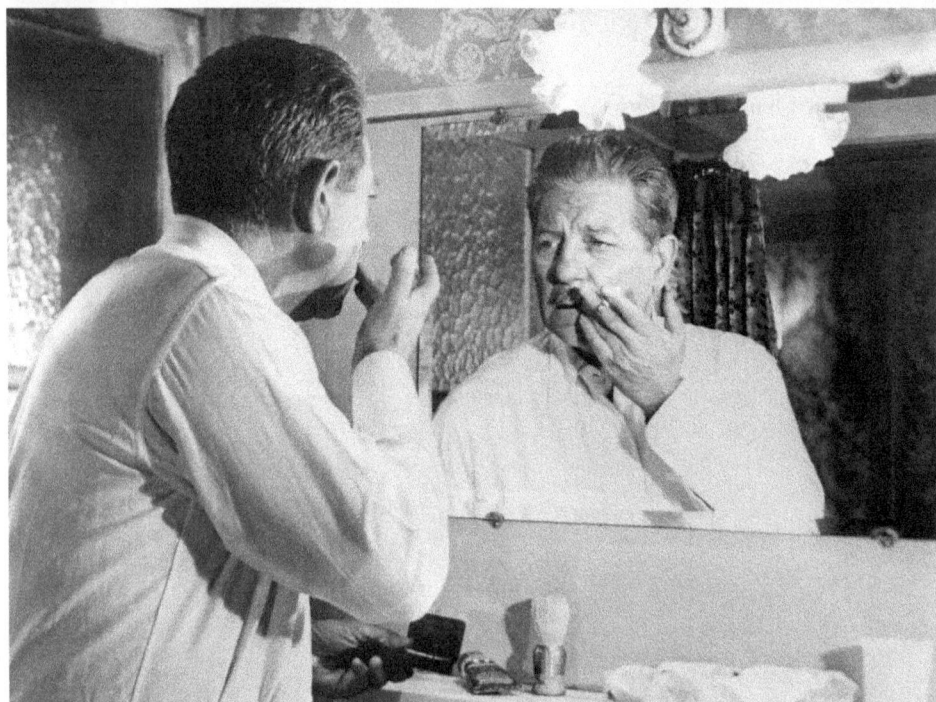

Top: With Cecile Didier. Above: Removing the mask.

FILM 45

LEUR DERNIERE NUIT

France, 1953

(Literal English Translation: "THEIR LAST NIGHT") Directed by Georges Lacombe. Produced by Edouard Harispuru. Screenplay by Jacques Celhay and Georges Lacombe. Based Upon a Story by Jacques Constant. Director of Photography (black and white), Philippe Agostini. Editor, Raymond Leboursier. Music by Francis Lopez. Production Designer, Leon Barsacq. (GENRES: ACTION/ SUSPENSE) A Production of Compagnie Commerciale Francaise Cinematographique (CCFC). Running Time, 1 hour 33 minutes. A Columbia Pictures Release in France, on October 23, 1953. Never Released Theatrically in the United States.

"I don't remember anything, and I don't know who I am. Now bring me a sandwich!"
— *Stoic Gabin's first and only words to the cops who have been interrogating him for more than eight hours, in "Leur derniere nuit"*

While the early 1950s would find Jean Gabin churning out a big stack of solidly-made (technically) yet narratively-insipid '*bourgeois* love-triangle pictures' (like *La Marie du port, Victor, Fille dangereuse, Bebe Donge*, and *La Minute de verite*), he'd also make some of his very best 'non-love triangle'/genre pictures in the early '50s—*Pour l'amour du ciel, Le Plaisir,* and now the mega-cool lost-classic, *Leur derniere nuit (Their Last Night)*, which is one of the most purely fun popcorn movies the actor ever made. *Nuit* will reunite J.G. with Georges Lacombe, the very capable and extremely underrated director who had already put him through his paces in two other great movies, *Martin Roumagnac* and *La Nuit est mon royaume*, and it's an amazing, fast-paced *film noir*, which is just as good as the best American *noir* thrillers which the big Hollywood studios had been churning out at the same time. The picture starts out as your typical 'Gabin+Brunette-Love-Story,' before it morphs into a full-blooded, white-knuckle, *E-ticket* crime picture, right before our '*yarbles*' (*per* Alex, in *A Clockwork Orange*).

As our film opens, pert-n'-perky young Madeleine (Madeleine Robinson, who had already appeared opposite Gabin on-stage, in 1949's Paris production of "*La Soif*"), is on her way to Paris, where she plans to seek employment as an English teacher. ("Those who can't do, teach"—even fifty years ago!) While she's on the train, a friendly old codger chats her up, in an avuncular and non-threatening way: "First time in Paris? I can tell you about a very nice boarding house, where you can rent a room inexpensively. And they have very nice people there."

She takes the old man up on his advice, and when she arrives at the hotel, all of the tenants are really super-friendly toward her, just like the old guy on the train told her they'd be. Many of them are older, and all of them feel instantly paternal—or maternal, as the case may be. One Older-Lady Tenant (Cecile Didier) is seated at the dining room table, reading tarot cards, and some of the other guests are sitting around, arguing about how stupid all of her psychic *mumbo-jumbo* is. Marceline (Francoise Soulie), the sweet-natured *hoteliere,* quickly gets Madeleine fixed up with a room of her very own.

Marceline announces that Madeleine's arrived just in time for dinner—and even though Marceline's tired, she agrees to join the whole group for the evening meal. One of the residents (all of them are more-or-less permanent) who's munching-out, is a nebbishy bespectacled/ mustached librarian, Mr. Ruffin (Jean Gabin) who, in this film, is going to be playing the only 'nerdy' role of his career. (And he really runs with it, too! 'Our J.G.' is hilarious, as a tight-assed bookworm.) Ruffin's reading everybody a newspaper article about a recent bank hold up, and the other residents are all rapt with attention, as he mentions how disappointed he is, in his own words, that "bad people" seem to be taking over Paris. When Madeleine sits down to join the others, one of them, the elderly judge Mr. Villard (Georges Vitray, an actor who already looked elderly twenty-two years before, when he played the jeweler Van Hoolst, in 1931's *Coeurs joyeux*), introduces her to their fellow diners: "Here at our hotel, we've got two students, a teacher, a librarian, and a lawyer." The hotel's Lawyer (George Baconnet), right on cue (and, no doubt, in an effort to impress her), now starts reeling off all of the fine points of his 'CV:' "I'm a criminal lawyer. And in my opinion, we need bad people here in Paris—otherwise, I'd be out of a job!"

At breakfast the next morning, Madeleine sits alone with Mr. Ruffin, and he's reading his newspaper out loud again, and this morning, he's got a bit of potential good news for Madeleine, as well: "I forgot to tell you, Miss: I don't want to promise anything, but I know a school nearby that just might need an English teacher. I owe the school's Director a call anyway, because he's a very good friend of mine." Ruffin, as he's now bragging to Madeleine, and to the rest of his tablemates, has just been nominated as Paris's Chief Librarian (!), and he also tells her that he doesn't plan on living here in the boarding house forever, and that soon, he's going to be buying a substantial piece of land from his school director-friend whom he next telephones on the hotel's payphone: "Your price is high, but I'm going to accept it. I'll send you the money, shortly. By the way, does your school need an English teacher? No? Well, okay. Thank you, anyway!" Ruffin 'Gabin-Shrugs,' and Madeleine looks happy anyway, because he's really tried for her.

Later on that same day, Ruffin's at a meeting at Paris's main public library, picking up his Chief Librarian of Paris Award at a small ceremony, and after making his acceptance speech, he sneaks out of the room, thanking everybody as he leaves. Madeleine's waiting outside the door for him, and he asks her if she was able to find a teaching job today—but no luck.

Ruffin tells Madeleine, sweetly, that he'll see her tonight at the hotel and, at this point, he heads into the local barber shop, where he orders Fernand the Barber (Georges Bever) to lock the door. Suddenly, and surprisingly, everything nerdy about Ruffin falls away—it was just an act! (You didn't think Jean Gabin would really play a nerd, did you?) Fernand owes Ruffin five hundred thousand francs, and our *faux*-librarian needs his money today, and *plus vite*. Of course, Fernand doesn't have it, and the guy wimpily pleads with Ruffin, telling him that his niece is going to be getting married next month, and that he *does* have some money on-hand, but that he's going to need to keep it around, to pay for the wedding. We know that Ruffin, who's really a tough guy, could take this little hairdresser apart in about one second if he really wanted to—but instead, he gives Fernand an extension.

Simultaneously, Madeleine's at a local employment agency, asking the Employment Lady if she knows of any English-teaching jobs in the area. Madeleine's brought no references with her, because this is going to be her first teaching job ever, so the lady tells her that, unfortunately, she has nothing to offer her. Finally though, as the days pass, and as Madeleine continues to pound the pavement, she's soon able to get an English class of her own, in a very prominent all-girl's school. Ruffin visits the school, under the guise of needing to bring over some library books, but he's really just come to say hi to Madeleine, on whom we can tell he's starting to develop a little crush. He walks her home that night, and she asks the older man why he doesn't have a family and kids of his own, and he replies, in 'that typically-cagey Jean Gabin Manner that we know and love,' that he's just never been interested in wedlock (*yup*, that's our Gabin!), and that he "likes to be alone a lot." She tells him sweetly that, in her opinion, he's not interested in children because he doesn't have any, and he smiles. At this point, she also tells Ruffin that she was married once, and very briefly, but that it didn't work out. Madeleine's very intelligent, and she has already figured out that there's a whole lot more to Ruffin than meets the eye.

Cut to the Hotel the following evening, and BANG!—we hear a shooting. Turns out, though, that it's just issuing from an "Inner Sanctum"-styled radio mystery, to which the hotel guests are listening. The *hotelière*, Marceline, a total mother-hen, is worried because both Madeleine and Ruffin haven't come home yet, and she likes to account for all of her boarders. She tells her other residents that she knows Madeleine and Ruffin walk home together sometimes, and she then wonders aloud if they're going to be coming home separately or together today.

About a minute later, Ruffin arrives at the hotel without Madeleine, and he looks pale, sweaty, and sick; *plus*, he's got a big (and mysterious) red blood-stain on the back of his shirt, which we'll see in greater detail when he gets up to his room alone and removes his jacket.

A few minutes later, Madeleine, who's now arrived home herself, bounds up to Ruffin's room to say hi, and when she sees the shirt, she immediately starts freaking. To calm her, he tells her (we don't know if this is true or not) that he was stabbed on his way home from work by a trio of street hoods. (Maybe they didn't return their overdue library books!) She knows Ruffin's not telling her the truth.

In a bar that evening, some thugs, who are led by Dede (Michel Barbey), play cards and discuss Ruffin who, according to what they're saying in this conversation, happens to be a legend in the Paris crime world! ("He acts like a meek little librarian," Didi intones, "but he's one tough bastard!") The next day, Ruffin stops over at Paris's Rodin Museum, and Dede meets him in the famous courtyard, next to a statue of Rodin's wife, the tortured sculptress Camille Claudel. "You look like someone who's looking for art," Dede mutters conspiratorially to Ruffin, and Ruffin whispers to Dede that he plans on heisting the office of the local power plant the following week, and that if Dede and his guys want in, there's always room for a few more. He tells Dede that if he and his men want to be involved in the heist, that they're going to have to provide a large vehicle to haul the money away in—possibly even a garbage truck, if Dede can make it happen.

On the appointed day the following week, Dede and one of his cohorts, 'Petit Louis' (in an American pic, they'd call him 'Little Louie'), who's played by an actor called Henri San Juan, pull up in a garbage truck and, wordlessly, Ruffin, hops onto the back. The trio of toughs makes haste over to the power plant, and immediately head-up to the executive offices, where the company's money men are in the middle of receiving their daily money-drop from the local armored car service. Suddenly, Ruffin, Dede, and Louis break the door down and hold the place up, and as they leave in the garbage truck, with the purloined giant bagful of cash firmly in Ruffin's mitts, two cop-motorcycles leap out of nowhere (Jerry Bruckenheimer/ *Bad Boys 2*-style) and begin chasing after them. Ruffin and Dede begin blasting away at the police officers with their 'heaters,' killing one of them in cold blood as they continue to make their getaway, and as more motorcycle cops appear now, to replace the ones that have just fallen away. (This American-movie-style car chase is accompanied by some very cool/ throbbing proto-Lalo Schiffrin-sounding American-movie-style chase music, courtesy of the film's composer, Francis Lopez.) The remaining *living* motorcycle cops, who are chasing the garbage truck, are now engaging our (anti)heroes in an amazing shoot-out, in which *popped-cops* on motorcycles spin out of control, smashing into buildings—bikes, and all. And just when Ruffin, Dede, and Louis have almost made a clean getaway, one of the more persistent moto-cops shoots out their tires, and hauls them down to the station.

In the interrogation room, Inspector Pierson (Jean Lanier) yanks Ruffin's librarian mustache off (it's fake), and it's now time for *Another Hilarious Jean Gabin Interrogation Scene,* in which our famously tight-lipped J.G. just won't talk. Ruffin won't tell the cops what his name is (they have no idea that they've just arrested Paris's Chief Librarian) and, in fact, one of the cops becomes so frustrated, he tells his superior, Inspector Dupre (Robert Dalban), "I've been interrogating this guy for eight solid hours, and he hasn't said a single word!" After eight hours, Ruffin finally decides to break the vaunted 'Gabin-Silence,' and gives the cops an ultra-brief statement, although he offers it up only in angry jest, and it doesn't help him out, too much: "I don't remember anything, I don't know who I am, *and you'd better give me a sandwich!"* *No-Bullshit* Inspector Dupre isn't about to take this kind of insolence off of any *interro-gee,* though: "Maybe you've lost your memory, Mister, but your fingerprints haven't lost theirs!" Pierson takes Ruffin's prints, and throws Ruffin, Dede, and Louis (the other two guys have been interrogated separately, in separate rooms, and by other cops) into a paddy wagon, which will now take them over to the *gray-bar hotel.*

But Ruffin doesn't look scared at all, and is quietly confident that he'll be able to get out of this mess with only the bare minimum of energy-expended. While the cops in the front seat of the paddy wagon are singing haplessly, and paying no attention to their dangerous cargo in the back, Ruffin, Dede, and Louis now cut their way out of the floor grill, escaping through the bottom of the truck and disappearing into a messy rush-hour traffic jam, and this is a scene which another director, Henri Verneuil, will repeat sixteen years later, almost to the letter, in another Gabin picture, 1969's Mafia thriller *Le Clan des Sicliens,* although in that picture, it will be Alain Delon (in the role of Gabin's young crime partner) who's going to be cutting his way out.

After Ruffin and his two crime-cohorts from the truck have escaped, and they all go their own separate ways, he now contacts Madeleine *via* telephone, and sets up a meeting with her in the park. A mousy girl who probably didn't experience a lot of excitement growing up, Madeleine's definitely *getting-off* on helping a criminal, especially a criminal whom she obviously finds attractive, as she finds Ruffin. The first thing he asks her, when they're together in the park, is if she's read about him in today's newspaper: "Guess the jig is up as far as my librarian [alibi] goes... Anyway, go up to my room at the hotel. Get me my room key, my trenchcoat, and the *three hundred-thousand francs* which I keep there. And grab as many of my clothes as you can carry. If I go back myself, it will raise suspicion."

Meanwhile, at Madame Marceline's Hotel, the residents are all busy, reading their own individual copies of the current day's newspaper, which happens to feature armed-robber Pierre Ruffin's picture right on the front page, and the Tarot-Lady seems especially shocked. ("Now I know why Mr. Ruffin didn't want me to read his cards!") While nobody is looking, Madeleine sneaks Ruffin's key out from behind the front desk, and sneaks up to Ruffin's room to liberate his possessions. And just as she's grabbing the stuff he requested, she also finds his business card: Besides being a librarian, Ruffin is also (at least, according to his business card) *a medical doctor!*

Ruffin meets Madeleine in the same park where they met before, and she gives him his things. He then tells her to head to the train station, and to buy him a ticket out of town. Meanwhile, Inspector Dupre and his men, knowing that Ruffin is on-the-loose, have blocked all of the streets which lead out of Paris. Dupre wonders aloud about whether Ruffin might be headed down south to Marseilles, but Pierson figures that he's probably not, because he knows that it would be too obvious for known criminals to be consorting in crime-filled Marseilles. At this point, the cops are also learning that Ruffin used to live at Marceline's hotel, so Dupre goes there, and she tells Dupre, even though she knows he's a criminal (and in the same way in which the good working-people sided with 'criminal Gabin' in some of his mid-to-late 1930s movies, like *Les Bas-fonds*), "I know Mr. Ruffin. And he is not a criminal."

Madeleine next arrives at a new hotel and, when she gets up to the room which she's booked, she has to sneak Ruffin in through the window, so that the cops won't be seeing him. Madeleine is definitely falling in love with Ruffin, even though they won't share any love scenes in the movie, and one of this otherwise impeccable film's only noticeable flaws, is that the director, Georges Lacombe, never shows us those all-important story beats in which Madeleine's filial fondness for older Ruffin morphs into romantic love. (In other words, her 100%-devotion to him is happening much too quickly.) She's also bought him a train ticket, *per* his request, to Angouleme, a town in southern France which he loves—a town which (importantly) happens to be very close to Spain, and once he gets to Angouleme, he'll be able to hop over the border, and the French cops won't be able to do anything about it. Ruffin thanks Madeline, and he tells her, warmly, that he doesn't want her to get any more mixed up with him than she already is, and that she should leave and forget she ever met him—but it's too late: Once a girl's met Gabin—she's hooked, forever!

At this new hotel, the Chambermaid (Genevieve Morel) sees Ruffin, and immediately recognizes him from the newspaper, and angry that he's been spotted, he now has to make a quick escape, before she can notify the cops. "That's the guy," she yells at the top of her lungs to anybody in the hotel who might be within earshot, as Ruffin scrambles out the window, *via* the fire escape.

The Hotel Clerk (Jean Sylvain) telephones the police, and Ruffin's now in a huge bind: He can't stay there anymore, but his train ticket out of Paris isn't valid for a few more hours, so instead, he high-tails it over to the apartment of Fernand, the barber who owes him money (an apartment, by the way, which happens to be located above a movie theater). "I know you saw me in the newspaper," he screams at Fernand. "Look: I'm leaving France, and I need that money you owe me—and I need it right now!" Since Fernand still doesn't have the money, Ruffin instantly (and this is very jarring, because it happens so suddenly) shoots him to death and (this is very cool), since Fernand lives over the theater, nobody can hear him getting blasted, over the din of the gunfire-packed cowboy movie that's playing.

Ruffin escapes into the alley, but it's crawling with cops, so instead, he ducks into a room with a middle-aged hooker who's played by Gaby Basset (a/k/a, the real-life 'ex-Mrs. Jean Gabin,' circa 1925—1931)! Ruffin hides in her bed, under the covers, and she's really excited that *a big, strappin' man* has just dropped into her lap, seemingly from the sky (is it 'manna from Heaven' or '*Gabinna from Heaven?*'): "You don't want to make love with me, you cute little rabbit?" she asks him playfully, and he waves her off with a plainitive cry of, "*I just want to sleep!*" Jean Gabin, who was nearly fifty years old when he made this movie, no longer needed to prove his masculinity on-screen, because it had already been proven, just like the laws of physics. Hilariously, he even pops his head out from beneath the covers, and screams-out, while showing off the biggest 'Gabin-Frown' of all time, "*And stop calling me 'rabbit!*'"

The police continue to comb Paris by night, as the manhunt for Ruffin is now in full-swing. A couple of cops ask a guy, who's wearing a trenchcoat which is similar to the one Ruffin has been seen wearing, if he can show them his ID, but of course, he's not Ruffin. About an hour later, when Ruffin feels secure that the police are no longer outside the hooker's pad, lying-in-wait for him, he takes his leave, heading for the train station and, when he gets there, Madeleine is waiting for him, and she looks plenty scared. She tells him that he'd better not get anywhere near the platform, since the cops are already there. (So, as it's now turning out, Angouleme is going to be out of the question.)

Madeleine next gets Ruffin a room at yet another (a third) hotel, and one which happens to be overlooking a local carnival. He walks around alone in the dark room, awaiting his fate, just as Gabin did fourteen years before in Carne's *Le Jour se leve*, as well as in director Lacombe's own *Martin Roumagnac*. Madeleine brings him groceries and flowers, and he jokes with her, knowing full-well that it's not going to be safe for him to leave the hotel, and that they should just go out dancing, at a nightclub. Instead, she opts to cook for him in the hotel room and, while they're eating, he makes a toast to her health. "To *our* health," she corrects him. The pair tries to ignore the noisy carnival sounds by talking about recipes and, at this point, they both hear what sounds like gunfire, emanating from outside the window. Ruffin, believing it to be the cops, steals a quick glance out of the window, and discovers that it's really just a group of teen-agers who are shooting off firecrackers, and he jokes (and this is one of the best lines in the movie), "*See! I knew humans were created in God's image!*" Madeleine, who's been very calm throughout this whole ordeal, is getting a major tension headache. He tells her that she should really go home to Marceline's rooming house, where it will be safer for her than it will be if she continues to remain here with him, but she tells him that she's afraid to leave him, because she obviously knows that if she does, she'll never see him again. The two hug goodbye tenderly, and she keeps her emotions in check, not crying like she really wants to. (It looks like her tears are about to start *squirting out*, but they don't.) We can tell that the main reason Ruffin likes Madeleine so much is because, like him, she is strong. (And it doesn't hurt that she also happens to be classically beautiful!)

Madeleine, against her own better judgment, finally returns to Marceline's hotel. Inspector Dupre is present and, in front of him, Marceline asks Madeleine where she's been for the last several hours, and she lyingly tells the concerned *hoteliere* that she was staying with a girlfriend. When Madeleine arrives up in her own room, she passes by the room which used to be occupied by Ruffin, and sees a bunch of cops who are turning it over, and making a giant mess. Meanwhile, since Ruffin is unable to take his planned train trip to Spain, because the terminal continues to be *crawling with fuzz*, Pierre now approaches the harbor master, and asks him if any boats will be leaving France over the next several hours.

Back at the police station, Dupre is poring through old newspapers, and this is where the Inspector is learning that Ruffin was arrested for the first time many years ago, and that, before he was a librarian, he was really the respected medical man, 'Dr. *Charles* Ruffin,' and that he was convicted in Angouleme for having performed illegal abortions. (What's funny about this movie, is that when Ruffin needed to change his identity, he didn't change his last name, but only his first. That's a sure sign that he knows Cruel Fate is going to be fucking with him, no matter what he does, or no matter where he goes. [*So!* That's why Ruffin wants to go to Angouleme: He committed his big medical crime there years ago, and he's smart enough to realize that the police would never dream of looking for him in the place where he had committed the biggest infraction of his life.])

Madeleine meets Ruffin by the docks, later that night, and she's brought him some more shirts, shoes, and socks. The two take refuge in still another hotel (a sailor hotel), where he confesses to her that, years ago, he was a young surgeon who, just like the young 'Poetic Realism'/'Drifter-Gabin'-characters of the '30s, dreamed that he'd one day travel to the end of the world, but that his whole medical career came to a halt in Angouleme when he was arrested, and that when the Medical Association took away his license, he became a librarian, not to mention, a *Smooth Criminal*. "I've always been on the run," he tells her. "But one also needs money." He Gabin-Shrugs helplessly and continues, "But now, everything in my life is ruined, for good."

Madeleine puts in an appearance down at the P.D., completely of her own volition, so that the cops won't continue to suspect that she's 'in' with Ruffin. Inspector Dupre is now questioning her and, this time, he's doing it more intensely than he did back at the boarding house, because of some new information which has just come to light: Dupre has just learned that, like Ruffin, Madeleine also has a secret past, and that she's not as much of a goody-goody as we originally thought she was: "You left Limoges, because your husband was a criminal!" (So: Ruffin wasn't her first scofflaw!) She tells him that she doesn't date Ruffin (which we already know is true, because they haven't slept together or even kissed, probably because, not-so-subconsciously, they both know that Ruffin's remaining time on earth is going to be short, and so it wouldn't behoove her to get any more attached to him than she already is). She tells Dupre, lyingly, that she hasn't seen Ruffin lately, which Dupre knows is pointedly untrue: "Well, just tell me where it was that you've been spending this past weekend, then. Because I know you weren't with a girlfriend!"

At a harbor bar, meanwhile, Ruffin's chatting-up a Belgian boat Captain (Arthur Devere), a guy who, when Ruffin meets him, is rubbing his sore shoulder in agony. Ruffin immediately fixes it for him, telling the guy that he "… used to be a doctor," and the way that Ruffin is saying 'used to' is a red flag to the Captain that Ruffin's in trouble (and boat captains love their 'colored flags!'), and that Ruffin's probably going to be needing to escape from France, and quickly! The Captain makes a deal with him, and it's the same deal which other boat captains already made with Gabin's other drifting characters in *Quai des brumes, Le Recif de corail,* and *Au-dela des grilles*: "Listen, Mr. Ruffin: In one hour, I'm sailing back to Belgium. Why don't you come with me? I've seen you walking around the harbor, and you look like you've got the weight-of-the-world on your shoulders. So come with me, okay? Anyway, since you fixed my shoulder, I owe you one."

Ruffin agrees to *split* for Belgium with the nice Captain, and he's definitely unhappy about leaving, because he knows that when he departs from France, he'll never see Madeleine again

With Arthur Devere.

(just as Gabin's character, Jean, didn't want to go to Venezuela in *Quai des brumes,* because he knew that he'd miss Michele Morgan too much). He tells the Captain that (and here comes a great crystallization of the recurring 'Gabin Movie Persona's Philosophy') he likes life a lot, but that he's also known, since he was a small boy, that life is often full of trouble—and *shitty people!* (The Jean Gabin Movie Philosophy About Life is just like the Woody Allen Movie Philosophy About Life, as espoused in *Annie Hall:* "It's horrible and miserable... and it's all over much too quickly.") The Captain, who is a more optimistic man than Ruffin, next philosophizes, "You know, there are nice people on earth too, mister. *Not just bastards.*"

A bit later, Ruffin meets Madeleine in a local seaside bar, and tells her that he's going to be leaving for Belgium, and when they leave the bar (of course) a cop car immediately springs out of nowhere like a bat out of hell, and starts tearing after them, and as they're being chased, Madeleine starts making with the 'I-Love-You-talk,' which the film's screenwriters had calculated, no doubt, to send the women in the movie theatre reaching for '*Les Kleenex*' ("Oh, Pierre! A few hours is not enough! Why can't love go on forever?")

(Why, indeed!)

Even though Ruffin and Madeleine have never consummated their mutual crush, she still treats the few days which they've just had together like the intense, Trevor Howard/Celia Johnson *luvfest* in David Lean's 1946 classic *Brief Encounter,* and she tells him that, even though she knows there's no chance this could ever happen, she still wishes for a future with him. He agrees, and invites her to sail away to Belgium with him.

Now, cops are starting to reproduce like rabbits. Dozens of cop cars, including Inspector Dupre's, are now chasing Madeleine and Ruffin's car, in a very exciting (not to mention *long*) chase sequence which seems to anticipate America's beloved 'O.J. Simpson Freeway-Chase' by more than forty years. As more and more police cars now begin converging on Ruffin's car, and as still other cops are glimpsed briefly, blocking the city's various ports-of-exit, the unassailable Ruffin (like all other Gabin characters, Ruffin is completely unafraid of anything, and everybody, on earth) next leaps out of the car and escapes, on foot, into the darkest corner of the docks, where he hides under some pylons. Police officers shine flashlights all over the harbor and, not knowing exactly where Ruffin is, start shooting willy-nilly all over creation, hoping that one of the bullets will find its way into him, wherever he is. Madeleine sees Ruffin and runs to him and, within a second, the entire harbor is bathed in flashlights and floodlights. Ruffin pops out of some pilings, and he's so adrenaline-powered, and totally unafraid, that the scene calls to mind both James Cagney's final, "Top of the world, Ma!"-moment in 1949's *White Heat,* as well as Al Pacino's Big Gundown in 1983's *Scarface.* He starts shooting-back at the cops, who are now filling him full of lead, and while his body is already (or should already be) dead, he continues to fire-away, ignoring the vast streams of blood which pulsate out of his mouth. Finally, Inspector Dupre fires the fateful shot, and Ruffin falls lifelessly into the water. Madeleine screams, as director Lacombe fades out, and as we get socked in the face by the giant end title-card, "*FIN,*" which springs toward us almost like it was filmed in 3-D. Of course in America, in 1953, while *Leur derniere nuit* was being made in Paris, the big 3-D movie craze was in full-swing. (It's too bad Jean Gabin never made a movie in 3-D. [But, come to think of it: Jean Gabin was already 3-D, so he didn't need any fancy optical tricks to make him any cooler!])

Leur derniere nuit is a very satisfying flick, and it also happens to be one of the most 'American-feeling' of Gabin's French pictures, which is to say that this movie, like most American studio-made movies (yesterday, today, and tomorrow) is plot-driven, as opposed to character-driven, which is what most European movies are (or at least what, in a lot of people's minds, they *used* to be). It's no surprise, then, that an American studio, Columbia Pictures, picked up the film's French distribution rights from its Paris-based production company, CCFC. (At the end of the pic, you even even get to see the famous Columbia-Lady logo, in all of her glory.) Columbia never released the picture in America, though, and this author believes that the studio's decision may some how have been connected to an unfairly harsh review of the film which was penned by *Variety's* Paris-based critic, George Moskowitz. (I've quoted from Moskowitz's review at the end of this chapter, and it's clear that this critic must have had some kind of personal axe to grind against Jean Gabin since, as you've probably already noticed, and as you will continue to notice throughout this book, Moskowitz gave a number of Gabin's wonderful movies only mediocre [and sometimes, even *downright shitty*] reviews.) At only 93 minutes in length, *Leur derniere nuit* is a great, fast-paced, American-style chase movie, and if you like *The French Connection, Serpico,* and *Dog Day Afternoon*, you'll totally get-off on this film, which you might want to consider as being 'those other movies' honorary birth-mother.' And if you like love stories, you'll love this movie too, because Gabin's 'Pierre Ruffin' and Madeleine Robinson's 'Madeleine' are two great screen lovers, in fact (and I'm not joking about this), I'd (almost) definitely put them right up there with Scarlett and Rhett.

Fun-Fact: The film's leading actress, Madeleine Robinson, who's right-name is 'Svoboda' (she was half-French and half-Czech) took her stage name, 'Robinson,' from Daniel Defoe's novel, *Robinson Crusoe*. She was married to a Gabin-movie regular, Robert Dalban who, in this film, played the character of 'Inspector Dupre'.

What a (Good) Critic Said at the Time: "An extraordinary film, very modest and fine. The film doesn't have any conventional morality, but it doesn't matter. Pierre and Madeleine's sorrow is the only thing that counts. Jean Gabin is transformed, in the first half of the movie, by a mustache, but he remains himself." (*Radio Cinema Televison Magazine*, Paris. 11-8-53 issue. Critic: Marcel Huret.)

What a (Wrongheaded) Critic Said at the Time: "Gabin plays with listlessness, as if he's done this before. This combo detective and character film hasn't enough development to make it a satisfactory entry for U.S. [theaters]." (*Variety*, 11-18-53 issue. Critic: "Mosk. [George Moskowitz.]" Reviewed in Paris.)

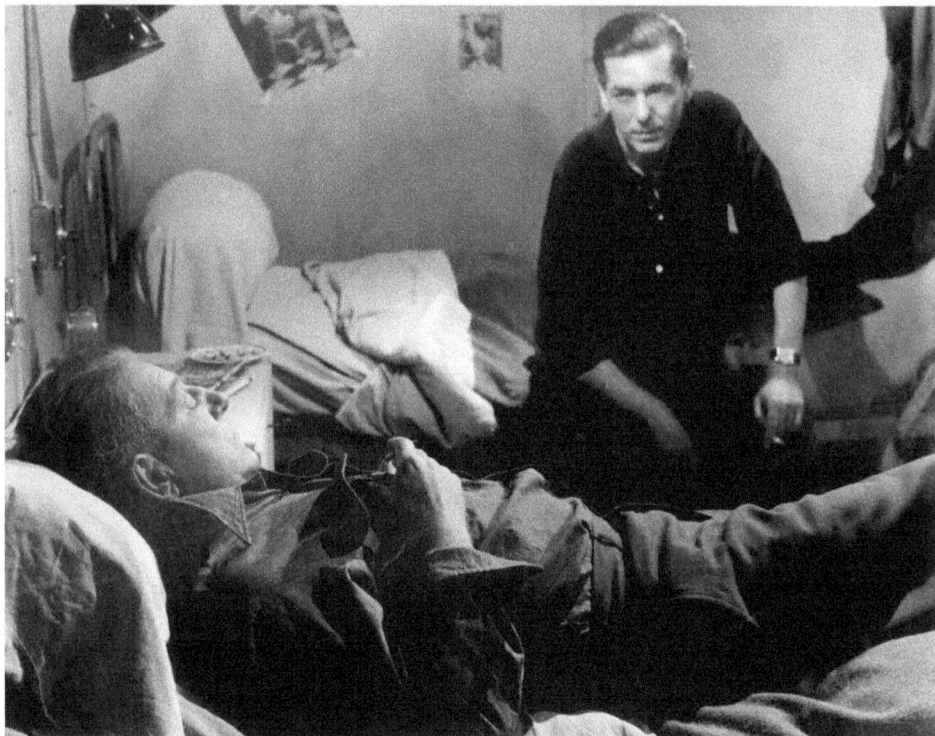

Top: With Claude Vernier. Above: Working Man.

FILM 46

La Vierge du Rhin

France, 1953

(Literal English Translation: "THE RHINE VIRGIN") Directed by Gilles Grangier. Produced by Evrard de Rouvre. Screenplay by Jacques Sigurd. Based Upon the Novel by Pierre Nord. Director of Photography (black and white), Marc Fossard. Editor, Paul Cayatte. Music by Joseph Kosma. Production Designer, Jacques Colombier. (GENRE: DRAMA) A Films Vega Production. Running Time, 1 hour 23 minutes. Released in France by La Societe des Films Sirius on November 13, 1953. Never Released Theatrically in the United States.

"I've seen worse things than prison…"
— *Mysterious loner Gabin, in "La Vierge du Rhin"*

The routine but well made *La Vierge du Rhin* combines the 1930s Gabin Movie Tropes (drifter/loner, hiding away so that the authorities can't catch him) with the 1950s Gabin Movie Tropes (*bourgeois* guy who's getting taken advantage of by a woman and not fighting back, even though we want him to) and unfortunately, I'm sorry to report that this movie is more *Marie du port* than it is *Quai des brumes*. It's the first of twelve pictures in which Gabin will star for his good friend, director Gilles Grangier, and it's also one of the least effective of their collaborations, because most of the others depict Grangier's trademark warmth and humanity, and this picture simply does not.

As the film opens, a fishing boat, *The Rhine Virgin*, which spends its life traveling up and down the river of the film's title (a river which links the Netherlands, France, Germany, and Switzerland), is docked in Dusseldorf (in southwestern Germany) near a mining camp. Meister (Oliver Hussenot), the boat's owner and captain, tells his daughter Maria (Nadia Gray), and his Second Mate Pietr (Claude Vernier), that after a few more hours of work, they'll begin their trip back home up the Rhine to their eastern-French home of Strasbourg. Pietr narrates the movie in voice-over narration which is directed not toward us, the film's audience, but instead, toward another character in the film, Meister's daughter Maria, upon whom he harbors (pun intended) a rather serious unrequited crush. (What other kind of crush is there?) Maria approaches Pietr, whom she notices gawking at her, and asks him,

"What's so fascinating?" Of course, he gives her the stock, too-cool-for-school/suave-guy answer: "*You.*" While they're talking, Meister's off on the pier, talking with a strange drifter. (And, of course: All French movie drifters are played by Jean Gabin!)

Meister returns to the *Rhine Virgin,* and clues his daughter in as to what he was talking about with The Stranger: "That guy asked if we'd take him with us, back to Strasbourg, but I said no. He's got a French accent, but he claims to be German. He looks like somebody with little hope." (That's Our Gabin, all right!) While the father-daughter conversation continues, we hear, but don't see, that a miner has just been stricken by a falling log. Our Mysterious Gabinian Stranger runs to the guy's aide, off-screen, and hefts the log off the guy's legs, both of which have snapped like twigs, and while he's helping the guy out, one longshoreman remarks to another that it's a miracle the guy wasn't killed. This life-saving incident, of course, endears the Stranger to Captain Meister, who is now starting to reconsider what he originally said about not letting the guy aboard his boat. (Meister has already mentioned to his daughter that they need an extra hand, anyhow.)

Meister next asks the Stranger, just like in *Casablanca,* if he's got a French passport, and *notre etranger* sidesteps the question neatly by changing the subject, and Meister then asks the Stranger, *apropos* of absolutely nothing, "Heyyy, weren't you in Brussels, in '39?" While Meister's a nice-enough fellow, *still,* he has to put his foot down, a bit: "Look, friend, you seem like a good man, and I'd like to take you with us. But if you don't have a French passport, I just can't. I don't want you take this the wrong way, because I like you, but I don't think you're really even French, although you've got that French accent—and, well, I just can't risk it. If I take you on my boat, we'll both wind up in prison." The Stranger just Gabin-Shrugs and monotones (and we totally believe this, when he says it), "I've seen worse things than prison."

Within minutes, Meister has been won-over for good, in spite of his better judgment, by a dose of the Good Ol' Gabinian Charisma, and he decides to take the Stranger along. The Stranger proves himself, immediately, to be a great deckhand—an absolute dynamo, in fact, when it comes to hull-cleaning and boat-maintenance. Young Pietr, who works alongside The Stranger, tries to get the tight-lipped guy to admit to something (anything!) about his life but, of course, as we already know, Jean Gabin's strong suit, is always going to be his extreme reticency to talk about himself unless he absolutely has to. As Michael Corleone famously said in *The Godfather,* and this maxim applies to most of the movie characters played by Jean Gabin, "Never tell anybody what you're thinking." Pietr says, in his voice-over, that he "asked the Stranger questions, but received no answers."

After a few days, when The Stranger figures that he can trust his new boat buddies, he finally opens up to them, inasmuch as any J.G. Character can really ever 'open up' to any other people, telling them that they were right to doubt his Frenchness, and he now apologizes sincerely for having lied to them. He's telling them now that he really is German, and that his real name is 'Martin Schmidt;' he even shows them his German passport, which we know, even if they don't, is probably a fake. Pietr, who's amazed that they've made headway in finding out even the slightest information about the Stranger, now sends Marie over to Martin's cabin privately, to see if she can cadge any more info out of him since, in Pietr's carefully studied opinion, "Whenever there is a mystery, a woman is best at checking it out!" Marie charms Schmidt, and is able to get a few more words out of the poker-faced guy, but nothing that's too useful, or that informative.

That night, Meister, Maria, Pietr, and Schimdt are all sitting down for dinner together. Meister's still nervous about the fact that they're about to cross into France, with the paperless Schmidt in tow and, as they munch-out on the evening meal, Meister and Maria talk about a Frenchman who's been very much in the news lately, the wealthy French captain-of-industry, Jacques Ledru, a 'proto-Onassis' who's built a magnificent shipping business in Strasbourg from the ground up—and a guy who has apparently died recently, and under mysterious circumstances. Meister mentions, also, that he's heard that the legendary Mr. Ledru was married to "a high-class prostitute" and that, as he's also heard it, Ledru was, in addition to being *a mega-gazillionaire* legitimate businessman, the woman's pimp. Has Meister brought Ledru's name up in front of Schmidt because he thinks that Martin Schmidt is really Ledru? Well, if Schimdt is Ledru, he certainly isn't letting on about it, and he changes the subject very promptly, telling his dinner companions about how he left Europe before WWII broke out, so that he wouldn't have to serve. In other words, Schimdt (who may, or may not, be Ledru) left Europe, at least this is what he's telling them, because he was a draft-dodger.

After dinner, Pietr and Schmidt are steering the tub together, and Pietr hands the wheel over to Schmidt, who pilots it with great precision. Pietr mentions, in his voice-over narration, that because of the way Schimdt is handling the boat, and because of the way that Schmidt seems to be on familiar terms with the complete geography of the area which they are navigating, that Schimdt really does know *a thing or three* about the seafaring world. Schimdt is also familiar with the names of the other boats which happen to be passing Meister's and, in fact, as the *Virgin* is passing one boat in particular, he tells Pietr that he knows it very well. (This other boat is called the *Montrachet,* which means that it comes from the Montrachet region of Burgundy in central-eastern France, where that *dee-licious* wine comes from!)

That night, Marie tries to pry more information out of Schmidt, who is able to throw her off her game very simply, by waxing poetically: "Some things in life are of no importance," he tells her. "Most of what life is all about, isn't winning or losing, anyway. *All life is about is the gaining of memories.*" She asks him, sweetly, if it's possible that he might be hiding something from herself and from her dad, and he replies that he doesn't have that much imagination, and that he's really just been traveling around lately "to forget," however he's not telling Marie what it is exactly that he's so keen on forgetting.

That night, the *Rhine Virgin* docks in Mannheim (it's about halfway to Strasbourg), and in his voice-over, Pietr mentions that he has been unable to pull any further backstory out of Schmidt, outside of what we already know about how Schmidt didn't want to serve in the military. He invites Schmidt to be his guest at a local boat bar, now telling Marie (and us, by default), in his voice-over, that he "thought alcohol would open Schmidt up a bit more." After Schmidt's downed a few, Peter casually asks him, "So, what is it that you want to forget? Do you have some troubles? Maybe I can help you!" Schimdt waves Pietr off though, telling him he's not interested in answering any more questions about himself. (This is exactly what Gabin's characters always do to nosy cops, during all of those pesky police interrogation-scenes.) Pietr's finally able to irk the unirkable Schimdt, when he blurts out, "Well, have it your way. But I'm just going to have to find out more about you on my own then, okay?" And while they're talking, a drunken American Sailor (French filmmakers love filling up their frames with dorky/crass American Seabees, who put on their little 'aww shucks-routines,' as they boob their ways across Europe) enters the bar and sits down with the two men, and he recognizes Schmidt, immediately: "Hey, wait a minute, feller! Don't I know you from somewhere? Well, sure I do! Hey, I've been looking for you!" (Now that he's recognizing Schimdt, this guy, who's speaking his dialogue in English, suddenly turns off his goofiness and becomes intense; obviously, this *swabbie* has had some kind of a bad business dealing with him in the past, and if Schmidt *is* Jacques Ledru, then maybe the two of them were involved in some kind of a bad pimp-client transaction and, just maybe, the American got screwed—*although not in the way he wanted to!* Schimdt, with 'Gabin Calm,' steps away from the Sailor, whose accusations cease immediately, the second the Sailor is approached by *a hot bar whore,* and Schmidt, next, buys a gun, at the bar. (Don't you love bars that sell booze, pickled eggs, and firearms?) A bit drunk, and therefore forgetful, Schimdt now leaves the tavern, but he's accidentally left his key ring on the table, and the initials on its surface aren't 'M.S.' (for Martin Schmidt), but 'J.L.,' which we know must stand for 'Jacques Ledru.' Pietr runs out of the bar to find Schmidt, but Schmidt (or Ledru, or whoever he is) has already vanished into the night. When Peter arrives back on the boat, he finds that Schmidt hasn't yet returned.

Then, it's Plot Twist Time: Even though Pietr's our narrator, and we're always supposed to trust a film's narrator implicitly (since he's the one who's supposed to be guiding us on our filmic voyage), he, like Martin Schmidt (or like 'Jacques Ledru,' as the case may be), is no angel, either: He trying to muck-up the *Rhine Virgin's* engine, so that the boat will be forced to stay in Mannheim for a few days, and also so that he'll be able to engage in some monkey business of his own—which, we can guess, is something that's probably illegal, simply because of the fact that he's doing it on his boss's dime: In this scene, not only does Pietr fuck up the engine, but he also steals a great deal of cash out of Meister's safe, which is also located below deck.

Not only is Pietr shady, but when he's been drinking, he becomes violent, as well: At this moment, Marie ventures below deck, and not only does he start manhandling her (without even as much as a polite hello!), but he even tries to rape her. But then (*"My hero!"*), Schmidt pops into the galley and saves her bacon, right on cue, and he then gets right up in Pietr's face: "You're going to regret this when you're sober. Now, let go of the girl!" Now that Schmidt has suddenly defended Marie's honor, she thanks him profusely; clearly, like other twenty-year-old girls in previous Gabin movies, and like more young girls, in more Gabin movies which will follow this one, she'd *drop trou* for this smooth older guy in a second. (It's like high school, where the high school girls don't want to hang out with *you;* they want to hang out with the older college guys!) Schimdt can see that Pietr's *cocked-up* the engine, so he fixes it very promptly, but Pietr doesn't run away. He's not afraid of Schmidt who, of course, he's already figured out is Jacques Ledru, and he holds Schimdt's keychain up (the keychain with the 'J.L.' insignia on it), right in front of Schimdt's ever-unchanging poker-face: "So—you left these keys in the bar last night. Wow, the cops sure would like to find that draft dodging-pimp Jacques Ledru, wouldn't they?" Schimdt makes no reply and, at that exact moment, Meister arrives in the galley. (*Hmm*: Maybe there's a reward for finding and capturing this 'lost' guy, and maybe, that's why the always-opportunistic Pietr is after him.)

When Meister sees Pietr and Schmidt in the middle of their little alpha-male-*vs.*-other alpha-male showcase/showdown, Pietr, very promptly, dummies-up. Meister announces that they're almost in Strasbourg, and Marie tells Schmidt that he should hide in the galley when the port authorities come on board, just like Gabin's character was forced to do in *Au-dela des grilles*, due to his lack of a French passport. But Schmidt doesn't seem to be too worried.

When the *Virgin* finally docks in Strasbourg, Marie uses her coy sexiness to lure the coast guard guys away from the boat, so that Schimdt (okay, okay, I'll start calling him 'Jacques Ledru' now, *since that's who he is*) can get off without a hitch, and when the coast is clear, he thanks both her, and her father, for putting him up. He lets them know that he'll definitely be in touch, and that he has genuinely appreciated their support in helping him get back home, to Strasbourg. Meanwhile, Ledru's spunky Gal Friday-secretary, Anna Berg (Andree Clement, an early-thirtysomething beauty), who definitely gives Marie Meister a run for her money in the Cute, Spunky-Girl-Who's-Hot-for-Gabin-Department, is already there and waiting for him, in Ledru's own Rolls-Royce.

And it's not just Anna who's shown up to meet Ledru: Ledru's Cruella DeVil-frightening ex-wife, Genevieve (Elina Labourdette), the one whom he had reportedly pimped-out in the past, is nearby, in the office of the Strasbourg harbor master, and it is here that the filmmakers are going to be shaking us up with Another Big Twist: Believing her husband to be dead, after Ledru disappeared mysteriously one year ago, she quickly got herself remarried, and to an oily young gigolo by the name of Maurice Labbe (Renaud Mary), and the two are living high-on-the-hog on Ledru's money, and in Ledru's Strasbourg mansion! Pietr's in the office too and, as it's turning out, he too already knows Genevieve: In fact, this is the scene in which we're going to be finding out that Genevieve has actually paid Pietr to find Ledru since, in the back of her mind, she knows that he's probably alive, and that if he ever comes back, her sham-of-a-second-marriage will be over. (Pietr hands Genevieve the 'J.L.' key-ring: "Okay, lady, I did it. I found him for you. You owe me ten thousand marks.") While they speak, unbeknownst to the both of them, Ledru and Anna are speeding away together, to the security of a small secret office which Jacques has always kept in Strasbourg, an office whose location is so secretive, even Genevieve is unaware of its existence.

Young Maurice, a typically-dead-eyed dilettante, is starting to get pretty mad at Genevieve because, when he married her—in fact, right up until this very moment—he had no idea that her ex-husband might still be alive-and-kicking. Based upon the fact that we've already seen a lot of American *films noirs*, like *Double Indemnity* and *The Postman Always Rings Twice*, we can now figure out that Genevieve and Maurice will probably soon be trying to kill Ledru for real, to make sure that they'll continue enjoying uninterrupted access to his millions.

Anna and Ledru arrive at Ledru's Secret Office. Shortly after they get there, Marie Meister comes to see them. (Before he got off the Meisters' boat, he told Marie where he'd be, since *he digs the young thing*.) Anna has known, for the whole time, that her esteemed boss Jacques Ledru was just pretending to be dead, and that he wasn't dodging the draft at all, but was actually just ditching town for a year while the residue of a bad business deal fell away, and she's been looking after his interests in his absence, hoping that he would soon be returning. Anna's like 'a cuter, younger Moneypenny' in the James Bond movies: She loves her boss Ledru, but he never gives her the time of day (which is weird, because she's hotter than Dutch love)! At the same time, though, it's also not so weird, because we know that sometimes, in his movies, Jean Gabin doesn't get involved with the women he really likes, because whenever he does, he's always leaving himself open to getting hurt—and we don't want that! Anna sees that Marie is checking her boss out, but she doesn't get too riled-up about it. (In other words, there's no catfight between the women.) She tells Ledru that, in his absence, Genevieve and her new hubby Maurice had been using his money to finance various local smuggling operations in Strasbourg, and she also tells him that she doesn't know where Genevieve met the young stud: "One day, this new guy took her. Nobody knows where she got him from."

Anna tells Ledru that she's seen his photo posted in the harbor master's office, on a missing persons-flyer, but that her beloved boss shouldn't worry about it: "Don't worry—I didn't tell the authorities that you were here. What you should do, is to just go away again. Go somewhere that nobody will ever look for you, and just be free. I will handle everything for you silently from here, just as I've been doing already. Your problems with your wife should be over, and I will see to it that the rest of your life is happy." Ledru now tells her (not cynically, but realistically), "Nothing in life is ever over," and it's just like that cool tag-line in the advertising campaign for P.T. Anderson's brilliant 1999 epic-film *Magnolia*, which read, "You may be done with the past… but the past isn't done with you!" Ledru tells Anna that he won't really be able to be at peace, until he gets revenge on Genevieve, because she's been living off of his bread, and he adds that, if Genevieve should come looking for him, Anna shouldn't tell Genevieve that he's returned. (Ledru has no idea that Genevieve already knows he's come back, and that Pietr's the one who told her about his return.) Anna next tells Ledru that he should go and talk to a second woman who used to be his secretary before she held that position (we won't see this other woman in the film), because not only might this other lady be able to help him, but she might even have some kind of damning evidence on Genevieve and Maurice, evidence which will get the two of them locked-up before they can get to him, and possibly even kill him. Anna and Marie both tell Ledru that they'll help him to exit the harbor safely, so that he won't run into the Harbor Patrol, and the two women, next, walk Jacques through Strasbourg, making sure that nobody can see him. After awhile, he tells them that he'll be okay, and that they should take off.

As Ledru walks through Strasbourg alone, suddenly—SCREECH! A car bolts out of the blue and attempts to mow him down; of course, Maurice is behind the wheel, and Genevieve is by his side. They've missed him, and Genevieve is frantic about it: "You've got to him run him down! If we let him live, we'll have no money!" Maurice might be an oily free-loader but, very pointedly, he's no killer and, at this point, she decides to set him straight about his wimpy, non-killing ways: "I love you, Maurice. But I will not start at the bottom again [meaning: with no money]." Maurice confirms to Genevieve that he loves her too, but he stands up for himself a bit, telling her that he will not kill Ledru for her, and that she should never ask him to do anything like this again.

That night, Maurice and Genevieve are partying-down in Ledru's mansion, and the phone rings: Whoever's called quickly hangs up, and Genevieve knows it's Ledru: "He probably wants us to know that he knows we're here," she tells Maurice, beginning to pale. Maurice then confesses something to Genevieve which he's known for a long time, but which he never told her—which is that he's always known, even if she didn't until today, that Ledru was still alive: "After he was reported missing, I saw your husband once, in a Strasbourg hospital, when I was there visiting a friend, but I never told anybody about it." Needless to say, she's furious: "You married me, knowing that my husband was alive?"

In a match-cut, we see that Ledru has now sneaked back into his own, 'legitimate' harbor office, by night, to confer with Anna. (It's a match-cut because, in this scene, Ledru and Anna are standing exactly in the same position in which Maurice and Genevieve were standing in the prior scene, and the moment has been edited very cleverly, so that it appears that Anna and Ledru are finishing Genevieve and Maurice's conversation.) Ledru now confirms for Anna what Maurice has just been saying to Genevieve: "I had an accident during the year I was gone [note: the film doesn't tell us what kind of accident it was], and I was in the hospital, semi-comatose. That Maurice-character recognized me, but he didn't say anything about it to Genevieve, obviously because he wanted it to appear that I was dead, so he could get his hooks into her, marry her, and get his hands on my money. He told the people in the hospital that I was German, so Germany is where I went. My wife truly didn't know I was alive." Anna tells Ledru that Genevieve even sold one of his favorite boats, just because she wanted a very expensive mink coat!

Back at *Maison* Ledru, meanwhile, Genevieve and Maurice are busily hiring a crew for their newest and latest smuggling operation, and we know that any time now, Ledru will be putting in a surprise appearance at his own house, to freak them out. Since Genevieve wasn't able to get Maurice to run Ledru over in the car, they're also conspiring, in this scene, about other fun ways in which they can kill him.

Of course, Maurice and Genevieve (neither of them are exactly MBA candidates), while they're trying to make money off of Ledru's businesses, are actually running them into the ground. ("Why do we have to pay the workers?" Maurice asks, truly baffled by the concept.) He and Genevieve get spooked, suddenly, when they look at a nearby ashtray, and discover a recently-stubbed-out cigarette—and it's Ledru's brand! "Someone has been here tonight," Maurice proclaims, knowing full well who that 'someone' was.

Now, about halfway through the movie, we're finally going to see the reunion of Ledru and Genevieve: Ledru's spending the twilight hours drinking, down at his favorite local bar, and since she's figured out that he's probably there, Genevieve sashays in, and when she now sees him, for the first time in over a year, she pretends that she's missed him in his absence, but he sees through that bullshit, right away: "Oh, Jacques, I'm feeling so many emotions right now. Why didn't you come back quicker? By the way, my friend, Maurice— he forced me to run you over! I had to force myself to pull the car back!" (This lady's so full of shit, she should telephone that household service, which the French must surely call, '*Le Roto Root-aire*')

And her dumb-show just keeps getting dumber: "Oh, Jacques! Why were you hiding? You know I've never been able to forget you!" He then submits a request, which is for her to cut out her free-flowing, patronizing stream of clichés, and he also asks her how long she's been married to Maurice for, to which she replies, "Oh, Jacques! I was so alone when I thought you died! And the responsibility of running your companies was too much for me to handle alone. And then I met Maurice and, well—he was sooo nice!"

Ledru has now heard enough. He tells Genevieve that he knows about all of the little businesses which she and Maurice have going, on his dime, and that they had better cut it out, and quick. She tells him that he should come to 'their' house (a/k/a, his house!) tonight at nine, and his reply is, at first, negative: "Nothing doing. If I come at nine o'clock, you and your new husband will kill me! But, you know what? Now that I'm thinking about it, maybe I *will* show up then, anyway. Because, guess what? I'm going to kill you and Maurice before you guys can kill me, and I've got to do it tonight, because I want to get all of the killing I have to do over with, and as quickly as possible!" So I want to warn you that if I show up, and the two of you try and do me in before I can do you in, you're both dead!" She remains calm, and tries to put a refreshing spin on his words: "Oh, Jacques! To see you in our house, again! If you still want me back, we can start all over again!" (This dried-up old ex-cutie is more delusional than Gloria Swanson, in *Sunset Blvd.*) When she leaves the bar, Maurice is outside in the car, ready to drive her home, and it's a good thing that Genevieve doesn't know Meister and Marie, because they've been in the bar the whole time, sitting at a table in the back while Genevieve and Jacques were talking. (Based on overhearing Ledru and Genevieve, they now know, incontrovertibly, that Ledru is a good guy.)

Meanwhile, Pietr shows up at Jacques' office for a confrontation with Ledru's secretary Anne, and he asks her where Ledru is, because, guess what: It's not just Genevieve and Maurice who want in on Jacques' businesses, but the *Rhine Virgin's* second-in-command, Pietr, has his eyes on the prize, as well! At this point, we're thinking that maybe he'll even try to rub Genevieve and Maurice out, so that he can get (or more accurately, rob) Ledru's fortune, for himself.

When 9:00 p.m. comes, Ledru arrives at his mansion for The Big Showdown. Will he kill Maurice and Genevieve? Will they kill him? Will Pietr kill everybody?

Ledru is way too smart to just ring the doorbell and just go in, because they'd surely kill him that way. So, instead, he first does a little re-con around his property, listening through the window at Genevieve and Maurice, whom he now sees continuing to conspire about his downfall in his study, just like he knew they'd be doing. As he looks through the window, he even sees that his safe is open, and that Maurice is rifling through his personal papers, and he also overhears Maurice telling Genevieve something which he hasn't expected to hear, which is that Maurice is going to be leaving her, and taking all of Ledru's money for himself. (So: Maurice isn't as dim as we thought he was.) When he gives her this information, she freaks instantly, and throws herself at his feet: "You can't leave me! You can't!" Maurice, who's way meaner than we originally thought him to be, now sniggers, snidely telling her, "I love money, just like you do. Maybe even more!" He also admits that, up until recently, he really *did* love her. ("When we got married last year, it wasn't just for money... but I'm just not feeling any love for you, anymore.") She screams at Maurice, letting him know that, in her estimation, he's nothing but a common pimp. Maurice knows that Genevieve used to be (*used to be?!*) a whore and that, therefore, her choice of vocabulary isn't *all that fantabulous*.

Genevieve now points a gun (the one she's been clutching the whole time, in case Ledru should happen to 'pop in') at Maurice, who starts laughing when he sees it because, clearly, she has no idea how to use the darned thing. ("If you're going to kill me, you'd better take that safety off the gun!") While Genevieve is working out her gun-problem, Ledru suddenly walks in, and tells the illicit couple that he's heard everything they've just been saying about him, and that both of them had better be 'hitting the road.' Without a thought, Genevieve instead tries to shoot Ledru, but her gun is jammed. Maurice suddenly turns into a wimpy crybaby (he actually starts bawling!) in the presence of 'real man' Ledru, and he weakly tries to save his own skin, telling Ledru that it was Genevieve who wanted to run him over that time, and not him. ("I'm the one who pulled the car back! I wanted to save your life! Please, Monsieur Ledru, if you let me live, I'll leave Strasbourg tomorrow! I promise!") A mirror then falls off the wall and smashes to the ground, and Ledru dispassionately deadpans, "Seven years of bad luck, for both of you!" (And you know Ledru's going to be enforcing that seven years of bad luck-policy.)

Maurice runs outside, to escape getting plugged by Jacques, and he's instantly shot to death by an Unseen Gunman who, we're pretty sure at this point, must be the loathsome Pietr.

Next, of course, it's a bit later (probably, about an hour or so) and, outside the house, two cops are busily checking out the murder scene. Genevieve is talking to the senior of the two officers, Inspector Guerin (Albert Dinan), and she's lying to the guy, telling him that it was Ledru who shot Maurice, and that if they want to find him, they should look aboard the *Rhine Virgin*.

The cops take Genevieve's lead, and when they get to the *Virgin*, they discover that Ledru's not aboard: "Undercover of the Night" (*per Mick n' Keef*), he has already sneaked-over to his dockside office, where Anna's at her desk, toiling away late into the night. Anna's heard through the grapevine that somebody was killed at Ledru's house, and she's relieved when she sees Ledru, because she thought it was him. "What stupid thing have you done?" she asks him. (Basically, she's the only person on God's green earth who is allowed to give him shit, because she's one of the few people on earth whom he really respects.) She tells him that he'd better not show himself around town: "Go hide away on that boat, again. I've been working for you for six years. This is my entire life. Now, go!" Only moments after Ledru sneaks out, Inspector Guerin enters the office, and interrogates Anna. Covering for her boss (what she's about to tell the investigating officer is true, only she doesn't know it), she tells the cop, "I don't think Mr. Ledru was the killer."

Inspector Guerin's next stop: The Meisters' boat, where he interrogates Father and Daughter-Meister, and they tell him that they both really like Jacques Ledru, in spite of whatever troubles he's having. "So, he really *is* loved by everybody," Guerin mutters, shaking his head, since a 'loved' person doesn't really fit with his idea of how a cold-blooded killer is supposed to behave. Guerin illuminates Meister and Marie on what he's already told Anna, which is that, in spite of how much everybody seems to like him, he still believes that Ledru is the one who's killed Maurice.

Guerin leaves and, after he does, we see that Ledru was really there the whole time, hiding in another room, and that Marie was in there with him. Anna advises her boss that he shouldn't be hanging by the window, since the cops, if any of them are indeed still around, will see him if he is. Marie lets him know that she and her father are going to do whatever it takes to help him out—but now, even Ledru himself is growing getting tired of all of this unconditional approbation. He tells both women that they don't have to help him, and that at the age of 45 (in real life, Gabin was 49 when he made this movie), he's growing tired of adventure. The three look out the window, discovering that the harbor is now positively swarming with cops, and he's ready to go outside, 'Gabin-Ready' to surrender himself to *Whatever Fate May Bring*, but his two protectively-adoring wimminfolk continue to warn him against it. Marie next leaves the office, returning not to the boat, but to Ledru's home.

This visit marks Marie's first time at Ledru's house, and she's going to be meeting Genevieve there. Marie thinks Genevieve is the one who killed Maurice, and she wants Genevieve to 'fess-up, to the cops, that she's the one who did it. Marie, not knowing that Genevieve wasn't Maurice's killer, and that, in fact, Pietr was the killer, which we, the audience, already knew anyway, now lies to Genevieve, to try and get her to admit to killing him, but she's not too effective at it: "I was out here in the garden when Maurice was killed, and I know that it was you, and not Jacques Ledru, who killed him!" But *you can't bullshit-a-bullshitter*, and Genevieve now shrieks, "I did not kill him! You weren't here, and you can't save Jacques, because you don't have any proof that he didn't shoot Maurice!" Standing up to Genevieve, who's much bigger, physically, than she is (Genevieve could probably take

With Elina Labourdette.

Marie two-out-of-three-falls), Marie now smirks: "And now, I think I'll call the police and tell them that you were your husband's [Maurice's] killer!" Genevieve asks Marie why she thinks she (Genevieve) killed Maurice, and Marie informs her (and this, too, is a lie), "Well, I was with Jacques when Maurice was murdered." Genevieve makes sure Marie knows full-well that, if she's blackmailing her, she's not going to be getting anything out of it, since she doesn't have any money, and this might be true: It's very possible that, when Ledru came back, he was able to retrieve whatever was left of his cash, from the safe. Marie next gives Genevieve a marching-order: "Jacques wants to see you. And you have no choice. If you don't go and see him right now, I'm calling the police." (Why isn't Genevieve just shooting Marie, and getting this over with?)

Marie phones Ledru at his office: "I'm here in your house, with your wife. She says she won't come to see you. And it's a pity, because I know for a fact that it was she who tried to run you over, in her car." Genevieve, who wants this whole, sorry inquisition to be over with, reluctantly decides to accompany Marie to Ledru's office, but as soon as she takes this decision, we see that it's all been for naught, because (surprise!) Ledru is already present in the house! Marie was just messing with Genevieve, telephoning Jacques not at his office, but from another extension on the same property.

All three are together now, and Ledru tells Genevieve what he knows: "Of course, you killed your lover. Maurice was leaving you for another woman, wasn't he? And that's why you killed him—didn't you!" Genevieve asks Ledru if he actually saw her kill Maurice, and just then, Inspector Guerin enters, and hears the tail-end of the bickering 'sort-of couple's,' argument; and when he hears them, he gets so confused that, now, he doesn't even know who the hell to arrest!

That's when Guerin tells them that he knows Maurice owed Pietr a lot of money (which is probably the money which Pietr was taking out of Ledru's safe), and that Pietr's got to be hiding somewhere in Strasbourg, with the bread. Ledru has now been cleared of any possible suspicion in Maurice's murder, and while he's relieved about that, he still wants to find Pietr and get his money back.

Anna, Ledru, and Inspector Guerin all high-tail it over to the pier, just in time to see the *Rhine Virgin* pulling away from the dock. They all think that Pietr's aboard, escaping with the money, and Guerin now yells out, over his megaphone, and demands that the vessel should return to port, and *stat!* (While the first hour-and-a-half of this movie was paced like *a decrepit, aged bivalve,* the last several minutes are incredibly action-packed, just like the final scenes of any number of American action movies which were made at the same time.)

The harbor cops stop the boat, and surprise—it's not Pietr who's on board, as they all suspected it was, but only Meister and his daughter Marie, and they weren't escaping at all: As it turns out, they were just heading for another town, to pick up some extra work. Meister tells the cops that he hasn't seen Pietr at all and, agreeably, he lets them search his boat.

Pietr, as we'll see in the next bit of the film, has been hiding out for the last several hours in some nearby Strasbourg trainyards, climbing girders with all of the loose-fingered skill of a Barbary Ape at the Rock of Gibraltar. Cops shoot up at him, and what guns can't accomplish—*giant cranes can:* One inventive cop even maneuvers a huge crane toward Pietr, smashing it into him, and knocking him off of the girder. Pietr's now dead on the ground, blood pooling around his head, as Ledru's purloined francs float around on the shiny surface of the crimson liquid, and we're going to be learning, in about one second, that Genevieve was planning on ripping Pietr off, too. (Yes, *La Vierge du Rhin* is one of those movies in which everybody is double-crossing everybody—just like they do in real life!)

Ledru walks away with Marie: It's clear that he's going to be winding-up with this 'nice girl,' in spite of their rather sizeable age difference. Meister now asks Ledru (sucking-up to his new, 'same-age son-in-law'), "So: You're the boss of this whole harbor?" Ledru just Gabin-Shrugs, and grins, "I'll tell you all about it, later." Director Gilles Grangier now superimposes a title card which reads, "Here stops the story of Jacques Ledru." (*Thank God! I was starting to worry that it would go on forever!*)

La Vierge du Rhin is 'just o.k.,' and the main reason that we lose interest in it is because, just like in *Fille Dangereuse* and *Bebe Donge,* Gabin's character isn't taking enough direct action against the characters who are ripping him off. (Another problem with the movie, is that it's too easy to figure out that Pietr is Maurice's killer, before the other characters figure it out, and when we, the audience, are smarter than a film's characters, it's hard to get too involved with the story. The most amusing thing about this movie, is that in French, the word '*ledru*' means, 'something cold and hard.' (That's our Gabin, all right!)

...

What a Critic Said at the Time: "Freshness in this film is missing. [It] has a slow-moving, melodramatic plot that never generates any suspense, and is lagging in interest. Gabin walks through his role, but manages to give it body, because of long experience." (*Variety*, 12-30-53 issue. Critic: "Mosk." [George Moskowitz.] Reviewed in Paris.)

In 1955, the blacklisted American 'ex-pat' filmmaker Jules Dassin, who would ultimately become known in the U.S. for his 1960 Melina Mercouri pic, *Never on Sunday*, went to Europe, where he made *Rififi*, a diamond-heist picture which many *cineastes* consider to be not only the best French *film noir* pictures ever, but also the best heist movie of all time. *Rififi* (in English, it means 'riff-raff') was so internationally popular, that it spawned fifty years worth of other heist pictures, a popular sub-genre to the suspense film which is still going strong to this day. (Some other great heist pictures include Jean-Pierre Melville's *Bob le flambeur* [1955, remade by Neil Jordan as *The Good Thief*, in 2003]; Kubrick's *The Killers* [1964]; Norman Jewison's *Thomas Crown Affair* [1968, remade in 2003]; *Ocean's 11, 12, and 13*; the De Niro/Brando epic, *The Score* [2001]; Guy Ritchie's *Snatch*, and David Mamet's *Heist* [2001].) All heist pictures typically deliver the same basic plot, which is as follows: "A group of misfit criminals has a designated amount of time to complete a massive robbery." Since all heist movies basically share the same exact plot, the joy in watching each individual film, always comes from seeing the subtle variations in character and story which each individual film's director and screenwriter chooses to present to us. In most heist movies, there's usually a 'double ending:' In the first ending, one of the criminal members of the heist mob double-crosses the others, takes the money for himself, and in the second ending, which follows the first one directly, *the winds of cruel fate* cause the heisters to lose the money which they've just carefully heisted. This trope of people working hard (or scheming hard) for something, and then suddenly losing it, is an incredibly existential one, and since the first heist pictures, like Dassin's *Rififi*, were French, we can see why that trope continues to be utilized even in American heist pictures, even if the directors of those pictures don't actually know that the paradigm of their stories' structures have come down the pike, over the years, from France. Over a fifteen-year period, between 1954 and 1969, Jean Gabin would star in three heist pictures—1954's *Touchez pas au grisbi*, 1966's *Soleil des voyous*, 1969's *Le Clan des Siciliens*, all of which are exceedingly cool movies.

And we'll talk about them all in Volume II...

www.ingramcontent.com/pod-product-compliance
Lightning Source LLC
Chambersburg PA
CBHW030421100426
42812CB00028B/3047/J